Principles and Practice of
AMERICAN POLITICS

Principles and Practice of
AMERICAN POLITICS

CLASSIC AND CONTEMPORARY READINGS

edited by

Samuel Kernell

Steven S. Smith

CQ PRESS

A Division of Congressional Quarterly Inc.
Washington, D.C.

CQ Press
A Division of Congressional Quarterly Inc.
1414 22nd St. N.W.
Washington, DC 20037
(202) 822-1475; (800) 638-1710
www.cqpress.com

Printed in the United States of America

04   03   02   01   00   5   4   3   2   1

Cover: Drafting of the Declaration of Independence (top left), copy of engraving by Alonzo Chappel, National Archives and Records Administrations. Photo of Tom Daschle and Trent Lott (top right) by Douglas Graham, CQ. Photo of Barbara Boxer (lower left) by R. Michael Jenkins, CQ. *The Declaration of Independence* (lower right), copy of painting by John Trumbull, National Archives and Records Administration. Background photo by Scott J. Ferrell, CQ.

LIBRARY OF CONGRESS CATALOGING-IN-PUBLICATION DATA

Principles and practice of American Politics / edited by Samuel Kernell, Steven S. Smith.
    p.   cm.
  Includes bibliographical references.
   ISBN 1-56802-577-7   ISBN 1-56802-576-9 (pbk.)
    1. United States—Politics and government. 2. Political culture—United States.
  I. Kernell, Samuel, date. II. Smith, Steven S., date.
JK21.P76 2000
320.973—dc21

                                                                00-024984

Principles and Practice of
AMERICAN POLITICS

CLASSIC AND CONTEMPORARY READINGS

edited by

Samuel Kernell

Steven S. Smith

CQ PRESS

A Division of Congressional Quarterly Inc.
Washington, D.C.

CQ Press
A Division of Congressional Quarterly Inc.
1414 22nd St. N.W.
Washington, DC 20037
(202) 822-1475; (800) 638-1710
www.cqpress.com

Printed in the United States of America

04 03 02 01 00   5 4 3 2 1

Cover: Drafting of the Declaration of Independence (top left), copy of engraving by Alonzo Chappel, National Archives and Records Administrations. Photo of Tom Daschle and Trent Lott (top right) by Douglas Graham, CQ. Photo of Barbara Boxer (lower left) by R. Michael Jenkins, CQ. *The Declaration of Independence* (lower right), copy of painting by John Trumbull, National Archives and Records Administration. Background photo by Scott J. Ferrell, CQ.

LIBRARY OF CONGRESS CATALOGING-IN-PUBLICATION DATA

Principles and practice of American Politics / edited by Samuel Kernell, Steven S. Smith.
    p. cm.
  Includes bibliographical references.
  ISBN 1-56802-577-7   ISBN 1-56802-576-9 (pbk.)
    1. United States—Politics and government. 2. Political culture—United States.
  I. Kernell, Samuel, date. II. Smith, Steven S., date.
JK21.P76 2000
320.973—dc21

00-024984

CONTENTS

Chapter 5. Civil Liberties   167

Chapter 6. Congress   244

Chapter 10. Public Opinion   502

Chapter 11. Voting, Campaigns, and Elections   598

PREFACE

ASSEMBLING THIS SET of readings for students of American politics has been a pleasure and a challenge. The pleasure has come in discovering so many articles that illuminate an important aspect of American politics. The challenge has come in finding far more than can be contained in a single volume. Consequently, despite its heft, *Principles and Practice* represents a small sampling of the literature.

The selection of articles has been guided by our common perspective on politics. Most of the readings concern the strategies of the major players in modern American politics—citizens, public officials, candidates for office, voters, parties, organized interests, and the media. The behavior of political actors is motivated by their own interests, though it is governed by the Constitution, the law, and institutional and organizational rules and is influenced by the strategies of others. Each chapter's readings introduce the interests, rules, and strategic context of political action in a major forum of national politics.

We have chosen the readings to serve two audiences. Many instructors will employ *Principles and Practice* as a supplement to an introductory American politics textbook. For others, this book may constitute the core reading material for the course. For the former, we looked to readings that will animate the institutional processes described in the text. For the latter, we have sought readings that do not assume more than an elementary knowledge of America's government and politics.

Some of the selections are classics that all instructors will recognize; others address contemporary political developments or proposals for reform and may be unfamiliar. Each article adds emphasis and depth to textbook coverage and illustrates an important theme; most introduce an important writer on American politics. We hope students' understanding of American politics is enriched by them all.

We have taken care to include as much of each original source as possible. In the interest of making them appropriate for use in the classroom, we have edited some of the pieces. Ellipses indicate where material has been excised, and brackets enclose editorial interpolations. Other changes are explained in the source note for the reading.

We wish to thank the editorial staff of CQ Press for its expertise, energy, and patience in helping us bring this project to completion. Brenda Carter and James Headley provided essential encouragement and guidance throughout the effort. Tom Roche provided superb editorial assistance, and Martha Hawley-Bertsch demonstrated persistence in gaining permission to reprint the selections. Several friends and colleagues have been helpful to us as well. Sarah Binder, Louis Fisher, Alan Houston, and John Zaller offered helpful suggestions that are reflected in the contents. Alan Abramowitz of Emory University, Scott Adler of the University of Colorado, Eric Lawrence of the University of California, Riverside, and several anonymous reviewers provided very helpful comments on our original outline.

Samuel Kernell
Steven S. Smith

1-

from *The Logic*

Ma

With the publication of .
Mancur Olson introduced the funu.
to all who study politics. When members .
gether to achieve a collective goal, each member u.
powerful disincentives, Olson showed, that can frustrau
the group as a whole. For example, when each can foresee that his .
relatively small contribution to a collective enterprise will not affect its
overall success, many will fail to contribute—a phenomenon known as
free riding—and leave to everyone else the burden of supplying the col-
lective good. As a consequence, collective enterprises based on coopera-
tion, and supported by the entire collectivity, nevertheless often fail.

IT IS OFTEN taken for granted, at least where economic objectives are involved, that groups of individuals with common interests usually attempt
to further those common interests. Groups of individuals with common interests are expected to act on behalf of their common interests much as single individuals are often expected to act on behalf of their personal
interests. This opinion about group behavior is frequently found not only in
popular discussions but also in scholarly writings. Many economists of diverse methodological and ideological traditions have implicitly or explicitly
accepted it. This view has, for example, been important in many theories of
labor unions, in Marxian theories of class action, in concepts of "countervailing power," and in various discussions of economic institutions. It has,
in addition, occupied a prominent place in political science, at least in the
United States, where the study of pressure groups has been dominated by a
celebrated "group theory" based on the idea that groups will act when necessary to further their common or group goals. Finally, it has played a significant role in many well-known sociological studies.

1

Designing Institutions

olitics is an ever-present social activity. It occurs whenever individuals seek to reach agreement on a course of common action despite their disagreement over the goals. Politics arises whenever people who have different, even opposing, interests accept that they must cooperate if their interest is to be served. Politics, so defined, occurs within the smallest, most intimate associations—as within families and among friends—as well as at city hall or in Washington, D.C. Successful politics almost always depends on bargaining and compromise as each side tries to get as much of what it wants from the agreement, whether friends are trying to decide on a restaurant or Congress and the president are wrangling over the budget. The essays in this book attest to the bargaining and compromise that occur in Washington, at least whenever politicians succeed in creating national policy.

By virtue of their size and complexity, national communities recurrently counter special problems in conducting political business. This is especially true when citizens participate in politics through voting and other activities. Every pect of a political choice presents a challenge: combining and ranking preferences bargaining and compromising to reach agreement, and implementing agreements. Each is based on recognizing the discrepancy between what we desire individuals and what is required of us as members of a collectivity. In this chapter we introduce American politics by taking inventory of some of the problems that we face when we try to act collectively. The commonly occurring collective action problems are known to economists and political scientists by some colorful names: free riding, the tragedy of the commons, externalities, and prisoner's dilemma. Each of these problems will be explored in the following lections.

1-1

from *The Logic of Collective Action*

Mancur Olson Jr.

With the publication of The Logic of Collective Action *in 1965, Mancur Olson introduced the fundamental dilemma of collective action to all who study politics. When members of a group agree to work together to achieve a collective goal, each member as an individual faces powerful disincentives, Olson showed, that can frustrate the efforts of the group as a whole. For example, when each can foresee that his or her relatively small contribution to a collective enterprise will not affect its overall success, many will fail to contribute—a phenomenon known as free riding—and leave to everyone else the burden of supplying the collective good. As a consequence, collective enterprises based on cooperation, and supported by the entire collectivity, nevertheless often fail.*

IT IS OFTEN taken for granted, at least where economic objectives are involved, that groups of individuals with common interests usually attempt to further those common interests. Groups of individuals with common interests are expected to act on behalf of their common interests much as single individuals are often expected to act on behalf of their personal interests. This opinion about group behavior is frequently found not only in popular discussions but also in scholarly writings. Many economists of diverse methodological and ideological traditions have implicitly or explicitly accepted it. This view has, for example, been important in many theories of labor unions, in Marxian theories of class action, in concepts of "countervailing power," and in various discussions of economic institutions. It has, in addition, occupied a prominent place in political science, at least in the United States, where the study of pressure groups has been dominated by a celebrated "group theory" based on the idea that groups will act when necessary to further their common or group goals. Finally, it has played a significant role in many well-known sociological studies.

1

Designing Institutions

Politics is an ever-present social activity. It occurs whenever individuals seek to reach agreement on a course of common action despite their disagreement over the goals. Politics arises whenever people who have different, even opposing, interests accept that they must cooperate if their interest is to be served. Politics, so defined, occurs within the smallest, most intimate associations—as within families and among friends—as well as at city hall or in Washington, D.C. Successful politics almost always depends on bargaining and compromise as each side tries to get as much of what it wants from the agreement, whether friends are trying to decide on a restaurant or Congress and the president are wrangling over the budget. The essays in this book attest to the bargaining and compromise that occur in Washington, at least whenever politicians succeed in creating national policy.

By virtue of their size and complexity, national communities recurrently encounter special problems in conducting political business. This is especially true when citizens participate in politics through voting and other activities. Every aspect of a political choice presents a challenge: combining and ranking preferences, bargaining and compromising to reach agreement, and implementing agreements. Each is based on recognizing the discrepancy between what we desire as individuals and what is required of us as members of a collectivity. In this chapter we introduce American politics by taking inventory of some of the problems that we face when we try to act collectively. The commonly occurring collective action problems are known to economists and political scientists by some rather colorful names: free riding, the tragedy of the commons, externalities, and the prisoner's dilemma. Each of these problems will be explored in the following selections.

The view that groups act to serve their interests presumably is based upon the assumption that the individuals in groups act out of self-interest. If the individuals in a group altruistically disregarded their personal welfare, it would not be very likely that collectively they would seek some selfish common or group objective. Such altruism is, however, considered exceptional, and self-interested behavior is usually thought to be the rule, at least when economic issues are at stake; no one is surprised when individual businessmen seek higher profits, when individual workers seek higher wages, or when individual consumers seek lower prices. The idea that groups tend to act in support of their group interests is supposed to follow logically from this widely accepted premise of rational, self-interested behavior. In other words, if the members of some group have a common interest or objective, and if they would all be better off if that objective were achieved, it has been thought to follow logically that the individuals in that group would, if they were rational and self-interested, act to achieve that objective.

But it is *not* in fact true that the idea that groups will act in their self-interest follows logically from the premise of rational and self-interested behavior. It does *not* follow, because all of the individuals in a group would gain if they achieved their group objective, that they would act to achieve that objective, even if they were all rational and self-interested. Indeed, unless the number of individuals in a group is quite small, or unless there is coercion or some other special device to make individuals act in their common interest, *rational, self-interested individuals will not act to achieve their common or group interests.* In other words, even if all of the individuals in a large group are rational and self-interested, and would gain if, as a group, they acted to achieve their common interest or objective, they will still not voluntarily act to achieve that common or group interest. The notion that groups of individuals will act to achieve their common or group interests, far from being a logical implication of the assumption that the individuals in a group will rationally further their individual interests, is in fact inconsistent with that assumption. . . .

A Theory of Groups and Organizations

The Purpose of Organization

Since most (though by no means all) of the action taken by or on behalf of groups of individuals is taken through organizations, it will be helpful to consider organizations in a general or theoretical way.[1] The logical place to begin any systematic study of organizations is with their purpose. But there are all types and shapes and sizes of organizations, even of economic organizations, and there is then some question whether there is any single purpose that would be characteristic of organizations generally. One purpose that is nonetheless characteristic of most organizations, and surely of practically all organizations with an important economic aspect, is the furtherance of the interests of their members. That would seem obvious, at least from the economist's perspective. To be sure, some organizations may out of ignorance fail to further their members' interests, and others may be enticed into serving only the ends of the leadership.[2] But organizations often perish if they do nothing to further the interests of their members, and this factor must severely limit the number of organizations that fail to serve their members.

The idea that organizations or associations exist to further the interests of their members is hardly novel, nor peculiar to economics; it goes back at least to Aristotle, who wrote, "Men journey together with a view to particular advantage, and by way of providing some particular thing needed for the purposes of life, and similarly the political association seems to have come together originally, and to continue in existence, for the sake of the *general* advantages it brings."[3] More recently Professor Leon Festinger, a social psychologist, pointed out that "the attraction of group membership is not so much in sheer belonging, but rather in attaining something by means of this membership."[4] The late Harold Laski, a political scientist, took it for granted that "associations exist to fulfill purposes which a group of men have in common."[5]

The kinds of organizations that are the focus of this study are *expected* to further the interests of their members.[6] Labor unions are expected to strive for higher wages and better working conditions for their members; farm organizations are expected to strive for favorable legislation for their members; cartels are expected to strive for higher prices for participating firms; the corporation is expected to further the interests of its stockholders;[7] and the state is expected to further the common interests of its citizens (though in this nationalistic age the state often has interests and ambitions apart from those of its citizens).

Notice that the interests that all of these diverse types of organizations are expected to further are for the most part *common* interests: the union members' common interest in higher wages, the farmers' common interest

in favorable legislation, the cartel members' common interest in higher prices, the stockholders' common interest in higher dividends and stock prices, the citizens' common interest in good government. It is not an accident that the diverse types of organizations listed are all supposed to work primarily for the *common* interests of their members. Purely personal or individual interests can be advanced, and usually advanced most efficiently, by individual, unorganized action. There is obviously no purpose in having an organization when individual, unorganized action can serve the interests of the individual as well as or better than an organization; there would, for example, be no point in forming an organization simply to play solitaire. But when a number of individuals have a common or collective interest—when they share a single purpose or objective—individual, unorganized action (as we shall soon see) will either not be able to advance that common interest at all, or will not be able to advance that interest adequately. Organizations can therefore perform a function when there are common or group interests, and though organizations often also serve purely personal, individual interests, their characteristic and primary function is to advance the common interests of groups of individuals.

The assumption that organizations typically exist to further the common interests of groups of people is implicit in most of the literature about organizations, and two of the writers already cited make this assumption explicit: Harold Laski emphasized that organizations exist to achieve purposes or interests which "a group of men have in common," and Aristotle apparently had a similar notion in mind when he argued that political associations are created and maintained because of the "general advantages" they bring. . . . As Arthur Bentley, the founder of the "group theory" of modern political science, put it, "there is no group without its interest."[8] The social psychologist Raymond Cattell was equally explicit, and stated that "every group has its interest."[9] This is also the way the word "group" will be used here.

Just as those who belong to an organization or a group can be presumed to have a common interest,[10] so they obviously also have purely individual interests, different from those of the others in the organization or group. All of the members of a labor union, for example, have a common interest in higher wages, but at the same time each worker has a unique interest in his personal income, which depends not only on the rate of wages but also on the length of time that he works.

Public Goods and Large Groups

The combination of individual interests and common interests in an organization suggests an analogy with a competitive market. The firms in a perfectly competitive industry, for example, have a common interest in a higher price for the industry's product. Since a uniform price must prevail in such a market, a firm cannot expect a higher price for itself unless all of the other firms in the industry also have this higher price. But a firm in a competitive market also has an interest in selling as much as it can, until the cost of producing another unit exceeds the price of that unit. In this there is no common interest; each firm's interest is directly opposed to that of every other firm, for the more other firms sell, the lower the price and income for any given firm. In short, while all firms have a common interest in a higher price, they have antagonistic interests where output is concerned. . . .

For these reasons it is now generally understood that if the firms in an industry are maximizing profits, the profits for the industry as a whole will be less than they might otherwise be.[11] And almost everyone would agree that this theoretical conclusion fits the facts for markets characterized by pure competition. The important point is that this is true because, though all the firms have a common interest in a higher price for the industry's product, it is in the interest of each firm that the other firms pay the cost—in terms of the necessary reduction in output—needed to obtain a higher price.

About the only thing that keeps prices from falling in accordance with the process just described in perfectly competitive markets is outside intervention. Government price supports, tariffs, cartel agreements, and the like may keep the firms in a competitive market from acting contrary to their interests. Such aid or intervention is quite common. It is then important to ask how it comes about. How does a competitive industry obtain government assistance in maintaining the price of its product?

Consider a hypothetical, competitive industry, and suppose that most of the producers in that industry desire a tariff, a price-support program, or some other government intervention to increase the price for their product. To obtain any such assistance from the government, the producers in this industry will presumably have to organize a lobbying organization; they will have to become an active pressure group.[12] This lobbying organization may have to conduct a considerable campaign. If significant resistance is encountered, a great amount of money will be required.[13] Public relations experts will be needed to influence the newspapers, and some advertising may

be necessary. Professional organizers will probably be needed to organize "spontaneous grass roots" meetings among the distressed producers in the industry, and to get those in the industry to write letters to their congressmen.[14] The campaign for the government assistance will take the time of some of the producers in the industry, as well as their money.

There is a striking parallel between the problem the perfectly competitive industry faces as it strives to obtain government assistance, and the problem it faces in the marketplace when the firms increase output and bring about a fall in price. *Just as it was not rational for a particular producer to restrict his output in order that there might be a higher price for the product of his industry, so it would not be rational for him to sacrifice his time and money to support a lobbying organization to obtain government assistance for the industry. In neither case would it be in the interest of the individual producer to assume any of the costs himself. A lobbying organization, or indeed a labor union or any other organization, working in the interest of a large group of firms or workers in some industry, would get no assistance from the rational, self-interested individuals in that industry.* This would be true even if everyone in the industry were absolutely convinced that the proposed program was in their interest (though in fact some might think otherwise and make the organization's task yet more difficult).

Although the lobbying organization is only one example of the logical analogy between the organization and the market, it is of some practical importance. There are many powerful and well-financed lobbies with mass support in existence now, but these lobbying organizations do not get that support because of their legislative achievements. . . .

Some critics may argue that the rational person will, indeed, support a large organization, like a lobbying organization, that works in his interest, because he knows that if he does not, others will not do so either, and then the organization will fail, and he will be without the benefit that the organization could have provided. This argument shows the need for the analogy with the perfectly competitive market. For it would be quite as reasonable to argue that prices will never fall below the levels a monopoly would have charged in a perfectly competitive market, because if one firm increased its output, other firms would also, and the price would fall; but each firm could foresee this, so it would not start a chain of price-destroying increases in output. In fact, it does not work out this way in a competitive market; nor in a large organization. When the number of firms involved is large, no one will notice the effect on price if one firm increases its output, and so no one will change his plans because of it. Similarly, in a large organization, the loss of one dues payer will not noticeably increase the burden for any other one dues payer, and so a rational person would not believe that if he were to withdraw from an organization he would drive others to do so.

The foregoing argument must at the least have some relevance to economic organizations that are mainly means through which individuals attempt to obtain the same things they obtain through their activities in the market. Labor unions, for example, are organizations through which workers strive to get the same things they get with their individual efforts in the market—higher wages, better working conditions, and the like. It would be strange indeed if the workers did not confront some of the same problems in the union that they meet in the market, since their efforts in both places have some of the same purposes.

However similar the purposes may be, critics may object that attitudes in organizations are not at all like those in markets. In organizations, an emotional or ideological element is often also involved. Does this make the argument offered here practically irrelevant?

A most important type of organization—the national state—will serve to test this objection. Patriotism is probably the strongest non-economic motive for organizational allegiance in modern times. This age is sometimes called the age of nationalism. Many nations draw additional strength and unity from some powerful ideology, such as democracy or communism, as well as from a common religion, language, or cultural inheritance. The state not only has many such powerful sources of support; it also is very important economically. Almost any government is economically beneficial to its citizens, in that the law and order it provides is a prerequisite of all civilized economic activity. But despite the force of patriotism, the appeal of the national ideology, the bond of a common culture, and the indispensability of the system of law and order, no major state in modern history has been able to support itself through voluntary dues or contributions. Philanthropic contributions are not even a significant source of revenue for most countries. Taxes, *compulsory* payments by definition, are needed. Indeed, as the old saying indicates, their necessity is as certain as death itself.

If the state, with all of the emotional resources at its command, cannot finance its most basic and vital activities without resort to compulsion, it would seem that large private organizations might also have difficulty in

getting the individuals in the groups whose interests they attempt to advance to make the necessary contributions voluntarily.[15]

The reason the state cannot survive on voluntary dues or payments, but must rely on taxation, is that the most fundamental services a nation-state provides are, in one important respect, like the higher price in a competitive market: they must be available to everyone if they are available to anyone. The basic and most elementary goods or services provided by government, like defense and police protection, and the system of law and order generally, are such that they go to everyone or practically everyone in the nation. It would obviously not be feasible, if indeed it were possible, to deny the protection provided by the military services, the police, and the courts to those who did not voluntarily pay their share of the costs of government, and taxation is accordingly necessary. The common or collective benefits provided by governments are usually called "public goods" by economists, and the concept of public goods is one of the oldest and most important ideas in the study of public finance. A common, collective, or public good is here defined as any good such that, if any person X_i in a group $X_1, \ldots, X_i, \ldots, X_n$ consumes it, it cannot feasibly be withheld from the others in that group.[16] In other words, those who do not purchase or pay for any of the public or collective good cannot be excluded or kept from sharing in the consumption of the good, as they can where noncollective goods are concerned.

Students of public finance have, however, neglected the fact that *the achievement of any common goal or the satisfaction of any common interest means that a public or collective good has been provided for that group.*[17] The very fact that a goal or purpose is *common* to a group means that no one in the group is excluded from the benefit or satisfaction brought about by its achievement. As the opening paragraphs of this chapter indicated, almost all groups and organizations have the purpose of serving the common interests of their members. As R. M. MacIver puts it, "Persons . . . have common interests in the degree to which they participate in a cause . . . which indivisibly embraces them all."[18] It is of the essence of an organization that it provides an inseparable, generalized benefit. It follows that the provision of public or collective goods is the fundamental function of organizations generally. A state is first of all an organization that provides public goods for its members, the citizens; and other types of organizations similarly provide collective goods for their members.

And just as a state cannot support itself by voluntary contributions, or by selling its basic services on the market, neither can other large organizations support themselves without providing some sanction, or some attraction distinct from the public good itself, that will lead individuals to help bear the burdens of maintaining the organization. The individual member of the typical large organization is in a position analogous to that of the firm in a perfectly competitive market, or the taxpayer in the state: his own efforts will not have a noticeable effect on the situation of his organization, and he can enjoy any improvements brought about by others whether or not he has worked in support of his organization.

There is no suggestion here that states or other organizations provide *only* public or collective goods. Governments often provide noncollective goods like electric power, for example, and they usually sell such goods on the market much as private firms would do. Moreover . . . large organizations that are not able to make membership compulsory *must also* provide some noncollective goods in order to give potential members an incentive to join. Still, collective goods are the characteristic organizational goods, for ordinary noncollective goods can always be provided by individual action, and only where common purposes or collective goods are concerned is organization or group action ever indispensable.[19]

NOTES

1. Economists have for the most part neglected to develop theories of organizations, but there are a few works from an economic point of view on the subject. See, for example, three papers by Jacob Marschak, "Elements for a Theory of Teams," *Management Science,* I (January 1955), 127–137, "Towards an Economic Theory of Organization and Information," in *Decision Processes,* ed. R. M. Thrall, C. H. Combs, and R. L. Davis (New York: John Wiley, 1954), pp. 187–220, and "Efficient and Viable Organization Forms," in *Modern Organization Theory,* ed. Mason Haire (New York: John Wiley, 1959), pp. 307–320; two papers by R. Radner, "Application of Linear Programming to Team Decision Problems, *Management Science,* V (January 1959), 143–150, and "Team Decision Problems," *Annals of Mathematical Statistics,* XXXIII (September 1962), 857–881; C. B. McGuire, "Some Team Models of a Sales Organization," *Management Science,* VII (January 1961), 101–130; Oskar Morgenstern, *Prolegomena to a Theory of Organization* (Santa Monica, Calif.: RAND Research Memorandum 734, 1951); James G. March and Herbert A. Simon, *Organizations* (New York: John Wiley, 1958); Kenneth Boulding, *The Organizational Revolution* (New York: Harper, 1953).

2. Max Weber called attention to the case where an organization continues to exist for some time after it has become meaningless because some official is making a living

out of it. See his *Theory of Social and Economic Organization,* trans. Talcott Parsons and A. M. Henderson (New York: Oxford University Press, 1947), p. 318.

3. *Ethics* viii.9.1160a.

4. Leon Festinger, "Group Attraction and Membership," in *Group Dynamics,* ed. Dorwin Cartwright and Alvin Zander (Evanston, Ill.: Row, Peterson, 1953), p. 93.

5. *A Grammar of Politics,* 4th ed. (London: George Allen & Unwin, 1939), p. 67.

6. Philanthropic and religious organizations are not necessarily expected to serve only the interests of their members; such organizations have other purposes that are considered more important, however much their members "need" to belong, or are improved or helped by belonging. But the complexity of such organizations need not be debated at length here, because this study will focus on organizations with a significant economic aspect. The emphasis here will have something in common with what Max Weber called the "associative group"; he called a group associative if "the orientation of social action with it rests on a rationally motivated agreement." Weber contrasted his "associative group" with the "communal group" which was centered on personal affection, erotic relationships, etc., like the family. (See Weber, pp. 136–139, and Grace Coyle, *Social Process in Organized Groups,* New York: Richard Smith, Inc., 1930, pp. 7–9.) The logic of the theory developed here can be extended to cover communal, religious, and philanthropic organizations, but the theory is not particularly useful in studying such groups. See Olson, pp. 61n17, 159–162.

7. That is, its members. This study does not follow the terminological usage of those organization theorists who describe employees as "members" of the organization for which they work. Here it is more convenient to follow the language of everyday usage instead, and to distinguish the members of, say, a union from the employees of that union. Similarly, the members of the union will be considered employees of the corporation for which they work, whereas the members of the corporation are the common stockholders.

8. Arthur Bentley, *The Process of Government* (Evanston, Ill.: Principia Press, 1949), p. 211. David B. Truman takes a similar approach; see his *The Governmental Process* (New York: Alfred A. Knopf, 1958), pp. 33–35. See also Sidney Verba, *Small Groups and Political Behavior* (Princeton, N.J.: Princeton University Press, 1961), pp. 12–13.

9. Raymond Cattell, "Concepts and Methods in the Measurement of Group Syntality," in *Small Groups,* ed. A. Paul Hare, Edgard F. Borgatta, and Robert F. Bales (New York: Alfred A. Knopf, 1955), p. 115.

10. Any organization or group will of course usually be divided into subgroups or factions that are opposed to one another. This fact does not weaken the assumption made here that organizations exist to serve the common interests of members, for the assumption does not imply that intragroup conflict is neglected. The opposing groups within an organization ordinarily have some interest in common (if not, why would they maintain the organization?), and the members of any subgroup or faction also have a separate common interest of their own. They will indeed often have a common purpose in defeating some other subgroup or faction. The approach used here does not ne-

glect the conflict within groups and organizations, then, because it considers each organization as a unit only to the extent that it does in fact attempt to serve a common interest, and considers the various subgroups as the relevant units with common interests to analyze the factional strife.

11. For a fuller discussion of this question see Mancur Olson, Jr., and David McFarland, "The Restoration of Pure Monopoly and the Concept of the Industry," *Quarterly Journal of Economics,* LXXVI (November 1962), 613–631.

12. Robert Michels contends in his classic study that "democracy is inconceivable without organization," and that "the principle of organization is an absolutely essential condition for the political struggle of the masses." See his *Political Parties,* trans. Eden and Cedar Paul (New York: Dover Publications, 1959), pp. 21–22. See also Robert A. Brady, *Business as a System of Power* (New York: Columbia University Press, 1943), p. 193.

13. Alexander Heard, *The Costs of Democracy* (Chapel Hill: University of North Carolina Press, 1960), especially note 1, pp. 95–96. For example, in 1947 the National Association of Manufacturers spent over $4.6 million, and over a somewhat longer period the American Medical Association spent as much on a campaign against compulsory health insurance.

14. "If the full truth were ever known . . . lobbying, in all its ramifications, would prove to be a billion dollar industry." U.S. Congress, House, Select Committee on Lobbying Activities, *Report,* 81st Cong., 2nd Sess. (1950), as quoted in the *Congressional Quarterly Almanac,* 81st Cong., 2nd Sess., VI, 764–765.

15. Sociologists as well as economists have observed that ideological motives alone are not sufficient to bring forth the continuing effort of large masses of people. Max Weber provides a notable example:

> All economic activity in a market economy is undertaken and carried through by individuals for their own ideal or material interests. This is naturally just as true when economic activity is oriented to the patterns of order of corporate groups. . . .
>
> Even if an economic system were organized on a socialistic basis, there would be no fundamental difference in this respect. . . . The structure of interests and the relevant situation might change; there would be other means of pursuing interests, but this fundamental factor would remain just as relevant as before. It is of course true that economic action which is oriented on purely ideological grounds to the interest of others does exist. But it is even more certain that the mass of men do not act this way, and it is an induction from experience that they cannot do so and never will. . . .
>
> In a market economy the interest in the maximization of income is necessarily the driving force of all economic activity. (Weber, pp. 319–320)

Talcott Parsons and Neil Smelser go even further in postulating that "performance" throughout society is proportional to the "rewards" and "sanctions" involved. See their *Economy and Society* (Glencoe, Ill.: Free Press, 1954), pp. 50–69.

16. This simple definition focuses upon two points that are important in the present context. The first point is that most collective goods can only be defined with respect to some specific group. One collective good goes to one group of people, another collective good to another group; one may benefit the whole world, another only two specific people. Moreover, some goods are collective goods to those in one group and at the same time private goods to those in another, because some individuals can be kept from consuming them and others can't. Take for example the parade that is a collective good to all those who live in tall buildings overlooking the parade route, but which appears to be a private good to those who can see it only by buying tickets for a seat in the stands along the way. The second point is that once the relevant group has been defined, the definition used here, like Musgrave's, distinguishes collective good in terms of infeasibility of excluding potential consumers of the good. This approach is used because collective goods produced by organizations of all kinds seem to be such that exclusion is normally not feasible. To be sure, for some collective goods it is physically possible to practice exclusion. But, as Head has shown, it is not necessary that exclusion be technically impossible; it is only necessary that it be infeasible or uneconomic. Head has also shown most clearly that nonexcludability is only one of two basic elements in the traditional understanding of public goods. The other, he points out, is "jointness of supply." A good has "jointness" if making it available to one individual means that it can be easily or freely supplied to others as well. The polar case of jointness would be Samuelson's pure public good, which is a good such that additional consumption of it by one individual does not diminish the amount available to others. By the definition used here, jointness is not a necessary attribute of a public good. As later parts of this chapter will show, at least one type of collective good considered here exhibits no jointness whatever, and few if any would have the degree of jointness needed to qualify as pure public goods. Nonetheless, most of the collective goods to be studied here do display a large measure of jointness. On the definition and importance of public goods, see John G. Head, "Public Goods and Public Policy," *Public Finance,* vol. XVII, no. 3 (1962), 197–219; Richard Musgrave, *The Theory of Public Finance* (New York: McGraw-Hill, 1959); Paul A. Samuelson, "The Pure Theory of Public Expenditure," "Diagrammatic Exposition of A Theory of Public Expenditure," and "Aspects of Public Expenditure Theories," in *Review of Economics and Statistics,* XXXVI (November 1954), 387–390, XXXVII (November 1955), 350–356, and XL (November 1958), 332–338. For somewhat different opinions about the usefulness of the concept of public goods, see Julius Margolis, "A Comment on the Pure Theory of Public Expenditure," *Review of Economics and Statistics,* XXXVII (November 1955), 347–349, and Gerhard Colm, "Theory of Public Expenditures," *Annals of the American Academy of Political and Social Science,* CLXXXIII (January 1936), 1–11.

17. There is no necessity that a public good to one group in a society is necessarily in the interest of the society as a whole. Just as a tariff could be a public good to the industry that sought it, so the removal of the tariff could be a public good to those who consumed the industry's product. This is equally true when the public-good concept is

applied only to governments; for a military expenditure, or a tariff, or an immigration restriction that is a public good to one country could be a "public bad" to another country, and harmful to world society as a whole.

18. R. M. MacIver in *Encyclopaedia of the Social Sciences,* VII (New York: Macmillan, 1932), 147.

19. It does not, however, follow that organized or coordinated group action is *always* necessary to obtain a collective goal.

1-2

from *Analyzing Politics*

Kenneth A. Shepsle and Mark S. Bonchek

A variety of related collective action problems, of which free riding is one example, arise whenever communities try to supply themselves with public goods. Public goods are goods that are non-excludable, or freely available to all, whether natural resources, such as fresh air or water, or goods produced for a collectivity, such as military protection. Communities provided with an abundance of public goods are faced with a seemingly benign situation. But embedded within it, warn Kenneth Shepsle and Mark Bonchek in the following article, are "socially destructive incentives" that lead to both the wasteful consumption and the underproduction of public goods.

Public Goods and Politics

POLITICS REARS its ugly head because . . . the provision of public goods is subject to socially destructive incentives. Because a public good is nonexcludable, it may be enjoyed without paying a price for it. But a producer will be loathe to provide a good if he cannot elicit payment for it. And even if there were some imperfect method by which a potential producer could extract a return from providing a public good, the amount supplied would likely be very much less than it would be if payment could be extracted directly. As a result, everyone is worse off.

Peasant farmers in a feudal world may well be willing to pay something for the lord's protection (certainly as much as they would have to pay, in terms of time, energy, and lost opportunities, to guard against predators themselves); but if the lord has no way of eliciting this payment from beneficiaries of his protection, then he will be less disposed to provide it, or very

From *Analyzing Politics: Rationality, Behavior, and Institutions*, by Kenneth A. Shepsle and Mark S. Bonchek. Copyright © 1997 by W. W. Norton & Company, Inc. Reprinted by permission of W. W. Norton & Company, Inc.

much of it at least, in the first instance. It was something like this that supported the enforcement of feudal arrangements in many parts of the world; accordingly, peasant families were coerced into contributing hours of labor in the lord's fields, a younger son to the lord's army, and a proportion of their crops to the lord's granary in exchange for the lord's safekeeping. Because protection is a public good, its supply by means of ordinary market exchange is problematic, necessitating the substitution of politics—the enforcement of coercive feudal institutions—for economic exchange. Political institutions, like feudalism, arise to fill the economic vacuum.

Sometimes the political arrangement is at one remove. The classic example of lighthouses illustrates this. The services of a lighthouse constitute a quintessential public good. If a lighthouse is erected on high ground near a shipping hazard, the warning it emits is available to every ship that passes (nonexcludability) and its use by one ship does not deny it to others (jointness of supply). No ship will willingly pay for lighthouse services, since nonpayment cannot lead to a refusal of service to nonpayers—if the service is provided at all. But if a private individual or firm cannot be compensated sufficiently to earn a normal return, it will not be inclined to invest in the provision of lighthouse services. For this reason, lighthouses turn up in introductory economics texts as the classic instance of a public goods problem—in which a public good is undersupplied owing to socially perverse incentives.

In a superb piece of economic detective work, the Nobel laureate Ronald Coase revealed that generations of undergraduates had been misled by the lighthouse example.[1] In England, at least, lighthouses were quite commonly provided along its western coastline by private entrepreneurs. But how could such entrepreneurs obtain a return on their investment? The ingenious answer Coase provided is that lighthouses typically were positioned near harbors, allowing ships to enter without crashing onto dangerous shoals. The lighthouse was primarily needed by precisely those ships coming into port. Ships not intending to put ashore would typically travel somewhat farther out to sea, thus not especially requiring the services of a lighthouse. Consequently, there was a way to discriminate between most users and nonusers. Was there a method for converting this capacity to discriminate into a capacity to extract payment? If a monopolist controlled the waterfront of the harbor, then he could jointly price lighthouse services together with docking privileges in a manner that captured a return for the former. Light-

house services, then, were part of a *tie-in-sale;* if a shipowner wanted to use wharf and warehousing facilities of the port, he would be required to pay for the lighthouse services he consumed as well.

The monopoly position of the entrepreneur is crucial here. If the lighthouse provider was but one of many owners of wharfs and warehouses, he could not charge extra because of competition for customers. Other wharf and warehouse owners could charge a price for their services lower than the tie-in sale price. So, in order for a lighthouse to be provided, an entrepreneur must enjoy the *political protection* of his monopoly position.[2]

Consider one last illustration, this one of more contemporary vintage. In the 1970s the entire industrialized world was held at ransom by a cartel known as OPEC—the Organization of Petroleum Exporting Countries. This organization, led by the oil ministers of the member states, conspired to jack up the price of petroleum by restricting the amount that would be available for export. The logic according to which they operated was quite straightforward and well known. From the simple law of supply and demand, for a given level of world demand for oil, if the supply were restricted, then its price would rise. Suppose the competitive price for and quantity of a barrel of oil—the ones that would emerge from competition among oil producers in the absence of a cartel—are P_c and Q_c, respectively, with total revenue, $R_c = P_c \times Q_c$. If the cartel could successfully restrict quantity to Q_{opec}, an amount less than Q_c, then the price would rise to P_{opec}, an amount higher than P_c. The new total revenue is $R_{opec} = P_{opec} \times Q_{opec}$. Under conditions prevailing in the 1970s, it was possible to find a Q_{opec} and its associated P_{opec} that produced a larger total revenue, i.e., $R_{opec} > R_c$. Thus, if the oil producers could agree on a system of quantity-restricting production quotas—one for each exporter—that added up to Q_{opec}, and could hang together by honoring these quotas, they would thereby reduce the amount of oil available on the world market and have a bigger revenue pie to slice up among themselves.

The higher price that prevails because of this restriction on oil supply is a public good for OPEC (and a public bad for everyone else). Let's see how this works. We said that a public good is, first of all, nonexcludable, and this is certainly true of a prevailing price. Every oil exporter gets the prevailing price. Second, a public good is jointly supplied, and this, too, is true of the prevailing price. One supplier selling its product at that price does not deny that same price for some other supplier.

The joint actions that sustain this price require each supplier to stick to its production quota (so that the total amount of oil for sale adds up to the optimal Q_{opec}, thus generating the optimal revenue, R_{opec}). But providing this particular public good, like the provision of public goods generally, is problematic. Each supplier will be tempted to cheat on the cartel by producing more than its quota. If the little bit extra is sufficiently small so as not to affect the prevailing price, then a cheater can sell more than its quota at the cartel-supported higher price than it would if it honored the quota. But if each member of OPEC cheats on the cartel, then there will be more oil on the market, the price will decline, revenues will drop, and each member will have incentives to begin a further round of cheating. In the end, like so many instances of collective action . . ., everything unravels and the cartel fails.

Indeed, this is what ultimately happened to OPEC. But it took quite a while for the cartel to break apart and, in the meantime, OPEC did very well while the rest of the world suffered immense economic hardship. Why did the cartel last as long as it did? The answer, like our answers to the provision of defense and lighthouses, is that a political understanding sustained OPEC's operation. In this case one petroleum exporter, Saudi Arabia, was dramatically larger than any of the other members of OPEC. Saudi Arabia vigilantly enforced the cartel agreement by using various carrots and sticks to induce compliance by its smaller cartel partners to previously set production quotas. Saudi Arabia (which was intent upon being the dominant state in the Arab world and, not uncoincidentally, also had the most to gain from cartel pricing, given its oil resources) took on the burdens of political leadership to hold the cartel together.[3]

We thus see that public goods will go underproduced, if produced at all, because individuals have private incentives at odds with those required to support their production. Individuals have private incentives to enjoy the benefits of defense and lighthouses without paying for them. Potential producers appreciate this prospect and, consequently, are discouraged from producing them unless they can find some means by which to elicit contributions. Potential cartel partners often forego cartel formation because they can anticipate that their various partners will cheat on the cartel, in effect seeking to enjoy cartel benefits without paying for them. Again, the public good—in this case a higher price for cartel products—will be produced only if members can assure one another that the behavior required to sustain the higher price will be forthcoming. . . . Perhaps the most common solution of all—the quintessential political solution—is the public supply of public goods. This solution requires a section all its own.

Public Supply

We have argued that the provision of public goods is poorly handled by ordinary market means. They are undersupplied relative to the levels that the members of society would prefer. Absent some sort of political intervention, there is, as we have just seen, too little protection from predators and too few lighthouses. Politically enforced feudal arrangements and monopoly rights in ports, respectively, are solutions to these problems (though not perfect solutions). An alternative is to turn to the state for public goods provision. Let the government build lighthouses and raise armies.

In many parts of the world, lighthouses, the protective services of the police and army, judicial services, public utilities like water, sewage, and power, and provision for public health, roads, and other infrastructure are commonly provided by government. Telephone and television are also often provided publicly in many countries. The argument is that, because they are public goods (or at least "public-like"), private market actors will not provide them (at least not in sufficient quantities) because they cannot be assured of adequate compensation. The state, on the other hand, may use its authority to *require* payment, either out of general revenue raised by taxation or from user charges of various sorts.[4]

However, there is a paradox associated with the public provision of public goods. Public provision does not just happen. Political pressure must be mobilized to encourage the institutions of government to make this provision a matter of public policy. Bills must be passed, appropriations enacted, and government agencies created. In short, political actors must be persuaded to act. But, if the provision of a public good distributes some benefit widely, and if the enjoyment of that benefit is unrelated to whether a contribution has been made toward mobilizing politicians to act, then we may reasonably ask: Why would any individual or interest group lobby the government for public goods? Why wouldn't they, instead, free-ride on the efforts of others, thereby freeing up their own resources either to lobby for some other private benefits or to deploy in the private sector for private gain? That is, if many public services are like public goods, then their supply depends upon individuals and groups successfully engaging in collective action to get the government to provide them. Since magic wands are not available, the "public supply" solution to the provision of public goods becomes a problem in collective action.

. . . First, we must distinguish between the *consumption* of a public good and its *production*.[5] When designating a good as public or private, we are really talking about consumption properties—whether you can exclude others from consuming the good or not and whether consumption diminishes the availability of the good. We have not remarked at all about production. In fact, in nearly every instance public goods are produced with substantial private input.

When the U.S. government began constructing a massive federal highway system in 1956, it was not intended for the government to get into the concrete business, the paint business, the sign- or guardrail-making business, or even the highway construction business. The government would use its taxing and borrowing powers to raise money, on the one hand, and its substantive political authority to make choices about highway routes and road attributes, on the other. But it would then request proposals for building highways from private contractors subject to these specifications. Successful contractors—actors from the market economy—would then make the concrete, pour it according to design, paint the yellow lines in the middle, assemble guardrails, signage, and overpasses, and so on.

The highway system, surely public in consumption, is in fact mostly *private* in production. Various aspects of the production process can be divvied up among contractors. The contract to provide concrete, for example, is excludable (the winning contractor gets the contract and can bar losing bidders from sharing in the associated profit) and is solitarily supplied (giving the contract to A eliminates its availability to B, C, D, . . .).

. . . So, who do you suppose lobbies for a highway system? On the consumption side, as we have seen, there are collective action problems. By conventional means they may be overcome to some extent. Thus, the American Automobile Association and the American Trucking Association, representing different segments of the consuming public, undoubtedly brought their political muscle to bear on legislators and executive branch officials in behalf of a highway program. Similarly, there are likely to have been political entrepreneurs taking up the cause—for example, legislators representing districts containing large transshipment centers (Chicago, Denver) and automobile and truck manufacturing facilities (Detroit, St. Louis, Akron, Toledo). But surely those most likely to gain *directly and im-*

mediately (and less likely to have been as plagued by collective action problems as groups on the consumption side) are those that would actually *produce* the public good. Concrete producers, highway contractors, makers of heavy equipment, manufacturers of guardrails and steel supports for overpasses, owners of rights-of-way, and many others all stood to make enormous sums of money from this multibillion-dollar project. In short, the politics of public supply is as much about the production of public goods as it is about their consumption.

The lesson here is that the politics of public supply cannot be adequately understood as a collective action phenomenon among those wishing to consume public goods. Consumers of public goods like good highways, clean air, lighthouses, and security from national defense, certainly play a role in providing political pressure. They are, however, limited by the collective-action obstacles with which the reader is now familiar. In fact, their interests often never materialize into group action; they remain latent. On the other hand, for every reference to consumers of national defense, to take one of the most important public goods, there are thousands of references to the "military-industrial complex," those who profit directly from the production of national defense. They are Olson's "privileged groups" who have the ability to surmount their own collective action problems and the incentive to do so (profits). They are found in the committee rooms and hallways of the Capitol, testifying, lobbying, and spreading campaign dollars around to any legislator who will take up their cause. In trying to understand the public supply of public goods, then, the astute observer will look to the supply side as well as the demand side of the "market."

Before concluding this discussion let us note several complaints lodged against public supply. The major concern with public supply as a solution to the problem of providing public goods is that public sector actors may not have "good" incentives. In this version of the "who will guard the guardians" problem, the question is not whether government is capable of supplying public goods, but rather is how well it does the job.

A classic instance of this involves the production of scientific knowledge. Many kinds of knowledge constitute public goods to the extent that they cannot be patented or copyrighted. Once it is known, for example, that $e = mc^2$, individuals cannot be excluded from this knowledge, on the one hand, and one person knowing it does not diminish its availability, on the other. . . .

The production of scientific knowledge is undertaken very substantially by the private sector—in places like California's Silicon Valley, Boston's

Route 128, and North Carolina's Research Triangle. But this kind of research tends to be very applied, tied to specific product development, conducted secretly, and often patentable (thereby preventing those who do not "own" it from making use of it). Thus, applied scientific research, to the degree that property rights may be assigned to its products, is essentially a private good. However, basic or fundamental research—research that often does not have immediate application—is not patentable and thus cannot be owned; it therefore tends to be underproduced by the private sector for all the public-goods reasons mentioned earlier.

Consequently, the U.S. government, through various agencies like the National Science Foundation, the National Institutes of Health, the National Aeronautics and Space Administration, the Department of Energy, and the Department of Defense, sponsor basic scientific research—a clear instance of the public provision of a public good. Some of this research is actually done in government laboratories. But much is contracted out to university scientists. Consider now the incentives facing, first, the legislators who provide the financial resources for, and oversee the execution of, this public good and, second, the bureaucrats that actually administer the programs.

As it happens, the universities that are best positioned to compete for basic research grants are not randomly distributed throughout the territorial United States. While many locations have the capability, there are discernible concentrations of excellence: the Bay Area, Los Angeles, and Seattle on the west coast; Chicago and Minneapolis in mid-America; Chapel Hill–Durham–Raleigh, Miami, and Atlanta in the south; and Washington, New York, and Boston on the east coast—to name some of the most prominent. If the National Science Foundation (NSF), for example, were to support research proposals strictly on the basis of merit, a disproportionate amount of its budget would be spent in these pockets of excellence.[6] Institutions in a great majority of the legislative districts of the nation would do rather poorly in the competition. And this, in turn, would not kindly dispose their representatives toward NSF. In short, while legislators may generally approve of producing public goods like scientific knowledge, they are much more focused on getting federal dollars for citizens and institutions in *their* districts. A government agency that flouted this concern of large numbers of legislators would undoubtedly not fare well in the annual appropriations process.

The administrators at NSF are not stupid. They can forecast the profound budgetary problems their agency would encounter if it did not attend to the conditions of representative government. So, they arrange for alternatives to merit-based allocation mechanisms. Instead of earmarking their entire budget for basic research—which would end up being spent chiefly in a small number of pockets of research excellence—they invent new categories and new programs in which less well-endowed parts of the country are competitive. Research in science education (as opposed to pure science), for example, may be quite competently conducted in many places around the country, places that do not require advanced research laboratories and cutting-edge scientists.

Constituency-oriented legislators and survival-oriented bureaucrats and administrators, not philosopher kings, support, finance and administer public programs that produce public goods. Their incentives dispose them to move away from what would be optimal if only the most effective production of public goods were motivating them. Public provision, then, is watered down by these competing, indeed distracting, objectives. Thus, while public provision may seem the best way to go in correcting for the underproduction of public goods, it is not without its shortcomings.

A second incentive distortion associated with public provision involves *time horizons*. Many scientific projects are years in the making. The initial phases are often relatively inexpensive and invisible, as ideas are examined, developed, and tested in small ways. Only after these initial hurdles are cleared are greater sums spent on large-scale testing and development. It is the latter, however, that involve new laboratory facilities, expensive high-tech equipment, or advanced testing sites—the sorts of things to which the local legislator can point with pride (and snip the ribbon at the dedication ceremony heavily covered by the local media). The political pressures associated with public provision, as a result, involve truncating the longer incubation and percolation process ideally associated with scientific research into a much shorter time horizon.[7]

To sum up, the production of public goods is a problem for communities because of the very nature of these products. Private incentives are typically insufficient to encourage their production voluntarily. Some sort of political fix is required, examples of which include grants of monopoly privilege, waivers of antitrust laws, public subsidy of private production, and outright public provision. None of these is ideal because each entails the grant of extraordinary privilege or authority to some individual—the lord of the manor, the firm granted a monopoly, a public-sector bureaucrat—whose incentives may not be aligned properly to the social objectives being sought. The lord of the manor wants prestige and glory, not public defense; the firm wants profits, not a national highway system; the bureaucrat wants turf and budget authority, not scientific discoveries. The public good is the incidental by-product of, not the motivation for, their behavior.

It is, therefore, not surprising that different communities at different times experiment with alternative (imperfect) solutions. In the past few years, for example, we have witnessed a tidal wave of change in which public sectors that formerly provided public goods directly are abandoning these activities. Under the rubric of *privatization,* both developing political economies and already developed ones are selling off state-owned assets to the private sector, hoping that, imperfect as they may be, private-sector incentives will be better aligned to social objectives than under the former arrangement of direct public provision. This may also entail technological enhancements that mitigate some of the "publicness" of the good.[8] We also observe the related phenomenon of *deregulation* in which heavy-handed bureaucratic oversight, command, and control are being relaxed or relinquished altogether. The imperfectness of any solution to the production of public goods stimulates this experimentation; but politico-economic change of this magnitude is, as we have emphasized, political through and through, with winners and losers determined at the end of the day in political arenas.

NOTES

1. Coase's essay first appeared in 1974, and has been reprinted in R. H. Coase, *The Firm, the Market, and the Law* (Chicago: University of Chicago Press, 1988), pp. 187–215.

2. . . . [T]he astute reader might wonder whether there are alternatives to granting an entrepreneur monopoly rights. That is, even if there were several wharfs and warehouses in port, their owners might arrange to jointly finance a lighthouse and cover their costs through charges on their port services. This is an interesting possibility that the reader might like to think through. Note, however, that this type of cooperation is, in a modern context, regarded as a violation of antitrust laws, because it essentially entails price-fixing. A waiver from antitrust prohibitions, like protection of monopoly power, is a *political* necessity.

3. A sophisticated strategic analysis of OPEC, with Saudi Arabia conceived of as a dominant member seeking to preserve its reputation, is found in James E. Alt, Randall Calvert, and Brian Humes, "Reputation and Hegemonic Stability," *American Political Science Review* 82 (1988): 445–466.

4. The reader should notice that public goods, as we have defined them, and publicly provided goods may not be the same. The latter *may* be public goods, like lighthouses and national defense; but the state provides lots of other goodies—like mail delivery, for

example—that are sufficiently like other private goods that they undoubtedly could be provided reasonably well in the marketplace. (Indeed, courier services, overnight mail delivery, and package delivery are provided privately in direct competition with the U.S. Postal Service.) Publicly provided goods and services—the activities in which governments engage—reflect the political advantages possessed by interests in the political process that are sufficient to induce the public sector to do their bidding. Surely some of these things are public goods, but not all of them.

5. This distinction is made persuasively by Peter Aranson and Peter Ordeshook, "Public Interest, Private Interest, and the Democratic Polity," in Roger Benjamin and Stephen Elkin, eds., *The Democratic State* (Lawrence, Kans.: University of Kansas Press, 1985).

6. If instead we were discussing the production of art and culture as financed by grants from the National Endowment for the Arts, merit-based concentration would be even more extreme with New York and Los Angeles securing the lion's share of support.

7. This argument is elaborated in Linda Cohen and Roger Noll, *The Technology Pork Barrel* (Washington: Brookings Institution, 1991).

8. For example, electronic lighthouses emit an electronic signal, rather than a light, which is received only by those ships that *purchase* the special signal detector. Cable television, likewise, requires a cable box and hookup that permits exclusion (thereby privatizing a public good). A public water supply may be metered at each household, thereby permitting user charges; so, too, may a firm's effluent (via sewer or smokestack), thus allowing for the pricing of its use of the environment as a dumping site.

1-3

Everything Must Go!

Beth Dickey

One possible solution to the problem of collective action is privatization, an idea that became increasingly attractive in the 1980s and 1990s as the federal government worked to extricate itself from annual budget deficits. By implementing incentives that reward those providing collective goods according to their performance, policy makers have tried to keep the problem of free riding to a minimum. In the following article Beth Dickey recounts one such instance—the privatization of many of the activities of NASA, the nation's space agency.

HISTORICALLY ON THE leading edge of technology, NASA now is on the leading edge of government privatization. The nation's premier research-and-development agency is rapidly selling itself off to the private sector, outsourcing everything from desktop computers to rocket science in its efforts to control or cut costs. Although the 40-year-old space agency has often been criticized for standing in the way of free enterprise, the pace, depth and theory of NASA's commercialization go far beyond what would be considered aggressive in other government agencies. This is a new frontier in privatized federal government, where almost anything is up for sale and little is considered sacrosanct—inherently governmental, that is.

"Every year, we tell the Congress that the goal of our government should be nothing short of opening the frontier of space to all Americans," says Ransom Wuller, an Illinois lawyer who presides over the nationwide ProSpace lobby and its annual "March Storm" of legislative offices on Capitol Hill. "We think that can happen if the government helps stimulate the private sector to take over the functions we think we could do better. I would propose putting the (space) shuttle up for auction—at least one of them," Wuller says, "and seeing what it would fetch."

With their exorbitant operating costs—not to mention the number of miles on them and their nearly obsolete early-1970s technology—none of the space shuttles would fetch close to the $2 billion it cost to build. But selling a taxpayer-financed shuttle to a private space company is just one of many options NASA is considering as it pushes to commercialize its day-to-day activities, guided in part by the 1998 Commercial Space Act.

Among other things, the law:

- requires the federal government to buy space-transportation services instead of building and operating its own vehicles;
- permits the use of surplus intercontinental ballistic missiles as low-cost disposable space launchers;
- authorizes the Transportation Department to issue atmospheric re-entry licenses for a new generation of space shuttles—privately developed reusable launch vehicles, or RLVs—that will fly back to land after completing commercial space missions;
- orders NASA to plan for the privatization of the space shuttle, the nation's only space transportation for humans;
- instructs NASA to evaluate markets for commercializing the international space station now under construction.

"The vast potential of the commercial space industry has been constrained by government regulations and laws that have not kept pace with the latest technology and changes in the marketplace," said Rep. James Sensenbrenner, R-Wis., a sponsor of the law, in a written statement upon passage of the bill in October. For NASA, which already considers itself 90 percent contracted, the new law is merely a navigational aid to be used on a course the agency already has charted.

. . . Recently, NASA lured back Daniel Tam, director of planning and investments for TRW's Space and Electronics Group, to be the agency's first commercialization czar. He had served as space station business manager from 1994 to 1997. Tam's new job is to look for opportunities to commercialize NASA's infrastructure, operations and technology. He will reach out to the broader public sectors, including industry, academia and other government organizations, to accelerate deployment of NASA-developed technologies outside the aerospace sector.

"We believe (that) by increasing and accelerating the commercial application and utilization of some of what we do, we'll help NASA focus on what we do best, which is the cutting-edge technologies—the going places where nobody has gone before," Tam says. . . .

Throughout government, the controversy about privatization and out-sourcing centers on what is inherently governmental—and, therefore, should remain in government hands—and what is not. The 1998 Federal Activities Inventory Reform Act (FAIR) requires executive agencies annu-ally to publish a list of their activities that are not inherently governmental and could be contracted out to federal or private bidders. The Pentagon is trying to put up for public–private competition some 230,000 civilian jobs from now through 2005—far more than the 90,000 it competed between 1979 and 1996.

NASA has taken a different path, one far beyond that contemplated by FAIR or even the Defense Department. Nonetheless, Tam's biggest chal-lenge will be to convince the entrenched bureaucracy that there should be no limits. "I personally don't have any desire or requirements to say that there are certain things that are holier than the others or more sacred than the others. It's all a matter of how and when," he says. "To me, the ultimate end game is to commercialize all of this.". . .

Last November, the 23,000-member National Space Society, a Washing-ton advocacy group, lauded NASA's commercial development plan for the international space station as "an encouraging step in the right direction." The society's statement said, "A body outside government bureaucracy will be better positioned to respond to the needs of industrial users, which should accelerate the rate of commercial customer sign-up for use of the station." The most significant proposal in the plan, the society said, is to shift from a cost-based pricing system to one based on value for research and manufacturing aboard the space station.

How Far, How Fast?

With all the talk of privatization at the Defense Department and elsewhere, the handing off of NASA chunk by chunk to contractors hasn't captured much attention in the mainstream press. But the handoffs raise interesting questions about the appropriate role of government in one of its last fron-tiers, pure science; about how privatization should be handled; and about what functions are inherently governmental and what are not. NASA already is one of the most contracted agencies in government. How far can, and should, privatization go?

Historically, NASA has contracted for support of its activities. The contracts specified a level of effort to be provided, not the results to be achieved. Without clearly stated contract objectives, civil servants had to maintain heavy surveillance of the work. But for the past three years, the goal has been to implement performance-based contracting "wherever it makes sense," says Ken Sateriale, a NASA procurement specialist. Performance-based contracts can give the contractor incentives to innovate, save the government money because it no longer pays a "marching army" of workers for a term of employment, and reduce the need for government surveillance. The new rule is insight, as opposed to oversight. "You're monitoring the contractor's activity, but you might be doing it through reports or data," Sateriale says.

But the gradual loss of control by civil servants has brought out concerns ranging from technical security to astronaut safety. NASA's Aerospace Safety Advisory Panel has urged caution in the commercialization of the human space flight program. In its annual report released in February, the panel repeated earlier warnings about the combined effect of workforce downsizing, a hiring freeze and the USA takeover of space shuttle operations. The situation "has raised the possibility that NASA senior managers in the future will lack the necessary hands-on technical knowledge and in-line experience to provide effective insight," according to the panel.

After almost three years under the new contract with USA, NASA civil servants still try to exercise well-intentioned, but not necessarily legal, oversight of shuttle work. Launch integration manager Don McMonagle, a former astronaut, acknowledges that for many civil servants, "it's difficult to step back and monitor the performance of this contract and only insert yourselves where you see a problem has developed." Contract monitor Jack Boykin in Houston dismisses such reactions as "human nature," but acknowledges that "this has been one of the problems with consolidation all across the board. People don't like (it) when they're not controlling the purse strings." . . .

Throughout history, government's role has been to underwrite the exploration of new frontiers. The railroads and the airlines began as government enterprises. "The government paid for lots of that early development and infrastructure," says Tam, "and now you see the whole thing truly is commercialized." The engineers of NASA's commercialization see public–private partnerships as the only way NASA will be able to venture deeper into space. "If we try to do it on public funding alone, we won't get there," says utilization manager Mark Uhran. "This is not as much NASA selling out its assets as it is NASA getting into public–private partnerships to allow us to continue to move out."

◂

1-4

The Tragedy of the Commons

Garrett Hardin

In this seminal article, Garrett Hardin identifies another class of collective action problems, the "tragedy of the commons." The concept—a "tragedy" because of the inevitability with which public goods, or the "commons," will be exploited—is generally applied to study cases in which natural resources are being misused. Unlike the problems we have already encountered, which concern the production of public goods, the tragedy of the commons affects their conservation. Because public goods are freely available, members of the community will be tempted to overly consume them—to overfish, to overuse national parks, to pollute public water or air—even as they realize their behavior and that of their neighbors is destroying the goods. Hardin discusses social arrangements that can substitute for the commons, or public ownership of scarce resources, and argues that that the tragedy of commons is becoming a more pressing concern as the population increases. As with the problem of free riding described by Mancur Olson, government authority offers one solution extricating participants from their bind.

AT THE END of a thoughtful article on the future of nuclear war, Wiesner and York concluded that: "Both sides in the arms race are . . . confronted by the dilemma of steadily increasing military power and steadily decreasing national security. *It is our considered professional judgment that this dilemma has no technical solution.* If the great powers continue to look for solutions in the area of science and technology only, the result will be to worsen the situation."[1]

I would like to focus your attention not on the subject of the article (national security in a nuclear world) but on the kind of conclusion they

Excerpted with permission from *Science*, December 3, 1968, pp. 1243–1248. Copyright 1968 American Association for the Advancement of Science.

reached, namely that there is no technical solution to the problem. An implicit and almost universal assumption of discussions published in professional and semipopular scientific journals is that the problem under discussion has a technical solution. A technical solution may be defined as one that requires a change only in the techniques of the natural sciences, demanding little or nothing in the way of change in human values or ideas of morality.

In our day (though not in earlier times) technical solutions are always welcome. . . . [Yet] it is easy to show that the class of human problems which can be called "no technical solution problems," is not a null class. Recall the game of tick-tack-toe. Consider the problem, "How can I win the game of tick-tack-toe?" It is well known that I cannot, if I assume (in keeping with the conventions of game theory) that my opponent understands the game perfectly. Put another way, there is no "technical solution" to the problem. I can win only by giving a radical meaning to the word "win." I can hit my opponent over the head; or I can drug him; or I can falsify the records. Every way in which I "win" involves, in some sense, an abandonment of the game, as we intuitively understand it. (I can also, of course, openly abandon the game—refuse to play it. This is what most adults do.)

The class of "No technical solution problems" has members. My thesis is that the "population problem," as conventionally conceived, is a member of this class. How it is conventionally conceived needs some comment. It is fair to say that most people who anguish over the population problem are trying to find a way to avoid the evils of overpopulation without relinquishing any of the privileges they now enjoy. They think that farming the seas or developing new strains of wheat will solve the problem—technologically. I try to show here that the solution they seek cannot be found. The population problem cannot be solved in a technical way, any more than can the problem of winning the game of tick-tack-toe.

What Shall We Maximize?

Population, as Malthus said, naturally tends to grow "geometrically," or, as we would now say, exponentially. In a finite world this means that the per capita share of the world's goods must steadily decrease. Is ours a finite world?

A fair defense can be put forward for the view that the world is infinite; or that we do not know that it is not. But, in terms of the practical problems that we must face in the next few generations with the foreseeable technology, it is clear that we will greatly increase human misery if we do not, during the immediate future, assume that the world available to the terrestrial human population is finite. "Space" is no escape.[2]

A finite world can support only a finite population; therefore, population growth must eventually equal zero. . . . When this condition is met, what will be the situation of mankind? Specifically, can [Jeremy] Bentham's goal of "the greatest good for the greatest number" be realized? . . .

The . . . reason [why not] springs directly from biological facts. To live, any organism must have a source of energy (for example, food). This energy is utilized for two purposes: mere maintenance and work. For man, maintenance of life requires about 1600 kilocalories a day ("maintenance calories"). Anything that he does over and above merely staying alive will be defined as work, and is supported by "work calories" which he takes in. Work calories are used not only for what we call work in common speech; they are also required for all forms of enjoyment, from swimming and automobile racing to playing music and writing poetry. If our goal is to maximize population it is obvious what we must do: We must make the work calories per person approach as close to zero as possible. No gourmet meals, no vacations, no sports, no music, no literature, no art. . . . I think that everyone will grant, without argument or proof, that maximizing population does not maximize goods. Bentham's goal is impossible. . . .

The optimum population is, then, less than the maximum. The difficulty of defining the optimum is enormous; so far as I know, no one has seriously tackled this problem. Reaching an acceptable and stable solution will surely require more than one generation of hard analytical work—and much persuasion. . . .

We can make little progress in working toward optimum population size until we explicitly exorcize the spirit of Adam Smith in the field of practical demography. In economic affairs, *The Wealth of Nations* (1776) popularized the "invisible hand," the idea that an individual who "intends only his own gain," is, as it were, "led by an invisible hand to promote . . . the public interest."[3] Adam Smith did not assert that this was invariably true, and perhaps neither did any of his followers. But he contributed to a dominant tendency of thought that has ever since interfered with positive action based on rational analysis, namely, the tendency to assume that decisions reached individually will, in fact, be the best decisions for an entire society. If this assumption is correct it justifies the continuance of our present policy of laissez-faire in reproduction. If it is correct we can assume that men will control their individual fecundity so as to produce the optimum population. If the assumption is not correct, we need to reexamine our individual freedoms to see which ones are defensible.

Tragedy of Freedom in a Commons

The rebuttal to the invisible hand in population control is to be found in a scenario first sketched in a little-known pamphlet in 1833 by a mathematical amateur named William Forster Lloyd (1794–1852).[4] We may well call it "the tragedy of the commons," using the word "tragedy" as the philosopher Whitehead used it: "The essence of dramatic tragedy is not unhappiness. It resides in the solemnity of the remorseless working of things."[5] He then goes on to say, "This inevitableness of destiny can only be illustrated in terms of human life by incidents which in fact involve unhappiness. For it is only by them that the futility of escape can be made evident in the drama."

The tragedy of the commons develops in this way. Picture a pasture open to all. It is to be expected that each herdsman will try to keep as many cattle as possible on the commons. Such an arrangement may work reasonably satisfactorily for centuries because tribal wars, poaching, and disease keep the numbers of both man and beast well below the carrying capacity of the land. Finally, however, comes the day of reckoning, that is, the day when the long-desired goal of social stability becomes a reality. At this point, the inherent logic of the commons remorselessly generates tragedy.

As a rational being, each herdsman seeks to maximize his gain. Explicitly or implicitly, more or less consciously, he asks, "What is the utility *to me* of adding one more animal to my herd?" This utility has one negative and one positive component.

1. The positive component is a function of the increment of one animal. Since the herdsman receives all the proceeds from the sale of the additional animal, the positive utility is nearly +1.

2. The negative component is a function of the additional overgrazing created by one more animal. Since, however, the effects of overgraz-

ing are shared by all the herdsmen, the negative utility for any particular decision-making herdsman is only a fraction of –1.

Adding together the component partial utilities, the rational herdsman concludes that the only sensible course for him to pursue is to add another animal to his herd. And another; and another. . . . But this is the conclusion reached by each and every rational herdsman sharing a commons. Therein is the tragedy. Each man is locked into a system that compels him to increase his herd without limit—in a world that is limited. Ruin is the destination toward which all men rush, each pursuing his own best interest in a society that believes in the freedom of the commons. Freedom in a commons brings ruin to all.

Some would say that this is a platitude. Would that it were! In a sense, it was learned thousands of years ago, but natural selection favors the forces of psychological denial.[6] The individual benefits as an individual from his ability to deny the truth even though society as a whole, of which he is a part, suffers. Education can counteract the natural tendency to do the wrong thing, but the inexorable succession of generations requires that the basis for this knowledge be constantly refreshed.

A simple incident that occurred a few years ago in Leominster, Massachusetts, shows how perishable the knowledge is. During the Christmas shopping season the parking meters downtown were covered with plastic bags that bore tags reading: "Do not open until after Christmas. Free parking courtesy of the mayor and city council." In other words, facing the prospect of an increased demand for already scarce space, the city fathers reinstituted the system of the commons. (Cynically, we suspect that they gained more votes than they lost by this retrogressive act.)

In an approximate way, the logic of the commons has been understood for a long time, perhaps since the discovery of agriculture or the invention of private property in real estate. But it is understood mostly only in special cases which are not sufficiently generalized. Even at this late date, cattlemen leasing national land on the western ranges demonstrate no more than an ambivalent understanding, in constantly pressuring federal authorities to increase the head count to the point where overgrazing produces erosion and weed-dominance. Likewise, the oceans of the world continue to suffer from the survival of the philosophy of the commons. Maritime nations still respond automatically to the shibboleth of the "freedom of the seas." Professing to believe in the "inexhaustible resources of the oceans," they bring species after species of fish and whales closer to extinction.[7]

The National Parks present another instance of the working out of the tragedy of the commons. At present, they are open to all, without limit. The parks themselves are limited in extent—there is only one Yosemite Valley—whereas population seems to grow without limit. The values that visitors seek in the parks are steadily eroded. Plainly, we must soon cease to treat the parks as commons or they will be of no value to anyone.

What shall we do? We have several options. We might sell them off as private property. We might keep them as public property, but allocate the right to enter them. The allocation might be on the basis of wealth, by the use of an auction system. It might be on the basis of merit, as defined by some agreed-upon standards. It might be by lottery. Or it might be on a first-come, first-served basis, administered to long queues. These, I think, are all the reasonable possibilities. They are all objectionable. But we must choose—or acquiesce in the destruction of the commons that we call our National Parks.

Pollution

In a reverse way, the tragedy of the commons reappears in problems of pollution. Here it is not a question of taking something out of the commons, but of putting something in—sewage, or chemical, radioactive, and heat wastes into water; noxious and dangerous fumes into the air; and distracting and unpleasant advertising signs into the line of sight. The calculations of utility are much the same as before. The rational man finds that his share of the cost of the wastes he discharges into the commons is less than the cost of purifying his wastes before releasing them. Since this is true for everyone, we are locked into a system of "fouling our own nest," so long as we behave only as independent, rational, free-enterprisers.

The tragedy of the commons as a food basket is averted by private property, or something formally like it. But the air and waters surrounding us cannot readily be fenced, and so the tragedy of the commons as a cesspool must be prevented by different means, by coercive laws or taxing devices that make it cheaper for the polluter to treat his pollutants than to discharge them untreated. We have not progressed as far with the solution of this problem as we have with the first. Indeed, our particular concept of private property, which deters us from exhausting the positive resources of the earth, favors pollution. The owner of a factory on the bank of a stream—whose property extends to the middle of the stream—often has difficulty seeing why it is not his natural right to muddy the waters flowing past his door. The law, always behind the times, requires elaborate stitching and fitting to adapt it to this newly perceived aspect of the commons.

The pollution problem is a consequence of population. It did not much matter how a lonely American frontiersman disposed of his waste. "Flowing water purifies itself every 10 miles," my grandfather used to say, and the myth was near enough to the truth when he was a boy, for there were not too many people. But as population became denser, the natural chemical and biological recycling processes became overloaded, calling for a redefinition of property rights.

How to Legislate Temperance?

Analysis of the pollution problem as a function of population density uncovers a not generally recognized principle of morality, namely: *the morality of an act is a function of the state of the system at the time it is performed.*[8] Using the commons as a cesspool does not harm the general public under frontier conditions, because there is no public; the same behavior in a metropolis is unbearable. A hundred and fifty years ago a plainsman could kill an American bison, cut out only the tongue for his dinner, and discard the rest of the animal. He was not in any important sense being wasteful. Today, with only a few thousand bison left, we would be appalled at such behavior.

In passing, it is worth noting that the morality of an act cannot be determined from a photograph. One does not know whether a man killing an elephant or setting fire to the grassland is harming others until one knows the total system in which his act appears. "One picture is worth a thousand words," said an ancient Chinese; but it may take 10,000 words to validate it. It is as tempting to ecologists as it is to reformers in general to try to persuade others by way of the photographic shortcut. But the essence of an argument cannot be photographed: it must be presented rationally—in words.

That morality is system-sensitive escaped the attention of most codifiers of ethics in the past. "Thou shalt not . . ." is the form of traditional ethical directives which make no allowance for particular circumstances. The laws of our society follow the pattern of ancient ethics, and therefore are poorly suited to governing a complex, crowded, changeable world. Our epicyclic solution is to augment statutory law with administrative law. Since it is practically impossible to spell out all the conditions under which it is safe to burn trash in the back yard or to run an automobile without smog-control, by law we delegate the details to bureaus. The result is administrative law, which is rightly feared for an ancient reason—*Quis custodiet ipsos custodes?*— "Who shall watch the watchers themselves?" John Adams said that we must have "a government of laws and not men." Bureau administrators, trying to evaluate the morality of acts in the total system, are singularly liable to corruption, producing a government by men, not laws.

Prohibition is easy to legislate (though not necessarily to enforce); but how do we legislate temperance? Experience indicates that it can be accomplished best through the mediation of administrative law. We limit possibilities unnecessarily if we suppose that the sentiment of *Quis custodiet* denies us the use of administrative law. We should rather retain the phrase as a perpetual reminder of fearful dangers we cannot avoid. The great challenge facing us now is to invent the corrective feedbacks that are needed to keep custodians honest. We must find ways to legitimate the needed authority of both the custodians and the corrective feedbacks.

Freedom to Breed Is Intolerable

The tragedy of the commons is involved in population problems in another way. In a world governed solely by the principle of "dog eat dog"—if indeed there ever was such a world—how many children a family had would not be a matter of public concern. Parents who bred too exuberantly would leave fewer descendants, not more, because they would be unable to care adequately for their children. David Lack and others have found that such a negative feedback demonstrably controls the fecundity of birds.[9] But men are not birds, and have not acted like them for millenniums, at least.

If each human family were dependent only on its own resources; *if* the children of improvident parents starved to death; *if*, thus, overbreeding brought its own "punishment" to the germ line—*then* there would be no public interest in controlling the breeding of families. But our society is deeply committed to the welfare state,[10] and hence is confronted with another aspect of the tragedy of the commons.

In a welfare state, how shall we deal with the family, the religion, the race, or the class (or indeed any distinguishable and cohesive group) that adopts overbreeding as a policy to secure its own aggrandizement?[11] To couple the concept of freedom to breed with the belief that everyone born has an equal right to the commons is to lock the world into a tragic course of action.

Unfortunately this is just the course of action that is being pursued by the United Nations. In late 1967, some 30 nations agreed to the following: "The Universal Declaration of Human Rights describes the family as the natural and fundamental unit of society. It follows that any choice and decision with regard to the size of the family must irrevocably rest with the family itself, and cannot be made by anyone else." [12] It is painful to have to deny categorically the validity of this right; denying it, one feels as uncomfortable as a resident of Salem, Massachusetts, who denied the reality of witches in the 17th century. At the present time, in liberal quarters, something like a taboo acts to inhibit criticism of the United Nations. There is a feeling that the United Nations is "our last and best hope," that we shouldn't find fault with it; we shouldn't play into the hands of the arch-conservatives. However, let us not forget what Robert Louis Stevenson said: "The truth that is suppressed by friends is the readiest weapon of the enemy." If we love the truth we must openly deny the validity of the Universal Declaration of Human Rights, even though it is promoted by the United Nations. We should also join with Kingsley Davis in attempting to get Planned Parenthood–World Population to see the error of its ways in embracing the same tragic ideal.[13] . . .

. . . The argument has here been stated in the context of the population problem, but it applies equally well to any instance in which society appeals to an individual exploiting a commons to restrain himself for the general good—by means of his conscience. To make such an appeal is to set up a selective system that works toward the elimination of conscience from the race.

Pathogenic Effects of Conscience

It is a mistake to think that we can control the breeding of mankind in the long run by an appeal to conscience. . . . If we ask a man who is exploiting a commons to desist "in the name of conscience," what are we saying to him? What does he hear?—not only at the moment but also in the wee small hours of the night when, half asleep, he remembers not merely the words we used but also the nonverbal communication cues we gave him unawares? Sooner or later, consciously or subconsciously, he senses that he has received two communications, and that they are contradictory: (i) (intended communication) "If you don't do as we ask, we will openly condemn you for not acting like a responsible citizen"; (ii) (the unintended communication) "If you *do* behave as we ask, we will secretly condemn you for a simpleton who can be shamed into standing aside while the rest of us exploit the commons." . . .

To conjure up a conscience in others is tempting to anyone who wishes to extend his control beyond the legal limits. Leaders at the highest level succumb to this temptation. Has any President during the past generation failed to call on labor unions to moderate voluntarily their demands for higher wages, or to steel companies to honor voluntary guidelines on prices? I can recall none. The rhetoric used on such occasions is designed to produce feelings of guilt in noncooperators.

For centuries it was assumed without proof that guilt was a valuable, perhaps even an indispensable, ingredient of the civilized life. Now, in this post-Freudian world, we doubt it.

Paul Goodman speaks from the modern point of view when he says: "No good has ever come from feeling guilty, neither intelligence, policy, nor compassion. The guilty do not pay attention to the object but only to themselves, and not even to their own interests, which might make sense, but to their anxieties." [14]

One does not have to be a professional psychiatrist to see the consequences of anxiety. We in the Western world are just emerging from a dreadful two-centuries-long Dark Ages of Eros that was sustained partly by prohibition laws, but perhaps more effectively by the anxiety-generating mechanisms of education. Alex Comfort has told the story well in *The Anxiety Makers;* it is not a pretty one. [15]

Since proof is difficult, we may even concede that the results of anxiety may sometimes, from certain points of view, be desirable. The larger question we should ask is whether, as a matter of policy, we should ever encourage the use of a technique the tendency (if not the intention) of which is psychologically pathogenic. We hear much talk these days of responsible parenthood; the coupled words are incorporated into the titles of some organizations devoted to birth control. Some people have proposed massive propaganda campaigns to instill responsibility into the nation's (or the world's) breeders. But what is the meaning of the word responsibility in this context? Is it not merely a synonym for the word conscience? When we use the word responsibility in the absence of substantial sanctions are we not trying to browbeat a free man in a commons into acting against his own interest? Responsibility is a verbal counterfeit for a substantial *quid pro quo*. It is an attempt to get something for nothing.

If the word responsibility is to be used at all, I suggest that it be in the sense Charles Frankel uses it.[16] "Responsibility," says this philosopher, "is the product of definite social arrangements." Notice that Frankel calls for social arrangements—not propaganda.

Mutual Coercion; Mutually Agreed Upon

The social arrangements that produce responsibility are arrangements that create coercion, of some sort. Consider bank-robbing. The man who takes money from a bank acts as if the bank were a commons. How do we prevent such action? Certainly not by trying to control his behavior solely by a verbal appeal to his sense of responsibility. Rather than rely on propaganda we follow Frankel's lead and insist that a bank is not a commons; we seek the definite social arrangements that will keep it from becoming a commons. That we thereby infringe on the freedom of would-be robbers we neither deny nor regret.

The morality of bank-robbing is particularly easy to understand because we accept complete prohibition of this activity. We are willing to say "Thou shalt not rob banks," without providing for exceptions. But temperance also can be created by coercion. Taxing is a good coercive device. To keep downtown shoppers temperate in their use of parking space we introduce parking meters for short periods, and traffic fines for longer ones. We need not actually forbid a citizen to park as long as he wants to; we need merely make it increasingly expensive for him to do so. Not prohibition, but carefully biased options are what we offer him. A Madison Avenue man might call this persuasion; I prefer the greater candor of the word coercion.

Coercion is a dirty word to most liberals now, but it need not forever be so. As with the four-letter words, its dirtiness can be cleansed away by exposure to the light, by saying it over and over without apology or embarrassment. To many, the word coercion implies arbitrary decisions of distant and irresponsible bureaucrats; but this is not a necessary part of its meaning. The only kind of coercion I recommend is mutual coercion, mutually agreed upon by the majority of the people affected.

To say that we mutually agree to coercion is not to say that we are required to enjoy it, or even to pretend we enjoy it. Who enjoys taxes? We all grumble about them. But we accept compulsory taxes because we recognize that voluntary taxes would favor the conscienceless. We institute and (grumblingly) support taxes and other coercive devices to escape the horror of the commons.

An alternative to the commons need not be perfectly just to be preferable. With real estate and other material goods, the alternative we have chosen is the institution of private property coupled with legal inheritance. Is this system perfectly just? As a genetically trained biologist I deny that it is. It seems to me that, if there are to be differences in individual inheritance, legal possession should be perfectly correlated with biological inheritance—that those who are biologically more fit to be the custodians of property and power should legally inherit more. But genetic recombination continually makes a mockery of the doctrine of "like father, like son" implicit in our laws of legal inheritance. An idiot can inherit millions, and a trust fund can keep his estate intact. We must admit that our legal system of private property plus inheritance is unjust—but we put up with it because we are not convinced, at the moment, that anyone has invented a better system. The alternative of the commons is too horrifying to contemplate. Injustice is preferable to total ruin.

It is one of the peculiarities of the warfare between reform and the status quo that it is thoughtlessly governed by a double standard. Whenever a reform measure is proposed it is often defeated when its opponents triumphantly discover a flaw in it. As Kingsley Davis has pointed out,[17] worshippers of the status quo sometimes imply that no reform is possible without unanimous agreement, an implication contrary to historical fact. As nearly as I can make out, automatic rejection of proposed reforms is based on one of two unconscious assumptions: (i) that the status quo is perfect; or (ii) that the choice we face is between reform and no action; if the proposed reform is imperfect, we presumably should take no action at all, while we wait for a perfect proposal.

But we can never do nothing. That which we have done for thousands of years is also action. It also produces evils. Once we are aware that the status quo is action, we can then compare its discoverable advantages and disadvantages with the predicted advantages and disadvantages of the proposed reform, discounting as best we can for our lack of experience. On the basis of such a comparison, we can make a rational decision which will not involve the unworkable assumption that only perfect systems are tolerable.

Recognition of Necessity

Perhaps the simplest summary of this analysis of man's population problems is this: the commons, if justifiable at all, is justifiable only under conditions of low-population density. As the human population has increased, the commons has had to be abandoned in one aspect after another.

First we abandoned the commons in food gathering, enclosing farm land and restricting pastures and hunting and fishing areas. These restrictions are still not complete throughout the world.

Somewhat later we saw that the commons as a place for waste disposal would also have to be abandoned. Restrictions on the disposal of domestic sewage are widely accepted in the Western world; we are still struggling to close the commons to pollution by automobiles, factories, insecticide sprayers, fertilizing operations, and atomic energy installations.

In a still more embryonic state is our recognition of the evils of the commons in matters of pleasure. There is almost no restriction on the propagation of sound waves in the public medium. The shopping public is assaulted with mindless music, without its consent. Our government is paying out billions of dollars to create supersonic transport which will disturb 50,000 people for every one person who is whisked from coast to coast 3 hours faster. Advertisers muddy the airwaves of radio and television and pollute the view of travelers. We are a long way from outlawing the commons in matters of pleasure. Is this because our Puritan inheritance makes us view pleasure as something of a sin, and pain (that is, the pollution of advertising) as the sign of virtue?

Every new enclosure of the commons involves the infringement of somebody's personal liberty. Infringements made in the distant past are accepted because no contemporary complains of a loss. It is the newly proposed infringements that we vigorously oppose; cries of "rights" and "freedom" fill the air. But what does "freedom" mean? When men mutually agreed to pass laws against robbing, mankind became more free, not less so. Individuals locked into the logic of the commons are free only to bring on universal ruin; once they see the necessity of mutual coercion, they become free to pursue other goals. I believe it was Hegel who said, "Freedom is the recognition of necessity."

The most important aspect of necessity that we must now recognize, is the necessity of abandoning the commons in breeding. No technical solution can rescue us from the misery of overpopulation. Freedom to breed will bring ruin to all. At the moment, to avoid hard decisions many of us are tempted to propagandize for conscience and responsible parenthood. The temptation must be resisted, because an appeal to independently acting consciences selects for the disappearance of all conscience in the long run, and an increase in anxiety in the short.

The only way we can preserve and nurture other and more precious freedoms is by relinquishing the freedom to breed, and that very soon. "Freedom is the recognition of necessity"—and it is the role of education to reveal to all the necessity of abandoning the freedom to breed. Only so, can we put an end to this aspect of the tragedy of the commons.

NOTES

1. J. B. Wiesner and H. F. York, *Sci. Amer.* 211 (No. 4), 27 (1964).

2. G. Hardin, *J. Hered.* 50, 68 (1959); S. von Hoernor, *Science* 137, 18 (1962).

3. A. Smith, *The Wealth of Nations* (Modern Library, New York, 1937), p. 423.

4. W. F. Lloyd, *Two Lectures on the Checks to Population* (Oxford Univ. Press, Oxford, England, 1833), reprinted (in part) in *Population, Evolution, and Birth Control,* G. Hardin, Ed. (Freeman, San Francisco, 1964), p. 37.

5. A. N. Whitehead, *Science and the Modern World* (Mentor, New York, 1948), p. 17.

6. G. Hardin, Ed. *Population, Evolution and Birth Control* (Freeman, San Francisco, 1964), p. 56.

7. S. McVay, *Sci. Amer.* 216 (No. 8), 13 (1966).

8. J. Fletcher, *Situation Ethics* (Westminster, Philadelphia, 1966).

9. D. Lack, *The Natural Regulation of Animal Numbers* (Clarendon Press, Oxford, 1954).

10. H. Girvetz, *From Wealth to Welfare* (Stanford Univ. Press, Stanford, Calif., 1950).

11. G. Hardin, *Perspec. Biol. Med.* 6, 366 (1963).

12. U. Thant, *Int. Planned Parenthood News,* No. 168 (February 1968), p. 3.

13. K. Davis, *Science* 158, 730 (1967).

14. P. Goodman, *New York Rev. Books* 10(8), 22 (23 May 1968).

15. A. Comfort, *The Anxiety Makers* (Nelson, London, 1967).

16. C. Frankel, *The Case for Modern Man* (Harper, New York, 1955), p. 203.

17. J. D. Roslansky, *Genetics and the Future of Man* (Appleton-Century-Crofts, New York, 1966), p. 177.

1-5

Quotas Might Save both Fish and Fishers

John McQuaid

A classic instance of what Garret Hardin called "the tragedy of the commons" can be seen in the devastating consequences that have followed from open access to ocean fisheries. In the following article, one of a Pulitzer Prize winning series published in the New Orleans Times-Picayune, *John McQuaid describes how this collective action problem has affected the surf clam fishery and details recent efforts by the government to solve it.*

FOR YEARS, surf clam fisherman Mike Garvilla was forced to shuffle paperwork under a bewildering array of regulations designed to protect the species from overfishing. Government agents told him which days and which hours he could fish, often regardless of the weather. Competition forced him to range far up the coast for days at a time. But six years ago, Garvilla, 36, became a rare phenomenon in these days of vanishing fish and eroding fishing jobs: a happy fisherman.

Now he fishes whenever and wherever he wants. He takes his boat, the *Betty C. II,* about 15 miles due east of Ocean City—an easy two-hour trip. He drops the stern-mounted, 22-foot dredge with a built-in hydraulic pump, blasts clams out of the sand and into the metal cage, then hauls them to the surface with electric winches. He's back by mid-afternoon. "It's a completely different situation," he said. "We have our freedom, and it feels good for a change."

Garvilla is part of a management experiment that could revolutionize fishing around the world by establishing property rights for fishers over the animals they catch for the first time in history. The program, proposed for the Gulf of Mexico red snapper, is called an Individual Transferable Quota (ITQ). It would assign each certified fisher a share of the year's preset total catch. He could fish any time he wanted to fill that quota, or sell or lease his share to someone else. The change would be this century's version of fencing the open range—a government-sanctioned takeover of an open resource, all in the name of saving it.

The theory is alluring: Giving fishers a direct financial stake in the resource would encourage conservation and end the mad rush to outfish rivals, a competition that has depleted many fish populations. But the reality would mean painful trade-offs.

"There is a tradition of wanting all fisheries to have open access. That's a cultural thing," said Carolyn Creed, a fishery anthropologist who co-authored a Rutgers University study of the several ITQ programs, including surf clams. "But the history of open access is pretty grim. So we're forced into the hard choices."

If it's widely implemented, as some experts predict, ITQs would transform commercial fishing in the Gulf into something unrecognizable. Only certified "professional" fishers could work. The lucky ones, however, would probably be better off. Creating property rights over fish would turn fishing into something closer to farming, with the crop effectively owned by the people who bring it in. ITQs are supposed to bring the free market to bear on fishing fleets, where normal market forces have been distorted by subsidies, overinvestment and the unconventional economics of a resource owned by no one.

In some places, they have had positive results. New Zealand has ITQs for 32 species of fish, part of a coordinated fishery development and management program. Fishing employment and ownership of quota shares has risen in the past 10 years, cutting against the trend of economic collapse elsewhere in the world. ITQs address the problem of overbuilt fleets by strictly limiting who may fish—usually those with a documented history of catching the fish being regulated. Managers assign a fraction of an annual quota to each fisher—or in some cases, each boat or fishing enterprise. The fisher must stop once the quota is reached. That eliminates the short seasons and derby fishing found in many fisheries, including the red snapper. Instead of seeing prices drop when everyone sells their catch at once during a derby, landings would be spread over time and the price would remain stable.

Finally, the T in ITQ means they can be transferred, creating a marketplace for the shares, a policy designed to consolidate them in the most economically efficient hands. Transferability would accelerate the slow shakeout of boats and employment occurring around the world, almost instantly creating winners and losers. And in many places, the losers would greatly outnumber the winners.

Revealing Experiment

The surf clam fishery was ideal for the ITQ experiment in ways many others are not. Surf clams are a small fishery. Boats sell only to a few companies that make processed fish products. The fleet size—about 135 boats—made it easier to arrive at a consensus among boat owners.

Still, its lessons are dramatic. Before the ITQ system took effect, the fleet was in bad shape. "Expenses had gone up, the fleet had become old, boats were unsafe, they'd lost people at sea. There was a knowledge that as things stood, many were going to go out of business. It just wasn't working," Creed said.

With an overall catch capped to preserve the stock, boats could fish only once every two weeks, for six hours. In Garvilla's case, it was every other Tuesday, from 8 A.M. to 2 P.M. If the weather on the designated day was bad, fishers could make it up the next day. But if bad weather continued, they had to wait another two weeks. That, and other mishaps such as engine trouble, often left them losing money.

When the ITQ program started in 1990, after a period of meetings and consensus-building among the boat owners and managers of the Mid-Atlantic Fishery Management Council, most boat owners ended up with small quotas. "I did not have enough allocation to make a living at it," said Joe Garvilla, Mike's father, who owns the *Betty C. II* along with his son. "If the quota is divided up properly at first, everybody is going to be unhappy. So when you come up with an ITQ plan, you've either got to buy or sell."

Over the next five years, the fleet size dropped by about 100 boats as their owners sold or leased their shares. Most of the boats ended up junked. Many people lost their jobs when companies and individuals consolidated their shares, though the number of jobs was shrinking even before the program began. But ITQs also provide a means for struggling boat owners to get out, something not easily accomplished before. "It allows them to leave the fishery with some resources," said Rutgers fishery anthropologist Bonnie McCay, who collaborated on the ITQ study with Creed. "If you quit farming you can sell the farm and move to Florida. In fishing, that's not the case because your boat has depreciated." With the experimental system, fishers have their quotas to sell.

But ITQs have sparked bitter opposition. Opponents say transferability would allow large entities to come in and dominate small operators—in effect eliminating the freedom that defines fishing, turning fishers into little better than sharecroppers. Even before the ITQ process started, big companies combining all the elements of seafood production—fishing, processing and marketing—dominated the surf clam fishery. ITQs accelerated the process.

Without limits on shares, critics say, ITQs could allow companies to corner a market and set the price, leaving consumers at their mercy. Proponents say the rules can be written to prevent concentrating too many shares in too few hands. Managers like the quota system because it's simpler than the current snarl of regulations. But whether it promotes conservation is unclear. McCay and Creed's study, for example, showed that in one Canadian fleet, it tended to increase the capture of bigger fish to ensure the largest profit margin—a practice that removes the best breeders from a stock. And under the U.S. system, the overall quotas would still be set by the regional Fishery Management Councils, which have often caved in to industry pressure to relax or delay conservation measures.

Meanwhile, Congress has gotten jittery on the issue. It appears poised to put off new ITQ programs for five years so they can be studied further, which may increase pressure on fish stocks. "There will be a mad rush by assorted fishing interests to acquire catch histories during the period of the moratorium so that they will be in a position to claim shares when it ends," said international fishery consultant Francis Christy, who is credited with introducing ITQs. "It will be the trumpet call for the start of a massive derby." ITQ proponents say it's transferability that makes the system work. Without it, they say, there is no way to consolidate shares, but also no incentive—and perhaps no way—for small operators to make their enterprises more profitable or even to get out of the business. "Without transferability, this is a crock," said Louisiana red snapper fisher Ron Anderson, who supports the ITQ snapper program, which was set to start this year but is now in political limbo.

1-6

The Prosperous Community

SOCIAL CAPITAL AND PUBLIC LIFE

Robert D. Putnam

The solutions to all of the problems presented in this chapter require participants to cooperate—to pay their taxes, to refrain from overfishing, to fix their polluting vehicles, and the like—even as each participant recognizes that he or she would be rewarded by failing to cooperate. This situation not only endangers a community's ability to achieve its collective goals; it engenders mutual suspicion and hostility among community members as well. In the article that follows, Robert Putnam argues persuasively that successful cooperation breeds success in the future. If we trust our neighbors to follow through on their commitments, then we are more likely to do the same.

> Your corn is ripe today; mine will be so tomorrow. 'Tis profitable for us both, that I should labour with you today, and that you should aid me tomorrow. I have no kindness for you, and know you have as little for me. I will not, therefore, take any pains upon your account; and should I labour with you upon my own account, in expectation of a return, I know I should be disappointed, and that I should in vain depend upon your gratitude. Here then I leave you to labour alone; You treat me in the same manner. The seasons change; and both of us lose our harvests for want of mutual confidence and security.
>
> —DAVID HUME

THE PREDICAMENT of the farmers in Hume's parable is all too familiar in communities and nations around the world:

- Parents in communities everywhere want better educational opportunities for their children, but collaborative efforts to improve public schools falter.

- Residents of American ghettos share an interest in safer streets, but collective action to control crime fails.
- Poor farmers in the Third World need more effective irrigation and marketing schemes, but cooperation to these ends proves fragile.
- Global warming threatens livelihoods from Manhattan to Mauritius, but joint action to forestall this shared risk founders.

Failure to cooperate for mutual benefit does not necessarily signal ignorance or irrationality or even malevolence, as philosophers since Hobbes have underscored. Hume's farmers were not dumb, or crazy, or evil; they were trapped. Social scientists have lately analyzed this fundamental predicament in a variety of guises: the tragedy of the commons; the logic of collective action; public goods; the prisoners' dilemma. In all these situations, as in Hume's rustic anecdote, everyone would be better off if everyone could cooperate. In the absence of coordination and credible mutual commitment, however, everyone defects, ruefully but rationally, confirming one another's melancholy expectations.

How can such dilemmas of collective action be overcome, short of creating some Hobbesian Leviathan? Social scientists in several disciplines have recently suggested a novel diagnosis of this problem, a diagnosis resting on the concept of *social capital*. By analogy with notions of physical capital and human capital—tools and training that enhance individual productivity— "social capital" refers to features of social organization, such as networks, norms, and trust, that facilitate coordination and cooperation for mutual benefit. Social capital enhances the benefits of investment in physical and human capital.

Working together is easier in a community blessed with a substantial stock of social capital. This insight turns out to have powerful practical implications for many issues on the American national agenda—for how we might overcome the poverty and violence of South Central Los Angeles, or revitalize industry in the Rust Belt, or nurture the fledgling democracies of the former Soviet empire and the erstwhile Third World. . . .

How does social capital undergird good government and economic progress? First, networks of civic engagement foster sturdy norms of generalized reciprocity: I'll do this for you now, in the expectation that down the road you or someone else will return the favor. "Social capital is akin to what Tom Wolfe called the 'favor bank' in his novel *The Bonfire of the Vanities*," notes economist Robert Frank. A society that relies on generalized reciprocity is more efficient than a distrustful society, for the same reason that money is more efficient than barter. Trust lubricates social life.

Networks of civic engagement also facilitate coordination and communication and amplify information about the trustworthiness of other individuals. Students of prisoners' dilemmas and related games report that cooperation is most easily sustained through repeat play. When economic and political dealing is embedded in dense networks of social interaction, incentives for opportunism and malfeasance are reduced. This is why the diamond trade, with its extreme possibilities for fraud, is concentrated within close-knit ethnic enclaves. Dense social ties facilitate gossip and other valuable ways of cultivating reputation—an essential foundation for trust in a complex society.

Finally, networks of civic engagement embody past success at collaboration, which can serve as a cultural template for future collaboration. The civic traditions of north-central Italy provide a historical repertoire of forms of cooperation that, having proved their worth in the past, are available to citizens for addressing new problems of collective action.

Sociologist James Coleman concludes, "Like other forms of capital, social capital is productive, making possible the achievement of certain ends that would not be attainable in its absence. . . . In a farming community . . . where one farmer got his hay baled by another and where farm tools are extensively borrowed and lent, the social capital allows each farmer to get his work done with less physical capital in the form of tools and equipment." Social capital, in short, enables Hume's farmers to surmount their dilemma of collective action.

Stocks of social capital, such as trust, norms, and networks, tend to be self-reinforcing and cumulative. Successful collaboration in one endeavor builds connections and trust—social assets that facilitate future collaboration in other, unrelated tasks. As with conventional capital, those who have social capital tend to accumulate more—them as has, gets. Social capital is what the social philosopher Albert O. Hirschman calls a "moral resource," that is, a resource whose supply increases rather than decreases through use and which (unlike physical capital) becomes depleted if *not* used.

Unlike conventional capital, social capital is a "public good," that is, it is not the private property of those who benefit from it. Like other public goods, from clean air to safe streets, social capital tends to be underprovided by private agents. This means that social capital must often be a by-product of other social activities. Social capital typically consists in ties, norms, and trust transferable from one social setting to another. . . .

Social Capital and Economic Development

Social capital is coming to be seen as a vital ingredient in economic development around the world. Scores of studies of rural development have shown that a vigorous network of indigenous grassroots associations can be as essential to growth as physical investment, appropriate technology, or (that nostrum of neoclassical economists) "getting prices right." Political scientist Elinor Ostrom has explored why some cooperative efforts to manage common pool resources, like grazing grounds and water supplies, succeed, while others fail. Existing stocks of social capital are an important part of the story. Conversely, government interventions that neglect or undermine this social infrastructure can go seriously awry.

Studies of the rapidly growing economies of East Asia almost always emphasize the importance of dense social networks, so that these economies are sometimes said to represent a new brand of "network capitalism." These networks, often based on the extended family or on close-knit ethnic communities like the overseas Chinese, foster trust, lower transaction costs, and speed information and innovation. Social capital can be transmuted, so to speak, into financial capital: In novelist Amy Tan's *Joy Luck Club*, a group of mah-jong–playing friends evolves into a joint investment association. China's extraordinary economic growth over the last decade has depended less on formal institutions than on *guanxi* (personal connections) to underpin contracts and to channel savings and investment. . . .

Bill Clinton's proposals for job-training schemes and industrial extension agencies invite attention to social capital. The objective should not be merely an assembly-line injection of booster shots of technical expertise and work-related skills into individual firms and workers. Rather, such programs could provide a matchless opportunity to create productive new linkages among community groups, schools, employers, and workers, without creating costly new bureaucracies. Why not experiment with modest subsidies for training programs that bring together firms, educational institutions, and community associations in innovative local partnerships? The latent effects of such programs on social capital accumulation could prove even more powerful than the direct effects on technical productivity.

Conversely, when considering the effects of economic reconversion on communities, we must weigh the risks of destroying social capital. Precisely because social capital is a public good, the costs of closing factories and destroying communities go beyond the personal trauma borne by individuals. Worse yet, some government programs themselves, such as urban renewal and public housing projects, have heedlessly ravaged existing social networks. The fact that these collective costs are not well measured by our current accounting schemes does not mean that they are not real. Shred enough of the social fabric and we all pay.

Social Capital and America's Ills

Fifty-one deaths and 1 billion dollars in property damage in Los Angeles . . . put urban decay back on the American agenda. Yet if the ills are clear, the prescription is not. Even those most sympathetic to the plight of America's ghettos are not persuaded that simply reviving the social programs dismantled in the last decade or so will solve the problems. The erosion of social capital is an essential and under-appreciated part of the diagnosis.

Although most poor Americans do not reside in the inner city, there is something qualitatively different about the social and economic isolation experienced by the chronically poor blacks and Latinos who do. Joblessness, inadequate education, and poor health clearly truncate the opportunities of ghetto residents. Yet so do profound deficiencies in social capital.

Part of the problem facing blacks and Latinos in the inner city is that they lack "connections" in the most literal sense. Job-seekers in the ghetto have little access, for example, to conventional job referral networks. Labor economists Anne Case and Lawrence Katz have shown that, regardless of race, inner-city youth living in neighborhoods blessed with high levels of civic engagement are more likely to finish school, have a job, and avoid drugs and crime, controlling for the individual characteristics of the youth. That is, of two identical youths, the one unfortunate enough to live in a neighborhood whose social capital has eroded is more likely to end up hooked, booked, or dead. Several researchers seem to have found similar neighborhood effects on the incidence of teen pregnancy, among both blacks and whites, again controlling for personal characteristics. Where you live and whom you know—the social capital you can draw on—helps to define who you are and thus to determine your fate.

Racial and class inequalities in access to social capital, if properly measured, may be as great as inequalities in financial and human capital, and no less portentous. Economist Glenn Loury has used the term "social capital" to capture the fundamental fact that racial segregation, coupled with socially inherited differences in community networks and norms, means that individually targeted "equal opportunity" policies may not eliminate racial inequality, even in the long run. Research suggests that the life chances of today's generation depend not only on their parents' social resources, but also on the social resources of their parents' ethnic group. Even workplace integration and upward mobility by successful members of minority groups cannot overcome these persistent effects of inequalities in social capital. William Julius Wilson has described in tragic detail how the exodus of middle-class and working-class families from the ghetto has eroded the social capital available to those left behind. The settlement houses that nurtured sewing clubs and civic activism a century ago, embodying community as much as charity, are now mostly derelict.

It would be a dreadful mistake, of course, to overlook the repositories of social capital within America's minority communities. . . . Historically, the black church has been the most bounteous treasure-house of social capital for African Americans. The church provided the organizational infrastructure for political mobilization in the civil rights movement. Recent work on American political participation by political scientist Sidney Verba and his colleagues shows that the church is a uniquely powerful resource for political engagement among blacks—an arena in which to learn about public affairs and hone political skills and make connections.

In tackling the ills of Americas cities, investments in physical capital, financial capital, human capital, and social capital are complementary, not competing alternatives. Investments in jobs and education, for example, will be more effective if they are coupled with reinvigoration of community associations.

Some churches provide job banks and serve as informal credit bureaus, for example, using their reputational capital to vouch for members who may be ex-convicts, former drug addicts, or high school dropouts. In such cases the church does not merely provide referral networks. More fundamentally, wary employers and financial institutions bank on the church's ability to identify parishioners whose formal credentials understate their reliability. At the same time, because these parishioners value their standing in the church, and because the church has put its own reputation on the line, they have an additional incentive to perform. Like conventional capital for conventional borrowers, social capital serves as a kind of collateral for men and women who are excluded from ordinary credit or labor markets.

In effect, the participants pledge their social connections, leveraging social capital to improve the efficiency with which markets operate.

The importance of social capital for America's domestic agenda is not limited to minority communities. Take public education, for instance. The success of private schools is attributable, according to James Coleman's massive research, not so much to what happens in the classroom nor to the endowments of individual students, but rather to the greater engagement of parents and community members in private school activities. Educational reformers like child psychologist James Comer seek to improve schooling not merely by "treating" individual children but by deliberately involving parents and others in the educational process. Educational policymakers need to move beyond debates about curriculum and governance to consider the effects of social capital. Indeed, most commonly discussed proposals for "choice" are deeply flawed by their profoundly individualist conception of education. If states and localities are to experiment with voucher systems for education or child care, why not encourage vouchers to be spent in ways that strengthen community organization, not weaken it? Once we recognize the importance of social capital, we ought to be able to design programs that creatively combine individual choice with collective engagement.

Many people today are concerned about revitalizing American democracy. Although discussion of political reform in the United States focuses nowadays on such procedural issues as term limits and campaign financing, some of the ills that afflict the American polity reflect deeper, largely unnoticed social changes.

"Some people say that you usually can trust people. Others say that you must be wary in relations with people. Which is your view?" Responses to this question, posed repeatedly in national surveys for several decades, suggest that social trust in the United States has declined for more than a quarter century. By contrast, American politics benefited from plentiful stocks of social capital in earlier times. Recent historical work on the Progressive Era, for example, has uncovered evidence of the powerful role played by nominally non-political associations (such as women's literary societies) precisely because they provided a dense social network. Is our current predicament the result of a long-term erosion of social capital, such as community engagement and social trust?

Economist Juliet Schorr's discovery of "the unexpected decline of leisure" in America suggests that our generation is less engaged with one another outside the marketplace and thus less prepared to cooperate for shared goals. Mobile, two-career (or one-parent) families often must use the market for child care and other services formerly provided through family and neighborhood networks. Even if market-based services, considered individually, are of high quality, this deeper social trend is eroding social capital. There are more empty seats at the PTA and in church pews these days. While celebrating the productive, liberating effects of fuller equality in the workplace, we must replace the social capital that this movement has depleted.

Our political parties, once intimately coupled to the capillaries of community life, have become evanescent confections of pollsters and media consultants and independent political entrepreneurs—the very antithesis of social capital. We have too easily accepted a conception of democracy in which public policy is not the outcome of a collective deliberation about the public interest, but rather a residue of campaign strategy. The social capital approach, focusing on the indirect effects of civic norms and networks, is a much-needed corrective to an exclusive emphasis on the formal institutions of government as an explanation for our collective discontents. If we are to make our political system more responsive, especially to those who lack connections at the top, we must nourish grass-roots organization.

Classic liberal social policy is designed to enhance the opportunities of *individuals,* but if social capital is important, this emphasis is partially misplaced. Instead we must focus on community development, allowing space for religious organizations and choral societies and Little Leagues that may seem to have little to do with politics or economics. Government policies, whatever their intended effects, should be vetted for their indirect effects on social capital. If, as some suspect, social capital is fostered more by home ownership than by public or private tenancy, then we should design housing policy accordingly. Similarly, as Theda Skocpol has suggested, the direct benefits of national service programs might be dwarfed by the indirect benefits that could flow from the creation of social networks that cross class and racial lines. In any comprehensive strategy for improving the plight of America's communities, rebuilding social capital is as important as investing in human and physical capital. . . .

Wise policy can encourage social capital formation, and social capital itself enhances the effectiveness of government action. From agricultural extension services in the last century to tax exemptions for community organizations in this one, American government has often promoted investments in social capital, and it must renew that effort now. A new administration that is, at long last, more willing to use public power and the public purse for public purpose should not overlook the importance of social connectedness as a vital backdrop for effective policy.

Students of social capital have only begun to address some of the most important questions that this approach to public affairs suggests. What are the actual trends in different forms of civic engagement? Why do communities differ in their stocks of social capital? What *kinds* of civic engagement seem most likely to foster economic growth or community effectiveness? Must specific types of social capital be matched to different public problems? Most important of all, how is social capital created and destroyed? What strategies for building (or rebuilding) social capital are most promising? How can we balance the twin strategies of exploiting existing social capital and creating it afresh? The suggestions scattered throughout this essay are intended to challenge others to even more practical methods of encouraging new social capital formation and leveraging what we have already.

We also need to ask about the negative effects of social capital, for like human and physical capital, social capital can be put to bad purposes. Liberals have often sought to destroy some forms of social capital (from medieval guilds to neighborhood schools) in the name of individual opportunity. We have not always reckoned with the indirect social costs of our policies, but we were often right to be worried about the power of private associations. Social inequalities may be embedded in social capital. Norms and networks that serve some groups may obstruct others, particularly if the norms are discriminatory or the networks socially segregated. Recognizing the importance of social capital in sustaining community life does not exempt us from the need to worry about how that community is defined—who is inside and thus benefits from social capital, and who is outside and does not. Some forms of social capital can impair individual liberties, as critics of comunitarianism warn. Many of the Founders' fears about the "mischiefs of faction" apply to social capital. Before toting up the balance sheet for social capital in its various forms, we need to weigh costs as well as benefits. This challenge still awaits.

Progress on the urgent issues facing our country and our world requires ideas that bridge outdated ideological divides. Both liberals and conservatives agree on the importance of social empowerment, as E. J. Dionne recently noted ("The Quest for Community (Again)," *TAP,* Summer 1992). The social capital approach provides a deeper conceptual underpinning for this nominal convergence. Real progress requires not facile verbal agreement, but hard thought and ideas with high fiber content. The social capital approach promises to uncover new ways of combining private social infrastructure with public policies that work, and, in turn, of using wise public policies to revitalize America's stocks of social capital.

2

The Constitutional Framework

A constitution can be thought of as the means by which a political community resolves the various collective action problems surveyed in the previous chapter. A constitution creates a nation's governing institutions and rules prescribing a political process these institutions must follow to reach and enforce collective agreements. A constitution may be an informal understanding based on years of accumulated laws and precedents, as with Great Britain's "unwritten" constitution, or, as with the United States, it can be a highly formal, legal statement of rights and responsibilities.

Other communities had on occasion convened a group of leaders to write or rewrite the rules governing the political process, but most scholars agree that the Constitutional Convention of 1787 was unique. Never before had a group assembled with the sole purpose of formulating a proposal for a new national government to be placed before the citizenry for ratification.

In designing the new Constitution, America's leaders were profoundly influenced by ideas fashionable in the Age of Reason. Isaac Newton had recently formulated laws of mechanics, Adam Smith had described the law-like properties of the marketplace under capitalism, and prominent political theorists—most important, John Locke and Montesquieu—were publishing essays on constitutional design, essays that read in some places as if the Framers had hired them as consultants. But the Constitution is not a simple product of sweet reason. Rather, every provision reflects the competition and ultimately compromise among political interests that were vying for advantage in the new institutions and rules. As a consequence, many of the Constitution's provisions have no theoretical rationale; they are simply the hammered out products of compromise. The following essays display the competition of ideas and interests that resulted in the Constitution.

2-1

James Madison Explains the Constitution
to Thomas Jefferson

Shortly after the Constitutional Convention adjourned and as both sides were gearing up for the ratification campaign, James Madison wrote Thomas Jefferson, America's ambassador in Paris, to report on the Convention's work. Madison and Jefferson, both Virginians, were friends and allies who corresponded frequently, sometimes in code in case their letters were intercepted by political adversaries. The topics and arguments Madison covers in their private correspondence offer insight into the issues that most interested and occupied the "father of the Constitution." In the following excerpt from his correspondence with Jefferson, Madison expresses his concern that the new national government lacked a veto over state laws.

YOU WILL HEREWITH receive the result of the Convention, which continued its session till the 17th of September. I take the liberty of making some observations on the subject, which will help to make up a letter, if they should answer no other purpose.

It appeared to be the sincere and unanimous wish of the Convention to cherish and preserve the Union of the States. No proposition was made, no suggestion was thrown out, in favor of a partition of the Empire into two or more Confederacies.

It was generally agreed that the objects of the Union could not be secured by any system founded on the principle of a confederation of Sovereign States. A voluntary observance of the federal law by all the members could never be hoped for. A compulsive one could evidently never be reduced to practice, and if it could, involved equal calamities to the innocent and guilty, the necessity of a military force, both obnoxious and dangerous, and, in general, a scene resembling much more a civil war than the administration of a regular Government.

Excerpted from a letter to Thomas Jefferson dated October 24, 1787. The volume editors have added footnotes, editorial interpolations in brackets, headings to indicate the divisions of Madison's commentary, and italics to emphasize key points.

Hence was embraced the alternative of a Government which, instead of operating on the States, should operate without their intervention on the individuals composing them; and hence the change in the principle and proportion of representation.

This ground-work being laid, the great objects which presented themselves were: 1. To unite a proper energy in the Executive, and a proper stability in the Legislative departments, with the essential characters of Republican Government. 2. To draw a line of demarkation which would give to the General Government every power requisite for general purposes, and leave to the States every power which might be most beneficially administered by them. 3. To provide for the different interests of different parts of the Union. 4. To adjust the clashing pretensions of the large and small States. Each of these objects was pregnant with difficulties. The whole of them together formed a task more difficult than can be well conceived by those who were not concerned in the execution of it. Adding to these considerations the natural diversity of human opinions on all new and complicated subjects, it is impossible to consider the degree of concord which ultimately prevailed as less than a miracle.

Designing the Presidency and Senate

Presidential Selection

The first of these objects, as respects the Executive, was peculiarly embarrassing. On the question whether it should consist of a single person or a plurality of co-ordinate members, on the mode of appointment, on the duration in office, on the degree of power, on the re-eligibility, tedious and re-iterated discussions took place. The plurality of co-ordinate members had finally but few advocates. Governor [of Virginia] Randolph was at the head of them. The modes of appointment proposed were various: as by the people at large, by electors chosen by the people, by the Executives of the States, by the Congress; some preferring a joint ballot of the two Houses; some, a separate concurrent ballot, allowing to each a negative on the other house; some, a nomination of several candidates by one House, out of whom a choice should be made by the other. Several other modifications were started. The expedient at length adopted seemed to give pretty general satisfaction to the members. As to the duration in office, a few would have preferred a tenure during good behaviour; a considerable number would have done so in case an easy and effectual removal by impeachment could be settled.

Pros and Cons of Presidential Term Limits

It was much agitated whether a long term, seven years for example, with a subsequent and perpetual ineligibility, or a short term, with a capacity to be re-elected, should be fixed. In favor of the first opinion were urged the danger of a gradual degeneracy of re-elections from time to time, into first a life and then hereditary tenure, and the favorable effect of an incapacity to be reappointed on the independent exercise of the Executive authority. On the other side it was contended that the prospect of necessary degradation would discourage the most dignified characters from aspiring to the office; *would take away the principal motive to the faithful discharge of its duties—the hope of being rewarded with a reappointment;*[1] would stimulate ambition to violent efforts for holding over the Constitutional term; and instead of producing an independent administration and a firmer defense of the constitutional rights of the department, would render the officer more indifferent to the importance of a place which he would soon be obliged to quit forever, and more ready to yield to the encroachments of the Legislature, of which he might again be a member.

The President's Appointment and Veto Authority

The questions concerning the degree of power turned chiefly on the appointment to offices, and the controul on the Legislature. An absolute appointment to all offices, to some offices, to no offices, formed the scale of opinions on the first point. On the second, some contended for an absolute negative, as the only possible mean of reducing to practice the theory of a free Government, which forbids a mixture of the Legislative and Executive powers. Others would be content with a revisionary power, to be overruled by three-fourths of both Houses. It was warmly urged that the judi-

---

1. Madison is employing precisely the same reasoning that many political scientists now use to argue against term limits for members of Congress and state legislatures. Jefferson responded to Madison with two complaints about the Constitution—the first and better known of which being the absence of a bill of rights, and the second being the

ciary department should be associated in the revision. The idea of some was, that a separate revision should be given to the two departments; that if either objected, two-thirds, if both, three-fourths, should be necessary to overrule.

Designing the Senate

In forming the Senate, the great anchor of the government, the questions, as they come within the first object, turned mostly on the mode of appointment, and the duration of it. The different modes proposed were: 1. By the House of Representatives. 2. By the Executive. 3. By electors chosen by the people for the purpose. 4. By the State Legislatures. On the point of duration, the propositions descended from good behaviour to four years, through the intermediate terms of nine, seven, six, and five years. The election of the other branch was first determined to be triennial, and afterwards reduced to biennial.

Distributing Power between the States and the National Goverment

The second object, the due partition of power between the General and local Governments, was perhaps, of all, the most nice and difficult. A few contended for an entire abolition of the States; some, for indefinite power of Legislation in the Congress, with a negative on the laws of the States; some, for such a power without a negative; some, for a limited power of legislation, with such a negative; the majority, finally, for a limited power without the negative. The question with regard to the negative underwent repeated discussions, and was finally rejected by a bare majority. As I formerly intimated to you my opinion in favor of this ingredient, I will take this occasion of explaining myself on the subject. Such a check on the States appears to me necessary—1. To prevent encroachments on the

---

absence of a term limit on the presidency. With the passage of the Twenty-second Amendment in 1951 limiting a president's tenure to two terms, the Constitution finally conformed to Jefferson's preferences.

General authority. 2. To prevent instability and injustice in the legislation of the States.[2]

National Veto to Resolve Interbranch Conflict and Protect the Nation's Collective Good

1. Without such a check in the whole over the parts, our system involves the evil of imperia in imperio. *If a complete supremacy somewhere is not necessary in every society, a controuling power at least is so, by which the general authority may be defended against encroachments of the subordinate authorities, and by which the latter may be restrained from encroachments on each other.* If the supremacy of the British Parliament is not necessary, as has been contended, for the harmony of that Empire, it is evident, I think, that without the royal negative, or some equivalent controul, the unity of the system would be destroyed.[3] The want of some such provision seems to have been mortal to the antient confederacies, and to be the disease of the modern. Of the Lycian confederacy little is known. That of the Amphictyons is well known to have been rendered of little use whilst it lasted, and, in the end, to have been destroyed by the predominance of the local over the federal authority. The same observation may be made, on the authority of Polybius, with regard to the Achaean League. The Helvetic System scarcely amounts to a confederacy, and is distinguished by too many peculiarities to be a ground of comparison.

The case of the United Netherlands is in point. The authority of a Statdholder, the influence of a standing Army, the common interest in the conquered possessions, the pressure of surrounding danger, the guarantee of foreign powers, are not sufficient to secure the authority and interest of the generality against the anti-federal tendency of the provincial sovereignties.

2. At this point, Madison shifts from explaining and justifying the Constitution to complaining that it does not include provision for a national veto over state laws. While the present state of federalism in America generally allows the national government supremacy over the states without this rule, one must remember that the balance of power greatly favored the states until the Civil War.

3. Always a political scientist, Madison recapitulates briefly a comparative analysis of confederations he had circulated to Virginia's fellow delegates to the upcoming Philadelphia convention.

The German Empire is another example. A Hereditary chief, with vast independent resources of wealth and power, a federal Diet, with ample parchment authority, a regular Judiciary establishment, the influence of the neighbourhood of great and formidable nations, have been found unable either to maintain the subordination of the members, or to prevent their mutual contests and encroachments. Still more to the purpose is our own experience, both during the war and since the peace. Encroachments of the States on the general authority, sacrifices of national to local interests, interferences of the measures of different States, form a great part of the history of our political system.

It may be said that the new Constitution is founded on different principles, and will have a different operation. I admit the difference to be material. It presents the aspect rather of a feudal system of republics, if such a phrase may be used, than of a Confederacy of independent States. And what has been the progress and event of the feudal Constitutions? In all of them a continual struggle between the head and the inferior members, until a final victory has been gained, in some instances by one, in others, by the other of them. In one respect, indeed, there is a remarkable variance between the two cases. In the feudal system, the sovereign, though limited, was independent; and having no particular sympathy of interests with the great Barons, his ambition had as full play as theirs in the mutual projects of usurpation. In the American Constitution, the general authority will be derived entirely from the subordinate authorities. The Senate will represent the States in their political capacity; the other House will represent the people of the States in their individual capacity. The former will be accountable to their constituents at moderate, the latter at short periods. The President also derives his appointment from the States, and is periodically accountable to them. . . .

We find the representatives of Counties and Corporations in the Legislatures of the States much more disposed to sacrifice the aggregate interest, and even authority, to the local views of their constituents, than the latter to the former. I mean not by these remarks to insinuate that an esprit de corps will not exist in the National Government, or that opportunities may not occur of extending its jurisdiction in some points. I mean only that the danger of encroachments is much greater from the other side, and that the impossibility of dividing powers of legislation in such a manner as to be free from different constructions by different interests, or even from ambiguity in the judgement of the impartial, requires some such expedient as I contend for.[4] Many illustrations might be given of this impossibility. How long has it taken to fix, and how imperfectly is yet fixed, the legislative power of corporations, though that power is subordinate in the most compleat manner? The line of distinction between the power of regulating trade and that of drawing revenue from it, which was once considered the barrier of our liberties, was found, on fair discussion, to be absolutely undefinable. No distinction seems to be more obvious than that between spiritual and temporal matters. Yet, wherever they have been made objects of Legislation, they have clashed and contended with each other, till one or the other has gained the supremacy. Even the boundaries between the Executive, Legislative, and judiciary powers, though in general so strongly marked in themselves, consist, in many instances, of mere shades of difference.

It may be said that the Judicial authority, under our new system, will keep the States within their proper limits, and supply the place of a negative on their laws. The answer is, that it is more convenient to prevent the passage of a law than to declare it void after it is passed; that this will be particularly the case where the law aggrieves individuals, who may be unable to support an appeal against a State to the Supreme Judiciary; that a State which would violate the Legislative rights of the Union would not be very ready to obey a Judicial decree in support of them; and that a recurrence to force, which, in the event of disobedience, would be necessary, is an evil which the new Constitution meant to exclude as far as possible.

National Veto to Prevent State Tyranny

2. *A Constitutional negative on the laws of the States seems equally necessary to secure individuals against encroachments on their rights.* The mutability of the laws of the States is found to be a serious evil. The injustice of them has been so frequent and so flagrant as to alarm the most stedfast friends of Republicanism. I am persuaded I do not err in saying that the evils issuing from these sources contributed more to that uneasiness which produced the Convention, and prepared the public mind for a general reform, than

---

4. Madison is referring to his repeated efforts to give the national government a veto over the states. Not only, as he says above, will the states be more inclined "to sacrifice the aggregate interest" of the nation; he also implies that differences of view on policy are normal, requiring that one side be given the final authority to decide the matter.

those which accrued to our national character and interest from the inadequacy of the Confederation to its immediate objects. A reform, therefore, which does not make provision for private rights, must be materially defective. The restraints against paper emissions and violations of contracts are not sufficient. Supposing them to be effectual as far as they go, they are short of the mark. Injustice may be effected by such an infinitude of legislative expedients, that where the disposition exists, it can only be controuled by some provision which reaches all cases whatsoever. The partial provision made supposes the disposition which will evade it.

It may be asked how private rights will be more secure under the Guardianship of the General Government than under the State Governments, since they are both founded on the republican principle which refers the ultimate decision to the will of the majority, and are distinguished rather by the extent within which they will operate, than by any material difference in their structure.[5] A full discussion of this question would, if I mistake not, unfold the true principles of Republican Government, and prove, in contradiction to the concurrent opinions of the theoretical writers, that this form of Government, in order to effect its purposes, must operate not within a small but an extensive sphere. I will state some of the ideas which have occurred to me on this subject.

Why State Majorities Are More Dangerous Than National Majorities

Those who contend for a simple democracy, or a pure republic, actuated by the sense of the majority, and operating within narrow limits, assume or suppose a case which is altogether fictitious. They found their reasoning on the idea that the people composing the Society enjoy not only an equality of political rights, but that they have all precisely the same interests and the same feelings in every respect. Were this in reality the case, their reasoning would be conclusive. The interest of the majority would be that of the minority also; the decisions could only turn on mere opinion concerning the good of the whole, of which the major voice would be the safest criterion;

5. Here Madison launches into an argument that he had made several times during floor debates at the Convention and would reappear inside the month in the famous *Federalist* no. 10.

and within a small sphere, this voice could be most easily collected, and the public affairs most accurately managed.

Society's Pluralism

We know, however, that no society ever did, or can, consist of so homogeneous a mass of Citizens. In the Savage state, indeed, an approach is made towards it, but in that state little or no Government is necessary. In all civilized societies, distinctions are various and unavoidable. A distinction of property results from that very protection which a free Government gives to unequal faculties of acquiring it. There will be rich and poor; creditors and debtors; a landed interest, a monied interest, a mercantile interest, a manufacturing interest. These classes may again be subdivided according to the different productions of different situations and soils, and according to the different branches of commerce and of manufactures. In addition to these natural distinctions, artificial ones will be founded on accidental differences in political, religious, or other opinions, or an attachment to the persons of leading individuals. However erroneous or ridiculous these grounds of dissention and faction may appear to the enlightened Statesman or the benevolent philosopher, the bulk of mankind, who are neither Statesmen nor philosophers, will continue to view them in a different light.

Majorities as Self-Interested Rulers

It remains, then, to be enquired, whether a majority having any common interest, or feeling any common passion, will find sufficient motives to restrain them from oppressing the minority. An individual is never allowed to be a judge, or even a witness, in his own cause. If two individuals are under to bias of interest or enmity against a third, the rights of the latter could never be safely referred to the majority of the three. Will two thousand individuals be less apt to oppress one thousand, or two hundred thousand one hundred thousand?

Three motives only can restrain in such cases: 1. A prudent regard to private or partial good, as essentially involved in the general and permanent good of the whole. This ought, no doubt, to be sufficient of itself. Experience, however, shews that it has little effect on individuals, and perhaps still less on a collection of individuals, and least of all on a majority with the public authority in their hands. If the former are ready to forget that honesty is the best policy, the last do more. They often proceed on the converse of the maxim, that whatever is politic is honest. 2. Respect for character. This motive is not found sufficient to restrain individuals from injustice, and loses its efficacy in proportion to the number which is to divide the pain or the blame. Besides, as it has reference to public opinion, which is that of the majority, the standard is fixed by those whose conduct is to be measured by it. 3. Religion. The inefficacy of this restraint on individuals is well known. The conduct of every popular assembly, acting on oath, the strongest of religious ties, shews that individuals join without remorse in acts against which their consciences would revolt, if proposed to them, separately, in their closets. When, indeed, Religion is kindled into enthusiasm, its force, like that of other passions, is increased by the sympathy of a multitude. But enthusiasm is only a temporary state of Religion, and whilst it lasts will hardly be seen with pleasure at the helm. Even in its coolest state, it has been much oftener a motive to oppression that a restraint from it.

Why Majorities Will Be Weaker in the National Government Than within the States

If, then, there must be different interests and parties in society, and a majority, when united by a common interest or passion, cannot be restrained from oppressing the minority, what remedy can be found in a republican Government, where the majority must ultimately decide, but that of giving such an extent to its sphere, that no common interest or passion will be likely to unite a majority of the whole number in an unjust pursuit? In a large society, the people are broken into so many interests and parties, that a common sentiment is less likely to be felt, and the requisite concert less likely to be formed, by a majority of the whole. The same security seems requisite for the civil as for the religious rights of individuals. If the same sect form a majority, and have the power, other sects will be sure to be depressed. *Divide et impera,* the reprobated axiom of tyranny is, under certain qualifications, the only policy by which a republic can be administered on just principles.[6]

6. The Latin phrase translates to "divide and conquer," which was a well-known strategy often employed by kings and dictators to defeat those who would overthrow their regime. By empowering those majorities that will be riddled by society's pluralism, Madison is "dividing" the power of the ruler and thereby placing the principle in defense of democracy.

It must be observed, however, that this doctrine can only hold within a sphere of a mean extent. As in too small a sphere oppressive combinations may be too easily formed against the weaker party, so in too extensive a one a defensive concert may be rendered too difficult against the oppression of those entrusted with the administration. The great desideratum in Government is so to modify the sovereignty as that it may be sufficiently neutral between different parts of the society to control one part from invading the rights of another, and at the same time sufficiently controlled itself from setting up an interest adverse to that of the entire society. In absolute monarchies, the prince may be tolerably neutral towards different classes of his subjects, but may sacrifice the happiness of all to his personal ambition or avarice. In small republics, the sovereign will is controlled from such a sacrifice of the entire society, but is not sufficiently neutral towards the parts composing it. In the extended Republic of the United States, the General Government would hold a pretty even balance between the parties of particular States, and be at the same time sufficiently restrained, by its dependence on the community, from betraying its general interests.

Begging pardon for this immoderate digression, I return to the third object above mentioned, the adjustments of the different interests of different parts of the continent.[7] Some contended for an unlimited power over trade, including exports as well as imports, and over slave as well as other imports; some, for such a power, provided the concurrence of two-thirds of both Houses were required; some, for such a qualification of the power, with an exemption of exports and slaves; others, for an exemption of exports only. The result is seen in the Constitution. South Carolina and Georgia were inflexible on the point of the Slaves.

The Large–Small State Disagreement
that Led to the Great Compromise

The remaining object created more embarrassment, and a greater alarm for the issue of the Convention, than all the rest put together. The little States

---

7. Here Madison briefly reports the different interests that led to the political dealings reported in William Riker's essay below. Without laying out the details—for he knows that Jefferson, a keen politician, will figure out what happened at the Convention—he notes tersely, "The result can be seen in the Constitution."

insisted on retaining their equality in both branches, unless a compleat abolition of the State Governments should take place; and made an equality in the Senate a *sine qua non*. The large States, on the other hand, urged that as the new Government was to be drawn principally from the people immediately, and was to operate directly on them, not on the States; and, consequently, as the States would lose that importance which is now proportioned to the importance of their voluntary compliance with the requisitions of Congress, it was necessary that the representation in both Houses should be in proportion to their size. It ended in the compromise which you will see, but very much to the dissatisfaction of several members from the large States.

2-2

Trading Votes at the Constitutional Convention

William Riker

The delegates deliberating a new constitution for the nation did not approach their task as disinterested constitutional architects. Rather, they came to Philadelphia representing the particular interests of their respective states, interests which sometimes brought them into conflict with representatives from other states. Even those who might have been inclined to subordinate their states' interests to some higher public good were disciplined by the knowledge that ultimately their constituents would decide whether to ratify the new constitution. Everyone is familiar with the Grand Compromise between large and small states that resulted in the House of Representatives being apportioned on the basis of population, while the states were allowed equal representation in the Senate. In this essay, William Riker examines another, particularly crass exchange between the dominant economic interests of the North and South, involving the slave trade and Congress's authority to pass navigation acts. He reminds us that the delegates' success in arriving at a deal was probably just as instrumental to the Constitution's ratification as were the convention's loftier deliberations.

IN THE PUBLIC imagination legislators are constantly trading votes. Just as in the case of describing other popular but slightly disreputable activities like drinking alcohol, we have coined a variety of synonyms for vote-trading, such as "log-rolling," "back-scratching," or "going along," as in the practical cynicism of Sam Rayburn's remark "To get along, go along." The proliferation of synonyms reveals our (possibly naive) belief in the universality as well as the mild vulgarity of trading votes. It is even possible, as it happens, to date our sensitivity to the practice. In the latter quarter of the nineteenth century, at least seven states prohibited vote-trading by constitution or statute. No one, so far as I know, was ever prosecuted, and surely the practice has not abated since then. . . .

Widespread as vote-trading is thought to be, it is difficult to find well-documented and admitted instances of it. For one reason, politicians do not like to talk about it. When they do so, they reveal both that they have bought another's vote and that they have, for instrumental reasons, voted contrary to what they truly believe. That is, the vote-traders, in persuading someone else to vote for what the trader most wants, buys this support by casting his own vote against something he (and his constituents) may hold slightly less dear. However nobly inspired such commerce may be, constituents and others may misunderstand it, resenting the vote cast against their interest without appreciating what was bought with it. Naturally, therefore, legislative traders are not eager to talk about potentially misunderstood arrangements.

The main reason actual instances of vote-trading are difficult to identify, however, is that most of them take place in necessarily nonpublic circumstances. Vote-trading is expensive to carry out, especially in large legislatures where significant groups must be persuaded to act in concert to do something that some of them may be disinclined to do. Consequently, in modern legislatures most vote-trading goes on in private in small committees where alternatives can be discussed discreetly and agreements reached in a reasonable amount of time. Thus, in American legislatures, committees write bills in "markup" sessions (usually closed to the public, though no longer so in Congress), and the process of writing is the successive discovery of themes or formulations that satisfy every element of a winning coalition. Naturally, some of the themes are contradictory in spirit: What satisfies group A harms group B, and what satisfies B harms A. Yet, in a well-written bill, both A and B are on balance satisfied because each has been satisfied by desired themes more than harmed by undesired ones. This is, of course, what vote-trading consists of; and it is, to a considerable degree, the informality and privacy of the markup that make the literary effort successful.

One location where vote-trading is clearly visible is, thus, in the record of a secret and relatively small decision-making body. The Philadelphia Convention of 1787 was relatively small (on most days, about forty delegates), left a good record of its discussions (namely, Madison's *Notes*), and was extraordinarily secret—hardly any of its daily details were leaked either in correspondence or casual conversation, and apparently no one out-of-doors (except printers) saw the working papers.* Fortunately, there were a number of implicit and explicit trades and one of them constitutes the example for this essay.

TOWARD THE END of the Convention, two unrelated questions, among others, remained unresolved:

1. Should Congress be authorized to prohibit the slave trade immediately or should it be restrained from prohibition until some later date, say 1800 or 1808? For convenience, let "A" stand for the power of immediate prohibition, and "a" stand for the power of future prohibition.
2. Should Congress be authorized to pass navigation acts (i.e., acts prohibiting foreign ships from loading cargo in American ports) by a simple majority ("B") or by only a two-thirds majority ("b")?

Although the two issues are unrelated, they were brought together into a single dimension of judgment in order to facilitate ratification of the Constitution. What made the junction possible was nothing, I think, inherent in these issues as issues, but rather the fortunate accident that dominant opinions in the two main regions, North and South, were arranged so that a trade was possible.

[Table 1] shows that delegates from the Northern states most of all wanted (AB)—that is, simple majority rule on navigation acts (B) and immediate prohibition of the slave trade (A), and that the simple majority was more important than prohibition. (That is, failing to get their way on both, they would rather have aB than Ab.)

---

* The remarkable degree of secrecy in the Convention is suggested in an anecdote written by William Pierce (Ga.). Early in the Convention, members made copies of "propositions brought forward as great leading principles" (probably the Virginia plan). A member dropped his handwritten copy and it was found and picked up by Thomas Mifflin (Pa.), who gave it to Washington as presiding officer. At the end of the day, Washington addressed the Convention thus (as reconstructed by Pierce): "I am sorry to find that some one Member of this Body, has been so neglectful of the secrets of the Convention as to drop in the State House a copy of their proceedings, which by accident was picked up and delivered to me this morning. I must entreat Gentlemen to be more careful, lest our transactions get into the News Papers, and disturb the public repose by premature speculations. I know not whose Paper it is, but there it is (throwing it down on the table), let him who owns it take it." Pierce continued: "At the same time he bowed, picked up his hat, and quitted the room with a dignity so severe that every Person seemed alarmed." Furthermore, Pierce concluded: "It is something remarkable that no Person ever owned the Paper."

Table 1

Preference orders of delegates	Eastern[a] and Middle[b] states	Southern[c] states	Virginia
Most desired outcome	AB	ab	Ab
	aB	aB	ab
	Ab	Ab	AB
Least desired outcome	ab	AB	aB

a. Eastern: New Hampshire, Massachusetts, Connecticut.
b. Middle: New Jersey, Pennsylvania, Delaware.
c. Southern: Maryland, North Carolina, South Carolina, Georgia.

Note: New York delegates had gone home and Rhode Island did not send delegates.

The rationale for this ordering was, first, that the shipping and shipbuilding in Philadelphia, Boston, and all the smaller New England coastal towns, which had been severely restricted during the Revolution, had not subsequently revived because British navigation acts excluded American bottoms from both British and West Indian ports. Consequently, Northern commercial interests were eager to retaliate by prohibiting British ships from ports in the United States. Their hope was, of course, that this retaliation would lead to negotiation and thence to reconciliation and free trade, at least between these nations, as indeed did eventually come about.

The second element of the rationale of the Northern preference was that opinion in many Northern states was, as early as 1787, opposed to slavery and especially to the slave trade. Comparing the two issues, however, that of navigation acts, which touched on pocketbooks, was probably more salient to the Eastern delegations than the issue of slavery, which touched only on souls.

Southern delegates most desired (ab), that is, delay of prohibition to the future (a) and passage of navigation acts by a two-thirds majority (b). Especially by South Carolina and Georgia, rapidly developing states in need of field hands, the opportunity to import slaves freely was thought to be a vital economic interest. A lesser, but still important, economic interest was the two-thirds rule. Most Southerners expected that a navigation act closing Southern ports to foreign ships would increase their shipping costs. But a two-thirds rule, which would require 18 out of 26 senators to carry, would give the five Southern states a veto on navigation acts. Compared with the issue of the importation of slaves, however, the rule on navigation acts was economically trivial, at least for South Carolina and Georgia. Thus, for them (aB) was preferred over (Ab). North Carolina and Maryland delegates were less dependent on importation, however, so their delegates may have preferred (Ab) to (aB).

Virginia was in a strikingly different position, however, which is why I have separated it from the rest of the South. Its staple was tobacco, and its citizens were especially sensitive to shipping costs. At the same time, it had far more slaves than any other state and they were swiftly and naturally increasing. It was indeed to Virginia's advantage to prohibit the importation of slaves because then it would have a monopoly in selling its excess slaves to South Carolina and Georgia. So Virginian delegates, especially George Mason and Governor Randolph, much desired both immediate prohibition (A) and a two-thirds rule (b), though, as we shall see, the two-thirds rule was their main concern (Ab).

Looking at the preference orders of the delegations, it is obvious that a trade was possible. The second-best outcome for both Northern and Southern states was the combination of future prohibition (a) and simple majority (B). Only Virginians, for whom (aB) was the worst outcome, would be severely hurt by the trade. This obvious second best made nearly everybody (but Virginians) pretty happy and so one might reasonably expect the second best to occur, especially since a minority of the Virginia delegation on these issues (certainly Madison and probably Washington) were also quite satisfied with the outcome of a trade (aB).

In a strict sense, no trade was necessary. The six Eastern and Middle states had an absolute majority of the eleven delegations present; so they could have imposed their favored outcome, immediate prohibition and simple majority. But they were convinced, I believe, by the repeated assertions made by Southerners that immediate prohibition would lead South Carolina and Georgia to reject the Constitution absolutely and even to secede from the federation. For the sake of peace and federacy, the Northerners were willing to trade.

One might think of the trade as a regional arrangement. Since the proposed Constitution was already opposed by Rhode Island and New York (and perhaps doubtful in Virginia if navigation acts were easy to pass), certainly it would not be viable in the South if importation were to be immediately prohibited. So a trade between the Eastern and Southern states was thought to be necessary to assure ratification, even though the Eastern and Middle states could have won without a trade in the Convention itself.

Looking backward from today's vantage point, one may criticize the Northern delegates for their trade. But they could not foresee the westward movement of slavery and the Civil War. . . .

Standing in the background of this trade was an earlier compromise on representation, and the form this earlier compromise took led inevitably to a dispute on importation. The greatest issue of the Convention was the argument over whether states would have equal votes in the legislature, as in the Articles. The ultimate compromise on that great issue was equal representation for states in the Senate and proportional representation in the House. During the shaping of that compromise, one important subsidiary issue was what the representation in the House would be proportional to, one possibility being population, another wealth. If population were to be the standard, then the further question arose: which people should be counted, just whites, or both whites and blacks? Easterners preferred just whites, and Gorham (Mass.) even argued that the white population itself was a measure of wealth. South Carolinians wanted blacks and whites counted equally, for that would greatly amplify the white Southern voice in the House. If, on the other hand, wealth were to be counted, how should it be measured? Might white population be a measure of Northern wealth and black population a measure of Southern wealth?

The compromise was one previously used to calculate state contributions under the Articles (by the Resolution of 18 April 1783): the count would include "the number of free persons" (including those indentured, but not including Indians not taxed) plus "three-fifths of all other persons" (i.e., slaves). But it was never clear which principle this compromise involved. At the same time (9 July) of the first attempt to apportion the House, Gorham explained that (even without the three-fifths rule) apportionment was based on "the number of whites and blacks with some regard to supposed wealth." Later (8 August), with the three-fifths rule in place, it was still unclear. Gouverneur Morris (Pa.), who of all the framers was most offended by slavery, asked: "Upon what principle is it that the slaves shall be computed in the representation? Are they men? Then make them Citizens and let them vote. Are they property? Why then is no other property included? . . . The admission of slaves into the Representation . . . comes to this: that the inhabitant of Georgia and S.C. who goes to the Coast of Africa, and in defiance of the most sacred laws of humanity tears away his fellow creatures from their dearest connections and damns them to the most cruel bondages, shall have more votes in a Govt. instituted for the protection of rights of mankind, than the Citizen of Pa. or N. Jersey who views with a laudable horror so nefarious a practice."

The issue of what the three-fifths were, other than a Southern advantage, was never satisfactorily resolved until the Thirteenth Amendment (1865). But once the three-fifths formula was accepted in the Convention, Northerners immediately concluded that some kind of limit on importation was necessary. . . . Such is the origin of the limit on importation. We know much less about the origin of the provision on navigation acts. It was not, apparently, discussed in the first two months of the Convention, and it appears suddenly (6 August) in the Report of the Committee on Detail. From Jefferson's record of a conversation (30 September 1792) with Mason (Va.), it seems that Mason remembered the two-thirds rule on navigation acts as being a central part of the agreement all along. The absence of discussion in Madison's *Notes* thus seems strange, until it is observed that other central issues were also undebated. For example, paper money was only occasionally mentioned until the Report of the Committee on Detail prohibited state bills of credit and legal tender laws. Most historians would agree, however, that one of the framers' main complaints about state legislatures was their proclivity to issue paper money as legal tender. Similarly, the prohibition of state imposts appeared initially in the Report, though the elimination of state tariffs was one of the main objectives of delegates from nonmaritime states. One concludes that the framers, conscious of writing for the future, concentrated on this work rather than on immediate political problems. Probably, however, they, like any other political men, incessantly discussed immediate issues and arrived at resolutions, which then showed up, for the first time in many cases, in the Report of the Committee on Detail.

This report provided, inter alia, in Article VII (VI), Sections 4–6:

> Sec. 4, clause 1: "No tax or duty shall be laid by the Legislature on articles exported from any State";
>
> Sec. 4, clause 2: "nor on the migration or importation of such persons as the several States shall think proper to admit";
>
> Sec. 4, clause 3: "nor shall such migration or importation be prohibited";
>
> Sec. 5: "No capitation tax shall be laid, unless in proportion to the census hereinbefore directed to be taken";
>
> Sec. 6: "No navigation act shall be passed without the assent of two-thirds of the members present in each House."

This was the set of provisions that led to the vote-trade here described.

To understand the trade, it is necessary, I believe, to understand the success of the Southern delegates in persuading the others that some importation of slaves was absolutely essential for ratification in the South. While Virginians and even some delegates from the deep South simply insisted on the rights of slaveholders in general, some Southerners made the real point frequently and bluntly. Williamson (N.C.), in most matters a moderate man, said "The S. States could not be members of the Union if the clause [i.e., Art. VII, Sec. 4, clauses 2 and 3] should be rejected." Charles Cotesworth Pinckney (S.C.), the most active delegate for the slaveholding interest, asserted that without Section 4, "if himself and all his colleagues were to sign the Constitution and use their personal influence, it would be of no avail towards obtaining the assent of their Constituents. S. Carolina and Georgia cannot do without slaves." And John Rutledge (S.C.), the dominant delegate from the deep South, was the bluntest of all: "The true question at present is whether the Southern States shall or shall not be parties to the Union."

The Northern response to these threats was to give in. Some Northerners had given in from the beginning, taking a high moral line against slavery but acquiescing in the slave trade. When George Mason (Va.), the owner of hundreds of slaves, denounced the African (but not, apparently, the domestic) slave trade and declared with amazing unconcern that "every master of slaves is a petty tyrant," Oliver Ellsworth (Conn.) replied rather drily that, "as he had never owned a slave [he] could not judge the effects of slavery on character," and urged that the Convention not "intermeddle" in what he saw as an internal squabble in the South between Virginia, where "slaves . . . multiply so fast . . . it is cheaper to raise than import them," and South Carolina, in the "sickly rice swamps" to which "foreign supplies are necessary."

Other Northerners at first opposed the slave interest in every way, only to capitulate. Wilson (Pa.) initially opposed counting slaves for representation, yet he was the one who proposed the three-fifths rule. King (Mass.) suggested that, if Southern states might leave the Union, so might Northern ones, but he ultimately became a spokesman for the vote-trade. Most astonishing of all was Gouverneur Morris (Pa.). His contempt for defenders of slavery was unbounded, and in this debate, just to embarrass them, he moved that the clause read "importation of slaves into N. Carolina, S. Carolina and Georgia." Once a few slow-witted delegates squirmed to defend the euphemisms, he withdrew his motion. Yet it was Morris . . . who proposed the vote-trade. After clause 1 of Article VII, Section 4, was adopted and debate wrangled on about the next two clauses, he "wished the whole subject to be committed including the clauses relating to taxes on exports and to a navigation act. *These things may form a bargain among the Northern and Southern States*" (emphasis added).

So Sections 4–6 were committed to a committee of eleven (one from each state) and it produced the required trade. This was its proposal (24 August):

> For Section 4, clauses 2 and 3: strike them out and insert "The migration or importation of such persons as the several States now existing shall think proper to admit, shall not be prohibited by the Legislature prior to the year 1800—but a tax or Duty may be imposed on such migration or importation at a rate not exceeding the average of Duties laid on Imports";
>
> for Section 5 (on capitation taxes): to remain;
>
> for Section 6 (on navigation acts): to be stricken out.

Thus it proposed (aB). And this is what the Convention adopted. The Northern delegates faithfully kept the bargain made in the committee, even though some had been initially dubious. . . . The report relative to Section 4 from 24 August was steamrollered through on 25 August, even extending 1800 to 1808 (thus giving South Carolina a full twenty years of unrestrained importation), on motion by C. C. Pinckney (S.C.) and Gorham (Mass.). The vote (#368, 25 August) to adopt the committee report on Section 4 was 7–4, with Massachusetts, New Hampshire, and Connecticut voting with the South.

When it came to the other half of the vote-trade, however, Charles Pinckney (S.C.) objected, proposing to delete that part relating to Section 6 in order to restore the two-thirds rule. But Pinckney was young and brash, and his three senior colleagues systematically rebuked him and in the process explained the full details of the vote-trade. Charles Cotesworth Pinckney revealed the most, so I quote his speech in full.

"Genl. Pinckney said it was the true interest of the S. States to have no regulation of commerce; but considering the loss brought on the commerce of the Eastern States by the revolution, their liberal conduct toward the views of South Carolina" [here Madison inserted a footnote: "He meant the permission to import slaves. An understanding on the two subjects of *navigation* and *slavery* (emphasis in original), had taken place between those parts of the Union, which explains the vote on the Motion depending, as well as the language of Genl. Pinckney and others."], ". . . and the interest the weak Southern States had in being united with the strong Eastern States, he thought it proper that no fetters should be imposed on the power of making commercial regulations; and that his constituents though prejudiced against the Eastern States, would be reconciled to [i.e., by] this liberality—He had himself, he said, prejudices agst the Eastern States before he came here, but he would acknowledge that he had found them as liberal and candid as any men whatever." So Charles Pinckney's motion to take up the two-thirds rule failed, 7–4, in vote 399, 29 August and (B) was then passed without opposition.

One can see the trade easily thus:

Vote 368		Vote 399	
To agree to the first clause of the report of the committee of eleven		To postpone the third clause of the report of the committee of eleven	
Yea (for a)	Nay (for A)	Yea (for b)	Nay (for B)
N.H. ←	————		N.H.
Mass. ←	————		Mass.
Conn. ←	————		Conn.
	N.J.		N.J.
	Pa.		Pa.
	Del.		Del.
Md.		Md.	
	Va.	Va.	
N.C.		N.C.	
S.C.		————————→	S.C.
Ga.		Ga.	

where the arrows indicate the trade-induced votes. Note that only South Carolina voted with the Eastern states on navigation acts, but its vote maintained the integrity of the trade. (Possibly Maryland and North Carolina were not fully committed to the bargain, and Georgia delegates may have believed their vote unnecessary.)

The consequences of the trade were straightforward. The Massachusetts ratifying convention ratified, under intense pressure from shipping interests in coastal towns. Elbridge Gerry, the Massachusetts delegate who refused to sign the Constitution and became an anti-Federalist leader, was not even elected to the Massachusetts convention; and Gerry's mentor, Samuel Adams, was silenced in the convention by the intense enthusiasm of Bostonians. Even though anti-Federalists began with a clear majority of delegates, the Federalists won—in no small part, in my opinion—because of the opportunity for a navigation act.

Similarly, South Carolina ratified—again in no small part—because the slavery issue was settled to slaveowners' satisfaction. In the South Carolina ratifying convention, Charles Cotesworth Pinckney, as extraordinarily candid as in Philadelphia, responded to a criticism of the compromise on importation with a survey of the settlement on slavery: "On this point your delegates had to contend with the religious and political prejudices of the Eastern and Middle States, and with the interested and inconsistent opinion of Virginia, who was warmly opposed to our importing more slaves. . . ." Turning to the vote-trade, he described the Eastern delegates as offering the bargain: " 'Show some period' . . . [they said] 'when it may be in our power to put a stop, if we please, to the importation of this weakness, and we will endeavor, for your convenience, to restrain the religious and political prejudice of our people on this subject.' " Then, without mentioning the rule on navigation acts, he described the committee report and recited the value of the settlement: ". . . we have secured an unlimited importation of negroes for twenty years. Nor is it declared that the importation shall then be stopped; it may be continued. We have a security that the general government can never emancipate them, for no such authority is granted; and it is admitted, on all hands, that the general government has no powers but what are expressly granted by the Constitution. . . . We have obtained a right to recover our slaves in whatever part of America they may take refuge, which is a right we had not before. In short, considering all circumstances, we have made the best terms for the security of this species of property it was in our power to make. We would have made better if we could; but, on the whole, I do not think them bad." Neither did his colleagues, and South Carolina ratified easily.

But what was gained in Massachusetts and South Carolina was almost lost in Virginia. Two of the Virginia delegates refused to sign the Constitution, and in both cases it was the simple majority on navigation acts (B) that turned them away. Randolph said, in the debate on Section 6, "There were features so odious in the Constitution as it stands, that he doubted whether he should be able to agree to it. A rejection of the motion [i.e., to postpone striking out the two-thirds rule] would compleat the deformity of the system. . . ." So the vote-trade was the marginal influence on Randolph's defection, although he was ultimately reconciled and supported the Constitution in the Virginia ratifying convention. Mason, on the other hand, was irreconcilable. As he told Jefferson five years later, it was the vote-trade and the loss of the two-thirds rule that turned him against the Constitution. And out of this parochial and petty economic interest, he fought the Constitution to the bitter end.

The battle in Virginia was very close, but it did ratify. So the judgment of the vote-traders was probably correct. South Carolina and Massachusetts were won and Virginia was not lost. The Constitution was ratified and the Union preserved, but with a terrible blot which it required a civil war to remove. Would it have been better to have no union at all than to have a civil war seventy years later?

3

Federalism

Federalism is deeply rooted in America's history. Its beginnings can be traced back to the British government's "home rule" policy, that gave each colony control over its internal affairs but allowed for no occasion on which the colonies would act in concert. After the revolution, the U.S. Constitution maintained the states' prerogatives to exercise something close to "home rule," both by formally allocating authority to the states and by providing for the election of senators by state legislatures instead of directly by the voters. Despite these early, seemingly irreversible guarantees of "states' rights," which reassured many delegates at the state ratification conventions, federalism has been engaged in a rear-guard action ever since. In fact, no feature of American government has undergone more dramatic transformation during the twentieth century than have federal–state relations.

The decline of state power has taken a variety of forms. In some instances, special interests have pressed for national action after failing in the state legislatures. In other instances, the states themselves have invited federal policy to solve their own collective action problems. The diminished role of the states in modern federalism is a by-product of the insistent growth of national policy.

3-1

The Rediscovery of American Federalism

Samuel Beer

In this essay, Samuel Beer examines the tension between the concept of federalism and the notion that Americans have constituted themselves into a single, national community. Throughout the nation's history this tension has been pondered and debated, but the terms of the discussion have changed with events and conditions, most notably the defeat of sectionalism in the Civil War and the rise of industrialism. Beer traces the history of discourse on the subject, which has shifted from a search for a role for the national government to play in a nation of semisovereign states to the present-day quest to identify and preserve a positive contribution for the states in the nation's civic life.

THE NATIONAL IDEA is a way of looking at American government and American society. It embraces a view of where the authority of government comes from and a view of what it should be used for. As a concept of authority, it identifies the whole people of the nation as the source of the legitimate powers of any and all governments. As a concept of purpose, it tells us that we are one people and guides us toward what we should make of ourselves as a people. The national idea envisions one people, at once sovereign and subject, source of authority and substance of history, affirming, through conflict and in diversity, our unity of being and becoming.

Because the national idea is also a democratic idea, these concepts of authority and purpose are interdependent. Self-government is reflexive. The people who govern are also the object of government. A government of the people, therefore, gets its legitimacy both from being a government by the people and from being a government for the people. Its citizens judge it by both standards, attaching value to the manner in which their government is carried on and to the policies which it pursues.

This theory of legitimacy is national and democratic. It is also federal. In the national perspective, although we are one people who enjoy a common life as one nation, we have set up not a unitary but a dual system of government. In establishing this system, the American people authorized and empowered two sets of governments: a general government for the whole, and state governments for the parts. The constitutional authority for the two sets of government is therefore coordinate. Neither created the other, and both are subject to the same ultimate legitimating power, the sovereign people. And periodically the people in this constituent capacity amend these institutions, by which in their governing capacity they direct the day-to-day affairs of the nation.

From our revolutionary beginnings the national idea has been widely accepted as a description of historical fact and a theory of legitimacy of American federalism. The American political tradition, however, has also sustained another view. In this opposing view, one of these levels of government, the federal government, was brought into existence not by the act of a sovereign people but by a compact among sovereign states. From this compact theory inferences follow that radically contradict the conclusions of the national theory. While the national theory has, on balance, had much the greater influence on thought and action, the compact theory has survived and continues even today to show itself in the feelings of citizens, the rhetoric of politicians, and the actions of governments.

When President Reagan took office in 1981, for instance, he proclaimed a "new federalism." Its central thrust was to cut back on the activities of the federal government by reducing or eliminating a vast number of programs, the principal cuts falling on federal aid to state and local governments. The President wished to do this because he judged these activities to be inefficient, unnecessary, and sometimes positively harmful. He also claimed that they were improper under the Constitution—not so much in the strict sense that they violated specific provisions of our fundamental law as in the larger philosophical and historical sense that they offended against the true meaning of the document.

In his first inaugural address on January 20, 1981, accordingly, President Reagan promised to "restore the balance between levels of government." And while he did not elaborate his political philosophy, he made clear in a phrase or two his reliance upon the compact theory of the Constitution to justify his new federalism. "The Federal government," he declared at one point in his address, "did not create the states; the states created the Federal government."

This allegation did not pass without comment. In response to President Reagan's use of the compact theory, eminent academic critics counterattacked in terms of the national theory. Richard P. Morris of Columbia University called the President's view of the historical facts "a hoary myth about the origins of the Union" and went on to summarize the evidence showing that "the United States was created by the people in collectivity, not by the individual states." No less bluntly, Henry Steele Commager of Amherst College said President Reagan did not understand the Constitution, which in its own words asserts that it was ordained by "We, the People of the United States," not by the states severally. An ardent liberal, he went on to argue that this view of the origin of the Constitution abundantly justified and even mandated the new purposes served by federal power in recent times.[1]

The argument between the President and the professors was not simply about history. Nor was it mainly about the constitutional authority of the federal and the state governments. Their primary disagreement was over public policy, specifically, the use of federal authority in recent years to expand the social and economic programs of the welfare state, especially those dating from the "new federalism" of Lyndon Johnson. President Reagan had taken office as the champion of conservative attitudes that had been gathering force around the country for a generation. He articulated these attitudes in a distinctive vision of American society at home and abroad and in a set of strategies for realizing that vision. Expressing in a new public philosophy the old and familiar values of rugged individualism, he sought to cut back the welfare state and to restore the free market—or in the language of political economy, to shift social choice from public choice toward market choice. Declaring in his first inaugural address that the excessive growth of the public sector in recent years meant that "government is not the solution to our problem; government is the problem," he proposed to "reverse" that growth. Intrinsic to this goal was his promise of another "new federalism" which would "restore the balance between levels of government." The reduction of federal grant programs would at once help restore the federal–state balance and promote the free market.

Some critics called him insincere, claiming that when he said he wanted to restore the federal–state balance, what he really wanted to do was to cut federal spending on social and economic programs. No doubt he was mainly interested in the impact of his policies on American society. But that is no reason for saying that he was not also interested in reducing what he thought was excessive centralization of power in the federal system. In American politics, thinking about federalism has usually had those two aspects: a concern with both the pattern of authority and the pattern of purpose, with the balance of power between levels of government and with the policies for which that power is used. When President Reagan called in the compact theory to lend support to his views on public policy, he was doing what its adherents before him had often done. In their way the nationalists had done the same, right from the days when Alexander Hamilton, as Secretary of the Treasury, set the course of the first administration of George Washington.

The Promise of Nationhood

Like the other founders, Hamilton sought to establish a regime of republican liberty, that is, a system of government which would protect the individual rights of person and property and which would be founded upon the consent of the governed. He was by no means satisfied with the legal framework produced by the Philadelphia Convention. Fearing the states, he would have preferred a much stronger central authority, and, distrusting the common people, he would have set a greater distance between them and the exercise of power. He was less concerned, however, with the legal framework than with the use that would be made of it.[2] He saw in the Constitution not only a regime of liberty, but also and especially the promise of nationhood.

He understood, moreover, that this promise of nationhood would have to be fulfilled if the regime of liberty itself was to endure. The scale of the country almost daunted him. At the Philadelphia Convention, as its chief diarist reported, Hamilton "confessed he was much discouraged by the amazing extent of Country in expecting the desired blessings from any general sovereignty that could be substituted."[3] This fear echoed a common opinion of the time. The great Montesquieu had warned that popular government was not suitable for a large and diverse country. If attempted, he predicted, its counsels would be distracted by "a thousand private views" and its extent would provide cover for ambitious men seeking despotic power.[4]

One reply to Montesquieu turned this argument on its head by declaring that such pluralism would be a source of stability. In his famous *Federalist 10* James Madison argued that the more extensive republic, precisely because of its diversity, would protect popular government by making oppressive combinations less likely. As elaborated by Madison, Hamilton, and other champions of the new regime, their hopes for a more extensive republic rested on more than its promise of a mechanical balance of groups. Hamilton summarized these views in the farewell address that he drafted for Washington in 1796. Its theme was the importance of union if the regime of liberty was to survive. This union would not consist merely in a balance of groups or a consensus of values, and certainly not merely in a strong central government or a common framework of constitutional law. It would be rather a condition of the American people, uniting them by sympathy as well as interest in what Washington termed "an indissoluble community of interest as one nation." [5]

Hamilton's nationalism was expressed not only in his belief that Americans were "one people" rather than thirteen separate peoples but even more emphatically in his commitment to governmental activism. This concern that the American people must make vigorous use of their central government for the tasks of nation-building separated him sharply from Thomas Jefferson, Washington's Secretary of State, who leaned toward the compact theory. The classic expression of this difference of opinion between the two members of the cabinet—the champion of federal power and the champion of states' rights—was their conflict over the proposed Bank of the United States. Jefferson feared that the bank would corrupt his cherished agrarian order and discovered no authority for it in the Constitution. Hamilton, believing that a central bank was necessary to sustain public credit, to promote economic development, and—in his graphic phrase—"to cement more closely the union of the states," found in a broad construction of the "necessary and proper" clause ample constitutional authorization. [6]

Should the words "necessary and proper" be construed narrowly, as Jefferson said, or broadly, as Hamilton advised? A generation later the question came before the Supreme Court in *McCulloch v. Maryland* (1819). [7] Speaking for the Jeffersonian reply, appellants advanced the theory that the Constitution was a compact of sovereign states and therefore should be strictly construed, in order to safeguard state power against the federal government. In the Court's decision, however, John Marshall argued from the national theory that the Constitution was "ordained and established" directly by the people of the United States and concluded in almost the same words used by Hamilton that the crucial phrase "necessary and proper" should be broadly construed to mean not "indispensable" but "appropriate."[8] Looking back today and recognizing that the words of the disputed clause could bear either construction, but that American government could never have adapted to the needs of a complex modern society in the absence of the doctrine of implied powers, the reader must feel relieved that at this critical moment in the development of our juristic federalism the national idea prevailed.

Hamilton was not only a nationalist and centralizer, he was also an elitist. Along with the bank, his first steps to revive and sustain the public credit were the full funding of the federal debt and the federal assumption of debts incurred by the states during the war of independence. These measures had their fiscal and economic purposes. Their social impact, moreover, favored the fortunes of those members of the propertied classes who had come to hold the federal and state obligations. This result, while fully understood, was incidental to Hamilton's ultimate purpose, which was political. As with the bank, that purpose was to strengthen the newly empowered central government by attaching to it the interests of these influential members of society. Hamilton promoted capitalism, not because he was a lackey to the capitalist class—indeed, as he once wrote to a close friend, "I hate moneying men"[9]—but just the opposite: his elitism was subservient to his nationalism.[10]

In the same cause he was not only an elitist but also an integrationist. I use that term expressly because of its current overtones, wishing to suggest Hamilton's perception of how diversity need not be divisive but may lead to mutual dependence and union. Here again he broke from Jefferson, who valued homogeneity. Hamilton, on the other hand, planned for active federal intervention to diversify the economy by the development of commerce and industry. His great report on manufactures is at once visionary and farseeing—"the embryo of modern America," a recent writer termed it.[11]

The economy he foresaw would be free, individualist, and competitive. The federal government, however, would take action to make it more likely that entrepreneurs invested their money in ways most advantageous to the national welfare. Bounties, premiums, and other aids, in addition to a moderately protective tariff, would be employed to develop industry, along with a federal commission to allocate funds. There would be federal inspection

of manufactured goods to protect the consumer and to enhance the reputation of American goods in foreign markets.[12] The purpose was to make
the country rich and powerful. At the same time, the interdependence of
agriculture and industry and especially of South and North would enhance
the union. The outcome, writes a biographer, would be to make the United
States "one nation indivisible, bound together by common wants, common
interests and common prosperity." [13]

Hamilton is renowned for his statecraft—for his methods of using the
powers of government for economic, political, and social ends. But that emphasis obscures his originality, which consisted in his conceptualization of
those ends. His methods were derivative, being taken from the theory and
practice of state-builders of the seventeenth and eighteenth centuries from
Colbert to Pitt. Hamilton used this familiar technology, however, to forward
the unprecedented attempt to establish republican government on a continental scale.[14] In his scheme, the unities of nationhood would sustain the authority of such a regime. By contrast, those earlier craftsmen of the modern
state in Bourbon France or Hohenzollern Prussia or Whig Britain could take
for granted the established authority of a monarchic and aristocratic regime.
They too had their techniques for enhancing the attachment of the people
to the prince. But in America the people *were* the prince. To enhance their attachment to the ultimate governing power, therefore, meant fortifying the
bonds that united them as a people. If the authority of this first nation-state
was to suffice for its governance, the purpose of the state would have to become the development of the nation. This was the essential Hamiltonian
end: to make the nation more of a nation.

The Trial of Sectionalism

The national idea, so launched by statesmen of the federalist persuasion,
confronted three great trials: the trial of sectionalism, culminating in the
Civil War; the trial of industrialism, culminating in the great depression and
the New Deal; and the trial of racism, which continues to rack our country
today.

In the course of the struggle with sectionalism, John C. Calhoun defined
the issue and threw down the challenge to nationalism when he said: "the
very idea of an *American People,* as constituting a single community, is a
mere chimera. Such a community never for a single moment existed—

neither before nor since the Declaration of Independence." This was a logical deduction from the compact theory, which in Calhoun's system made of each state a "separate sovereign community."[15]

His leading opponent, Daniel Webster, has been called the first great champion of the national theory of the union.[16] If we are thinking of speech rather than action, that was true, since Hamilton's contribution, while earlier, was more in the realm of deeds than words. Webster never won the high executive power that he sought, and the cause of union for which he spent himself frequently suffered defeat during his lifetime. But the impact on history of words such as his is not to be underestimated. "When finally, after his death, civil war did eventuate," concludes a biographer, "it was Webster's doctrine, from the lips of Abraham Lincoln, which animated the North and made its victory inevitable."[17] Webster gave us not only doctrine but also imagery and myth. He was not the narrow legalist and materialistic whig of some critical portraits. And if his oratory is too florid for our taste today, its effect on his audiences was overpowering. "I was never so excited by public speaking before in my life," exclaimed George Ticknor, an otherwise cool Bostonian, after one address. "Three or four times I thought my temples would burst with the gush of blood." Those who heard him, it has been said, "experienced the same delight which they might have received from a performance of *Hamlet* or Beethoven's Fifth Symphony."[18] Poets have been called the "unacknowledged legislators of the world." This legislator was the unacknowledged poet of the republic.

To say this is to emphasize his style. What was the substance of his achievement? Historians of political thought usually and correctly look first to his memorable debate with Senator Robert Hayne of South Carolina in January 1830.[19] Echoing Calhoun's deductions from the compact theory, Hayne had stated the doctrine of nullification. This doctrine would deny to the federal judiciary the right to draw the line between federal and state authority, leaving such questions of constitutionality to be decided—subject to various qualifications—by each state itself.

In reply, Webster set forth with new boldness the national theory of authority. Asking what was the origin of "this general government," he concluded that the Constitution is not a compact between the states. It was not established by the governments of the several states, or by the people of the several states, but by "the people of the United States in the aggregate." In Lincolnian phrases he called it "the people's Constitution, the people's government, made for the people, made by the people and answerable to the people," and clinched his argument for the dependence of popular government on nationhood with the memorable and sonorous coda, "Liberty and union, one and inseparable, now and forever."

These later passages of his argument have almost monopolized the attention of historians of political thought. Yet it is in an earlier and longer part that he developed the Hamiltonian thrust, looking not to the origins but to the purpose of government. These initial passages of the debate had not yet focused on the problems of authority and nullification. The question was rather what to do with a great national resource—the public domain, already consisting of hundreds of millions of acres located in the states and territories and owned by the federal government. Large tracts had been used to finance internal improvements—such as roads, canals, and schools—as envisioned by Hamilton and ardently espoused by the previous President, John Quincy Adams.[20]

When Webster defended such uses, citing the long-standing agreement that the public domain was for "the common benefit of all the States," Hayne made a revealing reply. If that was the rule, said he, how could one justify "voting away immense bodies of these lands—for canals in Indiana and Illinois, to the Louisville and Portland Canal, to Kenyon College in Ohio, to Schools for the Deaf and Dumb." "If grants of this character," he continued, "can fairly be considered as made for the common benefit of all the states, it can only be because all the states are interested in the welfare of each—a principle, which, carried to the full extent, destroys all distinction between local and national subjects."[21]

Webster seized the objection and set out to answer it. His task was to show when a resource belonging to the whole country could legitimately be used to support works on "particular roads, particular canals, particular rivers, and particular institutions of education in the West." Calling this question "the real and wide difference in political opinion between the honorable gentleman and myself," he asserted that there was a "common good" distinguishable from "local goods," yet embracing such particular projects. Senator Hayne, he said, "may well ask what interest has South Carolina in a canal in Ohio. On his system, it is true, she has no interest. On that system, Ohio and Carolina are different governments and different countries. . . . On that system, Carolina has no more interest in a canal in Ohio than in Mexico." For Webster, reasoning from the national theory, on the contrary, "Carolina and Ohio are parts of the same country, states, united under the same general government, having interests, common, associated, intermingled."[22]

In these passages the rhetoric is suggestive, but one would like a more specific answer: what is the difference between a local and a general good? Suddenly Webster's discourse becomes quite concrete. His approach is to show what the federal government must do by demonstrating what the states cannot do. Using the development of transportation after the peace of 1815 for illustration, he shows why a particular project within a state, which also has substantial benefits for other states, will for that very reason probably not be undertaken by the state within which it is located.

"Take the instance of the Delaware breakwater," he said. (This was a large artificial harbor then under federal construction near the mouth of Delaware Bay.)[23] "It will cost several millions of money. Would Pennsylvania ever have constructed it? Certainly never, . . . because it is not for her sole benefit. Would Pennsylvania, New Jersey and Delaware have united to accomplish it at their joint expense? Certainly not, for the same reason. It could not be done, therefore, but by the general government."[24]

The example illustrates a standard argument of political economy for centralization. Where the effects of government activity within one jurisdiction spill over into other jurisdictions, there is a case for central intervention to promote this activity, if it is beneficial, or to restrain it, if it is harmful. This spillover argument is one criterion of the "common good," and, as Webster pointed out, its logic calls for action in such cases by the government representing the whole country.

Hayne was right to shrink from the logic of this argument. For its logic does mean that in a rapidly developing economy such as that of America in the nineteenth century, increasing interdependence would bring more and more matters legitimately within the province of the federal government. But logic was not the only aspect of Webster's argument that Hayne was resisting. In the spirit of Hamilton, Webster did perceive the prospect of increasing interdependence and recognized that it could fully realize its promise of wealth and power only with the assistance of the federal government. Moreover, he looked beyond the merely material benefits that such intervention would bring to individuals, classes, and regions toward his grand objective, "the consolidation of the union."[25] This further criterion of the common good could under no circumstances be reconciled with Hayne's "system."

Like Hamilton, Webster sought to make the nation more of a nation. As he conceived this objective, however, turning his imagination toward the vistas of social possibility being opened by the rising romantic movement of his day, he portrayed far more perceptively than the Federalists the power of sympathy as well as interests to unite the nation. By "consolidation" Webster did not mean only attachment to the union arising from economic benefits. Indeed, he blamed Hayne for regarding the union "as a mere question of present and temporary expedience; nothing more than a mere matter of profit and loss . . . to be preserved, while it suits local and temporary purposes to preserve it; and to be sundered whenever it shall be found to thwart such purposes."[26]

The language brings to mind the imagery of another romantic nationalist, Edmund Burke, when in his famous assault upon the dry rationalism of the eighteenth century he proclaimed that "the state ought not to be considered as nothing better than a partnership agreement in a trade of pepper and coffee, calico or tobacco, or some other such low concern, to be taken up for a little temporary interest, and to be dissolved at the fancy of the parties," but rather as "a partnership in all science; a partnership in all art; a partnership in every virtue, and in all perfection."[27]

Setting forth his conception of the nation in a later formulation, Webster echoed Burke's words and phrasing even more exactly: "The Union," he said, "is not a temporary partnership of states. It is an association of people, under a constitution of government, uniting their power, joining together their highest interests, cementing their present enjoyments, and blending into one indivisible mass, all their hopes for the future."[28] For Webster as for Burke, the nation was held together not only by calculations of self-interest, but also by sentiments of "public affection."

Webster articulated this conception most vividly not in Congress or before the Supreme Court but at public gatherings on patriotic occasions. There the constraints of a professional and adversarial audience upon his imagination were relaxed and his powers as a myth-maker released. Consider what some call the finest of his occasional addresses,[29] his speech at the laying of the cornerstone of the Bunker Hill Monument on June 17, 1825. As in his advocacy and in his debates, his theme was the union. What he did, however, was not to make an argument for the union but to tell a story about it—a story about its past with a lesson for its future.[30]

The plot was simple: how American union foiled the British oppressors in 1775. They had thought to divide and conquer, anticipating that the other colonies would be cowed by the severity of the punishment visited on Massachusetts and that the other seaports would be seduced by the prospect of gain from trade diverted from Boston. "How miserably such

reasoners deceived themselves!" exclaimed the orator. "Everywhere the un-
worthy boon was rejected with scorn. The fortunate occasion was seized,
everywhere, to show to the whole world that the Colonies were swayed by
no local interest, no partial interest, no selfish interest." In the imagery of
Webster, the battle of Bunker Hill was a metaphor of that united people. As
Warren, Prescott, Putnam, and Stark had fought side by side; as the four
colonies of New England had on that day stood together with "one cause,
one country, one heart"; so also "the feeling of resistance . . . possessed the
whole American people." So much for Calhoun and his "system"!

From this myth of war Webster drew a lesson for peace. "In a day of
peace, let us advance the arts of peace and the works of peace. . . . Let us
develop the resources of our land, call forth its powers, build up its institutions, and see whether we also, in our day and generation, may not perform
something worthy to be remembered."

With his own matchless sensibility Abraham Lincoln deployed the doctrine and imagery of Webster to animate the North during the Civil War. In
his message to Congress of July 4, 1861, Lincoln justified his use of the "war
power" of the federal government to put down the rebellion in a lucid and
uncompromising version of the nationalist view of the origins of the Republic:

> Originally some dependent colonies made the Union, and, in turn,
> the Union threw off their old dependence for them, and made them
> States. . . . The Union, and not themselves separately, produced their in-
> dependence and liberty. By conquest or purchase the Union gave to each
> of them whatever independence or liberty it has. The Union is older than
> any of the States, and, in fact, it created them as States.[31]

From this it followed that "the States have their status in the Union, and
they have no other legal status. If they break from this, they can only do so
against the law and by revolution." There could therefore be no constitutional right of secession, nullification, interposition, or, indeed, of what was
called not many years ago "massive resistance" by any one or more states.
Short of revolution, as he had said in his first inaugural address, states, like
individuals, must rely on the democratic process under the Constitution for
the protection of their rights. "A majority held in restraint by constitutional
checks and limitations, and always changing easily with deliberate changes
of popular opinions and sentiments," he concluded in a memorable formulation, "is the only true sovereign of a free people." That people, in short,

was not only the sovereign authority which gave both states and nation a frame of government in the Constitution, it was also the authority which went on to govern them under that framework.[32]

No less for Lincoln than for his nationalist predecessors the national idea was also a perspective on public policy. In the same message of July 4, 1861, to Congress he further justified his use of the war power in this statement of purpose:

> This is essentially a people's contest. On the side of the Union it is a struggle for maintaining in the world that form and substance of government whose leading object is to elevate the condition of man—to lift artificial weights from all shoulders; to clear paths of laudable pursuit for all; to afford all an unfettered start, and a fair chance in the race of life.[33]

If this purpose were to be realized for "all" the nation, it was not enough simply to defeat secession. Positive steps had to be taken for "a new birth of freedom." During the very war years Lincoln not only gave slavery the death blow; as the heir of the Hamiltonian vision of commercial and industrial development, he also presided over the enactment of federal intervention in the fields of banking and currency, transportation, the tariff, land grants to homesteaders, and aid to higher education.[34]

In seeking to legitimize secession, Jefferson Davis replied with a forceful statement of compact theory. Like Lincoln, he identified the source of the Constitution's authority by a view of its origins. The federal government, he said, was not established directly by the people of the United States but by a compact among the several states. Under the Constitution, which sets forth the terms of this compact, as under the "close alliance" and "Confederation" among the rebellious colonies, "each state," he argued, "was, in the last resort, the sole judge as well of its wrongs as of the mode and measure of redress." For these reasons the nature of the Constitution itself justified the southern states, when, provoked by the northern states' "persistent abuse of the powers . . . delegated to Congress," they resumed "all their rights as sovereign and independent States and dissolved their connection with the other States of the Union."[35]

President Davis did not contend that no power to impose customs duties on imports had been vested in Congress by the Constitution. Relying on the compact theory, he charged that the Congress had abused its constitutional authority. The power to impose custom duties, he claimed, could properly be used only for revenue, not for protection. The northern states, however, exploiting their preponderance in Congress, had put through a protective tariff, which enriched their commercial and manufacturing classes at the expense of the agricultural South. By "the tyranny of an unbridled majority," they had invaded the "constitutional liberties" which the fundamental law, if properly construed, would protect. Finally, they had attacked interests of "transcendent magnitude" by "impairing the security of property in African slaves," whose labor had become "absolutely necessary for the wants of civilized man."

In the eyes of the South, the stakes were not only self-government, feasible only in a decentralized system, but also individual liberty, economic well-being, and civilization itself. For Jefferson Davis as for Abraham Lincoln, these wider perspectives gave meaning to the law of American federalism, lending it legitimacy, resolving its ambiguities, defining its purpose, and arousing passions that raised armies and sustained them at great sacrifice by soldiers and civilians through four years of war.

The Impact of Industrialism

The Lincolnian program set the course of national development for the next several generations. An enormous expansion of the economy propelled America into the age of industrialism, which in due course engendered its typical problems of deprivation, inequality, and class conflict.

A Republican, Theodore Roosevelt, first attempted to cope with these problems in terms of the national idea. Throughout his public career, an associate has written, Roosevelt "kept one steady purpose, the solidarity, the essential unity of our country. . . . All the details of his action, the specific policies he stated, arise from his underlying purpose for the Union." Like other progressives, Roosevelt was disturbed by the rising conflicts between groups and classes and sought to offset them by timely reform. In this sense integration was TR's guiding aim, and he rightly christened his cause "The New Nationalism." Effective advocacy of this cause, however, fell to another Roosevelt a generation later, when the failings of industrialism were raising far greater dangers to the union.

None of the main points in Franklin Roosevelt's famous inaugural address of March 4, 1933, can be summarized without reference to the nation. The emergency is national because of the "interdependence of the various elements in, and parts of, the United States." Our purpose must be, first, "the establishment of a sound national economy" and beyond that "the assurance of a rounded and permanent national life." The mode of action must be national, conducted by the federal government and carried out "on a national scale," helped "by national planning." No other thematic term faintly rivals the term "nation" as noun or adjective in emphasis. Democracy is mentioned only once; liberty, equality, or the individual not at all.[36]

Franklin Roosevelt's nationalism was threefold. First it was a doctrine of federal centralization, and in his administration, in peace as well as war, the balance of power in the federal system swung sharply toward Washington. Second, Roosevelt called not only for a centralization of government but also for a nationalization of politics. In these years a new kind of mass politics arose. The old rustic and sectional politics gave way to a new urban and class politics dividing electoral forces on a nationwide basis.[37]

The third aspect of Roosevelt's nationalism was expressed in his policies. Those policies do not make a neat package and include many false starts and failures and ad hoc expedients. Yet in their overall impact one can detect the old purpose of "consolidation of the union."

During the very first phase of the New Deal, based on the National Industrial Recovery Act, this goal was explicit. In its declaration of policy, the act, having declared a "national emergency," called for "cooperative action among trade groups" and "united action of labor and management" under "adequate government sanctions and supervision."[38] Engulfed in red, white, and blue propaganda, the NRA, after a first brief success, failed to achieve that coordinated effort and had virtually collapsed by the time it was declared unconstitutional in 1935. The second New Deal which followed, however, brought about fundamental and lasting changes in the structure of the American government and economy.

The paradox of the second New Deal is that although at the time it was intensely divisive, in the end it enhanced national solidarity. The divisiveness will be readily granted by anyone who remembers the campaign of 1936. The tone was set by Roosevelt's speech accepting the Democratic nomination. In swollen and abrasive hyperbole he promised that, just as 1776 had wiped out "political tyranny," so 1936 would bring "economy tyranny" to an end. The "economic royalist" metaphor that was launched into the political battle by this speech expressed the emerging purpose of the New Deal to create a new balance of power in the economy by means of a series of basic structural reforms.[39] The Wagner Act was the most important and characteristic. Utilizing its protections of the right to organize and to bargain collectively, trade unions swept through industry in a massive organizing effort. Despite bitter and sometimes bloody resistance in what can only be called class war, over the years not only practices but also attitudes were altered. The life of the working stiff was never again the same.

The Rooseveltian reforms expressed a "politics of civic inclusion."[40] In their material aspect they brought about a distribution of benefits and a redistribution of power in favor of certain groups. No less important was their symbolic significance as recognition of the full participation of these groups in the common life of the nation. Industrial labor and recent immigrants won a degree of acceptance in the national consciousness and in everyday social intercourse that they had not previously enjoyed. In Roosevelt's appointments to the judiciary, Catholics and Jews were recognized as never before. He named the first Italo-American and the first blacks ever appointed to the federal bench. As Joseph Alsop has observed, "the essence of his achievement" was that he "included the excluded."[41] "Remember, remember always," he reminded the DAR, "that all of us . . . are descended from immigrants and revolutionists."

By this time, a great switch in the attitude of the political parties toward federalism had taken place. The conservatives, who under the names of Federalist, Whig, and Republican had been partisans of national activism, took up the cause of the old Democrats, who from the days of Jefferson had espoused states' rights.

The Challenge of Racism

None of these conflicts in nation-building is ever wholly terminated. Sectionalism still flares up from time to time, as between frostbelt and sunbelt. So also does class struggle. Similarly today, the cleavages between ethnic groups that boiled up with a new bitterness in the 1960s are far from being resolved. In this nation of immigrants, "ethnicity" has been an old and fundamental feature of our politics. In the sixties the new word came into use to signify new facts as ethnic identity gained as a ground of claims and denials. "From the mid-sixties," one writer has reported, ". . . the ethnic identity began to gain on the general American identity. Indeed the very term 'American' became depreciated in the late 1960's."[42] Once again the question whether we were one nation and one people was put into doubt.

The issue is not just ethnicity but race. To be sure, ethnic pluralism is a fact—there are said to be ninety-two ethnic groups in the New York area alone—but this broad focus obscures the burning issue, which is the coexistence of blacks and whites in large numbers on both sides. That question of numbers is crucial. In other times and places one can find instances of a small number of one race living in relative peace in a society composed overwhelmingly of the other race. "Tokenism" is viable. But the facts rule out that solution for the United States. So also does the national idea. What we are attempting under its imperatives has never been attempted by any country at any time. It is to create within a liberal, democratic framework a society in which a vast number of both black and white people live in free and equal intercourse, political, economic, and social. It is a unique, a stupendous demand, but the national idea asks nothing less.

For John F. Kennedy and Lyndon Johnson, the question was, first of all, civil rights. This meant securing for blacks the legal and political rights that had been won for whites in other generations. But the problem of civil rights, which was mainly a problem of the South, merged with the problem of black deprivation, which was especially a problem of northern cities. Johnson's "poverty program" typified the main thrust of the Great Society measures which he built on the initiatives of Kennedy. To think of these measures as concerned simply with "the poor" is to miss the point. The actual incidence of poverty meant that their main concern would be with the living conditions and opportunities of blacks, and especially those who populated the decaying areas of the great urban centers swollen by migration from the South to the North during and after World War II.[43]

These programs were based on the recognition that membership in one ethnic group rather than another can make a great difference to your life chances. In trying to make the opportunities somewhat less unequal, they sought to bring the individuals belonging to disadvantaged groups—as was often said—"into the mainstream of American life." The rhetoric of one of Johnson's most impassioned speeches echoes this purpose. Only a few days after a civil rights march led by Martin Luther King had been broken up by state troopers in full view of national television, he introduced the Voting Rights Act of 1965 into Congress. Calling upon the myths of former wars, like other nationalist orators before him, he harked back to Lexington and Concord and to Appomattox Court House in his summons to national effort.

"What happend in Selma," he continued, "is part of a larger movement which reaches into every section and state of America. It is the effort of

American Negroes to secure for themselves the full blessings of American life." Then, declaring that "their cause must be our cause too," he closed with a solemn echo of the song of the marchers: "*And . . . we . . . shall . . . overcome.*" [44]

From the defeat of "massive resistance" mounted by the advocates of states' rights to the many victories for civil rights on the legal front, the effort of this new federalism to consolidate the union has made substantial progress. Still, no one would say that our statecraft—poverty programs, affirmative action, busing—has been adequate to the objective. Indeed, the very basis of that statecraft in our political culture has come under attack. In the name of "multiculturalism," activists claiming to speak for black and other ethnic groups have revived the ideal of segregation in a new form. In their rhetoric the metaphor of the "melting pot," in which the various ethnic identities are assimilated into an American identity, is rejected in favor of a "mosaic society" in which old identities are preserved and made central to the social, economic, and political life of those sharing them. "Instead of a nation composed of individuals making their own free choices," writes Arthur Schlesinger, Jr., "America increasingly sees itself as composed of groups more or less indelible in their ethnic character. The national ideal had once been *e pluribus unum*. Are we now to belittle *unum* and glorify *pluribus*? Will the center hold? Or will the melting pot yield to the Tower of Babel?" [45]

Federalism and Political Theory

So much for a brief sketch of the fortunes of the national idea in American political history. What is the connection of this idea with our federal arrangements?

Intrinsic to this way of looking at democratic nationalism in America is a theory of federalism. This theory is about the division of authority between the federal and the state governments and about the purposes which this distribution of power is expected to serve. It is a theory in the sense that it is a coherent body of thought describing and justifying the federal system in the light of certain fundamental principles. These are the principles of democracy and nationality on which the Constitution as a whole is based. The thrust of my argument is that this curious arrangement of a constitutionally protected vertical division of power is an intentional and functional institution—not an historical accident or the upshot of mere compromise—of the self-governing American people as they seek over time to make and remake themselves as a nation.

The significance of this theory as a choice among possible regimes is brought out by the contrast with compact theory. From the viewpoint of compact theory, federalism and nationalism, the states and the nation, are opposed. This is opposition in a quite fundamental sense: not merely a conflict between state government and federal government but between state and nation as political communities. For, if the center of political life is in each of the separate states of the nation, it cannot be in the nation as a whole. Or, to put the matter even more bluntly, in so far as the compact model is a correct description, the true nation in America is not the United States but the separate states of which it is composed. We are not one people but several.

Radically different conclusions follow from the opposing view of the location of our nationality, the source of our democracy, and the function of the federal–state division of authority. In contrast with compact theory, national theory takes a far more generous view of the powers and responsibilities of the federal government. Throughout our history, it has informed and supported the broad against the narrow construction of the constitutional power of the federal government. National theory, however, is not merely a doctrine of centralization. As its advocates at the time of the founding continually emphasized, the national point of view not only tolerates but indeed requires a federal arrangement.

In this conception the American republic is one nation served by two levels of government, the object of both being to protect and advance the well-being of the nation. The states are not rival communities carved out of the greater jurisdiction which, although they are incapable of real material or moral independence, seek to act on an exclusive and inward-looking concern for their distinct interests. Like the federal government, state governments also express the national will. The nation can use both levels or either level of government to make itself more of a nation: that is, to make the United States a freer, wealthier, more powerful, and indeed more virtuous human community.

Federalism is not a humdrum matter of public administration but a serious question of political philosophy. The conflict of ideas on federalism between the conservative President and liberal professors illustrates the point. . . . American federalism is at once a system of law and a structure of power. It has both a juristic and a behavioral aspect. As a system of law, it is a government in which the allocation of authority between levels is secured by some exceptional legal protection.[46] That last point is the crux. Federalism is not mere decentralization, even where decentralization is substantial and persistent. Any polity except the very smallest will have territorial subdivisions. In a unitary system the bodies governing these subdivisions will receive their authority from the ordinary statutory law of the central government. The distinctive thing about a federal system is that the authority of these bodies is assured by a law which is superior to the statutory law of the center and which indeed is also the source of authority of that law. Decentralization is constitutional, not merely statutory. That is, as in the United States, the division of authority between the two levels of government is set out in a legal document which can be amended only by a process of consent wider than and different from the process required for the ordinary statutory law of the central government.

By themselves, the words of this legal source, the Constitution, do not tell us what the law is. Our verbal federalism does not unambiguously determine our juristic federalism. A classic example is that fundamental controversy over the meaning of the "necessary and proper" clause. As we have seen, the Hamiltonian reading won out only with the aid of the national theory of authority and purpose.

But even when the words have been given a clear legal meaning, the result, our juristic federalism, still leaves open the question of how governments will actually use these constitutionally legal powers. As a structure of power, American federalism is this actual pattern of use of constitutional authority by the governments of different levels. The law of the Constitution, even when clearly determined, however, does not say whether or how far that authority should be exercised. . . . Jefferson Davis, as we observed, did not deny the power of Congress to levy custom duties. Construing those powers, however, in the light of the compact theory, he found the protective tariff so illegitimate and obnoxious as to support the case for secession.

A government may or may not use its duly authorized powers. They may lie dormant for years, only to be revived with transforming effect. For instance, the power conferred on Congress by the Constitution to spend for "the general welfare" was recognized by Alexander Hamilton and other worthies of the early republic.[47] It was not greatly used, however, until the twentieth century when, thanks especially to programs inaugurated by the

Great Society, federal grants in aid to state and local governments brought about a rapid and marked centralization of power. Without a significant change in our juristic federalism, a "new federalism" in the behavioral sense came into existence.[48]

A generation later, President Reagan proclaimed another "new federalism," although in a sense opposite to the "new federalism" of the Johnson years. By a reduction of intergovernmental aid, he achieved a significant shift in the federal–state balance of power.[49] Accepting much the same juristic federalism but calling upon two opposing strands of theory, the two Presidents found the rhetoric to legitimate two different patterns of power and policy.

Whether one tries to think about federalism or to do something about it, one cannot avoid acting on theory. . . . This reconstruction of nationalist thought presents, I believe, a past which is usable today, while remaining faithful to that past as it actually was.

NOTES

Full bibliographical information for the works cited in short form in the Notes appears in the References.

1. Report of comment by R. Morris, *New York Times*, January 31, 1981; by H. S. Commager, *Christian Science Monitor*, February 19, 1981.

2. McDonald, *Hamilton*, p. 3.

3. Farrand, *Records*, p. 283 (June 18, 1787).

4. *Spirit of the Laws*, Book 8, ch. 16.

5. Commager, *Documents*, p. 171.

6. The phrase comes in Hamilton's *Report on the Public Credit* (January 14, 1790), which will be found in his *Papers*, vol. 6, pp. 51–168. This report was concerned not specifically with the national bank but with the funding of the domestic and foreign debt at par and the federal assumption of debts incurred by the states during the Revolution. Hamilton's nation-building aim, however, was served by all the reports, as Lodge emphasizes in his biography where he quotes the phrase (p. 89), and goes on to elaborate the broad outlines of Hamilton's fiscal and economic policy. Although Lodge's work has been outdated by later scholarship, his judgments are worth considering since they come from a man who was a leading Republican in the days before his party switched from the nationalist to the states' rights position. Declaring that no single paper, except the Emancipation Proclamation, was of such importance in the history of the United States, Lodge called the report "the cornerstone of the Government of the United States and the foundation of the national movement" (p. 289).

7. *McCulloch v. Maryland* (1819) 4 Wheaton 316.

8. Ibid., at p. 421.

9. In a letter of May 22, 1779, to his intimate friend, Lt. Col. John Laurens. Quoted in Loss, "Alexander Hamilton and the Modern Presidency," p. 24, n. 53.

10. John C. Miller, noting that Hamilton sought to make the rich the pillars of the union, concludes that it was his nationalism that led to his elitism. *Growth of the New Nation,* p. 125. Also see Lodge, *Hamilton,* p. 89.

11. Miller, *Hamilton,* p. 289.

12. See especially *The Report on Manufactures* (December 1791), *Papers,* vol. 10, pp. 230–340.

13. Miller, *Hamilton,* p. 285.

14. Forrest McDonald points out that Hamilton used three institutions modeled on the British system—funding of the debt, a national bank, and a sinking fund—but for much broader ends. *Hamilton,* p. 161. Contrary to authoritative opinion, such as that of Adam Smith and David Hume, Hamilton believed that the public debt could be effectively used to enhance state power. See Park, *European Origins,* p. 161.

15. Report prepared for the South Carolina legislature's Committee on Federal Relations, November 1831. Calhoun, *Papers,* vol. 11, pp. 495–496.

16. Merriam, *American Political Theories,* p. 284.

17. Fuess, *Daniel Webster,* pp. 316–317.

18. Ibid., pp. 287–288, 290.

19. *Register* (1830), vol. 6, "First Session of the Twenty–first Congress." On January 18, Webster presented a petition in which the South Carolina Canal and Rail Road Co. requested a subsidy from the federal government. January 19 Senator Hayne objected. January 20 Webster replied. Hayne spoke again January 21 and 25. Webster made his famous speech January 26 and 27. Also on January 27 Hayne replied and Webster rebutted.

20. Bemis, *Adams and the Union,* ch. 4, "Liberty is Power," esp. on his public land policy, p. 78.

21. *Register,* pp. 44–45.

22. Ibid., pp. 45–46.

23. Scharf, *History of Delaware,* vol. 1, pp. 27, 28.

24. *Register,* p. 66.

25. *Register,* p. 38.

26. *Register,* p. 67.

27. "Reflections on the Revolution in France," Burke, *Writings and Speeches,* vol. 8, p. 147.

28. Speech of February 16, 1833, replying to Calhoun's Resolutions setting forth the compact theory of the Constitution.

29. Fuess, *Daniel Webster,* p. 31.

30. Webster, *Great Speeches,* pp. 123–135.

31. Lincoln, *Works,* vol. 4, pp. 434–435.

32. Lincoln, *Works*, vol. 4, p. 434. I have termed these two aspects of sovereignty "constituent" and "governmental."

33. Lincoln, *Works*, vol. 4, p. 438.

34. Lincoln's wartime messages were necessarily concerned mainly with the armed conflict. But he also showed his commitment to the Hamiltonian cause, or what Henry Cabot Lodge called "the national movement." In his second annual message of December 1, 1862, for instance, he dealt not only with "the fiery trial" but also with the consolidation of the union. Referring to "the vast extent" and "variety" of the United States, he observed that "steam, telegraphs, and intelligence have brought these to be an advantageous combination for one united people," and he went on to urge Congress to hasten the completion of "the Pacific Railroad" and to support the enlargement of "the great canals in New York and Illinois"; he also referred favorably to the activities of the newly created Department of Agriculture. Lincoln, *Works*, vol. 5, pp. 518–537.

35. Richardson, *Papers of Jefferson Davis*, vol. 1, p. 63.

36. Roosevelt, *Papers and Addresses*, vol. 2, p. 1.

37. Holcombe, *The New Party Politics*.

38. The National Recovery Act. U.S. Statutes at Large, vol. 48, p. 165.

39. Roosevelt, *Papers and Addresses*, vol. 5, pp. 230–236. See also Galbraith, *American Capitalism*.

40. Marshall, *Class, Citizenship, and Social Development*.

41. Alsop, *FDR*, pp. 10, 11.

42. Glazer, *Affirmative Discrimination*, pp. 177–178.

43. See President Johnson's speech to the graduating class of Howard University, June 4, 1965. Johnson, *Vantage Point*, p. 166.

44. Ibid., p. 165.

45. Schlesinger, *Disuniting of America*, p. 2.

46. So George C. Benson defines a federal government as "a government in which the written constitution, or an inviolable statutory precedent, specifies that certain fundamental authority adheres to a central government and that other governmental authority belongs to smaller areas." "Values of decentralized government." In Benson, ed., *Essays in Federalism*, p. 3.

47. Miller, *Hamilton*, p. 297.

48. See Walker, *Functioning Federalism*, pp. 7, 12, 173–180; and Beer, "Political Overload," pp. 6–7.

49. See Conlan, *New Federalism*, pp. 153–154.

REFERENCES

Alsop, Joseph. *FDR: A Centenary Remembrance.* London: Thames and Hudson, 1982.

Beer, Samuel H. "Political Overload and Federalism." *Polity,* vol. 10 (Fall 1977), pp. 5–17.

Bemis, Samuel Flagg. *John Quincy Adams and the Union.* New York: Knopf, 1956.

Benson, George C., ed. *Essays in Federalism.* Claremont, CA: Institute for Studies in Federalism, 1961.

Burke, Edmund. *The Writings and Speeches of Edmund Burke.* Gen. Ed. Paul Langford. Oxford: Clarendon Press, 1981–.

Calhoun, John C. *The Papers of John C. Calhoun.* Ed. Robert L. Meriwether et al. 19 vols. Columbia: University of South Carolina Press, 1959– .

Commager, Henry Steele, ed. *Documents of American History.* 7th ed. New York: Appleton-Century-Crofts, 1963.

Conlan, Timothy. *New Federalism: Intergovernmental Reform from Nixon to Reagan.* Washington: Brookings, 1988.

Davis, Jefferson. *The Messages and Papers of Jefferson Davis and the Confederacy, including Diplomatic Correspondence, 1861–1865.* Ed. James D. Richardson. New York: Chelsea House, 1966.

Farrand, Max, ed. *The Records of the Federal Convention of 1787.* 4 vols. New Haven: Yale University Press, 1911–1937, 1966.

Fuess, Claude. *Daniel Webster.* Boston: Little, Brown & Co., 1930.

Galbraith, John Kenneth. *American Capitalism: The Concept of Countervailing Power.* Boston: Houghton Mifflin, 1952.

Glazer, Nathan. *Affirmative Discrimination: Ethnic Inequality and Public Policy.* New York: Basic Books, 1975.

Hamilton, Alexander. *The Papers of Alexander Hamilton.* Ed. Harold C. Syrett. New York: Columbia University Press, 1961–1979.

Holcombe, Arthur H. *The New Party Politics.* New York: Norton, 1933.

Johnson, Lyndon Baines. *The Vantage Point: Perspectives on the Presidency, 1963–1969.* New York: Holt, Rinehart and Winston, 1971.

Lincoln, Abraham. *The Collected Works of Abraham Lincoln.* 8 vols. Ed. Roy P. Basler. New Brunswick: Rutgers University Press, 1953.

Lodge, Henry Cabot. *Alexander Hamilton.* New York: Greenwood Press, 1898, 1969.

Loss, Richard. "Alexander Hamilton and the Modern Presidency, Continuity or Discontinuity?" *Presidential Studies Quarterly,* vol. 12, no. 1 (Winter 1982), pp. 6–25.

Marshall, T. H. *Class, Citizenship, and Social Development.* Garden City, N.J. Anchor Books, 1965.

McDonald, Forrest. *Alexander Hamilton: A Biography.* New York: W. W. Norton, 1979.

Merriam, Charles E. *A History of American Political Theories.* New York: Macmillan, 1920.

Miller, John C. *Alexander Hamilton and the Growth of the New Nation.* New York: Harper & Row, 1959.

Montesquieu, Baron de. *The Spirit of the Laws.* Trans. Thomas Nugent. Introduction by Franz Neumann. New York: Collier-Macmillan, 1949.

Park, James. *The European Origins of the Economic Ideas of Alexander Hamilton.* New York: Arno Press, 1977.

Register of Debates in Congress. 14 vols. Washington: Gales and Seaton, 1825–1837.

Roosevelt, Franklin D. *The Public Papers and Addresses of Franklin D. Roosevelt.* Ed. Samuel I. Rosenman. 13 vols. New York: Random House, 1938–1950.

Scharf, John Thomas. *History of Delaware, 1608–1888.* Philadelphia, 1888.

Schlesinger, Arthur M., Jr. *The Disuniting of America: Reflections on a Multicultural Society.* New York: Whittle Books, 1991.

Walker, David B. *Toward a Functioning Federalism.* Cambridge, MA: Winthrop Publishers, 1981.

Webster, Daniel. *The Great Speeches and Orations of Daniel Webster.* Ed. Edwin P. Whipple. Boston: Little, Brown, & Co., 1879.

3-2

Federalism as an Ideal Political Order
and an Objective for Constitutional Reform

James M. Buchanan

In this essay Nobel laureate economist James M. Buchanan makes a case for federalism. Buchanan, a market-oriented economist, arrives at a solution to the threat of concentrated power nearly opposite to that proposed by Madison. Whereas Madison thought that the nation would be safe from such a threat if power were reposed in an inherently factious and weak national majority (see his letter to Jefferson in chapter 2), Buchanan prefers a more decentralized approach. He would give states greater authority and let market mechanisms regulate them—as in the residence decisions of a mobile citizenry, the subject of the excerpt below.

MY AIM HERE is to discuss federalism, as a central element in an inclusive political order, in two, quite different, but ultimately related, conceptual perspectives. First, I examine federalism as an ideal type, as a stylized component of a constitutional structure of governance that might be put in place ab initio, as emergent from agreement among citizens of a particular community before that community, as such, has experienced its own history. Second, the discussion shifts dramatically toward reality, and the critical importance of defining the historically determined status quo is recognized as a necessary first step toward reform that may be guided by some appreciation of the federalist ideal.

Ideal Theory

Federalism as an Analogue to the Market

An elementary understanding and appreciation of political federalism is facilitated by a comparable understanding and appreciation of the political function of an economy organized on market principles. Quite apart from

Excerpted from *Publius: The Journal of Federalism* 25 (spring 1995): 19–27. Reprinted by permission.

its ability to produce and distribute a highly valued bundle of "goods," relative to alternative regimes, a market economy serves a critically important political role. To the extent that allocative and distributive choices can be relegated to the workings of markets, the necessity for any politicization of such choices is eliminated.

But why should the politicization of choices be of normative concern? Under the standard assumptions that dominated analysis before the public choice revolution, politics is modeled as the activity of a benevolently despotic and monolithic authority that seeks always and everywhere to promote "the public interest," which is presumed to exist independently of revealed evaluations and which is amenable to discovery or revelation. If this romantic image of politics is discarded and replaced by the empirical reality of politics, any increase in the relative size of the politicized sector of an economy must carry with it an increase in the potential for exploitation.[1] The well-being of citizens becomes vulnerable to the activities of politics, as described in the behavior of other citizens as members of majoritarian coalitions, as elected politicians, and as appointed bureaucrats.

This argument must be supplemented by an understanding of why and how the market, as the alternative to political process, does not also expose the citizen-participant to comparable exploitation. The categorical difference between market and political interaction lies in the continuing presence of an effective exit option in market relationships and in its absence in politics. To the extent that the individual participant in market exchange has available effective alternatives that may be chosen at relatively low cost, any exchange is necessarily voluntary. In its stylized form, the market involves no coercion, no extraction of value from any participant without consent. In dramatic contrast, politics is inherently coercive, independently of the effective decision rules that may be operative.

The potential for the exercise of individual liberty is directly related to the relative size of the market sector in an economy. A market organization does not, however, emerge spontaneously from some imagined state of nature. A market economy must, in one sense, be "laid on" through the design, construction, and implementation of a political-legal framework (i.e., an inclusive constitution) that protects property and enforces voluntary contracts. As Adam Smith emphasized, the market works well only if these parameters, these "laws and institutions," are in place.[2]

Enforceable constitutional restrictions may constrain the domain of politics to some extent, but these restrictions may not offer sufficient protection against the exploitation of citizens through the agencies of governance. That is to say, even if the market economy is allowed to carry out its allocational-distributional role over a significant relative share of the political economy, the remaining domain of actions open to politicization may leave the citizen, both in person and property, vulnerable to the expropriation of value that necessarily accompanies political coercion.

How might the potential for exploitation be reduced or minimized? How might the political sector, in itself, be constitutionally designed so as to offer the citizen more protection?

The principle of federalism emerges directly from the market analogy. . . . Under a federalized political structure, persons, singly and/or in groups, would be guaranteed the liberties of trade, investment, and migration across the inclusive area of the economy. Analogously to the market, persons retain an exit option; at relatively low cost, at least some persons can shift among the separate political jurisdictions. Again analogously to the market, the separate . . . state governments would be forced to compete, one with another, in their offers of publicly provided services. The federalized structure, through the forces of interstate competition, effectively limits the power of the separate political units to extract surplus value from the citizenry.

Principles of Competitive Federalism

The operating principles of a genuinely competitive federalism can be summarized readily.[3] As noted, the central or federal government would be constitutionally restricted in its domain of action, severely so. Within its assigned sphere, however, the central government would be strong, sufficiently so to allow it to enforce economic freedom or openness over the whole of the territory. The separate states would be prevented, by federal authority, from placing barriers on the free flow of resources and goods across their borders.

The constitutional limits on the domain of the central or federal government would not be self-enforcing, and competition could not be made operative in a manner precisely comparable to that which might restrict economic exploitation by the separate states. If the federal (central) government, for any reason, should move beyond its constitutionally dictated mandate of authority, what protection might be granted—to citizens individually or to the separate states—against the extension of federal power?

The exit option is again suggested, although this option necessarily takes on a different form. The separate states, individually or in groups, must be constitutionally empowered to secede from the federalized political structure, that is, to form new units of political authority outside of and beyond the reach of the existing federal government. Secession, or the threat thereof, represents the only means through which the ultimate powers of the central government might be held in check. Absent the secession prospect, the federal government may, by overstepping its constitutionally assigned limits, extract surplus value from the citizenry almost at will, because there would exist no effective means of escape.[4]

With an operative secession threat on the part of the separate states, the federal or central government could be held roughly to its assigned constitutional limits, while the separate states could be left to compete among themselves in their capacities to meet the demands of citizens for collectively provided services. . . .

We should predict, of course, that the separate states of a federal system would be compelled by the forces of competition to offer tolerably "efficient" mixes of publicly provided goods and services, and, to the extent that citizens in the different states exhibit roughly similar preferences, the actual budgetary mixes would not be predicted to diverge significantly, one from the other. However, the point to be emphasized here (and which seems to have been missed in so much of the discussion about the potential European federalism) is that any such standardization or regularization as might occur, would itself be an emergent property of competitive federalism rather than a property that might be imposed either by constitutional mandate or by central government authority.

The Path Dependency of Constitutional Reform

From Here to There: A Schemata

The essential principle for meaningful discourse about constitutional-institutional reform (or, indeed, about any change) is the recognition that reform involves movement from some "here" toward some "there." The evaluative comparison of alternative sets of rules and alternative regimes of political order, as discussed above in the first section, aims exclusively at defining the "there," the idealized objective toward which any change must be turned. But the direction for effective reform also requires a definition of the "here." Any reform, constitutional or otherwise, commences from some "here and now," some status quo that is the existential reality. History matters, and the historical experience of a political community is beyond any prospect of change; the constitutional-institutional record can neither be ignored nor rewritten. The question for reform is, then: "How do we get there from here?"

These prefatory remarks are necessary before any consideration of federalism in discussion of practical reform. The abstracted ideal—a strong but severely limited central authority with the capacity and the will to enforce free trade over the inclusive territory, along with several separate "states," each one of which stands in a competitive relationship with all other such units—of this ideal federal order may be well-defined and agreed upon as an objective for change. However, until and unless the "here," the starting point, is identified, not even the direction of change can be known.

A simple illustration may be helpful. Suppose that you and I agree that we want to be in Washington, D.C. But, suppose that you are in New York and I am in Atlanta. We must proceed in different directions if we expect to get to the shared or common objective.

Constitutional reform aimed toward an effective competitive federalism may reduce or expand the authority of the central government relative to that of the separate state governments. . . . If the status quo is described as a centralized and unitary political authority, reform must embody devolution, a shift of genuine political power from the center to the separate states. On the other hand, if the status quo is described by a set of autonomous political units that may perhaps be geographically contiguous but which act potentially in independence one from another, reform must involve a centralization of authority, a shift of genuine power to the central government from the separate states.

Figure 1 offers an illustrative schemata. Consider a well-defined territory that may be organized politically at any point along the abstracted unidimensional spectrum that measures the extent to which political authority is centralized. At the extreme left of this spectrum, the territory is divided among several fully autonomous political units, each one of which possesses total "sovereignty," and among which any interaction, either by individuals or by political units, must be subjected to specific contractual negotiation and agreement. At the extreme right of this spectrum, the whole of the territory is organized as an inclusive political community, with this authority centralized in a single governmental unit. Individuals and groups may interact, but any such interaction must take place within the uniform limits laid down by the monolithic authority.

Figure 1. A Constitutional Reform Schemata

| Fully autonomous separate states | Competitive federalism | Centralized unitary polity |

An effective federal structure may be located somewhere near the middle of the spectrum, between the regime of fully autonomous localized units on the one hand and the regime of fully centralized authority on the other. This simple illustration makes it easy to see that constitutional reform that is aimed toward the competitive federal structure must be characterized by some increase in centralization, if the starting point is on the left, and by some decrease in centralization, if the starting point is on the right.

The illustration prompts efforts to locate differing regimes at differing places in their own separate histories on the unidimensional scalar. In 1787, James Madison, who had observed the several former British colonies that had won their independence and organized themselves as a confederation, located the status quo somewhere to the left of the middle of the spectrum, and he sought to secure an effective federalism by establishing a stronger central authority, to which some additional powers should be granted. Reform involved a reduction in the political autonomy of the separate units. In the early post–World War II decades, the leaders of Europe, who had observed the terrible nationalistic wars, located their status quo analogously to Madison. They sought reform in the direction of a federalized structure—reform that necessarily involved some establishment of central authority, with some granting of power independently of that historically claimed by the separate nation-states.

By comparison and contrast, consider the United States in 1995, the history of which is surely described as an overshooting of Madison's dreams for the ideal political order. Over the course of two centuries, and especially after the demise of any secession option, as resultant from the great Civil War of the 1860s, the U.S. political order came to be increasingly centralized. The status quo in 1995 lies clearly to the right of the spectrum, and any reform toward a federalist ideal must involve some devolution of central government authority and some increase in the effective independent power of the several states. . . .

Constitutional reform in many countries, as well as the United States, would presumably involve devolution of authority from the central government to the separate states.

Constitutional Strategy and the Federalist Ideal

The simple construction of Figure 1 is also helpful in suggesting that it may be difficult to achieve the ideal constitutional structure described as competitive federalism. Whether motivated by direct economic interest, by some failure to understand basic economic and political theory, or by fundamental conservative instincts, specific political coalitions will emerge to oppose any shift from the status quo toward a federal structure, no matter what the starting point. If, for example, the status quo is described by a regime of fully autonomous units (the nation-states of Europe after World War II), political groups within each of these units will object to any sacrifice of national sovereignty that might be required by a shift toward federalism. . . .

Similar comments may be made about the debates mounted from the opposing direction. If a unitary centralized authority describes the status quo ante, its supporters may attempt to and may succeed in conveying the potential for damage through constitutional collapse into a regime of autonomous units, vulnerable to economic and political warfare. The middle way offered by devolution to a competitive federalism may, in this case, find few adherents.[5] . . .

As the construction in Figure 1 also suggests, however, the fact that the federalist structure is, indeed, "in the middle," at least in the highly stylized sense discussed here, may carry prospects for evolutionary emergence in the conflicts between centralizing and decentralizing pressures. Contrary to the poetic pessimism of William Butler Yeats, the "centre" may hold, if once attained, not because of any intensity of conviction, but rather due to the location of the balance of forces.[6]

Federalism and Increasing Economic Interdependence

In the preceding discussion, I have presumed that the economic benefits of a large economic nexus, defined both in territory and membership, extend at least to and beyond the limits of the political community that may be constitutionally organized anywhere along the spectrum in Figure 1, from a regime of fully autonomous political units to one of centralized political authority. Recall that Adam Smith emphasized that economic prosperity and growth find their origins in the division (specialization) of labor and that this division, in turn, depends on the extent of the market. Smith placed no limits on the scope for applying this principle. But we know that the economic world of 1995 is dramatically different from that of 1775. Technological development has facilitated a continuing transformation of local to regional to national to international interactions among economic units. Consistently with Smith's insights, economic growth has been more rapid where and when political intrusions have not emerged to prevent entrepreneurs from seizing the advantages offered by the developing technology.

Before the technological revolution in information processing and communication, however, a revolution that has occurred in this half-century, politically motivated efforts to "improve" on the workings of market processes seemed almost a part of institutional reality. In this setting, it seemed to remain of critical economic importance to restrict the intrusiveness of politics, quite apart from the complementary effects on individual liberties. Political federalism, to the extent that its central features were at all descriptive of constitutional history, did serve to facilitate economic growth.

The modern technological revolution in information processing and communications may have transformed, at least to some degree, the setting within which politically motivated obstructions may impact on market forces. This technology may, in itself, have made it more difficult for politicians and governments, at any and all levels, to check or to limit the ubiquitous pressures of economic interdependence.[7] When values can be transferred worldwide at the speed of light and when events everywhere are instantly visible on CNN, there are elements of competitive federalism in play, almost regardless of the particular constitutional regimes in existence.

Finally, the relationship between federalism, as an organizing principle for political structure, and the freedom of trade across political boundaries must be noted. An inclusive political territory, say, the United States or Western Europe, necessarily places limits on its own ability to interfere politically with its own internal market structure to the extent that this structure is, itself, opened up to the free workings of international trade, including the movement of capital. On the other hand, to the extent that the internal market is protected against the forces of international competition, other means, including federalism, become more essential to preserve liberty and to guarantee economic growth.

Conclusion

The United States offers an illustrative example. The United States prospered mightily in the nineteenth century, despite the wall of protectionism that sheltered its internal markets. It did so because political authority, generally, was held in check by a constitutional structure that did contain basic elements of competitive federalism. By comparison, the United States, in this last decade of the twentieth century, is more open to international market forces, but its own constitutional structure has come to be transformed into one approaching a centralized unitary authority.

Devolution toward a competitive federal structure becomes less necessary to the extent that markets are open to external opportunities. However, until and unless effective constitutional guarantees against political measures to choke off external trading relationships are put in place, the more permanent constitutional reform aimed at restoring political authority to the separate states offers a firmer basis for future economic growth along with individual liberty. . . .

NOTES

1. James M. Buchanan, "Politics without Romance: A Sketch of Positive Public Choice Theory and Its Normative Implications," Inaugural Lecture, Institute for Advanced Studies, Vienna, Austria, *IHS Journal, Zeitschrift des Instituts für Höhere Studien* 3 (1979): B1–B11.

2. Adam Smith, *The Wealth of Nations* (1776; Modern Library ed.; New York: Random House, 1937).

3. See Geoffrey Brennan and James M. Buchanan, *The Power to Tax: Analytical Foundations of a Fiscal Constitution* (New York: Cambridge University Press, 1980), pp. 168–186, for more comprehensive treatment.

4. For formal analysis of secession, see James M. Buchanan and Roger Faith, "Secession and the Limits of Taxation: Towards a Theory of Internal Exit," *American Economic Review* 5 (December 1987): 1023–1031; for a more general discussion, see Allen Buchanan, *Secession: The Morality of Political Divorce from Fort Sumter to Lithuania and Quebec* (Boulder, Col.: Westview, 1991).

5. The theory of agenda-setting in public choice offers analogies. If the agenda can be manipulated in such fashion that the alternatives for choice effectively "bracket" the

ideally preferred position, voters are confronted with the selection of one or the other of the extreme alternatives, both of which may be dominated by the preferred option. See Thomas Romer and Howard Rosenthal, "Political Resource Allocation, Controlled Agendas, and the Status Quo," *Public Choice* 33 (Winter 1978): 27–43.

6. William Butler Yeats, "The Second Coming," *The Collected Works of W. B. Yeats,* vol. 1, *The Poems,* Ed. Richard J. Finneran (New York: Macmillan, 1989), p. 187.

7. Richard McKenzie and Dwight Lee, *Quicksilver Capital: How the Rapid Movement of Wealth Has Changed the World* (New York: Free Press, 1991).

3-3

Beyond the Welfare Clock

Jonathan Walters

*During the 1990s, when the national government's budget was wallow-
ing in red ink, politicians in Washington began warming to the idea
of restoring federalism by letting the states reassume responsibilities
that had in recent decades gravitated to Washington. The Republican-
controlled Congresses from 1995 through the end of the decade were especially enthusiastic about reducing the federal role. Nowhere were they
more successful than with welfare reform. The number of welfare
claimants is down, budgets for these programs are running a surplus,
but as the article below makes clear, the final verdict on the success of
the reform is not yet in.*

THE U.S. SENATORS who debated welfare reform two years ago didn't agree
on the merits of the bill before them, but they were unanimous about one
thing: It was an attempt at shock therapy. "A system that has failed in every
single respect will now be thrown away," said New Mexico Republican
Pete V. Domenici, "and we will start over." New York Democrat Daniel
Patrick Moynihan didn't disagree about that. But the proposed law, he said,
would be "the most brutal act of social policy we have known since Reconstruction."

Moynihan was referring specifically to the new time limits: 60 months of
welfare payments—that was it for the recipient's life. But as he spoke, many
states were writing their own provisions even tougher than the congressional ones. Florida went for a 24-month limit over any four-year period.
Tennessee passed a law forcing recipients off the rolls anytime they had
been there 18 months. The specifics varied from state to state, but the projected impact was the same everywhere: a drastic reduction or outright
elimination of benefits long before the 60-month federal cutoff had ever
been reached.

Originally published in *Governing*, April 1999, pp. 21–26. Reprinted by permission. Jonathan Walters
is a senior correspondent for *Governing* magazine.

Three years later, the deadlines are here. In Tennessee, the first ones arrived a year ago. In the period since then, some 5,000 families there have run out of time. But the result hasn't exactly been what was predicted. "About 2,800 were exempt from the time limit, either because they are disabled or for other reasons," says Mike O'Hara, assistant commissioner for family assistance in the Tennessee Human Services Division. "Of the remaining 2,200 cases, 1,400 have been extended for good cause, like illness or because they were cooperating in trying to find work." Which left 800, less than a fifth of those who had exhausted their benefits, who were actually cut off.

In Florida, where 1,000 families were on schedule to bump up against that state's 24-month limit on benefits on October 1, 1998, only 100 were actually dropped from the rolls. The others applied for and received benefit extensions, either due to hardship exemptions or the fact that they were cooperating in trying to find work but simply hadn't yet landed a job. On top of that, Florida had an even longer time limit—36 months—for long-term welfare recipients with poor job skills and little work experience.

Roughly the same scenario has unfolded in Connecticut, where welfare recipients started hitting that state's 21-month lifetime limit last fall. Of the roughly 23,000 who have used up their 21 months of benefits since time limits came into force in Connecticut, only around 500 have been dropped from the rolls, and those cases immediately become eligible for a state safety-net program that offers vouchers in lieu of cash payments.

Even staunch opponents of time limits such as Randy Albelda, a University of Massachusetts–Boston economics professor who has been tracking the impact of welfare reform, seem a little amazed by the Nutmeg State's performance. "Connecticut just turned to mush," says Albelda.

So it would seem that the verdict is in: While time limits had the hard ring of tough love when states adopted them, hard-liners are becoming social softies when time runs out on recipients. Across the country, states are turning to a host of exemptions and extensions that are allowing thousands of cases to continue, a policy approach that would seem to render the threat of time limits almost meaningless.

That would be an easy conclusion to come to if it weren't for the indisputable fact that caseloads have been plummeting. Because of time limits, caseworkers and clients alike are getting the message that welfare is no longer forever. "Time limits take a very complicated message about new programs and new expectations and make it simple for both the client and the caseworker," says Toby Herr, executive director of Project Match, the ground-breaking welfare-to-work program first established to work with clients from Chicago's hard-case Cabrini-Green housing project in the early 1980s: " 'The clock is ticking, and you have X amount of time until you lose your grant.' "

Some, like Jack Tweedie, who has been monitoring welfare reform for the National Conference of State Legislatures, believe that states aren't using time limits as a vehicle to close cases because the message is getting through. "Most of these time limits were adopted to enforce cooperation," says Tweedie. "So if a client is working or is looking for work, in most places they get an extension."

Tweedie's last point is central to the real reason why time limits have not been a huge issue so far: It's not so much that states haven't been tough about sticking with them; it's that, given the tremendous emphasis on work that is now central to almost every state welfare-reform program, most people are simply gone from the rolls long before they ever reach their limit, either because they've found jobs or because they have been sanctioned off welfare for failing to comply with work requirements.

"Time limits don't seem to be where the action's at, or to be the immediate cause of why people lose benefits," says Mark Greenberg, senior staff attorney for the Center on Law and Social Policy, a liberal think tank that has been critical of the 1996 welfare-reform measure. Where states have been tough is in enforcing work requirements, and in sanctioning those who fail to live up to them. "That's where we see lots of people losing benefits," says Greenberg.

Florida is a prime case in point. When the time-limit clock started ticking in October 1996, the state was carrying 150,000 cases, raising the specter of time-limit carnage come October 1998. But when the state's 24-month limit on benefits rolled around, an astounding 120,000 cases had already been closed: At a time when jobs are plentiful, Florida, like most states, has been insistent and consistent in signaling that welfare is now a two-way street and that to receive benefits, clients must look for and accept work. Such pacts are typically formalized through "personal responsibility agreements." Failure to live up to the conditions in those agreements invariably means an escalating series of sanctions, with 100 percent loss of benefits, known as a "full family sanction," for repeated non-compliance in most states.

And so Florida's version of work-first—its "Work and Gain Economic Self-sufficiency" (WAGES) program—has had the same impact as other similar state programs: huge numbers of clients off the rolls. Some found work, but some just never returned to the welfare office once the terms of the new deal had been explained to them.

It is through such immediate work requirements and sanction policies—as opposed to the somewhat distant threat of exhausted benefits due to time limits—that states have really sent the message that this time around, welfare reform is serious business. "This is a landmark shift in signalling, and the threat of sanctions has really gotten through to people," says Richard P. Nathan, director of the Rockefeller Institute of Government, which is studying the administrative response to welfare in 20 states.

While there is broad consensus that states and localities have indeed been fairly flexible when it comes to time limits, state and local policy on sanctions is another story. Client advocates charge that in some places sanctions are being used in an overly aggressive and punitive fashion. There is also anecdotal evidence that in many local welfare offices, caseworkers aren't doing a very good job of "signalling" to clients the bottom-line consequences of not living up to the new welfare-for-work equation or helping them get ready for and find work.

In Colorado, for example, a class-action suit filed against Denver and Adams counties charges that local officials have been unlawfully sanctioning clients in an overly aggressive effort to cut welfare rolls. New York City was recently slapped with a court order putting a hold on reorganization of its welfare system because judges ruled that city officials were actively discouraging applicants from signing up for any benefits—food stamps, Medicaid or cash assistance—as part of its conversion of "income support centers" into "job centers." In Arizona, which has been using sanctions to close a hefty 500 cases a month, field researchers with the Rockefeller Institute say caseworkers aren't doing a good job of communicating to clients the new expectations of welfare for work, perhaps in part because in Arizona there has been an old-style emphasis on tightening up error rates on food stamp eligibility rather than a new-style emphasis on helping clients find jobs. "In some states, it's just the same old bureaucracy with new rules," says Tom Gais, who is heading up the Rockefeller Institute study, "and that can be a bad combination."

It was inevitable, of course, that some states and localities would use the newfound flexibility handed to them under federal welfare reform to cut rolls more aggressively than might have been intended by reformers. It was also inevitable that in some states and localities, government's performance in implementing the new regimen would be uneven.

But clearly, sanctions have become a centerpiece of welfare reform in most places, regardless of how judiciously they are administered or how well they are explained to clients by caseworkers. According to an Urban Institute analysis of state welfare policy in the wake of federal reform, 36 states have adopted full family sanctions for repeated failure to comply with work requirements. Under a full sanction, families lose 100 percent of their cash benefit, rather than just the amount apportioned to adults. In most states, families that come back into compliance are once again eligible for benefits. Seven states, however, have lifetime bans for repeat offenders, according to the Urban Institute study.

Even as some states have been tough about sanctions, though, others have gone out of their way not to be. Rhode Island, which ranks 49th in closing cases, is emphasizing incentives rather than sanctions in its welfare-reform program. And in some states, caseworkers are concerned enough about the lifetime cutoff that they recommend to clients that they voluntarily leave welfare rather than suffer a lifetime sanction for non-compliance with work requirements. "Georgia has a lifetime ban on assistance once you've received a full set of sanctions," says LaDonna Pavetti, a senior researcher at Mathematica Policy Research Inc. who is studying state sanction policies. "The way some caseworkers handle that is they will call a client and ask them to either come in and comply with work requirements or voluntarily close their case."

But it isn't sanctions on active cases that have been the dramatic driver of tumbling welfare rolls. As was amply demonstrated in Florida—and in dozens of other states—it has been the closing of those cases where clients showed up for their initial post–welfare-reform interview and then just never came back. What nobody anticipated, say Pavetti and others on the welfare-reform front, was the huge number of people who would simply walk away from welfare upon learning about the new quid pro quo of work for benefits.

Since Durham County, North Carolina, started getting serious about workfare—which it did about 20 months ago—caseloads have tumbled 42 percent, says Dan Hudgins, the county's director of social services. Of the 3,500 cases that have been closed, Hudgins says 2,000 found jobs, but 1,500 simply took their entitlements—food stamps and Medicaid—and walked away from the $238 a month of cash assistance that now comes only with work.

What happens to people who just disappear like that? That's one of the major mysteries looming over sanctioning policies. Did they drop out because they decided "the juice wasn't worth the squeeze?" asks Linda Wolf, deputy director of the American Public Human Services Association (formerly the American Public Welfare Association). Or, she asks, "are they the hard-to-serve, multi-problem, more-than-one-barrier-to-employment clients," individuals who are so disorganized or have such poor social and work skills that they simply gave up in the face of the new requirements? It's a mystery that many in the social services world aren't comfortable with. "Now that we've achieved the numbers that make us look good," says Dan Hudgins, "I want to know what we've really accomplished."

While dozens of states and localities are in the process of studying what happened to families that left welfare, so far only a handful have done any research that is considered statistically reliable. Indiana, South Carolina and Washington state found that more than 60 percent of those who left welfare voluntarily found work; in Maryland, it was 55 percent. Montgomery County, Ohio, reports that virtually all the 10,000 clients who have left the rolls since 1996 left to take jobs; the county knows this because it placed them all in jobs.

There are also states that have tried to track clients who were dropped from welfare because of time limits. A study done by the Massachusetts Department of Transitional Assistance of those who left welfare because they had exhausted their 24 months of benefits—more than 2,000 families—found that 75 percent were working an average of 28 hours a week at $7 an hour.

A similar study in Florida suggests, likewise, that most of those who use up their benefits are coping. "Things for this group in general are tough, but not catastrophic," says Don Winstead, head of welfare reform for Florida's Children and Families Department. "Lots of people had some other safeguard to fall back on, either extended family or they had kids receiving SSI or they had some other income." What was difficult to tell, though, says Winstead, "was whether the people had other means and so decided to reach the end of their time limits or whether they reached the end of their time limit and then found other means."

Somewhat more troubling are the results of studies of those who were sanctioned off of welfare for failing to comply with or complete personal responsibility agreements. A New Jersey study found that only 30 percent had found jobs; in Tennessee it was 39 percent. A study of those sanctioned for non-compliance under Delaware's "Better Chance Program," done by Abt Associates Inc. for the Delaware Health and Social Services Department, suggests that sanction rates do tend to be higher for clients who either don't understand the new work requirements or who can't comply due to other circumstances. The study also notes that "caseworkers may be varyingly effective in communicating program requirements and helping clients meet those requirements." The report noted substantial differences in local office sanction rates, even controlling for caseload composition. That would seem to support Rockefeller Institute field research findings that caseworkers do indeed have significant influence over how individual cases and overall sanction rates play out.

Given the preliminary nature of all such studies, it might be tempting to defer conclusions about the effectiveness of welfare time limits and sanctions pending further study. But more than two years into the welfare-reform experiment, there is actually quite a bit that officials do know.

Most fundamental is that the end of the cash assistance entitlement under the old federal Aid to Families with Dependent Children program, combined with the work requirements under the new federal program, Temporary Assistance for Needy Families, are at least having the intended effect of pushing people into work. In Connecticut, a Manpower Demonstration Research Corp. study comparing welfare recipients who continue to collect benefits under AFDC (part of continuing research under a waiver granted to Connecticut prior to passage of federal welfare reform) with those enrolled in Connecticut's new Temporary Family Assistance program found that 16 percent of those on AFDC find work compared with 50 percent for those enrolled in TFA.

While it is generally agreed that the new law deserves credit for inspiring unprecedented numbers of welfare recipients to go to work, there also seems to be a growing awareness that the sanction policies underpinning the work requirements need to be pursued with the same care that states have shown toward time limits. Few states seem interested in "turning to mush" on work requirements, but in the wake of such studies as that done in Delaware, more states have recently been opting for some intense intervention before slapping families with full sanctions for work-requirement non-compliance. In January, Tennessee announced a program that requires a thorough review of cases that are about to be closed for non-cooperation with work requirements. Montana has already instituted an internal review of cases about to receive a full family sanction. Arizona's Department of Economic Security is backing a legislative request for $3 million to fund a program that would, likewise, provide for a formal review of cases about to suffer full sanction.

It is programs like those in Tennessee, Montana and Arizona that highlight the fundamental dilemma that is now being distilled out of welfare reform, a dilemma that grows increasingly pronounced as states and localities dig down into tougher-to-serve cases: how to work with a more entrenched and problem-plagued welfare population in a way that continues to signal that states and localities mean business when it comes to work requirements and time limits. "It's a difficult balance," says Project Match's Toby Herr. "Being tough while making exceptions."

In that regard, both the shorter state time limits on benefits and states' track record on sanctions have provided some valuable early lessons. And while states and localities have been working through those lessons, they also bear directly on future federal policy, which ultimately dictates time-limit and sanction policies for everybody.

Just as most states have taken less than a hard line on enforcing their own time limits, so might Congress choose to if cases start hitting the 60-month federal lifetime limit, especially if enough states appear to be struggling in meeting the more stringent federal work-participation requirements that arrive in 2002. Furthermore, Congress might have to consider adjusting what activities meet the definition of "work" for the purposes of continuing eligibility. Currently, so-called "family-building" activities—those focused on adults doing things for their kids, such as enrolling them in special programs or after-school activities—don't count. Yet for very dysfunctional families or problem-plagued adults, that may be as much as government can reasonably expect. "We may have to create a modest package of activities for clients who might not be able to work but who are willing to help their kids," says Herr. "Maybe it's enrolling their kids in an asthma education course, or taking them to the Scouts, or enrolling them in Special Olympics." Montana has already adopted such alternatives for work requirements, which the state has been allowed to do based on a waiver granted pre-federal reform.

Looming over the whole experiment, of course, are the intertwined issues of the U.S. economy's health and its ability to spawn living-wage jobs. Any economic downturn—or widespread evidence that there aren't enough living-wage jobs to sustain families off of assistance—could also quickly put serious pressure on Washington to reconsider its trickle-down time-limit and sanction policies. And the lesson that Washington can take from states and localities as it considers any potential policy adjustments is straightforward: There has been merit in being firm, but also wisdom in being flexible.

3-4

The Federalization of Criminal Laws

John J. Mountjoy

Politicians may sincerely support the principle of federalism in the abstract, but their decisions about whether to assign responsibility for a particular policy to the states or to Washington depend primarily on specific political objectives. Congressional Republicans enthusiastically dismantled national administration of welfare in the mid-1990s, but they were at the same time busy "federalizing" many crimes, such as numerous drug-related crimes, that had long fallen within the exclusive jurisdiction of the states and their local communities. In both instances, Congress acted in response to demands from the public rather than simply allowing the principle of federalism to guide policy.

WITH RARE EXCEPTION, crime traditionally has been a matter for states to address, according to a new report issued by the American Bar Association's Task Force on the Federalization of Criminal Law. Chaired by Edwin Meese, a former U.S. attorney general and adviser to President Reagan, the task force comprises various officials from the state and federal judicial systems, as well as noted legal scholars from across the nation. The report focuses on the trend for Congress to federalize crime laws, and how this trend is not answering the true needs of state and local residents and communities.

Since the adoption of the U.S. Constitution in 1789, states have defined and prosecuted nearly all criminal conduct. At the time, federal offenses and prosecutions were limited to treason, bribery of federal officials, perjury in federal courts, theft of government property and revenue fraud. All other crimes were the concern of states. According to the report, this was the case until the presidential election of 1928, in which crime was made a national issue.

Since then, and especially over the last three decades, there has been a dramatic increase in the assertion of federal jurisdiction. This expansion

Originally published in *Spectrum*, summer 1999, pp. 1–4. Copyright 1999 The Council of State Governments. Reprinted with permission from *Spectrum*.

Figure 1. Federal Criminal Statutes Enacted
(divided by time period, as a percentage of total)

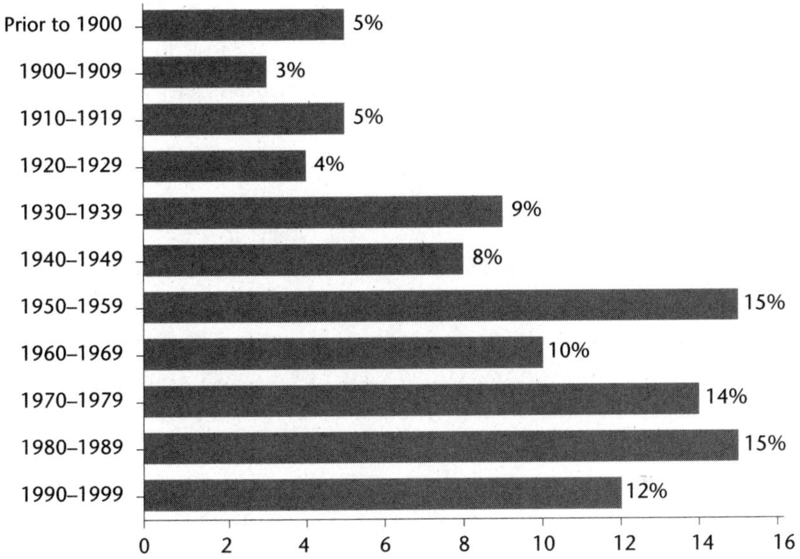

Source: American Bar Association, Task Force on the Federalization of Criminal Law.

largely has proceeded under the idea that Congress was better at regulating interstate commerce. In addition, federal programs have abounded during this time and have carried with them criminal sanctions for noncompliance. Public concern over organized crime, drugs, street violence and other social ills also has sharply increased, which the report says has resulted in a significant increase in federal legislation.

Task force research reveals some disturbing facts about this trend of federalization of criminal law. For example, 41 percent of federal criminal provisions enacted since the Civil War have been enacted since 1970 (see figure 1). In fact, a complete listing of all federal criminal laws, located together, is not available. The report further states that under these new federal criminal laws, it is clear that the amount of individual citizen behavior now subject to federal criminal laws has increased in astonishing proportions in the last few decades. And there are signs that this trend is growing. According to the report, more than 1,000 crime-related bills were introduced by the 105th Congress.

And not only is Congress passing more laws, the size of the federal criminal justice system has increased. Between 1982 and 1993, overall federal justice system expenditures increased at twice the rate of comparable state and local expenditures—317 percent to 163 percent. Over the same period, justice system personnel increased by 96 percent, while state and local levels increased only 42 percent.

In addition, the report points to the increased size of the federal prison population, which increased between 1982 and 1993 by 177 percent as compared to 134 percent for state and local levels. Finally, in the last 30 years, the number of U.S. attorney offices has grown from 3,000 to about 8,000.

One possible reason for this rise, the report says, is that in the face of more serious and more frequent incidents, citizens and legislators simply urge Congress to make more actions a federal crime. The public perceives the federal government to be a system that can right the wrongs, as far as law and order goes.

What perplexes some is the absence of an underlying principle governing congressional choice to criminalize conduct under federal law, the report says. Often Congress passes new criminal laws in response to newsworthy events, rather than as part of a planned and comprehensive criminal code. Police executives told the task force, "The trend [of federalization] has not declined, in part because federalization is politically popular. Herein lies the greatest danger in federalization: creating the illusion of greater crime control, while undermining an already over-burdened criminal justice system."

The task force concludes that the increase in legislation and criminal laws at the federal level has little measurable impact on violent crime at the state and local levels, because federal law enforcement only reaches a small percentage of such activity. Police executives also told the task force, "It is unrealistic to expect that federal authorities will have the resources and inclination to investigate and prosecute traditionally state and local offenses."

In effect, the federal system is enacting new laws without providing the resources needed to enforce them. The task force demonstrated this with its finding that federal prosecutions total less than 5 percent of the total nationwide.

The task force also found that even the most frequently prosecuted federal offense, drug trafficking (28 percent of all federal filings in 1997), accounted for only 2 percent of prosecutions of all crimes, including those at the state level. Of the 1 million-plus drug arrests in this country in 1997, about 1.5 percent were prosecuted federally, the report says. Furthermore, two crimes most recently federalized by Congress, drive-by shootings and interstate domestic violence, were not cited in a single prosecution in 1997. This rare use of federalization statutes, the report says, questions whether federalization can have a meaningful impact on street safety and local crime.

The task force cites many reasons for fundamental limitations on the federalization of criminal laws. For example, constitutional law recognizes that preventing and dealing with crime is more the business of states than the federal government. Criminal conduct is defined by state legislatures, investigated by state courts, prosecuted by state attorneys, tried in state courts and punished in state prisons. That general police power resides with states is a basic concept, the report says, established in the dual federal/state system. Inappropriate federalization undermines the strength of the states.

Federalization of criminal law also:

- *Undermines the role of states and their courts, which are constitutionally given the primary role of dealing with crime.* The report claims there is a perception that federal law officials prosecute only highly visible incidents of local crime, leaving the vast quantity of prosecutions to states.

- *Bestows new police powers upon federal agencies, broadening their powers in a system that specifically reserves these broad-policing powers to the states.* This is worrisome, the report says, since most of these agencies are subject only to a limited amount of executive oversight.

- *Increases the prosecutorial powers of the federal government.* This power increases the discretion with which prosecution decisions are made. It also supersedes the established system of using local and state judicial systems as the first line of public safety protection.

- *Takes a toll on the federal judicial system.* Federal justice personnel have almost doubled between 1982 and 1993, while the number of authorized judgeships has risen only by 26 percent, the report says. And from 1980 to 1994, while the number of federal prosecutors has grown by some 125 percent, federal judges in the district and appellate courts only grew by 17 percent. In addition, the resulting higher case load in the federal judicial system further taps already scarce resources.

- *Leads to competition between federal and state officials, notably in larger metropolitan areas.* Most state prosecutors are elected; most federal prosecutors are appointed. Many of each aspire to higher office. The competition to detect and then prosecute crime increases in direct proportion to the number of overlapping federal statutes that criminalize conduct traditionally held at the local level, the report says.

- *Scatters rather than focuses the resources needed to combat crime.* The federal courts should be reserved for use as a distinctive judicial forum. State courts should be given the responsibility for adjudicating all other matters.

Additionally, state law is easier to modify than is federal legislation. Public accountability in state and local government is higher, according to the report. The movement of laws to the federal level may leave local residents with the belief that they have less power to influence debate and less control over crime's impact on them.

Given its research and analysis, the task force emphasizes three points about the problem of inappropriate federalization.

- *Congress should use great caution when federalizing criminal law.* Federal criminal law should address crimes that affect: core functions of government, such as treason or national borders; national boundaries not governed by states, such as the seas; the Commerce Clause, such as Congress' assertion of jurisdiction over drive-by shootings and carjackings.

  The task force recommends one principle concerning the creation of a new federal crime: To create a federal crime, Congress should clearly show strong federal interest in the matter.

- *Congress should avoid the adverse effects on local crime it creates through inappropriate federalization.* Although many federalized laws rarely lead to prosecutions, they detract from the established allocation of responsibility between federal and state authorities.

  The task force says even one such law affects state courts, reduces state prosecutorial discretion, reduces the effectiveness of both the federal and state criminal justice systems, and forms a body of laws that require constant monitoring at all levels.

- *Congress should consider five recommendations to stem the flow of federalized criminal laws.*

  1) Recognize how best to fight crime within the federal system.

  2) Focus considerations on the true federal interests in crime control.

  3) Establish institutional mechanisms to foster restraint on further federalization.

  4) Include sunset provisions in federalized criminal laws to allow for their review over time.

  5) Respond to public safety concerns not with new federalized crimes, but with federal support for state and local crime control efforts.

The expanding trend of federalizing crime is detracting from the two parallel systems of justice established in this country by reducing the amount of resources available to fight crime, and by superseding the authority of state and local governments. The report recommends that Congress realize the long-range damage caused by these inappropriate laws and take steps to reduce their passage in the future.

4

Civil Rights

The politics of minority rights has been with the nation since its inception. William Riker's essay in chapter 2 reminds us that the issue surfaced at a critical juncture of the Constitutional Convention; it would later very nearly rip the nation apart, with only a bloody Civil War preserving the union. During the modern era, the politics of civil rights has branched out in two important directions: first, in the groups protected, moving beyond the rights of African Americans to those of women and other minorities, and second, in the kinds of protections encompassed by civil rights policy.

With the expansion of civil rights to new groups and jurisdictions, new controversies have emerged. The first and third essays in this chapter examine two such controversies: the use of racial preferences in hiring and admission to schools, and the creation of racially concentrated congressional districts as a means of guaranteeing minority representation. The second essay, by Megan Twohey, revisits recent developments in the issue that launched the civil rights movement of the 1960s—segregation in public education.

4-1

Understanding Whites' Resistance to Affirmative Action

THE ROLE OF PRINCIPLED COMMITMENTS AND RACIAL PREJUDICE

Laura Stoker

In recent years affirmative action policies have come under attack both in Washington and in the states. Large numbers of white voters have on occasion registered their dislike of preferential hiring and educational programs and have endorsed laws designed to end affirmative action. Supporters of affirmative action have argued that these sentiments reflect a veiled racism, while opponents respond that they are simply insisting that no one receive special consideration because of race. In the following essay Laura Stoker, drawing from survey experiments, reports on a more nuanced view held by some opponents of affirmative action programs. The opposition of many, she finds, is selective and depends on the principle upon which the programs are administered.

AFFIRMATIVE ACTION is an increasingly important and divisive issue in American society, so much so that it has been described by one recent commentator as "a time bomb primed to detonate in the middle of the American political marketplace."[1] It has figured prominently in numerous political campaigns, most notably Jesse Helms's 1990 race against Harvey Gantt in North Carolina, and David Duke's unsuccessful bid for the Senate in 1990. Its salience was heightened by legislative battles surrounding the failed 1990 and successful 1991 Civil Rights Acts, by the confirmation controversy surrounding Clarence Thomas's nomination to the Supreme Court, and most recently by the nationally visible campaign surrounding the 1996 California Civil Rights Initiative.

Excerpted from Jon Hurwitz and Mark Peffley, eds., *Perception and Prejudice: Race and Politics in the United States* (New Haven: Yale University Press, 1998), pp. 135–169. Copyright 1998 Yale University Press. Reprinted by permission.

In part because of its political importance, affirmative action has also played a pivotal, and sometimes controversial, role in scholarship on racial attitudes. The fact that whites have continued to resist affirmative action at the same time that they have increasingly come to endorse racial equality in principle and to disavow racially bigoted ideas has helped fuel two major (and related) developments in the literature on racial attitudes in America. The first concerns the so-called principle/policy gap, which has had scholars puzzling over why "white Americans increasingly reject racial injustice in principle but are reluctant to accept the measures necessary to eliminate the injustice" (Pettigrew 1979, p. 119). The second is the development of theories emphasizing "modern" or "symbolic" racism, which argue that although overt racial bigotry has waned, racial prejudice persists in a new guise, one that serves as the foundation for white opposition to racially egalitarian policies like affirmative action and busing. Controversially, some of this work has treated opposition to affirmative action as itself indicative of racial prejudice in its modern form.[2]

Despite the political importance of affirmative action and its significance to the development of the literature on racial attitudes, there have been relatively few direct inquiries into the determinants of public opinion on the issue. Several studies have examined the impact of racial prejudice, especially symbolic or modern variants, and most have concluded that it plays a substantial role in shaping whites' opinions.[3] Yet as with research on the principle/policy gap more generally, these and other studies have also found evidence of additional influences, especially beliefs about the causes of racial inequality (Kluegel 1985; Kluegel and Smith 1983, 1986), value commitments, particularly individualism and egalitarianism, generalized objections to government intervention, and judgments regarding the policy's fairness. As others have noted, the basis of whites' opposition to affirmative action remains poorly understood, particularly with regard to the importance of racial beliefs and attitudes on the one hand, and the importance of principled objections to the policy on the other.

The aim of this chapter is to shed new, if not definitive, light on these long-standing questions. The starting point for the analysis is two survey-based experiments, each of which manipulates features of affirmative action that bear on judgments of its fairness. The first experiment varies the circumstances in which racial quotas in hiring are to be implemented. The crucial issue here turns on whether or not they are to be introduced into settings that have been marked by identifiable practices of discrimination, a distinction that is at the heart of the Supreme Court rulings on the fairness, and thus the legality, of affirmative action measures. If they are to be just, says the Court, race-conscious hiring programs must be a remedial response undertaken by a company or governmental unit that had been previously engaging in a wrongful practice of discriminatory hiring, a response that is "narrowly tailored" to counterbalance the nature and extent of the wrong. As we will see, this is a concern about fairness to which the American public also responds.

The second experiment, this time focused on affirmative action in university admissions, varies according to whether the affirmative action program uses race as a selection criteria or instead employs race-targeted measures that operate before the selection stage. Here the crucial issue is the extent to which affirmative action opponents are specifically objecting to procedures that allocate goods on the basis of race, rather than resting allocation decisions solely on the basis of individual qualifications. Put in terms of popular rhetoric, this experiment assesses the importance of objections to "reverse discrimination"—objections that, as we will see, are powerful indeed.

Although the experimental results support the conclusion that whites' attitudes toward affirmative action are partly based on their judgments of the policy's fairness, they do not reveal how whites' racial beliefs and attitudes may also be entering in. White resistance to affirmative action may indeed be principled in part, but, as other analysts have suggested, it may also be grounded in thoughts and feelings that are far less sublime—racially charged feelings of resentment, bigoted and stereotypical beliefs about blacks, and the belief that racial inequality has arisen or persisted because of the failings of blacks themselves. In order to engage this issue, I build upon the earlier aggregate-level analysis of the experimental manipulations by turning to an individual-level analysis of the antecedents of opinions as rendered within each experimental condition. As the results demonstrate, white resistance to affirmative action is neither founded purely on principle nor fueled purely by racial perceptions and prejudice. In important and at times unexpected ways, it finds its roots in both.

Experiment 1: Context-Specific Support for Racial Quotas in Hiring

The typical survey question on affirmative action either generalizes over the contexts in which affirmative action policies are implemented or makes no reference to context whatsoever. The first case is illustrated by the questions below:

> Some large corporations are required to practice what is called affirmative action. This sometimes requires employers to give special preference to minorities or women when hiring. Do you approve or disapprove of affirmative action? (Cambridge Survey Research)
>
> The U.S. Supreme Court has ruled that employers may sometimes favor women and members of minorities over better-qualified men and whites in hiring and promoting, to achieve better balance in their workforces. Do you approve or disapprove of this decision? (Gallup)

The critical words in these questions are "some" and "sometimes." "*Some* corporations are *sometimes* required to implement preferential hiring programs," says the first. "The U.S. Supreme Court has ruled that employers may *sometimes* favor women and members of minorities over better-qualified men and whites in hiring and promoting," says the second. These questions treat the contexts in which affirmative action programs are implemented as irrelevant to the question of what the public thinks of them.

The second case, where the affirmative action opinion question makes no reference to context at all, is illustrated by the formulation used by the National Election Studies (NES):

> Some people say that because of past discrimination against blacks, preference in hiring and promotion should be given to blacks. Others say preferential hiring and promotion of blacks is wrong [Form A: because it discriminates against whites; Form B: because it gives blacks advantages they haven't earned]. What about your opinion—are you for or against preferential hiring and promotion of blacks?

This question abstracts its way away from the contexts in which affirmative action programs are implemented, treating any given affirmative action program as something that one might favor "because of past discrimination against blacks" or oppose "because it discriminates against whites" or "gives blacks advantages they haven't earned."

Such questions miss a key political feature of affirmative action policies in American society: that their legality depends upon the context in which they are implemented. In ruling after ruling over the past two decades, the Supreme Court has stipulated that race-conscious hiring policies are legitimate only when implemented by a business or governmental unit in response to a finding that the unit itself had been engaging in discriminatory hiring practices, and has clearly rejected race-conscious hiring policies whose aim is to compensate blacks for disadvantages rooted in historic or society-wide practices of discrimination in America or to promote racial balance in the workforce.[4] Thus, for example, in *Wygant v. Jackson Board of Education* Justice Lewis Powell wrote: "This Court never has held that societal discrimination alone is sufficient to justify a racial classification. Rather, the Court has insisted upon some showing of prior discrimination by the government unit involved before allowing limited use of racial classifications in order to remedy such discrimination" (1985 476 US 267, 274).

The Court rests its case here on an argument about just compensation: When it has been established that a given company or governmental unit has wrongfully discriminated against blacks, then justice demands that their discriminatory hiring practices be dismantled, and that compensatory or remedial actions be undertaken. Implementing race-conscious hiring policies in such circumstances is just, the Court argues, if it can be shown that they are narrowly tailored to the particular case at hand, and thus yield an appropriate form and level of compensation for the discriminatory practices that were in place. Prior findings as to the existence and nature of the discriminatory hiring practices, as Justice Sandra Day O'Connor put it in a 1988 opinion, are "necessary to define both the scope of the injury and the extent of the remedy necessary to cure its effects" (*Richmond v. J. A. Croson Co.,* 1988 488 US 497). In such cases, affirmative action policies then serve the "focused goal of remedying wrongs worked by specific instances of racial discrimination" rather than "the remedying of the effects of 'social discrimination,' an amorphous concept of injury that may be ageless in its reach to the past" (ibid., 469).[5] According to the compensatory logic, as one observer put it, it is "black *qua* victim and not black *qua* black person" that is significant (Simon 1977, p. 41).[6]

What makes the typical survey questions problematic is not that they simplify reality, as any survey question must do. Rather, the problem is in the nature of the simplifications that they introduce. If ordinary citizens are moved by the concerns about just compensation that inspire the Court, then we would expect their opinions about affirmative action programs to be sensitive to the context in which those programs are implemented, and specifically to depend upon whether racial preferences are to be introduced in settings marked by a history of discriminatory hiring. Correspondingly, if researchers are interested in knowing what the public thinks about affirmative action programs that the Court has deemed legitimate, then they should be asking affirmative action questions that situate the programs in the circumstances that the Court has identified. At the same time, if they want to know the public's view of affirmative action programs that are or might be found in circumstances that fail to meet the conditions that the Court has identified, then they should ask questions about the use of affirmative action in those circumstances too. Either way, questions that generalize across or ignore the contexts in which affirmative action programs are implemented, may (and, as we will see shortly, often do) yield results that misrepresent the level of public support for affirmative action programs that, as the Court puts it, serve as "narrowly tailored" remedial responses to wrongful practices of discrimination.[7]

The first affirmative action experiment was designed to evaluate the importance of context to opinions on affirmative action. Three different affirmative action questions, each concerning the implementation of a racial quota in hiring, were administered to random thirds of the respondents. The first question was context-free:

Question 1: No Context
Do you think that large companies should be required to give a certain number of jobs to blacks, or should the government stay out of this?

The second and third questions each locate the policy in a particular context. The second defines the policy as one that would be undertaken in companies where "blacks are underrepresented," whereas the third defines the policy as one that would be introduced in companies "with employment policies that discriminate against blacks":

Question 2: Underrepresentation Context
There are some large companies where blacks are underrepresented. . . . Do you think *these* large companies should be required to give a certain number of jobs to blacks, or should the government stay out of this?

Question 3: Discrimination Context
There are some large companies with employment policies that discriminate against blacks. . . . Do you think *these* large companies should be required to give a certain number of jobs to blacks, or should the government stay out of this?

Whereas the first question mimics the abstract framing that affirmative action ordinarily receives, the second locates the policy of race-conscious hiring

Figure 1. Distribution of Whites' Opinions on Affirmative Action in Hiring

a. No context

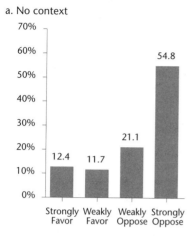

b. Underrepresentation context

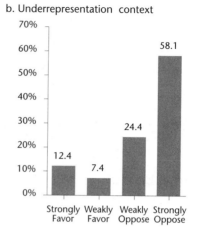

c. Discrimination context

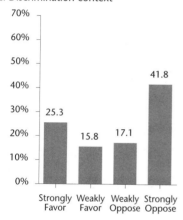

in companies where the workforce is racially imbalanced, and the third explicitly situates it in the context that the Supreme Court has judged legitimate—in companies whose hiring policies have discriminated against blacks.

Figures 1a–c present the distribution of whites' opinions as gauged by each version of the affirmative action opinion question, broken down into responses that range from "strongly favor" to "strongly oppose." Not surprisingly, in light of past research, responses to the context-free question show overwhelmingly opposition to racial hiring quotas (Figure 1a).

Seventy-six percent of the white respondents expressed opposition, and over 70 percent of those respondents identified their opposition as strong. In the second condition, when the context is described as one where "blacks are underrepresented," the portrait of opinion remains virtually unchanged (Figure 1b). We see a very different distribution of opinion, however, once the policy is situated as a response to identified practices of discrimination. Rather than revealing overwhelming opposition, opinion becomes polarized (Figure 1c). Whites opposing racial quotas (59 percent) still outnumber those who express support (41 percent), but the distribution shifts markedly—by roughly 18–20 percent—in the direction of greater support, with those expressing strong opinions outweighing those expressing weak opinions on both sides of the issue.[8]

There are three primary conclusions to draw from these results. First, the fact that racial hiring quotas garner less support when they are implemented by companies identified as having a racially imbalanced workforce (second condition) than when they are implemented by companies identified as having been discriminating against blacks (third condition) tells us that a significant fraction of the public does not consider racial imbalances in the workforce to be indicative of discriminatory hiring practices. Of course, this confirms by inference something about which we also have direct evidence. Research based upon the current survey, as well as previous surveys, has demonstrated that people draw upon a number of different ideas to explain racial differences in economic achievement, including the "lack of effort on the part of blacks, or the lack of skills and preparation, or as the result of a lack of holding the right values" (Kluegel 1985, p. 766) in addition to the forces of prejudice and discrimination.

Second, the enhanced level of support for affirmative action programs that *are*, in fact, situated in contexts where companies had been discriminating against blacks, which is evident for whites and blacks alike, supports the contention that public opinion on affirmative action is partly based on judgments regarding fairness. More specifically, the results suggest that the public is responding to the same concerns about fairness that have inspired the Supreme Court, which has sharply distinguished between race-conscious hiring programs that are introduced to compensate for established practices of discriminatory hiring and those that are implemented simply in order to achieve a racially balanced workforce or to compensate blacks for disadvantages wrought generally by the patterns of racism and prejudice in America.[9]

Finally, the results carry a lesson for how we depict public opinion on affirmative action. When it comes to affirmative action programs that actually meet the requirements set forth by the Supreme Court, programs that are implemented as a "narrowly tailored" remedial response to discriminatory hiring practices, it is not the case that "mass opinion remains invariably opposed to preferential treatment" (Lipset 1991, p. 14), or that "as a civil rights remedy, affirmative action has virtually no mass public support whatsoever" (Carmines and Champagne 1990, p. 197), or that there "is no ambiguity about where the majority stand" (Daniel Yankelovich, quoted in Bunzel 1986, p. 48)—the conventional wisdom about the matter. The portrait of opinion, instead, is of a public that is sharply divided.

Experiment 2: Preferential Treatment vs. Compensatory Action Policies

Race-conscious hiring or admissions policies—regardless of whether they are introduced to remedy established practices of discrimination, or to achieve racial balance, or to compensate blacks for disadvantages traced to the legacy of racism in America—violate the color-blind ideal of basing decisions solely on the applicants' merit, an ideal that judges race irrelevant to how prospective employees or college applicants should be treated (thus instantiating the principle of equal treatment), and where people of all races compete for jobs or admission slots on the basis of their individual qualifications (thus upholding the principle of equality of opportunity). Although these policies gain legitimacy and, as we have seen, public support when they are implemented to remedy ongoing practices of discrimination, they inevitably remain color-conscious, not blind. In this respect, many affirmative action opponents argue, they are patently unfair.

Yet not all affirmative action policies use race as a criteria for making selection decisions. In fact, the policies that best represent the affirmative action agenda as it was developed in the 1960s and 1970s aim to enhance blacks' educational and employment opportunities without introducing race at the selection stage, as, for example, programs that help blacks learn about available job opportunities or that provide them with educational or job-training assistance. Although such policies fall squarely under the mantle of affirmative action as set forth by the Equal Employment Opportunity Commission and continue to have a widespread presence today, they have become disassociated from the term "affirmative action," as Wilson (1992, p. 177) explains:

> The term "affirmative action" has changed in meaning since it was first introduced. Initially, the term referred primarily to special efforts to ensure that equal opportunities were available for members of groups that had been subject to discrimination. Those special efforts included public advertising for positions to be filled, active recruitment of qualified applicants from the formerly excluded groups, as well as special training programs designed to help them meet the standards for admission or appointment. More recently, the term has come to refer to the necessity of providing some degree of definite preference for members of these groups in determining access to positions from which they were formerly excluded.

Perhaps as a consequence, few studies have investigated the public's view of affirmative action in its preselection-stage guise.

In one of the few studies to do so, which was confined to a review of aggregate polling results on affirmative action, Lipset and Schneider (1978) noticed that the American public is more supportive of affirmative action programs that operate prior to the selection stage ("compensatory action" programs) than of those that introduce race as a selection criterion ("preferential treatment" programs).[10] Whereas American citizens in general, and whites in particular, tend to oppose programs that base selection decisions even partly on the basis of race, white majorities will back other race-conscious measures to enhance blacks' employment and educational opportunities.

The present study introduced an experiment that, by isolating the contrast between preferential treatment and compensatory action, was designed to reveal the extent to which opposition to affirmative action was uniquely tied to the use of racial preferences at the selection stage. Each respondent was asked, at random, one of two questions about affirmative action in university admissions. The first question described the policy as one that would give qualified blacks preference over whites, and the second described the policy as one that would involve making an extra effort to ensure that qualified blacks were considered for admission.

Question 1: Give Blacks Preference
Some people say that because of past discrimination, *qualified blacks should be given preference in university admissions.* Others say that this is

Figure 2. Distribution of Whites' Opinions on Affirmative Action in Admissions

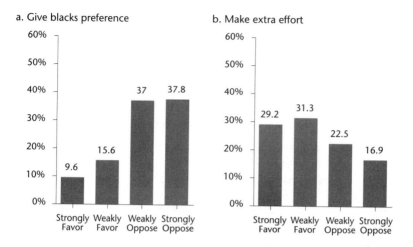

a. Give blacks preference

b. Make extra effort

wrong because it discriminates against whites. How do you feel—are you in favor of or opposed to *giving qualified blacks preference in admission to colleges and universities?*

Question 2: Make Extra Effort

Some people say that because of past discrimination, *an extra effort should be made to be sure that qualified blacks are considered in university admission.* Others say that this is wrong because it discriminates against whites. How do you feel—are you in favor of or opposed to *making an extra effort to make sure that qualified blacks are considered for admission to colleges and universities?*

Figures 2a–b contain the results for the sample of whites. When the question concerns policies that give qualified blacks preference in admission, we see a clear majority in opposition (75 percent), with opposition forces both more numerous and more intense than are the supporting forces (Figure 2a). This level of opposition is almost identical to that found when the question concerned racial preferences in hiring, where 76 percent of whites were opposed (Figure 1a), although is noticeably less intense (with 38 percent falling in the "strongly oppose" category, compared to 55 percent in Figure 1a).[11] The distribution of opinion shifts sharply, however, when the question concerns special efforts to make sure that qualified blacks are considered for admission (Figure 2b). The number of opponents drops sharply and the number of supporters more than doubles. In percentage terms, affirmative action support climbs by 35 points to where a clear majority (61 percent) backs the programs, of which half do so "strongly."[12]

As with the first experiment, these results demonstrate that whites' opinions on affirmative action have a principled basis. Whether whites are willing to support race-targeted programs designed to enhance blacks' educational opportunities depends on whether those programs specifically introduce race as a criterion for admissions. Although one sometimes finds political pundits claiming otherwise, it is not the race-targeted aspect of affirmative action programs, per se, that generates majority white opposition. What is crucial is whether they violate the principle of fairness specifying that selection decisions should be based upon applicant qualifications, not race. . . .

Conclusion

There is a noticeable discrepancy between how the typical survey question has framed affirmative action in employment and how it has been framed by the law that has emerged under the guidance of Supreme Court rulings. Survey questions usually pose the issue abstractly; they treat racial preferences in employment as a general measure designed to enhance the employment status of blacks, in light of discrimination generally experienced by blacks in the past. The Court, by contrast, has treated racial preferences in employment as a limited remedial measure designed to "eliminate those discriminatory practices and devices which have fostered racially stratified job environments to the disadvantage of minority citizens,"[13] appropriate only when implemented in occupational contexts marked by a history of racial discrimination. Their purpose is circumscribed—to remedy the effects of identifiable practices of discrimination; as are the circumstances in which they may legally be implemented—in companies where established practices of discrimination have left blacks disadvantaged.

The practice of studying public opinion on affirmative action through the use of abstract and general survey questions has several consequences, as demonstrated here. First, it fails to reveal that the American public, white and black alike, is sensitive to an issue of fairness that has preoccupied the courts: whether or not the programs are specifically tailored to respond to wrongful practices of discrimination and to compensate blacks for disadvantages suffered as a result. On the whole, Americans are significantly more supportive of programs that meet the "narrowly tailored" remedial purpose that the Supreme Court has established than of programs simply designed to eradicate racial stratification in the workforce, whatever its cause. Although it is standard practice to describe the American public as overwhelmingly and invariably opposed to racial quotas, that conventional wisdom should be revised.

Second, analyses based on responses to abstract affirmative action questions lead to an exaggerated sense of the opinion-shaping role played by whites' explanations for racial inequality—though exaggerated in one sense alone. These beliefs are indeed important to how whites evaluate affirmative action, but they are especially so when the program is framed as a general policy tool through which to enhance blacks' status. They become much less important, though not completely irrelevant, when the policy is treated as a limited measure only to be utilized in circumstances where discrimination against blacks has been operating. . . .

. . . [I]t is apparent that this study adds to the growing weight of evidence suggesting the importance of issue framing, an argument that has been developed by a number of analysts studying public opinion on affirmative action. The framing argument holds that the opinions citizens take on an issue are affected by the way the issue is "packaged" by elites or the mass media, and accordingly by our survey questions as well. In the survey context, however, this idea has usually been developed by thinking about the different ways in which a given policy stance—support or opposition—might be justified. Kinder and Sanders (1990), for example, experimentally manipulated the reason given for opposing a general policy of racial preferences, in one condition using the phrase "because it discriminates against whites," and in a second condition using the phrase "because it gives blacks advantages they haven't earned." What this investigation has emphasized, instead, is not how support or opposition to a given affirmative action policy is justified in our questions, but rather how our questions—and ultimately political elites—come to describe affirmative action policies themselves.

Affirmative action promises to remain a contested subject on the broader political agenda. As of this writing, the Republican majority in Congress is taking aim at affirmative action, hoping to use it as a "wedge issue" to elicit the conversion or defection of conservative white Democrats. New court cases challenging the legitimacy of race-conscious hiring and admissions programs continue to make their way through the legal system. Thinking about the broader political ramifications of the affirmative action debate provides a final way to put in perspective the findings and arguments presented here. In the electoral arena, the debate over affirmative action is typically waged in terms of symbols and slogans. It's about "quotas," "a color-blind society," "racism," "reverse discrimination," and the like. As Jesse Helms's infamous 1990 advertisement reminds us even more forcefully, it is often not about the parameters of actual policies at all.[14] There is every reason to believe that the controversies over affirmative action will continue to operate rhetorically in ways that fully ignore the policy distinctions I have focused upon here. As Theodore M. Shaw, associate director-counsel for the NAACP Legal Defense Fund, put it recently: "These issues are very complex and sensitive. The courts have struck a balance that allows affirmative action in limited circumstances. But the political process and the nature of political discourse these days do not insure these issues will be dealt with in a thoughtful and sensitive way."[15] To the extent that this is so, what will be of consequence to the electoral arena is not the fact that Americans will support this or that affirmative action policy, or support a given policy in one circumstance more than in another. Simplistic appeals and emotionally charged rhetoric may come to rule the day.

NOTES

1. Steven V. Roberts. "Affirmative Action on the Edge," *U.S. News and World Report,* February 13, 1995.

2. Kinder and Sears's (1981) index of "expressive racism," for example, included response to two questions tapping opinions on racial quotas in university admissions. Less blatant is the logic embodied in the implicit syllogism with which McConahay, Hardee, and Batts (1981) begin their article "Has Racism Declined in America?": "In recent years as public opinion polls have shown a decline in racist responses, white Americans have strongly resisted school desegregation and affirmative action programs. Hence, there has been a debate over the extent to which racism has really declined." See Sniderman and Tetlock (1986) for a critique of the thesis of symbolic racism in general, and the reading of opposition to affirmative action as equivalent to prejudice in particular.

3. The only study I am aware of that explicitly compares the effects of old-fashioned and modern versions of prejudice, Jacobson (1985), found smaller effects for the former than for the latter. This is consistent with what has been found for other race-policy opinions (Kinder 1986). Kinder and Sanders (1990) found that racial prejudice bore a moderately strong relationship to opinions on affirmative action, more so when the pol-

icy was framed as "giving blacks advantages they haven't earned" than when it was framed as "discriminating against whites." Although they do not describe their measure, it was presumably based on the symbolic racism items carried by the National Election Studies, as described in Kinder (1986). Kluegel and Smith's (1986) measure of racial prejudice, which combined "the perception of blacks' demands for change as legitimate or illegitimate, and evaluations of civil rights groups" (p. 160), proved to be one of the best predictors of opinions on affirmative action. Sniderman and Piazza (1993) examined the effects of a variety of racial stereotypes, finding effects for stereotypes that concern blacks' work ethic (e.g., the belief that blacks are lazy or undisciplined), but these effects were noticeably weaker with respect to affirmative action opinions than with respect to opinions concerning general social assistance programs for blacks. They conclude that "although it has become fashionable to assert that opposition to affirmative action is driven by racism, as though the reason so many whites object to racial quotas and preferential treatment is prejudice pure and simple, it turns out that the politics of affirmative action has remarkably little to do with whites' feelings toward blacks" (p. 109). Other studies of public opinion on affirmative action have not examined whites' racial beliefs and attitudes at all, because they focus either on aggregate polling results (e.g., Bunzel 1986; Lipset and Schneider 1978; Lipset 1990) or on the results of controlled experiments.

4. The Court has reached similar conclusions with respect to other areas in which affirmative action is practiced, although the legal details vary considerably. Discrimination throughout the construction industry, for example, has been judged relevant to the use of affirmative action in the awarding of government contracts (a point under contention in the 1995 case *Adarand Constructors v. Pena,* which otherwise affirmed the "narrowly tailored" rationale), and the value of diversity has been recognized in cases concerning university admissions. It is also worth noting that any business that voluntarily implements an affirmative action program must be able to provide evidence of prior discrimination if the legality of the program is challenged. Rosenfeld (1991) contains a useful review of affirmative action rulings from the 1970s and 1980s. Dansicker (1991) discusses more recent cases and legislation.

5. Here, Justice O'Connor is partially quoting from Justice Powell's opinion in *University of California Regents v. Baake* (1978 438 US 265). Court rulings also repeatedly warn about "the myriad of innocent causes that may lead to statistical imbalances in the composition of their work forces" (*Watson v. Fort Worth Bank and Trust,* 1988 487 US 977, 992; quoted in *Wards Cove Packing Co. v. Atonia,* 1989 490 US 642, 657).

6. Compensatory justice requires reparation or restitution to victims. One problematic issue that remains revolves around the question of whether preferential treatment policies are only acceptable if they compensate "actual victims" or whether they may apply to the entire "class of victims" (e.g., blacks) affected by the discriminatory practice. This continues to be debated by the Court (for example, see Justice Scalia's separate opinion in *Richmond v. J. A. Crosan Co.,* 1998 488 US 469), but in *Local 25, Sheet Metal Workers' Intern. Ass'n v. EEOC* the Court explicitly rejected the argument that Title VII, section 706(g) of the 1964 Civil Rights Act "authorizes a district court to award preferential relief

only to the actual victims of unlawful discrimination" and concluded that it "does not prohibit a court from ordering, in appropriate circumstances, affirmative race-conscious relief as a remedy for past discrimination. Specifically, we hold that such relief may be appropriate where an employer or a labor union has engaged in persistent or egregious discrimination, or where necessary to dissipate the lingering effects of pervasive discrimination" (1985 478 US 421, 444–445, opinion delivered by Justice Brennan).

7. Ironically, it is quite clear that affirmative action opinion questions have been formulated with Supreme Court decisions in mind. The first two questions listed above refer explicitly or implicitly to Court pronouncements. And, like the NES question, many others include such phrases as "because of past discrimination" or "to make up for past discrimination," language prominent in Supreme Court decisions on affirmative action. Yet, whereas the Court's use of the phrase "past discrimination" refers to past discrimination in the hiring unit in which the affirmative action policy serves as the remedial response, when it finds its way into abstract survey questions like that used by the NES, it instead evokes images of discrimination as a generalized social phenomenon, perhaps found only in the distant past.

8. It is important to note that although blacks exhibit much more support for racial quotas than do whites, they show a pattern of differences across the experimental conditions that is very similar to (and statistically indistinguishable from) that for whites. The percentage of blacks who express opposition to racial quotas drops from 33% and 37% in the first two conditions, respectively, to 19% in the third condition. For the sample as a whole, the comparable figures are 72%, 76%, and 54%.

9. Only two studies that I am aware of provide further evidence of this point, and do so only obliquely. The first was an experimental study undertaken by Rupert Nacoste (1985), where undergraduate subjects played the role of a female professor awarded a university grant through affirmative action, and which manipulated whether or not there was a history of discrimination against women in the awards committee. Subjects in the prior discrimination condition felt significantly more deserving of their grant, and Nacoste concluded that "overall, it appears that history of discrimination is an important contextual variable to consider within the domain of responses to affirmative action" (p. 240). The second study, undertaken by Francine Tougas, Ann Beaton, and France Veilleux, examined the attitudes of female workers in Canada. It found that perceptions regarding the extent to which women were disadvantaged by the organization's existing hiring and promotional practices strongly affected the level of support given to affirmative action programs.

10. The findings reported by Lipset and Schneider have also been noted by other analysts of public opinion on affirmative action, including Bunzel (1986), Kluegel and Smith (1983), and Lynch and Beer (1990).

11. Data from NES reported by Fine (1992) and from GSS reported by Kluegel and Smith (1986) have also shown that the American public responds similarly to quotas in hiring and in university admissions.

12. By way of comparison, the shift in blacks' opinions across the two conditions is not nearly as stark. Twenty-three percent of the black respondents expressed opposition

in the preferential treatment condition, dropping to 9% in the compensatory action case. The smaller experimental shift among blacks (14%) than among whites (35%), however, is apparently due to floor effects. Because the rate of black opposition to preferential treatment in university admissions is so low to begin with, there is not much further it could fall.

13. From Justice Brennan's opinion in *Local 25, Sheet Metal Workers' Intern. Ass'n v. EEOC* (1985 478 US 421, 450).

14. The advertisement showed "white hands holding a rejection slip, while a narrator intoned, `You needed that job, and you were the best qualified. But it had to go to a minority because of a racial quota.'" Priscilla Painton. "Quota Quagmire," *Time,* May 27, 1991.

15. *New York Times,* February 7, 1995.

REFERENCES

Achen, Christopher H. 1982. *Interpreting and Using Regression.* Beverly Hills, Calif.: Sage.

Bunzel, John H. 1986. "Affirmative Re-actions." *Public Opinion* February/March: 45–49.

Carmines, Edward G., and Richard A. Champagne, Jr. 1990. "The Changing Content of American Racial Attitudes: A Fifty-Year Portrait." *Journal of Micropolitics* 3:187–208.

Dansicker, Andrew M. 1991. "A Sheep in Wolf's Clothing: Affirmative Action, Disparate Impact, Quotas, and the Civil Rights Act." *Columbia Journal of Law and Social Problems* 25:1–50.

Fine, Terri Susan. 1992. "The Impact of Issue Framing on Public Opinion Toward Affirmative Action Programs." *Social Science Journal* 29:323–34.

Jacobson, Cardell. 1985. "Resistance to Affirmative Action: Self-interest or Racism?" *Journal of Conflict Resolution* 29:306–29.

Kinder, Donald R. 1986. "The Continuing American Dilemma: White Resistance to Racial Change 40 Years After Myrdal." *Journal of Social Issues* 42:151–71.

Kinder, Donald R., and Lynn M. Sanders. 1990. "Mimicking Political Debate with Survey Questions: The Case of White Opinion on Affirmative Action." *Social Cognition* 8:71–103.

Kinder, Donald R., and David O. Scars. 1981. "Symbolic Racism Versus Racial Threats to the Good Life." *Journal of Personality and Social Psychology* 40:414–31.

Kluegel, James R. 1985. "If There Isn't a Problem, You Don't Need a Solution: The Bases of Contemporary Affirmative Action Attitudes." *American Behavioral Scientist* 28:761–64.

Kluegel, James R., and Eliot R. Smith. 1983. "Affirmative Action Attitudes: Effects of Self-interest, Racial Affect, and Stratification Beliefs on Whites' Views." *Social Forces* 61:797–824.

_____. 1986. *Beliefs About Inequality.* New York: Aldine de Gruyter.

Lipset, Seymour Martin. 1991. "Two Americas, Two Value Systems: Blacks and Whites." Hoover Institution Working Paper P-91-1.

Lipset, Seymour Martin, and William Schneider. 1978. "The Bakke Case: How Would It Be Decided in the Bar of Public Opinion?" *Public Opinion* 1:38–44.

Lynch, Frederick R., and William R. Beer. 1990. "You Ain't the Right Color, Pal." *Policy Review* (Winter): 64–67.

McConahay, John B. 1986. "Modern Racism, Ambivalence, and the Modern Racism Scale." In *Prejudice, Discrimination, and Racism,* ed. John F. Dovidio and Samuel L. Gaertner. New York: Academic.

McConahay, John B., Betty B. Hardee, and Valerie Batts. 1981. "Has Racism Declined in America?" *Journal of Conflict Resolution* 25:563–79.

Nacoste, Rupert W. 1985. "Selection Procedure and Responses to Affirmative Action: The Case of Favorable Treatment." *Law and Human Behavior* 9:225–42.

Ottati, Victor C., and Robert S. Wyer, Jr. 1993. "Affect and Political Judgment." In *Explorations in Political Psychology,* ed. Shanto Iyengar and William J. McGuire. Durham, N.C.: Duke University Press.

Pettigrew, Thomas F. 1979. "Racial Change and Social Policy." *Annals of the American Academy of Political and Social Science* 44:114–31.

Rosenfeld, Michael. 1991. *Affirmative Action and Justice.* Hew Haven: Yale University Press.

Simon, Robert 1977. "Preferential Hiring: A Reply to Judith Jarvis Thomson." In *Equality and Preferential Treatment,* ed. Marshall Cohen, Thomas Nagel, and Thomas Scanlon. Princeton, N.J.: Princeton University Press.

Sniderman, Paul M., and Thomas Piazza. 1993. *The Scar of Race.* Cambridge, Mass.: Harvard University Press.

Sniderman, Paul M., and Philip E. Tetlock. 1986. "Symbolic Racism: Problems of Motive Attribution in Political Analysis." *Journal of Social Issues* 42:129–50.

Sniderman, Paul M., Philip E. Tetlock, Edward G. Carmines, and Randall S. Peterson. 1993. "The Politics of the American Dilemma: Issue Pluralism." In *Prejudice, Politics, and the American Dilemma,* ed. Paul M. Sniderman, Philip E. Tetlock, and Edward G. Carmines. Stanford, Calif.: Stanford University Press.

Wilson, Le Von E. 1992. "Affirmative Action: The Future of Race Based Preferences in Hiring." *The Western Journal of Black Studies* 16:173–179.

4-2

Desegregation Is Dead

Megan Twohey

Many observers believed that the Supreme Court's 1954 Brown v. Board of Education decision spelled the end of racial segregation in public schools. Especially after the Civil Rights Act of 1964 brought the full force of federal authority (including busing) to bear against segregation in the South, the end to segregated education appeared inevitable. But social policy is never easy to implement. In the following article Megan Twohey examines the countervailing social forces that appear to be reestablishing segregated schooling in many communities.

> Theoretically, the Negro needs neither segregated schools nor mixed schools. What he needs is Education. What he must remember is that there is no magic, either in mixed schools or in segregated schools. A mixed school with poor and unsympathetic teachers, with hostile public opinion, and no teaching of truth concerning black folk, is bad. A segregated school with ignorant placeholders, inadequate equipment, poor salaries, and wretched housing, is equally bad. Other things being equal, the mixed school is the broader, more natural basis for the education of all youth. . . . But other things seldom are equal. . . .
>
> —W. E. B. DUBOIS, 1935

RACIAL DESEGREGATION of the public schools was one of the hallmark victories of the civil rights struggles of the twentieth century—an accomplishment so strongly resisted that it often came only at the point of a gun, so painful that its consequences are still felt in cities across the nation. Now . . . America is abandoning the experiment. The idea that racial equality might be reached through racial proximity in schools is widely seen as an anachronism, and by some as an out-and-out mistake. The mandated programs intended to further that idea are shutting down.

Court-ordered busing—for three decades the primary tool to achieve racial integration in schools—has been rolling to a stop for the past several years. On Sept. 10 [1999], the full stop was reached, in the very place where busing began. In North Carolina, U.S. District Judge Robert Potter declared that busing was no longer necessary to remedy discrimination against blacks. Indeed, ruled Potter, any mechanism that assigns children to a school based on their race—whether through lotteries, quotas, preferences, or set-asides—is illegal. Potter's decision came in a lawsuit over busing in the Charlotte-Mecklenburg schools. Busing was born in this school district 30 years ago, when federal Judge James McMillan decreed, in *Swann v. Charlotte-Mecklenburg Board of Education,* that busing was a legitimate means to end segregation in the public schools.

What happened in Charlotte-Mecklenburg is the most recent example of an accelerating and overwhelming abandonment of mandated school integration. This past summer the Boston School Committee voted to stop desegregation there. Buffalo, Minneapolis, and Cleveland are among other Northern cities following a similar path. Mobile, Alabama, and Jacksonville, Florida, are phasing out their desegregation policies. Recent surveys show that across the South fewer and fewer black children are attending schools with white children, and vice versa. It is as if *Brown v. Board of Education*—the milestone 1954 Supreme Court decision that pronounced separate but equal education as, in fact, unequal and discriminatory education—had never existed.

The resegregation of the 1990s has many causes. Changing demographics in major cities, recent U.S. Supreme Court cases challenging the use of racial quotas, and shifting attitudes within the black community have all contributed to both the voluntary and the mandated abandonment of desegregation. There are many, including many black Americans, who argue that the change is inevitable.

But is this a good thing? Decades of research show that test scores of minority children improve when they attend school with substantial numbers of white children. Education experts fear that, as the tide turns, and as segregated neighborhood schools replace court-ordered integrated ones, the academic progress made by blacks could fade. No one knows whether all-black neighborhood schools, even well-funded ones in communities where blacks have enough political power to oversee them, can match the academic achievement of integrated schools. And there are broader questions too, beyond the goals of education. Some sociologists worry that the retreat from integrated schools could set back race relations by further cementing residential and social segregation. . . .

To be sure, not all cities or school districts are abandoning *Brown v. Board of Education*. Earlier this year, a group of mainly suburban middle-class school districts from around the country banded together in a new network dedicated to making integrated schools work. These districts intend to share knowledge of their successes and failures in an effort to ensure that the gap between white and black achievement continues to narrow. But these districts represent a conspicuous minority, a collective small voice raised against a trend that no one expects to see reversed in the near future.

The Demographics

According to a report by Harvard University sociologist Gary Orfield, released last June, resegregation is on the rise throughout the country, with the sharpest changes occurring in the South. After climbing for three decades and peaking in the late 1980s, the percentage of black and white students attending integrated schools began to decline steadily in the 1990s. The recent figures still show far more integration than during the pre-busing era. But the numbers are returning to levels not seen since the 1960s or 1970s.

In the 1996–97 school year, the average white public school student attended a school that was more than 80 percent white. Meanwhile, 69 percent of black students were attending a school defined as majority-minority—a school whose nonwhite population ranges from 50 percent to 100 percent of the student body. And 35 percent of black students were attending a school with a student body that was overwhelmingly minority—defined as 90 percent to 100 percent—a figure not seen since the mid-1970s.

Ironically, regions that initially required the most integration after *Brown v. Board of Education* are now seeing the most resegregation. In the South, after decades of growth, the portion of black students attending integrated schools with a majority-white population fell from a peak of 43.5 percent in 1988 to 34.7 percent in 1996, according to Orfield's report, which is based on data from the federal National Center for Education Statistics.

Yet the trend is not limited to the South. In Northern states, decades of white flight to the suburbs have left city school districts with few options. They simply do not have enough whites to effectively integrate the schools.

This is the case in Boston. Faced with a pending legal battle and a city population that went from 82 percent white in 1970 to 56 percent white in

1995, the Boston school board had to overhaul its racial desegregation plan this past summer. On the eve of the decision, the school population was only 17 percent white, down from 52 percent in 1974, when busing began.

Other demographic trends in the past 30 years have also added to the difficulty of integrating schools in cities, and some suburbs. Growth in non-European immigration—specifically a growing population of Hispanics in urban areas—has made it harder to achieve racial balance. Low birthrates among white women and continuing residential segregation in all parts of the country also impede desegregation.

Changing Black Attitudes

Another piece of the resegregation puzzle is a shift in attitudes among blacks. White support for integration has grown markedly over the past half-century. In recent years, however, increasing numbers of blacks—frustrated by the persistent gaps between black and white academic performance and fed up with the inconvenience of racial busing—have promoted a return to all-minority, nonbused neighborhood schools.

During the 1990s, black community leaders in several school districts pushed for an end to busing as a means of leveling the academic playing field for blacks and whites. In Yonkers, N.Y., Seattle, and Prince George's County, Md., school boards dominated by blacks have chosen to dismantle their desegregation plans in favor of better-financed neighborhood schools.

"Blacks were tired of being bused out of their communities," explains Alvin Thornton, professor of political science at Howard University and chairman of the school board in Prince George's County, a suburb of Washington, D.C., and home to one of the largest black middle-class populations in the country. "We signed a consent decree in 1998 in which we put in place a neighborhood schools plan. A key part was to rebuild schools in black areas to increase the sense of community," Thornton says. The plan also includes additional money from the state and county for the new schools.

Busing fatigue was accompanied by a rise in Afrocentric pride; in many black communities, the old notion that integration necessarily meant better came to be seen as a species of racism in itself. Black leaders began to re-evaluate and reject "the theory that racially identifiable (all-black) schools generate inferiority in African-American students and reduce their motivation to learn," Thornton wrote in an article titled "Academic Achievement vs. Busing," which appeared in a 1995 issue of the journal *Government and Politics*. Increasing numbers of black parents preferred to send their children to African-centered schools, where they might gain racial and cultural awareness—knowledge that, as Thornton puts it, "is not measured by SAT and other national test scores."

. . . The NAACP, which has been pro-integration since its founding 90 years ago, doesn't like the idea of going back to segregated schools. But even here, there are stirrings of dissent. In 1996, the board of the national NAACP fired Robert H. Robinson, the president of the Bergen County, N.J., branch, after he challenged the organization's stance on school integration. Similarly, Kenneth Jenkins was dismissed as president of the Yonkers branch in 1995 for questioning the use of racial busing.

NAACP leaders are determined to resist the trend toward resegregation. "Once the NAACP adopts a policy, all its members have to comply," says Maxine Waters, the chairwoman of the NAACP's National Education Committee. "After blacks reached a token state in the education system, we may have stopped pushing for integration. But we're not going to retreat. We can't go back to where we were before school desegregation. Resources have always followed the white child. If we go back to separate facilities, that will happen again."

Neighborhood Schools

If blacks are divided on the wisdom of returning to neighborhood schools, so, too, are the experts. Many thinkers, left and right, applaud the return to neighborhood schools as a way to strengthen communities and to use education resources for something more valuable than yellow buses. Bruno V. Manno, a senior fellow at the Annie E. Casey Foundation, a nonprofit, nonpartisan organization in Baltimore that promotes research about disadvantaged children, says that the shift away from racial busing will make schools better community institutions. "The issue is not race, it's community," Manno says. "Neighborhood schools create links between families and schools. Community involvement is an important ingredient to enhancing school performance and increasing family strength. If the community aspect is not there, it's pointless to bus kids across the city to boost performance."

Charles L. Glenn, a professor of education at Boston University, who oversaw Boston's original desegregation plan in 1974, says, "I'm quite comfortable moving beyond race in making decisions. Integration should be a goal, but there is no obligation to create diverse school systems."

Conservative think tanks generally agree that returning to neighborhood schools is appropriate. "Experience shows that integration doesn't work," says Nina S. Rees, an education policy analyst at the conservative Heritage Foundation. "Desegregation disrupts the system. We spend a lot of money busing blacks into white schools. . . . It's not a natural process. You're forcing integration. The first order of business is to make sure that you have good, quality schools." But Christopher Jencks, professor of social policy at Harvard University's John F. Kennedy School of Government and co-editor of *The Black–White Test Score Gap,* says: "A return to segregated schools is dangerous. Blacks who attend integrated schools do better than those in segregated schools. If you're committed to closing the gap between black and white students, you don't want to give ground."

Orfield of Harvard says, "There is considerable evidence that the resegregated schools of the 1990s are profoundly unequal," and "the costs of passively accepting them are likely to be immense."

Furthermore, liberals and education researchers say that integration is about more than academics. Jencks, for example, says, "There's more to worry about in segregated schools. Resegregation has all types of consequences that go beyond vocabulary scores. Such a trend leads to the general erosion of social ties in society. The more you let society pull itself apart, the less commitment the haves have to the have-nots."

The Law

The Supreme Court has been a major factor in the move away from busing and integrated schools; in several decisions during the 1990s, the Court has undermined the legal apparatus underpinning court-ordered desegregation plans.

In its 1991 decision *Board of Education of Oklahoma City v. Dowell,* the Court ruled that desegregation orders—some of which had been in effect in school districts for 25 years—should be temporary, not permanent, as long as cities tried to remedy past discrimination "as far as practicable." In 1992, the Court ruled in *Freeman v. Pitts* that individual components of desegregation plans, such as faculty or student assignment, could be evaluated separately and dismantled in stages. And in its 1995 decision *Missouri v. Jenk-*

ins, the high court rejected a lower-court decision that said desegregation must be maintained in Kansas City schools until it produces beneficial results for black students. These decisions encouraged other lawsuits challenging desegregation orders, and many school boards chose to settle out of court. That's what happened in Boston.

"The Supreme Court has shifted from being the leading edge of desegregation to being the leading edge of resegregation," says Orfield. "White parents who disapprove of desegregation can sue the school system. They have more power than the school boards, and that's dangerous."

The Supreme Court decisions have also been helped, and driven, by the fact that *Brown v. Board of Education* did not mandate integrated schools; it mandated only the dismantling of forced segregation. Legal experts say that desegregation and integration are not legally synonymous. "There has never been an obligation to create integrated, diverse school systems," says Glenn. "There has only been an obligation to cease and desist forced segregation. School systems only have to take remedial actions to undo the wrongs of segregation."

Indeed, the purpose of desegregation was to undo the damage done by legal segregation, not to mandate diversity. Diversity is not a compelling government purpose, says David J. Armor, research professor at the Institute of Public Policy at George Mason University and author of *Forced Justice: School Desegregation and the Law.* And racially unbalanced school districts are not illegal. "The only reason we had integration is because we first had legal segregation," says Armor, who advocates more school choice and magnet schools to accomplish desegregation. "Stopping racial busing plans brings us back to de facto segregation. . . . Some say that diversity should be a compelling government purpose, but the Supreme Court says no."

The legal future for mandatory desegregation does not look promising. The next question the high court is expected to face is whether school districts should be allowed to use race at all when deciding which schools children will attend—an issue at the heart of the affirmative action debate. In fact, the Sept. 10 ruling on the Charlotte-Mecklenburg schools in North Carolina could end up before the Supreme Court on appeal on that very issue, bringing the desegregation legal debate full circle. Busing as a tool to achieve school integration in the United States was first given the green light nationwide by the Supreme Court in 1971 in the landmark case *Swann v. Charlotte-Mecklenburg Board of Education.* In that case, black parents had sued the Charlotte schools in 1969 to force integration, on the ground that Charlotte's separate schools for whites and blacks were discriminatory.

But two years ago, after almost 30 years of forced integration, a white parent sued the Charlotte-Mecklenburg school system, charging that his daughter was twice denied admittance to a magnet school because she is not black. Six other white parents joined the case, arguing that race-based policies are discriminatory and that the district had successfully desegregated its schools. Judge Potter agreed, calling the argument for ongoing desegregation a "bizarre posture." He said that today's focus on "racial diversity" in education forces students to serve "as cogs in a social experiment." . . .

The school system, two black parents, and many of the original lawyers from the 1969 *Swann* case joined forces to fight the white parents, arguing that desegregation policies are still needed. After Potter's ruling, one of the black parents told *The Observer,* "This is a very sad, dark and dreary day in our history here in this community."

The Achievement Gap

As the Supreme Court and lower courts grapple with the legal issues surrounding racial quotas, resegregation continues to expand. And the academic achievement gap between black and white students, which narrowed in the 1970s and '80s, and remained constant during the early 1990s, may now be starting to grow. Education experts agree that many factors contribute to lower academic achievement among blacks, such as income and parents' level of education. But this is certain: When black children and white children attend the same schools, the achievement gap between them shrinks, and the performance of white children does not suffer. Although scholars disagree about exactly how much desegregation improves test scores for black students, data from the federal National Assessment of Educational Progress show that blacks made gains at the elementary school level during the 1970s and across all grade levels in the 1980s—the peak of desegregation.

Robert L. Crain at Columbia University's Teachers College studied the impact of school integration on black achievement during the 1970s. "We found that desegregation removed between one-quarter and one-third of the gap between black and white students," he says. "But the integration has to occur at the first-grade level. If it occurs later, the gains diminish."

Certainly other factors besides integration in the 1970s and 1980s helped shrink the gap between whites and blacks. According to Jencks, class sizes got smaller, curricula got better, and the disparity between the education levels of black and white parents narrowed during that period. Then, in the 1990s, the achievement gap began growing again. Black reading scores declined while white scores went up. Black math scores were stable or rose slightly, but white scores for math rose more. "There's been a retrogression of the gap," says Jencks. "Things have improved over the long run, but we've hit a plateau."

Is this wider gap caused by the resegregation of American schools? "No one can say exactly why the gap has grown in the 1990s, but a good hypothesis is that it's related to the decline in desegregation," says Meredith Phillips, assistant professor of policy studies and sociology at the University of California (Los Angeles) and co-editor of *The Black–White Test Score Gap.*

In 1996, Crain re-examined the relationship between integration and black test scores in 32 states. He reported that the gap between black and white fourth-grade reading scores was largest in Michigan and New York, states where the percentage of blacks in the schools was highest and blacks were more racially isolated, and smallest in West Virginia and Iowa, where blacks made up a much lower percentage of the school population and were the least isolated from whites.

In Prince George's County, where school board Chairman Thornton has pushed for neighborhood schools, even he acknowledges the black-white gap. "There is a twoness that has developed," says Thornton. "Poor black kids attending all-black schools are doing poorly. Black kids that can afford to get proximity to white students are doing better."

But Thornton says that returning to busing as a means of desegregation is not an option. "I don't have any choice in the matter," he says. "I don't have any white kids in my county, and I can't bus them in from other counties due to the Supreme Court's stance. When the demographics and jurisprudence of the Supreme Court have overwhelmed you, you have to use other strategies to integrate your community."

So Thornton and other black leaders have turned to campaigns to get more money for their neighborhood schools, usually from state legislatures or city councils. Indeed, research indicates that differences in funding and in community resources affect student achievement. Predominantly minority high schools are "on average, more than twice as large as predominantly white schools and reaching 3,000 students or more in most cities," reports

Linda Darling-Hammond in a 1998 paper, "Black America: Progress and Prospects," published by the Brookings Institution. "On average, class sizes are 15 percent larger overall; curriculum offerings and materials are lower in quality; and teachers are much less qualified in terms of levels of education, certification, and training in the fields they teach," according to Darling-Hammond.

To bring minority neighborhood schools up to the level of white schools will require urban school districts to undertake sustained efforts to obtain more money from state and local governments. In areas where blacks are politically powerful, such as in Maryland, that may indeed be possible.

A Different Approach

Not everyone is giving up on the integrated ideal. In some communities, school boards and administrators are fighting to narrow the academic achievement gap between black and white students and to maintain integrated classrooms. The best example is the Minority Student Achievement Network, a group of 15 middle-class, integrated school districts across the country that joined forces last February in an unprecedented effort to eliminate the disparity in test scores. Blacks in all of these districts generally perform above the national average for their racial group, but still at lower levels than their white counterparts.

The network has made a commitment to work with the College Board's National Task Force on Minority Achievement, which was established in 1997 to address the test-score gaps. The network plans to incorporate the board's research into its local curricula. In its mission statement, the network promises to share individual staff and district successes, and failures, through regular communications, exchange visits, special teacher seminars, and discussion focus groups. The network will also serve as a national clearinghouse for information about practices that are most effective in raising the achievements of minority students. Chapel Hill, N.C., White Plains, N.Y., and Evanston, Ill., are among the districts involved.

Allan Alson, superintendent at Evanston Township High School, launched the network after years of observing a racial divide between students in the school's honors and lower-level classes. Honors and advanced-placement classes are made up mainly of white students, and lower-level and special-education classes mainly of black students. "We recognized that the degree and scope of progress we were making on our own wasn't quick or good enough," Alson says. Evanston, with a population of 73,000, is 70 percent white and 23 percent black. The city has a long history of addressing white-black achievement gaps since self-imposed integration began in the 1960s. In any given primary school, a racial group cannot exceed 60 percent of the student body. Both white and black students are bused across town to achieve this goal at the elementary- and middle-school levels. The town has only one high school.

Evanston has consistently resisted the pressure to return to neighborhood schools. Changing demographics have periodically forced the Evanston school board to redraw the neighborhood lines used to shape busing plans. During several of the debates over these changes, black community leaders have suggested abandoning the city's integration plan in favor of neighborhood schools. In 1995, for example, Terri Sheppard, who later became a member of the school board, proposed an African-centered neighborhood school. Under consideration at the time was a new busing plan that would have required black and white students to literally crisscross town in order to uphold the racial guidelines. Sheppard, whose children would probably have been affected by the plan, said she was tired of "drive-by diversity." Yet the board stood firm and refused to OK the proposal.

In addition to working within the new nationwide network, the Evanston high school has implemented its own programs specifically aimed at boosting black achievement. Steps Toward Academic Excellence and Advancement Via Individual Determination are two of the programs that are up and running. The first strives to move black students into honors-level classes by providing tutorial support in English and math. The second targets minorities who are good students, but not likely to be considering college. To steer them toward a college career, they are enrolled in a midday learning-skills class. The school has also enriched the math curriculum in an attempt to address minority students' low test scores. Instead of enrolling in a single math class, students attend double periods of algebra and geometry.

Board members and Alson say that these programs are working. "We've seen gains," says Alson. "We are seeing increases in minority enrollment in honors and (advanced placement) English and history classes." And thus far, Evanston's education community, including Sheppard, is pleased with the superintendent's initiatives. "The board is fully supporting Alson's efforts," Sheppard says.

Polls on integration suggest that more communities would favor initiatives such as Alson's. Despite lawsuits brought by white parents against individual busing plans in cities across the country, national support for desegregation has grown over the past few decades and now appears to be strong and unwavering, according to a report released by the American Association for Public Opinion Research in 1998. In the 1960s, one-fifth of white parents objected to "a few" members of the other race in their child's school. In 1998, virtually all parents, black and white, express no objections. Fewer than 15 percent of whites object to having their children attend schools in which members of another race constitute half the student body. A Gallup Organization Inc. poll for CNN / USA Today released in July found that 59 percent of Americans say more, not less, should be done to integrate the nation's schools, up from 54 percent in 1994.

Growing public support for school desegregation may be the result of an increased interest in social mixing. Integration has a positive impact both inside and outside the classroom, says James McPartland of Johns Hopkins University. His tracking of both black and white students who have attended integrated schools indicates, he says, that "they are more likely to live in integrated neighborhoods, attend diverse colleges, and work in integrated job settings. That's the danger with abandoning desegregation. You can't rehearse living with other races."

Although some evidence suggests that a return to segregated school systems could hurt minority achievement, most education researchers say that the effects are unlikely to be catastrophic. Orfield, at the end of his report on resegregation, holds out some hope for natural integration because of the rapid suburbanization of the black and Latino middle class. "Whether or not this will produce lasting integration or merely a vast spread of suburban segregation is one of the great questions of the period," he wrote. . . .

4-3

High Court Upholds Minority Districts

Caroline E. Brown

During the decades since the 1954 Brown v. Board of Education de-
cision, the Supreme Court has repeatedly struck down policy and insti-
tutional barriers separating the races. Ironically, when it comes to equal
representation, the federal judiciary has been inclined to take the oppo-
site approach—that is, instructing states with large black populations
to create separate congressional districts for these populations, so as to
ensure black majorities in one or more districts. The following piece by
Caroline Brown examines a May 17, 1999, Supreme Court decision up-
holding the right of states to use race as a factor in creating congres-
sional districts. The policy remains controversial, even within the
courts, and the decision leaves future federal policy ambiguous.

THE SUPREME COURT has given a small but potentially pivotal amount of
leeway to states that want to create congressional districts with majorities
of racial minority groups.

The unanimous decision on May 17, 1999, makes it more difficult for
lower federal courts to invalidate districts when they suspect race was the
major factor in setting the boundaries. Conscious consideration of race is
not automatically unconstitutional, the court held in *Hunt v. Cromartie,* if
the state's primary motivation was potentially political rather than racial.

The decision could influence redistricting disputes nationwide after the
2000 census, when House seats will be reapportioned among the states and
then new district lines will be drawn for each of the 435 House seats in time
for the 2002 elections.

"A jurisdiction may engage in constitutional political gerrymandering,
even if it so happens that the most loyal Democrats happen to be black
Democrats and even if the state were conscious of that fact," Justice
Clarence Thomas wrote for the court. "Evidence that blacks constitute
even a supermajority in one congressional district while amounting to less

Originally published in *CQ Weekly*, May 22, 1999, p. 1202.

than a plurality in a neighboring district will not, by itself, suffice to prove that a jurisdiction was motivated by race in drawing its district lines when the evidence also shows a high correlation between race and party preference."

The ruling overturned the conclusion of a panel of three federal judges that North Carolina's 12th congressional district was unlawfully drawn by the General Assembly in 1997. The judges made the ruling without holding a trial, at which the state was expected to present evidence that its motive was political, not racial. The justices said the state should have been allowed to make that case and sent the case back to the three-judge panel.

Zee Lamb, general counsel for the state Board of Elections, said that he hopes the panel will issue a ruling by Feb. 2, the candidate filing date for the 2000 congressional elections. Otherwise, the state could face a repeat of the 1998 situation, when the three-judge panel's initial ruling came after the candidate filing period ended and forced the state to delay the primary from May to September.

The 12th District—which stretches from Charlotte to Winston-Salem and now has a 47 percent black population—is represented by Democrat Melvin Watt. When Watt was elected to the House in 1992 from a version of the district that was then 57 percent black, no African-American had represented the state in Congress since 1901. The boundaries were redrawn after 1993 in the court's *Shaw v. Reno* decision, which held that race may not be the "predominant factor" in drawing congressional lines. The Supreme Court struck down a second version of Watt's district three years later.

5

Civil Liberties

We tend to think of our rights and liberties as absolutes. "Life, liberty and the pursuit of happiness" are "unalienable," proclaimed Thomas Jefferson in the Declaration of Independence as he laid the groundwork for a revolution. The Constitution's Bill of Rights used similarly absolute language. In establishing freedom of speech, religion, and assembly, the First Amendment begins with the unequivocal declaration, "Congress shall make no law. . . ." Given this entrenched creed, one might understandably—albeit mistakenly—come to regard his or her individual liberties as lying beyond the jurisdiction of politicians and our neighbors. Rather than being fashioned in response to political pressures, our liberties change only as society more clearly discerns the truth about them and how they can best be ensured. Reinforcing this view is the common conception of the Supreme Court and its role in enunciating national policy on civil liberties. After weighing the pros and cons of an issue and deliberating the merits of a case, these men and women retire to their chambers to write reasoned judgments in which they apply philosophy to life.

Leaving aside the merits of such a process, the essays in this chapter (and in chapter 9, where we examine the judiciary) disabuse us of the notion that civil liberties lie beyond the reach of politics. The Supreme Court is just one of the many government institutions that participate in defining the current state of civil liberties in America. Even the judicial process, these essays make clear, is not far removed from politics. Judges have political preferences, litigants have policy agendas, and rarely do the decisions of the Supreme Court constitute the final word. Rather than being natural truths handed down by philosopher-kings, our civil liberties are the products of a political process that allows everyone who has a view to express it and to seek to influence civil liberties policy.

5-1

The Mysterious Case of
Establishment Clause Litigation

HOW ORGANIZED LITIGANTS FOILED LEGAL CHANGE

Joseph F. Kobylka

The First Amendment's ban on "religious establishment" remains one of the most controversial areas of civil liberties policy. The Supreme Court has held that the Establishment Clause prohibits almost anything the government might do to aid religious practice. The potential for conflict with the Court's establishment policy is great. Wherever the activities of government and religious organizations intersect, as in education, any coordination between them will likely run afoul of the Court.

Opponents of the Court, or "accommodationists," argue that the government should be allowed to encourage religious practice in general, so long as it does not favor a particular religious group or establish an official state church. Their efforts to change the Court's policy—which most agree is out of sync with public opinion—have met with only limited success. In the following essay Joseph Kobylka shows how the Court has managed to insulate itself from accommodationist pressures. Kobylka's analysis provides an informative tour of the Court's political environment.

ACCORDING TO Arthur Conan Doyle's classic literary figure Sherlock Holmes, in solving a crime, "when you have eliminated the impossible, whatever remains, *however improbable,* must be the truth" (Doyle 1930, 111). In important ways, Holmes also could have been describing the task confronting social scientists. Quite often scholarly research resembles detective work: when we observe patterns of social behavior that deviate from what we would normally expect, we set up a list of suspects (sometimes called hypotheses) that could explain the deviation. With those

Excerpted from Lee Epstein, ed., *Contemplating Courts* (Washington, D.C.: CQ Press, 1995), pp. 93–128. Some bibliographic references appearing in the original have been cut.

suspects in hand, we often proceed just as Holmes described: eliminate the impossible and accept whatever is left—however improbable—as the solution.

In this [essay], I seek to solve an intriguing puzzle involving the U.S. Supreme Court: Why has doctrine governing the Religious Establishment Clause of the First Amendment *failed* to experience major legal change? In what follows, I set out this mystery in some detail. For now it is enough to note that, with the onset of Ronald Reagan's presidency in 1981, observers expected the Court either to replace the relatively liberal standard it uses to assess these cases with a far more conservative one, or interpret it in such a way as to produce outcomes more tolerable to some religious interests. This expectation grew when Reagan gained an opportunity to replace some supporters of this liberal standard with justices who presumably would oppose it. The expectation became a near certainty with George Bush's appointments of David H. Souter and Clarence Thomas to replace the liberal stalwarts William J. Brennan, Jr., and Thurgood Marshall. The "sure thing," however, never happened. Although Reagan and Bush—through their appointees—sought and accomplished doctrinal shifts in some areas of the law, they had little effect on religious establishment litigation.

Why did the Court not shift gears in Establishment Clause litigation when virtually all informed observers expected that it would? To solve this mystery, I first map the course of Establishment Clause litigation over the past two decades. Next, I suggest that three possible suspects could explain the lack of legal change in this area: the justices on the Court, the political environment in which the Court rendered its decisions, and the configuration and arguments of organized litigants. By eliminating the "impossible," I come to an "improbable" answer, albeit one that seems to capture the truth. This answer says that even when empirical indicators (such as changes in the membership of the Court and a favorable political environment) suggest a looming change in judicial doctrine, interested litigators can use the *law*—in this case, precedents and the reasoning that supports them—to condition, channel, and, in some instances, frustrate the process of legal change. This group presence is significant, not only in itself, but also because it fosters a *pluralism of argument* that permits justices an opportunity to adjust constitutional doctrine in a fashion that maintains some continuity in "the law" while, at the same time, enabling them to pursue a gentle evolution that leads it toward its future.

The Mystery: A Brief Doctrinal and Political Account of the Establishment Clause

The words of the Establishment Clause of the First Amendment seem simple enough: "Congress shall make no law respecting an establishment of religion." This seeming simplicity, however, is deceptive. Indeed, perhaps no other clause of the Constitution has given the Court so much difficulty, with its resulting rulings marked by confusion, not clarity. Why? The answer lies in the basic difficulty of interpretation posed by the Establishment Clause: the permissible relation between government and religion. Should it resemble Thomas Jefferson's "wall of separation" or a picket fence of accommodation?

There are two general approaches to this problem. *Separationists,* arguing from assumptions grounded in the rationalism of the Enlightenment, posit that the spheres of church and state must be kept distinct and separate so that neither will contaminate the other. The First Amendment, under this argument, requires a high wall of separation between church and state. From an *accommodationist* perspective, government may use its authority to aid religion generally and acknowledge the role it plays in American life, so long as it does not establish an official state church or prefer one religion over others. This is the picket fence view of the Establishment Clause. Both arguments trace their constitutional roots to *Everson v. Board of Education* (1947).

Everson involved a challenge, sponsored by the American Civil Liberties Union (ACLU), to an Illinois statute permitting state reimbursement of transportation costs to the parents of all students, including those who attended sectarian schools. Writing for a bare majority, Justice Hugo L. Black held:

> The "establishment of religion" clause . . . means at least this: Neither a state nor the Federal Government can set up a church. Neither can pass laws which aid one religion, aid all religions, or prefer one religion over another. . . . No tax in any amount, large or small, can be levied to support any religious activities or institutions, whatever they may be called, or whatever form they may adopt to teach or practice religion. Neither a state nor the Federal Government can, openly or secretly, participate in the affairs of any religious organizations or groups and vice versa. In the words of Jefferson, the clause was intended to erect a "wall of separation" between church and state. (*Everson,* 1947, 15–16)

Black went on to suggest that the "wall" requires "the state to be a neutral in its relations with groups of religious believers and nonbelievers; it does not require the state to be their adversary." In this case, the Court held that the statute provided benefits to all children and their parents, and not to churches per se. This program went to the top of, but not over, the "wall." Four dissenting justices could not square Black's separationist *language* with his accommodationist *decision*. . . .

The seeming inconsistency of the majority opinion and decision in *Everson* weakened the separationist sentiment at the heart of Black's discussion. It also set the stage for a confused doctrinal legacy. This is seen vividly in the Court's cases immediately after *Everson: McCollum v. Board of Education* (1948) and *Zorach v. Clausen* (1952). In *McCollum,* the Court held that "released time" programs—allowing public school students to attend classes of religious instruction taught by volunteers on school premises during school hours—were unconstitutional. In *Zorach,* however, the Court upheld the ruling permitting a released time program that instructed students off-campus. Justice William O. Douglas, writing for the majority, penned what has become the accommodationist creed:[1]

> We are a religious people whose institutions presuppose a Supreme Being. . . . When the State encourages religious instruction or cooperates with religious authorities by adjusting the schedule of public events to sectarian needs, it follows the best of our traditions. . . . We cannot read into the Bill of Rights . . . a hostility to religion. (*Zorach,* 313–315)

McCollum and *Zorach* demonstrate that the *Everson* sword cuts both ways. The justices of the Warren Court era (1953–1968 terms), as shown in Table 1, continued to wield it to reach both separationist and accommodationist outcomes.

On becoming chief justice, Warren E. Burger sought to end this confusion by framing a comprehensive test to guide resolution of church-state issues. In *Lemon v. Kurtzman* (1971) Burger held that the Court would uphold laws if

- they have a *secular legislative purpose,*
- their principal or *primary effect* neither advances nor inhibits religion, and
- they do not foster "an *excessive entanglement* with religion." (Lemon, 1971, 612–613)

Table 1. The U.S. Supreme Court and Religious Establishment:
Selected Cases and Outcomes, 1948–1980

Case (year)	Issue	Outcome
McCollum v. Board of Education (1948)	Time-release programs	Separationist
Zorach v. Clausen (1952)	Time-release programs	Accommodationist
McGowan v. Maryland (1961)	Sunday closing laws	Accommodationist
Engel v. Vitale (1962)	School prayer	Separationist
Abington School District v. Schempp (1963)	School prayer	Separationist
Epperson v. Arkansas (1968)	Teaching evolutionary principles	Separationist
Board of Education v. Allen (1968)	Textbook loans to parochial schools	Accommodationist
Walz v. Tax Commissioner of the City of New York (1970)	Property tax exemptions for church land	Accommodationist
Lemon v. Kurtzman (1971)	State reimbursement for teachers and instructional materials	Separationist
Tilton v. Richardson (1971)	Construction grants for secular buildings on sectarian college campuses	Accommodationist
	20-year limit on nonsecular use of buildings on college campuses	Separationist
Committee for Public Education and Religious Liberty v. Nyquist (1973)	State grants for maintenance and repair of parochial school buildings and tuition reimbursements–tax credits for parents of children attending parochial school	Separationist
Meek v. Pittinger (1975)	State book loans to parochial schools	Accommodationist
	State-funded material loans, special programs, and counseling for parochial school children	Separationist

Table 1 *(continued)*

Case (year)	Issue	Outcome
Roemer v. Maryland (1976)	Annual state grants used by colleges for secular purposes	Accommodationist
Wolman v. Walter (1977)	State material and equipment loans and field trip assistance to parochial schools	Separationist
	State standardized testing and counseling services to parochial schools	Accommodationist

This new standard—dubbed the *Lemon* test—combined the "purpose and effect" approach favored by separationists with an accommodationist concept of "excessive entanglement." Soon, however, it became clear that Burger sought to use this three-pronged test to move the Court toward a generally accommodationist rendering of the Establishment Clause. In this he was stymied—at least throughout the 1970s—as the Court simply used *Lemon* as it had *Everson*: to support whatever holdings, separationist or accommodationist, it handed down.

By 1980, however, several factors coalesced to suggest a radical change in the Court's approach to Establishment Clause doctrine, a change that would establish a regime of accommodationism. First, commentators on both sides of the issue called on the Court to clarify this area of law. Second, in the late 1970s, the Court signaled that it too was growing weary of umpiring these controversies. As shown in Table 1, one can read decisions such as *Meek v. Pittinger* (1975), *Roemer v. Maryland* (1976), and *Wolman v. Walter* (1977) as gradually pulling *Lemon* doctrine toward a more accommodationist posture. Third, the energy unleashed by the "new right" in the electoral arena began to manifest itself in the courts as groups like the Christian Legal Society turned to litigation to promote a constitutional climate of accommodation.

The final and capping event was Ronald Reagan's election as the fortieth president of the United States. This, more than anything else, seemed to ensure the beginning of the end of a strict, judicially imposed, separation of church and state. The position he took on "the religion issue"—calling for the Court to reverse itself and for passage of a constitutional amendment to permit state-sponsored prayer in public schools—was a significant part of his campaign stump appeal. As president, he (and, later, George Bush) used the solicitors general to push this argument on the Court. Further, he was able to reshape the personnel of the Court. Reagan's three appointees— Sandra Day O'Connor, Antonin Scalia, and Anthony M. Kennedy—all *seemed* to fall in line with his philosophical position on the relation between church and state.

At first, the Court gave every indication that the expected legal change would in fact occur; its decisions of the early 1980s gave hope to those who wished to dismantle the stubbornly persisting "wall." The Court seemed on the verge of formally adopting an accommodationist reading of the *Lemon* test. In *Committee for Public Education and Religious Liberty (CPERL) v. Regan* (1980), a sharply divided Court upheld a New York statute that permitted the reimbursement of all nonpublic schools for costs incurred in performing certain state-mandated procedures (such as data on the state's pupil evaluation program, regents examinations, a state-wide student evaluation plan, and student attendance reports). Justice Byron R. White's majority opinion held that there was "no appreciable risk" that the aid would further the "transmission of religious values" (*CPERL v. Regan*, 1980, 846), and was thus constitutional under *Lemon*. With this, the Court, for the first time, upheld the ruling permitting a direct transfer of government funds to sectarian schools (Giacoma 1980, 406). Three terms later, in *Mueller v. Allen* (1983), the majority let stand a Minnesota law allowing tax deductions for costs associated with sectarian education. It also sustained Nebraska's use of a paid legislative chaplain in *Marsh v. Chambers* (1983). The majority did not even apply the *Lemon* test in *Marsh;* it sufficed that the Congress that wrote the First Amendment retained a paid chaplain.

Lynch v. Donnelly (1984) extended the logic of these accommodationist decisions. In upholding the constitutionality of a government-sponsored Christmas display that included a crèche, not only did a five-person majority say that it merely "acknowledged" a national holiday, but it held that the display conformed to *Lemon:* it had a secular purpose (depicting "the historical origins of the holiday"); its effect was only "indirect, remote, and incidental" to the advancement of religion; and it posed no danger of "the 'enduring entanglement' present in *Lemon.*" To rule otherwise, Burger concluded, would "impose a crabbed reading of the [Establishment] clause on the country" (*Lynch*, 1984, 1363–1366). The dissenters in these cases—Harry A. Blackmun, William Brennan, Thurgood Marshall, and John Paul Stevens—clung to the late-1970s version of the *Lemon* test, and came to contrary conclusions.

Just when it seemed that the Court would chart an accommodationist course and dispel the ambiguity that plagued this area of law it abruptly trimmed its sails. In three cases brought before the Court in 1984, five- and six-person majorities—made up of the dissenting justices in *Regan, Mueller, Marsh,* and *Lynch* plus Justices Lewis F. Powell, Jr., and sometimes O'Connor—applied new mortar to the crumbling wall. In *Wallace v. Jaffree* (1985), they struck down an Alabama law requiring public school teachers to start the day with a "moment of silence for prayer or meditation," and in *Grand Rapids v. Ball* (1985) and *Aguilar v. Felton* (1985) they voided state and federal programs providing public funds for remedial courses in secular subjects taught in sectarian schools. The majority applied the late 1970s separationist version of the *Lemon* test to reach these conclusions.

Following *Wallace, Aguilar,* and *Grand Rapids,* the Court returned to its dual-edged approach in Establishment Clause issues, upholding some accommodations of religion, striking others. Emblematic of this renewed strategy, and the interpretational confusion it generates, was the Court's decision in *County of Allegheny v. American Civil Liberties Union* (1989). The city of Pittsburgh and Allegheny County in Pennsylvania had erected seasonal displays celebrating Christmas and Chanukah. The Christmas display contained a crèche (with figures of the Christ child, Joseph, Mary, shepherds, the wise men, barn animals, and a manger), two evergreen trees, some white poinsettias, a surrounding fence, and an angel bearing a banner declaring "Gloria in Excelsis Deo!" at its apex. Designated as owned by a Catholic group called the Holy Name Society, the display "occupied a substantial amount of space on the Grand Staircase [of the County Courthouse]" (*County of Allegheny*, 1989, 3094). The city's display was outside of the city-county building and included a forty-five-foot decorated Christmas tree, a "Salute to Liberty" sign bearing the mayor's name, and an eighteen-foot menorah owned by Chabad, a Hasidic Jewish organization. Applying a "lemonized" *Lynch* case to these displays, a badly divided Court found the crèche display—but not the display of the menorah—violative of the Establishment Clause.[2]

The Court's interpretational odyssey continues to the present. Even though by 1992 Reagan and Bush appointees held six of the Court's nine seats, a five-justice majority found, in *Lee v. Weisman* (1992), that brief prayers offered by a rabbi at a high school graduation ceremony violated the Constitution. In his opinion for the Court, Justice Kennedy pointedly eschewed use of the *Lemon* test and ruled against the practice of such prayers on the basis of "the controlling precedents as they relate to prayer and religious exercise in primary and secondary public schools" (*Lee*, 1992, 2655). The following term, however, the Court held unconstitutional the decision of local school authorities to prohibit, based on Establishment Clause concerns, a church from access to school premises to show a movie about family and parenting issues (*Lamb's Chapel v. Center Moriches Union Free School District*, 1993) and the provision of a sign-language interpreter to a deaf boy attending a parochial high school (*Zobrest v. Catalina Foothills School District*, 1993). The latter decision was 5 to 4, used the *Lemon* test, and saw Kennedy join the *Lee* dissenters to form the majority. Most recently, by a vote of 6 to 3, the Court returned to a more separationist posture in striking down a public school district created by New York to assist a village composed exclusively of Orthodox Jews in *Board of Education of Kiryas Joel Village School District v. Grumet* (1994).[3] In his majority opinion, Justice Souter mentioned *Lemon* only twice and in passing, but he did not repudiate it. Thus, the only consistency in the Court's recent Establishment Clause litigation remains its ambiguity.

When viewed chronologically, as they are in Table 2, the Court's decisions since 1980 demonstrate that the justices failed to chart a new and clear course for confronting Establishment Clause issues. Although, on balance, accommodationists may have done somewhat better during this period than their separationist rivals . . . the doctrinal revolution that Reagan, Bush, and Court watchers expected did not occur. Thus, the mystery: why did the law not experience the abrupt change that was so widely anticipated?

The Suspects

To solve our mystery, we must assess the winding path of Establishment Clause litigation against a backdrop of the "usual suspects"—those factors that the literature suggests condition change in constitutional doctrine. A canvass of this literature reveals three "usual" suspects: the justices on the Court, the political environment in which the Court makes its decisions, and the configuration of organized litigators pressing their claims on the Court.

The Court

Scholars have reported on two essentially Court-centered explanations for legal change (or the lack thereof): changes in the thinking of individual justices and personnel turnover. Although the former is unusual, justices occasionally shift their position on the issues that come before them. An example is Justice Blackmun. Appointed by President Richard Nixon to strengthen a constitutional jurisprudence aligned with the "silent majority of law-abiding Americans," Blackmun began his career on the "pro-state" side of the judicial spectrum but at his retirement was considered to be one of the Court's strongest advocates of individual rights.

The appointment of new justices is more commonly noted as a path to legal change. . . . [W]hen presidents—be they Richard Nixon, Ronald Reagan, or Bill Clinton—turn their attention to filling vacancies in the high court, it is hardly surprising that they seek out candidates whose constitutional values (they think) coincide with their own. The power of nomination gives presidents an opportunity to try to influence the direction of the Court, an opportunity that few have passed by.

Obviously, the changes in the justices sitting on the Court must have, in some sense, contributed to the recent Establishment Clause odyssey because they decided the cases in question. Recall, however, that the Court's decisions were not unidirectional *even after* the Reagan and Bush appointments. The mystery thus remains: why did the Court continue to oscillate between the competing doctrinal approaches instead of clarifying and solidifying, once and for all, a single interpretation of the Establishment Clause?

The Court's applications of the *Lemon* test during the 1970s were driven by three blocs of justices (see Morgan 1973). First, there were the "super-separationists"—Brennan, Marshall, and Stevens.[4] *Their* understanding of *Lemon* viewed almost any state aid to religion as violative of its effect and entanglement prongs. As a result, they voted to support separationist outcomes almost exclusively.[5] In direct contrast was the "super-accommodationist" bloc. Its strongest members were White and Rehnquist, but Burger frequently joined them to favor state assistance to or "acknowledgement" of religion. *Their* reading of *Lemon* (although White and Rehnquist's attachment to the three-pronged test was never strong), allowed nearly total government accommodation of religion. Between these two extremes were the "moderates"—Potter Stewart, Blackmun, and Powell—who read

Table 2. U.S Supreme Court Votes and Outcomes in Establishment Clause Cases, 1979–1992

Case (year)	Subject	Vote	Outcome
CPERL v. Regan (1980)	Money for elementary and secondary schools	5–4	Accommodationist
Stone v. Graham (1980)	Prayer in elementary and secondary schools	5–4	Separationist
Widmar v. Vincent (1981)	Access to colleges	8–1	Accommodationist
Valley Forge Christian College v. Americans United (1982)	Money for colleges	5–4	Accommodationist
Larson v. Valents (1982)	Solicitations	5–4	Separationist
Larkin v. Grendel's Den (1982)	Zoning around schools and churches	8–1	Separationist
Mueller v. Allen (1983)	Money for elementary and secondary schools	5–4	Accommodationist
Marsh v. Chambers (1983)	Legislative chaplain	6–3	Accommodationist
Lynch v. Donnelly (1984)	Christmas	5–4	Accommodationist
Alamo Federation v. Secretary of Labor (1985)	Minimum wage	9–0	Accommodationist
Wallace v. Jaffree (1985)	Prayer in elementary and secondary schools	6–3	Separationist
Thornton v. Caldor (1985)	Sabbath exemptions	8–1	Separationist
Grand Rapids v. Ball (1985)	Money for elementary and secondary schools	5–4	Separationist
Aguilar v. Felton (1985)	Money for elementary and secondary schools	5–4	Separationist
Witters v. Washington (1986)	Money for colleges	9–0	Accommodationist
Edwards v. Aguillard (1987)	Prayer in elementary and secondary schools	7–2	Separationist
Corp. of Presiding Bishop v. Amos (1988)	Employment discrimination	9–0	Accommodationist
Bowen v. Kendrick (1988)	Birth control	5–4	Accommodationist
Texas Monthly v. Bullock (1989)	Taxes	6–3	Separationist

Case	Issue	Vote	Outcome
Hernandez v. Commissioner of Internal Revenue (1989)	Taxes	5–2	Accommodationist
County of Allegheny v. ACLU (1989)	Menorah and crèche displays	5–4	Mixed
Swaggart Ministries v. California (1990)	Taxes	9–0	Accommodationist
Board of Education of Westside Community Schools v. Mergens (1990)	Prayer in elementary and secondary schools	8–1	Accommodationist
Lee v. Weisman (1992)	Prayer in elementary and secondary schools	5–4	Separationist
Lamb's Chapel v. Center Moriches Union Free School District (1993)	Access to school building	9–0	Accommodationist
Zobrest v. Catalina Foothills School District (1993)	Money for elementary and secondary schools	5–4	Accommodationist

Lemon to prohibit "direct" state aid to religion, especially that aimed at "pervasively sectarian" elementary and secondary parochial schools. With the Court thus constituted, it was institutionally disposed to uphold, by a vote of 6 to 3, some state support of religious concerns and to strike down others by the same margin.[6]

These blocs began to crumble in 1977, when Powell announced that "the risk of significant religious or denominational control over our democratic processes—or even of deep political division along religious lines—is remote, and . . . seems entirely tolerable in light of the continuing oversight of this Court" (*Wolman v. Walter,* 1977, 262–263; see Table 1). In *CPERL v. Regan* (1980), the next significant *parochiaid* case, Powell and Stewart bolted from the moderate bloc to join a White opinion upholding broad state aid to sectarian schools.[7] Thus, even before the Reagan onslaught, the Court exhibited some signs of an accommodationist shift—a shift made possible by individual changes of thinking of a few justices.

One would expect the replacement of Stewart, Burger, and Powell with Reagan appointees to cement this shift. Reagan's position on church-state matters was clear. He had long opposed the Court's school prayer decisions—"I don't think that God should ever have been expelled from the classroom" (Reagan 1983, 603)—and made his general position on these issues plain in remarks at the National Prayer Breakfast in 1981: "Our nation's motto—'In God we trust'—was not chosen lightly. It reflects a basic recognition that there is a divine authority in the universe to which this Nation owes homage" (Reagan 1982, 268). Indeed, in replacing Stewart with O'Connor, Reagan switched a lukewarm accommodationist for a justice seemingly more sympathetic to accommodationist concerns.[8] His subsequent appointments, Scalia and Kennedy (both Roman Catholic), were yet more supportive of government acknowledgment of and support for religion.

. . . And yet . . . the Court ruled against a moment of silence (*Wallace*) and parochiaid legislation (*Grand Rapids* and *Aguilar*) the very next term over the dissents of Burger, White, Rehnquist, and, in part, O'Connor. Seven terms later, with the full complement of Reagan and Bush justices in place, a majority found unconstitutional prayers offered at a high school graduation in *Lee v. Weisman* (1992). Why?

The explanation lies, in a general sense, in the break from the super-accommodationist bloc by Powell and O'Connor in 1985 and by Kennedy in 1992. Powell's defection is difficult to assess, as is Kennedy's. O'Connor foreshadowed her shift, however, with the "endorsement" reading of *Lemon* offered in the *Lynch* concurrence. There she wrote, "The establishment clause prohibits government from making adherence to a religion relevant in any way to a person's standing in the political community" (*Lynch*, 1984, 687). This could happen if there was excessive government entanglement with religion or state "endorsement or disapproval of religion." She went on to explain that "endorsement sends a message to nonadherents that they are outsiders, not full members of the political community, and an accompanying message to adherents that they are insiders, favored members of the political community. Disapproval sends the opposite message" (*Lynch*, 1984, 688). The facts in *Wallace*—the moment-of-silence legislation included explicit mention of using the time to pray—violated O'Connor's endorsement test, and she voted to overrule it. . . .

Emerging from this analysis is the conclusion that the Reagan and Bush appointments did not *start* the latest cycle of interpretational confusion, nor did they *cement* the legal change that *Regan, Mueller, Marsh,* and *Lynch* seemed to promise. They *could* have—indeed, at first, they *appeared* to do so—but they did not. Thus, my analysis turns to other suspects.

The Political Environment

At the end of the nineteenth century, a popular fictional character named Mr. Dooley quipped that the Supreme Court "follows th' iliction returns" (Dunne 1938). While perhaps overstating his case, Dooley may have had a point. Jonathan Casper (1972, 293) notes that it is a mistake to depreciate "the importance of the political context in which the Court does its work. . . . [Dooley's] statement recognizes that the choices the Court makes are related to developments in the larger political system." Prominent among such factors are public opinion and the actions of government institutions designed to reflect it. Let us investigate these suspects in turn.

Scholars have demonstrated that there often seems to be a link between court decisions and public opinion. There are several reasons why this relation would exist. First, appointed and filtered by a political process, justices may reflect and, in some sense, represent majoritarian preferences. Second, aware of the difficulty of implementing their decisions, they might seek to practice "the art of the possible" by tailoring their decisions with an eye to satisfying the public. Third, the occasional ambiguity of constitutional text leads the justices to seek out the meaning of vague phrases in social sources.

In the Establishment Clause example, if the press of public opinion constrained accommodationist legal change, we would expect to find Americans largely supportive of separationist outcomes. This, as shown in Figure 1, is not the case: support for the Supreme Court's decisions forbidding organized prayer or Bible readings in public schools has always been a minority position. The data on parochiaid are more volatile but show a public rather consistently split over the expenditure of tax dollars to assist sectarian education.

These data suggest that the public is highly tolerant of government accommodation of religion (prayer in public schools) or, at the very least, divided over the issue (parochial aid). What is important, however, is that the perception existed on the Court that the former better characterized the viewpoint of Americans. In a 1980 dissent, Justice Blackmun charged that the Court's growing accommodationism was, in part, a reaction to public opinion. Referring to the shift of Stewart and Powell, he wrote: "I am able to attribute this defection only to a concern about the continuing and emotional controversy and to a persuasion that a good-faith attempt on the part of a state legislature is worth a nod of approval" (Regan, 1980, 664). Still, despite the perception that its litigation of church-state questions was occurring in a political climate generally supportive of accommodationist claims, the Court continued its decisional and doctrinal oscillations. Indeed, even with its ambivalent gyrations on these issues, it has stood against the press of public opinion urging a greater accommodation of religion. Consider that as recently as 1992 it stuck to its traditional prohibition against formal prayer in school, despite the fact that only about 38 percent of Americans support such a ban.

If public opinion does not help to solve our mystery, perhaps other suspects in the political environment do. Along these lines, political scientists assert that a host of institutionalized actors condition the direction of the decisions of the Court. Of particular interest here is the role of the president. Studies have shown that the president, through the solicitor general, can affect the Court's agenda and enjoy unusual success before it. Beyond this, the office is increasingly being used to advance the specific political values of the incumbent president.

As noted previously, court watchers expected Ronald Reagan's ascension to the presidency to prompt profound legal change: it placed a committed accommodationist in the White House. . . .

Reagan's attention to church-state issues was substantial, and it extended into legislative and judicial fora.[9] Legislatively, his attack took three routes.

Figure 1. Public Opinion on Religious Establishment Issues

Respondents Opposing Supreme Court Decisions Banning School Prayer

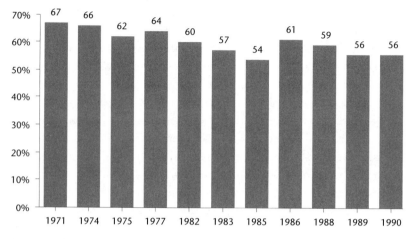

Source: Stanley and Niemi 1992, 21.

Respondents Approving Governmental Aid to Private/Sectarian Schools

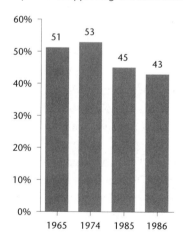

Source: Gallup Poll, 1959–1971, 1974, 1985, 1986 annual editions.

First, he proposed to Congress a constitutional amendment to overturn the prayer decisions.[10] Second, he pressed Congress for passage of legislation giving federal tuition tax credits to the parents of children who attended private schools. Finally, he achieved passage of the "Equal Access Act" of

1984—legislation that prohibited secondary public schools from denying "equal access to . . . any students who wish to conduct a meeting within that limited open forum on the basis of the religious, political, philosophical, or other content of the speech at such meetings" (Hertzke 1988; Moen 1989).[11]

Reagan's presidency also brought vigorous advocates of accommodationism to the solicitor general's office and kept an accommodationist perspective on the church-state question before the Court. Part of this office's agenda was to reverse the Court's perceived excessive separationism. Bush, as president, followed these tracks. Rex Lee, Charles Fried, and Kenneth Starr—their solicitors general—appeared before the Court in seventeen Establishment Clause cases (66 percent of the twenty-six decided during this period), arguing ten and filing as amicus curiae in seven.[12]. . . The arguments of the solicitors general were unrelentingly accommodationist. Also significant were the contentions of Edwin Meese who became attorney general in 1985. Meese took an especial interest in church-state cases and used the occasion of the Court's interpretational turn in the 1985 cases as an example of the utility of a jurisprudence of original intent—a belief that the Court should interpret the Constitution to mean *only* what the framers thought it meant. "One finds much merit in Justice Rehnquist's recent dissent in *[Wallace v.] Jaffree*. . . . To have argued . . . that the [First] Amendment demands a strict neutrality between religion and irreligion would have struck the founding generation as bizarre. The purpose was to prohibit religious tyranny, not to undermine religion generally." Meese's suggested replacement for the Court's "jurisprudence of idiosyncrasy" was a doctrine that prohibited the *formal establishment* of a *national* church or preference between religions (Meese 1985, 9). This approach was pressed on the solicitor general's office by, among others, Meese's lieutenant William Bradford Reynolds. The latter's goal was to force the Court to dismantle the "wall of separation" as the operative metaphor defining Establishment Clause doctrine (see Caplan 1987, 98–102). This caused frequent internecine battles at the Department of Justice: Rex Lee, the solicitor general at that time, and his assistant Paul Bator wanted to undermine *Lemon* but had no intention of losing the confidence of the Court or going on a legal "kamikaze mission" by pressing extreme arguments (Caplan 1987, 98–101).

Lee was no great friend of the *Lemon* test (see Lee 1981, 134), but he did have a lawyer's respect for precedent and a solicitor general's respect for the office he held. Not only would he lose an appeal and a case, but he would compromise long-term accommodationist goals if he pushed the Court too far, too fast. . . .

The closest Lee came to dismissing the relevance of *Lemon* was in cases like *Marsh*, *Lynch*, and *Wallace*, where he made an argument similar to the one made in *Lynch* that "[w]ooden application [of] legal tests devised for different situations" was inappropriate for issues outside the parochiaid contest.[13] Indeed, one of his major arguments in *Lynch* was that, although government "promotion" of it might be beyond the constitutional pale, government "acknowledgment" of religion—there, in the context of the Christmas display—was perfectly legitimate, *even under Lemon*. O'Connor adopted this language in that case and she still uses it, although in ways that often run counter to Lee's intent. . . .

Kenneth Starr, Bush's solicitor general, generally picked up where his predecessors left off, although he did explicitly call for "reconsideration" of the "so-called *Lemon* 'test' " in *Lee* (1992). He proposed that the Court replace it with "a single, careful inquiry into whether the practice at issue provides direct benefits to a religion in a manner that threatens the establishment of an official church or compels persons to participate in a religion or religious exercise contrary to their consciences."[14] The Court explicitly rejected this invitation and handed Starr his only loss in this area of law.

Scholars have long noted the significance of the participation of the Office of the Solicitor General in Supreme Court litigation. . . . This explanation, however, like that relying on public opinion, is not wholly moving. . . . Although the *Lemon* test may be going into eclipse, what Starr called its "constitutional underpinning" in his *Lee* brief stubbornly persists. Participation of Reagan and Bush's solicitors general, even before a Court largely appointed by their administrations, did not carry the day. This clears another suspect.

Group Presence, Argument, and Strategy

. . . [B]y sponsoring cases, filing amicus curiae briefs, coordinating research and publicity groups seek to influence judicial decisions. Although groups often have a variety of reasons for taking on the burden of litigation (Epstein and Kobylka 1992, 29–32), paramount among them is a desire to secure favorable judicial rulings that advance their policy goals. Because they bear the attributes of "repeat players" (Galanter 1974), many have succeeded in doing so. . . .

The organizational activity in church-state cases is immense. This is not surprising, given previous accounts of this litigation. Further, the density of this litigation environment—the number of groups involved in it and the frequency of their participation in any given case—is staggering. In the twenty-six cases decided by the Court in the fourteen terms from 1979 through 1992, arguments were presented by 128 groups. As noted in Table 3, 28 groups appeared in three or more cases, with 11 representing accommodationist interests and 17 articulating a separationist perspective. Did they affect the Court's adjudication of these issues? By structuring the arguments heard by the Court, and by demonstrating the pluralism of perspectives on these difficult questions, I think they did. Understanding the role they played provides a solution to the mysterious lack of legal change in this area of law.

Group involvement in Establishment Clause litigation has a long history. From the separationist perspective, it began with the ACLU consulting with the plaintiffs (Walker 1990, 169) and filing an amicus curiae brief in *Everson* (1947), and snowballed after that. The group again filed as an amicus in the first released time case (*McCollum*, 1948) and was closely involved with the American Jewish Congress (AJC) in the next released time case (*Zorach*, 1952) and in *Engel v. Vitale* (1962), the Court's initial tilt with school prayer. The ACLU and the AJC, joined recently by the Anti-Defamation League of B'nai B'rith (ADBB), are, by volume of cases (see Table 3) and expertise, the preeminent separationist litigators.[15]

The ACLU, AJC, and ADBB, while the most active separationist group litigators, are not the only organized separationist voices appearing before the Supreme Court. Americans United (AU), formerly called Protestants and Other Americans United for the Separation of Church and State, was formed in the immediate aftermath of the Court's decision in *Everson*. Since 1980, it has participated in thirteen (50 percent) of the Court's church-state decisions. Whereas the ACLU approaches these issues from the perspective of secular humanism, and the AJC and ADBB from that of mainstream Jewish thought, traditionally, the AU is more politically conservative and religiously Protestant. Although its greatest percentage of current contributors is Baptist, its "largest per capita contributions come from Christian Scientists, Seventh-day Adventists and Jews" (Hyer 1982). Even with this membership shift, however, it continues to seek to protect churches and believers from state interference, whereas the ACLU, AJC, and ADBB approach these issues from a more secular perspective.

Table 3. Frequent Group Litigators of Establishment Clause Issues, 1979–1992

Group	Instances of participation No.	Instances of participation Percentage	No. of sponsored instances of participation
Separationists (17)			
American Civil Liberties Union	21	81	7
AFL-CIO	5	19	0
American Jewish Committee	9	35	0
American Jewish Congress	16	62	0
Americans for Religious Liberty	6	23	0
Americans United for the Separation of Church and State	13	50	1
Anti-Defamation League of B'nai B'rith	16	62	1
Baptist Joint Committee on Public Affairs	9	35	0
Coalition for Public Education and Religious Liberty	12	46	1
Council on Religious Freedom	7	27	0
National Council of Churches of Christ	9	35	0
National Education Association	3	12	0
National Jewish Community Relations Council	5	19	0
National School Boards Association	5	19	0
People for the American Way	6	23	0
Seventh Day Adventists	4	15	0
Synagogue Council	3	12	3
Accommodationists (11)			
American Center for Law and Justice	4	15	3
Association for Public Justice	3	12	0
Catholic League for Religious and Civil Rights	8	31	0
Christian Legal Society	11	42	2
Concerned Women of America	7	27	1
Free Congress Research and Education Foundation	4	15	0
National Association of Evangelicals	10	38	0
National Jewish Commission on Law and Public Affairs	12	46	2

(continued)

Table 3 *(continued)*

Group	Instances of participation		No. of sponsored instances of participation
	No.	Percentage	
National Legal Foundation	3	12	1
Rutherford Institute and Freedom Council	8	31	1
United States Catholic Conference	10	38	0

The above-noted groups are the dominant separationist forces, but they are not alone. . . .

There was no organized accommodationist bar for much of the post-*Everson* period. Through the 1960s, with the exception of occasional amicus participation of the U.S. Catholic Conference, there was little nongovernment opposition to separationist claims. So paltry was the organized support for accommodationist legislation that Sorauf and Morgan, the best chroniclers of the pre-1970 period, could point to little concerted group presence in this area. The most they could locate was the existence of a determined group of attorneys (for example, William Ball, Porter Chandler, Edward Bennett Williams), who were occasionally dispatched by the American Catholic Church to help local attorneys defend accommodationist policies.

This situation changed after 1970, as groups advancing accommodationist arguments turned increasingly to litigation. Foremost here is the National Jewish Committee on Public Affairs (NJCPA) and its counsel Nathan Lewin. In its amicus brief in *Lemon* (1971), Lewin described the group as "a voluntary association organized to combat all forms of religious prejudice and discrimination and to represent the position of the Orthodox Jewish community on matters of public concern." The NJCPA filed its first amicus brief in *Walz v. Tax Commissioner of the City of New York* (1970). Since 1980, it has participated in twelve cases before the Supreme Court. Lewin also presented oral argument to the Court in *Levitt v. CPERL* (1973), *Regan* (1980), *Thorton v. Caldor* (1985), and *County of Allegheny* (1989). These instances represent involvement in 48 percent of the Court's twenty-six cases during this period and act as a counter to the separationist arguments of the AJC and the American Jewish Committee.

This fractionalization of the "Jewish position" presented to the Supreme Court has its parallel on the Protestant side. As noted, the Catholic Church and entities associated with it have pressed accommodationist arguments since *Everson,* but the NCC, the BJC, and the AU presented a relatively solid Protestant separationist front through the 1970s. Starting in 1980, two more Protestant groups entered the establishment fray: the Center for Law and Religion of the Christian Legal Society (CLS) and the National Association of Evangelicals (NAE). The Catholic League for Religious and Civil Rights provided yet another "perspective" on these questions. . . . These groups, especially the CLS and NAE, act as accommodationist counterparts to the NCC, BJC, and AU and perform a function akin to that of the NJCPA—they make the justices pointedly aware of the diversity of church-state perspectives in the Christian community.

In addition to these religious groups, other new accommodationist groups have sprung into action. Pat Robertson's National Legal Foundation filed amicus briefs in *County of Allegheny* and *Lee* (1992) and argued *Mergens* (1990)—the decision that upheld the Equal Access Act of 1984. More significantly, it created the American Center for Law and Justice in 1990. Its chief counsel, Jay Alan Sekulow, argued *Mergens* (1990), *Lee* (1992), and *Lamb's Chapel* (1993) and filed an amicus brief in *Zobrest* (1993) for the Deaf Community Center. Concerned Women of America, self-identified as a group "extremely concerned with government programs which deprive individuals and institutions of benefits because of their religious motivations or affiliations," has participated as amicus in seven cases since 1986—58 percent of the Court's cases since the group was founded. The Rutherford Institute, which "undertakes to assist litigants and to participate in significant cases relating to the protection and safeguarding of religious liberties," filed amicus briefs in eight cases, and its attorneys participated in oral arguments in the Louisiana creationism case *Edwards v. Aguillard* (1987). Table 3 notes other groups active as friends before the Court.

With the recent creation and activation of these groups, accommodationists are now able to counter the organized separationist perspective that previously enjoyed near-monolithic status before the Court. Added to this newly developed pluralism is the fact that schisms—at least on *some* issues—have formed on the separationist front. In a sense, these fissures find their genesis in different organizational (secular and religious) perspectives. They first became apparent to the Supreme Court in *Walz* (1970) when the AU filed an amicus brief urging the Court to sustain tax exemptions for church property. This put it in opposition to the ACLU. The AJC, unable to come to a position on the question, did not participate at all. This dissension, however, looked anomalous because these groups stayed together on the parochiaid issues that dominated the 1970s.

These separationist schisms grew in the 1980s, as "separationist" groups joined their usual opponents in many cases to urge an accommodationist interpretation of the Establishment Clause on the Court. A prime example is found in *Thorton* (1985). Here, a man who resigned from his job rather than work on his Sabbath filed a grievance with the Connecticut Board of Mediation and Arbitration against his previous employer for violating a state statute, which said that "[n]o person who states that a particular day of the week is observed as his Sabbath may be required by his employer to work on such day. An employee's refusal to work on his Sabbath shall not constitute grounds for his dismissal." The store from which Thorton resigned rather than accept a demotion or transfer argued that the statute violated the *Lemon* test and the Establishment Clause by providing Sabbath observers an absolute right not to work on their Sabbath—a claimed state advancement of religion.

The Court agreed with the store and struck the statute by a vote of 8 to 1. This decision, no doubt, pleased the groups—unions and business associations—that filed amicus briefs urging separation. It did not please Thorton's attorneys, the NJCPA's Lewin and Marc D. Stern of the AJC. Nor was the AJC the only separationist group urging an accommodationist result in this case. Filing amicus briefs on behalf of Thorton were the Seventh-Day Adventists, the ADBB, and the AU. They grounded their accommodationism here on the Free Exercise of Religion Clause of the First Amendment—arguing that the Establishment Clause should not promote hostility to religion—and this put them with groups whose claims they usually oppose and the solicitor general. Similar separationist slippage is also seen in other recent cases. . . .

The more often separationists split on the questions that come before the Court, and they did in ten of the twenty-six cases (38 percent) during this period, the more often they present the justices with mixed cues. This discordance changes the score read by the Court confronting these issues and can do little to advance the *core separationist values* that originally drew them to the courts; at a minimum it creates confusion about the coherence of the separationist understanding of the Establishment Clause. As such, over time it could undermine the ability of these groups to promote precedents favorable to their essentially separatist concerns. This pluralism of argument, coming from groups that previously sang together harmoniously, could give justices inclined to listen greater latitude in reworking, modifying, and recasting the precedents they ponder in deciding their cases.

Whatever confusion the proliferation of accommodationist groups and the occasional discordance of the separationists caused the justices, however, it is clear that neither of these occurrences dramatically affected the overall doctrinal development of the period. Accommodationist mobilization began with a vengeance in the early 1980s, but it did not deter the Court's separationist decisions in the 1984 term. Similarly, the most prominent discordance in the separationist chorus occurred after the Court's reassertion of separationism in *Wallace, Grand Rapids,* and *Aguilar* and did not keep the Court from deciding *Lee* (or, more recently, *Kiryas Joel*) in a separationist fashion. Although not irrelevant to the resolution of these issues— they clearly set part of the environment in which the Court considers them—changes in pluralistic participation do not account for the shifting tides of Establishment Clause doctrine. A more likely culprit are the arguments presented to the justices.

O'Connor's separate concurrence in *Lynch* made clear that she was the pivotal vote during the mid-1980s. Although she concurred in Burger's majority opinion, she argued that governments could "acknowledge" religion, but not "endorse" it. Since these concepts seemed to be drawn from Lee's accommodationist brief in *Lynch,* it was reasonable to assume that she understood them the way he meant them. Yet . . . this assumption was in error. Her votes and opinions in the cases of the 1984 term, especially in *Wallace,* made clear that her accommodationism, although robust, was less so than that of her fellow majority members in *Lynch.* Significantly, separationists picked up on this, as they had not done in the abortion case, and focused their subsequent arguments on getting her vote. Thus, the arguments of Jaffree's attorney and the ACLU's amicus brief specifically pointed to O'Connor's *Lynch* opinion to contend that the moment of prayer and meditation worked "to advance and express endorsement of religion."[16] They did not ask for reversal of *Lynch,* and they won their case and patched a "wall" on the verge of crumbling.[17]

Some accommodationists did not miss the significance of O'Connor's opinion in *Lynch,* either. Although attorneys for Alabama did not mention it in their briefs, Lee's brief explicitly did. O'Connor, however, concurring in the result reached by the majority (but not in its opinion), felt that the peculiar context that generated the moment-of-silence statute constituted an impermissible endorsement of religion.[18] But, even with her defection here, she did not recant her vote in *Lynch,* and she largely went along with the accommodationist bloc in *Grand Rapids* and *Aguilar.* Thus, even after *Wallace,* accommodationist interests remained in a good position: they simply needed to preserve and extend the legal and political gains achieved in *Regan, Mueller, Marsh,* and *Lynch.*

In *County of Allegheny,* accommodationists argued that the crèche-menorah context was no different from the Pawtucket fact setting that the Court previously sustained in *Lynch,* and that *Lynch* was the controlling precedent. The only new argument they advanced concerned the treatment of context in *Lynch.* Burger's opinion there said that the crèche, in the context of the display, raised no establishment problems. What was unclear was whether the relevant context was the physical layout of the display—the surrounding secular symbols—or the general context of a nationally recognized holiday. Accommodationists—an orthodox Jewish group, some conservative organizations, and the solicitor general—maintained that *Lynch* held the latter position: "Our nation is not secular, but pluralistic, and there is nothing wrong with the government attempting to recognize and commemorate the impact of religion in America's historical traditions and cultural heritage." Thus, the displays were merely a *Lynch*-style acknowledgment conveying no "special message of endorsement of religion."[19] If accepted by O'Connor and the Court, this would insulate all sectarian elements of public displays celebrating religious holidays, and another brick would fall from the "wall of separation."

Separationists countered with the revised litigation strategy they unveiled in *Wallace.* With the exception of the AJC, which, joined by the NCC and the AU, filed an amicus brief, none of these groups, including the ACLU, which argued the case, asked the Court to reverse *Lynch.* This strategic decision, grounded in a realization that the former majority remained intact, led them to argue that *Lynch*'s contextual elements should be read as closely tied to the *specific fact setting* that case presented. The Pittsburgh displays, adorning the seats of government, clearly constituted the kind of state "endorsement" of religion *Lynch* held beyond the pale. While the separationists argued that both the crèche and the menorah displays fell short of this understanding of *Lynch*—unlike Blackmun and O'Connor, they did not see the "Salute to Liberty" banner and Christmas tree that made up the rest of the menorah display to save its constitutionality—their scaled-down goals and the doctrinal argument that flowed from them clearly influenced the justice (O'Connor) they needed to salvage a partial victory in a case that certainly must have looked like a losing one as it made its way to the Court.

Because it allowed them to avoid the tyranny of absolutes, the separationists' acceptance of *Lynch* in their subsequent litigation was a strategic masterstroke. The argumentational flexibility it afforded enabled them to adapt to an altered Court that was clearly not particularly supportive of their broad claims and to manage, to the degree possible given the context, the process of legal change. This flexibility—and the moderateness of their response to the line of decisions that culminated in *Lynch*—stands in stark contrast to the pressures that *some* accommodationist forces placed on the Court. A good example is *Wallace*. In that case, attorneys for one of the appellants and the Center for Judicial Studies as an amicus endorsed Judge Hand's "wall-breaking" opinion and urged it on the Court. Although the solicitor general successfully dodged political pressures to take a similar stand before the Court (Caplan 1987, 96–103), the justices (particularly O'Connor)—if they were concerned that the Court and constitutional doctrine might appear to be simple pawns in a political game dominated by far-right conservatives—may have recoiled from pressing the accommodationist logic of the early 1980s and gutting long-prevailing doctrine. The separationist strategy provided them ready arguments to stem this tide.

Further, unlike the capital punishment example Lee Epstein and I examined elsewhere (Epstein and Kobylka 1992, chap. 4), none of the major groups involved in this litigation made the strategic error of assuming that *Lynch* absolutely settled the question before the Court. Even the accommodationists, who held a broad view of the contextual dimension of that decision and trivialized the physical context approach as "reindeer counting," [20] said that the display contained sufficient secular objects to save it under the more restrictive approach urged by the separationists. Blackmun and O'Connor accepted this logic, at least as it applied to the menorah.

This analysis supports a confident inference that the law—as explicated in precedents as diverse as *Zorach* and *Engel,* as encapsulated in the *Lemon* approach, and as framed in the legal arguments presented to the Court—mattered and is the culprit that stymied the expected legal change. Perhaps it is more accurate to say that the law mattered to the moderate justices—the separationist and accommodationist blocs were set in their own absolutes—and the major groups arguing before the Court behaved as if it did. Thus, neither side burned argumentational bridges here as the abolitionists had done in *Gregg v. Georgia* (1976) and the pro-choice forces did, to a lesser extent, in *Webster v. Reproductive Health Services* (1989). By accepting and operating in the pluralistic argumentational environment afforded by existing case law, these groups forestalled the kind of legal change characteristic of the abortion and capital punishment examples—a weaker abortion right and the reimposition of the death penalty.

What remains unclear is whether the argumentational pluralism that lurks amid the discordance among usual separationist allies will ultimately so erode the *Lemon* test that the Court will begin anew to fashion a coherent approach to Establishment Clause issues. The success of the accommodationists in the school access cases—*Widmar v. Vincent* (1981), *Mergens* (1990), and *Lamb's Chapel* (1993)—could foreshadow a growing trend among the justices to see establishment issues through the coercion-ground prism of free exercise doctrine. The separationist victory in *Lee* (1992), won largely by the argument that a graduation ceremony is constitutionally equivalent to a classroom, was based more on *Engel* and *Schempp* than on *Lemon*.[21] Further, Kennedy's majority opinion rested, in part, on the "coercive" nature of the event. This language, drawn from the Court's treatment of Free Exercise of Religion Clause cases, prompted Blackmun, Stevens, and O'Connor to issue a concurrence, noting, in part, that "our precedents make clear that proof of government coercion is not necessary to prove an establishment clause violation" (*Lee*, 1992, 2664). Their opinion concludes with a reference to settled law: "I remain convinced that our jurisprudence is not misguided, and that it requires the decision reached by the Court today" (*Lee*, 1992, 2267).

Part 2 of the dissenting opinion in *Lee* by Scalia, joined by Rehnquist, White, and Thomas, ridiculed the notion of any coercion present in the facts of the case. On this point, then, Kennedy and the four *Lee* dissenters agree: coercion is relevant to the resolution of establishment questions. Where they disagree is in what they count as coercive. Their agreement in the next term in *Zobrest* (1993)—over the dissents of Blackmun, Stevens, O'Connor, and Souter—and in *County of Allegheny* (1989) should give separationists pause; so should the retirements of White and Blackmun insofar as they unsettle the Court. The argumentational pluralism that promotes free exercise values over establishment precedents in some instances could end up with the Court's adopting an understanding of establishment with which all separationists would find it difficult to live.

Conclusion

Because the Supreme Court makes its decisions out of public view, the nature of constitutional adjudication seems surrounded by mystery. The process is, to be sure, political and politicized. The judges who decide the issues brought before them are people with partisan beliefs, values, and attitudes. Presidents know this, and this knowledge often guides their judicial nominations. Those who bring cases into the courts—both the attorneys and the groups—are policy entrepreneurs seeking to enshrine their values in the "law of the land." Thus, constitutional interpretation is a part of the political process; it is, in a sense, political decision making under the obscuring cloak of judicial robes. This is the core of our "conventional wisdom," and it is basically true. Yet, elements of the mystery persist.

Noting the political nature of constitutional adjudication does not fully capture the rich and unusual context in which it plays out—a context clearly relevant to constitutional adjudication. Article III of the Constitution provides federal judges considerable independence from the coarse politics of any given day. The "law," although never as clear and pristine as traditional jurisprudes or the advocates of "original intent" suggest, is a relevant "out there" for judges; it creates the formal legal context in which they make their decisions and in which they will be critiqued and understood by consumers for whom *the law* is a very real part of their day-to-day lives. At a minimum, judges have to fit their personal predilections into its fabric. At the other end of the spectrum are judges who seek to make their decisions in accordance with the law. The former describes the quintessential "political" judge; the latter, the conventional "legal" judge. Crucial, however, is the fact that both judicial "types" must account for the law in making their decisions.

This reality led C. Herman Pritchett to note that "political scientists who have done so much to put the 'political' in 'political jurisprudence' need to emphasize that it is still 'jurisprudence.' It is judging in a political context, but it is still judging; and, judging is something different from legislating or administering" (1969, 42). It is "something different" because judges must grapple with preexisting rules and precedents. How they do this sets the political field of play for interested litigants and affects the direction of legal development. For example, in *Payne v. Tennessee* (1991), Chief Justice Rehnquist discussed *stare decisis,* the doctrine of precedent, in this way:

> *Stare decisis* is the preferred course because it promotes the evenhanded, predictable, and consistent development of legal principles, fosters

reliance on judicial decisions, and contributes to the actual and perceived integrity of the judicial process. . . . Nevertheless, . . . *stare decisis* is not an inexorable command; rather, it "is a principle of policy and not a mechanical formula of adherence to the latest decision." (*Payne*, 1991, 2609–2610)

With this, his majority reversed two precedents that were less than five years old.[22]

Rehnquist's position noted, it was precedent that led Justices O'Connor, Kennedy, and Souter to reaffirm a woman's constitutional right to an abortion in *Planned Parenthood of Southeastern Pennsylvania v. Casey* (1992). Noting at the outset that "Liberty finds no refuge in a jurisprudence of doubt" (*Casey*, 1992, 2803), they rejected the Bush administration's invitation to overrule *Roe v. Wade* (1973):

> [W]hatever the premises of opposition [to a controversial precedent] may be, only the most convincing justification under accepted standards of precedent could suffice to demonstrate that a later decision overruling the first was anything but a surrender to political pressure, and an unjustified repudiation of the principle on which the Court staked its authority in the first instance. . . . The promise of constancy, once given, binds its maker for as long as the power to stand by the decision survives and the understanding of the issue has not changed so fundamentally as to render the commitment obsolete. (*Casey*, 1992, 2815–2816)

Stare decisis represents an effort to ease judging from the immediate political plane. In this sense, the law saved the basic holding of *Roe* from predicted reversal.

Obviously the law does not speak in the same voice to all people, lay or litigating. It is, however, an irreducible presence until a majority of the Court decides otherwise. This forces litigators to account for it in making their cases, even if they do not like or accept it. By doing so, litigators can encourage, and indeed facilitate, the growth and development of a pluralistically appropriate array of judicial doctrine. The mysterious case of recent Establishment Clause litigation demonstrates this point.

The accepted empirical indicators of modern political science suggest that the "wall of separation" would not survive the Reagan-Bush assault on it. Yet, even in the face of massive personnel changes, hostile public opinion, and concerted executive branch and group pressure, the Court held the shaky line that characterizes modern Establishment Clause litigation. In the pivotal cases of *Wallace* (1985), *County of Allegheny* 1989), and *Lee* (1992), the Court reaffirmed the law—as its predecessors laid it down—to maintain a constitutional regime, eschewing a too close relation between church and state. This is not to say that the balance on the Court is exactly as it was prior to 1980, for it is somewhat more supportive of elements of accommodation than it was previously. The point, rather, is that the legal development in these cases, viewed from the perspective of the 1980, 1984, and 1988 elections, is not what the conventional wisdom about legal change would have led one to expect. Eliminating the usual suspects, one is led to the conclusion that legal argument constrained legal change. . . .

Thus ends the mystery of the unsuccessful Reagan-Bush assault on the Establishment Clause. Our investigation has absolved the usual suspects of complicity and revealed the culprit that frustrated the legal change sought by these presidents. It also reminds us that in our investigations of things judicial we must not lose sight of something that was once taken for granted. However improbable it may seem, given our conventional wisdom about the political nature of the judicial process, the language and logic of the law—albeit shaped by an array of political factors—persists as an important element of legal change, conditioning its dynamics. In the hands of skillful attorneys and attentive jurists, this suspect foiled the expected alteration in Establishment Clause doctrine.

NOTES

1. Sometime after *Zorach* was decided, Douglas became something of a born-again separationist. By *Abington School District v. Schempp* (1963), his separationism was so extreme that he pondered the constitutional necessity of removing all vestiges of religion from governmental life. This included the motto "In God we trust" on American currency.

2. Blackmun delivered the judgment of the Court in an opinion largely joined by O'Connor. Justices Brennan, Marshall, and Stevens concurred in the judgment against the crèche display but dissented from that sustaining the menorah. Justices Kennedy, William H. Rehnquist, White, and Scalia voted to uphold the ruling permitting both displays, thus concurring in the judgment sustaining the menorah display.

3. Rehnquist, Scalia, and Thomas dissented, *Kiryas Joel* is the first Establishment Clause case on which Justice Ruth Bader Ginsburg, a Clinton appointee, sat. Because it was decided after the twelve-year period of the Reagan and Bush presidencies, it is not included in the formal analysis presented below. Its result, however, is consistent with the conclusions I offer here.

4. Douglas also was a member of the "super-separationist" bloc. His replacement by Stevens thus had no effect on its alignment.

5. They strayed from separationism only on questions of tax exemptions for church property (*Walz v. Tax Commission*, 1970) and secular book loans to sectarian schools (*Wolman v. Walter*, 1977).

6. Examples of the effects of these splits are *Meek* (1975) and *Wolman* (1977), where the super-accommodationists voted with the moderates to uphold some government assistance to sectarian schools, and the super-separationists cast the deciding votes to strike down other elements of the same legislation.

7. I use the term *parochiaid* here and elsewhere to refer to government efforts to aid sectarian schools.

8. Despite his seeming about-face in *Regan*, Stewart supported accommodationist values in only 44 percent of the cases decided between 1970 and his retirement (Kobylka 1985).

9. Reagan took his rhetorical trumpeting of accommodationism to the pulpit of the presidency. He frequented National Prayer Day ceremonies, and he regularly addressed groups like the National Religious Broadcasters, the National Association of Evangelicals, and the Women Leaders of Christian Organizations. He also devoted exclusive or substantial attention to this issue in at least five of his weekly Saturday radio addresses to the nation (September 18, 1982; January 22 and November 19, 1983; February 25, 1984; August 24, 1985).

10. "Nothing in this Constitution shall be construed to prohibit individual or group prayer in public schools or other public institutions. No person shall be required by the United States or by any State to participate in prayer." The amendment died after it failed to get the requisite two-thirds Senate approval in March 1984. Reagan, however, continued to submit it to the Senate throughout the rest of his presidency.

11. This act was upheld in *Board of Education v. Mergens* (1990) with only Stevens dissenting.

12. Of the ten cases, the solicitor general argued *Alamo Federation v. Secretary of Labor* (1985), *Corp. of Presiding Bishop v. Amos* (1988), and *Hernandez v. Commissioner of Internal Revenue* (1989), and intervened in *Lynch* (1984), *Wallace* (1985), *Aguilar* (1985), *Grand Rapids* (1985), *Bowen v. Kendrick* (1988), *Mergens* (1990), and *Lee* (1992). The seven cases in which amicus curiae briefs were filed were *Mueller* (1983), *Marsh* (1983), *Thorton v. Caldor* (1985), *Witters v. Washington* (1986), *County of Allegheny* (1989), *Lamb's Chapel* (1993), and *Zobrest* (1993).

13. Brief for the United States in *Lynch*, 1984, 1. Lee never asked the Court to reconsider or reverse *Lemon*. Indeed, his critics on the political right blasted him for exactly this. Note, for example, the comments of James McClellan (1984, 2), head of the Center for Judicial Studies: "Lee has not urged the Supreme Court to overrule a single prior decision, including *Roe v. Wade*, the New York prayer case, and *Mapp v. Ohio*." Caplan (1987, 99) notes that McClellan was linked to William Bradford Reynolds and was the inspiration for, if not the author of, Judge Learned Hand's district court opinion in *Wallace*. For more on McClellan's links to the Reagan Justice Department, see Schwartz (1988, 4–6).

14. Amicus curiae brief of the United States, requesting a gant of certiorari, *Lee v. Weisman* (1992, 15; a grant of certiorari formally dockets a case for argument before the Court.)

15. The linkages between the ACLU and the AJC cannot be overstated. Once the church-state issue was taken to the courts, these groups pursued a close and coordinated approach designed to erect and maintain a high "wall of separation." Indeed, scholars have pointed to Leo Pfeffer, a long-time counsel for the AJC, as "one of the most knowledgeable and experienced church-state lawyers in the country" (Morgan 1968, 55); we have no reason to dispute this claim. Pfeffer's reach was amazing. Not only was he active with the AJC, but he also served on the church-state committee of the ACLU, founded and directed the Committee for Public Education and Religious Liberty (CPERL), wrote briefs for other separationist interests (for example, the American Association of School Administrators, the Baptist Joint Committee on Public Affairs, and the Synagogue Council), appeared in untold numbers of cases as a plaintiff attorney, and wrote several books and articles on the constitutional status of religious freedom. He is as close to the historical architect and guide of the legal separationist position as can be imagined.

16. ACLU amicus brief in *Wallace*.

17. In its amicus brief, the AJC, joined by the NJCRC, the ADBB, and the American Jewish Committee, did not focus on either the *Lynch* precedent or O'Connor's "test." It argued that history and precedents demonstrated that the use of public schools to advance religious belief was inherently unconstitutional.

18. The Alabama state senator Donald G. Holmes, a self-described "prime sponsor" of the statute, testified before the district court that the statute was "an effort to return voluntary prayer to our public schools . . . it is a beginning and a step in the right direction," and that he supported it with "no other purpose in mind" than "returning voluntary prayer to our public schools" (*Wallace,* 1985, 2483).

19. Brief for the United States in *County of Allegheny* (1989, 18).

20. Brief for the United States, *County of Allegheny* (1989, 18).

21. The majority opinion in *Kiryas Joel* (1994) treats *Lemon* in much the same fashion.

22. *Booth v. Maryland* (1987) and *South Carolina v. Gathers* (1989).

REFERENCES

Caplan, Lincoln. 1987. *The Tenth Justice.* New York: Vintage Books.

Casper, Jonathan D. 1972. *The Politics of Civil Liberties.* New York: Harper and Row.

Doyle, Arthur Conan. 1930. *The Complete Sherlock Holmes.* Garden City, N.Y.: Doubleday.

Dunne, F. P. 1938. *Mr. Dooley at His Best.* New York: Charles Scribner's Sons.

Epstein, Lee, and Joseph F. Kobylka. 1992. *The Supreme Court and Legal Change.* Chapel Hill: University of North Carolina Press.

Galanter, Marc. 1974. "Why the 'Haves' Come Out Ahead: Speculations on the Limits of Legal Change." *Law and Society Review* 9:95–160.

Giacoma, James M. 1980. "Committee for Public Education and Religious Liberty v. Regan: New Possibilities for State Aid to Nonpuplic Schools." *Saint Louis University Law Journal* 24:406–424.

Hertzke, Allen D. 1988. *Representing God in Washington: The Role of Religious Lobbies in the American Polity.* Knoxville: University of Tennessee Press.

Hyer, Marjorie. 1982. "Americans United's Role in Church-State Separation." *Washington Post,* January 16.

Kobylka, Joseph F. 1985. "Justice Harry A. Blackmun and Church-State Questions: A 'Born-Again Separationist'?" Paper presented at the annual meeting of the Law and Society Association, San Diego.

Lee, Rex. 1981. *A Lawyer Looks at the Supreme Court.* Provo, Utah: Brigham Young University Press.

McClellan, James. 1984. "A Lawyer Looks at Rex Lee." *Benchmark* 1:1–16.

Meese, Edwin. 1985. "Remarks before the American Bar Association." In *The Great Debate: Interpreting Our Constitution.* Occasional Paper 2. Washington, D.C.: Federalist Society.

Moen, Matthew C. 1989. *The Christian Right and Congress.* Tuscaloosa: University of Alabama Press.

Morgan, Richard E. 1968. *The Politics of Religious Conflict.* New York: Pegasus.

_____. 1972. *The Supreme Court and Religion.* New York: Free Press.

_____. 1973. "The Establishment Clause and Sectarian Schools: A Final Installment?" *Supreme Court Review* 1973:57–97.

Pritchett, C. Herman. 1969. "The Development of Judicial Research." In *Frontiers of Judicial Research,* edited by Joel B. Grossman and Joseph Tanenhaus. New York: John Wiley and Sons.

Reagan, Ronald. 1982. *Public Papers of the President.* Washington, D.C.: U.S. Government Printing Office.

_____. 1983. *Public Papers of the President.* Washington, D.C.: U.S. Government Printing Office.

Shwartz, Herman. 1988. *Packing the Courts: The Conservative Campaign to Re-Write the Constitution.* New York: Charles Scribner's Sons.

Stanley, Harold W., and Richard G. Niemi. 1992. *Vital Statistics on American Politics.* Washington, D.C.: CQ Press.

Walker, Samuel. 1990. *In Defense of American Liberties: A History of the ACLU.* New York: Oxford University Press.

The Real World of Constitutional Rights

THE SUPREME COURT AND THE IMPLEMENTATION
OF THE ABORTION DECISIONS

Gerald N. Rosenberg

When one considers how exposed the Constitution's "religious estab-
lishment" clause is to continuous revision, it is not surprising to find
other, less established rights deeply enmeshed in politics as well. The
next essay examines the right to an abortion, a controversial aspect of
civil liberties policy that has been defended as an application of the
"right to privacy."

The Supreme Court began asserting the right to privacy in earnest
with Griswold v. Connecticut in 1965, when it ruled that a married
couple's decision to use birth control lay beyond the purview of the gov-
ernment. The 1973 Roe v. Wade decision establishing a woman's right
to an abortion—the best known and most controversial privacy right—
has further established privacy as a class of rights implicit in the Bill of
Rights. But, as Gerald Rosenberg explains, Roe v. Wade left many as-
pects of abortion rights unresolved, and a lively public debate on the
subject continues today.

IN *ROE V. WADE* and *Doe v. Bolton* (1973) the Supreme Court held unconstitutional Texas and Georgia laws prohibiting abortions except for "the purpose
of saving the life of the mother" (Texas) and where "pregnancy would en-
danger the life of the pregnant mother or would seriously and permanently
injure her health" (Georgia). The Court asserted that women had a fundamental right of privacy to decide whether or not to bear a child. Dividing
pregnancy roughly into three trimesters, the Court held that in the first
trimester the choice of abortion was a woman's alone, in consultation with
a physician. During the second trimester, states could regulate abortion for

Excerpted from Lee Epstein, ed., *Contemplating Courts* (Washington, D.C.: CQ Press, 1995), pp.
390–419. Some notes and bibliographic references appearing in the original have been cut.

the preservation and protection of women's health, and in approximately the third trimester, after fetal viability, could ban abortions outright, except where necessary to preserve a woman's life or health. Although responding specifically to the laws of Texas and Georgia, the broad scope of the Court's constitutional interpretation invalidated the abortion laws of almost every state and the District of Columbia.[1] According to one critic, *Roe* and *Doe* "may stand as the most radical decisions ever issued by the Supreme Court" (Noonan 1973, 261).

Roe and *Doe* are generally considered leading examples of judicial action in support of relatively powerless groups unable to win legislative victories. In these cases, women were that politically disadvantaged group; indeed, it has been claimed, "No victory for women's rights since enactment of the 19th Amendment has been greater than the one achieved" in *Roe* and *Doe* ("A Woman's Right" 1973, A4). But women are not the only disadvantaged interests who have attempted to use litigation to achieve policy ends. Starting with the famous cases brought by civil rights groups, and spreading to issues raised by environmental groups, consumer groups, and others, reformers have over the past decades looked to the courts as important producers of political and social change. Yet, during the same period, students of judicial politics have learned that court opinions are not always implemented with the speed and directness that rule by law assumes. This is particularly the case with decisions that touch on controversial, emotional issues or deeply held beliefs, such as abortion.

This chapter contains an exploration of the effect of the Court's abortion decisions, both *Roe* and *Doe,* and the key decisions based on them. How did the public, politicians, medical professionals, and interest groups react to them? Were the decisions implemented? Did they bring safe and legal abortions to all American women? To some American women? If the answer turns out to be only some, then I want to know why. What are the factors that have led a constitutional right to be unevenly available? More generally, are there conditions under which Court decisions on behalf of relatively powerless groups are more or less likely to be implemented.[2]

The analysis presented here shows that the effect and implementation of the Court's abortion decisions have been neither straightforward nor simple. Political response has varied and access to legal and safe abortion has increased, but in an uneven and nonuniform way. These findings are best explained by two related factors. First, at the time of the initial decisions there was widespread support for legal abortion from several sets of actors, including relevant political and professional elites on both the national and local level, the public at large, and activists. Second, the Court's decisions, by allowing clinics to perform abortions, made it possible for women to obtain abortions in some places where hospitals refused to provide them. Implementation by private clinics, however, has led to uneven availability of abortion services and has encouraged local political opposition.

The Abortion Cases

Roe and *Doe* were the Court's first major abortion decisions, but they were not its last.[3] In response to these decisions, many states rewrote their abortion laws, ostensibly to conform with the Court's constitutional mandate but actually with the goal of restricting the newly created right. Cases quickly arose, and continue to arise, challenging state laws as inconsistent with the Court's ruling, if not openly and clearly hostile to it. In general, the Court's response has been to preserve the core holding of *Roe* and *Doe* that a woman has a virtually unfettered constitutional right to an abortion before fetal viability, but to defer to legislation in areas not explicitly dealt with in those decisions. These cases require brief mention.

Areas of Litigation

Since *Roe* and *Doe,* the Court has heard three kinds of cases on abortion. One type involves state and federal funding for abortion. Here, the Court has consistently upheld the right of government not to fund abortion services and to prohibit the provision of abortions in public hospitals, unless the abortion is medically necessary. In perhaps the most important case, *Harris v. McRae* (1980), the Court upheld the most restrictive version of the so-called Hyde Amendment, which barred the use of federal funds for even medically necessary abortions, including those involving pregnancies due to rape or incest.

A second area that has provoked a great deal of litigation is the degree of participation in the abortion decision constitutionally allowed to the spouse of a pregnant married woman or the parents of a pregnant single minor. The Court has consistently struck down laws requiring spousal involvement but has upheld laws requiring parental notification or consent, as long as there is a "judicial bypass" option allowing minors to bypass their parents and obtain permission from a court.

A third area generating litigation involves the procedural requirements that states can impose for abortions. Most of these cases have arisen from state attempts to make abortion as difficult as possible to obtain. Regulations include requiring all post–first trimester abortions to be performed in hospitals; the informed, written consent of a woman before an abortion can be performed; a twenty-four-hour waiting period before an abortion can be performed; a pathology report for each abortion and the presence of a second physician at abortions occurring after potential viability; the preservation by physicians of the life of viable fetuses; and restrictions on the disposal of fetal remains. The Court's most recent pronouncement on these issues, *Planned Parenthood of Southeastern Pennsylvania v. Casey* (1992), found informed consent, a twenty-four-hour waiting period, and certain reporting requirements constitutional.

Trends in Court Treatment of Abortion Cases

Since the late 1980s, as *Casey* suggests, the Court has upheld more restrictions on the abortion right. In *Webster v. Reproductive Health Services* (1989), the Court upheld a 1986 restrictive Missouri law, and in 1991, in *Rust v. Sullivan,* it upheld government regulations prohibiting family-planning organizations that receive federal funds from counseling patients about abortion or providing abortion referrals. Most important, in *Casey* the Court abandoned the trimester framework of *Roe.* Although the justices did not agree on the proper constitutional standard for assessing state restrictions on abortion, Justices Sandra Day O'Connor, Anthony M. Kennedy, and David H. Souter adopted an "undue burden" standard. Under this standard, states may regulate abortion but may not place an undue burden on women seeking an abortion of a nonviable fetus.

Many commentators expected *Casey* to generate an avalanche of litigation centering directly on the abortion rights. Given the ambiguity of the undue burden standard, they expected expanded state activity to limit abortion. These expectations may yet be fulfilled, but, interestingly, Court cases since *Casey* have not specifically focused on the abortion right per se. Rather, in recent litigation the Court has been asked to resolve questions concerning access to abortion; namely, what steps can courts take to prevent antiabortion advocates from interfering with public access to family-planning and abortion clinics? The reason these kinds of questions arose is not difficult to discern; the 1990s has seen the rise of militant tactics—ranging from boisterous protests to harassment of clinic workers and even to the murder of physicians performing abortions—by certain segments of the antiabortion movement.

These "access" cases have generated mixed Court rulings. In *Bray v. Alexandria Women's Health Clinic* (1993), the Court rejected an attempt by pro-choice groups to use the 1871 Ku Klux Klan Act as a way to bring federal courts into this area. But, in *Madsen v. Women's Health Center* (1994), the Court upheld parts of a Florida trial court injunction permanently enjoining antiabortion protesters from blocking access to an abortion clinic and from physically harassing persons leaving or entering it. With the enactment by Congress of the Freedom of Access to Clinic Entrances Act in 1994, and the immediate filing of a legal challenge, it is likely that the Court will have another opportunity to address this issue.

Implementing Constitutional Rights

How have the public, politicians, medical professionals, and interest groups reacted to the Court decisions since *Roe* and *Doe*? How has access to legal and safe abortion changed in the wake of these decisions? In other words, when the Supreme Court announces a new constitutional right, what happens?

Legal Abortions: The Numbers

An obvious way to consider this question, at least in the abortion realm, is to look at the number of legal abortions performed before and after the 1973 decisions. For, if the Court has had an important effect on society in this area, we might expect to find dramatic increases in the number of legal abortions obtained after 1973. Collecting statistics on legal abortion, however, is not an easy task. Record keeping is not as precise and complete as one would hope. Two organizations, the public Centers for Disease Control and Prevention in Atlanta and the private Alan Guttmacher Institute in New York, are the most thorough and reliable collectors of the information. The data they have collected on the number of legal abortions

Figure 1. Legal Abortions, 1966–1992

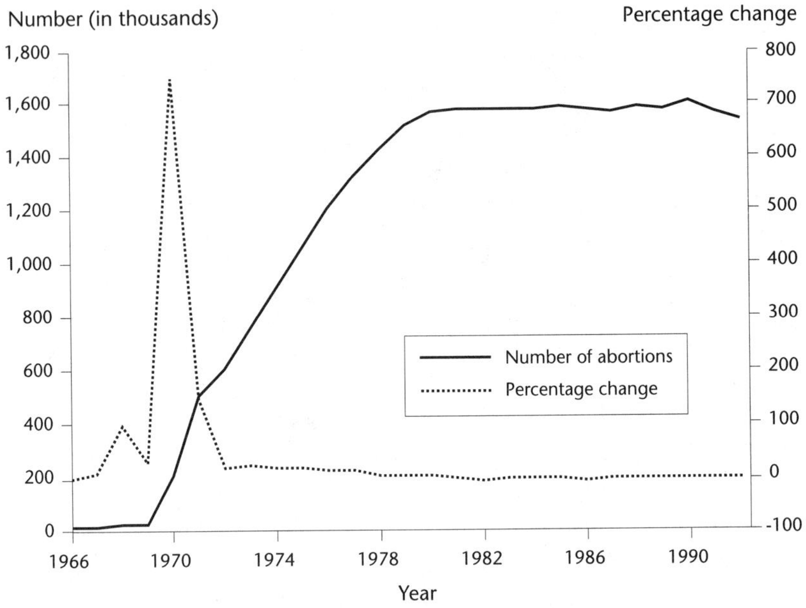

Sources: Estimates by the Alan Guttmacher Institute and the Centers for Disease Control and Prevention in Henshaw and Van Vort 1994, 100–106, 112; Lader 1973, 209; U.S. Congress 1974, 1976; Weinstock et al. 1975, 23. When sources differed, I have relied on data from the Alan Guttmacher Institute since its estimates are based on surveys of all known abortion providers and are generally more complete. Data points for 1983, 1986, and 1990 are estimates based on interpolations made by the Alan Guttmacher Institute.

performed between 1966 and 1992 and the yearly percentage change are shown in Figure 1.

Interestingly, these data present a mixed picture of the effect of the abortion decisions. On the one hand, they suggest that after *Roe* the number of legal abortions increased at a strong pace throughout the 1970s (the solid line in Figure 1). On the other hand, they reveal that the changes after 1973 were part of a trend that started in 1970, three years before the Court acted. Strikingly, the largest increase in the number of legal abortions occurs between 1970 and 1971, two years before *Roe*! In raw numerical terms, the increase between 1972 and 1973 is 157,800, a full 134,500 fewer than the pre-*Roe* increase in 1970–1971. It is possible, of course, that the effect of *Roe* was not felt in 1973. Even though the decision was handed down in January, perhaps the 1973–1974 comparison gives a more accurate picture. If this is the case, the increase, 154,000, is still substantially smaller than the change during 1970–1971. And while the number of legal abortions continued to increase in the years immediately after 1974, that rate eventually stabilized and by the 1990s had actually declined. The dotted line in Figure 1 (representing the percentage change in the number of legal abortions performed from one year to the next) shows, too, that the largest increases in the number of legal abortions occurred in the years prior to *Roe*. . . .

The data presented above show that the largest numerical increases in legal abortions occurred in the years prior to initial Supreme Court action. . . . There was no steep or unusual increase in the number of legal abortions following *Roe*. To be sure, it is possible that without constitutional protection for abortion no more states would have liberalized or repealed their laws and those that had done so might have overturned their previous efforts. And the fact that the number of legal abortions continued to increase after 1973 suggests that the Court was effective in easing access to safe and legal abortion. But those increases, while large, were smaller than those of previous years. Hence, the growth in the number of legal abortions can be only partially attributed to the Court; it might even be the case that the increases would have continued without the Court's 1973 decisions.

What Happened?

Particularly interesting about the data presented above is that they suggest that *Roe* itself failed to generate major changes in the number of legal abortions. This finding is compatible with political science literature, in which it is argued that Supreme Court decisions, particularly ones dealing with emotional and controversial issues, are not automatically and completely implemented. It also appears to fit nicely with an argument I have made elsewhere (Rosenberg 1991), which suggests that several factors must be present for new constitutional rights to be implemented. These include widespread support from political and professional elites on both the national and local level, from the public at large, and from activists and a willingness on the part of those called on to implement the decision to act accordingly. This is true, as Alexander Hamilton pointed out two centuries ago, because courts lack the power of "either the sword or the purse." To a greater extent than other government institutions, courts are dependent on both elite and popular support for their decisions to be implemented.

To fill out my argument in greater detail, I examine both pre- and post-1973 actions as they relate to the implementation of the abortion right. In so doing, I reach two important conclusions. First, by the time the Court reached its decisions in 1973, little political opposition to abortion existed on the federal level, relevant professional elites and social activists gave it widespread support, it was practiced on a large scale (see Figure 1), and public support for it was growing. These positions placed abortion reform in the American mainstream. Second, in the years after 1973, opposition to abortion strengthened and grew.

Pre-*Roe* Support

In the decade or so prior to *Roe,* there was a sea change in the public position of abortion in American life. At the start of the 1960s, abortion was not a political issue. Abortions, illegal as they were, were performed clandestinely, and women who underwent the procedure did not talk about it.[4] By 1972, however, abortion had become a public and political issue. While little legislative or administrative action was taken on the federal level, a social movement, organized in the mid- and late 1960s, to reform and repeal prohibitions on abortion met with some success at the state level, and public opinion swung dramatically from opposition to abortion in most cases to substantial support.

Elites and Social Activists

Although abortions have always been performed, public discussion did not surface until the 1950s. In 1962 the American Law Institute (ALI) published its Model Penal Code on abortion, permitting abortion if continuing the pregnancy would adversely affect the physical or mental health of the woman, if there was risk of birth defects, or if the pregnancy resulted from rape or incest. Publicity about birth defects caused by Thalidomide, a drug prescribed in the 1960s to cure infertility, and a German measles epidemic in the years 1962–1965 kept the issue prominent. By November 1965 the American Medical Association Board of Trustees approved a report urging adoption of the ALI law.

In 1966, reform activists began making numerous radio and television appearances.[5] By then there were several pro-choice groups, including the Society for Humane Abortion in California; the Association for the Study of Abortion in New York, a prestigious board of doctors and lawyers; and the Illinois Committee for Medical Control of Abortion, which advocated repeal of all abortion laws. Abortion referral services were also started. Previously, pro-choice activists had made private referrals to competent doctors in the United States and Mexico, who performed illegal but safe abortions. But by the late 1960s, abortion referral groups operated publicly. In New York City, in 1967, twenty-two clergy announced the formation of their group, gaining front-page coverage in the *New York Times* (Fiske 1967). The Chicago referral service took out a full page ad in the *Sun-Times* announcing its services. In Los Angeles, the referral service was serving more than a thousand women per month. By the late 1960s pro-choice organizations, including abortion-referral services, were operating in many major U.S. cities. And by 1971, the clergy referral service operated publicly in eighteen states with a staff of about 700 clergy and lay people (Hole and Levine 1971, 299).

In order to tap this emerging support, the National Association for the Repeal of Abortion Laws (NARAL) was founded.[6] Protesting in the streets, lecturing, and organizing "days of anger" began to have an effect. Women who had undergone illegal abortions wrote and spoke openly about them. Seventy-five leading national groups endorsed the repeal of all abortion laws between 1967 and the end of 1972, including twenty-eight religious and twenty-one medical groups. Among the religious groups, support ranged from the American Jewish Congress to the American Baptist Convention. Medical groups included the American Public Health Association, the American Psychiatric Association, the American Medical Association, the National Council of Obstetrics-Gynecology, and the American College of Obstetricians and Gynecologists. Among other groups, support included the American Bar Association and a host of liberal organizations. Even the YWCA supported repeal (U.S. Congress 1976, 4:53–91).

The Federal Government

In the late 1960s, while the abortion law reform battle was being fought in the states, the federal arena was quiet. For example, although states with less restrictive laws received Medicaid funds that paid for some abortions, for "six years after 1967, not a single bill was introduced, much less considered, in Congress to curtail the use of federal funds for abortion" (Rosoff 1975, 13). The pace momentarily quickened in 1968 when the Presidential Advisory Council on the Status of Women, appointed by President Lyndon Johnson, recommended the repeal of all abortion laws (Lader 1973, 81–82).

Still, abortion was not a major issue in the 1968 presidential campaign. Despite his personal beliefs, the newly elected president, Richard M. Nixon, did not take active steps to limit abortion, and the U.S. government did not enter *Roe* nor, after the decision, did it give support to congressional efforts to limit abortion.[7] Although it is true that in 1973 and 1974 President Nixon was occupied with other matters, his administration essentially avoided the abortion issue.

In Congress there was virtually no abortion activity prior to 1973. In April 1970, Sen. Bob Packwood (R-Ore.) introduced a National Abortion Act designed to "guarantee and protect" the "fundamental constitutional right" of a woman "to control her own fertility" (U.S. Congress 1970a). He also introduced a bill to liberalize the District of Columbia's abortion law (U.S. Congress 1970b). Otherwise, Congress remained essentially inactive on the abortion issue.

The States

It is not at all surprising that the president and Congress did not involve themselves in the abortion reform movement of the 1960s. Laws banning abortion were state laws, so most of the early abortion law reform activity was directed at state governments. In the early and middle parts of the decade there was some legislative discussion in California, New Hampshire, and New York. By 1967, reform bills were introduced in twenty-eight states, including California, Colorado, Delaware, Florida, Georgia, Maryland, Oklahoma, New Jersey, New York, North Carolina, and Pennsylvania (Rubin 1982). The first successful liberalization drive was in Colorado, which adopted a reform bill, modeled on the ALI's Model Penal Code. Interestingly, another early reform state was California, where Gov. Ronald Reagan, despite intense opposition, signed a reform bill.

These victories further propelled the reform movement, and in 1968, abortion legislation was pending in some thirty states. During 1968–1969 seven states—Arkansas, Delaware, Georgia, Kansas, Maryland, New Mexico, and Oregon—enacted reform laws based on or similar to the ALI model (Lader 1973, 84). In 1970, four states went even further. In chronological order, Hawaii, New York, Alaska, and Washington essentially repealed prohibitions on abortions in the first two trimesters.

To sum up, in the five or so years prior to the Supreme Court's decisions, reform and repeal bills had been debated in most states, and seventeen plus the District of Columbia acted to liberalize their laws (Craig and O'Brien 1993, 75). State action had removed some obstacles to abortion, and safe and legal abortions were thus available in scattered states. And, as indicated in Figure 1, in 1972, nearly 600,000 legal abortions were performed. Activity was widespread, vocal, and effective.

Public Opinion

Another important element in the effectiveness of the Court is the amount of support from the population at large. By the eve of the Court's decision in 1973, public opinion had dramatically shifted from opposition to abortion in most cases to substantial, if not majority, support. Indeed, in the decades that have followed, opinion on abortion has remained remarkably stable.[8]

Looking at the 1960s as a whole, Blake (1971, 543, 544) found that opinions on discretionary abortion were "changing rapidly over time" and polls were recording "rapidly growing support." For example, relying on data from Gallup polls, Blake (1977b, 49) found that support for elective abortion increased approximately two and one-half times from 1968 to 1972. One set of Gallup polls recorded a fifteen-point drop in the percentage of respondents disapproving of abortions for financial reasons in the eight months between October 1969 and June 1970 (Blake 1977a, 58). . . . [I]n 1971, a national poll taken for the Commission on Population Growth and the American Future found 50 percent of its respondents agreeing with the statement that the abortion "decision should be left up to persons involved and their doctor" (Rosenthal 1971, 22). Thus, in the words of one study, "[b]y the time the Supreme Court made its ruling, there was strong public support behind the legalization of abortion" (Ebaugh and Haney 1980, 493).

Much of the reason for the growth in support for the repeal of the laws on abortion, both from the public and from organizations, may have come from changes in opinion by the professional elite. Polls throughout the late 1960s reported that important subgroups of the American population were increasingly supportive of abortion law reform and repeal. Several nonscientific polls of doctors, for example, suggested a great deal of support for abortion reform. A scientific poll of nearly thirteen thousand respondents in nursing, medical, and social work schools in the autumn and winter of 1971 showed strong support for repeal. The poll found split opinions among nursing students and faculty but found that 69 percent of medical students, 71 percent of medical faculty, 76 percent of social work students, and 75 percent of social work faculty supported "freely accessible abortion" (Rosen et al. 1974, 165). And a poll by the American Council of Education of 180,000 college freshmen in 1970 found that 83 percent favored the legalization of abortion (Currivan 1970). It is clear that in the late 1960s and early 1970s, the public was becoming increasingly supportive of legal abortion.

Post-*Roe* Activity

The relative quiet of the early 1960s has yet to return to the abortion arena. Rather than settling the issue, the Court's decisions added even more controversy. On the federal level, legislative and administrative action dealing with abortion has swung back and forth, from more or less benign neglect prior to 1973 to open antipathy to modest support. State action has followed a different course. Legislative efforts in the 1960s and early 1970s to reform and repeal abortion laws gave way to efforts to limit access to abortions. Public opinion remained stable until the *Webster* decision, after which there was a noticeable shift toward the pro-choice position. Finally, the antiabortion movement grew both more vocal and more violent.

The Federal Government: The President

On the presidential level, little changed in the years immediately after *Roe*. Nixon, as noted, took no action, and Gerald R. Ford, during his short term, said little about abortion until the presidential campaign in 1976, when he took a middle-of-the-road, antiabortion position, supporting local option, the law before *Roe,* and opposing federal funding of abortion (Craig and O'Brien 1993, 160–161). His Justice Department, however, did not enter the case of *Planned Parenthood of Central Missouri v. Danforth,* in which numerous state restrictions on the provision of abortion were challenged, and the Ford administration took no major steps to help the antiabortion forces.[9]

The Carter administration, unlike its Republican predecessors, did act to limit access to abortion. As a presidential candidate Carter opposed federal spending for abortion, and as president, during a press conference in June 1977, he stated his support for the Supreme Court's decisions allowing states to refuse Medicaid funding for abortions (Rubin 1982, 107). The Carter administration also sent its solicitor general into the Supreme Court to defend the Hyde Amendment.

Ronald Reagan was publicly committed to ending legal abortion. Opposition to *Roe* was said to be a litmus test for federal judicial appointments, and Reagan repeatedly used his formidable rhetorical skills in support of antiabortion activists. Under his presidency, antiabortion laws enacted included prohibiting fetal tissue research by federal scientists, banning most abortions at military hospitals, and denying funding to organizations that counseled or provided abortion services abroad. His administration submitted amicus curiae cases in all the Court's abortion cases, and in two (*Thornburgh v. American College of Obstetricians and Gynecologists,* 1986, and *Webster*) urged that *Roe* be overturned. Yet, despite the rhetoric and the symbolism, these actions had little effect on the abortion rate. As Craig and O'Brien (1993, 190) put it, "in spite of almost eight years of antiabortion rhetoric, Reagan had accomplished little in curbing abortion."

The administration of George Bush was as, if not more, hostile to the constitutional right to abortion as its predecessor. It filed antiabortion briefs in several abortion cases and urged that *Roe* be overturned. During Bush's presidency, the Food and Drug Administration placed RU-486, a French abortion drug, on the list of unapproved drugs, making it ineligible to be imported for personal use. And, in the administration's most celebrated antiabortion action, the secretary of the Health and Human Services Department, Louis W. Sullivan, issued regulations prohibiting family-planning organizations that received federal funds from counseling patients about abortion or providing referrals (the "gag rule" upheld in *Rust*).

President Bill Clinton brought a sea change to the abortion issue. As the first pro-choice president since *Roe,* he acted quickly to reverse decisions of his predecessors. In particular, on the third day of his administration, and the twentieth anniversary of *Roe,* Clinton issued five abortion-related memos.

1. He rescinded the ban on abortion counseling at federally financed clinics (negating *Rust*).

2. He rescinded restrictions on federal financing of fetal tissue research.
3. He eased U.S. policy on abortions in military hospitals.
4. He reversed Reagan policy on aid to international family planning programs involved in abortion-related activities.
5. He called for review of the ban on RU-486, the French abortion pill (Toner 1993).

In addition, in late May 1994, he signed the Freedom of Access to Clinic Entrances Act, giving federal protection to facilities and personnel providing abortion services. And, in early August 1994, the U.S. Justice Department sent U.S. marshals to help guard abortion clinics in at least twelve communities around the country (Thomas 1994). Furthermore, his two Supreme Court appointees as of 1994, Ruth Bader Ginsburg and Stephen Breyer, are apparently both pro-choice.

The Federal Government: Congress

In contrast to the executive branch, Congress engaged in a great deal of antiabortion activity after 1973, although almost none of it was successful, and some supportive activity actually occurred in the late 1980s and early 1990s. By means of legislation designed to overturn *Roe,* riders to various spending bills, and constitutional amendments, many members of Congress made their opposition to abortion clear. Perhaps the most important congressional action was the passage of the Hyde Amendment, which restricted federal funding of abortion: First passed in 1976, and then in subsequent years, the amendment prohibited the use of federal funds for abortion except in extremely limited circumstances. Although the wording varied in some years, the least limited version allowed funding only to save the life of the woman, when rape or incest had occurred, or when some long-lasting health damage, certified by two physicians, would result from the pregnancy. The amendment has been effective and the number of federally funded abortions fell from 294,600 in 1977 to 267 in 1992 (Daley and Gold 1994, 250).

Despite the amount of congressional activity, the Hyde Amendment was the only serious piece of antiabortion legislation enacted.[10] And, in 1994, Congress actually enacted legislation granting federal protection to abortion clinics. Thus, Congress was hostile in words but cautious in action with abortion. While not supporting the Court and the right to abortion, congressional action did not bar legal abortion.[11]

The States

Prior to 1973 the states had been the main arena for the abortion battle, and Court action did not do much to change that. In the wake of the Court decisions, all but a few states had to rewrite their abortion laws to conform to the Court's constitutional mandate. Their reactions, like those on the federal level, varied enormously. Some states acted to bring their laws into conformity with the Court's ruling, while others reenacted their former restrictive laws or enacted regulations designed to impede access to abortion. Since abortion is a state matter, the potential for state action affecting the availability of legal abortion was high.

At the outset, a national survey reported that state governments "moved with extreme caution in implementing the Supreme Court's ruling" (Brody 1973, A1). By the end of 1973, Blake (1977b, 46) reports, 260 abortion-related bills had been introduced in state legislatures and 39 enacted. In 1974, 189 bills were introduced and 19 enacted. In total, in the two years immediately following the Court decisions, 62 laws relating to abortion were enacted by 32 states. And state activity continued, with more abortion laws enacted in 1977 than in any year since 1973 (Rubin 1982, 126, 136).

Many of these laws were hostile to abortion. "Perhaps the major share," Blake (1977b, 61 n. 2) believes, was "obstructive and unconstitutional." They included spousal and parental consent requirements, tedious written-consent forms describing the "horrors" of abortion, funding limitations, waiting periods, hospitalization requirements, elaborate statistical reporting requirements, and burdensome medical procedures. Other action undertaken by states was simple and directly to the point. North Dakota and Rhode Island, for example, responded to the Court's decisions by enacting laws allowing abortion only to preserve the life of the woman (Weinstock et al. 1975, 28; "Rhode Island" 1973). Virginia rejected a bill bringing its statutes into conformity with the Court's order (Brody 1973, 46). Arkansas enforced a state law allowing abortion only if the pregnancy threatened the life or health of the woman ("Abortions Legal for Year" 1973, A14). In Louisiana, the attorney general threatened to take away the license of any physician performing an abortion, and the state medical society declared that any physician who performed an abortion, except to save the woman's life, violated the ethical principles of medicine (Weinstock et al. 1975, 28). The Louisiana State Board of

Medical Examiners also pledged to prevent physicians from performing abortions (Brody 1973). In Pennsylvania, the state medical society announced that it did "not condone abortion on demand" and retained its strict standards (King 1973, 35). And in Saint Louis, the city attorney threatened to arrest any physician who performed an abortion (King 1973). Given this kind of activity, it can be concluded that in many states the Court's intent was "widely and purposively frustrated" (Blake 1977b, 60–61).

Variation in state response to the constitutional right to an abortion continues to this day. Although legal abortions are performed in all states, the availability of abortion services varies enormously. As noted, a variety of restrictions on abortion have been enacted across the country. In the wake of the Court's decision in *Webster* (1989), which upheld a restrictive Missouri law, a new round of state restrictions on abortion was generally expected. Indeed, within two years of the decision nine states and Guam enacted restrictions. Nevertheless, four states enacted legislation protecting a woman's right to abortion (Craig and O'Brien 1993, 280). The Pennsylvania enactments were challenged in *Casey* (1992), in which the "undue burden" standard was announced. The lack of clarity in this standard virtually ensures that restrictions will continue to be enacted.

Public Opinion

As shown in Figure 2, public opinion changed little from the early 1970s (pre-*Roe*) until the *Webster* decision in 1989, after which a small but important growth in pro-choice support occurred. Although differently worded questions produce different results, it is clear that the American public remains strongly supportive of abortion when the woman's health is endangered by continuing the pregnancy, when there is a strong chance of a serious fetal defect, and when the pregnancy is the result of rape or incest. The public is more divided when abortion is sought for economic reasons, by single unmarried women unwilling to marry, and by married women who do not want more children. "The overall picture that emerges is that a majority supports leaving abortion legal and available to women unfortunate enough to need it, though many in the majority remain concerned about the moral implications" (Craig and O'Brien 1993, 269). . . .

Figure 2. Public Opinion and Abortion, Selected Years, 1975–1992

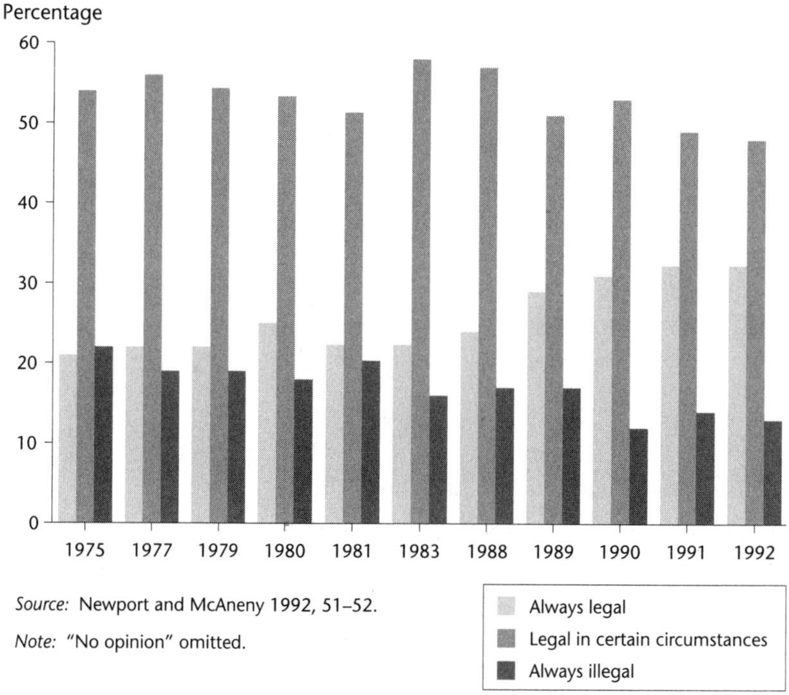

Percentage

Source: Newport and McAneny 1992, 51–52.

Note: "No opinion" omitted.

Always legal
Legal in certain circumstances
Always illegal

Anti-Abortion Activity

Organized opposition to abortion increased dramatically in the years following the Court's initial decisions. National groups such as the American Life Lobby, Americans United for Life, the National Right to Life Committee, the Pro-Life Action League, and Operation Rescue and numerous local groups have adopted some of the tactics of the reformers. They have marched, lobbied, and protested, urging that abortion be made illegal in most or all circumstances. In addition, in the 1980s, groups like Operation Rescue began to adopt more violent tactics. And, since 1982, the U.S. Bureau of Alcohol, Tobacco and Firearms has reported 146 incidents of bombing, arson, or attempts against clinics and related sites in thirty states,

Table 1. Abortion Clinics Reporting Harassment,
1985 and 1988 (in percentage)

Activity	1985	1988
Picketing	80	81
Picketing with physical contact or blocking	47	46
Demonstrations resulting in arrests	—	38
Bomb threats	48	36
Vandalism	28	34
Picketing homes of staff members	16	17

Note: Dash = question not asked.

Source: Surveys of all abortion providers taken by the Alan Guttmacher Institute in Henshaw (1991, 246–252, 263).

causing more than $12 million in damages (Thomas 1994). The high level of harassment of abortion clinics is shown in Table 1.

The level of harassment appears to have increased over time. In just 1992 and 1993 the U.S. Bureau of Alcohol, Tobacco and Firearms recorded thirty-six incidents, which resulted in an estimated $3.8 million in damages (Thomas 1994). The National Abortion Federation, representing roughly half of the nation's clinics, noted that incidents of reported vandalism at its clinics more than doubled from 1991 to 1992 (Barringer 1993). From May 1992 to August 1993 the U.S. Bureau of Alcohol, Tobacco and Firearms reported that 123 family-planning clinics were bombed or burned (Baum 1993). In 1992 more than forty clinics were attacked with butyric acid (a chemical injected through key holes, under doors, or into ventilation shafts) forcing clinic closures and requiring costly repairs (Anderson and Binstein 1993, C27). One of the aims of this violence appears to be to raise the cost of operating abortion clinics to such an extent as to force their closure. In 1992 and 1993, for example, arson destroyed clinics in Missoula and Helena, Montana, and in Boise, Idaho. The clinics have either been unable to reopen or have had great difficulty in doing so because of the difficulty of finding owners willing to rent to them and obtaining insurance coverage. In 1990, in the wake of such violence, one major insurer, Traveler's Insurance Company, decided not to insure any abortion-related concerns (Baum 1993).

Another tactic aimed at shutting down abortion clinics is to conduct large, sustained protests. During the summer of 1991, for example, Operation Rescue staged forty-six days of protest in Wichita, Kansas, resulting in the arrest of approximately 2,700 people. During the summer of 1993, Operation Rescue launched a seven-city campaign with similar aims. In addition, there have been individual acts of violence against abortion providers. Dr. David Gunn was murdered in March 1993 outside an abortion clinic in Pensacola, Florida; Dr. George Tiller was shot in August 1993 in Wichita, Kansas; and Dr. John Britton and his escort, James Barrett, a retired air force lieutenant colonel, were murdered in late July 1944, also in Pensacola. Commenting on the murders of Dr. Britton and James Barrett, Don Treshman, director of the antiabortion group Rescue America, issued an ominous warning: "Up to now, the killings have been on one side, with 30 million dead babies and hundreds of dead and maimed mothers. On the other side, there are two dead doctors. Maybe the balance is going to shift" (quoted in Lewin 1994, A7).[12] In sum, as Forrest and Henshaw (1987, 13) concluded, "antiabortion harassment in the United States is widespread and frequent."

Two important facts can be gleaned from the foregoing discussion. First, at the time of the 1973 abortion decisions, large segments of the political and professional elite were either indifferent to or supported abortion reform. Second, after the decisions, many political leaders vociferously opposed abortion. Congress enacted antiabortion legislation as did some of the states. In addition, activist opposition was growing. How this opposition affected the implementation of the decisions is the focus of the next section.

The Effect of Opposition on the Implementation of Abortion Rights

On the eve of the abortion decisions, there was widespread support from critical professional elites, growing public support, successful reform in many states, and indifference from most national politicians. Is this sufficient for the implementation of constitutional rights?

Constitutional rights are not self-implementing. That is, to make a right a reality, the behavior of individuals and the policies of the institutions in which they work must change. Because abortion is a medical procedure, and because safe abortion requires trained personnel, the implementation of abortion rights depends on the medical profession to provide abortion services. When done properly, first-term and most second-term abortions can be performed on an outpatient basis, and there is less risk of death in

Table 2. Hospitals Providing Abortions, Selected Years,
1973–1992 (percentage)

Year	Private, short-term non-Catholic, general	Public
1973	24	—
1974	27	17
1975	30	—
1976	31	20
1977	31	21
1978	29	—
1979	28	—
1980	27	17
1982	26	16
1985	23	17
1988	21	15
1992	18	13

Note: Dash = unavailable.

Sources: Forrest, Sullivan, and Tietze 1978, table 5; Henshaw 1986, 253; Henshaw et al. 1982, table 7; Henshaw, Forrest, and Van Vort 1987, 68; Henshaw and Van Vort 1990, 102–108, 142; Henshaw and Van Vort 1994, 100–106, 122; Rubin 1982, 154; Sullivan, Tietze, and Dryfoos, 1977, figure 10; Weinstock et al. 1975, 32.

the procedure than there is in childbirth or in such routine operations as tonsillectomies. Thus, no medical or technical reasons stand in the way of the provision of abortion services. Following Supreme Court action, however, the medical profession moved with "extreme caution" in making abortion available (Brody 1973, 1). Coupled with the hostility of some state legislatures, barriers to legal abortion remained.

These barriers have proved to be strong. Perhaps the strongest barrier has been opposition from hospitals. In Table 2, I track the response of hospitals to the Court's decisions. The results are staggering. Despite the relative ease and safety of the abortion procedure, and the unambiguous holding of the Court, both public and private hospitals throughout America have refused to perform abortions. *The vast majority of public and private hospitals have never performed an abortion!* In 1973 and the first quarter of 1974, for example, slightly more than three-quarters of public and private non-Catholic general care short-term hospitals did not perform a single abortion (Weinstock et al. 1975, 31). As illustrated in the table, the passage of time has not improved the situation. By 1976, three years after the decision, at least 70 percent of hospitals provided no abortion services. By 1992 the situation had further deteriorated: only 18 percent of private non-Catholic general care short-term hospitals and only 13 percent of public hospitals provided abortions. As Stanley Henshaw (1986, 253, emphasis added) concluded, reviewing the data in 1986, "most hospitals have *never* performed abortions."

These figures mask the fact that even the limited availability of hospital abortions detailed here varies widely across states. In 1973, for example, only 4 percent of all abortions were performed in the eight states that make up the East South Central and West South Central census divisions (Weinstock et al. 1975, 25).[13] Two states, on the other hand, New York and California (which are home to about 20 percent of all U.S. women), accounted for 37 percent of all abortions in 1974 (Alan Guttmacher Institute 1976). In eleven states, "not a single public hospital reported performance of a single abortion for any purpose whatsoever in all of 1973" (Weinstock et al. 1975, 31). By 1976, three years after Court action, no hospitals, public or private, in Louisiana, North Dakota, and South Dakota performed abortions. The Dakotas alone had thirty public and sixty-two private hospitals. In five other states, which had a total of eighty-two public hospitals, not one performed an abortion. In thirteen additional states, less than 10 percent of each state's public hospitals reported performing any abortions (Forrest, Sullivan, and Tietze 1979, 46). Only in the states of California, Hawaii, New York, and North Carolina and in the District of Columbia did more than half the public hospitals perform any abortions during 1974–1975 (Alan Guttmacher Institute 1976, 30). By 1992, the situation was little better, with five states (California, New York, Texas, Florida, and Illinois) accounting for 49 percent of all legal abortions (Henshaw and Van Vort 1994, 102).

This refusal of hospitals to perform abortions means that women seeking them, particularly from rural areas, have to travel, often a great distance, to exercise their constitutional rights. In 1973, for example, 150,000 women traveled out of their state of residence to obtain abortions. By 1982 the numbers had dropped, but more than 100,000 women were still forced to travel to another state for abortion services. . . .

Even when women can obtain abortions within their states of residence, they may still have to travel a great distance to do so. In 1974, the year after *Roe,* the Guttmacher Institute found that between 300,000 and 400,000 women left their home communities to obtain abortions (Alan Guttmacher

Institute 1976). In 1980, across the United States, more than one-quarter (27 percent) of all women who had abortions had them outside of their home counties (Henshaw and O'Reilly 1983, 5). And in 1988, fifteen years after *Roe,* an estimated 430,000 (27 percent) women who had abortions in non-hospital settings traveled more than fifty miles from their home to reach their abortion provider. This includes over 140,000 women who traveled more than 100 miles to obtain a legal abortion (Henshaw 1991, 248).[14]

The general problem that faces women who seek to exercise their constitutional right to abortion is the paucity of abortion providers. From the legalization of abortion in 1973 to the present, at least 77 percent of all U.S. counties have been without abortion providers. And the problem is not merely rural. In 1980, seven years after Court action, there were still fifty-nine metropolitan areas in which no facilities could be identified that provided abortions (Henshaw et al. 1982, 5). The most recent data suggest that the problem is worsening. In 1992, 84 percent of all U.S. counties, home to 30 percent of all women of reproductive age, had no abortion providers. Ninety-one of the country's 320 metropolitan (28 percent) areas have no identified abortion provider, and an additional 14 (4 percent) have providers who perform fewer than fifty abortions per year. . . .

Even when abortion service is available, providers have tended to ignore the time periods set out in the Court's opinions. In 1988, fifteen years after the decisions, only 43 percent of all providers perform abortions after the first trimester. More than half (55 percent) of the hospitals that perform abortions have refused to perform second-trimester procedures, a time in pregnancy at which hospital services may be medically necessary. Only at abortion clinics have a majority of providers been willing to perform abortions after the first trimester. Indeed, in 1988 a startling 22 percent of all providers refused to perform abortions past the tenth week of pregnancy, several weeks within the first trimester, during which, according to the Court, a woman's constitutional right is virtually all-encompassing (Henshaw 1991, 251).

Finally, although abortion is "the most common surgical procedure that women undergo" (Darney et al. 1987, 161) and is reportedly the most common surgical procedure performed in the United States, an *increasing* percentage of residency programs in obstetrics and gynecology do not provide training for it. A survey taken in 1985 of all such residency programs found that 28 percent of them offered no training at all, a nearly fourfold increase since 1976. According to the results of the survey, approximately one-half of the programs made training available as an option, while only 23 percent included it routinely (Darney et al. 1987, 160). By 1992 the percentage of programs requiring abortion training had dropped nearly to half, to 12 percent (Baum 1993). In a study done in 1992 of 216 of 271 residency programs, it was found that almost half (47 percent) of graduating residents had never performed a first-trimester abortion, and only 7 percent had ever performed one in the second trimester (Cooper 1993). At least part of the reason for the increasing lack of training is harassment by antiabortion activists. "Anti-abortion groups say these numbers prove that harassment of doctors, and in turn, medical schools which train residents in abortion procedures, is an effective tactic," Cooper reported. " 'You humiliate the school. . . . We hope that in 10 years, there'll be none' that train residents how to perform abortions" (Randall Terry, founder of Operation Rescue, quoted in Cooper 1993, B3) . . . .

It is clear that hospital administrators, both public and private, refused to change their abortion policies in reaction to the Court decisions. In the years since the Court's decisions, abortion services have remained centered in metropolitan areas and in those states that reformed their abortion laws and regulations prior to the Court's decisions. In 1976 the Alan Guttmacher Institute (1976, 13) concluded that "[t]he response of hospitals to the legalization of abortion continues to be so limited . . . as to be tantamount to no response." Jaffe, Lindheim, and Lee (1981, 15) concluded that "the delivery pattern for abortion services that has emerged since 1973 is distorted beyond precedent." Reviewing the data in the mid-1980s, Henshaw, Forrest, and Blaine (1984, 122) summed up the situation this way: "There is abundant evidence that many women still find it difficult or impossible to obtain abortion services because of the distance of their home to the nearest provider, the cost, a lack of information on where to go, and limitations on the circumstances under which a provider will make abortions available." Most recently, Henshaw (1991, 253) concluded that "an American woman seeking abortion services will find it increasingly difficult to find a provider who will serve her in an accessible location and at an affordable cost."

Implementing Constitutional Rights: The Market

The foregoing discussion presents a seeming dilemma. There has been hostility to abortion from some politicians, most hospital administrators, many doctors, and parts of the public. On the whole, in response to the Court, hospitals did not change their policies to permit abortions. Yet, as demonstrated in Figure 1, the number of legal abortions performed in the United States continued to grow. How is it, for example, that congressional and state hostility seemed effectively to prevent progress in civil rights in the 1950s and early 1960s but did not prevent abortion in the 1970s? The answer to this question not only removes the dilemma but also illustrates why the Court's abortion decisions were effective in making legal abortion more easily available. The answer, in a word, is *clinics*.

The Court's decisions prohibited the states from interfering with a woman's right to choose an abortion, at least in the first trimester. They did not uphold hospitalization requirements, and later cases explicitly rejected hospitalization requirements for second-trimester abortions.[15] Room was left for abortion reformers, population control groups, women's groups, and individual physicians to set up clinics to perform abortions. The refusal of many hospitals, then, to perform abortions could be countered by the creation of clinics willing to do the job. And that's exactly what happened.

In the wake of the Court's decisions the number of abortion providers sharply increased. In the first year after the decisions, the number of providers grew by nearly 25 percent. Over the first three years the percentage increase was almost 58 percent. The number of providers reached a peak in 1982 and has declined more than 18 percent since then. These raw data, however, do not indicate who these providers were.

. . . [T]he number of abortion providers increased because of the increase in the number of clinics. To fill the void that hospitals had left, clinics opened in large numbers. Between 1973 and 1974, for example, the number of nonhospital abortion providers grew 61 percent. Overall, between 1973 and 1976 the number of nonhospital providers grew 152 percent, nearly five times the rate of growth of hospital providers. In metropolitan areas . . . the growth rate was 140 percent between 1973 and 1976, five times the rate for hospital providers; in nonmetropolitan areas it was a staggering 304 percent, also about five times the growth rate for nonmetropolitan hospitals.

The growth in the number of abortion clinics was matched by the increase in the number of abortions performed by them. By 1974, nonhospital clinics were performing approximately 51 percent of all abortions, and nearly an additional 3 percent were being performed in physicians' offices. Between 1973 and 1974, the number of abortions performed in hospitals rose 5 percent, while the number performed in clinics rose 39 percent. By 1976, clinics accounted for 62 percent of all reported abortions, despite the fact that they were only 17 percent of all providers (Forrest, Sullivan, and Tietze 1979). From 1973 to 1976, the years immediately following Court action, the number of abortions performed in hospitals increased by only 8 percent, whereas the number performed in clinics and physicians' offices increased by a whopping 113 percent (Forrest et al. 1979a).[16] The percentages continued to rise, and by 1992, 93 percent of all abortions were performed in nonhospital settings. Clinics satisfied the need that hospitals, despite the Court's actions, refused to meet.

In permitting abortions to be performed in clinics as well as hospitals, the Court's decisions granted a way around the intransigence of hospitals. The decisions allowed individuals committed to safe and legal abortion to make use of the market and create their own structures to meet the demand. They also provided a financial incentive for services to be provided. At least some clinics were formed solely as money-making ventures. As the legal activist Janice Goodman put it, "Some doctors are going to see a very substantial amount of money to be made on this" (quoted in Goodman, Schoenbrod, and Stearns 1973, 31). Nancy Stearns, who filed a pro-choice amicus brief in *Roe,* agreed: "[In the abortion cases] the people that are necessary to effect the decision are doctors, most of whom are not opposed, probably don't give a damn, and in fact have a whole lot to gain . . . because of the amount of money they can make" (quoted in Goodman et al. 1973, 29). Even the glacial growth of hospital abortion providers in the early and mid-1970s may be due, in part, to financial considerations. In a study of thirty-six general hospitals in Harris County (Houston), Texas, the need for increased income was found to be an important determinant of whether hospitals performed abortions. Hospitals with low occupancy rates, and therefore low income, the study reported, "saw changing abortion policy as a way to fill beds and raise income" (Kemp, Carp, and Brady 1978, 27).

Although the law of the land was that the choice of an abortion was not to be denied a woman in the first trimester, and regulated only to the extent necessary to preserve a woman's health in the second trimester, American hospitals, on the whole, do not honor the law. By allowing the market to meet the need, however, the Court's decisions resulted in at least a continuation of some availability of safe and legal abortion. Although no one can be sure what might have happened if clinics had not been allowed, if the sole burden for implementing the decisions had been on hospitals, hospital practice suggests that resistance would have been strong. After all, the Court did find abortion constitutionally protected, and most hospitals simply refused to accept that decision.

The implementation of constitutional rights, then, may depend a great deal on the beliefs of those necessary to implement them. The data suggest that without clinics the Court's decisions, constitutional rights notwithstanding, would have been frustrated.

Court Decisions and Political Action

It is generally believed that winning a major Supreme Court case is an invaluable political resource. The victorious side can use the decision to dramatize the issue, encourage political mobilization, and ignite a political movement. In an older view, however, this connection is dubious. Writing at the beginning of the twentieth century, Thayer (1901) suggested that reliance on litigation weakens political organizing. Because there have been more than twenty years of litigation in regard to abortion, the issue provides a good test of these competing views.

The evidence suggests that *Roe* and *Doe* may have seriously weakened the political effectiveness of the winners—pro-choice forces—and inspired the losers. After the 1973 decisions, many pro-choice activists simply assumed they had won and stopped their activity. According to J. Hugh Anwyl, then the executive director of Planned Parenthood of Los Angeles, pro-choice activists went "on a long siesta" after the abortion decisions (quoted in Johnston 1977, 1). Alfred F. Moran, an executive vice president at Planned Parenthood of New York, put it this way: "Most of us really believed that was the end of the controversy. The Supreme Court had spoken, and while some disagreement would remain, the issue had been tried, tested and laid to rest" (Brozan 1983, A17). These views were joined by a NARAL activist, Janet Beals: "Everyone assumed that when the Supreme Court made its decision in 1973 that we'd got what we wanted and the battle was over. The movement afterwards lost steam" (quoted in Phillips 1980, 3). By 1977 a survey of pro-choice and antiabortion activity in thirteen states nationwide revealed that abortion rights advocates had failed to match the activity of their opponents (Johnston 1977).[17] The political organization and momentum that had changed laws nationwide dissipated in reaction to Court victory. This may help explain why abortion services remain so unevenly available.

Reliance on Court action seems to have harmed the pro-choice movement in a second way. The most restrictive version of the Hyde Amendment, banning federal funding of abortions even where abortion is necessary to save the life of the woman, was passed with the help of a parliamentary maneuver by pro-choice legislators. Their strategy, as reported the following day on the front pages of the *New York Times* and the *Washington Post,* was to pass such a conservative bill that the Court would have no choice but to overturn it (Russell 1977; Tolchin 1977). This reliance on the Court was totally unfounded. With hindsight, Karen Mulhauser, a former director of NARAL, suggested that "had we made more gains through the legislative and referendum processes, and taken a little longer at it, the public would have moved with us" (quoted in Williams 1979, 12). By winning a Court case "without the organization needed to cope with a powerful opposition" (Rubin 1982, 169), pro-choice forces vastly overestimated the power and influence of the Court.

By the time of *Webster* (1989), however, pro-choice forces seemed to have learned from their mistakes, while right-to-life activists miscalculated. In early August 1989, just after *Webster,* a spokesperson for the National Right to Life Committee proclaimed: "[F]or the first time since 1973, we are clearly in a position of strength" (Shribman 1989, A8). Pro-choice forces, however, went on the offensive by generating a massive political response. Commenting on *Webster,* Nancy Broff, NARAL's legislative and political director, noted, "It finally gave us the smoking gun we needed to mobilize people" (quoted in Kornhauser 1989, 11). Membership and financial support grew rapidly. "In the year after *Webster,* membership in the National Abortion Rights Action League jumped from 150,000 to 400,000; in the National Organization for Women [NOW], from 170,000 to 250,000" (Craig and O'Brien 1993, 296). Furthermore, NARAL "nearly tripled" its income in 1989, and NOW "nearly doubled" its income, as did the Planned Parenthood Federation of America (Shribman 1989, A8). In May 1989 alone, NARAL raised $1 million (Kornhauser 1989).

This newfound energy was turned toward political action. In gubernatorial elections in Virginia and New Jersey in the fall of 1989, pro-choice forces played an important role in electing the pro-choice candidates L. Douglas Wilder and James J. Florio over antiabortion opponents. Antiabortion legislation was defeated in Florida, where Gov. Bob Martinez, an opponent of abortion, called a special session of the legislature to enact it. Congress passed legislation that allowed the District of Columbia to use its own tax revenues to pay for abortions and that essentially repealed the so-called gag rule, but President Bush vetoed both bills, and the House of Representatives failed to override the vetoes. As Paige Cunningham, of the antiabortion group Americans United for Life, put it: "The pro-life movement has been organized and active for twenty years, and some of us are tired. The pro-choice movement is fresh so they're operating with a much greater energy reserve. They've really rallied in light of *Webster*" (quoted in Berke 1989, 1).

This new understanding was also seen in *Casey.* Although pro-choice forces had seen antiabortion restrictions upheld in *Webster* and *Rust,* and the sure antiabortion vote of Justice Clarence Thomas had replaced the pro-choice vote of Justice Thurgood Marshall on the Supreme Court in the interim, pro-choice forces appealed the lower-court decision to the Supreme Court. As the *New York Times* reported, this was "a calculated move to intensify the political debate on abortion before the 1992 election" (Berke 1989, 1). Further increasing the stakes, they asked the Court either to reaffirm women's fundamental right to abortion or to overturn *Roe.* Berke (1991, B8) declared that "[t]he action marked an adjustment in strategy by the abortion rights groups, who seem now to be looking to the Court as a political foil rather than a source of redress."

All this suggests that Thayer may have the stronger case. That is, Court decisions do seem to have a mobilizing potential, but for the losers![18] Both winners and losers appear to assume that Court decisions announcing or upholding constitutional rights will be implemented, but they behave in different ways. Winners celebrate and relax, whereas losers redouble their efforts. Note, too, that in the wake of *Webster,* public opinion moved in a pro-choice direction, counter to the tenor of the opinion. Court decisions do matter, but in complicated ways.

Conclusion

"It does no good to have the [abortion] procedure be legal if women can't get it," stated Gwenyth Mapes, the executive director of the Missoula (Montana) Blue Mountain Clinic destroyed by arson in March 1993 (quoted in Baum 1993, A1).

Courts do not exist in a vacuum. Supreme Court decisions, even those finding constitutional rights, are not implemented automatically or in any straightforward or simple way. They are merely one part of the broader political picture. At best, they can contribute to the process of change. In and of themselves, they accomplish little.

The implementation of the Court's abortion decisions, partial though it has been, owes its success to the fact that the decisions have been made in a time when the role of women in American life is changing dramatically. Out of the social turmoil of the 1960s grew a women's movement that continues to press politically, socially, and culturally for ending restrictions on women's opportunities. Access to safe and legal abortion is part of this movement. In 1973 the Supreme Court lent its support by finding a constitutional right to abortion. And in the years since, it has maintained its support for that core constitutional right. Yet, I have argued that far more important in making safe and legal abortion available are the beliefs of politicians, relevant professionals, and the public. When these groups are supportive of abortion choice, that choice is available. Where they have opposed abortion, they have fought against the Court's decisions, successfully minimizing access to abortion. Lack of support from hospital administrators and some politicians and intense opposition from a small group of politicians and activists have limited the availability of abortion services. On the whole, in states that were supportive of abortion choice before Court action, access remains good. In the states that had the most restrictive abortion laws before *Roe,* abortion services are available but remain difficult to obtain. As Gwenyth Mapes put it, "It does no good to have the [abortion] procedure be legal if women can't get it."

This analysis suggests that in general, constitutional rights have a greater likelihood of being implemented when they reflect the preexisting beliefs of politicians, relevant professionals, and the public. When at least some of these groups are opposed, locally or nationally, implementation is less likely. The assumption that the implementation of Court decisions and constitutional rights is unproblematic both reifies and removes courts from the political, social, cultural, and economic systems in which they operate. Courts are political institutions, and their role must be understood accordingly. Examining their decisions without making the political world central to that examination may make for fine reading in constitutional-law textbooks, but it tells the reader very little about the lives people lead.

NOTES

1. Alaska, Hawaii, New York, and Washington had previously liberalized their laws. The constitutional requirements set forth in *Roe* and *Doe* were basically, although not completely, met by these state laws.

2. For a fuller examination, see Rosenberg 1991.

3. In 1971, before *Roe* and *Doe*, the Court heard an abortion case (*United States v. Vuitch*) from Washington, D.C. The decision, however, did not settle the constitutional issues involved in the abortion controversy.

4. Estimates of the number of legal abortions performed each year prior to *Roe* vary enormously, ranging from 50,000 to nearly 2 million. See Rosenberg 1991, 353–355.

5. The following discussion, except where noted, is based on Lader 1973.

6. After the 1973 decisions, NARAL kept its acronym but changed its name to the National Abortion Rights Action League.

7. Nixon's "own personal views" were that "unrestricted abortion policies, or abortion on demand" could not be squared with his "personal belief in the sanctity of human life" (quoted in Lader 1973, 176–177).

8. Franklin and Kosaki (1989, 762) argue that in the wake of *Roe* opinions hardened. That is, those who were pro-choice before the decision became even more so after; the same held true for those opposed to abortion. Court action did not change opinions; abortion opponents did not become abortion supporters (and vice versa). See Epstein and Kobylka 1992, 203.

9. Ford did veto the 1977 appropriations bill containing the Hyde Amendment. He stated that he did so for budgetary reasons (the bill was $4 billion over his budget request) and reasserted his support for "restrictions on the use of federal funds for abortion" (quoted in Craig and O'Brien 1993, 161).

10. The Congressional Research Service reports that Congress enacted thirty restrictive abortion statutes during 1973–1982 (Davidson 1983).

11. The growth in violent attacks on abortion clinics, and illegal, harassing demonstrations in front of them, may demonstrate a growing awareness of this point by the foes of abortion.

12. Treshman is not the only antiabortion activist to express such views. Goodstein (1994, A1) writes that "there is a sizable faction among the antiabortion movement's activists . . . who have applauded Hill [the convicted killer of Dr. Britton and Mr. Barrett] as a righteous defender of babies."

13. The East South Central states are Kentucky, Tennessee, Alabama, and Mississippi. The West South Central states are Arkansas, Louisiana, Oklahoma, and Texas. Together, these eight states contained 16 percent of the U.S. population in 1973.

14. It is possible, of course, that some women had personal reasons for not obtaining an abortion in their home town. Still, that seems an unlikely explanation as to why 100,000 women each year would leave their home states to obtain abortions.

15. *Akron v. Akron Center for Reproductive Health* (1983); *Planned Parenthood v. Ashcroft* (1983). The vast majority of abortions in the United States are performed in the first trimester. As early as 1976, the figure was 90 percent. See Forrest et al. 1979, 32.

16. The percentage for clinics is not artificially high because there were only a small number of clinic abortions in the years preceding Court action. In 1973, clinics performed more than 330,000 abortions, or about 45 percent of all abortions (see Alan Guttmacher Institute 1976, 27).

17. Others in agreement with this analysis include Tatalovich and Daynes (1981, 101, 164), participants in a symposium at the Brookings Institution (in Steiner 1983), and Jackson and Vinovskis (1983, 73), who found that after the decisions "state-level pro-choice grounds disbanded, victory seemingly achieved."

18. This also appears to have been the case in 1954 with the Court's school desegregation decision, *Brown v. Board of Education.* After that decision, the Ku Klux Klan was reinvigorated and the White Citizen's Councils were formed, with the aim of preserving racial segregation through violence and intimidation.

REFERENCES

"Abortions Legal for Year, Performed for Thousands." 1973. *New York Times,* December 31, sec. A.

Alan Guttmacher Institute. 1976. *Abortion 1974–1975: Need and Services in the United States, Each State and Metropolitan Area.* New York: Planned Parenthood Federation of America.

Anderson, Jack, and Michael Binstein. 1993. "Violent Shift in Abortion Battle." *Washington Post,* March 18, sec. C.

Barringer, Felicity. 1993. "Abortion Clinics Said to Be in Peril." *New York Times,* March 6, sec. A.

Baum, Dan. 1993. "Violence Is Driving Away Rural Abortion Clinics." *Chicago Tribune,* August 21, sec. A.

Berke, Richard L. 1989. "The Abortion Rights Movement Has Its Day." *New York Times,* October 15, sec. 4.

———. 1991. "Groups Backing Abortion Rights Ask Court to Act." *New York Times,* November 8, sec. A.

Blake, Judith. 1971. "Abortion and Public Opinion: The 1960–1970 Decade." *Science,* February 12.

———. 1977a. "The Abortion Decisions: Judicial Review and Public Opinion." In *Abortion: New Directions for Policy Studies,* edited by Edward Manier, William Liu, and David Solomon. Notre Dame, Ind.: University of Notre Dame Press.

———. 1977b. "The Supreme Court's Abortion Decisions and Public Opinion in the United States." *Population and Development Review* 3:45–62.

Brody, Jane E. 1973. "States and Doctors Wary on Eased Abortion Ruling." *New York Times,* February 16, sec. A.

Brozan, Nadine. 1983. "Abortion Ruling: 10 Years of Bitter Conflict." *New York Times,* January 15, sec. A.

Cooper, Helene. 1993. "Medical Schools, Students Shun Abortion Study." *Wall Street Journal,* Midwest edition, March 12, sec. B.

Craig, Barbara Hinkson, and David M. O'Brien. 1993. *Abortion and American Politics.* Chatham, N.J.: Chatham House.

Currivan, Gene. 1970. "Poll Finds Shift to Left among College Freshmen." *New York Times,* December 20, sec. 1.

Daley, Daniel, and Rachel Benson Gold. 1994. "Public Funding for Contraceptive, Sterilization, and Abortion Services, Fiscal Year 1992." *Family Planning Perspectives* 25:244–251.

Darney, Philip D., Uta Landy, Sara MacPherson, and Richard L. Sweet. 1987. "Abortion Training in U.S. Obstetrics and Gynecology Residency Programs." *Family Planning Perspectives* 19:158–162.

Davidson, Roger H. 1983. "Procedures and Politics in Congress." In *The Abortion Dispute and the American System,* edited by Gilbert Y. Steiner. Washington, D.C.: Brookings Institution.

Ebaugh, Helen Rose Fuchs, and C. Allen Haney. 1980. "Shifts in Abortion Attitudes: 1972–1978." *Journal of Marriage and the Family* 42:491–499.

Epstein, Lee, and Joseph F. Kobylka. 1992. *The Supreme Court and Legal Change.* Chapel Hill: University of North Carolina Press.

Fiske, Edward B. 1967. "Clergymen Offer Abortion Advice." *New York Times,* May 22, sec. A.

Forrest, Jacqueline Darroch, and Stanley K. Henshaw. 1987. "The Harassment of U.S. Abortion Providers." *Family Planning Perspectives* 19:9–13.

Forrest, Jacqueline Darroch, Ellen Sullivan, and Christopher Tietze. 1978. "Abortion in the United States, 1976–1977." *Family Planning Perspectives* 10:271–279.

———. 1979. *Abortion 1976–1977: Need and Services in the United States, Each State and Metropolitan Area.* New York: Alan Guttmacher Institute.

Franklin, Charles H., and Liane C. Kosaki. 1989. "Republican Schoolmaster: The U.S. Supreme Court, Public Opinion, and Abortion." *American Political Science Review* 83:751–771.

Goodman, Janice, Rhonda Copelon Schoenbrod, and Nancy Stearns. 1973. "Doe and Roe." *Women's Rights Law Reporter* 1:20–38.

Goodstein, Laurie. 1994. "Life and Death Choices: Antiabortion Faction Tries to Justify Homicide." *Washington Post,* August 13, sec. A.

Henshaw, Stanley K. 1986. "Induced Abortion: A Worldwide Perspective." *Family Planning Perspective* 18:250–254.

———. 1991. "The Accessibility of Abortion Services in the United States." *Family Planning Perspectives* 23:246–252, 263.

Henshaw, Stanley K., and Kevin O'Reilly. 1983. "Characteristics of Abortion Patients in the United States, 1979 and 1980." *Family Planning Perspectives* 15:5.

Henshaw, Stanley K., and Jennifer Van Vort. 1990. "Abortion Services in the United States, 1987 and 1988." *Family Planning Perspectives* 22:102–108, 142.

———. 1994. "Abortion Services in the United States, 1991 and 1992." *Family Planning Perspectives* 26:100–106, 122.

Henshaw, Stanley K., Jacqueline Darroch Forrest, and Ellen Blaine. 1984. "Abortion Services in the United States, 1981 and 1982." *Family Planning Perspectives* 16:119–127.

Henshaw, Stanley K., Jacqueline Darroch Forrest, and Jennifer Van Vort. 1987. "Abortion Services in the United States, 1984 and 1985." *Family Planning Perspectives* 19:63–70.

Henshaw, Stanley K., Jacqueline Darroch Forrest, Ellen Sullivan, and Christopher Tietze. 1982. "Abortion Services in the United States, 1979 and 1980." *Family Planning Perspectives* 14:5–15.

Henshaw, Stanley K., Lisa M. Koonin, and Jack C. Smith. 1991. "Characteristics of U.S. Women Having Abortions, 1987." *Family Planning Perspectives* 23:75–81.

Hole, Judith, and Ellen Levine. 1971. *Rebirth of Feminism.* New York: Quadrangle.

Jackson, John E., and Maris A. Vinovskis. 1983. "Public Opinion, Elections, and the 'Single-Issue' Issue." In *The Abortion Dispute and the American System,* edited by Gilbert Y. Steiner. Washington, D.C.: Brookings Institution.

Jaffe, Frederick S., Barbara L. Lindheim, and Phillip R. Lee. 1981. *Abortion Politics.* New York: McGraw-Hill.

Johnston, Laurie. 1977. "Abortion Foes Gain Support as They Intensify Campaign." *New York Times,* October 23, sec. 1.

Kemp, Kathleen A., Robert A. Carp, and David W. Brady. 1978. "The Supreme Court and Social Change: The Case of Abortion." *Western Political Quarterly* 31:19–31.

King, Wayne. 1973. "Despite Court Ruling, Problems Persist in Gaining Abortions." *New York Times,* May 20, sec. 1.

Kornhauser, Anne. 1989. "Abortion Case Has Been Boon to Both Sides." *Legal Times,* July 3.

Lader, Lawrence. 1973. *Abortion II: Making the Revolution.* Boston: Beacon Press.

Lewin, Tamar. 1994. "A Cause Worth Killing For? Debate Splits Abortion Foes." *New York Times,* July 30, sec. A.

Newport, Frank, and Leslie McAneny. 1992. "Whose Court Is It Anyhow? O'Connor, Kennedy, Souter Position Reflects Abortion Views of Most Americans." *Gallup Poll Monthly* 322 (July): 51–53.

Noonan, John T., Jr. 1973. "Raw Judicial Power." *National Review,* March 2.

Phillips, Richard. 1980. "The Shooting War over 'Choice' or 'Life' Is Beginning Again." *Chicago Tribune,* April 20, sec. 12.

"Rhode Island Abortion Law Is Declared Unconstitutional." 1973. *New York Times,* May 17, sec. A.

Rosen, R. A. Hudson, H. W. Werley, Jr., J. W. Ager, and F. P. Shea. 1974. "Health Professionals' Attitudes toward Abortion." *Public Opinion Quarterly* 38:159–173.

Rosenberg, Gerald N. 1991. *The Hollow Hope: Can Courts Bring About Social Change?* Chicago: University of Chicago Press.

Rosenthal, Jack. 1971. "Survey Finds 50% Back Liberalization of Abortion Policy." *New York Times,* October 28, sec. A.

Rosoff, Jeannie I. 1975. "Is Support for Abortion Political Suicide?" *Family Planning Perspectives* 7:13–22.

Rubin, Eva R. 1982. *Abortion, Politics, and the Courts.* Westport, Conn.: Greenwood Press.

Russell, Mary. 1977. "House Bars Use of U.S. Funds in Abortion Cases." *Washington Post,* June 18, sec. A.

Shribman, David. 1989. "Abortion-Issue Foes, Preaching to the Converted in No Uncertain Terms, Step Up Funding Pleas." *Wall Street Journal,* December 26, sec. A.

Steiner, Gilbert Y., ed. 1983. *The Abortion Dispute and the American System.* Washington, D.C.: Brookings Institution.

Sullivan, Ellen, Christopher Tietze, and Joy G. Dryfoos. 1977. "Legal Abortion in the United States, 1975–1976." *Family Planning Perspectives* 9:116.

Tatalovich, Raymond, and Byron W. Daynes. 1981. *The Politics of Abortion.* New York: Praeger.

Thayer, James Bradley. 1901. *John Marshall.* Boston: Houghton, Mifflin.

Thomas, Pierre. 1994. "U.S. Marshals Dispatched to Guard Abortion Clinics." *Washington Post,* August 2, sec. A.

Tolchin, Martin. 1977. "House Bars Medicaid Abortions and Funds for Enforcing Quotas." *New York Times,* June 18, sec. A.

Toner, Robin. 1993. "Clinton Orders Reversal of Abortion Restrictions Left by Reagan and Bush." *New York Times,* January 23, sec. A.

United States. Congress. Senate. 1970a. *Congressional Record.* Daily ed. 91st Cong., 2d sess. April 23, S3746.

————. 1970b. *Congressional Record.* Daily ed. 91st Cong., 2d sess. February 24, S3501.

————. 1974. Committee on the Judiciary. *Hearings before the Subcommittee on Constitutional Amendments.* Vol. 2. 93d Cong., 2d sess.

————. 1976. Committee on the Judiciary. *Hearings before the Subcommittee on Constitutional Amendments.* Vol. 4. 94d Cong., 1st sess.

Weinstock, Edward, Christopher Tietze, Frederick S. Jaffe, and Joy G. Dryfoos. 1975. "Legal Abortions in the United States since the 1973 Supreme Court Decisions." *Family Planning Perspectives* 7:23–31.

Williams, Roger M. 1979. "The Power of Fetal Politics." *Saturday Review,* June 9.

"A Woman's Right." 1973. *Evening Star* (Washington, D.C.), January 27, sec. A.

5-3

Privacy, Please

THINKING ABOUT A TROUBLESOME CONCEPT

Richard A. Epstein

The right to privacy has been a political concern since before George Or-
well's time. As modern computer and telecommunications technology
have enhanced the ability of the government and private firms to moni-
tor our behavior and choices, privacy has increasingly become an urgent
matter of public policy. Advocates of privacy rights are demanding the
government's immediate intervention in constructing walls or zones of
privacy. Medical records and genetic data, mouse clicks on the Internet,
and bookstore purchases are just a few of the kinds of information for
which politicians and judges have begun deliberating privacy protec-
tions. In the following essay Richard Epstein presents the other side of
the issue, arguing that those who would be denied information in pro-
posed extensions of privacy rights—whether they be members of a com-
munity or an insurance company—frequently have legitimate claims to
this information.

WORRIED ABOUT privacy? You have good reason. But at the same time, you
may find it difficult to decide whether a strong privacy right is friend or foe.
Your privacy is fine, even sacrosanct. But the privacy of the other fellow
could easily cut you off from information you need for self-protection. The
tension between our dual role as information-hoarder and information-
seeker is inescapable. Just this past year, Intel was criticized for trying to
market a new chip with a serial number that critics claimed would allow
government agencies to follow a user's every online move. Elsewhere, the
federal government has been fighting a losing battle to get a backdoor key
to every confidential transmission of sensitive data over the telephone and
the Internet. How should we apply the traditional construct of privacy
rights to the lengthening list of challenges to privacy in the cyber-age?

Originally published in *National Review,* September 27, 1999, pp. 46–49. © 1999 by National Review,
Inc., 215 Lexington Avenue, New York, NY 10016. Reprinted by permission.

The privacy principle is invoked in so many different contexts that it is hard for us to know which claims to accept and which to reject. If you think abortion should be legal, it might be because you believe in a woman's constitutional right to privacy. If you want to make sure your employer or your insurer never sees your medical records, invoke privacy. If you want to keep unwanted solicitors and callers from your doorstep, privacy is the key principle yet again.

A neat resolution of the privacy issue will remain elusive. It is possible, however, to chart a rough path through the maze—but only by resisting the temptation to wallow in the novelty of recent manifestations of the privacy debate. What we must do is return to the fundamental principles that determine the rights and duties of individuals to each other and to the state.

Let us declare, as axiomatic, the libertarian presumption that all individuals should be free to do as they like. One crucial defense of that proposition was stated by John Stuart Mill: When we allow freedom of action, at least one individual will benefit, and no other person will be harmed. A freely chosen action thus results in a social gain that all should accept and none should oppose.

This presumption, however, is far from absolute. When the action of one person involves the use of force or fraud against another, the balance of gains and losses veers sharply in the opposite direction. In this context, we can find a loser to match up with the winner, and can be confident that the magnitude of the losses (as from a killing or wounding) dwarfs the potential gains. State intervention should therefore be invoked to ensure that the liberties we cherish are not undone. Individuals have a right to be protected in their persons and property against the aggression and machinations of others.

We should embrace, presumptively, the opposite attitude toward voluntary exchange. When two or more parties consent to a transaction, there is good reason to believe that all will benefit. Freedom of contract thus expands both liberty and property. To be sure, this presumption, too, can be overridden, as when two or more individuals plot to rig markets. The systematically negative effects of these arrangements lead us to rename them conspiracies and combinations—transactions to block, not to foster.

These strictures, however, do not cover the entire legal landscape. When substantial social gains can be achieved only through the cooperation of many individuals, one person can sometimes thwart the entire project by holding out for the lion's share of the gains. The use of the eminent-domain power brings that holdout in line, not by punishing him, but by forcing him to take just compensation for the property surrendered. When land is taken for a fort or a post office, the compensation will usually come in cash. But when a limitation restricts only one's freedom of action or property use, the compensation may come in the form of a like restriction on the freedom of other individuals. We do not give cash compensation to individuals who are thinking of rigging markets. We offer them, instead, the parallel protection against the market machinations of others.

The following basic principles will help us to sort out the various claims of privacy.

Cases Past and Present

The earliest judicial claim for invasion of privacy arose in 1902, when Franklin Mills Flour placed Mrs. Abigail Roberson's picture on its handbills over the name of the company, and under the words "Flour of the Family." So distraught was Mrs. Roberson that she rose from her sickbed, to sue for damages. She believed the advertisement constituted defamation. Also, the flour mill appropriated her picture for its use, but in ways that did not obviously fall within the usual prohibition against force and fraud.

The New York court sent her back to bed empty-handed. It feared that a finding of invasion of privacy would encourage individuals to sue whenever their name or likeness appeared in a news story, especially one containing comments of a critical nature. This would have been harmful to society, by deterring the publication of truthful information that helps individuals make judgments about whom to elect or throw out of office, or whom to imitate or disdain.

Although Mrs. Roberson's broader claim for privacy fell flat, her narrower commercial claim gave rise to a thriving industry. In the aftermath of her defeat, the New York state legislature promptly created a new property right, authorizing people to sue for damages and injunctions when their name or likeness has been used for "trade or advertising purposes." Other states soon fell into line.

Ironically, Mrs. Roberson's quest for solitude has led to a century-long procession of entertainers and athletes basking in highly lucrative publicity.

The right of privacy was transformed into a right of publicity, with name or likeness as just another form of intangible property to be sold to the highest bidder.

Today, this publicity right is taken for granted; only its limits are contested. Tiger Woods, for example, is suing painter Rick Rush for painting him. Rush isn't using the work of art in an advertisement—a clear no-no—but he's arguably using it for the purposes of trade, since he hopes to sell it without compensating Tiger. But Tiger doesn't collect tribute from a sportswriter who publishes an unauthorized account, so why here?

That's the troublesome "publicity" side of privacy law. But the other side of privacy, symbolized by the reclusive Mrs. Roberson, concerns what Justice Brandeis once termed "the right to be left alone." Privacy of this sort has long been protected by that old standby, "Do Not Trespass." The trespass laws keep folks from snooping around your backyard. An old tort protecting the exclusive possession of land has thus been happily refitted to protect personal privacy.

But the privacy interest runs deeper. To use Blackstone's example, what if a man hangs from the eaves of his house to overhear what goes on in yours? The libertarian can take comfort in this generalized principle for public regulation: Everyone is better off if all eavesdropping ceases. This principle covers not only Blackstone's ancient eavesdropper, but today's government agent or private investigator who beams a parabolic microphone into your window. The Warren Court did at least a few good things, and one of them was to hold that police uses of these distant listening devices are subject to the same constitutional restrictions as ordinary bedroom searches.

Lately, however, this principle has been eroded, even in trespass cases. In one case, a *New York Post* photographer sneaked onto the grounds of a psychiatric hospital to take a picture of Hedda Nussbaum, only to catch the plaintiff (whom I shall not name) in her party. Her doctors pleaded to no avail with the *Post* not to publish the picture, lest people outside her immediate family discover her whereabouts. But the New York court held that the First Amendment's news-gathering privilege protected its publication. But why? Freedom takes place within the limits of property; the *Post* could not publish confidential records listing the plaintiff as a hospital patient, even if they were true. It was up to the plaintiff to decide who should know of her confinement, and who not. In addition, the hospital could have enjoined the photographer's trespass. Why, then, can it not suppress the fruits of this illegal action, or at least have its patients recover damages for it?

If the privacy right is good against the government, it should be equally good against the press. Surely, the press has no greater reason to snoop on private property than the police.

This case shows that the privacy right lines up tolerably well with individual liberty and private property. The debate over FBI surveillance also illustrates this congruence. For a long time now, the FBI has taken the position that it should have a back door into every confidential telephone communication to conduct surveillance against potential criminal activity. The end is surely laudable, but the means are not. The privacy accorded confidential communications by strong encryption helps protect ordinary medical and financial records from the prying eyes of the state and other interlopers. If we weaken the encryption, criminals may be the first ones to take advantage of the weaker security. The appropriate rule is not a blanket weakening of privacy protections, but the continued demand that the police meet the time-honored constitutional standard of probable cause. It is not surprising that the government has backed away from its position, which was a clear overreach.

Complexity after Complexity

Thus far I have shown how traditional claims of privacy buttress a system of individual liberty and private property. But it is a sign of the complexity of privacy discourse that the same claims can be made in a completely antithetical cause. Some years ago, I worked briefly on a case in which a major credit-card company was sued for using its billing records to help target direct-mail campaigns by keying the solicitations to products similar to those the customers had previously bought. Some subscribers and privacy advocates opposed the program because it used confidential information for collateral purposes. But the objections were, in my view, wholly misplaced. Credit-card companies do not give out a list of names to potential advertisers, who could use them again and again. What of the response of customers? Generally, it is one of relief: Lots of junk mail never materializes, and the stuff that does arrive actually holds some interest. It is easy enough to allow any cardholder to withdraw from the program on demand, but few take the option. Here the claim of invasion of privacy is effectively overridden by a showing of individual consent.

And that gets us back to the much-criticized Intel chip, which was designed to give vendors and their consumers greater security for e-commerce. The embedded serial number helps establish that the buyer is who he says he is. Yet suppose some customers recoil at the thought of being so identified. Intel has reprogrammed its chip so that in its default mode the identification feature is in the off position. Customers who want the privacy may now have to pay the price in reduced convenience for online business. They may find fewer merchants to do business with, and those who remain may assess fees to cover their higher costs. Well and good. There's no abstract way to decide whether the loss of privacy is outweighed by the additional commercial security. Nor is there any need for privacy or commercial groups to make that decision for us on a one-size-fits-all basis. The chip feature is available, and the pressures of supply and demand should tell who will use it and when. The situation thus differs markedly from the government efforts for backdoor keys into private conversation, because, in this case, consent erects an important barrier against Big Brother.

The relationship of freedom to privacy gets even more complicated in other contexts. Consider the sensitive question of confidential medical records. People can instruct their hospitals and physicians to keep this information out of the hands of strangers. In large-scale clinical trials, it is customary to remove the names and other identifying marks of individuals whose cases are included. This protection of the privacy interest does little to impair the effectiveness of the studies.

But it hardly follows from this one example that medical information should always be kept confidential. The privacy interest seems strong enough when strangers just ask for your medical records. Yet the situation changes significantly when individuals wish to keep private information that is of value to their trading partners. Suppose, for example, that I want to obtain a job that requires good judgment, steady character, and the ability to work long hours. Can I keep from my prospective employer a medical history that indicates serious medical illness or a juvenile criminal record? The modern response to this question, all too often, is yes. Youthful criminal records are often expunged so that public authorities do not know what offenses individuals committed some years ago. Moreover, both federal and state disability-discrimination laws forbid employers to use information about health or criminal activities in making their decisions to hire and fire.

Where to Draw the Line?

In this context, we see privacy run amok. Rather than functioning as a bulwark of freedom, it becomes, not to put too fine a word on it, a handmaiden to private fraud and government domination. This concealment does not just protect privacy and tranquillity; it forces other people to part with hard cash against their will.

Take the simplest case: insurance. The traditional common-law view was that the potential insured was under a duty to volunteer all information material to the insurer's decision to take or to price the risk. Information was power, and the law helped to equalize the advantage possessed by the insured. Modern privacy advocates want to do a fast 180-degree turn on this question, by forbidding insurers to ask about medical conditions material to the risk, such as AIDS, a genetic predisposition to breast cancer, and preexisting medical conditions. The deliberate suppression of information leads to a large, implicit transfer of wealth: An expected $10,000 loss is covered for $500, forcing the employer or other insured parties to pay a huge surcharge. Some will simply decide that it is better to do without insurance altogether than to pay the subsidy. Others will seek to tailor the coverage in ways that minimize their outsized exposure. These countermeasures have at best fitful success, and often invite a tough regulatory response that tightens the noose further. It should come as no surprise that the number of people without health insurance has risen over the past generation.

When privacy teams up with genetic or employment anti-discrimination laws, it is invoked to defeat freedom of contract, not to support it. Far from extending the perimeter of one's person outward in ways consistent with the like liberty of others, it allows one group of individuals to deceive another, and through that deception to take the wealth of others. The tacit principle at work here is that undeniable cases of individual need justify theft from other individuals.

The better approach, by far, is to put aside the mantra of privacy altogether and ask one simple question: To what extent should healthy people be forced to subsidize the health care of their less-fortunate fellow citizens? Once that question is determined in an open and public debate, then we can use a transparent, on-budget tax expenditure to pick up all or some of the cost.

The Big Question: Abortion

Last, but not least, one comes to the question of abortion. Here the claim is that a woman's right to privacy (understood as the right to control her own body) drives us toward the constitutional protection of the right to terminate a pregnancy. The constant invocation of privacy in this context is odd, to say the least: The issue is not whether other individuals will learn about your behavior. Rather, the question goes to the reach of a woman's autonomy. Most pregnancies are the result of voluntary sexual relations, so the question boils down to whether the woman's autonomy right over her own body allows her to terminate a pregnancy.

The obvious limitation on this exercise of liberty is the classical Millian harm principle: You cannot exercise your liberty in ways that harm—in this case destroy—another person. The invocation of the privacy interest does nothing to address the question of whether abortion falls within the general rule of liberty or squarely within, as seems more likely, the harm exception, if the embryo after conception counts as a person. At this point, advocates of abortion could insist that termination of pregnancy is justified because of the undue strain it puts on the mother. In the world's worst analogy, Judith Jarvis Thomson claimed some years ago that carrying a child to term is a Kafkaesque experience—like waking up one morning to find yourself hooked up without consent to a distinguished violinist who uses you for a life-support system. The commonplace and the grotesque thus become one.

At this point, the argument raises serious moral and enforcement issues. How they should be resolved may be an open question. But even so, this short discussion should achieve at least one goal: The case for abortion is not clinched by the invocation of some "fundamental right" to privacy. It rests on a complex evaluation of competing issues of moral judgment and practical enforcement. My own sense is that the defenders of abortion cannot quite wriggle free of the Millian harm exception to the basic principle of individual freedom.

For the time being, we are in overdrive on the question of privacy. The term can be invoked by those who believe, as I do, in the classical virtues of limited government, and with equal earnestness by the champions of the modern welfare state—who first undermine the traditional use of state power to prevent harm and then, in the next breath, see no limits on the power of the state to take from A and to give to B in the name of redistribution. The classical liberal and the modern welfarist theories of government are utterly antithetical to each other in aspiration and effect. The equivocation over privacy takes us first to one side of the line, and then quickly to the other. Both in theory and in practice, however, we have to choose our definition of privacy as we choose our theory of government. I'll cast one vote for the classical liberal conception.

6

Congress

One of the staples of American politics is that most Americans like their own member of Congress but dislike Congress in general. The positive evaluations enjoyed by individual members of Congress are reflected in their very high re-election rates—higher than 90 percent, for most elections in recent decades. Incumbents are generally well attuned to the political inclinations of their constituents, as liberal districts and states return liberals to office and conservative districts and states return conservatives. The personal qualities of the incumbents are admired by their constituents as well. Constituents usually report that their own elected representatives and senators are hard-working, committed to their interests, and honest.

Evaluations of Congress as a whole are different. When Americans are asked whether they approve of the way the president, the Supreme Court, and Congress are doing their jobs, Congress nearly always receives the least approval of the three. Several factors contribute to Congress's dismal appraisal: sporadic scandals involving members of Congress, the partisanship of policy making, the compromising and slowness inherent in the legislative process, inaction on problems of importance, and so on. Members of Congress often reinforce the popular view in their campaigns, by running against Congress. "Reelect me and I'll return to fight the good fight against the forces of evil in Washington," the typical congressional candidate says. It is hard for an institution to look good when its own membership does not defend it.

The essays in this chapter encourage us to develop a more sophisticated view of Congress and its members. The policy making in which they are engaged is messy—real conflicts over the policies of government generate legislative battles that are sometimes partisan, often prolonged, and usually result in compromises that fully satisfy no one. The complexities of the legislative process frustrate even knowledgeable observers. And the system requires members to pay regular attention to the electoral process—which necessarily makes them look self-serving and often partisan.

6-1

The Senate in Bicameral Perspective

Richard F. Fenno Jr.

Rules matter, and constitutional rules often matter most. The Framers
of the Constitution created a bicameral national legislature and made
the two houses of Congress different in their constituencies, size, and
length of terms, with the expectation that they were shaping the way in
which the House and Senate would behave. In the following essay,
Richard Fenno introduces the differences between the House and the
Senate that originated in the Constitution. He then traces the influence
of the differences between the two chambers on the way representatives
and senators campaign and govern.

BICAMERALISM WAS A bedrock element of the constitutional arrangement of
1787. A resolution "that the national legislature ought to consist of two
branches" was the second one passed—"without debate or dissent"—at the
federal convention.[1] When, later in the proceedings, several delegates defended the adequacy of the one-chamber Congress then existing under the
Articles of Confederation, they did so as part of a strategic effort to secure
the equal representation of states in the new system. The principle of bicameralism was never challenged. Twelve of the thirteen states already had
bicameral legislatures. George Mason took this fact as evidence that "an attachment to more than one branch in the legislature" was—along with "an
attachment to republican government"—one of the two points on which
"the mind of the people of America . . . was well settled."[2] When James
Madison introduced the subject of a second chamber in *The Federalist*, he
declared it to be "founded on such clear principles, and now so well understood in the United States that it would be more than superfluous to enlarge
on it."[3] He and his colleagues did, of course, "enlarge" upon these "clear
principles" in their debates and writings. And I shall do so briefly, to expli-
cate the bicameral perspective.

Excerpted from Richard F. Fenno Jr., *The United States Senate: A Bicameral Perspective* (Washington,
D.C.: American Enterprise Institute, 1982), pp. 1–6, 26–46. Reprinted with the permission of the
American Enterprise Institute for Public Policy Research, Washington, D.C.

The framers wanted to create a government, but at the same time they distrusted the power of government. To protect individual liberty, they believed, it was necessary to control the power of government, first through the electoral process and second by dividing authority among and within political institutions. Madison described the "principles" this way:

> In framing a government which is to be administered by men over men, the great difficulty lies in this: you must first enable the government to control the governed; and in the next place oblige it to control itself. A dependence on the people is, no doubt, the primary control on the government; but experience has taught mankind the necessity of auxiliary precautions.[4]

Bicameralism should be viewed most broadly as one of those "auxiliary precautions." Indeed, it is the first one mentioned by Madison after the paragraph quoted above. It came first because the framers believed that the most powerful institution of government and the one most likely to run out of control was the legislature. And they believed that "in order to control the legislative authority, you must divide it."[5]

"Is there no danger of legislative despotism?" James Wilson asked his convention colleagues rhetorically:

> Theory and practice both proclaim it. If the legislative authority be not restrained, there can be neither liberty nor stability; and it can only be restrained by dividing it within itself into distinct and independent branches.[6]

Madison elaborated in *The Federalist*:

> In republican government, the legislative authority necessarily predominates. The remedy for this inconveniency is to divide the legislature into different branches; and to render them, by different modes of election and different principles of action, as little connected with each other as the nature of their common functions and their common dependence on the society will admit.[7]

(Here we have enunciated the basic ideas of bicameralism: that the legislature consist of two "distinct and independent" bodies and that these bodies be "different" from one another.)

The framers, of course, had ideas about just what differences should exist between the Senate and the House. For one thing, they believed that the differences ought to be substantial. In Madison's words:

As the improbability of sinister combinations will be in proportion to the dissimilarity in the genius of the two bodies, it must be politic to distinguish them from each other by every circumstance which will consist with a due harmony in all proper measures, and with the genuine principles of republican government.[8]

In pursuit of this goal, they determined that the Senate and the House should be structurally dissimilar with respect to their constituencies, their size, and the length of their terms. They also gave each chamber some distinctive policy prerogatives. The controversy over Senate and House constituencies very nearly broke up the entire enterprise. Once that was settled, however, the decisions of 1787 fixed the enduring agenda for discussions of bicameralism. For a long time the decision to establish different modes of election was also part of that agenda, but the Seventeenth Amendment, providing for the popular election of senators, removed it in 1913.

There is more, however, to the framers' conception of bicameralism than two legislative institutions differently constituted. They also believed that the two institutions should and would behave differently. The basic notion was simply that they would behave so as to check one another. In the very act of dividing power, the framers believed they had created two "different bodies of men who might watch and check each other."[9] Their favorite idea, that institutions should and would check one another, was a particularly strong element in their thinking about the Senate.

The House of Representatives was acknowledged to be "the grand repository of the democratic principle of the government."[10] That is why it was given the prerogative of initiating all legislation on taxes, where sensitivity to popular sentiment was deemed especially important. But the House was also thought likely to possess certain infirmities endemic to large, popularly elected legislatures—tendencies to instability in action, to impulsive, unpredictable, changeable decisions, and to a short-run view of good public policy. The Senate was thought of as providing a restraining, stabilizing counterweight, as being the source of a more deliberate, more knowledgeable, longer-run view of good public policy. Said Madison: "As a numerous body of Representatives was liable to err, also, from fickleness and passion, [a] necessary fence against this danger would be to select a portion of enlightened citizens, whose limited number, and firmness might reasonably interpose against impetuous councils." Madison also said: "The use of the Senate is to consist in its proceeding with more coolness, with more system and with more wisdom, than the popular branch."[11] On the basis of such a prediction, the Senate was granted prerogatives in foreign policy, where a steady view of the national interest and the respect of other nations was deemed especially important.

The framers based their predictions of House and Senate behavior on a set of assumptions about the importance of the structural differences they had prescribed. The superior "coolness," "system," and "wisdom" of the Senate, for example, were assumed to flow from its smaller size, the longer term of its members, and their election by state legislatures. If we ask whether the various predictions or their underlying assumptions have worked out as planned, the answer would be: not now—if ever. Some of the predicted differences—that the Senate would be "a more capable set of men" and would act with more "firmness"—seem almost quaint.[12] Research on the contemporary Congress has argued either that observable Senate-House differences do not follow the lines set forth by the framers or that those differences may be less important than the ever-growing similarities.[13] So there is evidence that the particular predictions and the particular linking assumptions of the framers do not hold true today.

Still, that is not a sufficient reason to abandon their original proposition: that structural differences would affect behavioral ones. The structural change to the popular election of senators, for instance, undoubtedly gave a major push to today's behavioral similarities. Other scholars, too, suggest that performance differences are related to structural differences.[14] So let us continue to assume that the enduring Senate-House differences—in constituency, size, and term—can have consequences for behavior, and let us consider such matters reasonable subjects for empirical investigation.

If encouragement be needed, it is provided by the existence of at least one crucial Senate-House difference in which the framers' assumptions about the effect of structures on behavior have been correct. By setting up two distinct and different bodies, they made it necessary that the Senate and the House take separate action. They wanted to make certain that the "concurrence of separate and dissimilar bodies is required in every public act."[15] Separate action means, at a minimum, sequential action, and sequential action very likely means different actions. That is because sequential action implies the passage of time and with it the changing of relevant contexts. Different contexts very likely lead to different behavior.

Not surprisingly, the exemplary anecdote about the Senate is an anecdote about sequence. It is the conversation between George Washington and Thomas Jefferson in which Jefferson, in France during the convention, asked Washington why he had consented to a second chamber. "Why," asked Washington, "did you pour that coffee into your saucer?" "To cool it," said Jefferson. "Even so," said Washington, "we pour legislation into the senatorial saucer to cool it." It was the Senate, of course, that was designed to contribute "coolness." But in the execution, it has been the existence of two separate legislative stages that has brought coolness to the legislative process. The anecdote is an exemplary one not just for the Senate, but for the Congress as a whole, for what it illustrates is the importance of separate, sequential action by the two chambers. The Senate is as likely to initiate heatedly as the House; the House is as likely to be the cooling saucer as the Senate.

If this is so, then the analysis of sequence becomes basic to an understanding of bicameral behavior—more basic than an analysis of whether the Senate is more liberal or more conservative than the House. The framers did not so much create one precipitate chamber and one stabilizing chamber as they did force decision making to move across two separate chambers, however those chambers might be constituted. The strategic maneuverings necessitated by such a process become a subject for empirical investigation—as in the analysis of conference committee behavior by Gerald Strom and Barry Rundquist.[16] For reasons of strategy, it would be important for members of the two chambers to assess each other's relative liberalism or conservatism. But analysts of sequencing strategies must recognize the more general proposition that the actions and reactions, the expectations and anticipations, of the two-stage process are as likely to flow one way across the two chambers as the other. The idea of two legislative institutions acting separately and sequentially and thereby having an effect on each other is another ingredient of a bicameral perspective. Although it is not pursued in this essay, it gives additional purpose to what is pursued here.

In sum, the framers of the constitution consciously created a bicameral legislature. They tried to create two different institutions, to construct them so that they would behave differently, and to provide for legislative action at two separate stages. Their legacy leaves us with two questions. What, if any, are the differences between the Senate and House? What, if any, difference do the differences make? To research these questions is a tall order. It calls for observation and description of both houses of Congress and of legislators both individually and collectively, both in and outside Washington.

This essay attempts a beginning. Because its ultimate interest is in the Senate, it treats the Senate more than the House. Further, it treats senators more individually than collectively, and it treats them more outside than inside Washington. But it tries to do what it does comparatively—in accordance with a bicameral perspective. . . .

A Bicameral Perspective: Campaigning and Governing

The Six-Year Term

. . . House members campaign continuously. Although an analytical distinction can be drawn between the campaign and the rest of their term, the activity of campaigning never stops. The typical House member's attitude was expressed by one who said, "If an incumbent doesn't have the election won before the campaign begins, he's in trouble. It's hard for me to step up my campaign. I've never been home less than forty times a year since I've been in Congress." When I traveled during the campaign with House members, I rarely had the sense that they were doing anything extraordinary. Their schedules might be a bit more crowded and might include a larger number of partisan events than during an off-year visit, but I felt that they were engaging in their familiar, year-round routines. Two weeks before election one of them remarked, typically, "We are doing now just about the same thing—I'll say the very same thing—I do when I come home weekends." My visits to their districts in nonelection years confirmed this view.

But a researcher does not get the same feeling during incumbent senators' campaigns. There one senses that they have geared up for a qualitatively different effort from anything they have engaged in recently. House members talk a lot about "last time." They campaign "the way we did it last time." Memories of "last time," that is, the last election, are vivid. In a senator's campaign, however, there is noticeably less talk about "last time." The campaign workers tend not to have been involved "last time." Last time is much less of a benchmark for this time; to the degree that it is, recollections of it are vague. In other words, although House members never stop campaigning, senators do. That is why it is impossible to make the easy inferences from campaign styles to home styles for senators that can be made for House members. For senators, campaign styles are not necessarily home styles. There is undoubtedly a relation between them, stronger in some instances than in others. I shall have something to say about this later. Now I propose to examine the underlying structural feature that gives rise to this observed House-Senate difference: the six-year term. It is another legacy of the decisions of 1787.

Traveling the two campaign trails sensitizes the researcher to the difference between the two-year term and the six-year term. It is a big difference. This statement may come as no surprise, but it is not self-evident. The most widely read and reprinted political science treatment of Senate-House differences, by Lewis Froman, contains not one word about the difference in the length of terms. In his chapter "Differences between the House and the Senate," Froman writes:

> Probably the two most important differences between the House and the Senate, and the two from which most of the others are derived, are that the House is more than four times as large as the Senate and that Senators represent sovereign states in a federal system, whereas most congressmen represent smaller and sometimes shifting parts of states.[17]

And in the chart that follows, entitled "Major Differences between the House and the Senate," Froman lists eleven major differences, not one of which has anything to do with the difference between the two-year term and the six-year term. It is largely a matter of research perspective. Froman studied the House and Senate from the inside, in Washington, and he saw only internal, organizational differences. One who begins research in the constituencies at campaign time sees other differences and carries other perspectives to Capitol Hill.

From the perspective of a Senate campaign, six years seems like a long time. Incumbent candidates talk less about last time precisely because it was so long ago—long enough to render the last campaign irrelevant, even if it could be remembered. A defeated senator discussed the six-year change in his state's policy climate:

> When I went in, the war was still on—Vietnam. The fellow I ran against was very closely associated with that. That was of interest to people. There was not building up, then, that avalanche of antigovernment feeling, in the sense that the government could not solve problems. There was a suspicion of people in government, the sense that government was remote. That feeling was there. But the lack of faith in government has grown enormously in six years. [Six years ago] there was a lot more support for farm price supports. There was more support for government

programs to help *me*. . . . Now there's the Goldwater spirit, that government never has done anything right and never will. . . . So the mood changed in six years. There's no doubt about that. The impact was very great, I think. People said about me, "He is not a bad guy. He works hard at it. He's honest. He comes back. But he's just too liberal. He hasn't kept up with this change and is holding out for old ideas. There's nothing wrong with him but his views."

This comment about change is not meant to explain an electoral outcome, although perhaps it does. Nor is it meant to explain why campaigning senators have difficulty delineating their supportive constituencies, although perhaps it may. It is meant, rather, to convey some sense of just how long a six-year term can be. Six years, especially six years without any electoral feedback, is plenty of time to get out of touch with one's constituency. Six years, in short, can be a political lifetime.

We cannot understand the Senate without examining the effects of this lengthy term. Six years between elections is long enough to encourage a senator to stop campaigning for a while and do something else with his or her time. House members, too, have this option, but they are constrained by the two-year term to a degree that senators are not—constrained to devote their time and energies fairly continuously and fairly heavily to campaigning for reelection. It is not happenstance that the hardest Senate campaigner I have traveled with was one who was serving a two-year term—a senator with a House member's term of office. "We started running four years ago and we have been running ever since," he said. "I have visited 165 cities and towns, places where no sitting senator has ever been." He came home every weekend for a year and a half. And he was introduced, everywhere, as "a man who is accessible." "Our campaign organization never shut down," said his campaign manager. He campaigned, in other words, like a House member; he did so because of the constraints of the two-year term. Like a House member, he had no choice. Even more, he had to cultivate a constituency much larger than that of a House member.

All senators, I assume, worry a lot about reelection, too. I also assume, however, that their reelection concerns are less immediate, less central, and less overwhelming than they are for House members, at least for some of the time. The amplitude of the six-year cycle gives senators more of a choice. To the degree that they choose to campaign less than continuously, it should be easier for outsiders to disentangle their campaign activities from their noncampaign activities. It gives us an incentive to analyze the effect of one kind of activity on the other and to examine the choices senators make about their noncampaign activity. That is what I propose to do. As I proceed, the focus of description will shift gradually from the constituencies to Washington, from outside the Senate into the Senate, and from the processes of campaigning to the processes of governing.

The Electoral Cycle

A two-year term compresses campaign activity and noncampaign activity so that they appear, to the observer, to proceed simultaneously. A six-year term makes it easier to separate the two kinds of activities and view them sequentially. It invites a view in which the mixture of campaign and noncampaign activity changes over the course of the six years, campaign activity visibly increasing as election time approaches and visibly decreasing afterward. Senators themselves speak in the language of cycles. "Your life has a six-year cycle to it," said one eighteen-year veteran:

> We say in the Senate that we spend four years as a statesman and two years as a politician. You should get cracking as soon as the last two years open up. You should take a poll on the issues, identify people to run your campaign in different parts of the states, raise money, start your PR, and so forth.

A five-term senator, Russell Long, said, "My usual pattern in the first three years of a term is to stick close to the job here and in the last three years to step up the pace in Louisiana." [18] Some evidence, both cross-sectional and longitudinal, exists in support of this cyclical view of senatorial behavior.

The presence of three distinct classes of senators, each with a different reelection date, makes possible some cross-sectional analysis. At the constitutional convention James Wilson noted, "As one-third would go out triennially, there would always be divisions holding their places for unequal terms and consequently acting under the influence of different views and different impulses." [19] Among those "different views and different impulses" is the impulse to campaign for reelection. In a cyclical view of the matter, the impulse would be strongest in that class for which election day was closest at hand.

Table 1. Average Amount Raised per Senator, 1977 and 1979 (in dollars)

	Reelection Date		
	One year away	Three years away	Five years away
1977	250,000 (22)	5,000 (34)	32,000 (30)
1979	391,000 (29)	64,000 (29)	112,000 (33)

Source: Federal Election Commission.

Note: Senators who did not file reports have been omitted. Numbers of senators in each group in parentheses.

I have examined the campaign contributions of all senators for the years 1977 and 1979, the years before the 1978 and 1980 Senate elections. The amount of money raised by each senator is taken to be a measure of that senator's campaign activity in that year. The results, reported in Table 1, do indeed indicate that the senators one year away from reelection campaign harder, that is, raise more money, than the senators for whom election day is either three years or five years away. The average amounts raised by the three classes (one year, three years, and five years away from reelection) were $250,000, $5,000, and $32,000 for 1978 and $391,000, $64,000, and $112,000 for 1980. In each year senators whose next election was furthest away ranked second in average amount collected. The pattern, then, is curvilinear. Those whose reelection was five years away "campaigned harder" than those whose reelection was only three years away. But they did so presumably because they were paying off the debts of a campaign just concluded. They were looking backward to the previous election, not forward to the next one.

Two changes between 1978 and 1980 are worth noting. Senators in all classes raised more money in 1979 than they did in 1977; campaigning is getting more expensive for everyone. The largest proportionate increase in fund raising occurred in the middle group, the class whose reelection was three years away. The average amount collected in this middle group jumped from $5,000 in 1977 to $64,000 in [1979], and the total amount collected by that one-third of the Senate jumped from $170,000 in 1977 to $1.9 million in 1979. This may indicate that senators are beginning their fund raising earlier than previously. As Robert Peabody has recently written:

> Few Senators can afford the proverbial luxury of serving as statesmen for four years, then reverting to the political role for the remaining two years of the term. Many of the younger group of Senators appear to be

following the practice of running hard through most of the six-year term, not unlike the experience of House incumbents.[20]

Table 1 contains some evidence of this change and at the same time demonstrates that some behavior still follows the electoral cycle.

The table indicates that there is a perceptible quickening of fund raising around the fifth year. Students of campaign finance have noted the same phenomenon. Herbert Alexander has observed, "It's becoming almost imperative for senators to spend the fifth year of their term to sew up the following year's elections."[21] Gary Jacobson has shown, for House races, that once a challenger starts spending large amounts of money, the incumbent cannot win simply by raising more money than the challenger.[22] It may be necessary, of course, for the incumbent to raise money in the sixth year to combat a strong challenger. But it can be even more important for an incumbent to use his or her fund-raising ability earlier, so as to keep a strong challenger from emerging. The appearance of electoral vulnerability can be disastrous for an incumbent, since potential challengers and the elites who fund them base their decisions partly on the perceived vulnerability of an incumbent.[23] Moreover, they will be making their calculations in the fifth year. One way to appear invulnerable is to raise a lot of money early. Such is the logic of fifth-year fund raising: at least, be prepared; at most, ward off a strong challenge. The logic of the preemptive strike may be even more important in the Senate than in the House, given the greater ability of Senate challengers to get media attention and to raise money once they have become committed to the race.

Two weeks before election, one incumbent senator talked about his fifth-year campaigning activity:

> Eighteen months ago, we started thinking about the strategy of the campaign. Our first strategy was to scare off other people from running by showing strength. And we did many interesting things to show our strength. . . . It worked in scaring off the governor and a congressman. It didn't work on my opponent. Whether or not we scared off the right people, we'll know on election day.

One of the "interesting things" this senator had done in the year before the election was to raise over $300,000. His press secretary talked about some of the others:

> In June of last year, we made a major strategic decision—to put an aura of invincibility around the senator. We collected money from all seg-

Table 2. Trips Home by Senate Class, 1977

Number of trips home	Reelection 1978		Reelection 1980		Reelection 1982		Retiring 1978	
	Number	Percent	Number	Percent	Number	Percent	Number	Percent
31+	5	23	3	9	5	18	0	0
21–30	7	32	6	19	4	14	2	29
11–20	9	41	13	41	12	43	1	14
0–10	1	5	10	31	7	25	4	57
Total	22	100	32	100	28	100	7	100
Average	23		16		18		12	

Source: Travel vouchers submitted to the secretary of the Senate.

Note: Excludes senators from Delaware, Maryland, and Virginia; senators who had served less than a full year; and senators whose records were obviously incomplete.

ments of the population of the state. We brought him and his family back home to the state. We ran a spring primary campaign as if we had an opponent—a heavy-schedule television campaign. In June of this year, we took a poll. He was ahead of his opponent by over twenty points.

This fifth-year activity may well have been the key to what turned out to be a narrow victory. Back in Washington after his reelection, the senator commented:

Here's something that would interest you from your professional standpoint. All the political leaders in the state, on both sides, thought my opponent was in a hopeless race. They believed the polls. The other party's leaders believed it so much that they gave up on him. They didn't dig down and help him. That may have hurt him more than anything else.

He believes the strategy worked. Although it is not my purpose to explain election outcomes, this case illustrates the rationale behind one cyclical pattern of campaign activity.

A second, less direct indicator of cyclical campaign activity might be the frequency with which the different classes of senators return to their home states. We would expect that those senators whose reelection was less than two years away would return home to campaign more often than those whose reelection was more than two years away. We have already noted that senators as a group return to their electoral constituencies a good deal less frequently than House members do. Among senators, however, do

Table 3. Trips Home by Senators, by Region, 1977

Number of trips home	East	South	Border	Midwest	Far West
31+	8	3	0	2	0
21–30	5	7	5	2	0
11–20	3	5	1	12	14
0–10	1	3	2	5	11
Total	17	18	8	21	25
Average	27	21	19	16	11

Source: Travel vouchers submitted to the secretary of the Senate.

Note: Excludes senators from Delaware, Maryland, and Virginia; senators who had served less than a full year; and senators whose records were obviously incomplete.

those up for reelection behave differently from those who are not? In general, there is some evidence that they do. Such patterns as there are run in the expected direction: more attentiveness to their constituencies by senators in the reelection class than by those in the other two classes. The differences are not overwhelming, however, and the small numbers in many categories argue against strong assertions. Still, the evidence is weakly supportive.

In 1977 the twenty-two incumbents facing reelection in 1978 averaged twenty-three trips to their home states, those whose reelection was three years away averaged sixteen trips, and those whose reelection was five years away averaged eighteen trips. Senators who retired in 1978, a group totally lacking in electoral incentives, averaged twelve trips home in 1977 (see Table 2). The difference between this group and their colleagues running for reelection is substantial. It surely testifies to a relationship between the proximity of reelection and trips home, if not to any great strength in its cyclical nature.

Among the three nonretiring groups, the findings resemble those for campaign finance activity. Senators up for reelection are most active, and recently elected senators seem to engage in more electorally related activity than senators in the middle of their term. In the area of campaign finance, the newly elected senators are still paying off their debts. In the matter of trips home, they are probably slow to throttle down from their recent campaigns. This might be particularly true of senators elected for the first time, whose sense of electoral insecurity might remain with them. In any case, it is the first-term senators whose performance accounts for the slightly higher average among the newly elected class. Veteran senators in that class, that is, those elected in 1976, did not go home any more frequently in 1977 than those senators who had been elected in 1974. There is thus some evidence, although it is not overwhelming, for a cyclical explanation of senatorial attentiveness to home.

Table 2 presents further evidence for an electoral cycle. The distribution of trips home within the reelection class differs from that of the other two classes and the retiring senators. Senators running for reelection are clustered more heavily in the top two categories than are senators in the other two classes or those who are retiring. The differences are greatest in the category of ten or fewer trips home; only one reelection-bound senator dared risk such infrequent visits. The retiring senators, of course, look very different from all other senators, but there is no clear pattern differentiating between the two classes of senators not running for reelection. Although reelection concerns have some effect on one class of senators, then, Table 2 conveys no information about other phases of a more defined electoral cycle.

A confounding circumstance affecting the distribution of trips home is the simple matter of distance from Washington, D.C. Among House members, it was found that distance, that is, the expenditure of time, money, and energy, was strongly related to trips home.[24] There is no reason to believe that this would not be true of the Senate, and it is. Table 3 presents a distribution of trips home by senators according to the region from which they come, region being employed as a surrogate for distance, as it was with House members. The farther senators live from Washington, the more difficult it is for them to get home. Senators from the East go home more often than any other group; those from the Far West go home less often than any other group. No senator from the Far West is to be found in the highest two categories of trips home. Senators from the Midwest also go home markedly less often than those from the East and South. So striking are these patterns that the question arises whether or not they overwhelm such evidence as supports the notion of a reelection effect. Perhaps region explains all the differences observed in Table 2. Senate classes may be skewed toward one region or another; thus an apparent reelection effect may mask what really is a distance effect.

The 1980 and 1982 Senate classes, for example, are more skewed toward the Far West, 31 percent and 32 percent respectively, than is the class of

1978, only 21 percent of whose members are from the Far West. These regional differences could account for the higher average number of trips among the group of senators running for reelection. One way to check for independent reelection effects would be to see whether, within each region, senators running for reelection were more attentive than senators in the two other classes to their home states. When this calculation is made, the effect of the electoral cycle remains. Of the twenty-two senators running for reelection, sixteen exceeded the average of all senators from their region, and six averaged fewer trips than their regional colleagues. Thus, although distance has an important effect on the frequency of senators' visits home, the proximity to reelection has an independent effect.

Other factors that might be thought to affect a cyclical-reelection explanation for trips home but do not do so—at least in terms of a bivariate relationship—include election margin, seniority, size of state, and previous service in the House. A more idiosyncratic factor, home style, probably does take an additional toll on the cyclical rationale of trips home. Consider, for example, the twenty cases where a senator faced reelection and his or her colleague from the same state did not. With distance thus held constant, we would expect, according to a cyclical rationale, that the campaigning senator would return home more often than his noncampaigning colleague. In ten cases he clearly did; but in six cases he clearly did not, and four cases were virtual ties. It seems likely, therefore, that some senators adopt and maintain a home style calling for frequent personal appearances back home and much personal attentiveness to the electorate. It is a decision having nothing to do with the amplitude of the electoral cycle or the proximity of reelection. Such a style may be adopted to make a deliberate contrast with the senator's same-state colleague. It is worth noting that in all six cases in the noncyclical pattern, it was the junior senator (five of whom were in their first term) who went home most often, even though the senior senator was the one running for reelection. Support for a cyclical-reelection explanation of behavior is weakened a bit more by this finding, and the importance of decisions about home style, taken independent of reelection proximity, is reasserted.

A final strand of research gives some support to a cyclical view of senatorial behavior. It is the body of work that demonstrates that the roll-call or other policy-related behavior of senators changes in the direction of the policy sentiments of their constituents as their reelection approaches. Since these changes are calculated to improve a senator's electoral prospects, we can think of this as another form of campaign activity. The prototype for this research is not about the U.S. Senate at all; it is James Kuklinski's study of California legislators. He found that the voting of state senators, who serve four-year terms, moved toward the policy preferences of their constituents as reelection time approached and moved away from those preferences after their reelection, while the voting of assemblymen, who serve two-year terms, showed no such cyclical change. Ryan Amacher and William Boyes argue a similar conclusion for the Senate. "Long terms, such as the U.S. Senate, seem to produce cycles in which the representative is able to behave independently when first elected and then becomes more representative as reelection approaches."[25] Their conclusion, unfortunately, rests on a methodology far less convincing than Kuklinski's.

John Jackson found that among senators whose 1963 constituency-related voting behavior was not consistent with their previously observed constituency-related voting behavior, the change could be explained by increased attention to the constituency among those whose reelection was closest at hand and decreased attention among those just reelected. Keith Poole has shown that senators' roll-call behavior, as measured by interest group ratings, becomes more ambiguous, or less consistent ideologically, the closer they get to reelection. Finally, Warren Kostroski and Richard Fleisher found that the voting behavior of senators up for reelection was more responsive to the policy wishes of their supportive constituencies than the voting behaviors of senators not up for reelection.[26]

In all these studies there is evidence, produced cross-sectionally, in support of a cyclical effect on campaign activity. Still, the evidence is not strong. The first study was not about the Senate at all. The second study, where the finding is the most applicable, used very questionable methods. The presence of cyclical effects was not the major finding of the last three studies but a subsidiary result. Their major findings emphasized behavioral consistency. Thus the body of evidence leaves us just about where we were at the conclusion of the discussion of trips home. There is weakly supportive evidence for the operation of an electoral cycle and for its systematic effect on campaign activity.

Evidence that constituency-related voting increases at the end of the cycle is buttressed a bit, however, by evidence that such voting can be diluted at the beginning of the electoral cycle. Evidence for the proposition—the "statesman" proposition—is fragmentary, but several senators talked about it. Said one in his first year, "I wouldn't have voted against food stamps as I did last Saturday if I had to run in a year. The six-year term gives you insurance. Well, not exactly—it gives you a cushion. It gives you some squirming room." Said another newcomer:

> It [the six-year term] helps you to take politically unpopular positions. Right now I'm trying to think of a way to change cost-of-living indexing. I'm convinced we've got to find a way of turning that process around. I don't know whether I'll get anywhere. Indexing is very popular. None of the people running for reelection next year will tackle it. I wouldn't either if I had to get reelected next year.

The idea is, of course, that such political actions would not be possible if the senator were near the end of his term. House members, by contrast, are always near the end of their term. As a House member put it, "You are tied down a lot closer to your constituency here than in the Senate. . . . Over there at least one-third of the senators can afford to be statesmen. Here you have to be a politician all the time because you have to run every two years." A third senator reflected, similarly, on the Senate's passage of the Panama Canal treaty:

> Two years is a much shorter leash. I think it makes a real difference. I don't think you would ever have gotten the Panama Canal treaty through the House. Not with the election coming up and the mail coming in so heavily against it. The sentiment in the House might not have been any different from what it was in the Senate. But you could never have passed it.

The implication is that some portion of the Senate was freed from the intense reelection pressure by the insulating effect of the length of term. Patterned action taken near the beginning of the cycle thus testifies to its existence as much as patterned action taken at the end of the cycle.

All this puts us a little bit in mind of an observation by H. Douglas Price: "Cycles have a deservedly bad reputation in most of the social sciences, but they seem to exercise an irresistible pull on explorers of poorly understood subjects."[27] Perhaps when we understand more about the Senate, the appeal of the electoral cycle will vanish. But until such time, it will continue to seem a useful way of exploring the consequences of the six-year term.

The Adjustment from Campaigning to Governing

There is a cycle-related admonition that senators repeat to one another: "Your most important years here are your first and your fifth." They sometimes argue over which is the more important. We know why the fifth year is important. It is the reelection year. We can guess why the first year is important. It is the adjustment year. Political scientists have devoted a great deal of attention to the adjustment period in the Senate, much more than they have paid to the reelection period. In the 1960s the writing about adjustment was dominated by the idea that newly elected senators had to attune themselves to the informal "folkways" of the institution. Especially prominent among those folkways was the notion that first-term senators should observe an apprenticeship. Donald Matthews, in his classic 1960 study, called it "the first rule of Senate behavior" that a newcomer "is expected to keep his mouth shut, not to take the lead in floor fights, to listen and to learn."[28] Recent writings on the Senate, however, have demonstrated beyond any doubt that this "norm of apprenticeship" is dead.[29] That does not mean, however, that the period of adjustment is any the less crucial for a newly elected senator—either in his eyes or in the eyes of those who make judgments about him. Political scientists, therefore, face the problem of confronting a crucial period in the life of a senator at the same time that they have undermined their favorite intellectual framework for studying it.

The suggestion offered here is to view the adjustment period from the perspective of the campaign and the electoral cycle. Newly elected senators can be seen as making a transition from campaign activity, during which time their noncampaign activity will be affected to varying degrees by their campaign activity. The adjustment they make is not so much something that takes place in Washington as it is an adjustment that takes place between constituency behavior and Washington behavior. The relationship, from this perspective, between campaign activity and noncampaign activity has long been deemed important by students of Congress. "It is difficult, really, to understand the Senators, how they act and why," asserted Matthews, "without considering what happens to them while they are running for office."[30] John Bibby and Roger Davidson have written, "The relationship of the campaign to the legislator's total world is of special fascination to students of the legislative process."[31] Yet both works make particular mention of the need for scholarly research into the relationship. Matthews, indeed, admits that his book has little to say on the subject.[32]

Senate newcomers are emerging from their campaigns and are positioned at the beginning of a six-year electoral cycle. From a cyclical view, they should be gearing down their campaign activity and stepping up their noncampaign activity. The six-year senatorial term relaxes their electoral constraints sufficiently so that they can, at some point, stop their campaigning and devote their time and energy to something else. Or, at least, they can alter the mixture of their activities. Indeed, it could be argued that all senators must make some such adjustment. If the amplitude of the electoral cycle is not a sufficient inducement, outsiders—particularly the media—will doubtless fix a set of noncampaign expectations for them. Just what is meant by "noncampaign activity" remains purposely vague, but it has something to do with the conduct of the legislature's business, with governing the country. Senators will make the adjustment from campaigning to governing at different rates of speed, in different ways, and with different consequences.

A senator's early days in office provide the observer with a natural setting in which to explore the variety of ways in which the campaign just concluded can impinge on the legislative behavior just taking shape. On the first visit to a newly elected senator's office, for example, an observer is struck by the number of familiar faces there, by the presence of acquaintances from the campaign trail. Whatever their ultimate adjustment to life in the Senate may be, newly elected senators want some people from the campaign with them in Washington.

I followed six neophyte senators from their campaigns into the Senate. On the average, one-third of their Senate staffs—in Washington and back home—were people who had worked in their campaigns. All six campaign managers became members of the Washington staffs, three as chief administrative assistants, two as chief legislative assistants. All six campaign press secretaries became senatorial press secretaries, five in Washington and one in the home state. This direct exchange of jobs, greater than for any other staff position, testifies to the continuing importance of the media for senators as well as for Senate candidates. One method, therefore, of coping with the adjustment period is to maintain some continuity in personnel, some "binding ties."[33]

The presence of people from the campaign ensures the continuance of some campaign activity throughout the six-year term—or if not campaign activity, at least what might be called a campaign metabolism. Senators want some people around who have the requisite metabolic makeup. They want people who have a first-hand sensitivity to electoral forces and electoral problems in the state. They want people who have proven political skill, proven political loyalty, and proven ability to function under pressure. They want people who can understand the senator's political obligations and assess his political risks. All these qualities are best discovered, developed, and tested in the crucible of a campaign. All will be needed to conduct whatever campaign activity is conducted over the next six years, and all will affect noncampaign activity as well. If we, on the outside, are to understand a senator's noncampaign activity, we shall have to know that some members of his staff possess this campaign metabolism. They will automatically factor into all their judgments perceptions of the last campaign and considerations of the next campaign, even as they go about their noncampaign activity. Looking back over six years, an administrative assistant to a first-term senator, the man who also managed the first campaign, provided an example:

> I started worrying the day after his election. He was the first member of the party elected from our state in many years. His reelection was never out of my mind. I thought everything we did here meant something could be done about our political situation or our political base. The senator may not have seen it that way. He's not a political guy. He's the least political senator around.

Staffers with a campaign metabolism will join the senator in making decisions about what is politically wise or politically feasible. Indeed, it may not even be possible to understand certain decisions made by senators unless we know that they have been made by people who had been campaigners.

Another set of continuing influences flows from the events and the rhetoric (I hesitate to say dialogue) of the campaign. At the most obvious level, there are the policy positions taken during the campaign that must now be addressed in office. "The problems I talked about in the campaign are the problems I'm still interested in—the auto industry," said one senator two months into his first term. "It's a continuum," said another, at the same stage:

> There are a lot of campaign promises to be fulfilled. We have to look after the export of coal, coal regulation, steel, pollution issues, Japanese imports, textiles. The NEA [National Education Association], which was a big help to me in the campaign, want more recognition on education matters. There are Jewish issues. There are the problems of [particular cities]. . . . I'm interested in a full plate of things.

John Bibby and Roger Davidson wrote of Senator Abraham Ribicoff that "the Senate campaign provided an important testing ground for the issues and themes that were to mark his early Senate career."[34] During their campaigns Senate candidates emphasize certain public policy concerns, and they carry the emphasis with them into the Senate.

How long the policy emphases of the campaign remain on the senator's "plate of things" is a matter of conjecture. Donald Matthews suggests that "the Senator's initial mandate—partly self-defined, partly reflecting popular sentiment . . . may be a major influence on his voting record many years after it was received."[35] One implication is that policy positions taken in the campaign may persist for so long that eventually the senator can get badly out of touch with his constituency—and, of course, lose. Another implication is that the duration of the campaign emphasis will depend on just how strong the senator believes the initial mandate to be. The finding of Alan Abramowitz that some Senate campaigns are more ideological than others and that voters respond ideologically to the more ideological campaigns may help to sort out the kinds of campaigns that have the most lasting effects on victorious senators.[36] I have already noted that Senate campaigns tend to be more policy oriented than House campaigns, but Senate campaigns can vary widely in the amount of policy controversy they contain.

One way to maintain a campaign policy interest is to institutionalize it by obtaining membership on the committee that deals with it. In an after-dinner campaign speech at a rural high school, I heard one Senate candidate say to the growers of a particular farm product, "I hope I become a member of the Agriculture Committee. I want to become a member of that committee. If I get to the Senate, I'm going to make the point loud and clear that in all the Department of Agriculture there's not one advocate of your industry." It was a campaign promise made to a group of his very strongest supporters. In Washington, in January, he was somewhat less enthusiastic. "The Agriculture Committee is a shambles. . . . When I told other senators I wanted it, they said 'too bad' or 'maybe we can reduce the size of the committee so you won't have to go on.'" But he felt constrained to do so. As his administrative assistant put it, "He's going to go on Agriculture whether he wants to or not." The first legislative staff person he hired was an agricultural expert. The first bill he introduced was an agricultural bill. Altogether it was a very direct, specific, and continuing influence of the campaign on this senator's subsequent legislative work.

To the degree that the adjustment period follows the presumed pattern of the electoral cycle, newly elected senators should gradually subordinate campaign-related behavior to behavior related to legislative work. But they will not all act to do so with the same speed or produce the same degree of subordination. We now know, for example, that some senators must remain active for a while in fund raising to pay off campaign debts. Moreover, some senators enjoy campaigning and are therefore less likely to ease up on it.

Candidate A—now Senator A—is such a person. He likes to campaign. During the campaign he had exclaimed at one point, "I like what we are doing here better than what I do in Washington. The House is a zoo. People say the Senate is much better. . . . [They say] 'you'll even enjoy it.' " Whereas a number of his former House colleagues saw in the six-year term a welcome opportunity to stop their incessant campaigning, he saw nothing attractive in that particular feature of Senate life. Three months into his term, he commented:

> I never gave the six-year term one minute's thought. People say to me, "Aren't you glad you're in for six years?" I say, "No." I always liked campaigning. I always won big in elections. I'll campaign just as often as a senator as I did in the House and in exactly the same way. I was back there over the recess, traveled over the state and made fifteen speeches in five days. Campaigning is the best part of the job. It's the most fun. The six-year term makes absolutely no difference to me.

It will be interesting to see whether, in spite of himself, the six-year term has some effect on his campaign rhythms. Certainly the mixture of activities will be far different for him than for some others, and the play of cyclical effects will be diminished. It seems very likely that, just as his established campaign style did not change when he ran for the Senate, his established home style will not change much while he is in the Senate.

Candidate B—now Senator B—experienced a different adjustment period. When I talked with him three months into his first term, he said, "Nobody talks about their campaigns. It's over. You start fresh. It's the same as your being in the House. That doesn't matter over here either. It's a clean slate." And that was the way he wanted it. Unlike Senator A, he was trying to establish a clean slate with his constituents. "I set a certain standard of expectation when I was in the House, going home every weekend, but I'm not going to do that now. One of the reasons I ran for the Senate was so I wouldn't have to go home every weekend." His determination to disengage quickly from campaign activities was not just a matter of personal preference. It was a decision that emerged out of the dynamics of the campaign itself. His election opponents had called him a "show horse" and had described the contest as "a show horse against a work horse." He was sufficiently affected by this campaign rhetoric that he worked hard to negate it during his early days in office. Two and a half months into his term, he commented:

> Yesterday I got a call from the editor of the state's largest paper asking me why I was keeping such a low profile back in the state. They are going to write a criticism of me for not appearing at every bean supper back home. I've been studying hard, doing my homework, showing up on time. During the campaign, I had to confront the show horse–work horse argument. I've been trying to be a work horse. I've been down here for a month and a half without going home.

Senator B was moving along the cycle in the direction we would normally expect, but his movement was accelerated by his experience in the campaign. It seems likely that Senator B's campaign may have an effect on his home style, changing it from what it was in the House; but we shall have to wait and see.

In general, when the campaign rhetoric emphasizes policy matters, policy concerns can be expected to have an important effect on the adjustment period. When the rhetoric of the campaign emphasizes stylistic matters, however, stylistic concerns can be expected to have an important effect on the adjustment period. Whether the effect is to speed up or retard the movement toward noncampaign activity by the newly elected senator depends entirely on the substantive content of the campaign rhetoric.

The case of candidate C—now Senator C—is instructive. Senator C was a person who wanted to gear down his campaigning during the adjustment period but found it nearly impossible to do so. When I originally asked candidate C why he wanted to leave the House, he answered, "You run for election all the time. You win one month, and a month later you find out who your opponent will be. You go to bean suppers eight days in a row." One month after his election, I asked him what he would miss least about the House. He answered quickly and with a smile. "The two-year term. Now I can do what I want to do well." He is a highly issue-oriented person, and he was impatient to begin some sustained legislative work. Yet, in the first four months of his tenure, he made thirteen trips home and spent thirty-one days there. Senator B, in that same period, went home five times and spent nine days there. Why the contrast?

Once again, we must look to the dynamics of the campaign itself. Candidate C's main line of attack against the incumbent senator had been a stylistic one—his lack of accessibility. "When was the last time you saw your senator?" he would ask. "He hasn't been in my district more than twice in six years. . . . He's very much of a Washingtonian and all that implies. He's on the Washington-overseas shuttle." The implied campaign promise was, of course, to be accessible—as accessible, he sometimes said, as he had been when he was in the House. "I will hold town meetings like I did as a congressman—twenty a year," he told a reporter in January. "I'll also do 'work days': spend a day doing what people do for a living. My wife will go back once a month and go around meeting people and giving speeches." It seemed easy to contemplate. "I was more involved in my congressional district than any congressman ever; so it's nothing more than an extension of what I'm into already. I'm comfortable with it, and I think it will work." In his early days, he tried to make it work. Indeed, he did not stop campaigning.

In May, he exclaimed:

> In the House, I tried to do everything I was asked to do, go everywhere I was invited. The problem is: How do you learn to say no? I'm doing fourteen commencements this spring. Can you believe it? Part of it is my own doing. After the campaign, I never stopped. I went around thanking everybody. So I never recouped from the campaign. And I haven't stopped since. The result is I'm tired all the time.

As we drove around the state one day in June, he revealed another reason for his continuing campaign activity—a degree of electoral insecurity evidenced by neither Senator A nor Senator B. They, however, represented states the same size and twice the size of their House districts whereas Senator C was trying to digest a vastly larger statewide constituency. "There are so many places I haven't been where I want to get established," he said that day. Passing through one small town, he said, "This could be a good place for a town meeting. They would appreciate it. I haven't been here before." In the car, he leafed through a pile of "thank you" letters. "When you accept appearances like these and do them well, the recognition is tremendous. So the temptation is to keep it up. . . . Politically it's fantastic; but personally it's devastating." He added, "I can't keep up the pace." A couple of years later he looked back on his adjustment period:

> There was a definite period of confusion and wandering. It lasted for about a year. We didn't know what we were doing. We didn't know what issues to work on. I was running around the state like a madman. The problem was that I still thought of myself as a congressman; but I wasn't

a congressman, and I had ten times the territory to cover. You need to make judgments about what you want to do here, and we began to do that.

Finally he had begun to enjoy the fruits of the six-year term he had so coveted in the beginning. In the Senate Office Building he told a group of college students that same day, "This is the best job there is. The six-year term gives you time to think. In the House, you just finish packing away the decorations from the victory celebration when someone announces against you, and you have to start campaigning all over again." By that time he had subordinated his campaign activity to his noncampaign activity. But as one of his chief campaigners and chief Senate staffers said, "It took us a long time to get over the campaign."

There is a lot more to any senator's adjustment period than the campaign effects I have discussed. There are a whole series of adjustments to be made to one's fellow senators, to the internal routines of legislative work, and to the other actors in the Washington political community. All adjustment problems, however, can be seen as matters of choice. Senators will choose—in accordance with their personal goals, their perception of their political world, and the objective constraints within which they operate—their modes of adjustment. They will decide what kind of senators they want to be and how they will spend their resources of time, intelligence, energy, and support. I have discussed a few such senatorial adjustment choices, concerning staff, policy, committee, style, as they are affected by the campaign. I have suggested that the campaign perspective will help us understand the adjustment period, but I suggest no more than that. Just as the senators themselves gradually subordinate campaign activity to noncampaign activity, so must the observer subordinate the campaign perspective to other perspectives in order to comprehend a fuller range of Senate activities. For us as for them, there is a transition from the matter of campaigning to the matter of governing. But that is for another essay.

NOTES

1. James Madison, *Notes of Debates in the Federal Convention of 1787* (New York: W. W. Norton, 1969), pp. 38–39.

2. Ibid., p. 158.

3. *The Federalist Papers* (New York: New American Library, 1969), no. 62, p. 379.

4. Ibid., no. 51, p. 322.

5. Madison, *Notes,* p. 127.

6. Ibid., pp. 126–27.

7. *Federalist,* no. 51, p. 322.

8. Ibid., no. 62, p. 379.

9. Madison, *Notes,* p. 193.

10. Ibid., p. 39.

11. Ibid., pp. 194, 83.

12. Ibid., pp. 113, 194.

13. Gary E. Gammon, "The Role of the United States: Its Conception and Its Performance" (Ph.D. diss., Claremont Graduate School, 1978); and Norman J. Ornstein, "The House and the Senate in a New Congress," in Thomas E. Mann and Norman J. Ornstein, eds., *The New Congress* (Washington, D.C.: American Enterprise Institute, 1981).

14. Joseph M. Bessette, "Deliberative Democracy: The Majority Principle in Republican Government," in Robert A. Goldwin and William A. Schambra, eds., *How Democratic Is the Constitution?* (Washington, D.C.: American Enterprise Institute, 1980); and Nelson W. Polsby, "Strengthening Congress in National Policymaking," *Yale Review* (Summer 1970), pp. 481–97.

15. *Federalist,* no. 63, p. 386.

16. Gerald S. Strom and Barry S. Rundquist, "A Revised Theory of Winning in House-Senate Conferences," *American Political Science Review* (June 1997).

17. Lewis A. Froman, Jr., *The Congressional Process: Strategies, Rules, and Procedures* (Boston: Little, Brown, 1967), pp. 7–8.

18. *New York Times,* April 15, 1979.

19. James Madison, *Notes of Debates in the Federal Convention of 1787* (New York: W. W. Norton, 1969), p. 198.

20. Robert Peabody, "Senate Party Leadership: From the 1950s to the 1980s" (unpublished manuscript, Baltimore, 1980), p. 27; see also, Norman J. Ornstein, "The House and the Senate in a New Congress," in Thomas E. Mann and Norman J. Ornstein, eds., *The New Congress* (Washington, D.C.: American Enterprise Institute, 1981).

21. *Congressional Quarterly Weekly Report,* July 28, 1979, p. 1539.

22. Gary Jacobson, *Money in Congressional Elections* (New Haven, Conn.: Yale University Press, 1980).

23. Gary Jacobson and Samuel Kernell, *Strategy and Choice in Congressional Elections* (New Haven, Conn.: Yale University Press, 1982).

24. Richard F. Fenno Jr., *Home Style: House Members in Their Districts* (Boston: Little, Brown, 1978).

25. James H. Kuklinski, "Representativeness and Elections: A Political Analysis," *American Political Science Review* (March 1978), pp. 165–77; and Ryan C. Amacher and William J. Boyes, "Cycles in Senatorial Voting Behavior: Implications for the Optimal Frequency of Elections," *Public Choice* (1978), pp. 5–13.

26. John Jackson, *Constituencies and Leaders in Congress* (Cambridge, Mass.: Harvard University Press, 1974), chap. 5; Keith T. Poole, "Dimensions of Interest Group Evaluation of the U.S. Senate, 1969–1978," *American Journal of Political Science* (February 1981),

pp. 49–67; and Warren Kostroski and Richard Fleisher, "Competing Models of Electoral Linkage: Senatorial Voting Behavior, 1963–1964" (unpublished manuscript, 1977?).

27. H. Douglas Price, " 'Critical Elections' and Party History: A Critical Review," *Polity* (1971), pp. 236–42, at p. 239.

28. Donald R. Matthews, *U.S. Senators and Their World* (Chapel Hill: University of North Carolina Press, 1960), pp. 92–99.

29. David Rohde, Norman Ornstein, and Robert Peabody, "Political Change and Legislative Norms in the U.S. Senate" (paper delivered at the annual meeting of the American Political Science Association, Chicago, 1974); Ross Baker, *Friend and Foe in the U.S. Senate* (New York: Free Press, 1980); and Michael Foley, *The New Senate* (New Haven, Conn.: Yale University Press, 1980).

30. Matthews, *U.S. Senators*, p. 68.

31. John Bibby and Roger Davidson, *On Capitol Hill* (New York: Holt, Rinehart, 1967), p. 51.

32. Matthews, *U.S. Senators*, p. 50; see also Bibby and Davidson, *On Capitol Hill*, p. 52.

33. Robert Salisbury and Kenneth Shepsle, "Congressional Staff Turnover and the Ties-That-Bind," *American Political Science Review* (June 1981), pp. 381–96.

34. Bibby and Davidson, *On Capitol Hill*, p. 52.

35. Matthews, *U.S. Senators*, pp. 234–35.

36. Alan Abramowitz, "Choices and Echoes in the 1978 U.S. Senate Elections: A Research Note," *American Journal of Political Science* (February 1981), pp. 112–18.

6-2

from *Congress: The Electoral Connection*

David R. Mayhew

Many unflattering stereotypes permeate public thinking about members of Congress. Legislators are sometimes viewed as partisans who are preoccupied with scoring political points against the opposition party. At other times, they are treated as ideologues pursuing their personal policy interests at the expense of the nation's collective interest. Sometimes they are even considered to be a special psychological type—power-hungry politicians. In the following essay, David Mayhew explores the implications of a more realistic assumption—that legislators seek reelection. He argues that legislators' efforts to gain reelection produce predictable behavior while in office. In particular, legislators seek to claim credit for legislation that sends money for projects in their constituencies back home, they find taking positions on issues more important than passing bills, and, of course, they advertise themselves.

THE DISCUSSION to come will hinge on the assumption that United States congressmen are interested in getting reelected—indeed, in their role here as abstractions, interested in nothing else. Any such assumption necessarily does some violence to the facts, so it is important at the outset to root this one as firmly as possible in reality. A number of questions about that reality immediately arise.

First, is it true that the United States Congress is a place where members wish to stay once they get there? . . .

In the modern Congress the "congressional career" is unmistakably upon us. Turnover figures show that over the past century increasing proportions of members in any given Congress have been holdovers from previous Congresses—members who have both sought reelection and won it. Membership turnover noticeably declined among southern senators as

Excerpted from David R. Mayhew, *Congress: The Electoral Connection* (New Haven: Yale University Press, 1974), pp. 13–27, 49–77. Copyright 1974 Yale University Press. Reprinted by permission. Notes appearing in the original have been cut.

early as the 1850s, among senators generally just after the Civil War. The House followed close behind, with turnover dipping in the late nineteenth century and continuing to decline throughout the twentieth. Average number of terms served has gone up and up, with the House in 1971 registering an all-time high of 20 percent of its members who had served at least ten terms. It seems fair to characterize the modern Congress as an assembly of professional politicians spinning out political careers. The jobs offer good pay and high prestige. There is no want of applicants for them. Successful pursuit of a career requires continual reelection.

A second question is this: even if congressmen seek reelection, does it make sense to attribute that goal to them to the exclusion of all other goals? Of course the answer is that a complete explanation (if one were possible) of a congressman's or any one else's behavior would require attention to more than just one goal. There are even occasional congressmen who intentionally do things that make their own electoral survival difficult or impossible. . . . The electoral goal has an attractive universality to it. It has to be the *proximate* goal of everyone, the goal that must be achieved over and over if other ends are to be entertained. One former congressman writes, "All members of Congress have a primary interest in getting re-elected. Some members have no other interest." Reelection underlies everything else, as indeed it should if we are to expect that the relation between politicians and public will be one of accountability. What justifies a focus on the reelection goal is the juxtaposition of these two aspects of it—its putative empirical primacy and its importance as an accountability link. . . .

. . . Congressmen must constantly engage in activities related to reelection. There will be differences in emphasis, but all members share the root need to do things—indeed, to do things day in and day out during their terms. The next step here is to present a typology, a short list of the *kinds* of activities congressmen find it electorally useful to engage in. The case will be that there are three basic kinds of activities. . . .

One activity is *advertising,* defined here as any effort to disseminate one's name among constituents in such a fashion as to create a favorable image but in messages having little or no issue content. A successful congressman builds what amounts to a brand name, which may have a generalized electoral value for other politicians in the same family. The personal qualities to emphasize are experience, knowledge, responsiveness, concern, sincerity, independence, and the like. Just getting one's name across is difficult enough; only about half the electorate, if asked, can supply their House members' names. It helps a congressman to be known. . . . A vital advantage enjoyed by House incumbents is that they are much better known among voters than their November challengers. They are better known because they spend a great deal of time, energy, and money trying to make themselves better known. There are standard routines—frequent visits to the constituency, nonpolitical speeches to home audiences, the sending out of infant care booklets and letters of condolence and congratulation. . . . Anniversaries and other events aside, congressional advertising is done largely at public expense. Use of the franking privilege has mushroomed in recent years; in early 1973 one estimate predicted that House and Senate members would send out about 476 million pieces of mail in the year 1974, at a public cost of $38.1 million—or about 900,000 pieces per member with a subsidy of $70,000 per member. By far the heaviest mailroom traffic comes in Octobers of even-numbered years. There are some differences between House and Senate members in the ways they go about getting their names across. House members are free to blanket their constituencies with mailings for all boxholders; senators are not. But senators find it easier to appear on national television—for example, in short reaction statements on the nightly news shows. Advertising is a staple congressional activity, and there is no end to it. For each member there are always new voters to be apprised of his worthiness and old voters to be reminded of it.

A second activity may be called *credit claiming,* defined here as acting so as to generate a belief in a relevant political actor (or actors) that one is personally responsible for causing the government, or some unit thereof, to do something that the actor (or actors) considers desirable. The political logic of this, from the congressman's point of view, is that an actor who believes that a member can make pleasing things happen will no doubt wish to keep him in office so that he can make pleasing things happen in the future. The emphasis here is on individual accomplishment (rather than, say, party or governmental accomplishment) and on the congressman as doer (rather than as, say, expounder of constituency views). Credit claiming is highly important to congressmen, with the consequence that much of congressional life is a relentless search for opportunities to engage in it.

Where can credit be found? If there were only one congressman rather than 535, the answer would in principle be simple enough. Credit (or blame) would attach in Downsian fashion to the doings of the government as a whole. But there are 535. Hence it becomes necessary for each congressman to try to peel off pieces of governmental accomplishment for which he can believably generate a sense of responsibility. For the average congressman the staple way of doing this is to traffic in what may be called "particularized benefits." Particularized governmental benefits, as the term will be used here, have two properties: (1) Each benefit is given out to a specific individual, group, or geographical constituency, the recipient unit being of a scale that allows a single congressman to be recognized (by relevant political actors and other congressmen) as the claimant for the benefit (other congressmen being perceived as indifferent or hostile). (2) Each benefit is given out in apparently ad hoc fashion (unlike, say, social security checks) with a congressman apparently having a hand in the allocation. A particularized benefit can normally be regarded as a member of a class. That is, a benefit given out to an individual, group, or constituency can normally be looked upon by congressmen as one of a class of similar benefits given out to sizable numbers of individuals, groups, or constituencies. Hence the impression can arise that a congressman is getting "his share" of whatever it is the government is offering. (The classes may be vaguely defined. Some state legislatures deal in what their members call "local legislation.")

In sheer volume the bulk of particularized benefits come under the heading of "casework"—the thousands of favors congressional offices perform for supplicants in ways that normally do not require legislative action. High school students ask for essay materials, soldiers for emergency leaves, pensioners for location of missing checks, local governments for grant information, and on and on. Each office has skilled professionals who can play the bureaucracy like an organ—pushing the right pedals to produce the desired effects. But many benefits require new legislation, or at least they require important allocative decisions on matters covered by existent legislation. Here the congressman fills the traditional role of supplier of goods to the home district. It is a believable role; when a member claims credit for a benefit on the order of a dam, he may well receive it. Shiny construction projects seem especially useful. In the decades before 1934, tariff duties for local industries were a major commodity. In recent years awards given under grant-in-aid programs have become more useful as they have become more numerous. Some quests for credit are ingenious; in 1971 the story broke that congressmen had been earmarking foreign aid money for specific projects in Israel in order to win favor with home constituents. It should be said of constituency benefits that congressmen are quite capable of taking the initiative in drumming them up; that is, there can be no automatic assumption that a congressman's activity is the result of pressures brought to bear by organized interests. Fenno shows the importance of member initiative in his discussion of the House Interior Committee.

A final point here has to do with geography. The examples given so far are all of benefits conferred upon home constituencies or recipients therein (the latter including the home residents who applauded the Israeli projects). But the properties of particularized benefits were carefully specified so as not to exclude the possibility that some benefits may be given to recipients outside the home constituencies. Some probably are. Narrowly drawn tax loopholes qualify as particularized benefits, and some of them are probably conferred upon recipients outside the home districts. (It is difficult to find solid evidence on the point.) Campaign contributions flow into districts from the outside, so it would not be surprising to find that benefits go where the resources are.

How much particularized benefits count for at the polls is extraordinarily difficult to say. But it would be hard to find a congressman who thinks he can afford to wait around until precise information is available. The lore is that they count—furthermore, given home expectations, that they must be supplied in regular quantities for a member to stay electorally even with the board. Awareness of favors may spread beyond their recipients, building for a member a general reputation as a good provider. "Rivers Delivers." "He Can Do More For Massachusetts." . . .

. . . Is credit available elsewhere for governmental accomplishments beyond the scale of those already discussed? The general answer is that the prime mover role is a hard one to play on larger matters—at least before broad electorates. A claim, after all, has to be credible. If a congressman goes before an audience and says, "I am responsible for passing a bill to curb inflation," or "I am responsible for the highway program," hardly anyone will believe him. There are two reasons why people may be skeptical of such claims. First, there is a numbers problem. On an accomplishment of a sort that probably engaged the supportive interest of more than one member it is reasonable to suppose that credit should be apportioned among them. But second, there is an overwhelming problem of information costs. For typical voters Capitol Hill is a distant and mysterious place; few have anything like a working knowledge of its maneuverings. Hence there is no easy way of knowing whether a congressman is staking a valid claim or not. The odds are that the information problem cuts in different ways on different kinds of issues. On particularized benefits it may work in a congressman's favor; he may get credit for the dam he had nothing to do with building. Sprinkling a district with dams, after all, is something a congressman is supposed to be able to do. But on larger matters it may work against him. For a voter lacking an easy way to sort out valid from invalid claims the sensible recourse is skepticism. Hence it is unlikely that congressmen get much mileage out of credit claiming on larger matters before broad electorates.

Yet there is an obvious and important qualification here. For many congressmen credit claiming on nonparticularized matters is possible in specialized subject areas because of the congressional division of labor. The term "governmental unit" in the original definition of credit claiming is broad enough to include committees, subcommittees, and the two houses of Congress itself. Thus many congressmen can believably claim credit for blocking bills in subcommittee, adding on amendments in committee, and so on. The audience for transactions of this sort is usually small. But it may include important political actors (e.g., an interest group, the president, the *New York Times,* Ralph Nader) who are capable of both paying Capitol Hill information costs and deploying electoral resources. There is a well-documented example of this in Fenno's treatment of post office politics in the 1960s. The postal employee unions used to watch very closely the activities of the House and Senate Post Office Committees and supply valuable electoral resources (money, volunteer work) to members who did their bidding on salary bills. . . .

The third activity congressmen engage in may be called *position taking,* defined here as the public enunciation of a judgmental statement on anything likely to be of interest to political actors. The statement may take the form of a roll call vote. The most important classes of judgmental statements are those prescribing American governmental ends (a vote cast against the war; a statement that "the war should be ended immediately") or governmental means (a statement that "the way to end the war is to take it to the United Nations"). The judgments may be implicit rather than explicit, as in: "I will support the president on this matter." But judgments may range far beyond these classes to take in implicit or explicit statements on what almost anybody should do or how he should do it: "The great Polish scientist Copernicus has been unjustly neglected"; "The way for Israel to achieve peace is to give up the Sinai." The congressman as position taker is a speaker rather than a doer. The electoral requirement is not that he make pleasing things happen but that he make pleasing judgmental statements. The position itself is the political commodity. Especially on matters where governmental responsibility is widely diffused it is not surprising that political actors should fall back on positions as tests of incumbent virtue. For voters ignorant of congressional processes the recourse is an easy one. . . .

The ways in which positions can be registered are numerous and often imaginative. There are floor addresses ranging from weighty orations to mass-produced "nationality day statements." There are speeches before home groups, television appearances, letters, newsletters, press releases, ghostwritten books, . . . articles, even interviews with political scientists. On occasion congressmen generate what amount to petitions; whether or not to sign the 1956 Southern Manifesto defying school desegregation rulings was an important decision for southern members. Outside the roll call process the congressman is usually able to tailor his positions to suit his audiences. A solid consensus in the constituency calls for ringing declarations; for years the late Senator James K. Vardaman (D., Miss.) campaigned on a proposal to repeal the Fifteenth Amendment. Division or uncertainty in the constituency calls for waffling; in the late 1960s a congressman had to be a poor politician indeed not to be able to come up with an inoffensive statement on Vietnam ("We must have peace with honor at the earliest possible moment consistent with the national interest"). On a controversial issue a Capitol Hill office normally prepares two form letters to send out to constituent letter writers—one for the pros and one (not directly contradictory) for the antis. . . .

. . . Versatility of this sort is occasionally possible in roll call voting. For example a congressman may vote one way on recommittal and the other on final passage, leaving it unclear just how he stands on a bill. Members who cast identical votes on a measure may give different reasons for having done so. Yet it is on roll calls that the crunch comes; there is no way for a member to avoid making a record on hundreds of issues, some of which are controversial in the home constituencies. Of course, most roll call positions considered in isolation are not likely to cause much of a ripple at home. But broad voting patterns can and do; member "ratings" calculated by the Americans for Democratic Action, Americans for Constitutional Action, and other outfits are used as guidelines in the deploying of electoral resources. And particular issues often have their alert publics. Some national interest groups watch the votes of all congressmen on single issues and ostentatiously try to reward or punish members for their positions; over the years some notable examples of such interest groups have been the Anti-Saloon League, the early Farm Bureau, the American Legion, the

American Medical Association, and the National Rifle Association. On rare occasions single roll calls achieve a rather high salience among the public generally. This seems especially true of the Senate, which every now and then winds up for what might be called a "showdown vote," with pressures on all sides, presidential involvement, media attention given to individual senators' positions, and suspense about the outcome. Examples are the votes on the nuclear test-ban treaty in 1963, civil rights cloture in 1964, civil rights cloture again in 1965, the Haynsworth appointment in 1969, the Carswell appointment in 1970, and the ABM in 1970. Controversies on roll calls like these are often relived in subsequent campaigns, the southern Senate elections of 1970 with their Haynsworth and Carswell issues being cases in point.

Probably the best position-taking strategy for most congressmen at most times is to be conservative—to cling to their own positions of the past where possible and to reach for new ones with great caution where necessary. Yet in an earlier discussion of strategy the suggestion was made that it might be rational for members in electoral danger to resort to innovation. The form of innovation available is entrepreneurial position taking, its logic being that for a member facing defeat with his old array of positions it makes good sense to gamble on some new ones. It may be that congressional marginals fulfill an important function here as issue pioneers—experimenters who test out new issues and thereby show other politicians which ones are usable. An example of such a pioneer is Senator Warren Magnuson (D., Wash.), who responded to a surprisingly narrow victory in 1962 by reaching for a reputation in the area of consumer affairs. Another example is Senator Ernest Hollings (D., S.C.), a servant of a shaky and racially heterogeneous southern constituency who launched "hunger" as an issue in 1969—at once pointing to a problem and giving it a useful non-racial definition. One of the most successful issue entrepreneurs of recent decades was the late Senator Joseph McCarthy (R., Wis.); it was all there—the close primary in 1946, the fear of defeat in 1952, the desperate casting about for an issue, the famous 1950 dinner at the Colony Restaurant where suggestions were tendered, the decision that "Communism" might just do the trick.

The effect of position taking on electoral behavior is about as hard to measure as the effect of credit claiming. Once again there is a variance problem; congressmen do not differ very much among themselves in the methods they use or the skills they display in attuning themselves to their diverse constituencies. All of them, after all, are professional politicians. . . .

There can be no doubt that congressmen believe positions make a difference. An important consequence of this belief is their custom of watching each other's elections to try to figure out what positions are salable. Nothing is more important in Capitol Hill politics than the shared conviction that election returns have proven a point. . . .

These, then, are the three kinds of electorally oriented activities congressmen engage in—advertising, credit claiming, and position taking. It remains only to offer some brief comments on the emphases different members give to the different activities. No deterministic statements can be made; within limits each member has freedom to build his own electoral coalition and hence freedom to choose the means of doing it. Yet there are broad patterns. For one thing senators, with their access to the media, seem to put more emphasis on position taking than House members; probably House members rely more heavily on particularized benefits. But there are important differences among House members. Congressmen from the traditional parts of old machine cities rarely advertise and seldom take positions on anything (except on roll calls), but devote a great deal of time and energy to the distribution of benefits. In fact they use their office resources to plug themselves into their local party organizations. . . .

. . . [A] difference appears if the initial assumption of a reelection quest is relaxed to take into account the "progressive" ambitions of some members—the aspirations of some to move up to higher electoral offices rather than keep the ones they have. There are two important subsets of climbers in the Congress—House members who would like to be senators (over the years about a quarter of the senators have come up directly from the House), and senators who would like to be presidents or vice presidents (in the Ninety-third Congress about a quarter of the senators had at one time or another run for these offices or been seriously "mentioned" for them). In both cases higher aspirations seem to produce the same distinctive mix of activities. For one thing credit claiming is all but useless. It does little good to talk about the bacon you have brought back to a district you are trying to abandon. And, as Lyndon Johnson found in 1960, claiming credit on legislative maneuvers is no way to reach a new mass audience; it baffles rather than persuades. Office advancement seems to require a judicious mixture of advertising and position taking. Thus a House member aiming for the Senate heralds his quest with press releases; there must be a new "image," sometimes an ideological overhaul to make ready for the new constituency.

Senators aiming for the White House do more or less the same thing—advertising to get the name across, position taking ("We can do better"). In recent years presidential aspirants have sought Foreign Relations Committee membership as a platform for making statements on foreign policy.

There are these distinctions, but it would be a mistake to elevate them over the commonalities. For most congressmen most of the time all three activities are essential. . . .

6-3

Party Leaders and the New Legislative Process

Barbara Sinclair

In recent years, summit negotiations between the president and top congressional leaders over the budget and other major issues have dominated policy making at the end of the annual sessions of Congress. Intensified partisanship, new issues, divided party control of Congress and the White House, and a reformed decision-making process have altered the context of congressional lawmaking, often contributing to policy deadlock. As a consequence, top party leaders have been forced to assume the role of negotiating the details of public policy. In the following essay, Barbara Sinclair details the recent changes in congressional policy making and provides a glimpse of the way party leaders have adapted to their new policy-making environment. Sinclair shows that few aspects of the policy-making role of committees, parties, and the parent chambers are chiseled in stone. The internal decision-making process of Congress is frequently adjusted as legislators adapt to changing political conditions.

As 1995 DREW to a close, President Bill Clinton, Speaker of the House Newt Gingrich, and Senate Majority Leader Bob Dole sat face-to-face attempting to negotiate a comprehensive budget agreement, a task that entailed making a host of major changes in policy. That this mode of policy making did not strike Americans as particularly out of the ordinary indicates just how much the legislative process has changed in recent years. Although it received less media attention, the legislative process on the budget bill in the months before the summit talks was also far from what would have been considered normal only a few years ago. In both chambers a large number of committees had a hand in drafting the legislation, and the resulting bill was an enormous omnibus measure. In the House, floor procedure was

Originally published in Lawrence C. Dodd and Bruce I. Oppenheimer, eds., *Congress Reconsidered*, 6th edition (Washington, D.C.: CQ Press, 1997), pp. 229–244. Some notes appearing in the original have been cut.

tailored especially to the specific problems this bill raised, and in both chambers majority party leaders were intensely involved throughout the process.

As this example suggests, the how-a-bill-becomes-a-law diagram that is a staple of American government textbooks in reality describes the legislative process on fewer and fewer of the major measures Congress considers. Rather than being sent to one committee in each chamber, a measure may be considered by several committees, and some measures bypass committees altogether. In addition, after a bill has been reported, but before it reaches the floor, substantive changes are often worked out via informal processes. Omnibus measures of great scope are a regular part of the legislative scene, and formal executive–congressional summits to work out deals on legislation are no longer considered extraordinary. On the House floor, most major legislation is considered under complex and usually restrictive rules, often tailored to deal with problems specific to that bill. In the Senate, bills are regularly subject to large numbers of not necessarily germane floor amendments, and filibuster threats are an everyday fact of life, affecting all aspects of the legislative process and making cloture votes a routine part of the process.

This essay explores how and why the legislative process in the U.S. Congress has changed and examines the consequences of that change. Because of their role in the development and deployment of a number of these unorthodox processes, majority party leaders are a special focus of the essay.

The Sources of Change

Why has the legislative process changed in such major ways? I hold that the modifications and innovations are responses to problems and opportunities that members of Congress—as individuals or collectively—confronted, problems and opportunities that arose from changes in institutional structure or challenges in the political environment. Majority party leaders' strivings to meet their members' expectations for legislation were an important but not the only source of procedural innovation, and many but by no means all of the special processes are used at their discretion.

Although the evolution of a new, more varied legislative process was complex, several factors can be isolated as pivotal: internal reforms that changed the distribution of influence in both chambers in the 1970s and a political environment in the 1980s and early 1990s characterized by divided control, big deficits, and ideological hostility to the legislative goals of congressional Democrats.

During the 1970s both the Senate and House distributed internal influence more broadly. As the incentives to exploit fully the great powers Senate rules confer on the individual senator increased in the 1960s and 1970s, the restraint senators had exercised in the use of their prerogatives gave way, and they began to offer more floor amendments and use extended debate—filibusters—more often. As a result, the Senate floor became a more active decision-making arena, and filibusters, or the threat of them, became a routine part of the legislative process.

The change in the Senate's legislative process brought about by senators' greater individualism and activism put heavy demands on party leaders, especially on the majority leader, who is in charge of scheduling legislation for the floor. The majority leader is also expected to help party members pass the legislation they need and want. The change in process increased the majority leader's involvement, often casting him in the role of head negotiator. But the Senate gave the majority leader no new powers to carry out his job.

In the House, reformers redistributed influence through a number of rules changes mostly instituted between 1969 and 1975. Powers and resources were shifted from committee chairs not only down to subcommittee chairs and rank and file members but also up to the party leadership. Junior members gained resources, especially staff, that boosted their ability to participate in the legislative process. The Speaker, as leader of the majority party, was given the power to select the Democratic members of the Rules Committee, a greater say in the assignment of members to other committees, and new powers over the referral of bills.

By reducing the power of the committees and facilitating greater participation by the rank and file, the reforms made legislating more difficult for the majority Democrats. Republicans quickly became adept at using floor amendments to make political points, confronting Democrats with a stream of politically difficult votes. Compromises carefully crafted in committee were being picked apart on the floor, and floor sessions were stretching on interminably.

Democrats began to look to their party leaders, the only central leaders in the chamber, to counter these problems. The leaders responded by innovating in ways that led to alterations in the legislative process. The leadership became more involved with legislation before it reached the floor, at times negotiating postcommittee adjustments to ease its passage. To respond to the barrage of amendments offered on the floor, the leadership developed special rules into devices for structuring floor decision making.

In the 1980s both the House and Senate were feeling the results of the changes in their internal distribution of influence. The highly individualistic Senate, in which each senator was accorded extraordinary latitude, was very good at agenda setting and publicizing problems, but poorly structured for legislative decision making. The House, which had expanded junior members' opportunities for participation, also had problems legislating, although its central leadership had begun to develop reasonably effective responses.

The political climate of the 1980s and early 1990s exacerbated the problems of legislating, especially for the Democratic House. Ronald Reagan was a conservative, confrontational president with policy views far from those of congressional Democrats. George Bush's policy preferences were not much closer. After 1981 large deficits became chronic and severely restricted the policy options seen as feasible. Partisan conflict and stalemate in Washington fed public cynicism about government's ability to handle effectively the problems facing the country. In such a climate the majority Democrats found it difficult to pass legislation they considered satisfactory. Just enacting the legislation necessary to keep the government going was often arduous, first, because of the ideological gulf between the congressional Democrats and the Republican president and, second, because of the unpalatable decisions they had to make.

In the 1980s and 1990s the battles over priorities and deficits were waged within the context of the budget process. Although instituted by the Budget and Impoundment Control Act of 1974, the budget process did not move to center stage until the early 1980s. Since then, the budget process, governed by complex rules and procedures, has had far-reaching effects on the legislative process. One reason is that the Reagan administration's use of it in 1981 showed that the mechanism could be used by central leaders to bring about comprehensive policy change.

The tough climate of the 1980s forced further innovation in the legislative process, especially in the House. Party leaders, as they tried to engineer passage of legislation that would satisfy their members, were more and more drawn into the substantive legislative process; in the House, leaders developed special rules into powerful and flexible tools for structuring floor decisions.

By the early 1990s the usefulness of many of the special processes for enacting legislation had become widely recognized, and congressional leaders continued to use them even though political circumstances changed. As the partisan climate intensified, individuals, especially in the Senate, stepped up their use of processes under their control. The 103d Congress (1993–1994) was the first in twelve years in which both houses of Congress and the White House were controlled by the same party. The 104th (1995–1996) was the first in forty years in which Republicans controlled both chambers. The two Congresses were similar in that both were under intense pressure to produce legislation; in the 103d, Clinton and congressional Democrats needed to show that the Democratic Party could govern; in the 104th, Gingrich and House Republicans needed to deliver on their promises in the Contract with America. The changes in the legislative process discussed here contributed significantly to their considerable success in the House and their lack of it in the Senate.

Omnibus Legislation, the Budget Process, and Summits

Omnibus legislation—bills with great substantive scope often involving, directly or indirectly, many committees—is now a regular part of the congressional agenda. Such measures increased as a proportion of the congressional agenda of major legislation from zero in the 91st Congress (1969–1970) to 8 percent in the 94th (1975–1976)—all budget resolutions—to 20 percent in the 97th (1981–1982) and 100th (1987–1988). In the Congresses of the 1990s, omnibus measures made up about 11 percent of major measures.*

Some omnibus measures are the result of the 1974 budget act. The act requires an annual budget resolution and, in the 1980s and 1990s, the budget resolution often called for a reconciliation bill. Beyond that, the decision

---

* Major legislation is defined as those measures Congressional Quarterly contemporaneously identifies as major legislation plus those measures on which key votes occurred, again according to CQ. This definition yields approximately forty-five to fifty-five major measures per Congress. The following Congresses have been coded: 91st (1969–1970), 94th (1975–1976), 97th (1981–1982), 100th (1987–1988), 101st (1989–1990), and 103d (1993–1994); when data are presented in the text, they are for these Congresses. Data for the 104th are based on all major measures as defined above that received floor consideration in at least one chamber in 1995.

to package legislation into an omnibus measure is discretionary, and it is principally the majority party leadership that decides. Measures may be packaged into an omnibus bill for several reasons: to pass unpalatable but necessary legislation; to force the president to accept legislative provisions that, were they sent to him in freestanding form, he would veto; or to raise the visibility of popular legislation and garner partisan credit. During the Reagan and Bush administrations, for example, House Democratic leaders packaged legislation on issues such as trade and drugs into high-profile omnibus measures to compete with the White House for media attention and public credit and to protect favored provisions from a veto. During the 103d Congress, congressional leaders did not need to pressure President Clinton into signing their legislation, but the usefulness of omnibus measures for enacting tough bills or for raising the visibility of popular measures led to their continued use. A number of modest provisions were packaged into a big anticrime bill, and omnibus budget measures were used to pass Clinton's economic program.

The most important and most prevalent omnibus measures in the 1980s and 1990s were budget related. The deficits that resulted from the Reagan tax cut guaranteed that budget politics would remain at center stage for the foreseeable future. In its attempts to control the deficit, Congress used the budget process, including in the budget resolution instructions to committees to change the laws under their jurisdiction to bring them into line with the budget resolution. The resulting provisions were then packaged into an omnibus reconciliation bill. Because the purpose was deficit reduction, the reconciliation instructions usually required committees to cut spending or raise taxes, confronting them with difficult decisions. Deep policy divisions between Republican presidents and House Democrats exacerbated the difficulties of reaching agreements.

In 1993 and 1995 central leaders used the budget process to try to enact comprehensive policy changes that in both years involved making some very difficult decisions. Clinton's economic program cut the deficit by $500 billion over five years and increased spending on high-priority programs; accomplishing that entailed tax increases, which are never popular, and a cut in spending for numerous lower-priority programs. The Republicans' 1995 program envisioned balancing the budget in seven years while also cutting taxes, which would require draconian cuts in domestic spending. It also included revamping major programs such as Medicare, Medicaid, and welfare. The budget process offered the only realistic hope for enacting either party's proposals. Wrapping the provisions into one omnibus bill cuts down the number of battles that need to be won—an important consideration in a system with a bias toward the status quo. Leaders can ask members to cast a handful of tough votes, but not dozens. With an omnibus bill, the stakes are so high, it is harder for members to vote against their party leaders. In 1993, for example, reluctant Democrats were warned that they would bring down the Clinton presidency if they contributed to the defeat of his economic program. In 1995 Newt Gingrich repeatedly warned his members that the Republican Party's ability to govern was at issue; that his own reputation and clout were at stake was clear to his members.

Divided government brought sharp differences in policy preferences between the president and the congressional majority. Combined with the painful decisions that huge budget deficits dictated, those differences have sometimes stalemated normal legislative processes. But the cost of failing to reach an agreement on budget issues was just too high, so when normal processes, even if supplemented by the more active role of majority party leaders, were incapable of producing legislation, the president and Congress had to find another way. The new device was the summit—relatively formal negotiations between congressional leaders and high-ranking administration officials representing the president or, as in 1995, the president himself. Between 1987 and 1990, four summits took place, and three concerned budget issues. Normal legislative processes foundered in the face of policy disagreements between the Democratic congressional majority and President Reagan in 1987 and between Congress and President Bush in 1989 and 1990, but the threat of severe automatic spending cuts dictated by the Gramm-Rudman Act, or the threat of an economic crisis, or both made a failure to reach agreement too costly. Aid to the Nicaraguan contras, another contentious issue, was the subject of the fourth summit.

When the congressional majority and the president are of the same party, normal processes, supplemented by informal consultation and negotiations, suffice to produce agreement on essential legislation such as budget bills. No summits were needed during the 103d Congress with the Democrats in control of both branches. Normal processes are more likely to fail when both policy and electoral goals are in conflict, as they tend to be when government is divided. The conflict between President Clinton and the conservative new Republican majority in the 104th Congress made agreement impossible through anything approaching normal processes. The Republicans attempted to use various legislative strategies to force

Clinton to accept their priorities: they threatened to include "must pass" legislation, such as the measure to increase the debt limit, in the reconciliation bill, and they sent Clinton appropriations bills with provisions he had vowed to veto, and, when he did, they refused to pass continuing resolutions to keep the government funded. Clearly, a summit was the only hope of resolving the impasse.

This time, however, the differences between the president and the congressional majority were just too great. Although not reaching a comprehensive agreement was costly for both, the compromises such an agreement would have required entailed sacrificing policy principles and the interests of important constituencies for one or both parties and so were more costly than no agreement.

New Processes and Procedures as Leadership Tools in the House

Traditionally, the legislative process would begin with the referral of a bill to a single committee, which would be largely responsible for its fate. In 1995 the Republicans' bill to abolish the Commerce Department was referred to eleven House committees. Although the number of committees was unusual, the fact that more than one committee was involved was not. In the contemporary House about one bill in five is referred to more than one committee. Major legislation is even more likely to be sent to several committees; between 1987 and 1995, about a third was.

Multiple referral of legislation was not possible before 1975, when the House passed a rule providing for it. The new rule came about for two reasons: the House's inability to realign outdated committee jurisdictions and reform-minded members' desire to increase opportunities for broad participation in the legislative process. The rule was amended in 1977 to give the Speaker the power to set deadlines for committees to report legislation. As revised in 1995, the rule directs the Speaker to designate a lead committee with the most responsibility for the legislation; once that committee has reported, the other committees are required to report under fairly strict deadlines.

For the Speaker, the frequency with which major legislation is multiply referred presents opportunities, but also problems. One problem is that when legislation is referred to several committees, the number of people who must come to agreement is multiplied, complicating and slowing down the legislative process. Often, multiple referral forces the Speaker to be the jurisdictional and substantive mediator, a role that brings with it influence as well as headaches. On contentious legislation, the leaders of the several committees involved may not be able to work out their differences without help. If the party leaders have to get involved, they gain influence over the substance of the legislation. Furthermore, when several committees work on the same piece of legislation, the committee process is more open to influence by party leaders; no one committee can consider such a bill its private business. Multiple referral also gives the Speaker the opportunity to set time limits for the reporting out of legislation. During the first one hundred days of the 104th Congress, when the new Republican majority was attempting to bring all the items in the Contract with America to the floor, that power gave added weight to Speaker Gingrich's stringent informal deadlines.

Although legislation is routinely considered by more than one committee, sometimes bills bypass committee consideration altogether. Skipping committee review was a rare occurrence before the 1980s; for example, in 1969 and 1970 and in 1975 and 1976, committees were bypassed on only 2 percent of the major legislation. By the late 1980s, however, almost 20 percent of major measures were never considered by a committee in the House. The frequency dropped to 6 percent in the 103d Congress; it then rose to 11 percent in 1995, but, as we shall see, that relatively low rate is somewhat misleading.

To force legislation to the floor for consideration, a majority of the House membership can bypass a nonresponsive committee by using the discharge procedure. Any member may file a discharge petition, and, when half the House members—218—have signed the petition, the measure is taken away from the committee and considered on the floor. In the 97th Congress, the 102d (1991–1992), and again in the 103d, a constitutional amendment to require a balanced federal budget was brought to the floor through the discharge procedure. Each time, the committee of jurisdiction—the House Judiciary Committee—opposed the measure and had refused to consider or report it. The discharge route, however, is seldom successful.

The majority party leadership usually makes the decision to bypass a committee, but the rationale for doing so varies widely. In early 1987, at the beginning of the 100th Congress, the Democratic Party leadership brought two big bills—a clean water bill and a highway–mass transit bill—directly to the floor because it wanted to score some quick victories. Both had gone through the full committee process and had passed by large margins in the preceding Congress, but had died because of President Reagan's opposition.

In some rare cases, the majority party leadership believes the issue to be too politically delicate for the committee or committees of jurisdiction to handle. In 1988 Speaker Jim Wright, D-Texas, entrusted the drafting of the House Democrats' plan for contra aid to a task force headed by the deputy whip; no committee was involved. The political risks inherent in opposing the president on a highly visible foreign policy issue, as House Democrats were doing, were too great to leave the decision making to a committee.

On the first day of the 104th Congress, knowing that press coverage would be at a maximum, the new Republican leadership wanted to make a big splash. The House passed the Congressional Accountability Act, which applied a number of federal laws to Congress itself. The bill was a part of the Contract with America, and it had passed the House during the previous Congress. Most of the items in the Republicans' contract went through the formal committee process—if very quickly—but they had actually been drafted before Congress began (the contract was put together in the summer of 1994), and the Republican leadership was unwilling to brook changes of any magnitude. The unfunded mandates bill, for example, was referred to four committees on January 4, the first day of the session. The Government Reform and Oversight Committee ordered it reported on January 10, having spent one meeting, its first of the session, marking up the bill; the Rules Committee followed suit two days later; on January 19 floor consideration began. The Republicans' promise of action on all the items in the first one hundred days allowed for little real deliberation in committee, and the leaders feared Republicans would be accused of not keeping their promises if significant changes were made.

This method of passing legislation is a radical change from the way things used to be done. In the prereform House, autonomous committees crafted legislation behind closed doors and usually passed it unchanged on the floor with little help from the party leadership. As a matter of fact, party leadership intrusion into the legislative process on matters of substance was considered illegitimate. As House members became less willing to defer to committees and more willing to question committee bills on the floor, as multiple referral destroyed committees' monopoly over legislation in their area of jurisdiction, and as the political climate became harsher and the political stakes higher, committees became less capable of crafting legislation that could pass the chamber without help. In responding to their members' demands for assistance, majority party leaders were drawn more deeply into the substantive aspects of the legislative process and, in effect, changed how the process works. Now party leaders often involve themselves well before legislation is reported from committee.

Moreover, party leaders frequently take a role in working out substantive adjustments to legislation *after* it has been reported from committee. In the prereform 91st Congress, no major legislation was subject to such postcommittee adjustments; in the 94th, 4 percent was—all budget resolutions. In the early 1980s, the frequency jumped to almost one major measure in four and, in the late 1980s and early 1990s, averaged a little more than one in three. In 1995 almost half of major measures underwent some sort of postcommittee adjustment.

When party leaders become involved in making postcommittee adjustments to legislation, their objective is to craft a bill that most majority party members can support and one that can pass the House. They may also want to amass enough votes to deter a veto or to send a message to the Senate. In addition, leaders must make sure that the legislation is defensible in the court of public opinion, that it enhances rather than harms the party's image.

Controversy and saliency often prompt the need for postcommittee adjustments. Supporters may find that their bill as it emerged from committee does not command enough votes to pass. For example, the leadership found that a majority of the House considered the 1988 welfare reform bill too expensive as reported from committee. The leaders realized the bill would be radically amended or fail if it went to the floor without change. This was a bill that many Democrats were committed to, that the committees had put a great deal of effort and time into drafting, and that the leadership believed would enhance the party's image. It could not just be allowed to die. After extensive negotiations, the leadership came up with a strategy: an amendment would be offered to cut the program enough to satisfy those Democrats who believed they needed to vote for cuts, but not so much that the legislation's erstwhile supporters could no longer vote for it. The amendment was offered on the floor and, once it passed, the bill did also.

During Clinton's first two years as president, the House leadership found it necessary to make some minor postcommittee adjustments to amass the necessary support for several of his programs; the national service program and the Goals 2000 education legislation, for example, required such fine-tuning. On the most important legislation of his second year, however, even major adjustments were not enough to win the day. Different versions of comprehensive health care legislation were reported by three committees (one committee reported two bills), and the party leadership attempted to put together a single bill that could pass, but was unsuccessful. The issue and the Clinton approach had become too controversial.

In the 104th Congress, the Republican majority leadership often found it necessary to make postcommittee adjustments in legislation. To pass a big rescission bill (a bill cutting already appropriated spending) in 1995, the leadership had to agree to drop restrictive anti-abortion language and to accept a "lockbox" provision mandating that the savings go to deficit reduction, not to fund tax cuts. The first was necessary to get the votes of GOP moderates, the second to pick up some votes from conservative Democrats. When the constitutional amendment imposing term limits on members of Congress emerged from the Judiciary Committee in a form that the majority of Republicans found unacceptable, the Rules Committee, at the direction of the leadership, dropped the committee draft and substituted another version.

Legislation that is multiply referred often requires postcommittee adjustments. When the committees involved cannot come to an agreement among themselves, the party leadership may have to negotiate enough of an agreement to avoid a bloody battle on the House floor. In 1990 the Ways and Means Committee and the Education and Labor Committee shared jurisdiction over child care legislation. The two committees took very different approaches to the problem and failed to reach an agreement. The party leadership intervened to break the stalemate, and that intervention involved making substantive adjustments to the legislation. In 1995 the House leadership produced a welfare reform bill by combining bills passed by three committees and, in the process, altered some controversial provisions.

The House considers most major legislation under a special rule that sets the conditions for floor debate. The variety in contemporary rules means that the legislative process differs quite substantially depending upon the choice of rule. Rules differ in many ways, but the most important is how amendments are to be treated. Rules can range from allowing no amendments, in which case the legislative battle is focused solely on the measure (or sometimes on the rule) and is clearly defined in time, to allowing all germane amendments, meaning that the amending process may stretch on for days and be unpredictable. Rules also can make otherwise nongermane amendments in order. Many rules allow some but not all germane amendments—sometimes listing them, sometimes requiring they be printed in the *Congressional Record* before floor consideration begins, and sometimes allowing all germane amendments that can be offered in a given time.

In the contemporary House, major legislation is likely to be brought to the floor under a complex, restrictive rule. In the prereform era, only tax bills were considered under a closed rule that allowed no amendments. As late as the 95th Congress (1977–1978), 85 percent of the rules were open, meaning that all germane amendments were allowed. As legislation became more vulnerable to alteration on the floor, Democrats began demanding that their leadership use the control over the Rules Committee they had been given in the reform era to protect legislation and, where possible, to shield members from having to cast difficult votes. In response, the Democratic leadership began to use restrictive rules more frequently. Rules that restrict the offering of germane amendments accounted for two-thirds of the rules granted for initial consideration of legislation in the 102d Congress and for 70 percent in the 103d.

When only major measures are examined, the trend is even stronger. In the 1970s more than 80 percent of the rules for major legislation were simple open rules. In the early 1980s about 60 percent of major measures received simple open rules; the rest were considered under closed or, more frequently, some form of hybrid complex rule. By the late 1980s and continuing in the 1990s, 75 percent or more of major measures were considered under complex (or, rarely, closed) rules. From the early 1980s on, almost all the complex rules restrict amending activity.

During the 1980s and early 1990s Democratic Party leaders developed special rules into powerful, flexible tools that can be tailored to the problem a particular bill presents. A rule that restricts amendments in any way reduces uncertainty and gives the bill's proponents the advantage. Strategy can be planned more efficiently. Carefully crafted rules can sometimes structure choices to bring about a particular outcome. . . . Most Democrats—enough to constitute a clear majority of the House—favored passing a welfare reform bill; they believed it constituted good public policy. Many, however, believed that for reelection reasons they had to go on record as favoring a reduction in what the program was going to cost. By allowing a vote on an amendment to make moderate cuts, but barring one on an amendment that slashed the program, the rule gave members the opportunity to demonstrate fiscal responsibility but ensured that legislation most Democrats favored would be enacted.

The power and flexibility of special rules as they have evolved make them useful in many circumstances. The uncertainty that the 1970s reforms begot and the problems that majority Democrats faced in legislating during the adverse political climate of the 1980s and early 1990s stimulated their development. But the upward trend in the use of special rules did not end when political circumstances changed. The legislative opportunity and the pressure to deliver under difficult circumstances that the election of a Democratic president represented led the Democratic leadership to intensify its employment of such rules during the 103d Congress.

The rule for the reconciliation bill implementing Clinton's economic program in 1993 provides an example of how useful a strategically structured rule can be. That rule allowed a vote only on a comprehensive Republican substitute; amendments to delete various unpopular elements of the package—the BTU tax and the tax on high income recipients' Social Security payments—were not made in order. Passage was crucial for the young Clinton administration and for the Democratic Party, but the constraints imposed by the huge deficit and the need to reduce it made it difficult to put a package together and hold it together. The rule was intended to focus debate on the broad philosophical differences between the two parties' approaches to the problem of reducing the deficit and to protect Democrats from having to cast one tough vote after another. Many would have found it hard to explain to the folks back home why they had voted against amendments striking unpopular tax provisions, especially in response to thirty-second attack ads. If the Republicans were allowed to offer amendments, the Democrats would be forced to choose between casting a series of politically dangerous votes or letting a carefully constructed compromise—the passage of which, most believed, was crucial to the future of the country and the party—be picked apart on the floor.

When in the minority, Republicans had labeled restrictive rules dictatorial and illegitimate and had promised not to use them if they took control. In the 104th Congress, however, they were committed to passing an ambitious agenda in a short time. The usefulness of restrictive rules for promoting the party's legislative objectives overcame any Republican objections based on principle or the fear of seeming hypocritical. To be sure, the restrictions were sometimes of a different nature: Republicans often limited amending activity by restricting the time for consideration rather than specifying the number or kind of amendments that could be offered. Overall, the proportion of restrictive rules declined. In 1995 about half of all rules for the initial consideration of legislation were restrictive. However, when only major measures are considered, the picture is different; in 1995, 77 percent of rules for the consideration of major measures were restrictive.

In 1995 Republicans used a cleverly constructed restrictive rule to protect their rescission bill. It specified that anyone wishing to restore a spending cut in the bill had to offset the cost by cutting something else in the same section of the bill; in other words, no money could be transferred to social programs from defense spending or from disaster relief for California.

The Triumph of Individualism and the New Legislative Process in the Senate

The contemporary legislative process in the Senate is shaped by senators' rampant individualism and their leaders' attempts to do their jobs within that context. Senators now routinely exploit the enormous prerogatives Senate rules give the individual to further their own agendas.

In an institutional setting where every member is able—and often willing—to impede the legislative process, leaders must accommodate individual members to legislate successfully. The increase in postcommittee adjustments to legislation in the Senate reflects this accommodation. Rare in the 1970s even on major legislation—only 2 percent of major measures underwent postcommittee adjustments in the 91st and 94th Congresses— the frequency jumped to about 20 percent in the 1980s and then to more than 33 percent in the early 1990s. In 1995 more than 60 percent of major legislation was subject to postcommittee adjustments. Although the negotiations that produce these modifications are sometimes undertaken by committee leaders or other interested senators, the party leaders often become involved.

Senate individualism is most evident on the floor. Senators can use their power to offer as many amendments as they choose to almost any bill, not only to further their policy preferences but also to bring up issues leaders might like to keep off the floor, to make political points, and to force their political opponents in the chamber to cast tough votes. Senators regularly use their amending prerogatives for all these purposes. Because, in most cases, amendments need not be germane, Barbara Boxer, D-Calif., was able to force onto the floor the issue of holding open hearings on the sexual harassment charges against Bob Packwood, R-Ore., even though Majority Leader Dole wanted to keep it off. Boxer offered it as an amendment to a defense authorization bill. For years, Jesse Helms, R-N.C., has been bringing up and forcing votes on amendments on hot button issues such as abortion, pornography, homosexuality, and school prayer. He often does not expect to win, but to provide ammunition for the electoral opponents of senators who disagree with him.

Senators' use of their amending prerogatives has resulted in many bills being subjected to a barrage of amendments on the floor. In the 1950s the proportion of legislation subject to high amending activity (ten or more amending roll calls) was tiny: for the 84th (1953–1954) and 86th (1959–1960) Congresses, it averaged 2.7 percent. In the 1960s and 1970s it rose to a mean of 8.2 percent per Congress, and in the 1980s it averaged 14.9 percent. In the 1980s and 1990s major legislation was considerably more likely to be subject to such amending marathons; on about 30 percent of major legislation, more than ten amendments were offered on the floor and pushed to a roll call vote.

Bills that are controversial or broad in scope or that, at least in the view of the majority party, have to pass are most likely to be the target of large numbers of amendments. For example, more than forty amendments were offered and pushed to a recorded vote on each of the following: the Democrats' major trade bill in 1988, the 1993 budget resolution that carried Clinton's economic program, and the Republicans' unfunded mandates bill in 1995. Such high amending activity presents problems for the Senate as a legislature and for its majority leadership, which is charged with floor scheduling and coalition building. It creates uncertainty about the schedule and about policy outcomes. How long floor consideration of a contentious measure will take may be impossible to predict. Under a barrage of amendments, compromises can be difficult to hold together. Opponents, after all, attempt to write amendments that will split the majority coalition. The majority leader has no mechanism such as the House special rule that can be used to fend off these amendments.

To lend some predictability to floor proceedings, the majority leader frequently negotiates unanimous consent agreements to govern the consideration of major legislation. Such an agreement limits floor time and may limit the amendments allowed; however, one senator's objection can kill a proposed unanimous consent agreement, so all senators' interests must be accommodated.

Senators' willingness to use their privilege of unlimited debate has had a major impact on the legislative process in the Senate. In the 1950s, filibusters occurred at a rate of about one per Congress; the rate rose to just under five per Congress in the 1960s and continued to rise at an accelerated pace in the 1970s and 1980s. The 103d Congress saw thirty filibusters. Major legislation often encounters some extended debate-related problem identifiable from the public record. In the late 1980s and early 1990s just under 30 percent did; in the first Congress of the Clinton presidency, almost 50 percent of major measures encountered such problems, and in 1995, 44 percent did.

Written into the budget act are rules limiting debate on budget resolutions and reconciliation bills. Because such measures are protected from a filibuster, they become even more attractive as a vehicle for major policy change. The budget act, however, also restricts that strategy through the Byrd rule, named for Sen. Robert Byrd, D-W.Va. The rule prohibits "extraneous matter" in a reconciliation bill.

Given senators' willingness to exploit their right of extended debate, the majority leader, in scheduling legislation and often in crafting it, has little choice but to be responsive to small groups of members or even to individuals. On legislation of secondary importance, before a recess, or late in the session, one senator's objection will suffice to keep a bill off the floor. When a great deal of legislation is awaiting floor consideration, the majority leader cannot afford the time for a filibuster, so even an ambiguous threat to filibuster serves as a veto. This reality has become semi-institutionalized in the practice of holds. Any senator can inform the leader that he or she wishes to place a hold on a measure—a bill, a presidential nomination, or a treaty. Leaders assert that use of this device only guarantees that the senator will be informed before the measure is scheduled for floor consideration; however, if the hold represents a veiled threat to filibuster the measure and if other matters are more pressing, it often constitutes a de facto veto.

The mere threat to filibuster is often sufficient to extract concessions from the supporters of a measure. A number of the Contract with America items that sped through the House were held up in the Senate until their supporters made significant compromises—for example, a bill to impose a moratorium on all new regulations was transformed, under a filibuster threat, into a measure giving Congress forty-five days to review new regulations. In the 103d Congress a number of Clinton's priorities also ran into troubles in the Senate, not because they lacked the support of a majority but because the sixty votes to cut off debate could not be amassed. Supporters had to make concessions on national service legislation and the voter registration bill (motor voter), for example, to overcome a filibuster or a filibuster threat.

Sometimes a large minority defeats outright legislation supported by a majority. Clinton's stimulus package succumbed to this fate in 1993. Senate Majority Leader George Mitchell, D-Maine, attempted to invoke cloture a number of times, but, even though majorities supported cutting off debate, he was not able to put together the necessary sixty votes. In 1995 Senate Democrats forced Majority Leader Dole to abandon his own bill overhauling federal regulatory procedures; he mustered a majority on several cloture votes but fell short of the sixty needed. In the 103d Congress, of nineteen major measures that failed to become law, twelve were killed by the Senate alone; eight of those ran into filibuster-related problems.

The majority leader's leverage depends not on procedural powers, of which he has few, but on his central position in the chamber; on really difficult and contentious issues, he has a better chance than anyone else in the chamber of negotiating a deal that can get the necessary votes. Consequently his leverage is dependent on senators wanting legislation, but if a substantial minority prefers no legislation to a deal, he has little recourse.

New Legislative Processes: An Assessment

By the end of the first hundred days of the 104th Congress, the House had voted on every measure in the Contract with America, as Republicans had promised, and had passed all but the term limits constitutional amendment, which required a two-thirds vote. In the Senate only five measures—some parts of the preface and of two of the ten planks of the contract—had reached the floor, and only four, mostly relatively uncontroversial measures, had passed. By the end of 1995 just five contract items had become law.

The contract items fared differently in the House and Senate in part because the distribution of preferences differed in the two chambers: moderates made up a larger proportion of the Senate Republican membership than of the House Republican membership, and Senate Republicans had not endorsed the contract. Even more important, however, are the differences in chamber rules and in the tools leaders have available. In the House many of the modifications and innovations in the legislative process allow the party leadership to tailor the process to the problems a particular measure raises and use them to get the measure passed. In the Senate changes in the legislative process have created more problems than opportunities for the majority party leadership.

A brief examination of the legislative process on welfare reform, one of the major contract items, illustrates the differences. In the House three committees—Ways and Means, Education and Economic Opportunity, and Agriculture—reported their provisions by early March. Under strict instructions from the party leadership, Republican committee chairs had pushed the measures through their committees with limited debate and on largely party line votes. The leadership then combined the provisions from the three committees, making alterations where they seemed advisable. The bill was brought to the floor under a tight rule barring votes on several amendments that would have split Republicans. Pro-life Republicans, who feared that provisions cutting off benefits to teenage unwed mothers would encourage abortions, were denied a chance to offer amendments deleting such provisions. The rule was narrowly approved, and the bill passed on a 234–199 party line vote.

The Senate Finance Committee did not report a bill until May 26. Problems within the majority party quickly became apparent: Republicans from the South and Southwest, who represent fast-growing states that offer relatively low welfare benefits, objected to funding formulas based on past welfare expenditures; some conservative senators decried the dropping of House provisions barring unwed teenage mothers from receiving welfare; and Republican moderates believed the legislation did not provide enough money for child care and would allow states to cut their own welfare spending too much.

Because of the saliency and hot-button character of the issue, no one, including most Democrats, wanted to vote against a welfare reform bill, and, had the Republican leadership been able to force an up-or-down vote, the committee bill might well have passed. But because Dole had no way of protecting the legislation from a filibuster or a barrage of amendments on the floor, he had to deal. He, along with Finance Committee Chairman Packwood, took on the task of rewriting the bill. In early August, after several months of negotiations, Dole unveiled a revised bill aimed at satisfying the various factions. The new proposal was a modified version of the Finance Committee bill and incorporated in revised form three other pieces of legislation—the food stamps overhaul from the Agriculture Committee and the child care and job training bills approved by the Labor and Human Resources Committee. Adding these provisions provided a greater scope for compromise.

Floor debate began August 7, and it soon became evident that problems still existed and the bill would not pass before the scheduled recess. Republicans blamed the Democrats, charging that they intended to offer fifty amendments. In fact, the GOP was still split. On September 6, after the recess, Dole brought the bill back to the floor, but he still lacked a secure winning coalition and continued to make changes to placate various groups of Republicans. He began talking with Democrats and moderate Republicans, and on September 15 a compromise was reached; among other provisions, it added substantial funds for child care. On September 19 Dole offered for himself and the minority leader the Dole-Daschle amendment, which incorporated the compromise, and it passed, 87–12, with mostly hardline conservative Republicans opposed. Acceptance of the amendment moderated the Senate welfare bill, which was already more moderate than the House bill. The Senate passed the bill as amended 87 to 12, with only one Republican voting in opposition.

In the House, then, the new legislative process has on balance provided the majority party leadership with effective tools for facilitating the passage of legislation. Backed by a reasonably cohesive majority party, House leaders can engineer passage of legislation quickly and in a form consonant with the preferences of the members of the majority party. In the Senate, as in the House, the party leadership has become more central to the legislative process, but, unlike the Speaker, the Senate majority leader has gained few new tools for dealing with a more unruly membership. The need to accommodate most senators and to build supermajority coalitions to pass legislation in the Senate almost always means the process is slower and often results in more broadly based (or weakening) compromises. Sometimes, it results in no legislation at all. In the contemporary Congress, the legislative process in the two chambers is more distinct in form and in results than ever before.

6-4

Toward More Accountable Members

Fred R. Harris

*Public interest in term limits for members of Congress has faded in re-
cent years. The Supreme Court has ruled that states cannot impose term
limits on their own congressional delegations. To institute such limits,
proponents would have to amend the Constitution, but they have been
unable to muster the two-thirds majority in both houses of Congress
necessary to recommend a constitutional amendment. For the time
being, reformers have few options. Yet the issues raised in the debate
about term limits remain very much alive. In the following essay, former
New Mexico senator Fred Harris argues that the Framers were right in
opposing term limits. In Harris's view, too much of what is good about
the modern Congress would be lost if term limits were imposed.*

JAMES MADISON wrote in *Federalist 57* that the aim of a country's constitution should be, first, "to obtain for rulers, men who possess most wisdom to
discern, and most virtue to pursue the common good of society" and, then,
"to take the most effectual precautions for keeping them virtuous." Madison believed that the best precaution for keeping members of the House of
Representatives virtuous was to require all of them to stand for election
every two years. Election, he wrote, is "the characteristic policy of republican government."

Members of the Senate were also meant to be accountable to the people,
of course, though initially only indirectly; senators were at first chosen by
state legislatures. But the Seventeenth Amendment, adopted in 1913, provided that senators, too, should be elected directly (though still only a third
of them each two years and all for six-year terms).

Two presumptions underlie such a system of holding senators and representatives accountable through periodic elections: first, the presumption

Excerpted from Fred R. Harris, *In Defense of Congress* (New York: St. Martin's Press, 1995).
Reprinted with permission of Bedford/St. Martin's Press, Inc. Copyright © December 1999 by Bed-
ford/St. Martin's Press, Inc. Some notes appearing in the original have been cut.

that the voters will be able to get the information they need to judge the performance and virtues of incumbent members of Congress, and second, the presumption that sitting senators and representatives will be electorally challengeable, that there will, in other words, be a real potential for competitive elections. Until the congressional reforms of the 1970s, the first presumption about voter access to information remained far from realization. Congress was a very closed institution. First, unrecorded voice votes and teller votes were commonplace in the House of Representatives. Unless citizens happened to be in the House gallery when such a vote was taken, they usually had no way of knowing how a particular representative voted.

Second, prior to the 1970s reforms, mark-up sessions in congressional committees and subcommittees—where the crucial final decisions are taken on amendments to pending legislation and on whether to report the legislation to the full House or Senate—were closed as a matter of course. Thus what individual senators and representatives did in their committees, how they voted, went largely unreported and unnoticed. Further, television cameras were not allowed into even the *public* hearings of House committees, nor were they allowed to cover the full sessions of either chamber.

All that changed, as Congress began to apply sunshine laws to itself. House rules were amended to require recorded votes, and a system of public, electronic voting was also adopted in that body. Committee and subcommittee mark-up sessions in both houses were opened up to the public as a matter of routine, and radio and television were allowed to cover such sessions, the same as the writing press could. The Senate and House began to televise their plenary sessions, too.

Congress became much more open to the public and the press, then, just at a time, incidentally, when the public was becoming more attentive to congressional operations. Simultaneously, there were two significant developments in the press: an enormous growth in the number of reporters covering Congress and the assumption by reporters of a much more aggressive role.

In the sixteen years between 1960 and 1976, for example, the number of radio and television journalists reporting on Congress tripled, and the number of print journalists increased by a third. This kind of growth continued so that by the mid-1980s, around ten thousand reporters were working in Washington.

Nationally, both the number and length of television network news programs expanded. Cable news networks were launched. Continuous, twenty-four-hour-a-day radio and television news programs appeared. Two new national cable channels began to cover Congress live. Local newspapers and television stations opened their own Washington bureaus or hired stringers for regular capital reports.

The number of spotlights on Congress multiplied and so did their intensity. "In the old days," former Senate parliamentarian Floyd Riddick said, "no reporter would dare stop a senator on his way to or from the Senate and ask for a comment. The Senator would have said, 'See me in my office.' Senators are now more accessible." Representatives are, too. And nothing—neither public decision making nor personal peccadillos—is off limits for today's reporters.

It is much more likely, these days, that U.S. voters will get the information they need to judge senators and representatives at election time. But, if the voters are dissatisfied because of what they know, can they really do anything about it? Critics say that the answer is often no, that frequently no real electoral challenge or competition exists, because the incumbent has too great an advantage.

Abuse of the franking privilege and the use of staff for campaign purposes are listed as two "grossly unfair" advantages enjoyed by congressional incumbents. After reporting on a 1992 ABC News "Nightline" show that a former congressional aid "says almost all congresspeople and senators regularly abuse the franking privilege, just as he says almost all of them use their professional staffers to campaign," television journalist Dave Marash concluded on his own that Congress thereby "buys itself a better chance to get reelected" and that, thus, "the biggest cost of keeping Congress may not be to taxpayers, but to democracy."

House and Senate campaigns cost tremendous amounts of money today, and incumbents have a much better chance of raising it than potential challengers do. This advantage is seen by congressional critics not only as an enormous one for the incumbent, making real electoral competition more unlikely, but also as a source of potential corruption of senators and representatives, making them too beholden to the special interests. And critics also charge that the ethics of many members of Congress are somewhere between questionable and rotten.

A burgeoning and increasingly vociferous group of anti-Congress activists say that a quick cure-all that they advocate would deal with all these problems at once: the imposition of limits on how long each senator and representative can serve in Congress.

Term Limits

The term limit movement has a decidedly conservative and Republican cast, and it springs from a kind of throw-the-rascals-out disapproval of Congress *as a whole,* as an institution. Never mind that nothing about term limits would prevent the voters from electing new senators and representatives just as "bad" as those that limited terms would discard. Never mind, either, as James Sundquist said, that the voters of each district and state can already reject their *own* members of Congress:

> Each voter can act to throw out one rascal, but the others are beyond reach. And it is the others who have aroused the citizens; the single one on whom the individual voter is permitted to pass judgment is, in all likelihood, one with whom he or she usually agrees and who is often, too, a friend, neighbor, or at least a casual acquaintance to whom the citizen has access when it may be needed, and one who may have brought tangible benefits to the state or district—and, with reelection and greater seniority, will be able to bring more.[1]

Antagonism in Colorado toward Congress as a whole caused that state to be the first, in 1990, to adopt term limits for its own U.S. senators and representatives. The voters in fourteen other states adopted similar congressional term limits two years later, in the elections of November 1992. Despite such growing support, the idea of term limits is still one whose time has not yet—and should never—come. In the first place, it is unconstitutional.

The Founders' Decision against Term Limits

Legislative term limits, or "rotation" in office, as it was then called, was neither a new nor acceptable concept for the Founders when they met in Philadelphia in 1787. Thirty-two of the thirty-nine eventual signers of the Constitution had earlier been delegates at one time or another to the old Continental Congress, in which, under the Articles of Confederation, service had been limited to "three years in any term of six years." The Founders knew that the old Congress had gotten itself into such a bitter internal fight in 1784 over the question of enforcing these term limits against sitting members that the whole matter had had to be dropped.

The Founders decided against term limits for federal officials, and later argued against them in the ratification fight, on three grounds. First, they did so because term limits would be an unreasonable restriction on the power of the people—would unacceptably "abridge the privilege of the people," as Roger Sherman put it.[2] Robert R. Livingston made the same argument when he wrote: "The people are the best judges of who ought to represent them. To dictate and control them, to tell them whom they shall not elect, is to abridge their natural rights."[3]

Second, the Founders argued that term limits for federal officials, by limiting reelection possibilities, would reduce incentive for good conduct in office. Limiting terms "would be a diminution of the inducements to good behavior," according to Alexander Hamilton,[4] would "remove one great motive to fidelity in office," as Roger Sherman put it.[5] Robert R. Livingston stated the argument even more strongly: "This rotation is an absurd species of ostracism—a mode of proscribing eminent merit, and banishing from stations of trust those who have filled them with the greatest faithfulness. Besides it takes away the strongest stimulus to public virtue—the hopes of honors and rewards."[6]

The third argument of the Founders against term limits was that they would deny people the right to retain experienced public officials, as Livingston had said, and would "render persons incapable of serving in offices, on account of their experience, which would best qualify them for usefulness in office," as Roger Sherman wrote.[7]

Can States Adopt Term Limits?

Since the writers of the Constitution, then, unlike those who drafted the earlier Articles of Confederation, rejected term limits, can states, by amendments to their own constitutions, now adopt limits on how long their members of Congress can serve? The U.S. Supreme Court has never squarely decided this question, but it is fairly clear that the answer should be no. The Court may soon have to face the issue. The League of Women Voters, joined by Democratic U.S. House Speaker Thomas Foley of Washington, has filed a lawsuit in federal court to nullify the 1992 initiative adopted in Foley's home state that would limit the terms of that state's members of Congress.[8]

The U.S. Constitution, in Article I, Sections 2 and 3, is quite specific about the requisite qualifications for serving in the U.S. House and Senate, in each case prescribing only requirements of age, citizenship, and residence. Senators and representatives must be "inhabitants" of the states from which they are elected. A representative must be at least twenty-five years of age and must have been a U.S. citizen for at least seven years. A senator must be at least thirty years old and at least nine years a citizen. Section 4 of the same article gives the state legislatures the power to decide only on the "times, places, and manner of holding elections" for senators and representatives (subject to change in such regulations by Congress). Section 5 makes each house of Congress the sole judge of the "elections, returns, and qualifications" of its own members.

Can a state require a certain number of voter signatures on a petition for a person to become a candidate for the House or Senate, regulate political party nominations generally, and prohibit, say, a person from running as an independent candidate who has been affiliated with a political party within the preceding year? Certainly, it can. Such state laws are "an essential part of its overall mechanism" of traditional election regulation, and, as such, are permissible under the U.S. Constitution.[9]

But suppose the declaration of candidacy form for the U.S. House of Representatives from Washington state, for example, were to call not only for affirmations that the prospective candidate meets the constitutional age, citizenship, and residency qualifications for the office, but also were to require a fourth affirmation, such as, "I certify that I have not previously served twelve or more years as a member of the U.S. House of Representatives"?

That new requirement would obviously amount to more than mere state "regulation" of elections. It would constitute an additional qualification for the office, and a state has no power to add new qualifications for membership in the U.S. House and Senate to those already set forth in the U.S. Constitution. Constitutional experts such as Duke University law professor Walter Dellinger hold this view.[10]

In the 1969 case of *Powell v. McCormack*,[11] the U.S. Supreme Court recounted how those who wrote the U.S. Constitution considered, and rejected, any qualifications for the U.S. Senate and House of Representatives other than those related to age, citizenship, and residence. The Court then held in that case that an attempt by the House of Representatives, itself, to tack on an additional qualification for membership in that body was unconstitutional.

The same should also be true for states. An early decision by the U.S. House of Representatives, at a time when its members were still contemporaries of the writers of the Constitution, gives us some further insight into the Founders' intent on this matter. The decision grew out of a 1790 Maryland statute that required a year's prior residence for U.S. House candidates from that state. One William McCreery had been elected without meeting this Maryland requirement. His election was challenged in the House of Representatives, where he was eventually seated by a vote of 89 to 18. A part of the report of the House Committee of Elections on that occasion stated:

> The committee proceeded to examine the Constitution, with relation to the case submitted to them, and find that qualifications of members are therein determined, without reserving any authority to the State Legislatures to change, add to, or diminish those qualifications; and that, by that instrument, Congress is constituted the sole judge of the qualifications prescribed by it, and are obliged to decide agreeably to the Constitutional rules.[12]

In his remarks on the House floor, the committee chair in the McCreery matter amplified:

> The Committee of Elections considered the qualifications of members to have been unalterable determined by the Federal Convention, unless changed by an authority equal to that which framed the Constitution at first; that neither the State nor the Federal Legislatures are vested with authority to add to those qualifications so as to change them.[13]

After all, senators and representatives hold federal offices, not state offices, and, as the eminent Justice Joseph Story wrote in his early, landmark constitutional treatise: "The states have just as much right, and no more, to prescribe new qualifications for a representative, as they have for a president. Each is an officer of the Union, deriving his powers and qualifications from the Constitution, and neither created by, dependent upon, nor controllable by, the states."[14]

Theoretically, the U.S. Constitution could be amended to limit congressional terms, but, in reality, there is virtually no chance that proponents of such an amendment could put together the two-thirds majority necessary in both houses of Congress to refer it to the people for vote. Congress cannot pass a simple law to limit the terms of senators and representatives. That would surely be unconstitutional. So, too, the Supreme Court is highly likely to rule in the near future, would be state attempts to do so.[15] Constitutional or not, though, term limits are neither necessary nor wise.

Current Turnover in Congress

Both because of incumbent defeats in recent times (forty-three members of Congress defeated in the big year of 1992, for example) and voluntary retirements (sixty-six in 1992), a large turnover in Congress already occurs. Senior members of Congress have been more likely to go down to defeat in recent elections than first termers.[16] Again, in the 1992 congressional elections, representatives who were defeated in the general election averaged nearly ten and a half years of House service; those who lost in the primaries, fourteen.[17] These primary-defeat numbers prompted one congressional observer to write: "The prototypical incumbent who has lost a House primary this year is not a relatively inexperienced first- or second-termer who has trouble raising money. He is, on average, a fifty-eight-year-old Hill veteran with fourteen years' seniority and a substantial financial advantage over his primary opposition."[18]

The median number of terms in office for members of the U.S. House of Representatives has fluctuated between four and five since 1953. In 1991, the median was five terms, the same as it was in 1957, 1961, 1963, 1969, 1971, 1973, 1987, and 1989. In the other years since 1957, including 1993, the median was four.[19] "The image of a House top heavy with long-term incumbents is false," Representative Pat Schroeder (D., Colo.) pointed out in 1990. "Since 1980, more than half of the House has turned over due to defeat, resignation, retirement or death. The average length of service is 5.8 terms."[20]

Similarly, political scientist Marjorie Randon Hershey wrote:

> It is ironic that ... the average member of the House now serves no longer than he or she would be allowed to serve by many term-limitation measures: six two-year terms. And largely because of retirements, between 10 and 20 percent of House members in any given Congress are serving their first term—a larger proportion than one might expect after listening to arguments for limits. It seems clear, then, that term limits are no more—and no less—than a symbolic expression of public frustration.[21]

Along the same line, after noting that a twelve-year limit on House service would produce at least 100 percent turnover every twelve years, a little over 16 percent every two years, political scientist John Hibbing observed: "Such a limit would constitute a small increase over turnover rates in the 1980s but would be about equal to turnover rates in the 1970s—and possibly less than those of the 1990s, if 1992 is any indication. . . . So term limits would stimulate less additional turnover than most people realize."[22]

The question, then, as James L. Sundquist put it, is "whether senators and representatives who are competent, energetic, and representative should be cast out of Congress along with their colleagues who may lack those qualities, simply on the ground of length of service."[23] Term limiters, in effect, say yes. They want to substitute new, younger members for old ones, regardless of merit. Their hope is that doing so would change the internal workings of Congress, too. Less of a case can be made for this argument today than formerly, according to Sundquist, again:

> Were this being written thirty years ago, one could easily come down on the side of youth, for the critical repositories of legislative power in the two houses—specifically, committee chairmanships—were then bestowed automatically on the basis of seniority, and members who were ideologically rigid, unrepresentative of their bodies' membership, worn out, or even senile could gain and retain immense power. But since then Congress has reformed itself. First, committee chairs have been stripped of much of their arbitrary authority and subjected to democratic control, both by the committee members acting collectively and by the majority party caucuses and the leaders and leadership bodies elected by them. Second, the automatic seniority system has been jettisoned; although seniority is still the principal criterion in choosing committee chairs, enough senior chairmen have been rejected by their party caucuses to make clear that competence, energy, and a reasonable degree or representativeness are requisites for leadership position.[24]

Sundquist specifically noted that the requirement of competence was reaffirmed in 1992, when the threat of removal caused Democratic Representative Jamie Whitten of Mississippi, who had suffered a stroke, to give up the chair of the House Appropriations Committee. What Sundquist wrote generally about committee chairs being deposed actually applies only to House chairs, but in the Senate, too, the power and formerly autocratic behavior of committee chairs have been seriously curtailed by, among other changes, the establishment of permanent subcommittees for all the standing committees and by rules changes that facilitate caucus votes on the retention of committee chairs in their positions.

Term Limits and Accountability

Limiting congressional terms would be bad policy. The Founders were right when they decided that term limits would unreasonably restrict the power of the people to elect whomever they might choose to public office, would deny the people the opportunity to retain in elective posts those most experienced and expert, and would limit an important incentive for good conduct by incumbent public officials, the desire for reelection.

On this latter point, proponents of term limits frequently bog into logical quicksand. As R. Douglas Arnold wrote:

> Many proponents of term limits for legislators have fallen into this trap, arguing that legislators operate beyond the control of constituents—the evidence being that so few legislators are ever defeated at the polls. The problem with this argument is that the contrary hypothesis is observationally equivalent. A setting in which legislators responded perfectly to constituency opinion would produce no defeats at the polls as certainly as one in which legislators operated independently of constituency opinion.[25]

We need term limits, proponents argue, because senators and representatives do not concern themselves enough with the public interest, since they are too worried about running for reelection. We need term limits, proponents also argue, because incumbent members are not sufficiently accountable to the people, since they are so secure in their jobs and enjoy such advantages of incumbency, that they are invulnerable to defeat and know it.

Which is it? Are incumbent senators and representatives too *little* worried about being reelected, or are they too *much* worried about being reelected? If they are too little worried about reelection, it is hard to see how limiting their opportunity for reelection through term limits is the proper remedy. If incumbents are too much worried about reelection, can that desire be curbed through term limits? Should it be?

Take the first question first: even if controls ought to be placed on the electoral ambitions of senators and representatives, is that possible? The fact is that if too great a concern with reelection is an incumbent sickness that term limits are meant to heal, it is likely that the remedy will produce an equally objectionable side effect: too much concern with running for some *other* elective post. In other words, term limits might replace "reelection behavior with pre-election behavior," as a couple of experts have phrased it well.[26] Most people who run for high public office—such as that of governor or U.S. senator or representative—are people who have decided on elective public service as a career. Is it not unreasonable to suppose that their political ambitions would abruptly wither and die, simultaneously with the expiration of their limited congressional terms?

A reverse case demonstrates the point. Back in the 1950s and earlier, former governors nearly always accounted for close to a fourth of the membership of the Senate, but not any more. Nowadays, usually no more than a tenth of the 100 senators have previously been governors. What changed? State constitutions did. They were amended to allow state chief executives to succeed themselves, and more of these governors thereafter began to run for reelection, rather than for the Senate.[27] Put a limit on Senate terms, and, just as certainly, a certain number of additional senators, most of whom would not now quit to be governor back home, will in their last years as senators begin to focus their election sights on state capitals. The electoral ambitions of a good many senators will not automatically be snuffed out by term limits.

The same would also clearly apply to many more incumbent U.S. representatives. At any one time, now, about a third of the Senate is usually made up of former House members,[28] even though, with two-year terms, these individuals had to give up their House seats to run for the Senate. No one doubts that more House members would launch campaigns for the Senate were this unnecessary. Cap their House careers, and representatives will have nothing to lose by concentrating during their last, limited terms on getting elected to the Senate and, in the process, incidentally, on making themselves more attractive to state-wide, rather than district-wide, electorates.

Now, for the other question: *should* the electoral ambitions of members of Congress be curtailed by term limits? The Founders rightly thought that no such curtailment should be attempted. Those who wrote our Constitution were convinced that the desire for reelection would operate as a salutary restraint on officeholders. The removal of that incentive for conscientious service—through term limits—would encourage officeholders to "sordid views" and "peculation," said Alexander Hamilton, to "make hay while the sun shines," declared Gouverneur Morris.[29]

A popular Mexican couplet is instructive in this respect. The Constitution of Mexico incorporates a major theme of the 1910 Mexican Revolution— *"¡No Reeleccíon!"* It limits that country's president to one six-year term, or *sexenio* (as some have unwisely advocated should be done here in the United States). Today in Mexico, many laughingly call the last year of a president's term "the year of the hidalgo," in an apparent allusion to the often-corrupt noblemen sent by Spain to govern Mexico during colonial times. Referring to the supposed thinking of the president and his term in the final year of a *sexenio*, cynical Mexicans recite a rhyming couplet that says:

> Éste es el año del hidalgo;
> Bueyes los que no roban algo.
>
> *This is the year of the hidalgo;*
> *Dumb oxen, those who don't rob something.*

Would it really be advisable to make members of Congress less answerable to the people by imposing an unbreachable ceiling on their prospects for reelection? Perhaps, as proponents hope, incumbents so limited would turn their attention more assiduously to the public's business; but is it not just as logical to assume the opposite? Might some not, freed from the restraint of having to face reelection, turn their attention more enterprisingly to their own personal interests—for example, to making money, in a few cases, or, in others, to spending their final terms ingratiating themselves with corporations or special interest groups or the law firms and lobbyists of either so as to lock up good private jobs to replace the ones the incumbents would soon be forced to vacate?

Political scientist Linda Fowler has called attention to the fact that a good many members of Congress stay on in Washington after leaving office, using their knowledge of the system and their contacts to make money. She thinks that this "de-recruitment," as she calls it, by the special interests, heightened by term limits, "could mean even more, rather than less, influence peddling" in Washington.[30] Political scientist Nelson Polsby touched somewhat on this same point in this way:

> It is a delusion to think that good public servants are a dime a dozen in each congressional district, and that only the good ones would queue up to take their twelve-year fling at congressional office. But suppose they did. In case they acquired expertise, what would they do next? Make money, I suppose. Just about the time that their constituents and the American people at large could begin to expect a payoff because of the knowledge and experience that these able members had acquired at our expense, off they would go to some Washington law firm.[31]

Inexperienced Legislators and Special Interest Influence

We neither can nor should set rigid time boundaries on the electoral ambitions of members of Congress. But perhaps an even greater concern about congressional term limits, from a good government standpoint, is one expressed by two congressional experts, Edward Schneier and Bertram Gross, having to do with the balance of power in Washington. "To lose the knowledge that comes with legislative experience is to relinquish influence to those who have subject-matter expertise, especially lobbyists and civil servants," they wrote. "Term limitation proposals should probably be called bureaucratic empowerment acts."[32] What about the usefulness, then, of senators and representatives with limited terms? asked Nelson Polsby—and then he answered his own question in this way:

> It would be limited, I'm afraid, by the greater expertise and better command of the territory by lobbyists, congressional staff, and downtown bureaucrats—career people one and all. So this is, once again, a proposal merely to weaken the fabric of Congress in the political system at large, and thereby to limit the effectiveness of the one set of actors most accessible to the citizens.[33]

It stands to reason that the Speaker of the House in Oklahoma was right when he said that "entrenched interests" will gain from new term limits for state legislators in that state:

> Entrenched interests such as the bureaucracy may gain. They'll always be there. . . . Interest groups, special interests, organized interests are a steady source of influence and that influence will increase. They will be there and the legislature will not. Those who stay around will have more influence than those who are new to the scene.[34]

In the halls of Congress, too, the lobbyists would still be on the scene, if term-limited senators and representatives were forced out, and, as always, the lobbyists would be only too happy to help "educate" the new members who replace those leaving. In Oklahoma, state capital lobbyists think their jobs are going to be harder as a result of legislative term limits because they will have to "spend all of [their] time educating people just to bring them up to speed." This difficulty will be offset, though, one said, by greater effectiveness: "It's easier to influence a freshman. They won't know the ropes. I'll be able to say I was there."[35]

The same effect would apply in a Washington, D.C., with term limits. The headline of a front page *New York Times* article during the 1993 fight on President Clinton's budget announced that a strategy of its lobbyist opponents was to "Go After the Greenhorns," an internal subhead reporting: "The theory: it's easier to win over inexperienced legislators." It was stated in the body of the article that lobbyists "are hoping that the relative inexperience of the new members will leave them open to special entreaties," and the head of one lobbying group was quoted as saying, "The new members tend to be more responsive to our efforts."[36]

With term limits, there would presumably be more such inexperienced and lobbyist-vulnerable new senators and representatives. Reduce the expertise and experience of members of Congress, and you will enhance the influence of the special interests. That seems obvious. It is equally obvious that the balance of governmental power in Washington would undoubtedly be tipped away from Congress toward the bureaucracy.

Conclusion

Term limit advocates are like the old country doctor who threw all his patients into convulsions, no matter what their initial complaints, because he thought he knew how to cure convulsions. Term limits are the wrong medicine, and the remedy would be worse than the presumed malady. . . .

The Power of Incumbency

Service in the U.S. House of Representatives became a career for its members as long ago as the turn of the century.[37] Since the mid-1960s, though, incumbents running for reelection have enjoyed a strong advantage over other candidates.

This House member advantage has been manifested in a number of ways. First, more than 90 percent of representatives seeking renomination and election since 1980 have indeed been successful. Second, until quite recently, the incumbent winner's average share of the two-party, general election vote has been going up, and the number of *marginals,* incumbents who win with less than 55 percent of that vote, has been going down. Finally, studies reveal a "sophomore surge" and a "retirement slump" in house races: the first reelection, or sophomore, victory by a new House member is by a margin that is, on average, 6 percent better than his or her initial winning margin; and in an open election after an incumbent retires, the district vote for the House candidate of that party drops, or slumps, by an average of 11 percent.[38]

Incumbency matters, then. But some political scientists feel that its benefits have been overstated,[39] and others think that the incumbent-advantage increase in recent times has been exaggerated.[40] Certainly, incumbents did not fare as well as formerly in the House elections of 1990 and 1992, both with respect to the increased number of defeats for incumbents in 1992 and the decreased average margins of victory in both elections for those incumbents who did win.[41]

Margins of victory for House incumbents have become more unstable; a representative may win in one election and then get defeated or just squeak by in the next. For example, although only six formerly safe, or nonmarginal, House members were defeated in 1990, twenty-six such representatives suffered drops in their margins of victory of 14 percentage points or more below those of the previous election.[42] And, in the last decade and a half, senior representatives have proved at least as vulnerable to defeat as more junior members.[43]

Also, the power of incumbency is considerably less in the Senate than in the House.[44] All Senate seats are now potentially two-party competitive. Since more of a media spotlight is on senators, and there are only one hundred of them, senators' positions on controversial national issues are generally better known by their constituents than House members' are, which can cause Senate incumbents a lot of extra political trouble. The Senate's greater prestige and visibility, as well as the six-year term, attract more high-quality, well-financed challengers, and it is the quality and financing of the challenger that, more than anything else, determine whether an incumbent will lose. Finally, it is much easier for Senate challengers than House challengers to become well-known rapidly—first, because a Senate race attracts a great deal more free media attention than a House race, and, second, because statewide Senate campaigns fit and can afford paid advertisements in television and newspaper markets, while House campaigns generally fit only a piece of such media markets, making advertisement in them cost-ineffective.

Whatever the facts about incumbency are, though, and no doubt the power is substantial, most House and Senate incumbents do not *feel* electorally safe. Why is this important? It is important because of the impression, particularly on the part of congressional critics, that a member who feels invulnerable, sure of always winning reelection, will grow increasingly unresponsive and unaccountable to constituents.

"But that impression would be quite mistaken," Robert Erikson and Gerald Wright wrote. "Even though House members know they are unlikely to lose the next election, they know that their chances are roughly one in three that they will *eventually* lose and be sent home by the voters."[45] And, according to Thomas Mann, members of Congress evaluate their electoral vulnerability differently from outsiders: "Their subjective assessments of electoral safety are dominated but uncertainty—the threat of redistricting, of population shifts, of external events like recession or Watergate, but most important the unpredictability of the challenger."[46]

Members of Congress also feel electorally vulnerable because they are acutely aware that today's well-financed media campaigns, using negative television ads and direct mail, can almost overnight explode some earlier, obscure vote of theirs into a colossal, killer issue. Democratic Majority Leader George Mitchell of Maine has said that senators are now frequently heard talking before a vote about what kind of negative ad might be made out of it: "Watch out for this one, guys; this could really be made into an effective 30-second spot."[47]

WHAT ABOUT ATTENTION to constituents, then? Do long-serving members of Congress, in fact, "go Washington" and forget the folks back home. The answer is no, according to John Hibbing. He says that when you look at the individual behavior of members, such as their trips back home and the percentage of staff they assign to their home districts, House members "do not greatly reduce their constituency-oriented behavior" over time.[48]

What about the way they vote? Do members, the longer they serve, drift away from the policy views of their constituents? Again, Hibbing has found, the answer is no: "For most members, how they vote the first year is now an incredibly accurate guide to how they will vote fifteen years hence."[49] Without respect to seniority, the most liberal House districts have the most liberal representatives; the most conservative districts, the most conservative members.[50]

Incidentally, what *does* change with seniority is legislative effectiveness. "Senior members are more active, more focused, and more successful legislatively than junior members," John Hibbing reported, and he added that now, more than ever, if we value that type of legislative service and competence, "we should value senior legislators."[51]

Incumbent Advantages

Still, there is no doubt that the odds are usually against challengers who run against sitting senators or representatives. And awareness of this often discourages good challengers from even announcing their candidacies in the first place.

Incumbent advantages spring from several sources. First, an incumbent is known and has name recognition, which is of considerable importance in a campaign. Most people know or can pick out the names of their own senators and representatives. The average challenger may have to spend hundreds of thousands of dollars to match such recognition. The incumbent, on the other hand, most likely has already laid out that kind of advertising money, at least once, in an earlier campaign. And, in office, the incumbent has kept up a drumbeat of news releases and public and media appearances back home, announcing local federal projects, taking credit, holding town meetings.

Little or nothing can be done about the incumbent name recognition advantage. It is just a fact of political life. We could not, for example, require that incumbents run for reelection under different names each time, just as we could not bar famous nonpoliticians—astronauts or basketball players, for example—from running for Congress. Nor could we demand that incumbent senators or representatives remain mute during their terms, declining to report to constituents.

The value of incumbent name recognition is enhanced by another advantage House members have—the uniqueness of their districts. Nothing in the Constitution requires that House district lines correspond to the boundaries of other local entities—to those of a county, city, or ward, for example. Because a congressional district therefore often crosses or ignores such local lines and usually has no natural coherence or intrinsic reason for being, except that it contains the requisite number of people, it is not an easy entity to organize; frequently, no reason in fact exists for it to be politically organized at all, save as a congressional district. And the incumbent already has the district organized—because, of course, he or she has earlier run a campaign in it, and has won there, at least once.

The average House district is unique in another way: it usually does not fit a television broadcast area, as noted earlier, and often not even the circulation area of a daily newspaper. A House challenger in south Chicago, say, or in southern New Mexico is not likely to be able to afford costly television advertising, when most of that expense would be wasted; the voters would only amount to a fraction of the viewers reached. The incumbent House member in such a district, on the other hand, has the advantage of already being well-known there from earlier campaigns and from being in office.

How Incumbency Became Increasingly Important in Elections

Most observers feel that something happened in the mid-1960s and later, as noted earlier, that began to make incumbency an increasingly important factor in congressional elections. What was it? Some critics of Congress have charged that it was redistricting on the basis of favoritism, state legislatures redrawing congressional district lines after each decennial census so as to produce districts tailor-made for the incumbent House members from the state.

Questions are, indeed, raised every ten years about redistricting by this or that state legislature, and often the questions raised are very serious ones, questions involving equal protection of the laws, civil rights, and gerrymandering, particularly. But redistricting favoritism does not explain the growth in the reelection advantage of House incumbents. This explanation is "clearly incorrect," a couple of congressional experts, John Alford and David Brady, stated, because Senate incumbent advantage trends are, according to them, similar to those for the House, "and, of course, no redistricting takes place to affect the Senate." [52]

Edward Schneier and Bertram Gross went further. They pointed out other important reasons why redistricting does not explain the modern power of incumbency. First, "gerrymanders of earlier years were at least as outrageous as those of today." Second, there are just as many "safe" seats in nonredistricted states and in redistricted ones. And third, incumbent security is not found to be greatest immediately following redistricting, with an erosion thereafter as district populations begins to change; in fact, redistricting was a major factor in the retirements and defeats of a good many incumbent House members in 1992. [53]

What did occur in the mid-1960s, and even earlier, was a slippage in political party loyalty in America. This change came as a part of whole series of other developments that amounted to a kind of "nationalization" of American society—rapid mass communications and transportation, a markedly raised standard of living, much higher levels of education, greater citizen mobility, and increased urbanization. Candidates found that they could go over the heads of party leaders and make their pitches directly to the voters, and they began to do so. Senate and House candidates developed their own personal, cottage industry parties, in a sense. "They ran vigorous campaigns, sometimes supplanting the old party organization, sometimes simply ignoring it," John Alford and David Brady wrote. "Their goal was to win office, not simply to carry the party banner, and they chose their races and ran them accordingly."[54]

Among the voters, split-ticket voting increased significantly: in the same election, a person might vote for a Republican for president, a Democrat for U.S. representative, and a Republican, again, for U.S. senator—or some similar partisan split. Between 1952 and 1988, for example, the proportion of voters who reported that they had split their tickets between presidential and House candidates increased from 12 percent to 25 percent, and those who said that they had voted a split ticket between House and Senate races increased from 9 percent to 27 percent.[55]

As the effectiveness of the party label weakened as a cue, then, for how people ought to vote, the cue of incumbency gained countervailing strength.[56] A congressional candidate's appeal and following became more personal. Challenger nominees got less of a boost from their party labels. They were more on their own, which was a disadvantage for them against a known incumbent.

All these developments combined to make the name recognition value of congressional incumbency worth more. The nationalization of American society also produced great numbers of additional citizens who were more aware of, and attentive to, what Congress was doing and who were much more activist—constituents who wrote letters and made calls, who organized, and who campaigned. There was an "advocacy explosion," too, an enormous increase in the numbers of Washington-based interest groups and in the scope and intensity of their activities. And the federal government grew tremendously.

With these added pressures and with all the fresh issues and government programs, the newer members of Congress, especially, began to demand more participation in congressional decision-making. They also had to deal with the burgeoning activism and attention and growing demands of their constituents. They started to feel, too, an elevated sense of political exposure and electoral vulnerability, a sense that campaigning had to be virtually perpetual if they were to survive. Senators and representatives, as a result, made demands on the House and Senate, and they largely got what they wanted. They got more visibility and more subcommittees. They got more staff, more free mail, more paid trips home.

Each member needed more staff and more free, franked mail in order, among other things, to handle a greatly increased load of casework—personal requests by constituents for help with social security claims, veterans' pensions, or immigration matters, for example. Is this a part of the job of a senator or House member? It nearly always has been and certainly is now. Did members themselves cause the increase in casework by going around their districts or states or sending out bushels of letters to drum up more of this business, announcing in effect, "I hope you have a social security problem that I can help you with"? Perhaps they did in some cases, but, mostly, casework increased on its own.

Is casework a part of good government? Probably it is. Somewhere an ombudsman service ought to be available to citizens as a kind of court of last resort to help them deal with, cope with, an often faceless, impersonal, mammoth, and complex federal government. The people have picked out senators and representatives for this chore. Handling casework sometimes helps make members of Congress more aware of the way programs they have passed are actually working, or are not working, and how the programs might be improved.

Can senators and representatives now refuse to deal with these personal problems of their constituents? Not likely. Is a history of performing this kind of constituency service an advantage for an incumbent member of Congress? Without a doubt. If you had been a candidate against a long-time, service-oriented member of Congress like New Mexico Republican Manuel Lujan, before he quit in 1989 to become Secretary of the Interior, you would have heard several times a day, until you were nearly sick of it, something like, "I'd like to vote for you, but Manuel Lujan helped us with the VA to get Dad's disability established as service connected." You would have wanted to respond, "But that's his job, and, if you put me in there, I'll do the same thing." Maybe, but Lujan was already there, and he had already done it.

A record of constituency service is an advantage that an incumbent member of Congress has over a challenger. Do critics want to force senators and representatives to cut down on casework and similar service to constituents? Do they want them to turn their backs and walk away when water and sewer projects, defense contracts, airport funds, or university programs that might go to their districts or states are being handed out in Washington—pork, as it is called if it is going to somebody else's state or district? Let critics tell us how they would do that. Term limits, some say. But would not the new, replacement senators and representatives help on casework, too, and go after so-called pork just as much? The answer, of course, is yes, they would.

Voters in 1992 elected the largest group of new House members in forty years. But, even before they were sworn in, the *New York Times* reported: "After a campaign focused on fighting the status quo, it did not take long for the freshmen in Congress to start wheeling and dealing for coveted positions in the insider network." The new members, the *Times* said, were already "falling into the clutches of incumbency—fighting like political pros for the committee assignments" that would determine how much influence they would wield.[57] And, later, after these new members had been in office a few months, *Congressional Quarterly* related that they had "turned out to differ little from the veterans," an outcome probably to be expected "considering that 72 percent of them previously held office."[58]

It is interesting that one study shows that the reelection vote margins of incumbent House members do not seem to be boosted by increases in the constituent services performed by their offices, the number of trips home members take, or the volumes of grants and contracts obtained for the districts.[59] And tighter electoral competition apparently would not cause members to reduce such efforts. In fact, just the opposite seems to be true; the more narrow their margins of electoral victory, the more incumbents seem to be scared into increasing constituent service and attention.[60]

Is it fair, though, for members to use travel allowances, staff, and franked mail for political purposes? Paid trips home during their terms can, it is true, help incumbent members of Congress get reelected, no question about it. But do we really want to argue that the number of such trips should be substantially reduced—that members should go home fewer times, stay less in touch with their constituents? Surely that argument would be hard to sustain. And it raises the same old question again: is the complaint that incumbent members pay too much attention to constituents or too little?

Taxpayer-Financed Campaigning

The main trouble, critics say, is that senators and representatives use their taxpayer-paid perks to campaign. But the line between legitimate congressional work and campaigning is always a hard one to draw. Former congressional staffer Mark Bisnow wrote:

[Congress] by its nature is so intensely political that it becomes a practical impossibility to say in many instances where the discharge of official duties leaves off and aspirations to higher office (or reelection) begin. A congressman and his staff, for example, are not supposed to use office typewriters, photocopy machines, and phone lines to solicit financial contributions for election campaigns, but who is to judge their ulterior motives in taking positions, proposing bills and amendments, writing speeches, or issuing press releases that happened to be of value in both legislative and campaign contexts?[61]

President Clinton flies on Air Force One to St. Louis to view flood damage: is he just doing his job or already campaigning for reelection? Doing a good job is itself the best campaigning, both for presidents and for members of Congress, and both would undoubtedly say, with reason, that staying in touch is an integral part of their jobs.

But what about paid staff actually campaigning for a member's reelection on official time? That would be wrong. For some time, now, there has been a low and declining number of congressional staff members who got their jobs because of their political contacts.[62] Furthermore, it is the usual, and better, practice today for congressional staff members who are engaged in campaigning to go off the staff payroll, wholly or in part, and be placed on the payroll of the campaign.

No law requires them to do so, though.[63] And a federal appeals court has refused to go into the matter, saying it involves a "political question," to be decided by the Senate and House themselves. There surely ought to be a law—or at least very clear Senate and House rules—on this issue. House and Senate staffers should not be permitted to engage in campaigning while on a congressional payroll.

Members are already prevented from using franked mail to campaign. For official business, though, senators and representatives can send mail with facsimiles of their signatures in place of postage stamps. That has been true in the United States since the Continental Congress first established the franking privilege in 1776.[64]

Franked mail is not free, though. Congress makes appropriations for this expense, and individual members are given mail allowances. The franking privilege cost taxpayers $85.3 million in 1989, up from $52 million in 1981 and just $11.2 million in 1971.[65] Even with postage for the average unit mailed having gone up from eight cents to nearly fifteen cents during that period, the figures still show quite an increase in franked mail and its cost.

Experts on Congress have found that a major reason for the increased use of the frank before 1981 was a liberalization of the law that permitted members to send mass mailings—such as newsletters, questionnaires, and the like—addressed only to "occupant." After 1981, the same experts reported, increased franking costs resulted from the "explosive growth" in grass-roots lobbying. "In other words," they say, "the first wave of growth was stimulated by members, the second by constituents."[66]

A senator or representative cannot use the frank for personal business nor send franked holiday greetings or sympathy messages. And the law says that franked mailings must not be used, either, for partisan, political, or campaign purposes. Yet a study found that the volume of franked mail in the election years from 1976 to 1988 was half again higher than in the non-election years during that period. After that, both houses adopted restrictions limiting franked mass mailings (500 or more identical pieces) to three a year (down from six) and prohibiting such mailings altogether during the sixty-day period prior to a primary or general election. Furthermore, as a result of a court decision, followed by their own action, House members may not now send any mass mailings outside their own districts.[67]

Both houses now allot each member a specific mail budget (equal to three first-class mailings to every residence) and require full public disclosure of each member's expenditures for franked mail. This change has already had a significant effect on costs. Moreover, for fiscal 1994—an election year, when the volume of franked mail has in the past gone up—the House has actually reduced appropriations for such mailings by its members by $8 million below the preceding year's figure, and the Senate has frozen such expenditures by its members at the 1993 figure.[68]

Both houses should go further and prohibit mass franked mailings by a senator or representative any time during a year when the member appears on the ballot, a provision included, incidentally, in a Senate-passed 1993 campaign reform bill.[69] And the House should adopt the Senate's present proscription against sending franked mail that is addressed only to "postal patron" or "occupant."

Conclusion

It is true that incumbent senators and representatives have certain advantages over their challengers. Most such advantages inevitably result from the incumbent having gotten elected in the first place and from their trying to do a good job thereafter. A tight prohibition against staff campaigning and the enactment of further restrictions on the franking privilege would expand the potential for electoral competition and thus the greater accountability of incumbents.

But the most valuable advantage incumbents have is their ability to raise great sums of campaign money. Something must be done about this problem.

Campaign Finance Reform

The costs of congressional campaigns are enormous, and for nearly the last thirty years, these costs have been growing markedly faster than the rate of inflation. For the 1992 elections—with an unusually large number of open seats (where no incumbent was running) and, therefore, an increased number of candidates—total spending by all House and Senate campaigns came to $678 million, 52 percent more than for 1990.[70]

In 1992 the average victorious House candidate spent about $550,000; the average winning Senate candidate, approximately $3.85 million.[71] Including both winners and losers, fifty of the 1992 House candidates spent more than $1 million each in their campaigns, six of them more than $1.75 million.[72] Fourteen of the 1992 Senate candidates, including both winners and losers, spent in excess of $5 million each; three Senate victors that year (Republican incumbents Alfonse D'Amato of New York and Arlen Specter of Pennsylvania and Democrat Barbara Boxer, winner of an open California seat) spent more than $10 million each to achieve their victories.[73]

Where does all this money come from? It comes from those who have money—both individuals and, increasingly, Political Action Committees (PACs), the campaign financing arm of corporations, interest groups, and lobbies. Why do they give it? Not just because they have taken to heart their high school civics lesson about the duty of everyone to take part in politics. Money buys—and is intended to buy—access to power and policy-making. It can buy influence. Here are off-the-record statements on the subject by three senators:

> It is difficult to maintain a sense of integrity and self-worth when asking for money, and then trying to separate that from your decisions.
>
> In some cases, you feel one way, and vote the other.

Congress will listen to big contributors. They have a direct influence. It is demeaning and wasteful [to solicit contributions] and the money makes us ripe for corruption.[74]

The 1991 Senate Ethics Committee hearings concerning the so-called Keating Five (Republican John McCain of Arizona and Democrats Alan Cranston of California, Dennis DeConcini of Arizona, John Glenn of Ohio, and Donald Riegle, Jr., of Michigan) revealed that they had intervened with the Federal Savings and Loan Insurance Corporation on behalf of Charles Keating and his rapidly unraveling savings and loan swindles. They had done so after Keating had made campaign contributions to them, as well as registration and get-out-the-vote, "soft money" donations for their benefit. Keating, who was later convicted of criminal felonies for his financial manipulations, told the press candidly, if arrogantly, why he had made these contributions. "One question, among many others raised in recent weeks, had to do with whether financial support in any way influenced several political figures to take up my cause. I want to say in the most forceful way I can: I certainly hope so."[75]

PAC contributions are an increasing share of congressional campaign contributions, totaling $189 million for Senate and House candidates in the 1992 elections, up from $150 million two years earlier.[76] "Alarming, outrageous, and downright dangerous" are the words Fred Wertheimer, president of the citizen lobby Common Cause, used to characterize what he called "the threat posed by the torrents of special interest campaign cash being offered up to our Representatives and Senators by the special interest political action committees."[77]

The Gap between Incumbent and Challenger

Whether it comes from individuals or PACs, congressional campaign money is, for the most part, axe-to-grind money. And most of it goes to incumbents, both because they are known quantities and because they are seen as good investments since they have the best chances of winning. This money, in turn, of course, gives incumbents even more of an advantage. Thus, if you want to know why incumbent members of Congress win, Marjorie Randon Hershey said, "Money is one of the primary culprits."[78]

Incumbents are always worried, and, week after week, month after month, year in and year out, during all their terms, they are always raising money. And they can raise almost any amount they think they may need. After the 1990 election campaigns, for example, House incumbents still had on hand leftover, unspent campaign funds totaling $77 million, a sum more than twice as much as the $37 million that all House challengers, together, had been able to raise and spend in that campaign.[79]

The gap between incumbent and challenger spending has been greatly widening. Between 1972 and 1990, the amount spent (in constant dollars) by the average House incumbent increased by nearly 300 percent, while the amount spent by the average House challenger during that period went up only 12 percent.[80] For the 1992 election, 72 percent of all PAC contributions to House and Senate campaigns went to incumbents, while only 12 percent went to challengers (with 16 percent going to candidates in open-seat contests).[81] House incumbents that year received 44 percent of their total campaign contributions from PACs.[82] Senate incumbents in 1992 outspent their challengers an average of two to one and enjoyed an advantage over them in PAC contributions of nearly six to one.[83] In mid-1993, more than a year ahead of the 1994 elections, ten senators already had campaign cash on hand in the amount of $1 million or more each; in 1994 one senator, Republican Phil Gramm of Texas, not even up for reelection until two years later, already had a campaign war chest totaling $6.2 million cash.[84]

Reform Bills

It is clear that the greatest advantage enjoyed by congressional incumbents, as well as the greatest potential for political corruption, is found in the present system of campaign financing. In this case something *is* broke, and it very much needs fixing.

Strict limits should be placed on total congressional campaign spending in each state and district, and no candidate should be able to contribute more than $25,000 to his or her own campaign. PACs should be abolished altogether (or, if this measure is found to be unconstitutional, should be restricted to contributions of $1,000 for each campaign, down from $5,000). Candidates should get the benefit of discount broadcast and postage rates for the general election. And candidates who abide by the spending and contribution limits should receive public financing for their campaigns, similar to that provided to presidential campaigns since 1974. Party spending, too, should be restricted, and uncontrolled "soft money" should be eliminated.

All these goals are very much what the bill that Congress passed in 1992, which President George Bush vetoed, would have accomplished. With the exception of the public funding part, which had to be dropped in order to bring an end to a Republican filibuster, these provisions were also contained in the 1993 campaign reform bill passed by the Senate.

The earlier, 1992 bill had offered public funding as a carrot to entice candidates to agree to comply with spending and contribution limits. The final 1993 Senate bill substituted threatened elimination of the present income tax exemption on campaign receipts as a kind of compliance stick. The House's own 1993 campaign finance reform bill provided for vouchers for up to $200,000 in federal funds to match individual contributions and to be used for general election advertising, postage, and materials.[85] It was hoped that House and Senate measures would be reconciled in conference. "If you combine the best features of both bills," Fred Wertheimer, president of Common Cause, said, "you can wind up with fundamental reform."[86]

The reinstitution of elections that provide sufficient potential for competition, the kind Madison thought would keep incumbent members of Congress virtuous and accountable, requires the immediate adoption of one or the other of these campaign reform bills, preferably the one that provides for public financing.

Summary

The term limit movement is a mistaken and misguided one. Congress is a more open place, now, and the press is more vigilant than ever as a watchdog over its congressional members and operations. The ethical standards of senators and representatives are high, higher than in the past. Incumbent members of Congress do have unfair advantages against challengers. Some further tightening is needed against the use of staff and the franking privilege for campaigning. But the greatest incumbency advantage is the ability to raise almost unlimited sums of campaign money. Campaign finance reform is greatly needed and long overdue.

NOTES

1. James L. Sundquist, *Constitutional Reform and Effective Government,* rev. ed. (Washington, D.C.: Brookings Institution, 1992), pp. 178, 179.

2. Jonathan Elliot, ed., *Debates on the Adoption of the Federal Constitution,* Vol. 2 (New York: Burt Franklin, 1988), p. 292.

3. Paul Leicester Ford, *Essays on the Constitution of the United States* [1892] (New York: Burt Franklin, 1970), p. 234.

4. Quoted in Mark P. Petracca, "Rotation in Office: The History of an Idea," in Gerald Benjamin and Michael J. Malbin, eds., *Limiting Legislative Terms* (Washington, D.C.: Congressional Quarterly Press, 1992), p. 30.

5. Paul Leicester Ford, *Essays on the Constitution of the United States,* p. 234.

6. Jonathan Elliot, ed., *Debates on the Adoption of the Federal Constitution,* Vol. 1 (New York: Burt Franklin, 1988), pp. 292, 293.

7. Paul Leicester Ford, *Essays on the Constitution of the United States,* p. 234.

8. "Foley Joins in Effort Against Term Limits," *Congressional Quarterly Weekly Report* (June 12, 1993), p. 1504.

9. See, for example, *Storer v. Brown,* 415 U.S. 726 (1974).

10. See "Voters Embrace Congressional Term Limits," *Congressional Quarterly Almanac 1992* (Washington, D.C.: Congressional Quarterly Press, 1992), p. 71.

11. 415 U.S. 726 (1969).

12. 17 *Annals of Congress* 871 (1807), quoted in *Powell v. McCormack,* 395 U.S. 486 (1969), p. 542.

13. Ibid., *Annals* 872, *Powell v. McCormack,* p. 543.

14. Joseph Story, *A Familiar Exposition of the Constitution of the United States* [1840] (New York: Harper and Brothers, 1893), quoted in Steven R. Ross and Charles Tiefer, "Brief of the *Amicus Curiae* United States Representative Lawrence J. Smith," in Gerald Benjamin and Michael J. Malbin, eds., *Limiting Legislative Terms,* p. 256.

15. An Arkansas circuit court in 1993 ruled in *Hill v. Tucker* that the state's term limits for members of Congress violated the U.S. Constitution because they attempted to add a new qualification for congressional membership, and this case may be the first on the question to go to the U.S. Supreme Court. See Jennifer S. Thompson, "Judge in Arkansas Declares Measure Unconstitutional," *Congressional Quarterly Weekly Report* (August 7, 1993), p. 2181.

16. Marjorie Randon Hershey, "The Congressional Elections," in Gerald M. Pomper, ed., *The Election of 1992* (Chatham, N.J.: Chatham House, 1992), pp. 166, 177.

17. Ibid., p. 174.

18. Rhodes Cook, "Incumbency Proves Liability in '92," *Congressional Quarterly Weekly Report* (September 12, 1992), p. 2774.

19. Norman J. Ornstein, Thomas E. Mann, and Michael J. Malbin, *Vital Statistics on Congress 1993–1994* (Washington, D.C.: Congressional Quarterly Press, 1992), pp. 19, 20.

20. Quoted in John Fund, "Term Limitation: An Idea Whose Time Has Come," in Gerald Benjamin and Michael J. Malbin, eds., *Limiting Legislative Terms* (Washington, D.C.: Congressional Quarterly Press, 1992), p. 232.

21. Marjorie Randon Hershey, "The Congressional Elections," pp. 184, 185.

22. John R. Hibbing, "Careerism in Congress: For Better or for Worse?" in Lawrence C. Dodd and Bruce I. Oppenheimer, eds., *Congress Reconsidered*, 5th ed. (Washington, D.C.: Congressional Quarterly Press, 1993), pp. 67, 68.

23. James L. Sundquist, *Constitutional Reform and Effective Government*, rev. ed., pp. 184, 185.

24. Ibid., p. 183.

25. R. Douglas Arnold, "Can Inattentive Citizens Control Their Elected Representatives?" in Lawrence C. Dodd and Bruce I. Oppenheimer, eds., *Congress Reconsidered*, 5th ed., pp. 407, 408.

26. This statement was made concerning state legislatures and term limits that might encourage "musical chairs." Michael J. Malbin and Gerald Benjamin, "Legislatures After Term Limits," in Gerald Benjamin and Michael J. Malbin, eds., *Limiting Legislative Terms*, p. 211.

27. On this point, see Fred R. Harris, *Deadlock or Decision: The U.S. Senate and the Rise of National Politics* (New York: Oxford University Press, 1993), p. 97.

28. Ibid.

29. Quoted in Charles R. Kesler, "Bad Housekeeping: The Case Against Congressional Term Limits," in Gerald Benjamin and Michael J. Malbin, eds., *Limiting Legislative Terms*, p. 248.

30. Linda L. Fowler, "A Comment on Competition and Careers," in Gerald Benjamin and Michael J. Malbin, eds., *Limiting Legislative Terms*, p. 183.

31. Nelson W. Polsby, "Congress-Bashing for Beginners," *Public Interest* (1990), 100, pp. 20, 21.

32. Edward V. Schneier and Bertram Gross, *Congress Today* (New York: St. Martin's Press, 1993), p. 501.

33. Ibid., p. 21.

34. Quoted in Gary Copeland, "Term Limits and Political Careers in Oklahoma: In, Out, Up, or Down," in Gerald Benjamin and Michael J. Malbin, eds., *Limiting Legislative Terms*, p. 154.

35. Ibid.

36. Joel Brinkley, "A Strategy on the Budget: Go After the Greenhorns," *New York Times* (July 23, 1993), pp. A1, A7.

37. Nelson W. Polsby, "The Institutionalization of the U.S. House of Representatives," *American Political Science Review* (1968), 62, pp. 144–168.

38. Information in this paragraph is taken from John R. Alford and David W. Brady, "Personal and Partisan Advantage in U.S. Congressional Elections, 1846–1990," in Lawrence C. Dodd and Bruce I. Oppenheimer, eds., *Congress Reconsidered*, 5th ed., pp. 141–157.

39. See James L. Sundquist, *Constitutional Reform and Effective Government,* rev. ed., p. 185.

40. Melissa Collie and Gary Jacobson, cited in John R. Alford and David W. Brady, "Personal and Partisan Advantage in U.S. Congressional Elections, 1846–1990," p. 154.

41. Ibid., 155; and Marjorie Randon Hershey, "The Congressional Elections," pp. 160–166.

42. Edward V. Schneier and Bertram Gross, *Congress Today,* pp. 93, 94.

43. John R. Hibbing, "Careerism in Congress: For Better or for Worse?" p. 72.

44. On this point, see Fred R. Harris, *Deadlock or Decision: The U.S. Senate and the Rise of National Politics,* pp. 57–59; and Robert S. Erikson and Gerald C. Wright, "Voters, Candidates, and Issues in Congressional Elections," in Lawrence C. Dodd and Bruce I. Oppenheimer, eds., *Congress Reconsidered,* 5th ed., pp. 110, 111.

45. Robert S. Erikson and Gerald C. Wright, "Voters, Candidates, and Issues in Congressional Elections," p. 103.

46. Thomas E. Mann, *Unsafe at Any Margin: Interpreting Congressional Elections* (Washington, D.C.: American Enterprise Institute, 1978), pp. 23, 24.

47. Quoted in "Candidates and Process Wounded in 'Total War,' " *New York Times* (March 19, 1990), p. A14.

48. John R. Hibbing, "Careerism in Congress: For Better or for Worse?" p. 78.

49. Ibid., p. 76.

50. Robert S. Erikson and Gerald C. Wright, "Voters, Candidates, and Issues in Congressional Elections," p. 108.

51. John R. Hibbing, "Careerism in Congress: For Better or for Worse?" p. 80.

52. John R. Alford and David W. Brady, "Personal and Partisan Advantage in U.S. Congressional Elections, 1846–1990," p. 151.

53. Edward M. Schneier and Bertram Gross, *Congress Today,* p. 80.

54. James R. Alford and David W. Brady, "Personal and Partisan Advantage in U.S. Congressional Elections, 1846–1990," p. 153.

55. Martin P. Wattenberg, *The Decline of American Political Parties 1952–1988* (Cambridge, Mass.: Harvard University Press, 1990), p. 165.

56. See David Mayhew, "Congressional Elections: The Case of the Vanishing Marginals," *Polity* (Spring 1974), 7, p. 311; and John R. Alford and David W. Brady, "Personal and Partisan Advantage in U.S. Congressional Elections, 1846–1990," pp. 151–154.

57. Clifford Kraus, "Political Memo: Vying for Committees, Freshmen Mimic Elders," *New York Times* (November 30, 1992), p. A9.

58. "Freshman Class: No Reform Juggernaut," *Congressional Quarterly Weekly Report* (April 24, 1993), p. 99. See also Beth Donovan, "Factures in Freshman Class Weaken Impact on House," *Congressional Quarterly Weekly Report* (April 3, 1993), pp. 807–810.

59. See Alan I. Abramowitz, "Incumbency, Campaign Spending, and the Decline of Competition in U.S. House Elections," *Journal of Politics* (August 1991), 53, p. 35.

60. See Kenneth N. Bickers and Robert M. Stein, "Congressional Elections and the Pork Barrel," paper delivered at the annual meeting of the American Political Science Association, Chicago, September 1992.

61. Mark Bisnow, *In the Shadow of the Dome: Chronicles of a Capitol City Aide* (New York: Morrow, 1990), quoted in Congressional Quarterly, *Congressional Ethics: History, Facts, and Controversy* (Washington, D.C.: Congressional Quarterly Press, 1992), p. 104.

62. See Harrison W. Fox, Jr., and Susan W. Hammond, *Congressional Staffs: The Invisible Force in American Lawmaking* (New York: The Free Press, 1977), p. 66.

63. Material in this paragraph is taken from Congressional Quarterly, *Congressional Ethics: History, Facts, and Controversy*, pp. 104, 105.

64. This and other information about the franking privilege, unless indicated otherwise, is taken from Congressional Quarterly, *Congressional Pay and Perquisites: History, Facts, and Controversy* (Washington, D.C.: Congressional Quarterly, 1992), pp. 27–36.

65. These and related figures concerning the franking privilege are taken from Norman J. Ornstein, Thomas E. Mann, and Michael J. Malbin, *Vital Statistics on Congress 1991–1992*, pp. 122, 139, 160, 161.

66. Ibid., p. 122.

67. "House Tightens Limits on Franked Mail," *Congressional Quarterly Almanac 1992*, p. 61.

68. See Beth Donovan, "Congress Avoids Battles Over Its Own Funding," *Congressional Quarterly Weekly Report* (August 7, 1993), p. 2143.

69. "Highlights of Campaign Finance Bill As Passed by the Senate on June 17," *Congressional Quarterly Weekly Report* (June 19, 1993), p. 1537.

70. See Jennifer S. Thompson, "With So Many Seats Open in '92, Campaign Spending Rose 52%," *Congressional Quarterly Weekly Report* (March 20, 1993), p. 691.

71. See "Research & Readings: Congressional Candidates Spending Up 52% in '92," *Campaigns & Elections* (April/May 1993), p. 76; Beth Donovan, "'92 Numbers Suggest Big Changes If Campaign Finance Bill Passes," *Congressional Quarterly Weekly Report* (February 27, 1993), p. 693; and "FEC Reports: Senate Candidates," *Congressional Quarterly Weekly Report* (March 20, 1993), p. 692.

72. Beth Donovan, "'92 Numbers Suggest Big Changes If Campaign Finance Bill Passes," p. 437.

73. Ibid.

74. From interviews with U.S. Senators by the Center for Responsive Politics, Washington, D.C., compiled April 30, 1987, and made available to the author with the understanding that the identities of the senators would not be disclosed.

75. Quoted in Jack W. Germond and Jules Whitcover, "Inside Politics: Looking for a Smoking Gun on Campaign Funds?" *National Journal* (December 12, 1989), p. 2956.

76. Federal Election Commission report, cited in Charles R. Babcock, "Leaders of the PACs: NRA, UPS and Dentists," *Washington Post National Weekly Edition* (May 10–16, 1993), p. 13.

77. Direct-mail letter, quoted in Larry J. Sabato, *PAC Power: Inside the World of Political Action Committees* (New York: W. W. Norton, 1985), p. xi.

78. Marjorie Randon Hershey, "The Congressional Elections," p. 159.

79. Gary C. Jacobson, "The Misallocation of Resources in House Campaigns," in Lawrence C. Dodd and Bruce I. Oppenheimer, eds., *Congress Reconsidered*, 5th ed., p. 119.

80. Ibid.

81. Federal Election Commission report, cited in Charles R. Babcock, "Leaders of the PACs: NRA, UPS and Dentists," p. 13.

82. Beth Donovan and Ilyse J. Veron, "Freshman Got to Washington with Help of PAC Funds," *Congressional Quarterly Weekly Report* (March 27, 1993), p. 723.

83. Beth Donovan, "Delay, Controversy Certain as Senate Takes Up Plan," *Congressional Quarterly Weekly Report* (May 22, 1993), p. 1273.

84. Federal Election Commission report, cited in "Planning Ahead: What Senators Raised in the First Half of 1993," *New York Times* (August 13, 1993), p. A9.

85. Concerning the 1993 House campaign-finance reform bill, see Beth Donovan, "House Will Vote on Limits Nearing $1 Million in '96," *Congressional Quarterly Weekly Report* (November 13, 1993), pp. 3091–3093; and Beth Donovan, "House Takes First Big Step in Overhauling System," *Congressional Quarterly Weekly Report* (November 27, 1993), pp. 3246–3249.

86. Quoted in Kenneth J. Cooper and David S. Broder, "Campaign Reform, On the House," *Washington Post National Weekly Edition* (November 29–December 5, 1993), p. 13.

7

The Presidency

When the president and Congress try to exercise their power, they face problems that are opposite in nature. Congress encounters numerous difficulties in reaching collective agreements, which is to be expected of a large, bifurcated institution representing diverse interests. Yet if it does act in concert, it enjoys an excellent prospect of redirecting government policy. The president, conversely, enjoys a single individual's capacity for making decisions but may not have the authority to enact them. The Framers of the Constitution sought to control the presidency's authority by giving it full rein when the nation required speedy, decisive action but otherwise tightly restricting the office's capacity to act alone. As the nation's commander in chief, the president has extraordinary authority to respond to foreign threats. But during normal circumstances, when decisiveness is unnecessary, the office's unilateral authority is limited. The president can propose legislation to Congress and veto bills he does not favor, but the Constitution carefully denies him the authority or resources to commit the nation to a course of action.

If this characterization of a constrained presidency seems at odds with the image of the office's modern occupant, who appears nightly on the news behaving as if he were single-handedly solving the nation's problems, there are two reasons why this might be. The first has to do with the difference between appearance and reality. Modern presidents undertake a substantial amount of public activity, but much of it, rather than being direct action, consists of persuading other politicians who possess real authority—particularly, members of Congress—to adopt preferred policies. Also, the above characterization is somewhat out of date. The modern presidency has evolved more authority to act than the Framers initially provided. With the growth of government, Congress delegated to the president a sizable share of day-to-day administrative responsibility and the policy discretion that goes with it. Congress also finds it necessary, even when controlled by the opposition party, to continually seek information and advice from the nation's chief executive and his agents to do its work.

7-1

Presidential Power

Richard E. Neustadt

In his classic treatise Presidential Power, *Richard E. Neustadt presents a problem that confronts every occupant of the White House: His authority does not match the expectations for his performance. We expect our presidents to be leaders, Neustadt tells us, but the office guarantees no more than that they will be clerks. In the following excerpt, Neustadt explains that the key to presidential success lies in persuasion, and shows how the ability to persuade depends on bargaining.*

THE LIMITS ON command suggest the structure of our government. The Constitutional Convention of 1787 is supposed to have created a government of "separated powers." It did nothing of the sort. Rather, it created a government of separated institutions *sharing* powers.[1] "I am part of the legislative process," Eisenhower often said in 1959 as a reminder of his veto.[2] Congress, the dispenser of authority and funds, is no less part of the administrative process. Federalism adds another set of separated institutions. The Bill of Rights adds others. Many public purposes can only be achieved by voluntary acts of private institutions; the press, for one, in Douglass Cater's phrase, is a "fourth branch of government."[3] And with the coming of alliances abroad, the separate institutions of a London, or a Bonn, share in the making of American public policy.

What the Constitution separates our political parties do not combine. The parties are themselves composed of separated organizations sharing public authority. The authority consists of nominating powers. Our national parties are confederations of state and local party institutions, with a headquarters that represents the White House, more or less, if the party has a President in office. These confederacies manage presidential nominations. All other public offices depend upon electorates confined within the states.[4] All other nominations are controlled within the states. The President and congressmen who bear one party's label are divided by dependence upon different sets of voters. The differences are sharpest at the stage of nomination. The White House has too small a share in nominating congressmen, and Congress has too little weight in nominating presidents for party to erase their constitutional separation. Party links are stronger than is frequently supposed, but nominating processes assure the separation.[5]

The separateness of institutions and the sharing of authority prescribe the terms on which a President persuades. When one man shares authority with another, but does not gain or lose his job upon the other's whim, his willingness to act upon the urging of the other turns on whether he conceives the action right for him. The essence of a President's persuasive task is to convince such men that what the White House wants of them is what they ought to do for their sake and on their authority. (Sex matters not at all; for *man* read *woman.*)

Persuasive power, thus defined, amounts to more than charm or reasoned argument. These have their uses for a President, but these are not the whole of his resources. For the individuals he would induce to do what he wants done on their own responsibility will need or fear some acts by him on his responsibility. If they share his authority, he has some share in theirs. Presidential "powers" may be inconclusive when a President commands, but always remain relevant as he persuades. The status and authority inherent in his office reinforce his logic and his charm.

Status adds something to persuasiveness; authority adds still more. When Truman urged wage changes on his secretary of commerce [Charles Sawyer] while the latter was administering the [recently seized] steel mills, he and Secretary Sawyer were not just two men reasoning with one another. Had they been so, Sawyer probably would never have agreed to act. Truman's status gave him special claims to Sawyer's loyalty or at least attention. In Walter Bagehot's charming phrase, "no man can *argue* on his knees." Although there is no kneeling in this country, few men—and exceedingly few cabinet officers—are immune to the impulse to say "yes" to the President of the United States. It grows harder to say "no" when they are seated in his Oval Office at the White House, or in his study on the second floor, where almost tangibly he partakes of the aura of his physical surroundings. In Sawyer's case, moreover, the President possessed formal authority to intervene in many matters of concern to the secretary of commerce. These matters ranged from jurisdictional disputes among the defense agencies to legislation pending before Congress and, ultimately, to the tenure of the secretary, himself. There is nothing in the record to suggest that Truman voiced specific threats when they negotiated over wage increases. But given his formal powers and their relevance to Sawyer's other interests, it is safe to assume that Truman's very advocacy of wage action conveyed an implicit threat.

A President's authority and status give him great advantages in dealing with the men he would persuade. Each "power" is a vantage point for him in the degree that other men have use for his authority. From the veto to appointments, from publicity to budgeting, and so down a long list, the White House now controls the most encompassing array of vantage points in the American political system. With hardly an exception, those who share in governing this country are aware that at some time, in some degree, the doing of *their* jobs, the furthering of *their* ambitions, may depend upon the President of the United States. Their need for presidential action, or their fear of it, is bound to be recurrent if not actually continuous. Their need or fear is his advantage.

A President's advantages are greater than mere listing of his "powers" might suggest. Those with whom he deals must deal with him until the last day of his term. Because they have continuing relationships with him, his future, while it lasts, supports his present influence. Even though there is no need or fear of him today, what he could do tomorrow may supply today's advantage. Continuing relationships may convert any "power," any aspect of his status, into vantage points in almost any case. When he induces other people to do what he wants done, a President can trade on their dependence now and later.

The President's advantages are checked by the advantages of others. Continuing relationships will pull in both directions. These are relationships of mutual dependence. A President depends upon the persons whom he would persuade; he has to reckon with his need or fear of them. They too will possess status or authority, or both, else they would be of little use to him. Their vantage points confront his own; their power tempers his.

Persuasion is a two-way street. Sawyer, it will be recalled, did not respond at once to Truman's plan for wage increases at the steel mills. On the contrary, the secretary hesitated and delayed and only acquiesced when he was satisfied that publicly he would not bear the onus of decision. Sawyer had some points of vantage all his own from which to resist presidential pressure. If he had to reckon with coercive implications in the President's "situations of strength," so had Truman to be mindful of the implications underlying Sawyer's place as a department head, as steel administrator, and as a cabinet spokesman for business. Loyalty is reciprocal. Having taken on a dirty job in the steel crisis, Sawyer had strong claims to loyal support. Besides, he had authority to do some things that the White House could ill afford. . . . [H]e might have resigned in a huff (the removal power also works two ways). Or . . . he might have declined to sign necessary orders. Or he might have let it be known publicly that he deplored what he was told to do and protested its doing. By following any of these courses Sawyer almost surely would have strengthened the position of management, weakened the position of the White House, and embittered the union. But the whole purpose of a wage increase was to enhance White House persuasiveness in urging settlement upon union and companies alike. Although Sawyer's status and authority did not give him the power to prevent an increase outright, they gave him capability to undermine its purpose. If his authority over wage rates had been vested by a statute, not by revocable presidential order, his power of prevention might have been complete. So Harold Ickes [Sr.] demonstrated in the famous case of helium sales to Germany before the Second World War.[6]

The power to persuade is the power to bargain. Status and authority yield bargaining advantages. But in a government of "separated institutions sharing power," they yield them to all sides. With the array of vantage points at his disposal, a President may be far more persuasive than his logic or his charm could make him. But outcomes are not guaranteed by his advantages. There remain the counter pressures those whom he would influence can bring to bear on him from vantage points at their disposal. Command has limited utility; persuasion becomes give-and-take. It is well that the White House holds the vantage points it does. In such a business any President may need them all—and more.

THIS VIEW OF POWER as akin to bargaining is one we commonly accept in the sphere of congressional relations. Every textbook states and every legislative session demonstrates that save in times like the extraordinary Hundred Days of 1933—times virtually ruled out by definition at mid-century—a President will often be unable to obtain congressional action on his terms or even to halt action he opposes. The reverse is equally accepted: Congress often is frustrated by the President. Their formal powers are so intertwined that neither will accomplish very much, for very long, without the acquiescence of the other. By the same token, though, what one demands the other can resist. The stage is set for that great game, much like collective bargaining, in which each seeks to profit from the other's needs and fears. It is a game played catch-as-catch-can, case by case. And everybody knows the game, observers and participants alike.

The concept of real power as a give-and-take is equally familiar when applied to presidential influence outside the formal structure of the federal government. . . . When he deals with [governors, union officials, company executives and even citizens or workers] a President draws bargaining advantage from his status or authority. By virtue of their public places or their private rights they have some capability to reply in kind.

In spheres of party politics the same thing follows, necessarily, from the confederal nature of our party organizations. Even in the case of national nominations a President's advantages are checked by those of others. In 1944 it is by no means clear that Roosevelt got his first choice as his running mate. In 1948 Truman, then the President, faced serious revolts against his nomination. In 1952 his intervention from the White House helped assure the choice of Adlai Stevenson, but it is far from clear that Truman could have done as much for any other candidate acceptable to him.[7] In 1956 when Eisenhower was President, the record leaves obscure just who backed Harold Stassen's efforts to block Richard Nixon from renomination as vice president. But evidently everything did not go quite as Eisenhower wanted, whatever his intentions may have been.[8] The outcomes in these instances bear all the marks of limits on command and of power checked by power that characterize congressional relations. Both in and out of politics these checks and limits seem to be quite widely understood.

Influence becomes still more a matter of give-and-take when Presidents attempt to deal with allied governments. A classic illustration is the long unhappy wrangle over Suez policy in 1956. In dealing with the British and the French before their military intervention, Eisenhower had his share of bargaining advantages but no effective power of command. His allies had their share of counterpressures, and they finally tried the most extreme of all: action despite him. His pressure then was instrumental in reversing them. But had the British government been on safe ground at home, Eisenhower's wishes might have made as little difference after intervention as before. Behind the decorum of diplomacy—which was not very decorous in the Suez affair—relationships among allies are not unlike relationships among state delegations at a national convention. Power is persuasion, and persuasion becomes bargaining. The concept is familiar to everyone who watches foreign policy.

In only one sphere is the concept unfamiliar: the sphere of executive relations. Perhaps because of civics textbooks and teaching in our schools, Americans instinctively resist the view that power in this sphere resembles power in all others. Even Washington reporters, White House aides, and congressmen are not immune to the illusion that administrative agencies comprise a single structure, "the" executive branch, where presidential word is law, or ought to be. Yet . . . when a President seeks something from executive officials his persuasiveness is subject to the same sorts of limitations as in the case of congressmen, or governors, or national committeemen, or private citizens, or foreign governments. There are no generic differences, no differences in kind and only sometimes in degree. The incidents preceding the dismissal of [General Douglas] MacArthur and the incidents surrounding seizure of the steel mills make it plain that here as elsewhere influence derives from bargaining advantages; power is a give-and-take.

Like our governmental structure as a whole, the executive establishment consists of separated institutions sharing powers. The President heads one of these; cabinet officers, agency administrators, and military commanders head others. Below the departmental level, virtually independent bureau chiefs head many more. Under mid-century conditions, federal operations spill across dividing lines on organization charts; almost every policy entangles many agencies; almost every program calls for interagency collaboration. Everything somehow involves the President. But operating agencies owe their existence least of all to one another—and only in some part to him. Each has a separate statutory base; each has its statutes to administer; each deals with a different set of subcommittees at the Capitol. Each has its own peculiar set of clients, friends, and enemies outside the formal government. Each has a different set of specialized careerists inside its own bailiwick. Our Constitution gives the President the "take-care" clause and the appointive power. Our statutes give him central budgeting and a degree of personnel control. All agency administrators are responsible to him. But they also are responsible to Congress, to their clients, to their staffs, and to themselves. In short, they have five masters. Only after all of those do they owe any loyalty to each other.

"The members of the cabinet," Charles G. Dawes used to remark, "are a president's natural enemies." Dawes had been Harding's budget director,

Coolidge's vice president, and Hoover's ambassador to London; he also had been General Pershing's chief assistant for supply in World War I. The words are highly colored, but Dawes knew whereof he spoke. The men who have to serve so many masters cannot help but be somewhat the "enemy" of any one of them. By the same token, any master wanting service is in some degree the "enemy" of such a servant. A President is likely to want loyal support but not to relish trouble on his doorstep. Yet the more his cabinet members cleave to him, the more they may need help from him in fending off the wrath of rival masters. Help, though, is synonymous with trouble. Many a cabinet officer, with loyalty ill rewarded by his lights and help withheld, has come to view the White House as innately hostile to department heads. Dawes's dictum can be turned around.

A senior presidential aide remarked to me in Eisenhower's time: "If some of these cabinet members would just take time out to stop and ask themselves, 'What would I want if I were President?' they wouldn't give him all the trouble he's been having." But even if they asked themselves the question, such officials often could not act upon the answer. Their personal attachment to the President is all too often overwhelmed by duty to their other masters.

Executive officials are not equally advantaged in their dealings with a President. Nor are the same officials equally advantaged all the time. Not every officeholder can resist like a MacArthur or Sawyer. . . . The vantage points conferred upon officials by their own authority and status vary enormously. The variance is heightened by particulars of time and circumstance. In mid-October 1950, Truman, at a press conference, remarked of the man he had considered firing in August and would fire the next April for intolerable insubordination:

> Let me tell you something that will be good for your souls. It's a pity that you . . . can't understand the ideas of two intellectually honest men when they meet. General MacArthur . . . is a member of the Government of the United States. He is loyal to that Government. He is loyal to the President. He is loyal to the President in his foreign policy. . . .There is no disagreement between General MacArthur and myself.[9]

MacArthur's status in and out of government was never higher than when Truman spoke those words. The words, once spoken, added to the general's credibility thereafter when he sought to use the press in his campaign against the President. And what had happened between August and October? Near victory had happened, together with that premature conference on postwar plans, the meeting at Wake Island.

If the bargaining advantages of a MacArthur fluctuate with changing circumstances, this is bound to be so with subordinates who have at their disposal fewer powers, lesser status, to fall back on. And when officials have no powers in their own right, or depend upon the President for status, their counterpressure may be limited indeed. White House aides, who fit both categories, are among the most responsive men of all, and for good reason. As a director of the budget once remarked to me, "Thank God I'm here and not across the street. If the President doesn't call me, I've got plenty I can do right here and plenty coming up to me, by rights, to justify my calling him. But those poor fellows over there, if the boss doesn't call them, doesn't ask them to do something, what *can* they do but sit?" Authority and status so conditional are frail reliances in resisting a President's own wants. Within the White House precincts, lifted eyebrows may suffice to set an aide in motion; command, coercion, even charm aside. But even in the White House a President does not monopolize effective power. Even there persuasion is akin to bargaining. A former Roosevelt aide once wrote of cabinet officers:

> Half of a President's suggestions, which theoretically carry the weight of orders, can be safely forgotten by a Cabinet member. And if the President asks about a suggestion a second time, he can be told that it is being investigated. If he asks a third time, a wise Cabinet officer will give him at least part of what he suggests. But only occasionally, except about the most important matters, do Presidents ever get around to asking three times.[10]

The rule applies to staff as well as to the cabinet, and certainly has been applied *by* staff in Truman's time and Eisenhower's.

Some aides will have more vantage points than a selective memory. Sherman Adams, for example, as the assistant to the President under Eisenhower, scarcely deserved the appellation "White House aide" in the meaning of the term before his time or as applied to other members of the Eisenhower entourage. Although Adams was by no means "chief of staff" in any sense so sweeping—or so simple—as press commentaries often took for granted, he apparently became no more dependent on the President than Eisenhower on him. "I need him," said the President when Adams turned out to have been remarkably imprudent in the Goldfine case, and delegated to him, at least nominally, the decision on his own departure.[11] This instance is extreme, but the tendency it illustrates is common enough. Any aide who demonstrates to others that he has the President's consistent confidence and a consistent part in presidential business will acquire so much business on his own account that he becomes in some sense independent of his chief. Nothing in the Constitution keeps a well-placed aide from converting status into power of his own, usable in some degree even against the President—an outcome not unknown in Truman's regime or, by all accounts, in Eisenhower's.

The more an officeholder's status and his powers stem from sources independent of the President, the stronger will be his potential pressure on the President. Department heads in general have more bargaining power than do most members of the White House staff; but bureau chiefs may have still more, and specialists at upper levels of established career services may have almost unlimited reserves of the enormous power which consists of sitting still. as Franklin Roosevelt once remarked:

> The Treasury is so large and far-flung and ingrained in its practices that I find it almost impossible to get the action and results I want—even with Henry [Morgenthau] there. But the Treasury is not to be compared with the State Department. You should go through the experience of trying to get any changes in the thinking, policy, and action of the career diplomats and then you'd know what a real problem was. But the Treasury and the State Department put together are nothing compared with the Na-a-vy. The admirals are really something to cope with—and I should know. To change anything in the Na-a-vy is like punching a feather bed. You punch it with your right and you punch it with your left until you are finally exhausted, and then you find the damn bed just as it was before you started punching.[12]

In the right circumstances, of course, a President can have his way with any of these people. . . . [But] as between a President and his "subordinates," no less than others on whom he depends, real power is reciprocal and varies markedly with organization, subject matter, personality and situation. The mere fact that persuasion is directed at executive officials signifies no necessary easing of his way. Any new congressman of the Administration's party, especially if narrowly elected, may turn out more amenable (though less useful) to the President than any seasoned bureau chief "downtown." *The probabilities of power do not derive from the literary theory of the Constitution.*

THERE IS A widely held belief in the United States that were it not for folly or for knavery, a reasonable President would need no power other than the logic of his argument. No less a personage than Eisenhower has subscribed to that belief in many a campaign speech and press-conference remark. But faulty reasoning and bad intentions do not cause all quarrels with Presidents. The best of reasoning and of intent cannot compose them all. For in the first place, what the President wants will rarely seem a trifle to the people he wants it from. And in the second place, they will be bound to judge it by the standard of their own responsibilities, not his. However logical his argument according to his lights, their judgment may not bring them to his view.

Those who share in governing this country frequently appear to act as though they were in business for themselves. So, in a real though not entire sense, they are and have to be. When Truman and MacArthur fell to quarreling, for example, the stakes were no less than the substance of American foreign policy, the risks of greater war or military stalemate, the prerogatives of Presidents and field commanders, the pride of a proconsul and his place in history. Intertwined, inevitably, were other stakes as well: political stakes for men and factions of both parties; power stakes for interest groups with which they were or wished to be affiliated. And every stake was raised by the apparent discontent in the American public mood. There is no reason to suppose that in such circumstances men of large but differing responsibilities will see all things through the same glasses. On the contrary, it is to be expected that their views of what ought to be done and what they then should do will vary with the differing perspectives their particular responsibilities evoke. Since their duties are not vested in a "team" or a "collegium" but in themselves, as individuals, one must expect that they will see things for themselves. Moreover, when they are responsible to many masters and when an event or policy turns loyalty against loyalty—a day-by-day occurrence in the nature of the case—one must assume that those who have the duties to perform will choose the terms of reconciliation. This is the essence of their personal responsibility. When their own duties pull in opposite directions, who else but they can choose what they will do?

When Truman dismissed MacArthur, the latter lost three posts: the American command in the Far East, the Allied command for the occupation of Japan, and the United Nations command in Korea. He also lost his status as the senior officer on active duty in the United States armed forces.

So long as he held those positions and that status, though, he had a duty to his troops, to his profession, to himself (the last is hard for any man to disentangle from the rest). As a public figure and a focus for men's hopes he had a duty to constituents at home, and in Korea and Japan. He owed a duty also to those other constituents, the UN governments contributing to his field forces. As a patriot he had a duty to his country. As an accountable official and an expert guide he stood at the call of Congress. As a military officer he had, besides, a duty to the President, his constitutional commander. Some of these duties may have manifested themselves in terms more tangible or more direct than others. But it would be nonsense to argue that the last negated all the rest, however much it might be claimed to override them. And it makes no more sense to think that anybody but MacArthur was effectively empowered to decide how he himself would reconcile the competing demands his duties made upon him.

. . . Reasonable men, it is so often said, *ought* to be able to agree on the requirements of given situations. But when the outlook varies with the placement of each man, and the response required in his place is for each to decide, their reasoning may lead to disagreement quite as well—and quite as reasonably. Vanity, or vice, may weaken reason, to be sure, but it is idle to assign these as the cause of . . . MacArthur's defiance. Secretary Sawyer's hesitations, cited earlier, are in the same category. One need not denigrate such men to explain their conduct. For the responsibilities they felt, the "facts" they saw, simply were not the same as those of their superiors; yet they, not the superiors, had to decide what they would do.

Outside the executive branch the situation is the same, except that loyalty to the President may often matter *less*. There is no need to spell out the comparison with governors of Arkansas, steel company executives, trade union leaders, and the like. And when one comes to congressmen who can do nothing for themselves (or their constituents) save as they are elected, term by term, in districts and through party structures differing from those on which a President depends, the case is very clear. An able Eisenhower aide with long congressional experience remarked to me in 1958: "The people on the Hill don't do what they might *like* to do, they do what they think they *have* to do in their own interest as *they* see it." This states the case precisely.

The essence of a President's persuasive task, with congressmen and everybody else, is to induce them to believe that what he wants of them is what their own appraisal of their own responsibilities requires them to do in their interest, not his. Because men may differ in their views on public policy, because differences in outlook stem from differences in duty—duty to one's office, one's constituents, oneself—that task is bound to be more like collective bargaining than like a reasoned argument among philosopher kings. Overtly or implicitly, hard bargaining has characterized all illustrations offered up to now. This is the reason why: Persuasion deals in the coin of self-interest with men who have some freedom to reject what they find counterfeit.

A PRESIDENT DRAWS influence from bargaining advantages. But does he always need them? . . . [S]uppose most players of the governmental game see policy objectives much alike, then can he not rely on logic (or on charm) to get him what he wants? The answer is that even then most outcomes turn on bargaining. The reason for this answer is a simple one: Most who share in governing have interests of their own beyond the realm of policy objectives. The sponsorship of policy, the form it takes, the conduct of it, and the credit for it separate their interest from the President's despite agreement on the end in view. In political government the means can matter quite as much as ends; they often matter more. And there are always differences of interest in the means.

Let me introduce a case externally the opposite of my previous examples: the European Recovery Program of 1948, the so-called Marshall Plan. This is perhaps the greatest exercise in policy agreement since the Cold War began. When the then secretary of state, George Catlett Marshall, spoke at the Harvard commencement in June 1947, he launched one of the most creative, most imaginative ventures in the history of American foreign relations. What makes this policy most notable for present purposes, however, is that it became effective upon action by the Eightieth Congress, at the behest of Harry Truman, in the election year 1948.[13]

Eight months before Marshall spoke at Harvard, the Democrats had lost control of both houses of Congress for the first time in fourteen years. Truman, whom the secretary represented, had just finished his second troubled year as President-by-succession. Truman was regarded with so little warmth in his own party that in 1946 he had been urged not to participate in the congressional campaign. At the opening of Congress in January 1947, Senator Robert A. Taft, "Mr. Republican," had somewhat the attitude of a President-elect. This was a vision widely shared in Washington, with Truman relegated thereby to the role of caretaker-on-term. Moreover, within just two weeks of Marshall's commencement address, Truman was to veto two prized accomplishments of Taft's congressional majority: the Taft-Hartley Act and tax reduction.[14] Yet scarcely ten months later the Marshall Plan was under way on terms to satisfy its sponsors, it authorization completed, its first-year funds in sight, its administering agency in being: all managed by as thorough a display of executive-congressional cooperation as any we have seen since the Second World War. For any President at any time this would have been a great accomplishment. In years before mid-century it would have been enough to make the future reputation of his term. And for a Truman, at this time, enactment of the Marshall Plan appears almost miraculous.

How was the miracle accomplished? How did a President so situated bring it off? In answer, the first thing to note is that he did not do it by himself. Truman had help of a sort no less extraordinary than the outcome. Although each stands for something more complex, the names of Marshall, Vandenberg, Patterson, Bevin, Stalin tell the story of that help.

In 1947, two years after V-J Day, General Marshall was something more than secretary of state. He was a man venerated by the President as "the greatest living American," literally an embodiment of Truman's ideals. He was honored at the Pentagon as an architect of victory. He was thoroughly respected by the secretary of the Navy, James V. Forrestal, who that year became the first secretary of defense. On Capitol Hill, Marshall had an enormous fund of respect stemming from his war record as Army chief of staff, and in the country generally no officer had come out of the war with a higher reputation for judgment, intellect, and probity. Besides, as secretary of state, he had behind him the first generation of matured foreign service officers produced by the reforms of the 1920s, and mingled with them, in the departmental service, were some of the ablest of the men drawn by the war from private life to Washington. In terms both of staff talent and staff use, Marshall's years began a State Department "golden age" that lasted until the era of McCarthy. Moreover, as his under secretary, Marshall had, successively, Dean Acheson and Robert Lovett, men who commanded the respect of the professionals and the regard of congressmen. (Acheson had been brilliantly successful at congressional relations as assistant secretary in the war and postwar years.) Finally, as a special undersecretary Marshall had Will Clayton, a man highly regarded, for good reason, at both ends of Pennsylvania Avenue.

Taken together, these are exceptional resources for a secretary of state. In the circumstances, they were quite as necessary as they obviously are relevant. The Marshall Plan was launched by a lame-duck Administration "scheduled" to leave office in eighteen months. Marshall's program faced a congressional leadership traditionally isolationist and currently intent upon economy. European aid was viewed with envy by a Pentagon distressed and virtually disarmed through budget cuts, and by domestic agencies intent on enlarged welfare programs. It was not viewed with liking by a Treasury intent on budget surpluses. The plan had need of every asset that could be extracted from the personal position of its nominal author and from the skills of his assistants.

Without the equally remarkable position of the senior senator from Michigan, Arthur H. Vandenberg, it is hard to see how Marshall's assets could have been enough. Vandenberg was chairman of the Senate Foreign Relations Committee. Actually, he was much more than that. Twenty years a senator, he was the senior member of his party in the chamber. Assiduously cultivated by FDR and Truman, he was a chief Republican proponent of bipartisanship in foreign policy and consciously conceived himself its living symbol to his party, to the country, and abroad. Moreover, by informal but entirely operative agreement with his colleague Taft, Vandenberg held the acknowledged lead among Senate Republicans in the whole field of international affairs. This acknowledgment meant more in 1947 than it might have meant at any other time. With confidence in the advent of a Republican administration two years hence, most of the gentlemen were in a mood to be responsive and responsible. The war was over, Roosevelt dead, Truman a caretaker, theirs the trust. That the senator from Michigan saw matters in this light his diaries make clear.[15] And this was not the outlook from the Senate side alone; the attitudes of House Republicans associated with the Herter Committee and its tours abroad suggest the same mood of responsibility. Vandenberg was not the only source of help on Capitol Hill. But relatively speaking his position there was as exceptional as Marshall's was downtown.

Help of another sort was furnished by a group of dedicated private citizens who organized one of the most effective instruments for public information seen since the Second World War: the Committee for the Marshall Plan, headed by the eminent Republicans whom FDR in 1940 had brought to the Department of War: Henry L. Stimson as honorary chairman and Robert P. Patterson as active spokesman. The remarkable array of bankers, lawyers, trade unionists, and editors, who had drawn together in defense of "internationalism" before Pearl Harbor and had joined their talents in the war itself, combined again to spark the work of this committee. Their efforts generated a great deal of vocal public support to buttress Marshall's arguments, and Vandenberg's, in Congress.

But before public support could be rallied, there had to be a purpose tangible enough, concrete enough, to provide a rallying ground. At Harvard, Marshall had voiced an idea in general terms. That this was turned into a hard program susceptible of presentation and support is due, in major part, to Ernest Bevin, the British foreign secretary. He well deserves the credit he has sometimes been assigned as, in effect, coauthor of the Marshall Plan. For Bevin seized on Marshall's Harvard speech and organized a European response with promptness and concreteness beyond the State Department's expectations. What had been virtually a trial balloon to test reactions on both sides of the Atlantic was hailed in London as an invitation to the Europeans to send Washington a bill of particulars. This they promptly organized to do, and the American Administration then organized in turn for its reception without further argument internally about the pros and cons of issuing the "invitation" in the first place. But for Bevin there might have been trouble from the secretary of the treasury and others besides.[16]

If Bevin's help was useful at that early stage, Stalin's was vital from first to last. In a mood of self-deprecation Truman once remarked that without Moscow's "crazy" moves "we would never have had out foreign policy . . . we never could have got a thing from Congress."[17] George Kennan, among others, had deplored the anti-Soviet overtone of the case made for the Marshall Plan in Congress and the country, but there is no doubt that this clinched the argument for many segments of American opinion. There also is no doubt that Moscow made the crucial contributions to the case.

By 1947 events, far more than governmental prescience or open action, had given a variety of publics an impression of inimical Soviet intentions (and of Europe's weakness) and a growing urge to "do something about it." Three months before Marshall spoke at Harvard, Greek-Turkish aid and promulgation of the Truman Doctrine had seemed rather to crystallize than to create a public mood and a congressional response. The Marshall planners, be it said, were poorly placed to capitalize on that mood, nor had the secretary wished to do so. Their object, indeed, was to cut across it, striking at the cause of European weakness rather than at Soviet aggressiveness, per se. A strong economy in Western Europe called, ideally, for restorative measures of continental scope. American assistance proffered in an anti-Soviet context would have been contradictory in theory and unacceptable in fact to several of the governments that Washington was anxious to assist. As Marshall, himself, saw it, the logic of his purpose forbade him to play his strongest congressional card. The Russians then proceeded to play it for him. When the Europeans met in Paris, Molotov walked out. After the Czechs had shown continued interest in American aid, a Communist coup overthrew their government while Soviet forces stood along their borders within easy reach of Prague. Molotov transformed the Marshall Plan's initial presentation; Czechoslovakia assured its final passage, which followed by a month the takeover in Prague.

Such was the help accorded Truman in obtaining action on the Marshall Plan. Considering his politically straitened circumstances he scarcely could have done with less. Conceivably some part of Moscow's contribution might have been dispensable, but not Marshall's or Vandenberg's or Bevin's or Patterson's or that of the great many other men whose work is represented by their names in my account. Their aid was not extended to the President for his own sake. He was not favored in this fashion just because they liked him personally or were spellbound by his intellect or charm. They might have been as helpful had all held him in disdain, which some of them certainly did. The Londoners who seized the ball, Vandenberg and Taft and the congressional majority, Marshall and his planners, the officials of other agencies who actively supported them or "went along," the host of influential private citizens who rallied to the cause—all these played the parts they did because they thought they had to, in their interest, given their responsibilities, not Truman's. Yet they hardly would have found it in their interest to collaborate with one another or with him had he not furnished them precisely what they needed from the White House. Truman could not do without their help, but he could not have had it without unremitting effort on his part.

The crucial thing to note about this case is that despite compatibility of views on public policy, Truman got no help he did not pay for (except Stalin's). Bevin scarcely could have seized on Marshall's words had Marshall not been plainly backed by Truman. Marshall's interest would not have comported with the exploitation of his prestige by a president who undercut him openly or subtly or even inadvertently at any point. Vandenberg, presumably, could not have backed proposals by a White House that begrudged him deference and access gratifying to his fellow partisans (and satisfying to himself). Prominent Republicans in private life would not have found it easy to promote a cause identified with Truman's claims on 1948—

and neither would the prominent New Dealers then engaged in searching for a substitute.

Truman paid the price required for their services. So far as the record shows, the White House did not falter once in firm support for Marshall and the Marshall Plan. Truman backed his secretary's gamble on an invitation to all Europe. He made the plan his own in a well-timed address to the Canadians. He lost no opportunity to widen the involvements of his own official family in the cause. Averell Harriman, the secretary of commerce; Julius Krug, the secretary of the interior; Edwin Nourse, the Economic Council chairman; James Webb, the director of the budget—all were made responsible for studies and reports contributing directly to the legislative presentation. Thus these men were committed in advance. Besides, the President continually emphasized to everyone in reach that he did not have doubts, did not desire complications and would foreclose all he could. Reportedly his emphasis was felt at the Treasury, with good effect. And Truman was at special pains to smooth the way for Vandenberg. The senator insisted on "no politics" from the Administration side; there was none. He thought a survey of American resources and capacity essential; he got it in the Krug and Harriman reports. Vandenberg expected advance consultation; he received it, step by step, in frequent meetings with the President and weekly conferences with Marshall. He asked for an effective liaison between Congress and agencies concerned; Lovett and others gave him what he wanted. When the senator decided on the need to change financing and administrative features of the legislation, Truman disregarded Budget Bureau grumbling and acquiesced with grace. When, finally, Vandenberg desired a Republican to head the new administering agency, his candidate, Paul Hoffman, was appointed despite the President's own preference for another. In all these ways Truman employed the sparse advantages his "powers" and his status then accorded him to gain the sort of help he had to have.

Truman helped himself in still another way. Traditionally and practically, no one was placed as well as he to call public attention to the task of Congress (and its Republican leadership). Throughout the fall and winter of 1947 and on into the spring of 1948, he made repeated use of presidential "powers" to remind the country that congressional action was required. Messages, speeches, and an extra session were employed to make the point. Here, too, he drew advantage from his place. However, in his circumstances, Truman's public advocacy might have hurt, not helped, had his words seemed directed toward the forthcoming election. Truman gained advantage for his program only as his own endorsement of it stayed on the right side of that fine line between the "caretaker" in office and the would-be candidate. In public statements dealing with the Marshall Plan he seems to have risked blurring this distinction only once, when he called Congress into session in November 1947 asking both for interim aid to Europe and for peacetime price controls. The second request linked the then inflation with the current Congress (and with Taft), becoming a first step toward one of Truman's major themes in 1948. By calling for both measures at the extra session he could have been accused—and was—of mixing home-front politics with foreign aid. In the event no harm was done the European program (or his politics). But in advance a number of his own advisers feared that such a double call would jeopardize the Marshall Plan. Their fears are testimony to the narrowness of his advantage in employing his own "powers" for its benefit.[18]

It is symptomatic of Truman's situation that bipartisan accommodation by the White House then was thought to mean congressional consultation and conciliation on a scale unmatched in Eisenhower's time. Yet Eisenhower did about as well with opposition congresses as Truman did, in terms of requests granted for defense and foreign aid. It may be said that Truman asked for more extraordinary measures. But it also may be said that Eisenhower never lacked for the prestige his predecessor had to borrow. It often was remarked, in Truman's time, that he seemed a split personality, so sharply did his conduct differentiate domestic politics from national security. But personality aside, how else could he, in his first term, gain ground for an evolving foreign policy? The plain fact is that Truman had to play bipartisanship as he did or lose the game.

HAD TRUMAN LACKED the personal advantages his "powers" and his status gave him, or if he had been maladroit in using them, there probably would not have been a massive European aid program in 1948. Something of the sort, perhaps quite different in its emphasis, would almost certainly have come to pass before the end of 1949. Some American response to European weakness and to Soviet expansion was as certain as such things can be. But in 1948 temptations to await a Taft plan or a Dewey plan might well have caused at least a year's postponement of response had the outgoing Administration bungled its congressional or public or allied or executive relations. Quite aside from the specific virtues of their plan. Truman and his helpers gained that year, at least, in timing the American response. As European time was measured then, this was a precious gain. The President's own share in this accomplishment was vital. He made his contribution by exploiting his advantages. Truman, in effect, lent Marshall and the rest the perquisites and status of his office. In return they lent him their prestige and their own influence. The transfer multiplied his influence despite his limited authority in form and lack of strength politically. Without the wherewithal to make this bargain, Truman could not have contributed to European aid.

Bargaining advantages convey no guarantees. Influence remains a two-way street. In the fortunate instance of the Marshall Plan, what Truman needed was actually in the hands of men who were prepared to "trade" with him. He personally could deliver what they wanted in return. Marshall, Vandenberg, Harriman, et al., possessed the prestige, energy, associations, staffs essential to the legislative effort. Truman himself had a sufficient hold on presidential messages and speeches, on budget policy, on high-level appointments, and on his own time and temper to carry through all aspects of his necessary part. But it takes two to make a bargain. It takes those who have prestige to lend it on whatever terms. Suppose that Marshall had declined the secretaryship of state in January 1947; Truman might not have found a substitute so well equipped to furnish what he needed in the months ahead. Or suppose that Vandenberg had fallen victim to a cancer two years before he actually did; Senator Wiley of Wisconsin would not have seemed to Taft a man with whom the world need be divided. Or suppose that the secretary of the treasury had been possessed of stature, force, and charm commensurate with that of his successor in Eisenhower's time, the redoubtable George M. Humphrey. And what if Truman then had seemed to the Republicans what he turned out to be in 1948, a formidable candidate for President? It is unlikely that a single one of these "supposes" would have changed the final outcome; two or three, however, might have altered it entirely. Truman was not guaranteed more power than his "powers" just because he had continuing relationships with cabinet secretaries and with senior senators. Here, as everywhere, the outcome was conditional on who they were and what he was and how each viewed events, and on their actual performance in response.

Granting that persuasion has no guarantee attached, how can a President reduce the risks of failing to persuade? How can he maximize his prospects for effectiveness by minimizing chances that his power will elude him? The

Marshall Plan suggests an answer: He guards his power prospects in the course of making choices. Marshall himself, and Forrestal and Harriman, and others of the sort held office on the President's appointment. Vandenberg had vast symbolic value partly because FDR and Truman had done everything they could, since 1944, to build him up. The Treasury Department and the Budget Bureau—which together might have jeopardized the plans these others made—were headed by officials whose prestige depended wholly on their jobs. What Truman needed from those "givers" he received, in part, because of his past choice of men and measures. What they received in turn were actions taken or withheld by him, himself. The things they needed from him mostly involved his own conduct where his current choices ruled. The President's own actions in the past had cleared the way for current bargaining. His actions in the present were his trading stock. Behind each action lay a personal choice, and these together comprised his control over the give-and-take that gained him what he wanted. In the degree that Truman, personally, affected the advantages he drew from his relationships with other men in government, his power was protected by his choices.

By "choice" I mean no more than what is commonly referred to as "decision": a President's own act of doing or not doing. Decision is so often indecisive, and indecision is so frequently conclusive, that *choice* becomes the preferable term. "Choice" has its share of undesired connotations. In common usage it implies a black-and-white alternative. Presidential choices are rarely of that character. It also may imply that the alternatives are set before the choice maker by someone else. A President is often left to figure out his options for himself. . . .

If Presidents could count upon past choices to enhance their current influence, as Truman's choice of men had done for him, persuasion would pose fewer difficulties than it does. But Presidents can count on no such thing. Depending on the circumstances, prior choices can be as embarrassing as they were helpful in the instance of the Marshall Plan. . . . Truman's hold upon MacArthur was weakened by his deference toward him in the past.

Assuming that past choices have protected influence, not harmed it, present choices still may be inadequate. If Presidents could count on their own conduct to provide them enough bargaining advantages, as Truman's conduct did where Vandenberg and Marshall were concerned, effective bargaining might be much easier to manage than it often is. In the steel crisis, for instance, Truman's own persuasiveness with companies and union, both, was burdened by the conduct of an independent wage board and of government attorneys in the courts, to say nothing of Wilson, Arnall, Sawyer, and the like. Yet in practice, if not theory, many of *their* crucial choices never were the President's to make. Decisions that are legally in others' hands, or delegated past recall, have an unhappy way of proving just the trading stock most needed when the White House wants to trade. One reason why Truman was consistently more influential in the instance of the Marshall Plan than in the steel case or the MacArthur case is that the Marshall Plan directly involved Congress. In congressional relations there are some things that no one but the President can do. His chance to choose is higher when a message must be sent, or a nomination submitted, or a bill signed into law, than when the sphere of action is confined to the executive, where all decisive tasks may have been delegated past recall.

But adequate or not, a President's choices are the only means in his own hands of guarding his own prospects for effective influence. He can draw power from continuing relationships in the degree that he can capitalize upon the needs of others for the Presidency's status and authority. He helps himself to do so, though, by nothing save ability to recognize the preconditions and the chance advantages and to proceed accordingly in the course of the choice making that comes his way. To ask how he can guard prospective influence is thus to raise a further question: What helps him guard his power stakes in his own acts of choice?

NOTES

1. The reader will want to keep in mind the distinction between two senses in which the word *power* is employed. When I have used the word (or its plural) to refer to formal constitutional, statutory, or customary authority, it is either qualified by the adjective "formal" or placed in quotation marks as "power(s)." Where I have used it in the sense of effective influence on the conduct of others, it appears without quotation marks (and always in the singular). Where clarity and convenience permit, *authority* is substituted for "power" in the first sense and *influence* for power in the second.

2. See, for example, his press conference of July 22, 1959, as reported in the *New York Times*, July 23, 1959.

3. See Douglass Cater, *The Fourth Branch of Government* (Boston: Houghton Mifflin, 1959).

4. With the exception of the vice presidency, of course.

5. See David B. Truman's illuminating study of party relationships in the Eighty-first Congress, *The Congressional Party* (New York: Wiley, 1959), especially chaps. 4, 6, 8.

6. As secretary of the interior in 1939, Harold Ickes refused to approve the sale of helium to Germany despite the insistence of the State Department and the urging of President Roosevelt. Without the Secretary's approval, such sales were forbidden by statute. See *The Secret Diaries of Harold L. Ickes* (New York: Simon & Schuster, 1954), vol. 2, especially pp. 391–93, 396–99.

In this instance the statutory authority ran to the secretary as a matter of his discretion. A President is unlikely to fire cabinet officers for the conscientious exercise of such authority. If the President did so, their successors might well be embarrassed both publicly and at the Capitol were they to reverse decisions previously taken. As for a President's authority to set aside discretionary determinations of this sort, it rests, if it exists at all, on shaky legal ground not likely to be trod save in the gravest of situations.

7. Truman's *Memoirs* indicate that having tried and failed to make Stevenson an avowed candidate in the spring of 1952, the President decided to support the candidacy of Vice President Barkley. But Barkley withdrew early in the convention for lack of key northern support. Though Truman is silent on the matter, Barkley's active candidacy nearly was revived during the balloting, but the forces then aligning to revive it were led by opponents of Truman's Fair Deal, principally Southerners. As a practical matter, the President could not have lent his weight to their endeavors and could back no one but Stevenson to counter them. The latter's strength could not be shifted, then, to Harriman or Kefauver. Instead the other Northerners had to be withdrawn. Truman helped withdraw them. But he had no other option. See Harry S Truman, *Memoirs*, vol. 2, *Years of Trial and Hope* (Garden City, N.Y.: Doubleday, Time Inc., 1956), pp. 495–96.

8. The reference is to Stassen's public statement of July 23, 1956, calling for Nixon's replacement on the Republican ticket by Governor Herter of Massachusetts, the later secretary of state. Stassen's statement was issued after a conference with the President. Eisenhower's public statements on the vice-presidential nomination, both before and after Stassen's call, permit of alternative inferences: either that the President would have preferred another candidate, provided this could be arranged without a showing of White House dictation, or that he wanted Nixon on condition that the latter could show popular appeal. In the event, neither result was achieved. Eisenhower's own remarks lent strength to rapid party moves that smothered Stassen's effort. Nixon's nomination thus was guaranteed too quickly to appear the consequence of popular demand. For the public record on this matter see reported statements by Eisenhower, Nixon, Stassen, Herter, and Leonard Hall (the National Republican Chairman) in the *New York Times* for March, 1, 8, 15, 16; April 27; July 15, 16, 25–31; August 3, 4, 17, 23, 1956. See also the account from private sources by Earl Mazo in *Richard Nixon: A Personal and Political Portrait* (New York: Harper, 1959), pp. 158–87.

9. Stenographic transcript of presidential press conference, October 19, 1950, on file in the Truman Library at Independence, Missouri.

10. Jonathan Daniels, *Frontier on the Potomac* (New York: Macmillan, 1946), pp. 31–32.

11. Transcript of presidential press conference, June 18, 1958, in *Public Papers of the Presidents Dwight D. Eisenhower, 1958* (Washington, D.C.: National Archives, 1959), p. 479. In the summer of 1958, a congressional investigation into the affairs of a New England textile manufacturer, Bernard Goldfine, revealed that Sherman Adams had accepted various gifts and favors from him (the most notoriety attached to a vicuña coat). Adams also had made inquiries about the status of a Federal Communications Commission proceeding in which Goldfine was involved. In September 1958 Adams was allowed to resign. The episode was highly publicized and much discussed in that year's congressional campaigns.

12. As reported in Marriner S. Eccles (*Beckoning Frontiers,* New York: Knopf, 1951), p. 336.

13. In drawing together these observations on the Marshall Plan, I have relied on the record of personal participation by Joseph M. Jones, *The Fifteen Weeks* (New York: Viking, 1955), especially pp. 89–256; on the recent study by Harry Bayard Price, *The Marshall Plan and Its Meaning* (Ithaca: Cornell University Press, 1955), especially pp. 1–86; on the Truman *Memoirs*, vol. 2, chaps. 7–9; on Arthur H. Vandenberg, Jr., ed., *The Private Papers of Senator Vandenberg* (Boston: Houghton Mifflin, 1952), especially pp. 373 ff.; and on notes of my own made at the time. This is an instance of policy development not covered, to my knowledge, by any of the university programs engaged in the production of case studies.

14. Secretary Marshall's speech, formally suggesting what became known as the Marshall Plan, was made at Harvard on June 5, 1947. On June 20 the President vetoed the Taft-Hartley Act; his veto was overridden three days later. On June 16 he vetoed the first of two tax reduction bills (HR 1) passed at the first session of the Eightieth Congress; the second of these (HR 3950), a replacement for the other, he also disapproved on July 18. In both instances his veto was narrowly sustained.

15. *Private Papers of Senator Vandenberg,* pp. 378–79, 446.

16. The initial reluctance of secretary of the treasury, John Snyder, to support large-scale spending overseas became a matter of public knowledge on June 25, 1947. At a press conference on that day he interpreted Marshall's Harvard speech as a call on Europeans to help themselves, by themselves. At another press conference the same day, Marshall for his own part had indicated that the United States would consider helping programs on which Europeans agreed. The next day Truman held a press conference and was asked the inevitable question. He replied, "General Marshall and I are in complete agreement." When pressed further, Truman remarked sharply, "The secretary of the treasury and the secretary of state and the President are in complete agreement." Thus the President cut Snyder off, but had programming gathered less momentum overseas, no doubt he would have been heard from again as time passed and opportunity offered.

The foregoing quotations are from the stenographic transcript of the presidential press conference June 26, 1947, on file in the Truman Library at Independence, Missouri.

17. A remark made in December 1955, three years after he left office, but not unrepresentative of views he expressed, on occasion, while he was President.

18. This might also be taken as testimony to the political timidity of officials in the State Department and the Budget Bureau where that fear seems to have been strongest. However, conversations at the time with white House aides incline me to believe that there, too, interjection of the price issue was thought a gamble and a risk. For further comment see my "Congress and the Fair Deal: A Legislative Balance Sheet," *Public Policy,* vol. 5 (Cambridge: Harvard University Press, 1954), pp. 362–64.

7-2

from *Going Public*

Samuel Kernell

Richard Neustadt, writing in 1960, judged that the president's ability to lead depended on skill at the bargaining table in cutting deals with other politicians. In the following essay Samuel Kernell examines how the leadership strategy of modern presidents has evolved. He finds that, rather than limiting their leadership to quiet diplomacy with fellow Washingtonians, modern presidents often "go public," a set of activities borrowed from presidential election campaigns and directed toward persuading other politicians to adopt their policy preferences. Some examples of going public are a televised press conference, a special prime-time address to the nation, traveling outside Washington to deliver a speech to business or professional convention, or a visit to a day care center with network cameras trailing behind.

Introduction: Going Public in Theory and Practice

WHEN PRESIDENT BUSH delivered his State of the Union address to the joint assembly of the mostly Democratic Congress in January 1992, he assumed what has become a familiar stance with Congress:

> I pride myself that I am a prudent man, and I believe that patience is a virtue. But I understand that politics is for some a game. . . . I submit my plan tomorrow. And I am asking you to pass it by March 20. And I ask the American people to let you know they want this action by March 20.
> From the day after that, if it must be: The battle is joined.
> And you know when principle is at stake, I relish a good fair fight.

Once upon a time, these might have been fighting words, but in this era of divided government, with the legislative and executive branches con-

Excerpted from Samuel Kernell, *Going Public: New Strategies of Presidential Leadership*, 3d edition (Washington, D.C.: CQ Press, 1997), pp. 1–12, 17–26, 34–38, 57–64.

trolled by different parties, and presidents who therefore routinely enlist public support in their dealings with other Washington politicians, such rhetoric caused hardly a ripple in Congress.

By 1992, presidential appeals for public support had, in fact, become commonplace. Jimmy Carter delivered four major television addresses on the energy crisis alone and was about to give a fifth when his pollster convinced him that he would be wasting his time. Richard Nixon employed prime-time television so extensively to promote his policies on Vietnam that the Federal Communications Commission (FCC) took an unprecedented step when it applied the "fairness doctrine" to a presidential appeal and granted critics of the war response time on the networks.[1] (In the past, the FCC had occasionally invoked the "equal time" rule during presidential campaigns.) More than any other of Bush's predecessors, Ronald Reagan excelled in rallying public opinion behind presidential policies, but by the end of his second term, he had worn out his welcome with the networks, who stood to lose at least $200,000 in advertising each time he delivered one of his prime-time addresses. They instituted an independent assessment of the likely newsworthiness of the president's address, thereby managing to pare down the frequency of Reagan's televised speeches.[2]

I call the approach to presidential leadership that has come into vogue at the White House "going public." It is a strategy whereby a president promotes himself and his policies in Washington by appealing to the American public for support. Forcing compliance from fellow Washingtonians by going over their heads to appeal to their constituents is a tactic not unknown during the first half of the century, but it was seldom attempted. Theodore Roosevelt probably first enunciated the strategic principle of going public when he described the presidency as the "bully pulpit." Moreover, he occasionally put theory into practice with public appeals for his Progressive reforms. During the next thirty years, other presidents also periodically summoned public support to help them in their dealings with Congress. Perhaps the most famous such instance is Woodrow Wilson's ill-fated whistle-stop tour of the country on behalf of his League of Nations treaty. Another historic example is Franklin D. Roosevelt's series of radio "fireside chats," which were designed less to subdue congressional opposition than to remind politicians throughout Washington of his continuing national mandate for the New Deal.

These historical instances are significant in large part because they were rare. Unlike President Nixon, who thought it important "to spread the

White House around" by traveling and speaking extensively,[3] these earlier presidents were largely confined to Washington and obliged to speak to the country through the nation's newspapers. The concept and legitimizing precedents of going public may have been established during these years, but the emergence of presidents who *routinely* do so to promote their policies in Washington awaited the development of modern systems of transportation and mass communications. Going public should be appreciated as a strategic adaptation to the information age.

The regularity with which recent presidents have sought public backing for their Washington dealings has altered the way politicians both inside and outside the White House regard the office. The following chapters of this book present numerous instances of presidents preoccupied with public relations, as if these activities chiefly determined their success. Cases are recounted of other Washington politicians intently monitoring the president's popularity ratings and his addresses on television, as if his performance in these realms governed their own behavior. Also examined are testimonials of central institutional figures, such as those from various Speakers of the House of Representatives, citing the president's prestige and rhetoric as they explain Congress's actions. If the public ruminations of politicians are to be believed, the president's effectiveness in rallying public support has become a primary consideration for those who do business with him.

Presidential Theory

Going public merits study because presidents now appeal to the public routinely. But there is another reason as well. Compared with many other aspects of the modern presidency, scholarship has only recently directed its attention toward this feature of the president's repertoire. Although going public had not become a keystone of presidential leadership in the 1950s and 1960s when much of the influential scholarship on the subject was written, sufficient precedents were available for scholars to consider its potential for presidential leadership in the future.

Probably the main reason presidential scholarship has shortchanged going public is its fundamental incompatibility with bargaining. Presidential power is the "power to bargain," as Richard E. Neustadt taught a generation of students of the presidency.[4] When Neustadt gave this theme its most evocative expression in 1960, the "bargaining president" had already become a centerpiece of pluralist theories of American politics. Nearly a decade earlier, Robert A. Dahl and Charles E. Lindblom had described the politician in America generically as "the human embodiment of a bargaining society." They made a special point to include the president in writing that despite his possessing "more hierarchical controls than any other single figure in the government . . . like everyone else . . . the President must bargain constantly."[5] Since Neustadt's landmark study, other major works in the field have reinforced and elaborated on the concept of the bargaining president.[6]

Going public violates bargaining in several ways. First, it rarely includes the kinds of exchanges necessary, in pluralist theory, for the American political system to function properly. At times, going public will be merely superfluous—fluff compared with the substance of traditional political exchange. Practiced in a dedicated way, however, it can threaten to displace bargaining.

Second, going public fails to extend benefits for compliance, but freely imposes costs for noncompliance. In appealing to the public to "tell your senators and representatives by phone, wire, and Mailgram that the future hangs in balance," the president seeks the aid of a third party—the public— to force other politicians to accept his preferences.[7] If targeted representatives are lucky, the president's success may cost them no more than an opportunity at the bargaining table to shape policy or to extract compensation. If unlucky, they may find themselves both capitulating to the president's wishes and suffering the reproach of constituents for having resisted him in the first place. By imposing costs and failing to offer benefits, going public is more akin to force than to bargaining. Nelson W. Polsby makes this point when he says that members of Congress may "find themselves ill disposed toward a president who prefers to deal indirectly with them [by going public] through what they may interpret as coercion rather than face-to-face in the spirit of mutual accommodation."[8] The following comment of one senator may well sum up commonly felt sentiments, if not the actions, of those on Capitol Hill who find themselves repeatedly pressured by the president's public appeals: "A lot of Democrats, even if they like the President's proposal, will vote against him because of his radio address on Saturday."[9]

Third, going public entails public posturing. To the extent that it fixes the president's bargaining position, posturing makes subsequent compromise with other politicians more difficult. Because negotiators must be prepared

to yield some of their clients' preferences to make a deal, bargaining prover-
bially proceeds best behind closed doors. Consider the difficulty Ronald
Reagan's widely publicized challenge "My tax proposal is a line drawn in
dirt" posed for subsequent budget negotiations in Washington.[10] Similarly,
during his nationally televised State of the Union address in 1994, President
Bill Clinton sought to repair his reputation as someone too willing to compromise away his principles by declaring to the assembled joint session of
Congress, "If you send me [health care] legislation that does not guarantee
every American private health insurance that can never be taken away, you
will force me to take this pen, veto the legislation, and we'll come right
back here and start all over again."[11] Not only did these declarations
threaten to cut away any middle ground on which a compromise might be
constructed, they probably stiffened the resolve of the president's adversaries, some of whom would later be needed to pass the administration's
legislative program.

Finally, and possibly most injurious to bargaining, going public undermines the legitimacy of other politicians. It usurps their prerogatives of office, denies their role as representatives, and questions their claim to reflect
the interests of their constituents. For a traditional bargaining stance with
the president to be restored, these politicians would first have to reestablish
parity, probably at a cost of conflict with the White House.[12]

Given these fundamental incompatibilities, one may further speculate
that by spoiling the bargaining environment, going public renders the president's future influence ever more dependent upon his ability to generate
popular support for himself and his policies. The degree to which a president draws upon public opinion determines the kind of leader he will be.

Presidential Practice

Bargaining and going public have never been, in principle, particularly congenial styles of leadership. One can imagine, however, that in an earlier era,
when technology limited the capacity and tendency of presidents to engage
in public relations, these two strategies of leadership might have coexisted
in quiet tension. In modern times, though, when going public is likely to
take the form of a political campaign which engages the energies of numerous presidential aides and the president's attention, the choice has become clear: to choose one strategy of leadership makes it increasingly
difficult to undertake the other. And since they cannot be naively combined,

the decision to go public at one juncture may preclude and undermine the opportunity to bargain at another, and vice versa. All this means that the decision to bargain or to go public must be carefully weighed.

The two case studies below reveal that modern presidents and their advisers carefully attend to this strategic issue. As we shall do throughout this book, we compare instances of presidential success and failure in order to understand the potential gains and losses embedded in presidents' choices.

Ronald Reagan Enlists Public Opinion as a Lever

No president has enlisted public strategies to better advantage than did Ronald Reagan. Throughout his tenure, he exhibited a full appreciation of bargaining and going public as the modern office's principal strategic alternatives. The following examples from a six-month survey of White House news coverage show how entrenched this bifurcated view of presidential strategy has become. The survey begins in late November 1984, when some members of the administration were pondering how the president might exploit his landslide victory and others were preparing a new round of budget cuts and a tax reform bill for the next Congress.

November 29, 1984. Washington Post columnist Lou Cannon reported the following prediction from a White House official: "We're going to have confrontation on spending and consultation on tax reform." The aide explained, "We have somebody to negotiate with us on tax reform, but may not on budget cuts."[13] By "confrontation" he was referring to the president's success in appealing to the public on national television, that is, in going public. By "consultation" he meant bargaining.

January 25, 1985. The above prediction proved accurate two months later when another staffer offered as pristine an evocation of going public as one is likely to find: "We have to look at it, in many ways, like a campaign. He [Reagan] wants to take his case to the people. You have a constituency of 535 legislators as opposed to 100 million voters. But the goal is the same— to get the majority of voters to support your position."[14]

February 10, 1985. In a nationally broadcast radio address, President Reagan extended an olive branch inviting members of Congress to "work with us in the spirit of cooperation and compromise" on the budget. This public statement probably did little to allay the frequently voiced suspicion of House Democratic leaders that such overtures were mainly intended for public consumption. One Reagan aide insisted, however, that the president simply sought to reassure legislators that "he would not 'go over their heads' and campaign across the country for his budget without trying first to reach a compromise."[15] In this statement the aide implicitly concedes the harm public pressure can create for bargaining but seeks to incorporate it advantageously into the strategic thinking of the politicians with whom the administration must deal by not forswearing its use.

March 9, 1985. After some public sparring, the administration eventually settled down to intensive budget negotiations with the Republican-led Senate Finance Committee. Failing to do as well as he would like, however, Reagan sent a message to his party's senators through repeated unattributed statements to the press that, if necessary, he would "go to the people to carry our message forward."[16] Again, public appeals, though held in reserve, were threatened.

March 11, 1985. In an interview with a *New York Times* correspondent, a senior Reagan aide sized up his president: "He's liberated, he wants to get into a fight, he feels strongly and wants to push his program through himself. . . . Reagan never quite believed his popularity before the election, never believed the polls. Now he has it, and he's going to push . . . ahead with our agenda."[17]

May 16, 1985. To avoid entangling tax reform with budget deliberations in Congress, Reagan, at the request of Republican leaders, delayed unveiling his tax reform proposal until late May. A couple of weeks before Reagan's national television address on the subject, White House aides began priming the press with leaks on the proposal's content and promises that the president would follow it with a public relations blitz. In the words of one White House official, the plan was to force Congress to make a "binary choice between tax reform or no tax reform."[18] The administration rejected bargaining, as predicted nearly six months earlier by a White House aide, apparently for two strategic reasons. First, Reagan feared that in a quietly negotiated process, the tax reform package would unravel under the concerted pressure of the special interests. Second, by taking the high-profile approach of "standing up for the people against the special interests," in the words of one adviser, tax reform might do for Republicans what social security did for Democrats—make them the majority party.[19]

During these six months when bargaining held out promise—as it had during negotiations with the Senate Finance Committee—public appeals were held in reserve. The White House occasionally, however, threatened an appeal in trying to gain more favorable consideration. On other occasions, when opponents of the president's policies appeared capable of extracting major concessions—House Democrats on the budget and interest groups on tax reform, for example—the White House disengaged from negotiation and tried through public relations to force Congress to accept his policies. Although by 1985 news items such as the preceding excerpts seemed unexceptional as daily news, they are a recent phenomenon. One does not routinely find such stories in White House reporting twenty years earlier when, for example, John Kennedy's legislative agenda was stalled in Congress.

President Clinton Snares Himself by Bargaining

Shortly after assuming office, President Clinton received some bad news. The Bush administration had underestimated the size of the next year's deficit by $50 billion. The president's campaign promises of new domestic programs and a middle-class tax cut would have to be put on hold in favor of fulfilling his third, now urgent pledge to trim $500 billion from the deficit over the next five years. On February 17, 1993, President Clinton appeared before a joint session of Congress and a national television audience to unveil his deficit reduction package. The president's deficit-cutting options were constrained by two considerations: he wanted to include minimal stimulus spending to honor his campaign promise, and he faced a Congress controlled by fellow Democrats who were committed to many of the programs under the budget ax. Even with proposed cuts in defense spending, the only way the budget could accommodate these constraints was through a tax increase. The package raised taxes on the highest income groups and introduced a broad energy consumption tax. During the following weeks, the president and his congressional liaison team quietly lobbied Congress. He would not again issue a public appeal until the eve of the final vote in August.

The president soon learned that Republicans in both chambers had united in opposition to the administration proposal. Led by Newt Gingrich in the House of Representatives and Bob Dole in the Senate, Republicans retreated to the sidelines and assumed the role of Greek chorus, ominously chanting "tax and spend liberals." This meant that the administration needed virtually every Democratic vote to win. Democratic members appreciated this, and many began exploiting the rising value of their votes to extract concessions that would make the legislation more favorable to their constituents.

By June the president's bargaining efforts had won him a watered down bill that even he had difficulty being enthusiastic about. Meanwhile, the Republicans' public relations campaign had met with success. The American public had come to regard President Clinton as a "tax and spend liberal." Whereas shortly after the speech, the *Los Angeles Times* had found half of their polling respondents willing to describe the president's initiative as "bold and innovative" and only 35 percent of them willing to describe it as "tax and spend," by June these numbers had reversed. Now, 53 percent labeled it "tax and spend" and only 28 percent still regarded it as "bold and innovative." [20] Given this turnaround in the public's assessment of the initiative, it was not surprising that the public also downgraded its evaluation of the initiative's sponsor. During the previous five months, President Clinton's approval rating had plunged from 58 to 41 percent.

This was the situation when several of Clinton's senior campaign consultants sounded the alarm in a memo: in only six months the president had virtually exhausted his capacity for leadership. If he did not turn back the current tide of public opinion, he would be weakened beyond repair. In response, the president assembled his senior advisers to evaluate current strategy. This set the stage for a confrontation between those advisers who represented the president in bargaining with other Washingtonians and those staffers who manned the White House public relations machinery. The argument that erupted between these advisers should disabuse anyone of the notion that bargaining and cultivating public support are separate, self-contained spheres of action that do not encroach on one another. [21]

The president's chief pollster, Stanley Greenberg, opened the discussion by stating his and his fellow consultants' position: "We do not exaggerate when we say that our current course, advanced by our economic team and Congressional leaders, threatens to sink your popularity further and weaken your presidency." "The immediate problem," Greenberg explained, "is that thanks to the Republican effort no one views your economic package as anything other than a tax scheme. You must exercise a 'bold zero option,' which is consultant talk for 'rid your policy of any taxes that affect the middle class.' " (In fact, the only tax still in the bill was a 4.3-cent-per-gallon gasoline tax that would raise a modest $20 billion.) Greenberg then unveiled polling data that found broad public support for such a move. He closed by warning everyone in the room, "We have a very short period of time. And if we don't communicate something serious and focused in the period, we're going to be left with what our detractors used to characterize our plan. . . . Don't assume we can fix it in August." This concluded the case for going public. And in order to use this strategy, Clinton had to change course on taxes.

According to those present, the economic and congressional advisers had listened to this argument "with a slow burn." Finally, the president's chief lobbyist, Howard Paster, blurted out, "This isn't an election! The Senate breaks its ass to get a 4.3-cent-a-gallon tax passed, and we can't just abandon it." Besides, they needed the $20 billion provided by the tax to offset other concessions that would be necessary to get the bill passed. "I need all the chips that are available," Paster pleaded. "Don't bargain them away here. Let me have maximum latitude."

From here, the discussion deteriorated into name calling and assignment of blame. It stopped when Clinton started screaming at everyone—"a purple fit" is the way one participant described it. In the end the president decided that he had to stay the course but that he would begin traveling around the country to explain to the public that his economic package was the "best" one that could be enacted. In mid-August, after a concerted public relations campaign that concluded with a nationally televised address, the legislation barely passed. (In the Senate, Vice President Al Gore cast the tie-breaking vote.) The new administration's first legislative initiative had drained its resources both in Congress and across the nation. From here, the Clinton administration limped toward even more difficult initiatives represented by the North American Free Trade Agreement (NAFTA) and health care reform.

Clearly, as both case studies show, going public appears to foster political relations that are quite at odds with those traditionally cultivated through bargaining. One may begin to examine this phenomenon by asking, what is it about modern politics that would inspire presidents to go public in the first place?

How Washington and Presidents Have Changed

The incompatibility of bargaining and going public presents a pressing theoretical question. Why should presidents come to favor a strategy of leadership that appears so incompatible with the principles of pluralist theory? Why, if other Washington elites legitimately and correctly represent the interests of their clients and constituents, would anything be gained by going over their heads? The answers to these questions are several and complex, having to do with the ways Washington and presidents have changed. All in all, bargaining has shown declining efficiency, and opportunities to go public have increased. . . .

There is another, more fundamental reason for the discrepancy between theory and current practice. Presidents have preferred to go public in recent years perhaps because the strategy offers a better prospect of success than it did in the past. Politicians in Washington may no longer be as tractable to bargaining as they once were. We are in an era of divided government, with one party controlling Congress and the other holding the presidency. Each side frequently finds political advantage in frustrating the other. On such occasions, posturing in preparation for the next election takes precedence over bargaining.

The decoupling of voters from political parties across the nation, which makes possible the occurrence of divided government, has also had more pervasive consequences for political relations among politicians in Washington. Weaker leaders, looser coalitions, more individualistic politicians, and stronger public pressure are among the developments reworking political relations in Washington that may inspire presidents to embrace a strategy of leadership antithetical to that prescribed by theory. . . .

The President's Place in Institutionalized Pluralism

Constructing coalitions across the broad institutional landscape of Congress, the bureaucracy, interest groups, courts, and state governments requires a politician who possesses a panoramic view and commands the resources necessary to engage the disparate parochial interests of Washington's political elites. Only the president enjoys such vantage and resources. Traditional presidential scholarship leaves little doubt as to how they should be employed. . . .

> Status and authority yield bargaining advantages. But in a government of "separated institutions sharing powers," they yield them to all sides. With the array of vantage points at his disposal, a President may be far more persuasive than his logic or his charm could make him. But outcomes are not guaranteed by his advantages. There remain the counter pressures those whom he would influence can bring to bear on him from vantage points at their disposal. Command has limited utility; persuasion becomes give-and-take. . . .[22]

Bargaining is thus the essence of presidential leadership, and pluralist theory explicitly rejects unilateral forms of influence as usually insufficient and ultimately costly. The ideal president is one who seizes the center of the Washington bazaar and actively barters with fellow politicians to build winning coalitions. He must do so, according to this theory, or he will forfeit any claim to leadership. . . .

The President's Calculus

. . . No politician within Washington is better positioned than the president to go outside of the community and draw popular support. With proto-coalitions in disarray and members more sensitive to influences from beyond Washington, the president's hand in mobilizing public opinion has been strengthened. For the new Congress—indeed, for the new Washington generally—going public may at times be the most effective course available.

Under these circumstances, the president's prestige assumes the currency of power. It is something to be spent when the coffers are full, to be conserved when low, and to be replenished when empty. As David Gergen remarked when he was President Reagan's communications director, "Everything here is built on the idea that the President's success depends on grassroots support."[23]

Sixteen years later White House officials continue to adhere to this view. Early in 1997, when asked by campaign-weary news reporters why President Clinton maintained such a heavy travel schedule after the election victory, press secretary Michael D. McCurry lectured them on modern political science: "Campaigns are about framing a choice for the American people. . . . When you are responsible for governing you have to use the same tools of public persuasion to advance your program, to build public support for the direction you are attempting to lead."[24]

Modern presidents must be attentive to the polls, but they need not crave the affection of the public. Their relationship with it may be purely instrumental. However gratifying public approval may be, popular support is a resource the expenditure of which must be coolly calculated. As another Clinton aide explained, "Clinton has come to believe that if he keeps his approval ratings up and sells his message as he did during the campaign, there will be greater acceptability for his program. . . . The idea is that you have to sell it as if in a campaign."[25]

Bargaining presidents require the sage advice of politicians familiar with the bargaining game; presidents who go public need pollsters. Compare the relish with which President Nixon was reported by one of his consultants to have approached the polls with the disdain Truman expressed. "Nixon had all kinds of polls all the time; he sometimes had a couple of pollsters doing the same kind of survey at the same time. He really studied them. He wanted to find the thing that would give him an advantage."[26] The confidant went on to observe that the president wanted poll data "on just about anything and everything" throughout his administration.

Indicative of current fashion, presidents from Carter through Clinton have all had in-house pollsters taking continuous—weekly, even daily—readings of public opinion.[27] When George Bush reportedly spent $216,000 of Republican National Committee money on in-house polling in one year, many Washington politicians probably viewed the president's use of this resource as excessive. But this figure looked modest after Bill Clinton spent nearly ten times that amount in 1993. That year he averaged three or four polls and an equal number of focus groups each month.[28]

Pollsters vigilantly monitor the pulse of opinion to warn of slippage and to identify opportunities for gain. Before recommending a policy course, they assess its costs in public support. Sometimes, as with Clinton's pollsters, they go so far as to ask the public whether the president should bargain with Congress's leaders or challenge them by mobilizing public opinion.[29] These advisers' regular and frequently unsolicited denials that they affected policy belie their self-effacement.

To see how the strategic prescriptions of going public differ from those of bargaining, consider the hypothetical case of a president requiring additional votes if he is to prevail in Congress. If a large number of votes is needed, the most obvious and direct course is to go on prime-time television to solicit the public's active support. Employed at the right moment by a popular president, the effect may be dramatic. This tactic, however, has considerable costs and risks. A real debit of lost public support may occur when a president takes a forthright position. There is also the possibility that the public will not respond, which damages the president's future credibility. Given this, a president understandably finds the *threat* to go public frequently more attractive than the *act*. To the degree such a threat is credible, the anticipated responses of some representatives and senators may suffice to achieve victory.

A more focused application of popular pressure becomes available as an election nears. Fence-sitting representatives and senators may be plied with promises of reelection support or threats of presidential opposition. This may be done privately and selectively, or it may be tendered openly to all who may vote on the president's program. Then there is the election itself. By campaigning, the president who goes public can seek to alter the partisan composition of Congress and thereby gain influence over that institution's decisions in the future.

All of these methods for generating publicity notwithstanding, going public offers fewer and simpler stratagems than does its pluralist alternative. At the heart of the latter lies bargaining, which above all else involves choice: choice among alternative coalitions, choice of specific partners, and choice of the goods and services to be bartered. The number and variety of choices place great demands upon strategic calculation, so much so that pluralist leadership must be understood as an art. In Neustadt's schema, the president's success ultimately reduces to intuition, an ability to sense "right choices." [30]

Going public also requires choice, and it leaves ample room for the play of talent. (One need only compare the television performance of Carter and Reagan.) Nonetheless, public relations appears to be a less obscure matter. Going public promises a straightforward presidency—its options fewer, its strategy simpler, and consequently, its practitioner's behavior more predictable.

Thus there is a rationale for modern presidents to go public in the emerging character of Washington politics. As Washington comes to depend on looser, more individualistic political relations, presidents searching for strategies that work will increasingly go public.

So far, I have said little about the individual in the White House or the personal character of leadership. To consider these ingredients important does not violate any of the assumptions made here. Rationality does not leave choice to be determined strictly by the environment. To the degree occupants of the Oval Office differ in their skills and conceptions of leadership, one may expect that similar circumstances will sometimes result in different presidential behavior.

Perhaps, as has frequently been suggested, presidents go public more today because of who they are. What did Jimmy Carter and Ronald Reagan have in common? The answer is their lack of interest in active negotiation with fellow politicians and their confidence in speaking directly to the voters.

The Calculus of Those Who Deal with the President

Those Washingtonians who conduct business with the president observe his behavior carefully. Their judgment about his leadership guides them in their dealings with him. Traditionally, the professional president watchers have asked themselves the following questions: What are his priorities? How much does he care whether he wins or loses on a particular issue? How will he weigh his options? Is he capable of winning?

Each person will answer these questions about the president's will and skill somewhat differently, of course, depending upon his or her institutional vantage. The chief lobbyist for the United Auto Workers, a network White House correspondent, and the mayor of New York City may size up the president differently depending upon what they need from him. Nonetheless, they arrive at their judgments about the president in similar ways. Each observes the same behavior, inspects the same personal qualities, evaluates the views of the same recognized opinion leaders—columnists and commentators, among others—and tests his or her own tentative opinions with those of fellow community members. Local opinion leaders promote a general agreement among Washingtonians in their assessments of the president. Their agreement is his reputation.[31]

A president with a strong reputation does better in his dealings largely because others expect fewer concessions from him. Accordingly, he finds them more compliant; an orderly marketplace prevails. Saddled with a weak reputation, conversely, a president must work harder. Because others expect him to be less effective, they press him harder in expectation of greater gain. Comity at the bargaining table may give way to contention as other politicians form unreasonable expectations of gain. Through such expectations, the president's reputation regulates community relations in ways that either facilitate or impede his success. In a world of institutionalized pluralism, bargaining presidents seldom actively traded upon their prestige, leaving it to influence Washington political elites only through their anticipation of the electorate's behavior. As a consequence, prestige remained largely irrelevant to other politicians' assessments of the president.[32] Once presidents began going public and interjecting prestige directly into their relations with fellow politicians, and once these politicians found their resistance to this pressure diminished because of their own altered circumstances, the president's ability to marshal public opinion soon became an important ingredient of his reputation. New questions were added to traditional ones. Does the president feel strongly enough about an issue to go public? Will he follow through on his threats to do so? Does his standing in the country run so deep that it will likely be converted into mail to members of Congress, or is it so shallow that it will expire as he attempts to use it?

In today's Washington, the answers to these questions contribute to the president's reputation. As a consequence, his prestige and reputation have lost much of their separateness. The community's estimates of Carter and Reagan rose and fell with the polls. Through reputation, prestige has begun to play a larger role in regulating the president's day-to-day transactions with other community members. Grappling with the unclear causes of Carter's failure in Washington, Neustadt arrived at the same conclusion:

> A President's capacity to draw and stir a television audience seems every bit as interesting to current Washingtonians as his ability to wield his formal powers. This interest is his opportunity. While national party organizations fall away, while congressional party discipline relaxes, while interest groups proliferate and issue networks rise, a President who wishes to compete for leadership in framing policy and shaping coalitions has to make the most he can out of his popular connection. Anticipating home reactions, Washingtonians . . . are vulnerable to any breeze from home that presidential words and sights can stir. If he is deemed effective on the tube they will anticipate. That is the essence of professional reputation.[33]

The record supports Neustadt's speculation. In late 1978 and early 1979, with his monthly approval rating dropping to less than 50 percent, President Carter complained that it was difficult to gain Congress's attention for his legislative proposals. As one congressional liaison official stated, "When you go up to the Hill and the latest polls show Carter isn't doing well, then there isn't much reason for a member to go along with him."[34] A member of Congress concurred: "The relationship between the President and Congress is partly the result of how well the President is doing politically. Congress is better behaved when he does well. . . . Right now, it's almost as if Congress is paying no attention to him."[35]

NOTES

1. Newton N. Minow, John Bartlow Martin, and Lee M. Mitchell, *Presidential Television* (New York: Basic Books, 1973), 84–87.

2. Peter J. Boyer, "Networks Refuse to Broadcast Reagan's Plea," *New York Times,* February 3, 1988.

3. Robert B. Semple Jr., "Nixon Eludes Newsmen on Coast Trip," *New York Times,* August 3, 1970, 16.

4. Richard E. Neustadt, *Presidential Power* (New York: John Wiley and Sons, 1980).

5. Robert A. Dahl and Charles E. Lindblom, *Politics, Economics, and Welfare* (New York: Harper and Row, 1953), 333.

6. Among them are Aaron Wildavsky, *The Politics of the Budgetary Process* (Boston: Little, Brown, 1964); Graham T. Allison, *The Essence of Decision: Explaining the Cuban Missile Crisis* (New York: HarperCollins, 1987); Hugh Heclo, *The Government of Strangers* (Washington, D.C.: Brookings Institution, 1977); and Nelson W. Polsby, *Consequences of Party Reform* (New York: Oxford University Press, 1983).

7. From Ronald Reagan's address to the nation on his 1986 budget. Jack Nelson, "Reagan Calls for Public Support of Deficit Cuts," *Los Angeles Times,* April 25, 1985, 1.

8. Nelson W. Polsby, "Interest Groups and the Presidency: Trends in Political Intermediation in America," in *American Politics and Public Policy,* ed. Walter Dean Burnham and Martha Wagner Weinbey (Cambridge: MIT Press, 1978), 52.

9. Hedrick Smith, "Bitterness on Capitol Hill," *New York Times,* April 24, 1985, 14.

10. Ed Magnuson, "A Line Drawn in Dirt," *Time,* February 22, 1982, 12–13.

11. William J. Clinton, *Public Papers of the Presidents of the United States: William J. Clinton, 1994,* vol. 1 (Washington, D.C.: Government Printing Office, 1995), 126–135.

12. See David S. Broder, "Diary of a Mad Majority Leader," *Washington Post,* December 13, 1981, C1, C5; David S. Broder, "Rostenkowski Knows It's His Turn," *Washington Post National Weekly Edition,* June 10, 1985, 13.

13. Lou Cannon, "Big Spending-Cut Bill Studied," *Washington Post,* November 29, 1984, A8.

14. Bernard Weinraub, "Reagan Sets Tour of Nation to Seek Economic Victory," *New York Times,* January 25, 1985, 43.

15. Bernard Weinraub, "Reagan Calls for 'Spirit of Cooperation' on Budget and Taxes," *New York Times,* February 10, 1985, 32. On Democratic suspicions of Reagan's motives see Hedrick Smith, "O'Neill Reflects Democratic Strategy on Budget Cuts and Tax Revisions," *New York Times,* December 6, 1984, B20; and Margaret Shapiro, "O'Neill's New Honeymoon with Reagan," *Washington Post National Weekly Edition,* February 11, 1985, 12.

16. Jonathan Fuerbringer, "Reagan Critical of Budget View of Senate Panel," *New York Times,* March 9, 1985, 1. Senate Majority Leader Bob Dole told reporters that if the president liked the Senate's final budget package he would campaign for it "very vigorously . . . going to television, whatever he needs to reduce federal spending." Karen

Tumulty, "Reagan May Get Draft of Budget Accord Today," *Los Angeles Times,* April 4, 1985, 1.

17. Bernard Weinraub, "In His 2nd Term, He Is Reagan the Liberated," *New York Times,* March 11, 1985, 10.

18. David E. Rosenbaum, "Reagan Approves Primary Elements of Tax Overhaul," *New York Times,* May 16, 1985, 1.

19. Robert W. Merry and David Shribman, "G.O.P. Hopes Tax Bill Will Help It Become Majority Party Again," *Wall Street Journal,* May 23, 1985, 1. See also Rosenbaum, "Reagan Approves Primary Elements of Tax Overhaul," 14. Instances such as those reported here continued into summer. See, for example, Jonathan Fuerbringer, "Key Issues Impede Compromise on Cutting Deficit," *New York Times,* June 23, 1985, 22.

20. These figures are reported in Richard E. Cohen, *Changing Course in Washington* (New York: Macmillan, 1994), 180.

21. The account of this meeting comes from Bob Woodward, *The Agenda* (New York: Simon and Schuster, 1994).

22. Richard E. Neustadt, *Presidential Power,* 28–29. Compare with Dahl and Lindblom's earlier observation: "The President possesses more hierarchical controls than any other single figure in the government; indeed, he is often described somewhat romantically and certainly ambiguously as the most powerful democratic executive in the world. Yet like everyone else in the American policy process, the President must bargain constantly—with Congressional leaders, individual Congressmen, his department heads, bureau chiefs, and leaders of nongovernmental organizations" (Dahl and Lindblom, *Politics, Economics, and Welfare,* 333).

23. Sidney Blumenthal, "Marketing the President," *New York Times Magazine,* September 13, 1981, 110.

24. Alison Mitchell, "Clinton Seems to Keep Running Though the Race Is Run and Won," *New York Times,* February 12, 1997, A1, A12.

25. Ibid., A12.

26. Cited in George C. Edwards III, *The Public Presidency* (New York: St. Martin's Press, 1983), 14.

27. B. Drummond Ayres Jr., "G.O.P. Keeps Tabs on Nation's Mood," *New York Times,* November 16, 1981, 20.

28. These figures are cited in George C. Edwards III, "Frustration and Folly: Bill Clinton and the Public Presidency," in *The Clinton Presidency: First Appraisals,* ed. Colin Campbell and Bert A. Rockman (Chatham, N.J.: Chatham House, 1996), 234.

29. In 1993 Clinton's chief pollster, Stanley Greenberg, added such a question to one of his national surveys. Unsurprisingly, a sizable majority favored cooperation with Congress. Bob Woodward, *The Agenda* (New York: Simon and Schuster, 1994), 268–269.

30. Neustadt, *Presidential Power,* especially chap. 8; and Peter Sperlich, "Bargaining and Overload: An Essay on Presidential Power," in *Perspectives on the Presidency,* ed. Aaron Wildavsky (Boston: Little, Brown, 1975).

31. This discussion of reputation follows closely that of Neustadt in *Presidential Power* (New York: John Wiley and Sons, 1980), chap. 4.

32. Neustadt observed that President Truman's television appeal for tighter price controls in 1951 had little visible effect on how Washington politicians viewed the issue. This is the only mention of a president going public in the original eight chapters of the book. Neustadt, *Presidential Power,* 45.

33. Neustadt, *Presidential Power,* 238.

34. Cited in Gary C. Jacobson, *The Politics of Congressional Elections,* 4th ed. (New York: Longman, 1997), 193–194.

35. Statement by Rep. Richard B. Cheney cited in Charles O. Jones, "Congress and the Presidency," in *The New Congress,* eds. Thomas E. Mann and Norman J. Ornstein (Washington, D.C.: American Enterprise Institute, 1981), 241.

What Seemed Like a Good Idea
Haunts the GOP Establishment

Gerald F. Seib and John Harwood

*Normally one can assume that politicians adjust their strategies to ac-
commodate the institutions and electoral rules under which they compete. This is not always necessary when it comes to presidential
primaries. Ever since the presidential nomination reforms in the early
1970s required all state parties to select their convention delegates
through primaries or open caucuses, each state's election schedule and
rules have been in flux, subject to the strategies of state politicians and
the presidential candidates. The former jockey for a date on the election
calendar that they think would give their state's voters the best chance of
determining the winner. Similarly, the candidates and their allies try to
adjust the calendar and rules to gain a competitive edge. The following
article shows how George W. Bush's supporters succeeded in fashioning
the 2000 Republican primaries as they thought would best suit their
candidate. Their handiwork very nearly cost their man the nomination.*

IF JOHN MCCAIN sweeps aside the Republican establishment to win his
party's presidential nomination this year, the establishment won't have to
look far to assign blame. It can just look in a mirror.

There are many factors fueling the McCain challenge to the GOP establishment's favorite, George W. Bush: the captivating war-hero story, the
image as a forthright outsider, the message of government reform. But as
Mr. McCain prepares for a crucial stretch of primaries starting with South
Carolina's Saturday [February 19], he could get an unintended boost from
the very party establishment hoping to stop him.

In the 1970s, following the Democrats' example, GOP leaders began expanding the primary system to remove power from party insiders and hand
it to voters. Across the country, and particularly in the South, Republican

Originally published in the *Wall Street Journal*, February 16, 2000. Reprinted by permission.

leaders saw the shift as a way to broaden the GOP's reach and help it over-take Democrats to become the nation's majority party. Republicans invited Democrats and independent voters to cross over into their primaries. More recently, GOP leaders changed the primary schedule to enlarge the role of states run by governors friendly to the party establishment and to make it easier for a mainstream Republican presidential contender to wrap up the nomination quickly.

Miscalculation and Arcana

For two decades it all worked. But suddenly, through a combination of strategic miscalculation and the arcana of each party's rules, it is all threat-ening to go awry. The changes party leaders once designed to consolidate their positions could instead cost them control of their nominating process.

Going into this election season, top Republicans assumed that Mr. Bush's more moderate "compassionate conservatism" would attract swing voters to the GOP. In reality, it has been the maverick Mr. McCain, running explic-itly against the party establishment, who has served as a magnet for new and non-Republican voters. On the heels of Mr. McCain's New Hampshire victory, the primary calendar now moves to three important states with wide-open primaries—South Carolina, Michigan and Virginia—where non-GOP voters can boost Mr. McCain. Even worse for Mr. Bush, Democratic Party rules preventing those same states from hosting early Democratic contests have enhanced the temptation to cross over.

Big Mistake?

"Maybe that was a big mistake," concedes Gov. John Engler of Michigan, which has jumped ahead on the primary schedule by a month since 1996 to enhance its role in the 2000 race. The staunch Bush ally still predicts victory but adds, "If we don't win, it was a terrible idea."

Mr. Bush himself says in an interview that some Democratic leaders in Michigan are urging their party members to show up and vote for Mr. McCain simply to foil Mr. Engler's plans. "I don't think we anticipated that," Mr. Bush says.

The McCain high command savors the irony. "The idea," spokesman Howard Opinsky says wryly, "wasn't to open the front door to new people so the party establishment would get kicked out the back door."

It is possible, of course, that the system may work exactly as designed. Mr. Bush's establishment allies in South Carolina, Virginia and Michigan now have a special incentive to hold off Mr. McCain and prove that their decisions didn't backfire. Virginia Gov. James Gilmore, a Bush backer who pushed to have his state's primary revived and moved up on the calendar ahead of other big states, believes that Mr. Bush "will do quite well in this primary, even though independents and even Democrats will be able to vote." In any event, he insists, "I absolutely have no regrets."

Pressure for Change

Still, the twists in the party's story line are already fueling pressure to reconfigure the system again after 2000. Even before Mr. McCain's emergence, the "front-loading" produced by the scramble for advantage among states was amplifying calls for a new approach to the primary system.

Now, "it really screams for change," says Alabama Republican Chairman Winton Blount III. Though he is officially neutral, his father, a principal architect of the Alabama GOP, is backing Mr. Bush. Declares the younger Mr. Blount: "We need to look at a whole different way of reaching consensus on who our nominee is."

As the current GOP trauma suggests, the most consistent feature of all electoral reforms is the law of unintended consequences—which Democrats know as surely as do Republicans. When left-leaning reformers pressed the Democratic Party to open up the nominating process in 1972, for example, Michigan Democrats held their first primary—and watched in horror as conservative George Wallace crushed liberal George McGovern by a margin of nearly 2 to 1. Mr. Wallace's support from thousands of independent and Republican crossover voters, who then as now could participate under the open-primary rules, is an eerie reminder for GOP regulars of what could happen for Mr. McCain in Michigan's February 22 contest.

In many ways, the predicament Mr. Bush faces this week in South Carolina can be traced to the evolution of the modern GOP in the South. For much of the past century, the legacy of the Civil War kept the region so uniformly Democratic that partisan competition was irrelevant; in eight of the eleven states of the old Confederacy, voters still don't register by party. Instead of holding primaries, Republican insiders for years would simply "draft a candidate" who in turn would lose the general election, recalls Clarke Reed of Mississippi, a founding father of the modern Southern GOP and current backer of Mr. Bush.

But the civil-rights revolution helped fuel the growth of Southern Republicans, and by the 1970s the party began holding primaries and using them as a party-building tool. By the 1980s, the GOP leaders had taken two important steps to try to accelerate their progress.

Reagan Vanquishes

The first was South Carolina's GOP primary, established in 1980 and placed early in the calendar. That year, GOP leaders watched as Ronald Reagan discovered that a win in the state helped him vanquish a Republican field that included his eventual vice president, George Bush.

Eight years later, South Carolinian Lee Atwater was running Mr. Bush's campaign, and he convinced the state GOP to again schedule an early primary. He then set out to lock up the state for the elder Mr. Bush, the candidate of the party's mainstream, and turn it into a "firewall" to protect him from any early campaign mishaps. Mr. Bush did suffer an early loss to Bob Dole in Iowa. Sure enough, South Carolina gave Mr. Bush an easy win and pushed him on to the presidency.

The second step also came in 1988, when Haley Barbour, a member of the Republican National Committee from Mississippi who later became the party's national chairman, launched a full-bore effort to persuade Southern independents and Democrats to vote in Republican primaries. His "Southern Primary Project" aimed to encourage ideologically conservative Democrats to begin considering themselves Republicans.

The goal was twofold. First, Republicans figured that voters who came into their primaries were likely to continue voting Republican and therefore would help turn the region toward the GOP more quickly. "Over the last 30 years, people who vote Republican in the primary almost always vote Republican no matter what," Mr. Barbour says today. "We thought the larger the universe who voted in the Republican primary in March, the stronger our nominee would be in November."

Foiling the Democrats

Second, Republicans wanted to foil the Democrats' own aims in the region. Southern Democrats had set up "Super Tuesday," a collection of Southern primaries all run on the same day, in the hope of giving the party's moderate Southern wing the increased clout necessary to pick one of its own as a nominee rather than a liberal Northerner. But by sucking conservative Democrats into the Republican primaries, Mr. Barbour and his colleagues hoped to leave only liberal Democrats behind to pick their party's nominee.

The project succeeded on both counts. In the Democratic Super Tuesday contests, most delegates were won by the more liberal candidates, the Rev. Jesse Jackson and Massachusetts Gov. Michael Dukakis, who went on to win the Democratic nomination. Meanwhile, Mr. Bush swept the GOP's Southern primaries that day—and went on to beat Mr. Dukakis nationally while carrying every state in the old Confederacy.

Fast-forward to this year. Eyeing President Bush's son as the hope for recapturing the White House, top Republicans seemed to make their system even more congenial to the party establishment. New Hampshire's first-in-the-nation primary loomed as a potential obstacle for the front-runner, but his main threat there figured to come from bedrock antitax conservatives—not from moderate, independent crossover voters. And in any case, South Carolina—where Mr. Bush enjoyed the support of two former GOP governors and the venerable Sen. Strom Thurmond—was poised to play its typical role of boosting the establishment favorite.

In addition, following South Carolina's lead, GOP leaders in Michigan and Virginia decided to move up their primaries to magnify their states' roles. "We didn't do it strictly to help a particular candidate," Gov. Gilmore says. "We did it so the people of Virginia would have a stronger voice in the selection process." But when Mr. Bush entered the race, Messrs. Gilmore and Engler emerged as strong Bush supporters, and set out to use their states to help him lock up the nomination as soon as possible.

Two Things Unforeseen

The fact that these primaries would be open to independents and Democrats didn't initially seem a big issue. Mr. Bush was running on his record in

Texas of reaching across party lines, and bracing for a challenge from wealthy publisher Steve Forbes and others on his party's right wing. "They thought the open primaries would help Bush," says Mike Murphy, a political consultant who was influential in the decision to move forward Michigan's primary and who now advises Mr. McCain.

But the party's leaders failed to take into account two things. One was the power of Mr. McCain's message, which emphasized a more moderate approach to tax-cutting and a more aggressive stance toward shaking up the Washington establishment. The other was the way in which the new economy has changed the face of the key early states. High-technology and international businesses have drawn in waves of transplanted new voters. They tend to be more independent-minded, rather than falling into the comfortable voting patterns of their adopted states.

In New Hampshire, they flocked to Mr. McCain—and now he is actively courting them in South Carolina and beyond. If it works again, these new voters could upend not just Mr. Bush, but also a generation of GOP orthodoxy on issues ranging from tax cuts to tobacco to campaign finance.

Mr. Barbour still doubts that will happen. Even with a rush of new voters, he says, ideological conservatives will continue to be decisive in GOP primaries—and will "come home" as Mr. Bush exposes Mr. McCain's more-moderate views.

But the threat has been enough to rattle GOP regulars. Already the national organization of secretaries of state—the officials in the 50 states who administer elections—has endorsed a plan for rotating regional primaries to even out disparities in the way individual states affect the nominating process. An alternative proposal known as the "Delaware Plan" would schedule primaries by population, starting with the smallest state.

Achieving national consensus for such plans in either party will be a huge challenge. Not surprisingly, Mr. Blount of Alabama (pop. 4.3 million) prefers the small-states-first approach; Mr. Engler of Michigan (pop. 9.6 million) dismisses it as a bad idea. And while both men fret about primaries that blur partisan lines, some states are expressing interest in following the example of giant California. The state this year has adopted a confusing "jungle primary" in which presidential contenders of both parties appear on a single ballot provided to all voters, but only the votes of registered Democrats and Republicans will count toward picking their parties' convention delegates.

To some of Mr. McCain's new Southern backers, all these primary maneuvers sound like an attempt to slam shut an electoral process that throughout the past century has grown progressively more open. "It's a free country," says Patricia Gill, 23 years old, a self-styled independent who backed President Clinton's 1996 reelection. After hearing Mr. McCain at a town meeting last week in Spartanburg, S.C., she now intends to cast her first-ever presidential primary vote for the Arizona senator.

But that's just what worries retiree Betty Parker, secretary of the Cherokee County Republican Women's club, who was on hand for a Bush appearance in Gaffney, S.C. A GOP elephant pin on her lapel, Mrs. Parker shakes her head at the prospect of wayward Democrats crossing over to back Mr. McCain's "liberal" views this week.

"If you want the Democrats to vote for you," she says impatiently of Mr. McCain, "you ought to run under the Democratic name."

8

The Bureaucracy

The modern federal bureaucracy is large, and its regulatory reach is tremendous. About two million civilian employees work for the federal government. The Federal Register, in which federal regulations are recorded, exceeds 70,000 pages in length. Many, if not most, new policies—passed by Congress or ordered by the president—entail expansion of agency responsibilities. Some call for the addition of a new department, bureau, or office, and most add to the body of administrative rules and regulations. There has been a measurable reduction in the size of the federal workforce and regulations in the past two decades. But the federal bureaucracy remains a powerful influence on the lives of all Americans, an influence so pervasive and familiar that it has become an object of ridicule. Americans long ago coined the term "red tape" to describe the often frustrating rules, regulations, and processes—and the associated paperwork and forms—created by government agencies. Politicians today often decry the bureaucracy's "waste, fraud, and abuse"—a standard phrase used to label the most obvious problems of agencies.

The bureaucracy affects policy outcomes and influences who wins and who loses in politics. Because of its importance—as an instrument of policy, as a political resource, and as a scapegoat in everyday politics—it draws the keen interest of organized interests and elected officials. The essays in this chapter address the nature of problems associated with bureaucracies and portray aspects of the struggle among Congress, the president, and other players for control over the bureaucratic agencies.

8-1

from *Bureaucracy*

James Q. Wilson

*When Congress and the president create new programs and assign re-
sponsibility for implementing them to executive agencies, they are delegating power that might be used arbitrarily by unelected bureaucrats.
To avoid the arbitrary use of power—one of the prime objectives of
democracy—they impose rules on agencies. These rules, which serve as
beneficial constraints, may limit bureaucrats' options and create inefficiencies in the implementation of policy. In the following essay James Q.
Wilson examines the causes and consequences of discretion and arbitrariness, and of rules and inefficiencies.*

ON THE MORNING of May 22, 1986, Donald Trump, the New York real estate
developer, called one of his executives, Anthony Gliedman, into his office.
They discussed the inability of the City of New York, despite six years of effort and the expenditure of nearly $13 million, to rebuild the ice-skating
rink in Central Park. On May 28 Trump offered to take over the rink reconstruction, promising to do the job in less than six months. A week later
Mayor Edward Koch accepted the offer and shortly thereafter the city appropriated $3 million on the understanding that Trump would have to pay
for any cost overruns out of his own pocket. On October 28, the renovation
was complete, over a month ahead of schedule and about $750,000 under
budget. Two weeks later, skaters were using it.

For many readers it is obvious that private enterprise is more efficient
than are public bureaucracies, and so they would file this story away as simply another illustration of what everyone already knows. But for other readers it is not so obvious what this story means; to them, business is greedy
and unless watched like a hawk will fob off shoddy or overprices goods on
the American public, as when it sells the government $435 hammers and
$3,000 coffeepots. Trump may have done a good job in this instance, but

perhaps there is something about skating rinks or New York City government that gave him a comparative advantage; in any event, no larger lessons should be drawn from it.

Some lessons can be drawn, however, if one looks closely at the incentives and constraints facing Trump and the department of Parks and Recreation. It becomes apparent that there is not one "bureaucracy problem" but several, and the solution to each in some degree is incompatible with the solution to every other. First there is the problem of accountability—getting agencies to serve agreed-upon goals. Second there is the problem of equity—treating all citizens fairly, which usually means treating them alike on the basis of clear rules known in advance. Third there is the problem of responsiveness—reacting reasonably to the special needs and circumstances of particular people. Fourth there is the problem of efficiency—obtaining the greatest output for a given level of resources. Finally there is the problem of fiscal integrity—assuring that public funds are spent prudently for public purposes. Donald Trump and Mayor Koch were situated differently with respect to most of these matters.

Accountability. The Mayor wanted the old skating rink refurbished, but he also wanted to minimize the cost of the fuel needed to operate the rink (the first effort to rebuild it occurred right after the Arab oil embargo and the attendant increase in energy prices). Trying to achieve both goals led city hall to select a new refrigeration system that as it turned out would not work properly. Trump came on the scene when only one goal dominated: get the rink rebuilt. He felt free to select the most reliable refrigeration system without worrying too much about energy costs.

Equity. The Parks and Recreation Department was required by law to give every contractor an equal chance to do the job. This meant it had to put every part of the job out to bid and to accept the lowest without much regard to the reputation or prior performance of the lowest bidder. Moreover, state law forbade city agencies from hiring a general contractor and letting him select the subcontractors; in fact, the law forbade the city from even discussing the project in advance with a general contractor who might later bid on it—that would have been collusion. Trump, by contrast, was free to locate the rink builder with the best reputation and give him the job.

Fiscal Integrity. To reduce the chance of corruption or sweetheart deals the law required Parks and Recreation to furnish complete, detailed plans to every contractor bidding on the job; any changes after that would require renegotiating the contract. No such law constrained Trump; he was free to give incomplete plans to his chosen contractor, hold him accountable for building a satisfactory rink, but allow him to work out the details as he went along.

Efficiency. When the Parks and Recreation Department spent over six years and $13 million and still could not reopen the rink, there was public criticism but no city official lost money. When Trump accepted a contract to do it, any cost overruns or delays would have come out of his pocket and any savings could have gone into his pocket (in this case, Trump agreed not to take a profit on the job).

Gliedman summarized the differences neatly: "The problem with government is that government can't say, 'yes' . . . there is nobody in government that can do that. There are fifteen or twenty people who have to agree. Government has to be slower. It has to safeguard the process."

Inefficiency

The government can't say "yes." In other words, the government is constrained. Where do the constraints come from? From us.

Herbert Kaufman has explained red tape as being of our own making: "Every restraint and requirement originates in somebody's demand for it." Applied to the Central Park skating rink Kaufman's insight reminds us that civil-service reformers demanded that no city official benefit personally from building a project; that contractors demanded that all be given an equal chance to bid on every job; and that fiscal watchdogs demanded that all contract specifications be as detailed as possible. For each demand a procedure was established; viewed from the outside, those procedures are called red tape. To enforce each procedure a manager was appointed; those managers are called bureaucrats. No organized group demanded that all skating rinks be rebuilt as quickly as possible, no procedure existed to enforce that demand, and no manager was appointed to enforce it. The political process can more easily enforce compliance with constraints than the attainment of goals.

When we denounce bureaucracy for being inefficient we are saying something that is half true. Efficiency is a ratio of valued resources used to valued outputs produced. The smaller that ratio the more efficient the production. If the valued output is a rebuilt skating rink, then whatever process uses the fewest dollars or the least time to produce a satisfactory rink is the most efficient process. By this test Trump was more efficient than the Parks and Recreation Department.

But that is too narrow a view of the matter. The economic definition of efficiency (efficiency in the small, so to speak) assumes that there is only one valued output, the new rink. But government has many valued outputs, including a reputation for integrity, the confidence of the people, and the support of important interest groups. When we complain about skating rinks not being built on time we speak as if all we cared about were skating rinks. But when we complain that contracts were awarded without competitive bidding or in a way that allowed bureaucrats to line their pockets we acknowledge that we care about many things besides skating rinks; we care about the contextual goals—the constraints—that we want government to observe. A government that is slow to build rinks but is honest and accountable in its actions and properly responsive to worthy constituencies may be a very efficient government, *if* we measure efficiency in the large by taking into account *all* of the valued outputs.

Calling a government agency efficient when it is slow, cumbersome, and costly may seem perverse. But that is only because we lack any objective way for deciding how much money or time should be devoted to maintaining honest behavior, producing a fair allocation of benefits, and generating popular support as well as to achieving the main goal of the project. If we could measure these things, and if we agreed as to their value, then we would be in a position to judge the true efficiency of a government agency and decide when it is taking too much time or spending too much money achieving all that we expect of it. But we cannot measure these things nor do we agree about their relative importance, and so government always will appear to be inefficient compared to organizations that have fewer goals.

Put simply, the only way to decide whether an agency is truly inefficient is to decide which of the constraints affecting its action ought to be ignored or discounted. In fact that is what most debates about agency behavior are all about. In fighting crime are the police handcuffed? In educating children are teachers tied down by rules? In launching a space shuttle are we too concerned with safety? In building a dam do we worry excessively about endangered species? In running the Postal Service is it important to have many post offices close to where people live? In the case of the skating rink, was the requirement of competitive bidding for each contract on the basis of detailed specifications a reasonable one? Probably not. But if it were abandoned, the gain (the swifter completion of the rink) would have to be balanced against the costs (complaints from contractors who might lose business and the chance of collusion and corruption in some future projects).

Even allowing for all of these constraints, government agencies may still be inefficient. Indeed, given the fact that bureaucrats cannot (for the most part) benefit monetarily from their agencies' achievements, it would be surprising if they were not inefficient. Efficiency, in the large or the small, doesn't pay. . . .

Military procurement, of course, is the biggest source of stories about waste, fraud, and mismanagement. There cannot be a reader of this book who has not heard about the navy paying $435 for a hammer or the air force paying $3,000 for a coffeepot, and nobody, I suspect, believes Defense Department estimates of the cost of a new airplane or missile. If ever one needed evidence that bureaucracy is inefficient, the Pentagon supplies it.

Well, yes. But what kind of inefficiency? And why does it occur? To answer these questions one must approach the problem just as we approached the problem of fixing up a skating rink in New York City: We want to understand why the bureaucrats, all of whom are rational and most of whom want to do a good job, behave as they do.

To begin, let us forget about $435 hammers. They never existed. A member of Congress who did not understand (or did not want to understand) government accounting rules created a public stir. The $3,000 coffeepot existed, but it is not clear that it was overpriced. But that does not mean there are no problems; in fact, the real problems are far more costly and intractable than inflated price tags on hammers and coffeemakers. They include sticking too long with new weapons of dubious value, taking forever to acquire even good weapons, and not inducing contractors to increase their efficiency. What follows is not a complete explanation of military procurement problems; it is only an analysis of the contribution bureaucratic systems make to those problems.

When the military buys a new weapons system—a bomber, submarine, or tank—it sets in motion a procurement bureaucracy comprised of two key actors, the military program manager and the civilian contract officer, who must cope with the contractor, the Pentagon hierarchy, and Congress. To understand how they behave we must understand how their tasks get defined, what incentives they have, and what constraints they face.

Tasks

The person nominally in charge of buying a major new weapon is the program manager, typically an army or air force colonel or a navy captain. Officially, his job is to design and oversee the acquisition strategy by establishing specifications and schedules and identifying problems and tradeoffs. Unofficially, his task is somewhat different. For one thing he does not have the authority to make many important decisions; those are referred upward to his military superiors, to Defense Department civilians, and to Congress. For another, the program he oversees must constantly be sold and resold to the people who control the resources (mostly, the key congressional committees). And finally, he is surrounded by inspectors and auditors looking for any evidence of waste, fraud, or abuse and by the advocates of all manner of special interests (contractors' representatives, proponents of small and minority business utilization, and so on). As the Packard Commission observed, the program manager, "far from being the manager of the program . . . is merely one of the participants who can influence it."

Under these circumstances the actual task of the program manager tends to be defined as selling the program and staying out of trouble. Harvard Business School professor J. Ronald Fox, who has devoted much of his life to studying and participating in weapons procurement, found that a program manager must spend 30 to 50 percent of his time defending his program inside DOD and to Congress. It is entirely rational for him to do this, for a study by the General Accounting Office showed that weapons programs with effective advocates survived (including some that should have been terminated) and systems without such advocates were more likely to be ended (even some that should have been completed). Just as with the New York City skating rink, in the Pentagon there is no one who can say "yes" and make it stick. The only way to keep winning the support of the countless people who must say "yes" over and over again is to forge ahead at full speed, spending money at a rate high enough to prevent it from being taken away.

The program manager's own background and experience reinforce this definition of his task. He is a military officer, which means he cares deeply about having the best possible airplane, tank, or submarine. In recommending any tradeoffs between cost and performance, his natural inclination is to favor performance over savings. After all, someday he may have to fly in that airplane or sail on that ship. This often leads to what is commonly called "goldplating": seeking the best possible, most sophisticated weapon and making frequent changes in the contract specifications in order to incorporate new features. The program manager, of course, does not make these decisions, but he is an integral part of a user-dominated process that does make them.

The civilian counterpart to the program manager is the contracting officer. What is clear is that he or she, and not the program manager, is the only person legally authorized to sign the contract. In addition, the contracting officer administers the contract and prepares a report on contractor performance. Everything else is unclear. In principle, contracting officers are supposed to be involved in every step of the acquisition process, from issuing an invitation to bid on the contract through the completion of the project. In practice, as Ronald Fox observes, contracting officers often play only a small role in designing the acquisition strategy or in altering the contracts (this tends to be dominated by the program manager) and must share their authority over enforcing the terms of the contract with a small army of auditors and advocates.

What dominates the task of the contract officer are the rules, the more than 1,200 pages of the Federal Acquisition Regulation and Defense Acquisition Regulation in addition to the countless other pages in DOD directives and congressional authorization legislation and the unwritten "guidance" that arrives with every visit to a defense plant where a contracting officer works. Contract officers are there to enforce constraints, and those constraints have grown exponentially in recent years.

Incentives

In theory, military program managers are supposed to win promotions if they have done a good job supervising weapons procurement. In fact, promotions to the rank of general or admiral usually have been made on the basis of their reputation as combat officers and experience as military leaders. . . . The perceived message is clear: Traditional military specialties are a surer route to the top than experience as a program manager.

Reinforcing this bias against acquisition experience is the generalist ethos of the armed services—good officers can do any job; well-rounded officers have done many jobs. As a result, the typical program manager has a brief tenure in a procurement job. In 1986, the GAO found that the average program manager spent twenty-seven months on the job, and many spent less than two years. By contrast, it takes between eleven and twenty years to procure a major new weapons system, from concept to deployment. This means that during the acquisition of a new aircraft or missile, the identity of the program will change five or ten times.

In 1987, the services, under congressional prodding, established career paths for acquisition officers so that they could rise in rank while continuing to develop experience in procurement tasks. It is not yet clear how significant this change will be. If it encourages talented officers to invest ten or twenty years in mastering procurement policies it will be a major gain, one that will enable program managers from DOD to deal more effectively with experienced industry executives and encourage officers to make tough decisions rather than just keeping the program alive.

Civilian contract officers do have a distinct career path, but as yet not one that produces in them much sense of professional pride or organizational mission. Of the more than twenty thousand civilian contract administrators less than half have a college degree and the great majority are in the lower civil-service grades (GS-5 to GS-12). Even the most senior contract officers rarely earn (in 1988) more than $50,000 a year, less than half or even one-third of what their industry counterparts earn. Moreover, all are aware that they work in offices where the top posts usually are held by military officers; in civil-service jargon, the "head room" available for promotions is quite limited. . . .

The best evidence of the weakness of civilian incentives is the high turnover rate. Fox quotes a former commander of the military acquisition program as saying that "good people are leaving in droves" because "there is much less psychic income today" that would make up for the relatively low monetary income. The Packard Commission surveyed civilian procurement personnel and found that over half would leave their jobs if offered comparable jobs elsewhere in the federal government or in private industry.

In short, the incentives facing procurement officials do not reward people for maximizing efficiency. Military officers are rewarded for keeping programs alive and are encouraged to move on to other assignments, civilian personnel have weak inducements to apply a complex array of inconsistent constraints to contract administration.

Constraints

These constraints are not designed to produce efficiency but to reduce costs, avoid waste, fraud, and abuse, achieve a variety of social goals, and maintain the productive capacity of key contractors.

Reducing costs is not the same thing as increasing efficiency. If too little money is spent, the rate of production may be inefficient and the managerial flexibility necessary to cope with unforeseen circumstances may be absent. Congress typically appropriates money one year at a time. If Congress wishes to cut its spending or if DOD is ordered to slash its budget requests, the easiest thing to do is to reduce the number of aircraft, ships, or missiles being purchased in a given year without reducing the total amount purchased. This stretch-out has the effect of increasing the cost of each individual weapon as manufacturers forgo the economies that come from large-scale production. As Fox observes (but as many critics fail to understand), the typical weapons program in any given year is not overfunded, it is *under*funded. Recognizing that, the Packard Commission called for adopting a two-year budget cycle.

Reducing costs and eliminating fraud are not the same as increasing efficiency. There no doubt are excessive costs and there may be fraud in military procurement, but eliminating them makes procurement more efficient only if the costs of eliminating the waste and fraud exceed the savings thereby realized. To my knowledge no one has systematically compared the cost of all the inspectors, rules, and auditors with the savings they have achieved to see if all the checking and reviewing is worth it. Some anecdotal evidence suggests that the checking does not always pay for itself. In one case the army was required to spend $5,400 to obtain fully competitive bids for spare parts that cost $11,000. In exchange for the $5,400 and the 160 days it took to get the bids, the army saved $100. In short, there is an optimal level of "waste" in any organization, public or private: It is that level below which further savings are worth less than the cost of producing them.

The weapons procurement system must serve a number of "social" goals mandated by Congress. It must support small business, provide opportunities for minority-owned businesses, buy American-made products whenever possible, rehabilitate prisoners, provide employment for the handicapped, protect the environment, and maintain "prevailing" wage rates. One could lower the cost of procurement by eliminating some or all of the social goals the process is obliged to honor; that would produce increases in efficiency, narrowly defined. But what interest group is ready to sacrifice its most cherished goal in the name of efficiency? And if none will volunteer, how does one create a congressional majority to compel the sacrifice?

Weapons procurement also is designed to maintain the productive capacity of the major weapons builders. There is no true market in the manufacture of missiles, military aircraft, and naval vessels because typically there is only one buyer (the government) and no alternative uses for the production lines established to supply this buyer. Northrop, Lockheed, Grumman, McDonnell Douglas, the Bath Iron Works, Martin Marietta—these firms and others like them would not exist, or would exist in very different form, if they did not have a continuous flow of military contracts. As a result, each new weapons system becomes a do-or-die proposition for the executives of these firms. Even if the Pentagon cared nothing about their economic well-being it would have to care about the productive capacity that they represent, for if it were ever lost or much diminished the armed services would have nowhere else to turn when the need arose for a new airplane or ship. And if by chance the Pentagon did not care, Congress would; no member believes he or she was elected to preside over the demise of a major employer.

This constraint produces what some scholars have called the "follow-on imperative": the need to give a new contract to each major supplier as work on an old contract winds down. If one understands this it is not necessary to imagine some sinister "military-industrial complex" conspiring to keep new weapons flowing. The armed services want them because they believe, rightly, that their task is to defend the nation against real though hard to define threats; the contractors want them because they believe, rightly, that the nation cannot afford to dismantle its productive capacity; Congress wants them because its members believe, rightly, that they are elected to maintain the prosperity of their states and districts.

When these beliefs encounter the reality of limited resources and the need to make budget choices, almost everyone has an incentive to overstate the benefits and understate the costs of a new weapons system. To do otherwise—to give a cautious estimate of what the weapon will achieve and a candid view of what it will cost—is to invite rejection. And none of the key actors in the process believe they can afford rejection.

The Bottom Line

The incentives and constraints that confront the military procurement bureaucracy push its members to overstate benefits, understate costs, make frequent and detailed changes in specifications, and enforce a bewildering array of rules designed to minimize criticism and stay out of trouble. There are hardly any incentives pushing officials to leave details to manufacturers or delegate authority to strong program managers whose career prospects will depend on their ability to produce good weapons at a reasonable cost.

In view of all this, what is surprising is that the system works as well as it does. In fact, it works better than most people suppose. The Rand Corporation has been studying military procurement for over thirty years. A summary of its findings suggests some encouraging news, most of it ignored amidst the headlines about hammers and coffeepots. There has been steady improvement in the performance of the system. Between the early 1960s and the mid-1980s, cost overruns, schedule slippages, and performance shortfalls have all decreased. Cost overruns of military programs on the average are now no greater than they are for the civil programs of the government such as highway and water projects and public buildings. Moreover, there is evidence that for all its faults the American system seems to work as well or better than that in many European nations. . . .

Arbitrary Rule

Inefficiency is not the only bureaucratic problem nor is it even the most important. A perfectly efficient agency could be a monstrous one, swiftly denying us our liberties, economically inflicting injustices, and competently expropriating our wealth. People complain about bureaucracy as often because it is unfair or unreasonable as because it is slow or cumbersome.

Arbitrary rule refers to officials acting without legal authority, or with that authority in a way that offends our sense of justice. Justice means, first, that we require the government to treat people equally on the basis of clear rules known in advance: If Becky and Bob both are driving sixty miles per hour in a thirty-mile-per hour zone and the police give a ticket to Bob, we believe they also should give a ticket to Becky. Second, we believe that justice obliges the government to take into account the special needs and circumstances of individuals: If Becky is speeding because she is on her way to the hospital to give birth to a child and Bob is speeding for the fun of it, we may feel that the police should ticket Bob but not Becky. Justice in the first sense means fairness, in the second it means responsiveness. Obviously, fairness and responsiveness often are in conflict.

The checks and balances of the American constitutional system reflect our desire to reduce the arbitrariness of official rule. That desire is based squarely on the premise that inefficiency is a small price to pay for freedom and responsiveness. Congressional oversight, judicial review, interest-group participation, media investigations, and formalized procedures all are intended to check administrative discretion. It is not hyperbole to say that the constitutional order is animated by the desire to make the government "inefficient."

This creates two great tradeoffs. First, adding constraints reduces the efficiency with which the main goal of an agency can be attained but increases the chances that the agency will act in a nonarbitrary manner. Efficient police departments would seek out criminals without reading them their rights, allowing them to call their attorneys, or releasing them in response to a writ of habeas corpus. An efficient building department would issue construction permits on demand without insisting that the applicant first show that the proposed building meets fire, safety, sanitation, geological, and earthquake standards.

The second great tradeoff is between nonarbitrary governance defined as treating people equally and such governance defined as treating each case on its merits. We want the government to be both fair and responsive, but the more rules we impose to insure fairness (that is, to treat all people alike) the harder we make it for the government to be responsive (that is, to take into account the special needs and circumstances of a particular case).

The way our government manages these tradeoffs reflects both our political culture as well as the rivalries of our governing institutions. Both tend toward the same end: We define claims as rights, impose general rules to insure equal treatment, lament (but do nothing about) the resulting inefficiencies, and respond to revelations about unresponsiveness by adopting new rules intended to guarantee that special circumstances will be handled with special care (rarely bothering to reconcile the rules that require responsiveness with those that require equality). And we do all this out of the best of motives: a desire to be both just and benevolent. Justice inclines us to treat people equally, benevolence to treat them differently; both inclinations are expressed in rules, though in fact only justice can be. It is this futile desire to have a rule for every circumstance that led Herbert Kaufman to explain "how compassion spawns red tape."

Discretion at the Street Level

We worry most about arbitrary rule at the hands of those street-level bu-reaucracies that deal with us as individuals rather than as organized groups and that touch the more intimate aspects of our lives: police, schools, pris-ons, housing inspectors, mental hospitals, welfare offices, and the like. That worry is natural; in these settings we feel helpless and The State seems om-nipotent. We want these bureaucracies to treat us fairly but we also want them to be responsible to our particular needs. The proper reconciliation of these competing desires requires a careful understanding of the tasks of these organizations.

There are at least two questions that must be answered: What consti-tutes in any specific organization the exercise of arbitrary or unjust power? Under what circumstances will the elaboration of rules reduce at an ac-ceptable cost the unjust use of power? Police officers act unjustly when they arrest people without cause. "Equality before the law" is the bedrock prin-ciple of our criminal justice system, however imperfectly it may be realized. And so we create rules defining when people can be arrested. . . .

Discretion at the Headquarters Level

Interest groups also complain about arbitrariness, especially when they deal with regulatory agencies that have either no clear rules (and so the groups do not know whether policies in effect today will be in effect tomorrow) or rules so clear and demanding that there is no freedom to adjust their activ-ities to conform to economic or technological imperatives.

The exercise of discretion by regulatory agencies does not occur because their activities are invisible or their clients are powerless but because these agencies and their legislative supporters have certain beliefs about what constitutes good policy. For many decades after the invention of the regula-tory agency, Progressives believed that good decisions were the result of empowering neutral experts to decide cases on the basis of scientifically de-termined facts and widely shared principles. No one took it amiss that these "principles" often were so vague as to lack any meaning at all. The Federal Communications Commission (FCC) was directed to issue broadcast li-censes as the "public interest, convenience, and necessity" shall require. A similar "standard" was to govern the awarding of licenses to airline com-panies by the now-defunct Civil Aeronautics Board (CAB). The Antitrust

Division of the Justice Department was charged with enforcing the Sherman Act that made "combinations in restraint of trade" illegal.

What the statute left vague "experts" were to imbue with meaning. But expert opinion changes and some experts in fact are politicians who bow to the influence of organized interests or ideologues who embrace the enthusiasms of zealous factions. The result was an invitation for interests to seek particular results in the absence of universal standards.

One might suppose that the agencies, noticing the turmoil caused by having to decide hard cases on the basis of vacuous standards, would try to formulate and state clear policies that would supply to their clients the guidance that the legislature was unwilling to provide; but no. For the most part regulatory agencies with ambiguous statutes did not clarify their policies. I conjecture that this is because the agencies realized what Michel Crozier has stated: Uncertainty is power. If one party needs something from another and cannot predict how that second party will behave, the second party has power over the first. In the extreme case we will do almost anything to please a madman with life-or-death power over us because we cannot predict which behavior will produce what reaction. . . .

Conclusions

Neither inefficiency nor arbitrariness is easily defined and measured. Inefficiency in the small, that is, the excessive use of resources to achieve the main goal of an agency, is probably commonplace; but inefficiency in the large—the excessive use of resources to achieve all the goals, including the constraints—may not be so common. To evaluate the efficiency of a government agency one first must judge the value of the constraints under which it operates; to improve its efficiency one must decide which constraints one is willing to sacrifice. The best way to think about this is to ask whether we would be willing to have the same product or service delivered by a private firm.

If we decide that the constraints are important then we should be clear-eyed about the costs of retaining them. Those costs arise chiefly from the fact that most bureaucrats will be more strongly influenced by constraints than by goals. Constraints apply early in the process: You know from day one what will get you into trouble. Goals apply late in the process (if then): You must wait to see if the goal is achieved, assuming (a big assumption) that you can state the goal or confirm its achievement. Constraints are strongly enforced by attentive interest groups and their allies in Congress, the White House, the courts, and the media; goal attainment is weakly enforced because an agency head can always point to factors beyond one's control that prevented success. Constraints dissipate managerial authority; every constraint is represented in the organization by someone who can say no. Goals, if they exist and can be attained, are the basis for increasing managerial authority; a clear and attainable goal provides an opportunity for one person to say yes.

Bureaucracies will differ in their vulnerability to the tradeoff between goal attainment and constraint observance. Production organizations, having clear and attainable goals, are more easily evaluated from the standpoint of economic efficiency and thus the cost of any given constraint is more easily assessed. Coping and procedural organizations are impossible to evaluate in terms of economic efficiency and so the cost of a constraint is hard to assess. Craft organizations are a mixed case; because their outputs are observable, we know if they are attaining their goal, but because their work is hard to observe we may think mistakenly that we can alter those work procedures without paying a cost in goal attainment.

The Social Security Administration and the Postal Service are not hard to judge in efficiency terms, though the latter presents a more difficult case than the former because we want the USPS to serve a number of partially inconsistent purposes. The State Department and public schools are impossible to evaluate in efficiency terms, and so we regularly pile on more constraints without any sense that we are paying a price. Police detectives or the Army Corps of Engineers can be evaluated, but only after the fact—the crook is caught, the bridge completed—but we are at somewhat of a loss to know what alteration in procedures would have what effect on these outcomes. Prisons can be evaluated in terms of the resources they consume and the complaints they engender, but ordinarily we have little information as to whether changes in resources or complaints have any effect on such objectives as security, rehabilitation, or deterrence.

Arbitrariness means acting without legal authority, or with such authority in ways that treat like cases in an unlike manner or unlike cases in a similar manner. Deciding what constitutes a "like case" is the heart of the problem. Prisons require rules, but what ends should the rules serve—custody? Security? Self-governance? Rehabilitation? Regulatory agencies formulate rules, but under what circumstances can those rules be clear and comprehensive as opposed to vague and partial? The next [section] will not answer all these questions, but it will suggest how Americans have tried to use rules, as well as the problems with rule-oriented bureaucracy.

Rules

On February 8, 1967, Robert H. Weaver, the secretary of the Department of Housing and Urban Development, announced that henceforth persons applying for apartments in federally financed public housing projects would be given such apartments on a first-come, first-serve basis. Weaver, who is black, issued the new rule in response to the criticism of civil-rights organizations (including a group he once headed) that the local managers of these projects practiced or condoned segregation.

Under the old rules the city agencies that ran these projects gave to individual project managers great discretion to pick their tenants. The effect of that discretion, combined with the preferences of the tenants, was that projects tended to be all-white or all-black. In Boston, for example, there were twenty-five public housing projects built for low-income tenants. Thirteen of these were more than 96 percent white, two were entirely black, and the rest were predominately of one race or the other. These differences could not be explained entirely by neighborhood considerations. The Mission Hill project was 100 percent white; across the street from it, the Mission Hill Extension project was 80 percent black.

Weaver's order became known as the "1-2-3 Rule." It worked this way: All housing applicants would be ranked in numerical order based on the date they applied for housing, their need for housing, and the size of their families. When a vacancy became available it would be offered to the family at the top of the list. If there were more than one vacancy the one offered first would be drawn from the project with the most vacancies. If the family turned it down it would be offered another, and then a third. If all three vacancies were rejected the family would go to the bottom of the list and the next family in line would receive the offer. The Weaver order was an effort, typical of many in government, to prevent the arbitrary use of discretion by replacing discretion with a rule.

Eight years later a group of tenants sued the Boston Housing Authority (BHA). In his findings, the Housing Court judge determined that public housing in Boston still was being allocated in a way that perpetuated racial segregation, a view confirmed by a 1976 report of the Department of

Housing and Urban Development. What had gone wrong? How could a discriminatory pattern of tenant assignment persist for so long after the BHA had implemented, albeit reluctantly, a clear federal rule that on its face did not allow race to be taken into account in choosing tenants?

The answer, supplied by the research of Jon Pynoos and Jeffrey M. Prottas, suggests the limit to rules as a means for controlling the discretion of bureaucrats. First, the 1-2-3 Rule combined three criteria: date, need, and family size. To rank applicants by these criteria someone had to decide how to measure "need" and then how much weight to give to need as opposed to family size or date of application. The evaluation of need inevitably was subjective. Moreover, the neediest families almost by definition were those who had been on the waiting list for the least time. For example, a family living on the street because its home had burned down the night before clearly is going to be regarded as needier than one whose home is livable but who may have been on the waiting list for many months. Second, the rules were inconsistent with the incentives facing the applicants. Applicants wanted to live in the "nicest" projects, but these usually had few vacancies. The worst projects, those with the most crime, litter, and graffiti, had the most vacancies. Applicants would rather turn down a bad project, even if it meant going to the bottom of the list. Since the bad projects often were all-black, this meant that hardly any families, especially any white families, were willing to move in, and so they tended to remain all-black. Third, the rules were inconsistent with the incentives facing the project managers. Managers were exposed to pressure from the tenants in the buildings they operated to keep out the "bad element"—drug users, prostitutes, families with noisy children—and to attract the "good element," such as retired couples and the elderly. The managers bent to these pressures by various stratagems such as concealing the existence of vacancies from the central office or finding ways to veto the applications of certain tenants.

Rules and Discretion

Max Weber said that the great virtue of bureaucracy—indeed, perhaps its defining characteristic—was that it was an institutional method for applying general rules to specific cases, thereby making the actions of government fair and predictable. Weber's belief in the superiority of rule-based governance has been echoed by Theodore J. Lowi, who has criticized the exercise of administrative discretion in the modern American state on the grounds that it leads to the domination of the state by interest groups, thereby weakening popular control and creating new structures of privilege. To restore democratic accountability he called for replacing discretionary authority with what he termed "juridical democracy": governance based on clear legislative standards for bureaucratic action or, failing that, on clear rules formulated by the bureaucracies themselves. When rules are clear, governance is better. Lawrence Friedman has argued that welfare and public housing programs are especially suitable for governance by rule because they involve the simple allocation of resources on an equitable basis. . . .

On occasion, Americans have temporarily abandoned their fear of discretion and their insistence on rules. During the New Deal a number of regulatory agencies—the Securities and Exchange Commission, the National Labor Relations Board, the Federal Communications Commission—were endowed with great powers and vague standards. But in time we have returned to our natural posture, insisting that the powers of any new agencies carefully be circumscribed by law (as they were with the Environmental Protection Agency) and that the powers of existing agencies be if not precisely defined then at least judicially reviewable. But the love of rules has obscured the question of the circumstances under which rules will work. Clearly, an apparently simple rule did not solve the problems of the Boston Housing Authority.

As we saw, the first-come, first-served rule had several defects. Those defects suggest some of the properties a workable and fair rule should have. First, a good rule should treat equals equally. The BHA rule attempted to allocate dissimilar things among dissimilar claimants. Not all apartments were the same: They varied in size, amenity, and, above all, location. Not all clients were the same: Some were law-abiding, some lawless; some were orderly, some disorderly. Second, an effective rule will specify the tradeoffs to be made among the criteria governing the application of the rule. The BHA rule did not do this and in fact could not have done it. Need and time on the waiting list often were in conflict and there was no nonarbitrary way to resolve the conflict. Third, a workable rule will be consistent with the incentives operating on the administrators and on at least some of the clients. Neither the BHA clients nor its managers had many incentives to conform to the rules. The clients wanted to move into "nice" housing; very few wanted to integrate housing, whatever the cost in amenity. The managers wanted to get "nice" clients; very few wanted problem families. We want rules to be clear, but the BHA rule only seemed to be clear.

Rules and Tasks

When the work and the outcomes of a government agency are observable and unambiguous some but not all of the conditions for management by rule are present. I have called such bureaus production agencies. . . . Processing claims for old-age and survivors' insurance in the Social Security Administration (SSA) is subject to very detailed rules. These rules seem to work well. This happens not only because the work (processing claims) and the outcomes (who gets how much money) are easily observed, but also because the rules meet or come very close to meeting the tests described in the preceding section: They refer to comparable cases (people of a defined age and marital status), they do not involve difficult tradeoffs (unless the Social Security Trust Fund runs out of money, everybody who meets certain tests gets money), and they conform to the natural incentives of the agency members (the service ethos of the SSA leads its employees to want to give money to every eligible person).

SSA also manages the disability insurance program. This makes the use of rules a bit more complicated because the definition of a disabled person is much more ambiguous than that of an elderly or retired one. In his excellent book on SSA management of the disability program [*Bureaucratic Justice: Managing Social Security Claims* (1983)], Jerry Mashaw concluded that despite the ambiguity the program works reasonably well. One reason is that every disabled person is entitled to benefits whatever his or her financial need; thus the definition of "disabled," although vague, does not have to be traded off against an even vaguer definition of need. Moreover, the lack of clarity in the rules defining disability is made up for by the working environment of the operators. The examiners who review claims for disability payments work elbow-to-elbow with their peers and supervisors. The claims are all in writing, there is no need to make snap judgments, and the decisions are reviewable by quality assurance inspectors. Dissatisfied claimants can appeal the decisions to administrative law judges. Out of this deliberate process there has emerged a kind of common law of disability, a set of precedents that reflects pooled experience and shared judgments.

The use of rules becomes more difficult in local welfare offices. These agencies administer the federal Aid to Families with Dependent Children program that, until it was changed in 1988, authorized the states to pay money to needy women who had children but no husbands and were otherwise fit but unemployable parents. It is very hard to make clear rules on these matters. What is a "fit" or an "employable" parent? How much does a given woman "need"? Some countries such as Great Britain do not try to solve these problems by rule; instead they empower welfare workers to make a judgment about each case and to use their discretion in approving payments.

In the United States, we use rules—up to a point. Since many of the rules are inevitably vague, the welfare workers who administer them have a significant amount of discretion. An intake worker could use that discretion to deny benefits to women on grounds of fitness or employability. But in fact they rarely do. Joel Handler, who studied welfare administration in Wisconsin in the 1960s, described how welfare workers used the rules they were given: In essence they focused on what was measurable. In each of the six counties investigated by Handler, the questions asked of applicants chiefly involved assessing the women's financial resources. The rule that was enforced was the means test: "Are your resources sufficiently inadequate as to justify your participation in this program?" If the applicant passed the means test the rest of the interview was about her budget—how much money she needed and for what. In only a minority of the cases were any questions asked about employability, marriage plans, or child-care practices. Though the federal government once tried by a law passed in 1962 to get welfare workers to deliver "social services" to their clients, the workers did not deliver them.

Welfare workers could get in trouble for allowing ineligible clients to get on the welfare rolls. But only *financial* ineligibility was easily determined, and so the rules governing money were the rules that were enforced. The workers had little incentive to find out how the clients led their lives and even less to tell them how they ought to lead those lives.

If rules are such an imperfect guide to action even in welfare and housing agencies (where according to Friedman their application was supposed to be straightforward), it is not hard to imagine how much more imperfect their use will be in coping, procedural, or craft agencies. Consider police patrol officers. We expect them to prevent disorderly conduct, but it is virtually impossible to define disorderly (or orderly) conduct. Behavior that is frightening to an old woman or nerve-wracking to a diamond-cutter is fun to a teenager or necessary to a garbage collector. Because we cannot produce a clear rule by which to guide the police control of disorderly conduct does not mean that the police should do nothing about disorder. But what they will do always will be a matter of dispute.

Or consider the "rules" contained in the Education for All Handicapped Children Act passed by Congress in 1975. It required each state to guarantee by a certain date a free and appropriate education for all handicapped children between the ages of three and twenty-one. That goal, however laudable, strained the capacity of every state's educational system. But if tight timetables and scarce resources were the only problems the law would not have raised any fundamental administrative problems. What made matters worse was that the law did not leave the selection of means to local authorities; instead it required the schools to develop for each eligible child an Individualized Education Program, or IEP, that specified short-term and annual instructional goals as well as the services that were to be supplied to attain those goals. Each IEP was to be developed jointly by a team comprised of the child's teacher and parents together with specialists in education for the handicapped and others "as necessary." If a parent disagreed with the IEP, he or she was afforded a due-process hearing. Here, a bureaucracy—the public school—the work and outputs of which can barely be observed (much less measured) was obliged to follow a rule that called for the education of every handicapped child (but not every normal one) on the basis of an individual plan that could be shaped and enforced by going to court.

Rules, like ideas, have consequences. When there is a mismatch between legal rules and bureaucratic realities, the rules get subverted. The subversion in this case took two forms. First, teachers struggling to find the time and energy for their daily tasks would not refer potentially eligible children to the special-education program. And when they did refer them they often made the decision on the basis not of which child most needed special education but of which child was giving the teacher the most trouble in the classroom. Second, some parents but not others took advantage of their due-process rights. Most observers agree that competent, middle-class parents were more effective at using the legal system than less competent, lower-class parents.

Because of the law, more is being done today for handicapped children than was once the case, but how it is being done cannot readily be inferred from the IEP rules. If some critics are right the insistence on defining education by means of formal, legally enforceable rules has led to substituting paperwork and procedure for services and results. This should not be surprising. A rule is a general statement prescribing how a class of behaviors should be conducted. Using a general statement to produce an individualized result is almost a contradiction in terms. We tailor behavior in accordance with individual circumstances precisely in those cases when the circumstances defy classification by rule.

The bureaucratic behaviors that most easily can be defined by rule tend to be those that are frequent, similar, and patterned—those that are routine. SSA easily applied rules in advance to its retirement benefits; with somewhat more difficulty it began to develop rules for disability claims. By contrast, the National Labor Relations Board (NLRB) has few rules. "Neither the fulminations of commentators nor the prodding of courts," Mashaw writes, "has convinced it that any of its vague adjudicatory doctrines can bear particularization or objectification in regulatory form." The Federal Communications Commission (FCC) for a long time resisted demands that it formulate into clear rules the standards it would use for awarding broadcast licenses. The NLRB and the FCC saw themselves as quasi-judicial bodies that decided each unique case on its individual merits. In fact, many NLRB and FCC policies probably could have been reduced to rule. The FCC did this when it finally announced what it had long practiced: that broadcast licenses routinely would be renewed absent some showing that they should not be. Commissions, like courts, resist routinization, perhaps because they delve so deeply into the matters before them that they see differences where others see similarities.

Rules and Impermissible Outcomes

Even where bureaucratic behavior is not so routinized that it can be conveniently prescribed by rule, we insist on rules when there is a significant risk of an impermissible outcome. There is no reason in principle why we could not repeal the laws against homicide and create in their stead a Commission on Life Enhancement and Preservation (CLEP) that would hear complaints about persons who had killed other persons. It would consider evidence about the character of the deceased: Was he lazy or dutiful, decent or disorderly, likable or hateful? On the basis of this evaluation of the lost life and relying on the professional judgment of its staff, the CLEP would decide whether the life lost was worth losing and, if not, whether the person who took it was justified in doing so. By thus decriminalizing homicide, we surely would experience a reduction in the number of events officially labeled murders since the CLEP would undoubtedly conclude that many who had been killed richly deserved their fate.

Most of us would not vote for such a proposal because we attach so high a value to human life that we are unwilling to trust anyone, especially any bureaucrat employed by CLEP, to decide who should die and who should live. We hold this view despite our belief that there are probably some (perhaps many) that the world would be better off without. In short, the risk of error—in this case, wrongly deciding that a worthy life had been a worthless one—is so great that we allow no discretion to the government. If a person who kills another is to escape punishment, it must be for particular excusing conditions (for example, self-defense) and not because of a government-assessed valuation of the lost life.

The laws of this country have multiplied beyond measure the number of outcomes that are deemed impermissible. From 1938 to 1958, the Food and Drug Administration (FDA) had the authority to prevent the sale or distribution of any drug unless it was shown by "adequate tests" to be safe. In 1958 new legislation was passed that directed it to bar from sale or distribution any food additive, food color, or drug administered to food animals if "it is found to induce cancer when ingested by man or animal." This was the so-called Delaney Amendment, named after the New York congressman who sponsored it.

Ignoring for the moment certain exceptions, the Delaney Amendment implied that we should swallow nothing that might cause cancer in the kinds of laboratory animals on which scientists test foods. In principle, this meant that the FDA was hostage to progress in analytical chemistry: As scientists improved their ability to detect cancer-causing chemicals, the FDA would be obliged to ban those chemicals (and the foods they contained) from the supermarket shelves. Cancer was a risk, the FDA was told, that it was impermissible to run, whatever the costs. Thus it was to enforce the rule, "no cancer."

But when the FDA in 1979 used this rule to ban saccharin, the artificial sweetener used in such products as "Sweet 'n Low," it suddenly discovered that Congress did not mean what it had said—at least in this case. "All hell broke loose," recalled one representative. Consumers wanted to use saccharin in order to lose weight, even if scientists had discovered that in very high dosages it induced bladder cancer in laboratory animals. Faced with this popular revolt, Congress swiftly passed a law delaying (and ultimately prohibiting) the FDA ban on saccharin. But Congress did not review the Delaney Amendment: It stood as a rule that could not (with certain minor exceptions) be traded off against any other rule. . . .

The United States relies on rules to control the exercise of official judgment to a greater extent than any other industrialized democracy. The reason, I think, has little to do with the kinds of bureaucrats we have and everything to do with the political environment in which those bureaucrats must work. If we wish to complain about how rule-ridden our government agencies seem to be, we should direct those complaints not to the agencies but to the Congress, the courts, and the organized interests that make effective use of Congress and the courts

Rules: Gains and Losses

The difficulty of striking a reasonable balance between rules and discretion is an age-old problem for which there is no "objective" solution any more than there is to the tension between other competing human values such as freedom and order, love and discipline, or change and stability. At best we can sensitize ourselves to the gains and losses associated with governance by rule rather than by discretion.

Rules, if they are clear, induce agencies to produce certain observable outcomes: nursing homes must have fire sprinklers, hotels must have smoke alarms, dairy products may not contain polychorinated biphenyls (PCBs), automobiles must be equipped with crashworthy bumpers and steering wheels. But rules often cannot induce organizations to improve hard-to-observe processes. A nursing home may be safer because it has certain equipment installed, but it will not be well run unless it has competent head nurses. Eugene Bardach and Robert Kagan make this point by comparing public and private factory inspections. An inspector from OSHA charged with enforcing rules will evaluate the physical aspects of a factory: the ventilation, guardrails, and safety devices. By contrast, an inspector from an insurance company charged with assessing the insurability of the firm will evaluate the attitude and policies of management: its safety consciousness. The difference in approaches is important because, if John Mendeloff is correct, "most workplace injuries are not caused by violations of standards [i.e., rules], and even fewer are caused by violations that inspectors can detect."

Rules create offices, procedures, and claims inside an organization that can protect precarious values. An automobile company is required to comply with OSHA rules. If the only effect of the rules were the company's fear of inspectors, not much would happen. But to cope with the inspectors the company will hire its own industrial safety experts, and these in turn will establish procedures and generate pressures that alter the company's behavior even when it is not being inspected. At the same time, rules generate paperwork and alter human relationships in ways that can reduce the ability of the organization to achieve its goals and its incentives to cooperate with those who enforce the rules. To verify that military aircraft are built according to government specifications, hundreds of pounds of forms must be filled out that document each operation on each aircraft; these forms, one set for every individual airplane, must be stored for twenty years. Nurses must record every step in medical treatments. Personnel officers must document the grounds for every hiring and promotional decision. Teachers must fill out sign-in sheets, absence slips, attendance records, textbook requests, lesson plans, student evaluations, questionnaires, ethnic and language surveys, free-lunch applications, time cards, field-trip requests, special-needs assessments, and parental conference reports. Rarely does anybody read these forms. They are, after all, what Bardach and Kagan call a "declaration of innocence"; no aircraft company, charge nurse, personnel officer, or schoolteacher will use these forms to admit their wrongdoing, and so no government inspector will read them. The rules and the forms contribute to the adversarial relationship that so often characterizes the relationship between regulator and regulatee.

Rules specify minimum standards that must be met. This is a clear gain when an organization, public or private, is performing below the minimum. But minimum standards often become maximum standards. Alvin Gouldner first noticed this in his study of a private firm, the General Gypsum Company (a pseudonym). Suppose workers were expected to "get the day's job done." Some would work less than eight hours, some much longer. Now suppose that a rule is announced—"everybody will work eight hours"—and a device (the time clock) is installed to enforce it. Laggards would now work eight hours but zealots would stop working more than eight. Bardach and Kagan observed this in the case of OSHA rules: At one time, a company would improve ventilating or lighting systems when workers or union leaders complained about these matters; later, the company would make no changes unless required by OSHA rules.

To decide whether the gains from imposing a rule outweigh the costs you must carefully judge the particular circumstances of a given organization. In other words, no rule can be promulgated that tells you when promulgating rules is a good idea. But at least the tensions highlighted in this section should make you aware that rules have risks and teach you to be sensitive to the fact that the American political system is biased toward solving bureaucratic problems by issuing rules. Given that bias, people who worry about the costs of rules usually will not be heard very clearly in the hubbub of concern about an unmet need or a bureaucratic failure.

Talented, strongly motivated people usually will find ways of making even rule-ridden systems work. This is especially the case when complying with the rules is seen as a mere formality; a form to be filled out, a box to be checked, a file to be kept. Teachers, nurses, police officers, and housing project managers can find ways of getting the job done—if they want to.

The managerial problem arises from two facts: First, talented, strongly motivated workers are a minority in any organization. People who can cope with rules will be outnumbered by people who hide behind them. . . .

Second, whatever behavior will get an agency executive in trouble will get a manager in trouble; whatever gets a manager in trouble will get an operator in trouble. Or put another way: Agency executives have a strong incentive to enforce on their subordinates those rules the violation of which create external political difficulties for the executive. This means that even talented and motivated operators will not be free to violate rules that threaten their agency, even if the rule itself is silly. Many agency executives do not understand this. They are eager to deflect or mollify critics of their agencies. In their eagerness they suppose that announcing a rule designed to forbid whatever behavior led to the criticism actually will work. Their immediate subordinates, remote from field pressures (and perhaps eager to ingratiate themselves with the executive) will assure their bosses that the new rule will solve the problem. But unless the rule actually redefines the core tasks of the operators in a meaningful and feasible way, or significantly alters the incentives those operators value, the rule will be seen as just one more constraint on getting the job done (or, more graphically, as "just another piece of chicken——t").

8-2

The Politics of Bureaucratic Structure

Terry M. Moe

Legislators, presidents, and other political players care about the content and implementation of policy. They also care about the way executive agencies are structured: Where in the executive branch are new agencies placed? What kind of bureaucrat will be motivated to aggressively pursue, or to resist the pursuit of, certain policy goals? Who should report to whom? What rules should govern bureaucrats' behavior? In the following essay, Terry Moe observes that these questions are anticipated and answered by politicians as they set policy. They are the subjects of "structural" politics. The federal bureaucracy is not structured on the basis of a theory of public administration, Moe argues, but should instead be viewed as the product of politics.

AMERICAN PUBLIC bureaucracy is not designed to be effective. The bureaucracy arises out of politics, and its design reflects the interests, strategies, and compromises of those who exercise political power.

This politicized notion of bureaucracy has never appealed to most academics or reformers. They accept it—indeed, they adamantly argue its truth—and the social science of public bureaucracy is a decidedly political body of work as a result. Yet, for the most part, those who study and practice public administration have a thinly veiled disdain for politics, and they want it kept out of bureaucracy as much as possible. They want presidents to stop politicizing the departments and bureaus. They want Congress to stop its incessant meddling in bureaucratic affairs. They want all politicians to respect bureaucratic autonomy, expertise, and professionalism.[1]

The bureaucracy's defenders are not apologists. Problems of capture, inertia, parochialism, fragmentation, and imperialism are familiar grounds for

Excerpted from John E. Chubb and Paul E. Peterson, eds., *Can the Government Govern?* (Washington, D.C.: Brookings Institution Press, 1989), pp. 267–285. Reprinted by permission. Some notes appearing in the original have been cut.

criticism. And there is lots of criticism. But once the subversive influence of politics is mentally factored out, these bureaucratic problems are understood to have bureaucratic solutions—new mandates, new rules and procedures, new personnel systems, better training and management, better people. These are the quintessential reforms that politicians are urged to adopt to bring about effective bureaucracy. The goal at all times is the greater good: "In designing any political structure, whether it be the Congress, the executive branch, or the judiciary, it is important to build arrangements that weigh the scale in favor of those advocating the national interest."[2]

The hitch is that those in positions of power are not necessarily motivated by the national interest. They have their own interests to pursue in politics—the interests of southwest Pennsylvania or cotton farmers or the maritime industry—and they exercise their power in ways conducive to those interests. Moreover, choices about bureaucratic structure are not matters that can be separated off from all this, to be guided by technical criteria of efficiency and effectiveness. Structural choices have important consequences for the content and direction of policy, and political actors know it. When they make choices about structure, they are implicitly making choices about policy. And precisely because this is so, issues of structure are inevitably caught up in the larger political struggle. Any notion that political actors might confine their attention to policymaking and turn organizational design over to neutral criteria or efficiency experts denies the realities of politics.

This essay is an effort to understand bureaucracy by understanding its foundation in political choice and self-interest. The central question boils down to this: what sorts of structures do the various political actors—interest groups, presidents, members of Congress, bureaucrats—find conducive to their own interests, and what kind of bureaucracy is therefore likely to emerge from their efforts to exercise political power? In other words, why do they build the bureaucracy they do? . . .

A Perspective on Structural Politics

Most citizens do not get terribly excited about the arcane details of public administration. When they choose among candidates in elections, they pay attention to such things as party or image or stands on policy. If pressed, the candidates would probably have views or even voting records on structural issues—for example, whether the Occupational Safety and Health Administration should be required to carry out cost-benefit analysis before proposing a formal rule or whether the Consumer Product Safety Commission should be moved into the Commerce Department—but this is hardly the stuff that political campaigns are made of. People just do not know or care much about these sorts of things.

Organized interest groups are another matter. They are active, informed participants in their specialized issue areas, and they know that their policy goals are crucially dependent on precisely those fine details of administrative structure that cause voters' eyes to glaze over. Structure is valuable to them, and they have every incentive to mobilize their political resources to get what they want. As a result, they are normally the only source of political pressure when structural issues are at stake. Structural politics is interest group politics.

Interest Groups: The Technical Problem of Structural Choice

Most accounts of structural politics pay attention to interest groups, but their analytical focus is on the politicians who exercise public authority and make the final choices. This tends to be misleading. It is well known that politicians, even legislators from safe districts, are extraordinarily concerned about their electoral popularity and, for that reason, are highly responsive to their constituencies. To the extent this holds true, their positions on issues are not really their own, but are induced by the positions of others. If one seeks to understand why structural choices turn out as they do, then, it does not make much sense to start with politicians. The more fundamental questions have to do with how interest groups decide what kinds of structures they want politicians to provide. This is the place to start.

In approaching these questions about interest groups, it is useful to begin with an extreme case. Suppose that, in a given issue area, there is a single dominant group (or coalition) with a reasonably complex problem—pollution, poverty, job safety, health—it seeks to address through governmental action, and that the group is so powerful that politicians will enact virtually any proposal the group offers, subject to reasonable budget constraints. In effect, the group is able to exercise public authority on its own by writing legislation that is binding on everyone and enforceable in the courts.

The dominant group is an instructive case because, as it makes choices about structure, it faces no political problems. It need not worry about losing its grip on public authority or about the influence of its political opponents—considerations which would otherwise weigh heavily in its calculations. Without the usual uncertainties and constraints of politics, the group has the luxury of concerning itself entirely with the technical requirements of effective organization. Its job is to identify those structural arrangements that best realize its policy goals.

It is perhaps natural to think that, since a dominant group can have anything it wants, it would proceed by figuring out what types of behaviors are called for by what types of people under what types of conditions and by writing legislation spelling all this out in the minutest detail. If an administrative agency were necessary to perform services, process applications, or inspect business operations, the jobs of bureaucrats could be specified with such precision that they would have little choice but to do the group's bidding.

For simple policy goals—requiring, say, little more than transfer payments—these strategies would be attractive. But they are quite unsuited to policy problems of any complexity. The reason is that, although the group has the political power to impose its will on everyone, it almost surely lacks the knowledge to do it well. It does not know what to tell people to do.

In part, this is an expertise problem. Society as a whole simply has not developed sufficient knowledge to determine the causes of or solutions for most social problems; and the group typically knows much less than society does, even when it hires experts of its own. These knowledge problems are compounded by uncertainty about the future. The world is subject to unpredictable changes over time, and some will call on specific policy adjustments if the group's interests are to be pursued effectively. The group could attempt to specify all future contingencies in the current legislation and, through continuous monitoring and intervention, update it over time. But the knowledge requirements of a halfway decent job would prove enormously costly, cumbersome, and time-consuming.

A group with the political power to tell everyone what to do, then, will typically not find it worthwhile to try. A more attractive option is to write legislation in general terms, put experts on the public payroll, and grant them the authority to "fill in the details" and make whatever adjustments are necessary over time. This compensates nicely for the group's formidable knowledge problems, allowing it to pursue its own interests without knowing exactly how to implement its policies and without having to grapple with future contingencies. The experts do what the group is unable to do for itself. And because they are public officials on the public payroll, the arrangement economizes greatly on the group's resources and time.

It does, however, raise a new worry: there is no guarantee the experts will always act in the group's best interests. Experts have their own interests—in career, in autonomy—that may conflict with those of the group. And, due largely to experts' specialized knowledge and the often intangible nature of their outputs, the group cannot know exactly what its expert agents are doing or why. These are problems of conflict of interest and asymmetric information, and they are unavoidable. Because of them, control will be imperfect.

When the group's political power is assured, as we assume it is here, these control problems are at the heart of structural choice. The most direct approach is for the group to impose a set of rules to constrain bureaucratic behavior. Among other things, these rules might specify the criteria and procedures bureaucrats are to use in making decisions; shape incentives by specifying how bureaucrats are to be evaluated, rewarded, and sanctioned; require them to collect and report certain kinds of information on their internal operations, and set up oversight procedures by which their activities can be monitored. These are basic components of bureaucratic structure.

But some slippage will remain. The group's knowledge problems, combined with the experts' will and capacity to resist (at least at the margins), make perfect control impossible. Fortunately, though, the group can do more than impose a set of rules on its agents. It also has the power to choose who its agents will be—and wise use of this power could make the extensive use of rules unnecessary.

The key here is reputation. Most individuals in the expert market come with reputations that speak to their job-relevant traits: expertise, intelligence, honesty, loyalty, policy preferences, ideology. "Good" reputations provide reliable information. The reason is that individuals value good reputations, they invest in them—by behaving honestly, for instance, even when they could realize short-term gains through cheating—and, having built up reputations, they have strong incentives to maintain them through consistent behavior. To the group, therefore, reputation is of enormous value because it allows predictability in an uncertain world. And predictability facilitates control.

To see more concretely how this works, consider an important reputational syndrome: professionalism. If individuals are known to be accountants or securities lawyers or highway engineers, the group will immediately know a great deal about their "type." They will be experts in certain issues. They will have specialized educations and occupational experiences. They will analyze issues, collect data, and propose solutions in characteristic ways. They will hew to the norms of their professional communities. Particularly when professionalism is combined with reputational information of a more personal nature, the behavior of these experts will be highly predictable.

The link between predictability and control would seem especially troublesome in this case, since professionals are widely known to demand autonomy in their work. And, as far as restrictive rules and hierarchical directives are concerned, their demand for autonomy does indeed pose problems. But the group is forced to grant experts discretion anyway, owing to its knowledge problems. What professionalism does—via reputation—is allow the group to anticipate how expert discretion will be exercised under various conditions; it can then plan accordingly as it designs a structure that takes best advantage of their expertise. In the extreme, one might think of professionals as automatons, programmed to behave in specific ways. Knowing how they are programmed, the group can select those with the desired programs, place them in a structure designed to accommodate them, and turn them loose to exercise free choice. The professionals would see themselves as independent decisionmakers. The group would see them as under control. And both would be right.

The purpose of this illustration is not to emphasize professionalism per se, but to clarify a general point about the technical requirements of organizational design. A politically powerful group, acting under uncertainty and concerned with solving a complex policy problem, is normally best off if it resists using its power to tell bureaucrats exactly what to do. It can use its power more productively by selecting the right types of bureaucrats and designing a structure that affords them reasonable autonomy. Through the judicious allocation of bureaucratic roles and responsibilities, incentive systems, and structural checks on bureaucratic choice, a select set of bureaucrats can be unleashed to follow their expert judgment, free from detailed formal instructions.

Interest Groups: The Political Problem of Structural Choice

Political dominance is an extreme case for purposes of illustration. In the real world of democratic politics, interest groups cannot lay claim to unchallenged legal authority. Because this is so, they face two fundamental problems that a dominant group does not. The first I will call political uncertainty, the second political compromise. Both have enormous consequences for the strategic design of public bureaucracy—consequences that entail substantial departures from effective organization.

Political uncertainty is inherent in democratic government. No one has a perpetual hold on public authority nor, therefore, a perpetual right to control public agencies. An interest group may be powerful enough to exercise public authority today, but tomorrow its power may ebb, and its right to exercise public authority may then be usurped by its political opponents. Should this occur, they would become the new "owners" of whatever the group had created, and they could use their authority to destroy—quite legitimately—everything the group had worked so hard to achieve.

A group that is currently advantaged, then, must anticipate all this. Precisely because its own authority is not guaranteed, it cannot afford to focus entirely on technical issues of effective organization. It must also design its creations so that they have the capacity to pursue its policy goals in a world in which its enemies may achieve the right to govern. The group's task in the current period, then, is to build agencies that are difficult for its opponents to gain control over later. Given the way authority is allocated and exercised in a democracy, this will often mean building agencies that are insulated from public authority in general—and thus insulated from formal control by the group itself.

There are various structural means by which the group can try to protect and nurture its bureaucratic agents. They include the following:

• It can write detailed legislation that imposes rigid constraints on the agency's mandate and decision procedures. While these constraints will tend to be flawed, cumbersome, and costly, they serve to remove important types of decisions from future political control. The reason they are so attractive is rooted in the American separation-of-powers system, which sets up obstacles that make formal legislation extremely difficult to achieve— and, if achieved, extremely difficult to overturn. Should the group's opponents gain in political power, there is a good chance they would still not be able to pass corrective legislation of their own.

• It can place even greater emphasis on professionalism than is technically justified, since professionals will generally act to protect their own autonomy and resist political interference. For similar reasons, the group can be a strong supporter of the career civil service and other personnel systems that insulate bureaucratic jobs, promotion, and pay from political intervention. And it can try to minimize the power and number of political appointees, since these too are routes by which opponents may exercise influence.

- It can oppose formal provisions that enhance political oversight and involvement. The legislative veto, for example, is bad because it gives opponents a direct mechanism for reversing agency decisions. Sunset provisions, which require reauthorization of the agency after some period of time, are also dangerous because they give opponents opportunities to overturn the group's legislative achievements.

- It can see that the agency is given a safe location in the scheme of government. Most obviously, it might try to place the agency in a friendly executive department, where it can be sheltered by the group's allies. Or it may favor formal independence, which provides special protection from presidential removal and managerial powers.

- It can favor judicialization of agency decisionmaking as a way of insulating policy choices from outside interference. It can also favor making various types of agency actions—or inactions—appealable to the courts. It must take care to design these procedures and checks, however, so that they disproportionately favor the group over its opponents.

The driving force of political uncertainty, then, causes the winning group to favor structural designs it would never favor on technical grounds alone: designs that place detailed formal restrictions on bureaucratic discretion, impose complex procedures for agency decisionmaking, minimize opportunities for oversight, and otherwise insulate the agency from politics. The group has to protect itself and its agency from the dangers of democracy, and it does so by imposing structures that appear strange and incongruous indeed when judged by almost any reasonable standards of what an effective organization ought to look like.

But this is only part of the story. The departure from technical rationality is still greater because of a second basic feature of American democratic politics: legislative victory of any consequence almost always requires compromise. This means that opposing groups will have a direct say in how the agency and its mandate are constructed. One form that this can take, of course, is the classic compromise over policy that is written about endlessly in textbooks and newspapers. But there is no real disjunction between policy and structure, and many of the opponents' interests will also be pursued through demands for structural concessions. What sorts of arrangements should they tend to favor?

- Opponents want structures that work against effective performance. They fear strong, coherent, centralized organization. They like fragmented authority, decentralization, federalism, checks and balances, and other structural means of promoting weakness, confusion, and delay.
- They want structures that allow politicians to get at the agency. They do not want to see the agency placed within a friendly department, nor do they favor formal independence. They are enthusiastic supporters of legislative veto and reauthorization provisions. They favor onerous requirements for the collection and reporting of information, the monitoring of agency operations, and the review of agency decisions—thus laying the basis for active, interventionist oversight by politicians.
- They want appointment and personnel arrangements that allow for political direction of the agency. They also want more active and influential roles for political appointees and less extensive reliance on professionalism and the civil service.
- They favor agency decisionmaking procedures that allow them to participate, to present evidence and arguments, to appeal adverse agency decisions, to delay, and, in general, to protect their own interests and inhibit effective agency action through formal, legally sanctioned rules. This means that they will tend to push for cumbersome, heavily judicialized decision processes, and that they will favor an active, easily triggered role for the courts in reviewing agency decisions.
- They want agency decisions to be accompanied by, and partially justified in terms of, "objective" assessments of their consequences: environmental impact statements, inflation impact statements, cost-benefit analysis. These are costly, time-consuming, and disruptive. Even better, their methods and conclusions can be challenged in the courts, providing new opportunities for delaying or quashing agency decisions.

Political compromise ushers the fox into the chicken coop. Opposing groups are dedicated to crippling the bureaucracy and gaining control over its decisions, and they will pressure for fragmented authority, labyrinthine procedures, mechanisms of political intervention, and other structures that subvert the bureaucracy's performance and open it up to attack. In the politics of structural choice, the inevitability of compromise means that agencies will be burdened with structures fully intended to cause their failure.

In short, democratic government gives rise to two major forces that cause the structure of public bureaucracy to depart from technical rationality. First, those currently in a position to exercise public authority will often face uncertainty about their own grip on political power in the years ahead, and this will prompt them to favor structures that insulate their achievements from politics. Second, opponents will also tend to have a say in structural design, and, to the degree they do, they will impose structures that subvert effective performance and politicize agency decisions.

Legislators and Structural Choice

If politicians were nothing more than conduits for political pressures, structural choice could be understood without paying much attention to them. But politicians, especially presidents, do sometimes have preferences about the structure of government that are not simple reflections of what the groups want. And when this is so, they can use their control of public authority to make their preferences felt in structural outcomes.

The conduit notion is not so wide of the mark for legislators, owing to their almost paranoid concern for reelection. In structural politics, well-informed interest groups make demands, observe legislators' responses, and accurately assign credit and blame as decisions are made and consequences realized. Legislators therefore have strong incentives to do what groups want—and, even in the absence of explicit demands, to take entrepreneurial action in actively representing group interests. They cannot satisfy groups with empty position taking. Nor can they costlessly "shift the responsibility" by delegating tough decisions to the bureaucracy. Interest groups, unlike voters, are not easily fooled.

This does not mean that legislators always do what groups demand of them. Autonomous behavior can arise even among legislators who are motivated by nothing other than reelection. This happens because politicians, like groups, recognize that their current choices are not just means of responding to current pressures, but are also means of imposing structure on their political lives. This will sometimes lead them to make unpopular choices today in order to reap political rewards later on.

It is not quite right, moreover, to suggest that legislators have no interest of their own in controlling the bureaucracy. The more control legislators are able to exercise, the more groups will depend on them to get what they want; and this, in itself, makes control electorally attractive. But the attractiveness of control is diluted by other factors. First, the winning group—the more powerful side—will pressure to have its victories removed from political influence. Second, the capacity for control can be a curse for legislators in later conflict, since both sides will descend on them repeatedly. Third, oversight for purposes of serious policy control is time-consuming, costly, and difficult to do well; legislators typically have much more productive ways to spend their scarce resources.

The result is that legislators tend not to invest in general policy control. Instead, they value "particularized" control: they want to be able to intervene quickly, inexpensively, and in ad hoc ways to protect or advance the interests of particular clients in particular matters. This sort of control can be managed by an individual legislator without collective action; it has direct payoffs; it will generally be carried out behind the scenes; and it does not involve or provoke conflict. It generates political benefits without political costs. Moreover, it fits in quite nicely with a bureaucratic structure designed for conflict avoidance: an agency that is highly autonomous in the realm of policy yet highly constrained by complex procedural requirements will offer all sorts of opportunities for particularistic interventions.

The more general point is that legislators, by and large, can be expected either to respond to group demands in structural politics or to take entrepreneurial action in trying to please them. They will not be given to flights of autonomous action or statesmanship.

Presidents and Structural Choice

Presidents are motivated differently. Governance is the driving force behind the modern presidency. All presidents, regardless of party, are expected to govern effectively and are held responsible for taking action on virtually the full range of problems facing society. To be judged successful in the eyes of history—arguably the single most important motivator for presidents—they must appear to be strong leaders. They need to achieve their policy initiatives, their initiatives must be regarded as socially valuable, and the structures for attaining them must appear to work.

This raises two basic problems for interest groups. The first is that presidents are not very susceptible to the appeals of special interests. They want to make groups happy, to be sure, and sometimes responding to group demands will contribute nicely to governance. But this is often not so. In general, presidents have incentives to think in grander terms about what is best for society as a whole, or at least broad chunks of it, and they have their own agendas that may depart substantially from what even their more prominent group supporters might want. Even when they are simply responding to group pressures—which is more likely, of course, during their first term—the size and heterogeneity of their support coalitions tend to promote moderation, compromise, opposition to capture, and concern for social efficiency.

The second problem is that presidents want to control the bureaucracy. While legislators eagerly delegate their powers to administrative agencies, presidents are driven to take charge. They do not care about all agencies equally, of course. Some agencies are especially important because their programs are priority items on the presidential agenda. Others are important because they deal with sensitive issues that can become political bombshells if something goes wrong. But most all agencies impinge in one way or another on larger presidential responsibilities—for the budget, for the economy, for national defense—and presidents must have the capacity to direct and constrain agency behavior in basic respects if these larger responsibilities are to be handled successfully. They may often choose not to use their capacity for administrative control; they may even let favored groups use it when it suits their purposes. But the capacity must be there when they need it.

Presidents therefore have a unique role to play in the politics of structural choice. They are the only participants who are directly concerned with how the bureaucracy as a whole should be organized. And they are the only ones who actually want to run it through hands-on management and control. Their ideal is a rational, coherent, centrally directed bureaucracy that strongly resembles popular textbook notions of what an effective bureaucracy, public or private, ought to look like.

In general, presidents favor placing agencies within executive departments and subordinating them to hierarchical authority. They want to see important oversight, budget, and policy coordination functions given to department superiors—and, above them, to the Office of Management and Budget and other presidential management agencies—so that the bureaucracy can be brought under unified direction. While they value professionalism and civil service for their contributions to expertise, continuity, and impartiality, they want authority in the hands of their own political appointees—and they want to choose appointees whose types appear most conducive to presidential leadership.

This is just what the winning group and its legislative allies do not want. They want to protect their agencies and policy achievements by insulating them from politics, and presidents threaten to ruin everything by trying to control these agencies from above. The opposing groups are delighted with this, but they cannot always take comfort in the presidential approach to bureaucracy either. For presidents will tend to resist complex procedural protections, excessive judicial review, legislative veto provisions, and many other means by which the losers try to protect themselves and cripple bureaucratic performance. Presidents want agencies to have discretion, flexibility, and the capacity to take direction. They do not want agencies to be hamstrung by rules and regulations—unless, of course, they are presidential rules and regulations designed to enhance presidential control.

Legislators, Presidents, and Interest Groups

Obviously, presidents and legislators have very different orientations to the politics of structural choice. Interest groups can be expected to anticipate these differences from the outset and devise their own strategies accordingly.

Generally speaking, groups on both sides will find Congress a comfortable place in which to do business. Legislators are not bound by any overarching notion of what the bureaucracy as a whole ought to look like. They are not intrinsically motivated by effectiveness or efficiency or coordination or management or any other design criteria that might limit the kind of bureaucracy they are willing to create. They do not even want to retain political control for themselves.

The key thing about Congress is that it is open and responsive to what the groups want. It willingly builds, piece by piece—however grotesque the pieces, however inconsistent with one another—the kind of bureaucracy interest groups incrementally demand in their structural battles over time. This "congressional bureaucracy" is not supposed to function as a coherent whole, nor even to constitute one. Only the pieces are important. That is the way groups want it.

Presidents, of course, do not want it that way. Interest groups may find them attractive allies on occasion, especially when their interests and the presidential agenda coincide. But, in general, presidents are a fearsome presence on the political scene. Their broad support coalitions, their grand perspective on public policy, and their fundamental concern for a coherent, centrally controlled bureaucracy combine to make them maverick players in the game of structural politics. They want a "presidential bureaucracy" that is fundamentally at odds with the congressional bureaucracy everyone else is busily trying to create.

To the winning group, presidents are a major source of political uncertainty over and above the risks associated with the future power of the group's opponents. This gives it even greater incentives to pressure for structures that are insulated from politics—and, when possible, disproportionately insulated from presidential politics. Because of the seriousness of the presidency's threat, the winning group will place special emphasis on limiting the powers and numbers of political appointees, locating effective authority in the agency and its career personnel, and opposing new hierarchical powers—of review, coordination, veto—for units in the Executive Office or even the departments.

The losing side is much more pragmatic. Presidents offer important opportunities for expanding the scope of conflict, imposing new procedural constraints on agency action, and appealing unfavorable decisions. Especially if presidents are not entirely sympathetic to the agency and its mission, the losing side may actively support all the trappings of presidential bureaucracy—but only, of course, for the particular case at hand. Thus, while presidents may oppose group efforts to cripple the agency through congressional bureaucracy, groups may be able to achieve much the same end through presidential bureaucracy. The risk, however, is that the next president could turn out to be an avid supporter of the agency, in which case presidential bureaucracy might be targeted to quite different ends indeed. If there is a choice, sinking formal restrictions into legislative concrete offers a much more secure and permanent fix.

Bureaucracy

Bureaucratic structure emerges as a jerry-built fusion of congressional and presidential forms, their relative roles and particular features determined by the powers, priorities, and strategies of the various designers. The result is that each agency cannot help but begin life as a unique structural reflection of its own politics.

Once an agency is created, the political world becomes a different place. Agency bureaucrats are now political actors in their own right. They have career and institutional interests that may not be entirely congruent with their formal missions, and they have powerful resources—expertise and delegated authority—that might be employed toward these selfish ends. They are new players whose interests and resources alter the political game.

It is useful to think in terms of two basic types of bureaucratic players:

political appointees and careerists. Careerists are the pure bureaucrats. As they carry out their jobs, they will be concerned with the technical requirements of effective organization, but they will also face the same problem that all other political actors face: political uncertainty. Changes in group power, committee composition, and presidential administration represent serious threats to things that bureaucrats hold dear. Their mandates could be restricted, their budgets cut, their discretion curtailed, their reputations blemished. Like groups and politicians, bureaucrats cannot afford to concern themselves solely with technical matters. They must take action to reduce their political uncertainty.

One attractive strategy is to nurture mutually beneficial relationships with groups and politicians whose political support the agency needs. If these are to provide real security, they must be more than isolated quid pro quos; they must be part of an ongoing stream of exchanges that give all participants expectations of future gain and thus incentives to resist short-term opportunities to profit at one another's expense. This is most easily done with the agency's initial supporters. Over time, however, the agency will be driven to broaden its support base, and it may move away from some of its creators—as regulatory agencies sometimes have, for example, in currying favor with the business interests they are supposed to be regulating. All agencies will have a tendency to move away from presidents, who, as temporary players, are inherently unsuited to participation in stable, long-term relationships.

Political appointees are also unattractive allies. They are not long-term participants, and no one will treat them as though they are. They have no concrete basis for participating in the exchange relationships of benefit to careerists. Indeed, they may not want to, for they have incentives to pay special attention to White House policy, and they will try to forge alliances that further those ends. Their focus is on short-term presidential victories, and relationships that stabilize politics for the agency may get in the way and have to be challenged.

As this begins to suggest, the strategy of building supportive relationships is inherently limited. In the end, much of the environment remains out of control. This prompts careerists to rely on a second, complementary strategy of uncertainty avoidance: insulation. If they cannot control the environment, they can try to shut themselves off from it in various ways. They can promote further professionalization and more extensive reliance on civil service. They can formalize and judicialize their decision procedures. They can base decisions on technical expertise, operational experience, and precedent, thus making them "objective" and agency-centered. They can try to monopolize the information necessary for effective political oversight. These insulating strategies are designed, moreover, not simply to shield the agency from its political environment, but also to shield it from the very appointees who are formally in charge.

All of this raises an obvious question: why can't groups and politicians anticipate the agency's alliance and insulationist strategies and design a structure ex ante that adjusts for them? The answer, of course, is that they can. Presidents may push for stronger hierarchical controls and greater formal power for appointees than they otherwise would. Group opponents may place even greater emphasis on opening the agency up to political oversight. And so on. The agency's design, therefore, should from the beginning incorporate everyone's anticipations about its incentives to form alliances and promote its own autonomy.

Thus, however active the agency is in forming alliances, insulating itself from politics, and otherwise shaping political outcomes, it would be a mistake to regard the agency as a truly independent force. It is literally manufactured by the other players as a vehicle for advancing and protecting their own interests, and their structural designs are premised on anticipations about the roles the agency and its bureaucrats will play in future politics. The whole point of structural choice is to anticipate, program, and engineer bureaucratic behavior. Although groups and politicians cannot do this perfectly, the agency is fundamentally a product of their designs, and so is the way it plays the political game. That is why, in our attempt to understand the structure and politics of bureaucracy, we turn to bureaucrats last rather than first.

Structural Choice as a Perpetual Process

The game of structural politics never ends. An agency is created and given a mandate, but, in principle at least, all of the choices that have been made in the formative round of decisionmaking can be reversed or modified later.

As the politics of structural choice unfolds over time, three basic forces supply its dynamics. First, group opponents will constantly be on the lookout for opportunities to impose structures of their own that will inhibit the agency's performance and open it up to external control. Second, the winning group must constantly be ready to defend its agency from attack—but it may also have attacks of its own to launch. The prime reason is poor performance: because the agency is burdened from the beginning with a structure unsuited to the lofty goals it is supposed to achieve, the supporting group is likely to be dissatisfied and to push for more productive structural arrangements. Third, the president will try to ensure that agency behavior is consistent with broader presidential priorities, and he will take action to impose his own structures on top of those already put in place by Congress. He may also act to impose structures on purely political grounds in response to the interests of either the winning or opposing group.

All of this is going on all the time, generating pressures for structural change that find expression in both the legislative and executive processes. These are potentially of great importance for bureaucracy and policy, and all the relevant participants are intensely aware of it. However, the choices about structure that are made in the first period, when the agency is designed and empowered with a mandate, are normally far more enduring and consequential than those that will be made later. They constitute an institutional base that is protected by all the impediments to new legislation inherent in separation of powers, as well as by the political clout of the agency's supporters. Most of the pushing and hauling in subsequent years is likely to produce only incremental change. This, obviously, is very much on everyone's minds in the first period.

NOTES

1. Harold Seidman and Robert Gilmour, *Politics, Position, and Power: From the Positive to the Regulatory State*, 4th ed. (Oxford University Press, 1986); and Frederick C. Mosher, *Democracy and the Public Service*, 2d ed. (Oxford University Press, 1982).

2. Seidman and Gilmour, *Politics, Position, and Power*, p. 330.

8-3

from *The True Size of Government*

Paul C. Light

Between 1984 and the late 1990s the American government, by all appearances, shrunk by a substantial amount. About one million fewer people are budgeted to work for the federal government in 2000 than fifteen years earlier. However, if we take into account the number of jobs created by government contracts—that is, jobs created by companies doing work for the government—the government has not shrunk. Nearly as many private sector jobs, created under government contracts, were added during the same period. The contracting of government jobs has produced an "illusion of smallness" in the government. In the following essay Paul Light describes the privatized sector of government, or the "shadow government," and explains why Congress, presidents, and interest groups have been eager to create it.

ONLY THREE YEARS after Republicans swept control of Congress in 1994 and barely two after Bill Clinton declared the era of big government over, the conservative press had concluded that the era of big government was still alive and well. The *Economist* and *American Enterprise* both featured cover stories on the death of downsizing, the former under the title "The Visible Hand: Big Government Is Still in Charge," and the latter under the title "What Ever Happened to Downsizing Government?"

Neither magazine questioned the declining number of federal civil servants, but neither used that number in measuring the true size of government, either. The reliably conservative *Economist* used gross domestic product, for example, in arguing that big government was still in charge across the globe. Despite years of promised spending cuts, most government spending, at least as measured in gross domestic product, had gone up. And even where it had gone down, as in Sweden and Britain, even the

Excerpted from Paul C. Light, *The True Size of Government* (Washington, D.C.: Brookings Institution Press, 1999), pp. 46–98. Reprinted by permission. Notes appearing in the original have been cut.

deepest of cuts produced only modest reductions. Twenty years of unrelenting budget cutting in Britain drove government spending all the way down from 43 percent of gross domestic product to 42 percent. "Sickened in the end by this remorseless brutality," wrote the *Economist*, "the British electorate earlier this year swept Labour back into power with a landslide majority."

In contrast, the *American Enterprise* used the increased dependence of American citizens on federal funding as its measure. "Remember 1994?" asked editor in chief Karl Zinsmeister, as he introduced the issue. "It seems like another world now. . . . It is somewhere between amusing and nauseating to note that under Republican leadership the House of Representatives Public Works Committee (Pork Barrel Central for highway projects, dams, etc.) has ballooned to a record membership of 73 congressmen. Seventy-three! Ideal for clipped debate and crisp decision-making, I guess." By 1997 fully 40 percent of Americans were net recipients of government aid, he added. "That is to say, they suck more dollars out of the dish than they put in. Many of these people have the same relationship to our lords in Washington and other seats of government that a household pet has to its keeper." Over the next couple of decades, the magazine predicted, half of all Americans would be net recipients.

How one measures the true size of government depends on where one sits. There is no doubt that the two magazines chose their measures to emphasize the growth of government. The numbers were not inaccurate per se, just not the only numbers available. Just as one can criticize Bill Clinton for declaring the era of big government over on the basis of civil service head counts, one can also criticize the *Economist* and *American Enterprise* analysts for declaring the era still alive by using gross domestic product or dependency ratios.

The two magazines were not the only ones to question the illusion of smallness, however. *Governing* entered the era-of-big-government debate in 1998 in studiously nonpartisan fashion with a detailed assessment of state and local head count. After noting that nothing seemed more certain in the wake of the 1994 Republican sweep than a wholesale downsizing of state government, *Governing* concluded that just the opposite had occurred, even in states headed by tough-talking Republican governors such as Michigan's John Engler and Texas's George Bush Jr. "In the mid-1990s, as the words 'freeze,' 'shrink,' 'cap' and 'cut' have become staples of the executive lexicon," wrote *Governing* reporter Jonathan Walters, "state government employment has continued to go up almost everywhere. Nationally, in the years from 1990 to 1996, it increased by 5 percent." Local government employment went up, too, rising 11 percent. "All told, between 1990 and 1996, state and local government accounted for more than one-seventh of all the new jobs in the U.S. non-farm economy."

But for the shrinking of civil service employment, most of the promised cuts never took place. One can easily argue that the shadow of government includes a significant number of workers who would have been federal civil servants in the absence of head count constraints. If Washington could not cut its budget or reduce its mission, it most certainly could reduce its full-time-permanent head count, driving those jobs into service contracts, grants, and mandates, while creating a government that looks smaller but delivers at least as much. . . .

The Market for Smallness

The political economy of shadow casting starts with a simple conclusion: there would be no illusion of smallness if the American public were willing to accept a federal work force that is big enough to cover the government's mission. The fact is that Americans want at least as much, if not more, of virtually everything the federal government delivers, but they also believe that just about everything the federal government delivers is wasteful and inefficient. The vast majority of Americans want a high or very high priority given to almost anything the federal government runs, but they also believe that anything run by the federal government is doomed to create more problems than it solves. Before asking how the contradiction produces support for the illusion of smallness, however, it is first useful to understand the two sides of the contradiction.

A Government that Delivers at Least as Much

The first half of the contradiction is clearly revealed in a 1997 survey by The Pew Research Center for The People & The Press. If the sample of 1,762 respondents is representative, a significant majority of Americans wants the federal government to continue delivering at least as much as it ever has.

Three-quarters of the Pew respondents said the federal government should be primarily responsible for ensuring that food and medicines are safe, two-thirds for managing the economy to prevent another recession or depression, three-fifths for ensuring that every American has access to affordable health care, and just over half for conserving the country's natural resources. . . .

Moreover, Americans are mostly favorable toward both government employees and the agencies that deliver the goods. Roughly 70 percent of the Pew sample voiced a favorable opinion of government workers in general, a number that was up 15 points from 1981. When asked who they trusted more to do the right thing, politicians who lead the federal government or the civil service employees who run departments and agencies, the civil servants won hands down, by a margin of nearly five to one.

The Pew respondents also felt favorable toward most federal departments and agencies. The U.S. Postal Service topped the favorable ratings at 89 percent, prompting the postmaster general to run nationwide ads in late spring 1998 congratulating his work force on its performance, with the Park Service second at 85 percent, the Centers for Disease Control third at 79 percent, the Defense Department fourth at 76 percent, and the Food and Drug Administration fifth at 75 percent. . . .

Not only are Americans reasonably favorable toward their frontline departments, but they also are mostly confident that government can handle significant problems. A total of 60 percent of the Pew sample had a great deal or fair amount of confidence in the federal government's ability to handle domestic problems, up from 51 percent at the height of the Watergate crisis, while three-quarters had similar levels of confidence in the federal government's ability to handle international affairs, up only slightly from the mid 1970s. Confidence was up at the state and local level, too, where Americans were more confident in 1997 than they had been in twenty-five years. According to the Pew survey, 78 percent of Americans had a great deal or fair amount of trust and confidence in their local government to handle problems, a gain of 15 percent from 1972. State government did slightly better, with 81 percent of Americans having a great deal or fair amount of trust and confidence in 1997, up from 63 percent in 1972. The numbers confirm the longstanding notion that Americans are more trusting toward the governments they know, meaning the ones closest to home. . . .

A Government that Looks Smaller

Americans may still support a mostly activist federal government, but they have serious doubts about how that government performs. They may love their bureaucrats and agencies, but they do not give government much credit for success. Asked how well the federal government is running its programs, only a quarter of the Pew respondents answered excellent or good, half said only fair, and a fifth said poor. Asked whether criticism of government was justified, three-fifths said yes. And asked whether something run by the government is bound to be wasteful and inefficient, two-thirds said yes, a number that has remained roughly constant since the Pew Research Center began asking the question in 1987 (the high was 69 percent in 1992, the low 63 percent in 1987). All in all, it was not a particularly enthusiastic portrait.

More troubling perhaps, the Pew respondents were mostly underwhelmed with the federal government's actual performance in delivering public value. Asked to rate the federal government's success on eight policy issues, they gave only one, ensuring that food and medicines are safe, an "excellent/good" endorsement. The other seven fell well short, with reducing poverty and juvenile delinquency each earning less than 15 percent of an "excellent/good" rating. . . .

When pressed to explain the poor performance on each of the eight policy issues, roughly half of the Pew respondents blamed the government while the other half said the given issue was just too difficult or too complicated to solve. There were only three areas where Americans said good performance was beyond the government's reach: ensuring an affordable college education, reducing juvenile delinquency, and reducing poverty. Juvenile delinquency was seen as the most difficult issue of all. . . .

. . . [I]t is not surprising that confidence in Washington's ability to do the right thing all or most of the time was just 39 percent in 1997, up ever so slightly from a modern low of just 21 percent in 1994, but far below the modern high of 76 percent in 1964. If this is as good as confidence gets at the end of five years of unrelenting attention to reinventing government, perhaps Congress and the president are right to worry about how to convince the public that government can do good. Moreover, even the modest gains were gone after a year of unrelenting attention to stories of scandal and impeachment. By November 1998 the number of Americans who trusted Washington to do the right thing had fallen from 39 percent to 26 percent.

The Core Constituents of Reinventing Government

The question is how the general contradiction described above might create a market for illusions. A first answer is that the positives tend to tone down the public's demand for radical reform. Americans may think government is bound to be inefficient and wasteful, but they do not think it needs much more than a tweak or two to work much better. Asked how much reform is enough, only 37 percent of the Pew sample said the federal government needs major reform, while 58 percent said the federal government is basically sound and needs only some reform. Granted, only 4 percent said the federal government does not need much change at all, but most prefer a more cautious course.

A second answer is that Americans are just as reluctant to hurt people as are Congresses and presidents. Asked what kind of reform might make them trust government again, most Americans recommend changing how government works, not who works there. . . .

The market for shadow government appears to reside, therefore, in the intersection between public demands for more of what government delivers, continued doubts about what government can actually deliver, and the general reluctance to undertake radical reform of any kind. Americans ask their government to do the impossible, as Charles Goodsell puts it, giving it "inconsistent, contradictory, and hence unachievable goals and tasks," demanding that it "achieve results indirectly, through the efforts of others," evaluating it "not by how much it *tries* to move ahead on an impossible front but whether or not 'success' is achieved," and "both overselling and underselling what it can do." Under great pressure to deliver the goods without bulking up, government has little choice but to create shadows.

Not all Americans favor the shadow course, however. Indeed, the Pew survey suggests that there are at least four different philosophies of government reform. These four types are produced when two key questions from the survey are combined into a single measure. The first question asked respondents to place themselves on a six-point scale of government activism, the number one representing "someone who generally believes that, on the whole, federal government programs should be cut back greatly to reduce the power of government," and the number six representing "someone who feels that federal government programs should be maintained to deal with important problems." The second question asked respondents what they personally felt was the bigger problem with government: "Government has the wrong priorities, OR government has the right priorities but runs programs inefficiently?" After collapsing the first question into two categories, antigovernment (numbers one through three on the six-point scale) and progovernment (numbers four through six) respondents can be divided into four cells: (1) devolvers (antigovernment and wrong priorities), (2) realigners (progovernment and wrong priorities), (3) downsizers (antigovernment and right priorities, but inefficiency), and (4) reinventors (progovernment and right priorities, but inefficiency). Table 1 shows the resulting combination.

As Table 1 shows, the number of Americans who might be moved by promises of a government that looks smaller and delivers at least as much is remarkably large. Four out of ten Pew respondents simultaneously expressed a demand for maintaining government programs to deal with important problems and believed the bigger problem with government was not the wrong priorities, but inefficiency. Although these reinventors would most certainly respond to the "works better and costs less" message of Vice President Al Gore's first reinventing government report, they would oppose any reduction in the core programs of government. They also would have been the first to criticize the back-to-back 1995 government shutdowns. Unlike the devolvers, who would have seen the shutdowns as a way to get government off their backs, if only for a moment, the reinventors would have seen peril in any effort to undermine essential services. . . .

The Core Leaders of Reinventing Government

Even if the public were to resolve its ambivalence in favor of deep cuts or vast expansions, Congress and the presidency would still face substantial institutional incentives for creating the illusion of smallness. As will be discussed shortly, the illusion of smallness allows Congress and the president to have their cake and eat it too. They can claim a shrinking government, even as they satisfy the demand for government goods and services.

Gore certainly understood that reinventing government was good politics when he accepted the reinventing government assignment in 1993. According to journalist Elizabeth Drew, Gore had been given the reinventing government issue in March as a "consolation prize" instead of the lead role on welfare reform. If Gore was disappointed by the outcome, he never showed it. He approached the National Performance Review with unprecedented fervor, collecting a staff of nearly a hundred federal managers to

Table 1. Where the Public Stands on Reform

Government reform philosophy	Bigger problem with government[a]	
	Has the wrong priorities	Right priorities, but runs programs inefficiently
Cut federal programs to greatly reduce government power (1–3 on 6-point scale)	Devolvers 16	Downsizers 22
Maintain federal programs to deal with important issues (4–6 on 6-point scale)	Realigners 14	Reinventors 39

a. Percentage of total respondents who occupy given cell; 9 percent of the total was in the don't know / not ascertained categories.

Source: The Pew Research Center for The People & The Press, secondary analysis of data released in *Deconstructing Distrust: How Americans View Government* (Washington, D.C.: The Pew Research Center for The People & The Press, 1998), N = 1,762.

investigate every facet of federal management. "There are not going to be any sacred cows," Gore said at the outset. "At the end of the month, we'll have real results and real proposals to offer. Write it down. Check back with us."

Six months later, the National Performance Review produced the first of what would become annual reports. Standing next to Clinton and backed by two forklifts piled high with government regulations, Gore said "Mr. President, if you want to know why government doesn't work, look behind you." . . .

Clinton and Gore shared a common concern about making government more effective. Both also shared an interest in restoring their party after twelve years of Republican tax-and-spend pounding. As the *Wall Street Journal* reported on the day of the release, "Much as it was easier for Republican President Nixon to overcome conservative opposition and go to China, an attempt to streamline government is more powerful coming from a Democrat, whose party generally likes government. President Clinton will be especially eager to push his plan to remake government as a way of offsetting the image that he is just an old-fashioned tax-and-spend democrat, an image some Republicans tried to pin on him during the summer budget debate."

Nevertheless, as Table 2 suggests, reinventing government fits with the prevailing view of government reform among the presidential appointees, senior civil servants, and members of Congress interviewed by the Pew

Table 2. Where Government Officials Stand on Reform

Government reform philosophy	Bigger problem with government[a]	
	Has the wrong priorities	Right priorities, but runs programs inefficiently
Cut federal programs to greatly reduce government power (1–3 on 6-point scale)	*Devolvers*	*Downsizers*
All leaders[b]	6	14
Only executive	3	9
Only Congress	14	28
Public employees	13	21
Maintain federal programs to deal with important issues (4–6 on 6-point scale)	*Realigners*	*Reinventors*
All leaders	8	46
Only executive	13	50
Only Congress	4	31
Public employees	16	39

a. Percentage of total respondents who occupy given cell; figures do not include don't knows/not ascertained.

b. All leaders includes members of Congress, presidential appointees, and career members of the Senior Executive Service; "only executive" includes presidential appointees and career members of the Senior Executive Service.

Sources: For leaders, The Pew Research Center for The People & The Press, secondary analysis of data released in *Washington Leaders Wary of Public Opinion* (Washington, D.C.: The Pew Research Center for The People & The Press, 1998), $N = 98$ presidential appointees, 81 members of Congress, and 151 members of the career Senior Executive Service; for public employees, The Pew Research Center for The People & The Press, secondary analysis of data released in *Deconstructing Distrust: How Americans View Government* (Washington, D.C.: The Pew Research Center for The People & The Press, 1998), $N = 542$.

Research Center in 1997, as well as among the public employees at all levels of government interviewed at roughly the same time. Devolution has even less support in the halls of Congress or executive branch than it does in the general public writ large. (Readers are cautioned that the sample of leaders interviewed by Pew had a higher percentage of refusals to answer the two questions that form the basis of the typology than of responses.)

It is impossible to know, of course, whether Congress and the president are leading or following public opinion on government reform. What is clear is that there is a remarkable coincidence of opinion between the governed and the government. Interestingly, however, all three sets of leaders interviewed underestimated the public's trust in government while overestimating the degree to which the public would say government could act to increase trust. . . .

Presidential Incentives

Ordinarily, presidents have good reason to keep every last person delivering services within government. To the extent shadows dilute their control, presidents must theoretically resist. "While legislators eagerly delegate their powers to administrative agencies, presidents are driven to take charge," writes Terry Moe in outlining his theory of public bureaucracy [see selection 8-2]. "They do not care about all agencies equally, of course. . . . But most agencies impinge in one way or another on larger presidential responsibilities—for the budget, for the economy, for national defense—and presidents must have the capacity to direct and constrain agency behavior in basic ways if these larger responsibilities are to be handled successfully."

The desire for control is why presidents have long supported what organizational theorists call scientific management, which favors what Moe describes as the presidential ideal of "a rational, coherent, centrally directed bureaucracy that strongly resembles popular textbook notions of what an effective bureaucracy, public or private, ought to look like." Given its focus on the president as the one true master of government, as Luther Gulick once described the chief executive, it is not surprising that scientific management would be the tide of reform most likely to emanate from the White House.

The desire for control is also why presidents have long resisted efforts to cut the number of political appointees. They simply believe in leadership by layering. Whether Democrat or Republican, they adamantly defend the penetration of political appointees ever deeper into the executive hierarchy. To paraphrase Senator Daniel Patrick Moynihan (D-N.Y.), they have defined leadership downward. The result has been a steady thickening of government. More layers of leaders, more leaders at each layer. Occurring under head count pressure, the thickening gives agencies cause to cast shadows. . . .

Finally, the desire for control is why presidents resisted the head count pressure for as long as they did. . . . Congress, not the president, was the source of most head count ceilings and hiring freezes during the 1950s and 1960s. Presidents resisted and Congress insisted.

Ordinarily, therefore, we would expect presidents to fight any efforts to flatten the hierarchy, decentralize control, and impose head counts. Such resistance fits perfectly with the prevailing incentives described by Moe's theory of public bureaucracy. "Governance is the driving force behind the modern presidency," Moe writes. "All presidents, regardless of party, are expected to govern effectively and are held responsible for taking action on virtually the full range of problems facing society. To be judged successful in the eyes of history—arguably the single most important motivator for presidents—they must appear to be strong leaders, active and in charge." They must have organizations that appear to work.

These are not ordinary times, however. Recent presidents have done all of the above: they have fought at least two battles of the bulge (Reagan and Clinton), pushed for decentralization (Nixon and Clinton), and become steadfast advocates of reducing overall head count (Nixon, Carter, Reagan, and Clinton). Even when they have abandoned head count as a budget-making tool, as the Clinton administration did in the mid 1990s, they have only done so because they knew that departments and agencies did not have the money to hire the employees to threaten the head count ceilings they had established. But for their continued support for politicization, which may be weak evidence of affection for centralization, they have behaved as if they are adversaries of the very organizations they lead.

Congress Now Proposes

The question is what might lead presidents to favor organizational structures that are contrary to their hypothetical self-interest. The answer may be that Congress, not the presidency, has become the central force in government reform. At least as far as statutory efforts go, Congress now proposes and the president disposes.

. . . Watergate was the unmistakable turning point. Congress authored ten of the thirteen management reforms passed in 1974, including the Congressional Budget and Impoundment Control Act, marking a successful resurgence after nearly a half century of decline. . . .

. . . From 1945 to 1974 presidents accounted for three-quarters of all management reforms enacted into law, drawing heavily on scientific management for their legislative inspiration. From 1974 to 1995, however, Congress became the dominant source of reforms, accounting for three-quarters of all reform ideas in the wake of Watergate. Adding in the eleven statutes passed in the 1993–96 period, Congress accounted for seventy of the ninety-three reforms enacted since Nixon's resignation.

The trends actually accelerated after Reagan entered office. Of the sixty management reforms enacted since 1981, fifty originated in Congress, including a host of reforms more traditionally associated with presidential control. It was Congress, not the president, that authored the 1990 Chief Financial Officers Act, which created chief financial officers across government and mandated annual financial statements for every department and agency. It was Congress, not the president, that authored the 1993 Government Performance and Results Act, which established an entirely new binding process for holding individual departments and agencies to a government-wide process. And it was Congress, not the president, that authored the 1996 Information Technology Management Reform Act, also called the Clinger-Cohen act in honor of its House and Senate cosponsors, which established chief information officers across government and imposed a new process for integrated information planning.

Fifty years ago these statutes would have almost certainly come from the president—indeed, post–World War II commissions headed by Herbert Hoover recommended elements of all three. Today Congress is the author in what is becoming a presidential spectator sport.

The consequences of the growing congressional involvement are clear. Making government work has become a distrustful business, focusing on procedural compliance with tightly written statutes. . . .

Presidents still pursue reform from time to time, of course, just not with the traditional elements of rational, centralized scientific management. Liberating government from the rules has become the president's preferred reform, represented by the 1994 Acquisition Streamlining Act. The act produced a sharp reduction in procurement paperwork, while raising the threshold for simplified procurement from $25,000 to $100,000 and encouraging departments and agencies to become smarter buyers of goods and services. But for occasional congressional forays into the tide, scientific management has been out of fashion for the better part of two decades. My research suggests that scientific management had mostly played out in the 1940s and 1950s with the two Hoover commissions. The days of department and agency building are now over, as are the days of tight central control.

As Congress has become more dominant in shaping government reform, presidents have struggled to regain a semblance of control. But for occasional looks back at scientific management, the latest example being Gore's endorsement of chief operating officers in 1993, presidents have been led away from scientific management and toward a new set of tactics. Their strategic advantage today lies with informal networks and exhortative demands that render statutes less important for shaping organizational structure. . . .

If not quite adversaries of the agencies they oversee, presidents are no longer quite allies, either. To win control of government, presidents must dismantle the very control structures that have served them so well over the years, even if that means pushing work outward and downward, while embracing the head count ceilings of the war on waste. In short, they must adopt a new set of tactics that weaken congressional control largely through deregulation, decentralization, and, where necessary, shadow casting.

Thus Gore has argued strenuously against the very systems that once assured presidential responsiveness: "In Washington's highly politicized world, the greatest risk is not that a program will perform poorly, but that a scandal will erupt. Scandals are front-page news, while routine failure is ignored. Hence control system after control system is piled up to minimize the risk of scandal. The budget system, the personnel rules, the procurement process, the inspectors general—all are designed to prevent the tiniest misstep."

Gore has also supported decentralization, a favored tool of those out of power. According to Moe, it is opponents of those in power who "like fragmented authority, decentralization, federalism, checks and balances, and other structural means of promoting weakness, confusion, and delay." Edit out the weakness, confusion, and delay, and Moe has the first principle of reinventing government: cutting red tape. As Gore argued,

> Effective, entrepreneurial governments cast aside red tape, shifting from systems in which people are accountable for following rules to systems in which they are accountable for achieving results. They streamline their budget, personnel, and procurement systems—liberating organizations to pursue their missions. They reorient their control systems to prevent problems rather than simply punish those who make mistakes. They strip away unnecessary layers of regulation that stifle innovation. And they deregulate organizations that depend upon them for funding, such as lower levels of government.

Freedom, not control, is the preferred option.

Finally, Gore has championed the concept of the creation of dozens of performance-based organizations, which would be freed from government control systems under performance-based contracts. Creating agile, highly responsive organizations headed by senior executives on short-term contracts might give the president maximum short-term authority, but it would also expose the agency to immediate manipulation by adversaries who might win a future election. A similar critique could be made of Gore's focus on customer satisfaction, which opens an agency to the kind of external sunshine that adversaries favor. Can it be that the theory of public bureaucracy simply cannot tolerate reality?

Before rejecting the theory, however, it is useful to note that party politics and public opinion also play a significant role in shaping presidential incentives for action. Gore entered office first and foremost a Democrat who wanted to be part of an activist administration. Given his own desires to ascend to the presidency and his party's lingering reputation for tax-and-spend government, his political fortunes rested heavily on proving to the public that government could perform. The political incentives thus far outweighed the traditional structural pressures that Moe describes. Decentralization makes perfect sense, therefore, as a defense against further congressional encroachment on executive prerogative. Far better to hide the work force or diffuse authority than to risk congressional meddling, which has been growing under Republican and Democratic majorities alike, and under divided and unified party control of the two branches.

One can also argue, as Moe probably would, that the performance-based organizations and customer service actually fit quite nicely with presidential control. By changing the basis of the relationship with Congress from one of budgets and incremental adjustment to hard measures of performance, the performance-based organizations would gain significant control of their own destinies. And who would select and negotiate the contracts at hand? The president, of course. The very first contracts written would establish precedents of their own for the future. Little wonder then that the new Republican Congress would reject the performance-based organization concept out of hand. Democrats would have, too.

Politics is very much a part of Moe's theory of public bureaucracy. As he writes, "Winning groups, losing groups, legislators, and presidents combine to produce bureaucratic arrangements that, by economic standards, appear to make no sense at all. Agencies are not built to do their jobs well. Strange and incongruous structures proliferate. Presidential bureaucracy is layered on top of congressional bureaucracy. No one is really in charge." If that is not a description of the tides of reform, what is? Offensive though such organizations might be to economics, they are perfectly comfortable for democracy, which writes its conflicts in the structures of government just as certainly as it does in the statute books. . . .

Still Thickening after All These Years

Not everything in the illusion of smallness is contrary to Moe's theory of political bureaucracy. Even as presidents invent new tactics for wresting control from Congress, they continue to heed the bureaucratic incentives on political appointments. The definition of leadership by layering began with Franklin Roosevelt's 1937 Brownlow Committee, which argued that the president needs help, and continued into the Eisenhower administration, which created Schedule C of the federal general service to give cabinet officers greater freedom to hire their own personal and confidential assistants, through Nixon's unprecedented effort to pack the executive branch with loyal aides, and into the more recent centralization of all political appointments in the White House Office of Presidential Personnel. Although the politicization has prompted a substantial amount of lower level layering, as departments and agencies follow Moynihan's Iron Law of Emulation, the incentives for centralization are overwhelming. Much as I still believe that thickening undermines presidential leadership, it continues to exist because it allows presidents to simultaneously fulfill their perceived constitutional obligation to command the government and their political obligation to reward contributors and allies.

Presidents are right to believe that their appointees can make a difference, a point well made by B. Dan Wood and Richard Waterman. Examining Reagan's efforts to dominate administrative decisionmaking in seven agencies—EPA, Equal Employment Opportunity Commission, FTC, FDA, National Highway Traffic Safety Administration, Nuclear Regulatory Commission, and Office of Surface Mining—Wood and Waterman concluded that presidential appointees can have "extraordinary influence" over agency policy. "In five of the seven programs we examined, agency outputs shifted immediately after a change in agency leadership. In four of these cases (the NRC, the EEOC, the FTC and the FDA), change followed an appointment at the beginning of a presidential administration. The direction and magnitude of these responses reflects the increased power of a chief executive in

Table 3. The Thickening of Government, 1960–1998

Title[a]	Number of departments where title exists			Number of positions open for occupancy		
	1960	1992	1998	1960	1992	1998
Secretary	10	14	14	10	14	14
Chief of staff to the secretary	—	11	13	—	11	13
Deputy chief of staff to the secretary	—	2	9	—	2	10
Deputy secretary	3	14	14	6	20	23
Chief of staff to the deputy secretary	—	2	5	—	2	5
Deputy deputy secretary	—	—	3	—	—	4
Principal associate deputy secretary	1	—	1	2	13	1
Associate deputy secretary	—	6	6	—	—	12
Deputy associate deputy secretary	—	—	1	—	—	1
Assistant deputy secretary	—	—	3	—	—	5
Under secterary	8	9	10	15	32	41
Chief of staff to the under secretary	—	—	4	—	—	4
Principal deputy under secretary	1	2	2	1	8	2
Deputy under secretary	4	11	8	9	52	8
Principal associate deputy under secretary	—	1	—	—	1	—
Associate deputy under secretary	—	6	—	—	11	—
Principal assistant deputy under secretary	—	—	1	—	—	1
Assistant deputy under secretary	—	1	1	—	11	1
Associate under secretary	—	1	1	—	1	1
Assistant under secretary	—	—	1	—	—	1
Assistant secretary	10	14	14	87	225	212
Chief of staff to the assistant secretary	—	4	8	—	5	21
Principal deputy assistant secretary	1	8	7	1	76	64
Associate principal deputy assistant secretary	—	—	1	—	—	1
Deputy assistant secretary	7	14	14	78	518	484
Principal deputy deputy assistant secretary	—	—	1	—	—	5
Deputy deputy assistant secretary	—	—	1	—	—	1

Title[a]	Number of departments where title exists			Number of positions open for occupancy		
	1960	1992	1998	1960	1992	1998
Associate deputy assistant secretary	5	4	6	20	50	42
Assistant deputy assistant secretary	—	3	2	—	26	16
Principal associate assistant secretary	—	—	2	—	—	6
Associate assistant secretary	1	14	12	4	208	148
Chief of staff to the associate assistant secretary	—	—	1	—	—	2
Deputy associate assistant secretary	—	—	8	—	121	66
Assistant assistant secretary	3	14	14	16	177	220
Chief of staff to the assistant assistant secretary	—	—	1	—	—	1
Deputy assistant assistant secretary	—	11	13	—	57	82
Administrator	9	11	9	90	128	140
Chief of staff to the administrator	—	2	5	—	7	12
Assistant chief of staff to the administrator	—	—	1	—	—	1
Principal deputy administrator	—	3	2	—	9	4
Deputy administrator	8	10	9	52	190	193
Associate deputy administrator	—	1	2	—	15	30
Deputy associate deputy administrator	—	—	1	—	—	1
Assistant deputy administrator	1	4	3	2	48	42
Deputy assistant deputy administrator	—	—	1	—	—	1
Associate administrator	2	9	9	3	105	138
Chief of staff to the associate administrator	—	—	1	—	—	1
Deputy Associate Administrator	—	6	4	—	28	24
Assistant administrator	7	8	8	55	159	146
Chief of staff to the assistant administrator	—	—	1	—	—	1
Deputy assistant administrator	—	8	5	—	66	54
Associate assistant administrator	—	1	—	—	12	—
Total	17	33	49	451	2,408	2,462[b]
Absolute increase	—	16	16	—	1,957	54
Percentage increase	—	88	49	—	434	2.2

(continued)

Table 3 *(continued)*

a. This table includes all titles in the 14 federal departments that are listed as Executive Levels I, II, III, IV, and V of Title 5, United States Code, as well as titles that are variations of all titles at Executive Levels I–V, including, for example, the secretaries of the Army, Air Force, and Navy, Administration and Federal Highway Administration at Executive Level II, and assorted commisioners, directors, administrators, inspectors general, general counsels, chief information officers, and chief financial officers at Executive Level IV.

b. 1998 figures include the Social Security Administration, which was elevated to independent status in 1994, but was part of the Department of Health and Human Services until then. With Social Security excluded, the totals for 1996 would have fallen by 54 to 2,384, for a decrease of 24 positions or 1 percent from 1992.

Sources: 1960 and 1992 data are from Paul C. Light, *Thickening Government: Federal Hierarchy and the Diffusion of Accountability* (Brookings/Governance, 1995); 1998 data are from further coding of the *Federal Yellow Book,* Winter 1998 edition.

the period after a presidential election." Presidents can hardly be expected to give up that kind of influence.

Although the Gore reinventors considered a token cut in the number of presidential appointees as part of what would become a downsizing of 272,900 jobs under the Workforce Restructuring Act of 1994, the White House Office of Presidential Personnel scuttled the recommendation, eventually leading the effort to defeat a Senate-passed bill that would have imposed a more substantial cut from 3,000 to 2,000 appointees. Once again, the desire for presidential control outweighed all arguments for what would have been at most a symbolic thinning at the top of the hierarchy. . . .

Given the prevailing incentives, it is no surprise that the Clinton administration would fight any cuts. What is more surprising perhaps is the degree to which the Clinton administration lost control of the senior hierarchy through a steady and largely accidental title creep. Notwithstanding its rhetoric about leaner, meaner bureaucracy and its determined attack on the midlevel bulge, the administration added as many new titles to the seniormost levels of government in its first five years as the seven administrations before it had added over their three decades combined. Table 3 shows the changing height (number of layers) and width (number of occupants) between 1960, 1992, and 1998. . . .

By itself, the new height will not lengthen the shadow of government. The new titles simply have not spread far enough to cast light. Nevertheless, the height does confirm the central incentives for thickening, whether driven by the president's own demand for control or by agency preferences for institutional similarity. As those sixteen new titles start to spread, as they most certainly will given the hostility of liberation management toward meddlesome central oversight, the federal hierarchy will continue to go circular.

Congressional Incentives

Unlike the presidency, where casting shadows is a mostly counterintuitive expression of institutional self-interest, Congress has ample incentive to favor a government that looks smaller and delivers at least as much. Simply stated, head count constraints give individual members substantial electoral advantages back home, whether by providing protection against opponents who charge that members have been captured by the federal bureaucracy, creating significant opportunities for crediting nonfederal jobs with federal dollars, and generating a steady flow of the campaign funding needed for reelection. In short, shadow casting is a substantial source of incumbency advantage.

Before turning to the argument in more detail, however, it is important to note that the shadow of government fits perfectly with the incentives described by Moe's theory of public bureaucracy. Unlike presidents, who must balance short-term pressures to produce against longer term incentives to balkanize, legislators have a very simple incentive to do what interest groups want by way of structural choice. Because of what Moe describes as "their almost paranoid concern for reelection," and because "interest groups, unlike voters, are not easily fooled," legislators are not given to "flights of autonomous action or statesmanship." Harsh and unforgiving as Moe's characterizations might be, his description fits well with the history of head counts. . . . Most of the early thaws in the head count freezes were prompted by heavy lobbying from the postal unions, while most of the resistance to a more deliberate work force policy reflected continuing pressure from private contractors and consulting firms.

It is easy to understand why interest groups, both those that are favorable toward an agency and those that are unfavorable, would endorse the use of shadows. Those that favor a given agency or program can do everything Moe recommends by way of complicating administrative systems, even as they use shadows to produce the desired goods. To protect their agency from outside influence, they can write detailed legislation that constrains future action, impose specific deadlines for action as a device for front-loading benefits, demand greater professionalism than technically justified, limit congressional opportunities for oversight, and enhance judicial review of agency decisionmaking.

Such tactics can also be applied to contracts, grants, and mandates. What better way to assure long-term protection than to give a favored program to intensely loyal, self-interested firms? What better way to confuse congressional overseers than to place a favored program deep within a web of contracts, subcontracts, grants, and mandates? What better way to judicialize the delivery of public goods than to write a legally binding contract that can be defended in court? The very things that allies would favor, meaning "designs that place detailed formal restrictions on bureaucratic discretion, impose complex procedures for agency decisionmaking, minimize opportunities for oversight, and otherwise insulate the agency from politics," fit perfectly with a shadow work force governed by tight performance-based contracts, grants, and mandates. Shadow casting is an obvious defense strategy.

At the same time, groups that oppose a given agency or program can use the shadow of government to weaken delivery. Adversaries can fragment internal structures, write ambiguous mandates that confuse more than clarify, resist formal deadlines, open the agency to maximum external inspection, pursue appointment and personnel policies that enhance political direction of the agency, impose time-consuming procedures for making decisions, require endless justifications for even minor action, and demand procedures that allow them to participate, appeal, and delay.

Such tactics can easily produce an increase in shadow casting. What better way to drive an agency to contracting than to set the price of internal action so high that nothing can be done in house? What better way to frustrate accountability and create the potential for scandal than to load an agency with so many regulations that it cannot properly oversee the contracts it lets? What better way to assure maximum feasible conflict than to impose head count constraints that might lead to unfunded mandates? The very things adversaries favor, meaning "fragmented authority, labyrinthine procedures, mechanisms of political intervention, and other structures that subvert the bureaucracy's performance and open it up to attack," inevitably create incentives for casting shadows as agencies struggle to fulfill their missions.

Even if interest groups were agnostic about bureaucratic structure, which they most certainly are not, shadow casting creates enormous congressional benefits back home. For most members of Congress, as Thomas Mann argues, elections will always be *Unsafe at Any Margin*. The fear of defeat is so great that members do all they can to assure reelection. If that means creating an occasional shadow through pork barrel legislation, no problem.

That Congress cares about credit claiming back home is hardly in dispute. A host of political scientists have written about the phenomenon, none ever so persuasively as Richard Fenno in *Home Style*. Nor is there any doubt that pork barrel projects, and the shadows they create, generate credit-claiming opportunities. As Morris Fiorina writes, "The average constituent may have some trouble translating his congressman's vote on some civil rights issue into a change in his personal welfare. But the workers hired and supplies purchased in connection with a big federal project provide benefits that are widely appreciated."

That is why, for example, all fifty governors, the American Automobile Association, environmental groups, the Chamber of Commerce, and even the American Planning Association (highways need planners, too) endorsed the $217 billion transportation bill passed by Congress in May 1998. Congress most certainly understood that the Transportation Equity Act for the Twenty-First Century (TEA 21) would create jobs back home. Although never discussed as anything but good old fashioned pork, the shadow effects featured prominently in the House debate leading to final passage. It was a debate led by twelve-term House member E. G. "Bud" Shuster (R-Pa.), chairman of the House Transportation and Infrastructure Committee and arguably the most effective pork producer since Jamie Whitten (D-Miss.). . . .

There is nothing new about transportation pork, of course. Congress has been taking home the projects for decades, usually through funding formulas that allow each member to claim a fair share of the credit for new highways and the jobs they create. What makes the past decade interesting perhaps is the growing use of earmarks to make the credit claiming easier. Both the number and amount of earmarks has been rising steadily, whether in transportation, higher education, veterans health care, or environmental protection. The number of transportation earmarks has gone up from just 10 projects and $362 million in 1982 to 152 projects and $1.4 billion in 1987, 538 projects and $6.2 billion in 1991, and 1,850 projects and $9.3 billion in 1998. Although higher education pork dipped briefly in the mid-1990s because of a determined campaign by California Democrat George Miller, it appears to be on its way back up, too.

No one talks about the shadow-casting effects of such legislation in explicit terms, of course, and no one would ever recommend that the highway construction jobs be nationalized. Even staunch critics of the federal downsizing such as Eleanor Holmes Norton (D-D.C.) can find ample reason to support transportation earmarks. "Mr. Speaker, this is not pork," Norton argued in support of the transportation package. "This is steak. If we want to continue to be a prime rib country, we better pass this bill quick." But the shadow-casting effects exist nonetheless. Assuming that all $217 billion goes directly into grants to state and local government, TEA 21 will create almost six million shadow jobs with its six years of funding. . . .

A Debt Repaid?

. . . Looking back over the past decade, the top contractors have showered both lobbying attention and campaign contributions on Congress and the presidency. In the first half of 1997, for example, the top twenty-five federal contractors spent over $38 million on lobbying, with General Motors at $5.2 million in lobbying expenditures, United Technologies at $4.2 million, General Electric at $4.1 million, Northrop Grumman at $3.6 million, and Boeing at $2.9 million. Although it is impossible to know how much or little was spent lobbying Congress for specific products such as new fighter jets or new computer systems, the more general purpose of the lobbying was to create a generally favorable climate toward the individual corporations involved, which in turn might create a specifically favorable climate toward their products and services.

The top twenty-five contractors also provided significant amounts of campaign support to candidates for federal office. Although there is no evidence that such campaign financing purchases specific votes on legislation, there can be little doubt that the dollars helped remind incumbent members of Congress that contractors care about their reelection. As Table 4 shows, the top twenty-five contractors contributed just over $10 million in 1992 and $15 million in 1996. AT&T led the group on campaign contributions at almost $4 million, followed by Lockheed Martin at $2.5 million, General Electric at $1.8 million, Northrop-Grumman at $1.5 million, and Boeing at $1.3 million.

As the contribution figures show, contractors clearly favor incumbents. Congress may have changed majority parties in 1994, but incumbents got exactly 86 percent of top twenty-five contributions immediately before and after the congressional elections. The major difference between 1992 and

Table 4. Contractor Campaign Contributions, 1992 and 1996
(in percentages, unless otherwise specified)

Measure	1992	1996
Total contributions from the top 25 contractors (dollars)	10,023,000	15,137,000
Political action committee and individual contributions to Democrats	53	35
Political action committee and individual contributions to Republicans	46	65
Political action committee and individual contributions to incumbents	86	86
Political action committee and individual contributions to House candidates	67	70
Political action committee and individual contributions to Senate candidates	31	27
Political action committee and individual contributions to presidential candidates	2	3
Total contributions from political action committees	80	55
Total contributions in soft money	13	38
Total contributions from individuals	7	7

Source: Analysis of databases maintained by the Center for Responsive Politics.

1996 is the rising tide of soft campaign contributions. Because soft money contributions are unregulated, contributions can rise well beyond the meager limits imposed on political action committees and individual contributions by the Federal Election Campaign Act. That means that contributors can make themselves even more visible. That the top contractors would drift toward more soft money is merely a reminder that campaign cash is a potent tool for thanking incumbents for what they may have done in the past and for creating a favorable climate in the future.

Party Incentives

. . . Presidential elections rarely turn on debates about bureaucratic reform. Looking back over the years, the size and structure of government have never come close to making the list of most important problems about which citizens care. Jobs, inflation, international crisis, war, scandal, schools, children, the elderly, health care, the environment, and a host of other issues are infinitely more interesting to most voters than government operations.

Nevertheless, campaigns do help explain why both parties might favor shadow government. In theory, Democrats should seek to advertise the benefits of activist government, while Republicans should keep the focus on inefficiency and the need for solid business sense. Given their support from organized labor, it would be surprising if Democrats talked much about the need for contracting out. And given their support from big and small business alike, it would be equally surprising if Republicans promised to create new departments and agencies, increase government pay, or improve life in the career civil service.

Until just recently, however, there has been almost no systematic evidence to support either hypothesis. Lacking solid data to the contrary, most public administration and management scholars have concluded that bureaucrat bashing is on the rise in both parties. "Countless politicians run for office (including the highest posts in the land) on platforms that blame society's problems on 'the bureaucrats' and their burdensome rules, lack of entrepreneurship, wasteful extravagance, social experimentation, intervention in business, and whatever else nettles," writes Charles Goodsell in *The Case for Bureaucracy*. "Candidates promise that when elected they will sternly deal with the bureaucratic enemy. When, after the election, neither the bureaucrats nor the problems disappear, voters conclude that the survival of the former has caused the perpetuation of the latter."

Goodsell is quite right in emphasizing the political benefits of bureaucrat bashing. Incumbents and challengers have long seen the value in running against government. In reality, however, the actual rhetoric from the 1960, 1980, 1992, and 1996 presidential campaigns suggests a more nuanced message. Looking at the inventory of every campaign advertisement, speech, and debate in each campaign, all of which have been collected and coded by the University of Pennsylvania's Annenberg School for Communication, the conversation about government appears to have changed radically twice: first in 1980 and again in 1992. As Table 5 shows, whereas Republicans owned the antigovernment issue in 1980, Democrats were able to shift the conversation to much safer ground by 1992, even to the point of making bureaucracy almost lovable again. . . .

Table 5.   Presidential Campaign Rhetoric about Government,
1960, 1980, 1992, 1996 (number of words)

Word spoken about government	1960		1980[a]		1992[a]		1996		Total
	Dem.	Rep.	Dem.	Rep.	Dem.	Rep.	Dem.	Rep.	
Bureaucrat	0	3	0	2	2	23	0	15	45
Bureaucratic	0	2	2	9	9	10	16	0	48
Bureaucracy	6	0	1	6	54	33	16	37	153
Waste, fraud, or abuse	0	0	1	82	28	20	6	31	168
Size of government	0	2	0	4	0	0	28	6	40
Big government	4	0	1	2	17	27	11	21	83
Public employee/ employment	0	0	2	1	1	0	0	0	4
Public servant/service	2	0	8	2	10	5	15	4	46
Civil servant/service	1	0	1	1	1	0	0	0	4
Total words spoken	13	7	16	109	122	118	92	114	591
Total no. of campaign speeches, ads, and debates	173	57	179	88	106	145	161	111	1,020

a. Does not include third party candidates.

Source: Annenberg Campaign Data Base.

Conclusion

It is one thing for Congress and the president, Democrats and Republicans, even civil servants to prefer an illusion of smallness, and quite another to make the illusion real. After all, few members of Congress understand the mechanics of public personnel, and fewer still have the patience for legislative hearings and bill drafting. As Representative Patricia Schroeder (D-Colo.) once complained to her Civil Service Committee colleagues, "the civil service is a very difficult concept for most people to know about, and once you get beyond this committee, if you did a test on the House floor about the difference between RIFs and freezes and buyouts and everything, their eyes glaze over, and they stare at you like a deer staring in the headlights."

9

The Judiciary

In a Federalist Papers *essay promoting the Constitution's ratification, Alexander Hamilton allayed concerns that judges would be unelected and life-tenured by characterizing the federal judiciary as the "least dangerous branch." At the time few foresaw that the Supreme Court would establish judicial review, the authority to declare state and national laws unconstitutional, or that it would establish a pyramidal organizational structure comprising thirteen courts of appeals and ninety-four district courts. On paper, the modern federal judiciary looks like a formidable and resourceful branch of government. Unlike Congress, it appears to have solved problems in coordinating its members' activities by hierarchically organizing its subunits. Unlike the presidency, its authority within its sphere of protecting and upholding the Constitution appears unassailable.*

Yet there are chinks in the judiciary's armor. First, the appearance of hierarchy within the branch is deceptive. Federal judges are appointed to lifetime posts by the president and confirmed by the Senate. This means that the Supreme Court has no control over judicial appointments and only a tenuous influence over the actions of lower-court judges. The guarantee of life tenure, designed to insulate the judges from political pressures, also effectively insulates them from the influence of fellow judges. Second, the Court has weak enforcement mechanisms. It makes decisions and trusts other actors to comply.

These weaknesses have two notable effects. First, they serve to keep judicial policy from straying too far from national opinion. Second, because the judiciary remains tethered to the political system, judges must weigh their policies to ensure that they remain closely aligned with those of the elected branches of government.

9-1

from *The Choices Justices Make*

Lee Epstein and Jack Knight

When deciding cases before the Supreme Court, the justices weigh the arguments offered by the plaintiffs and defendants. But, Lee Epstein and Jack Knight tell us below, the merits of the case are rarely all that the justices consider. Since the outcome will be decided by a majority of the Court, rather than by an individual justice, each justice can be expected to strategically adapt his or her expressed preferences to attract the support and votes of the other justices. In a very real sense, successful Supreme Court justices must be good "politicians."

DRIVING WHILE INTOXICATED (DWI) and driving under the influence (DUI) are now familiar terms to most Americans, but that was not true during the 1960s. With the Vietnam War and the civil rights movement monopolizing the media, drunk driving was just not one of the pressing issues of the day.

Even so, various researchers and government agencies began to explore the problem as early as 1968.[1] Although these initial studies differed in design and sampling, they reached the same general conclusion: teens, particularly males, had a greater tendency than the general population to be involved in alcohol-related traffic incidents. A 1972 FBI report, for example, indicated that between 1967 and 1972 national drunk driving arrests among those under eighteen increased 138 percent and that 93 percent of those arrested were males.

Despite the accumulation of statistical evidence, another decade elapsed before most states even considered raising the legal drinking age. Oklahoma was a notable exception. In 1972 it passed a law prohibiting men from purchasing beer until they reached the age of twenty-one, but allowing women to buy low alcohol-content beer at eighteen.

Regarding the Oklahoma law as a form of sex discrimination, Curtis Craig, a twenty-year-old male who wanted to buy beer, and Carolyn

Excerpted from Lee Epstein and Jack Knight, *The Choices Justices Make* (Washington, D.C.: CQ Press, 1998), pp. 1–21.

Whitener, a beer vendor who wanted to sell it, brought suit in a federal trial court. Among the arguments they made was that laws discriminating on the basis of sex should be subject, at least according to rulings by the U.S. Supreme Court, to a "strict scrutiny" test.[2] Under this standard of review, as Table 1 shows, a court presumes a law to be unconstitutional, and, to undermine that assumption, the government must demonstrate that its legislation is the least restrictive means available to achieve a *compelling* state interest. As one might imagine, laws reviewed under this standard almost never survived tests in court.[3] In Craig and Whitener's opinion, the Oklahoma statute was no exception: no compelling state interest was achieved by establishing different drinking ages for men and women.

In response, the state argued that the U.S. Supreme Court had never explicitly applied the strict scrutiny test to laws discriminating on the basis of sex. Rather, the justices had ruled that such laws ought to be subject to a lower level of review—a test called "rational basis" (Table 1). Under this test the state need demonstrate only that the law is a *reasonable* measure designed to achieve a *legitimate* (as opposed to compelling) government purpose. Surely, Oklahoma contended, its law met this standard because statistical studies indicated that men "drive more, drink more, and commit more alcohol-related offenses."

The trial court held for the state. While it acknowledged that U.S. Supreme Court precedent was murky, it felt that the weight of case law supported the state's reliance on the lower standard.* Moreover, the state had met its obligation of establishing a rational basis for the law: given the sta-

---

*The problem was that a majority of the justices had not backed a particular standard of review since 1971, when a unanimous Court used the rational basis test to strike down an Idaho law that gave preference to men as estate administrators. *Reed v. Reed,* 404 U.S. 71 (1971). Two years later, however, a plurality adopted the strict scrutiny approach saying that the military could not force women officers to prove that their husbands were dependent on them while presuming that wives were financially dependent on their male officer spouses. *Frontiero v. Richardson,* 411 U.S. 677 (1973). But, in *Stanton v. Stanton,* 421 U.S. 7 (1975), the case most proximate to *Craig,* the Court seemed to give up the search for an appropriate standard. At issue in *Stanton* was a Utah law specifying that, for purposes of receiving child support payments, boys reach adulthood at age twenty-one and girls at eighteen. The Court held that the law constituted impermissible sex discrimination, but it failed to articulate a standard of review. Instead, the majority opinion

Table 1. Arguments in *Craig v. Boren* over the Appropriate Test
to Assess Sex-Based Classifications

Party	Test Advanced	Policy Implications
Craig/Whitener	*Strict Scrutiny:* The law must be the least restrictive means available to achieve a compelling state interest.	If adopted, the Court would almost never uphold a sex-based classification. It would (presumably) strike down the Oklahoma law.
Oklahoma	*Rational Basis:* The law must be a reasonable measure designed to achieve a legitimate government purpose.	If adopted, the Court would (presumably) uphold most sex-based classifications, including the Oklahoma law.
ACLU	Something "in between" strict scrutiny and rational basis.[a]	If adopted, the Court would sometimes strike down laws discriminating on the basis of sex and sometimes uphold them. The ACLU argued that application of this test should lead the Court to strike down the Oklahoma law.

a. This test is now called "heightened scrutiny": the law must be substantially related to the achievement of an important government objective.

tistical evidence, Oklahoma's goal of reducing drunk driving seemed legitimate.

Refusing to give up the battle, Craig and Whitener appealed to the U.S. Supreme Court. While they and the state continued to press the same claims they had at trial, a third party advanced a somewhat different approach. The American Civil Liberties Union entered the case as an amicus

---

concluded that "under any test—compelling state interest, rational basis, or something in between—[the Utah law] does not survive . . . attack."

It is no wonder that trial court judges were confused over the appropriate standard of review. As one district court judge wrote, "Lower courts searching for guidance in the 1970s Supreme Court sex discrimination precedents [prior to *Craig*] have 'an uncomfortable feeling'—like players at a shell game who are 'not absolutely sure there is a pea.'" Quoted in Herma H. Kay, *Sex-Based Discrimination* (St. Paul: West, 1981), 70.

curiae, a friend of the court, on behalf of Craig (see Table 1).* ACLU attorneys Ruth Bader Ginsburg and Melvin Wulf argued that the Oklahoma law "could not survive review whatever the appropriate test": strict scrutiny or rational basis or "something in between." This argument, which Ginsburg and Wulf had taken directly from the Court's decision in *Stanton v. Stanton,* was interesting in two regards: it suggested that (1) the Court could apply the lower rational basis standard and still hold for Craig, or (2) the Court might consider developing a standard "in between" strict scrutiny and rational basis.

What would the Supreme Court do? That question loomed large during the justices' conference, held a few days after oral arguments.[4] As it is traditional for the chief justice to speak first, Warren Burger led off the discussion. He asserted that *Craig* was an "isolated case" that the Court should dismiss on procedural grounds. The problem was that, because Curtis Craig had turned twenty-one after the Court agreed to hear the case, his claim was moot. So, to Burger, the . . . issue was whether Whitener, "the saloon keeper," had standing to bring the suit. Burger thought that she did not.[†] But, if his colleagues disagreed and thought Whitener had standing, Burger said he was willing to find for Craig if the majority opinion was narrowly written. By this, Burger meant that he did not want to apply strict scrutiny to classifications based on sex.[‡]

---

*Despite the literal meaning of amicus curiae, most amici are not friends of the court; rather, they support one party over the other. Nearly 85 percent of all orally argued Supreme Court cases contain at least one amicus curiae brief, and the average is 4.4. See Lee Epstein, "Interest Group Litigation During the Rehnquist Court Era," 9 *Journal of Law and Politics* (1993): 639–717. In *Craig,* however, the ACLU was the only group to file an amicus curiae brief.

†The doctrine of standing prohibits the Court from resolving a dispute if the party bringing the litigation is not the appropriate one. The Court has said that Article III of the U.S. Constitution requires that litigants demonstrate "such a personal stake in the outcome of the controversy as to assure that concrete adverseness which sharpens the presentation of issues upon which the Court so largely depends for illumination of difficult constitutional questions." *Baker v. Carr,* 369 U.S. 186 at 204 (1962). In *Craig,* Burger felt that Whitener, being over the age of twenty-one and female, did not have the requisite personal stake.

‡He made this point again in an October 18, 1976, memo to Brennan: "I may decide to join you in reversal, particularly if we do not expand the 'equal advantage' clause or

Once Burger had spoken, the other justices presented their views in order of seniority, another of the Court's norms.* They were, as Table 2 shows, all over the map. Lewis Powell and Harry Blackmun agreed with the chief justice: both would dismiss on the standing issue, and both thought they could find for Craig. William Rehnquist also wanted to dismiss on standing, but would hold for Oklahoma should the Court resolve the dispute. The remaining five justices would rule in Craig's favor, but disagreed on the appropriate standard. Thurgood Marshall favored strict scrutiny, as did William Brennan, but Brennan suggested that a standard in between rational and strict might be viable.[5] Byron White seemed to go along with Brennan. Potter Stewart intimated that the Court need only apply the rational basis test to find in Craig's favor. John Paul Stevens argued that some "level of scrutiny above mere rationality has to be applied," but he was not clear on what that standard should be.

According to the Court's procedures, if the chief justice is in the majority after the conference vote, he decides who will write the opinion of the Court. If he is not part of the majority, the most senior member of the majority—Brennan, in the *Craig* case—takes on that responsibility. According to Court records, Brennan assigned the *Craig* opinion to himself. When he took on the responsibility, Brennan knew, as do all justices, that he needed to obtain the signatures of at least four others if his opinion was to become the law of the land. If he failed to get a majority to agree to its contents, his opinion would become a judgment of the Court and would lack precedential value.

The majority requirement for precedent is another of the Court's many norms, which for Brennan, in *Craig*, must have seemed imposing. Only three others—Marshall and possibly White and Stevens—tended to agree with his *most* preferred positions in the case: (1) Whitener had standing; (2) a strict scrutiny standard should be used; and (3) the Court should rule in Craig's favor. From whom would the fourth vote come? Rehnquist seemed

---

'suspect' classifications! In short, I am 'available.' " He reiterated this position in two subsequent memos dated November 11 and November 15.

*The order of speaking is a norm, as is the tradition of the chief justice speaking first at conference. Norms structure social interactions (here, among the justices) and are known to the community (the justices) to serve this function. See Jack Knight, *Institutions and Social Conflict* (Cambridge: Cambridge University Press, 1992).

Table 2. Justices' Conference Positions on the Issues in *Craig v. Boren*

Justice	Standing	Standard	Disposition
		Conference Position	
Burger	No	Rational?	Dismiss/Lean toward Craig if decided on merits
Brennan	Yes	[Strict]/ In-between*	Craig
Stewart	Yes	Rational	Craig
White	Yes	Strict/ In-between?	Craig
Marshall	Yes	Strict	Craig
Blackmun	No	Undeclared	Dismiss/Lean toward Craig if decided on merits
Powell	No	Rational?	Dismiss/Lean toward Craig if decided on merits
Rehnquist	No	Rational	Dismiss/Lean toward Oklahoma if decided on merits
Stevens	Yes	Above rational	Craig

? = Implicit but not explicit from conference discussion. * "Strict" represented Brennan's most preferred position, but at conference he offered the "in-between" standard.

Data Sources: Docket sheets and conference notes of Justice William J. Brennan Jr., Library of Congress; and conference notes and vote tallies of Justice Lewis F. Powell Jr., Washington and Lee University School of Law.

out of the question because his position was diametrically opposed to Brennan's on all the main points, and he would surely dissent. Blackmun, Powell, and Burger also favored dismissal but were closer to Brennan on point 3.

That left Stewart. He, as do all justices, had several feasible courses of action, as shown in Table 3: join the majority opinion, concur "regularly," concur "specially," or dissent. Based on his conference position—he had voted in favor of both standing and Craig, but was not keen on the strict scrutiny approach—it was possible that Stewart, as well as Blackmun, Powell, and Burger, might join Brennan's disposition of the case (that Craig should win) but disagree with the strict scrutiny standard the opinion articulated. This situation would not be good news from Brennan's perspective because such (dis)agreement—called a "special" concurrence—meant that Stewart would fail to provide the crucial fifth signature. Stewart might,

Table 3. Major Voting and Opinion Options

Option	Meaning
1. Join the majority or plurality	The justice is a "voiceless" member of the majority or plurality; the justice writes no opinion but agrees with the opinion of the Court.[a]
2. Write or join a regular concurrence	The justice writes or joins an opinion and is also a member of the majority or plurality opinion coalition.
3. Write, join, or note[b] a special concurrence	The justice agrees with the disposition made by the majority or plurality but disagrees with the reasons in the opinion. The justice is not a member of the majority or plurality opinion coalition.[c]
4. Write, join, or note a dissent	The justice disagrees with the disposition made by the majority or plurality. The justice is not a member of the majority or plurality opinion coalition.

Note: A justice may be assigned to write the opinion of the Court. But, with the exception of self-assignment, a justice does not make this decision for himself or herself. It is the responsibility of the chief justice, if he is in the majority, or the senior associate in the majority, if the chief justice is not, to assign the opinion of the Court.

a. Or the judgment of the Court, which results when the opinion writer cannot get a majority of the participating justices to agree to the opinion's contents.

b. To note is to speak, without opinion, as in "Justice Stewart concurs in the judgment of the Court."

c. At least one justice must cast such a concurrence to produce a judgment of the Court.

Source: Jeffrey A. Segal and Harold J. Spaeth, *The Supreme Court and the Attitudinal Model* (New York: Cambridge University Press, 1993), 276.

however, join the majority opinion coalition and write a regular concurrence. A regular concurrence, in contrast to a special concurrence, counts as an opinion "join," and Brennan would have his fifth vote.*

After several opinion drafts, all revised to accommodate the many suggestions of his colleagues, Brennan succeeded in marshaling a Court. The final version took up the ACLU's invitation, as well as Brennan's conference alternative, and articulated a new test for sex discrimination cases. Called "heightened" or midlevel scrutiny, it lies somewhere between strict scrutiny

---

*When justices agree to sign on to an opinion draft, they typically write a memo to the writer saying that they "join" the opinion. Many simply write "I join" or "Join me."

Table 4. Comparison of Justices' Conference and
Final Positions in *Craig v. Boren*

Justice	Conference Position			Final Position		
	Standing	Standard	Disposition	Standing	Standard	Disposition
Burger	No	Rational?	Dismiss/Craig	No	Rational	Oklahoma[a]
Brennan	Yes	[Strict]/In-between*	Craig	Yes	Heightened	Craig
Stewart	Yes	Rational	Craig	Yes	Unclear	Craig[b]
White	Yes	Strict/In-between?	Craig	Yes	Heightened	Craig
Marshall	Yes	Strict	Craig	Yes	Heightened	Craig
Blackmun	No	Undeclared	Dismiss/Craig	Yes	Heightened	Craig[c]
Powell	No	Rational?	Dismiss/Craig	Yes	Heightened[d]	Craig[e]
Rehnquist	No	Rational	Dismiss/Oklahoma	No	Rational	Oklahoma[a]
Stevens	Yes	Above rational	Craig	Yes	Heightened[d]	Craig[e]

? = Implicit but not explicit from conference discussion. * "Strict" represented Brennan's most preferred position, but, at conference, he offered the "in-between" standard.
  a. Wrote dissenting opinion.
  b. Wrote opinion concurring in judgment (special concurrence).
  c. Wrote opinion concurring in part.
  d. With reservations or qualifications.
  e. Wrote concurring opinion (regular concurrence).

Data Sources: Docket sheets and conference notes of Justice William J. Brennan Jr., Library of Congress; and conference notes and vote tallies of Justice Lewis F. Powell Jr., Washington and Lee University School of Law.

and rational basis.* From there, the votes and positions fell out as Table 4 indicates. Note that Powell, Burger, and Blackmun did not join opinions that coincided with their conference positions; that Marshall signed an opinion advocating a standard that was less than ideal from his point of view; and that Brennan's writing advanced a sex discrimination test that fell short of

*Brennan outlined the heightened scrutiny approach as follows: "classifications by gender must serve important governmental objectives and must be substantially related

his most preferred standard. Even the votes changed. Powell, Blackmun, and Burger switched their positions, but in different directions.

In the end, *Craig* leaves us with many questions. Why did Powell, Blackmun, and Burger alter their votes? Why did Brennan advance the heightened scrutiny test when he clearly favored strict scrutiny? Why did Marshall join Brennan's opinion, when it adopted a standard he found less than appealing? More generally, why did *Craig* come out the way it did?

These questions become more interesting when we consider that *Craig* is not an anomaly. In more than half of all orally argued cases, the justices switch their votes, make changes in their opinions to accommodate the suggestions of colleagues, and join writings that do not necessarily reflect their sincere preferences.[6]

Overview of the Strategic Account

How might we answer the questions raised by *Craig* and many other Court cases? Certainly, we should begin by acknowledging the voluminous body of literature that has attempted to address them. For more than fifty years scholars have tried to develop theories to explain why justices behave in particular ways, and they have had a modicum of success or, at the very least, they have come to some agreement over the fundamentals. Among the most important of these is the primacy of policy preferences; that is, judicial specialists generally agree that justices, first and foremost, wish to see their policy preferences etched into law. They are, in the opinion of many, "single-minded seekers of legal policy."[7]

Craig illustrates this point. During conference discussion, almost every justice expressed some preference about the way he wanted the case to come out and what he hoped the opinion would say. For example, we know that Marshall wanted the Court to hold that Whitener had standing, to apply a strict scrutiny standard to sex discrimination claims, and to rule in Craig's favor. But, as we also know, his preferences alone did not drive

---

to the achievement of those objectives." *Craig v. Boren*, 429 U.S. 190 at 197 (1976). Using this approach, the Court sometimes strikes down sex-based classifications, such as the law in *Craig*, and sometimes upholds them. One law it upheld is the federal policy limiting the military draft to men. See *Rostker v. Goldberg*, 453 U.S. 57 (1981).

Marshall's behavior: he signed an opinion articulating a standard of review that fell short of his most preferred position.

So it seems that something is missing from this basic story of Court decisions. Even after we take preferences into account, important questions linger, suggesting the need for a more comprehensive approach—a strategic account of judicial decisions. This account rests on a few simple propositions: justices may be primarily seekers of legal policy, but they are not unconstrained actors who make decisions based only on their own ideological attitudes. Rather, justices are strategic actors who realize that their ability to achieve their goals depends on a consideration of the preferences of other actors, the choices they expect others to make, and the institutional context in which they act. We call this a *strategic account*. . . .

Major Components of the Strategic Account

As we have set it out, the strategic account of judicial decision making comprises three main ideas: justices' actions are directed toward the attainment of goals; justices are strategic; and institutions structure justices' interactions. . . .

Goals

A central assumption of strategic explanations is that actors make decisions consistent with their goals and interests. We say that an actor makes a rational decision when she takes a course of action that satisfies her desires most efficiently. What this means is that when a political actor chooses between two courses of action, she will select the one she thinks is most likely to help her attain her goals. . . . [I]n terms of *Craig*, because Marshall preferred the establishment of a strict scrutiny standard more than a heightened scrutiny standard, and heightened scrutiny more than a rational basis standard, we would say he acted rationally if he made those individual choices that led to a decision by the full Court that established a standard closest to the strict scrutiny criterion. . . .

Strategic Interaction

The second part of the strategic account is tied to the first: for justices to maximize their preferences, they must act strategically in making their choices. By "strategic," we mean that judicial decision making is interdependent. From *Craig,* we learn that it is not enough to say that Justice Brennan chose heightened scrutiny over rational basis or strict scrutiny because he preferred heightened scrutiny; we know he actually preferred strict scrutiny. Rather, interdependency suggests that Brennan chose heightened scrutiny because he believed that the other relevant actors—including his colleagues—would choose rational basis, and, given this choice, heightened scrutiny led to a better outcome for Brennan than the alternatives.[8]

To put it plainly, strategic decision making is about *interdependent* choice: an individual's action is, in part, a function of her expectations about the actions of others.* To say that a justice acts strategically is to say that she realizes that her success or failure depends on the preferences of other actors and the actions she expects them to take, not just on her own preferences and actions.[9]

Occasionally, strategic calculations lead justices to make choices that reflect their sincere preferences. Suppose, in *Craig,* that all of the justices agreed on all of the important issues: Whitener had standing; a strict scrutiny standard should be used; and the Court should rule in Craig's favor. If those conditions held, Brennan would have been free to write an opinion that reflected his true preferences, for they were the same as the Court's. In other instances, strategic calculations lead a justice to act in a sophisticated fashion; that is, he acts in a way that does not accurately reflect his true preferences so as to avoid the possibility of seeing his colleagues reject his most preferred policy in favor of his least preferred. Brennan may have followed this line of thinking in *Craig.* We know that he had to choose among three possible standards, but preferred strict scrutiny over heightened scrutiny over rational basis. Yet, he did not select his most preferred standard, opting instead for his second choice. Why? A possibility is that Brennan thought an opinion advancing strict scrutiny would be completely unacceptable to certain members of the Court, who would push for a rational basis standard, his least preferred standard. He may have chosen heightened scrutiny because, based on his knowledge of the preferences of

---

*Some believe that such a broad (and simple) conception of strategic decision making undermines the value of the approach. See, for example, Howard Gillman, "Placing Judicial Motives in Context," 7 *Law and Courts* (1997): 10–13. We, however, see it as what underlies its importance because it acknowledges the breadth of the phenomena that might be explained.

other justices, it allowed him to avoid his least preferred position, not because it was his first choice.

Brennan chose the course of action that any justice concerned with maximizing his policy preferences would take. In other words, for Brennan to set policy as close as possible to his ideal point, strategic behavior was essential. In *Craig* he needed to act in a sophisticated fashion, given his beliefs about the preferences of the other actors and the choices he expected them to make. . . .

Institutions

According to the strategic account, we cannot fully understand the choices justices make unless we also consider the institutional context in which they operate. By institutions, we mean sets of rules that "structure social interactions in particular ways.". . . [I]nstitutions can be formal, such as laws, or informal, such as norms and conventions.[10]

To see how central institutions are to this account of judicial decisions, consider two examples. First, think about how the norm governing the creation of precedent—a majority of justices must sign an opinion for it to become the law of the land—affected the resolution of *Craig*. Had Brennan believed that four other justices shared his preference for the strict scrutiny standard, he would have written an opinion that adopted that standard. However, only three justices at the most were firmly behind him. If a different threshold for the establishment of precedent had existed, if four justices were enough, perhaps Brennan would have pushed for strict scrutiny. But such was not the case, which may explain, in part, why he was willing to consider the heightened standard: given the norm for precedent, he thought heightened was the best he could do.

Second, another institution of some importance is Article III of the U.S. Constitution, which states that justices "hold their Offices during good Behaviour." What this phrase means is that, barring an impeachment by Congress, justices have life tenure; unlike members of legislatures and even judges in many states, they do not have to face the voters to retain their jobs. The institution of life tenure also influences justices' goals. Instead of acting to maximize their chances for reelection, justices act to maximize policy.[11] To understand the effect of this institution, one has only to think about the kinds of activities in which a justice running for office would engage as opposed to a justice attempting to influence policy. In deciding *Craig,* for example, rather than considering the preferences of his colleagues and Congress over what test to use in sex discrimination cases, Justice Brennan would have been taking the pulse of his "constituents," talking with lobbyists, holding press conferences, and otherwise behaving in the ways we associate with members of Congress, not justices of the Supreme Court.[12]

Conclusion

As we have set it out, the strategic account of judicial decisions has several implications for the way we think about the development of law in American society. We argue that it suggests that law, as it is generated by the Supreme Court, is the result of short-term strategic interactions among the justices and between the Court and other branches of government.[13] But before we think about the implications of the strategic account, we must consider whether it is plausible and whether it provides us with any real leverage to understand judicial decisions.

To accomplish these tasks, we follow essentially the same path that David Mayhew did in *Congress: The Electoral Connection:* we develop a "picture" of justices as strategic seekers of legal policy and explore how justices so motivated go about making choices.[14] . . .

NOTES

1. See Mark Wolfson, "The Legislative Impact of Social Movement Organizations: The Anti-Drunken-Driving Movement and the 21-Year-Old Drinking Age," 76 *Social Science Quarterly* (1995): 311–327.

2. The material in the next few paragraphs comes from *U.S. Supreme Court Records and Briefs,* BNA's Law Reprints, no. 75-628.

3. Susan Gluck Mezey, *In Pursuit of Equality* (New York: St. Martin's, 1992), 17.

4. The next few paragraphs draw on the papers, including case files, docket books, and transcriptions of conference discussions, of Justices William J. Brennan Jr., Lewis F. Powell Jr., and Thurgood Marshall. The Brennan and Marshall collections are located in the Library of Congress; the Powell papers, in the Law Library at Washington and Lee University.

5. Typically, Brennan's case files contain memos of the remarks he made at conferences. Unfortunately, his *Craig* conference memo was missing, so we rely on Bernard Schwartz, who writes that Brennan wanted to adopt the strict scrutiny approach (see Brennan's opinion for the Court in *Frontiero v. Richardson*), but at conference he offered

the "in between" standard. See Bernard Schwartz, *The Ascent of Pragmatism* (Reading, Mass.: Addison-Wesley, 1990), 226. For now, the important point is that "strict scrutiny" represented Brennan's most preferred position.

6. See, for example, Lee Epstein and Jack Knight, "Documenting Strategic Interaction on the U.S. Supreme Court" (paper presented at the 1995 annual meeting of the American Political Science Association, Chicago). Vote shifts are already the object of extensive investigation. For the latest and best installment, see Forrest Maltzman and Paul J. Wahlbeck, "Strategic Considerations and Vote Fluidity on the Burger Court," 90 *American Political Science Review* (1996): 581–592.

7. Tracey E. George and Lee Epstein, "On the Nature of Supreme Court Decision Making," 86 *American Political Science Review* (1990): 325.

8. See, generally, Peter C. Ordeshook, *A Political Theory Primer* (New York: Routledge, 1992).

9. See Charles M. Cameron, "Decision-Making and Positive Political Theory (Or, Using Game Theory to Study Judicial Politics)" (paper presented at the 1994 Columbus Conference, Columbus, Ohio).

10. See Jack Knight, *Institutions and Social Conflict* (Cambridge: Cambridge University Press, 1992), 2–3.

11. See Jeffrey A. Segal and Harold J. Spaeth, *The Supreme Court and the Attitudinal Model* (New York: Cambridge University Press, 1993), 69–72.

12. See, generally, David Mayhew, *Congress: The Electoral Connection* (New Haven: Yale University Press, 1974).

13. Knight makes this argument in *Institutions and Social Conflict,* and we explore it in an essay on *Marbury v. Madison,* 1 Cr. 137 (1803). Jack Knight and Lee Epstein, "On the Struggle for Judicial Supremacy," 30 *Law and Society Review* (1996): 87–130.

14. After proclaiming that representatives and senators were "single-minded seekers of reelection," Mayhew (*Congress: The Electoral Connection,* 9) went on to develop a "picture of what the United States Congress looks like if the reelection quest is examined seriously."

9-2

from *The Supreme Court*

Lawrence Baum

Lee Epstein and Jack Knight described how Supreme Court justices often craft their arguments to attract the support of others. This is one way in which the justices behave strategically. Another strategic consideration in deciding cases arises from the realization that the Court has limited wherewithal to implement its decisions as public policy. In the following essay, Lawrence Baum considers how justices must at times adapt their decisions to the likely response of other government actors—from police to presidents—to improve the chance that their prescriptions will meet with compliance.

IN TWO DECISIONS in 1962 and 1963, the Supreme Court ruled that prayer and Bible reading exercises in public schools violate the constitutional prohibition of an establishment of religion.[1] These decisions seemed to resolve the issue of organized religious observances in public schools.

As it turned out, the Court did not resolve that issue. While many school districts eliminated the practices that the Court had held unconstitutional, many others retained them. Some states enacted laws that were intended to get around the Court's rulings, such as a requirement of a "moment of silence" that could be used by teachers as an occasion for prayer. Other states simply mandated prayer in contradiction of the Supreme Court. When noncompliant districts and state governments were taken to court, federal judges generally struck down practices that conflicted with the Court's decisions. But one Alabama district judge announced in an opinion that the Supreme Court had "erred" and refused to apply its rulings.[2]

Opposition extended to Congress.[3] Members denounced the Court for its school prayer rulings. Over the years, several hundred resolutions were introduced to overturn the Court's decisions through a constitutional

Excerpted from Lawrence Baum, *The Supreme Court*, 6th edition (Washington, D.C.: CQ Press, 1998), pp. 225–277. Some notes appearing in the original have been cut.

amendment. Other proposals would have eliminated the Court's jurisdiction to hear cases in this field.

The controversy has continued in the 1990s. New disputes arose over religious observances at school graduations and athletic events, and there are signs that compliance with the Court's decisions has declined.[4] After the 1994 elections, when the Republican party gained majorities in both houses of Congress, there was a renewed drive for a constitutional amendment on school prayer. In 1997 a resolution for a "religious freedom amendment" was introduced in the House.[5] One effect of the draft amendment would be to allow organized prayers in schools so long as the prayers were not initiated or designated by "the government." The prospects for this proposal were uncertain, but its introduction with 116 cosponsors underlined the fact that the school prayer issue is far from settled thirty-five years after the Supreme Court seemingly resolved it.

THE SUPREME COURT is the highest interpreter of federal law, and people often think of it as the final arbiter of the issues it addresses. But as the school prayer controversy illustrates, this image of the Court is misleading. It is more useful to think of the Court as one of many institutions that participate in a fluid process of policy making.

Often the Court's decisions decide only one aspect of an issue or offer general guidelines that other policy makers have to fill in. Even when the Court seems to rule decisively on an issue, other institutions may limit the impact of that ruling or negate it altogether. Congress and the president can write a new statute to override the Court's interpretation of an old one. Congress and the states can amend the Constitution to overcome a constitutional decision. Judges and administrators can choose not to carry out a Supreme Court policy fully. And the Court's ultimate impact on society is mediated by the actions of other institutions in and out of government. The Court may influence the strength of the labor movement or the status of women, but so do many other forces—including some that are likely to be far more powerful than the Court. . . .

Responses by Legislatures and Chief Executives

After the Supreme Court hands down its decisions, Congress, the president, and their state counterparts can respond in various ways. They may help or hinder the implementation of decisions, they may act to change the Court's interpretations of the law, and they may attack the Court or its members.

Congress

Statutory Interpretation. Congress is supreme in statutory law: it can override the Supreme Court's interpretation of a statute simply by adopting a new statute with different language that supersedes the Court's reading of the old statute. Congress can also ratify or extend the Court's interpretation of a statute, but overrides of statutory decisions are especially significant.

A substantial proportion of statutory decisions receive some congressional scrutiny, and proposals to override decisions are common. Most of these proposals fail, for the same reasons that most bills of any type fail: legislation must navigate successfully through several decision points at which it can be killed, and there is usually a presumption in favor of the status quo. Still, overrides are far from rare. Over the past three decades, on average, more than ten statutory decisions have been overturned in each two-year Congress. Of the statutory decisions in the Court's 1978–1989 terms, Congress had overridden more than five percent by 1996.[6] As Table 1 illustrates, overrides range across a wide array of issues and areas of law. The table also shows that some overrides follow quickly after a decision, while others come considerably later.

In most respects, the politics of congressional response to the Court's statutory decisions resembles congressional politics generally.[7] The initiative for bills to overturn decisions often comes from interest groups. Just as groups that fail to achieve their goals in Congress frequently turn to the courts for relief, groups whose interests suffer in the Supreme Court frequently turn to Congress.

The success of efforts to overturn statutory decisions depends on the same broad array of factors that influence the fates of other bills in Congress. The political strength of the groups that favor or oppose overrides is important. Not surprisingly, the federal executive branch enjoys considerable success in getting Congress to overturn unfavorable decisions, while nearly all decisions that work to the detriment of criminal defendants are left standing.[8] When a significant group favors action and organized opposition does not exist, Congress may override a decision quickly and easily. Many successful overrides are enacted not as separate bills but as provisions of broader bills such as appropriations, and members of Congress who vote

Table 1. Selected Congressional Legislation Overturning
Supreme Court Statutory Decisions, 1995–1996

Migrant Worker Protection (enacted 1995)
Overturned *Adams Fruit Co. v. Barrett* (1990) by prohibiting migrant farm workers from
suing employers for injuries when they could obtain workers' compensation benefits for
those injuries.

False Statements Accountability Act of 1996
Overturned *Hubbard v. United States* (1995) by making it a criminal offense to make a
false statement in a judicial proceeding.

Federal Courts Improvement Act of 1996
Overturned *Pulliam v. Allen* (1984) by giving judges immunity from lawsuits for injunc-
tive relief and from the payment of costs in lawsuits; also overturned *Primate Protection
League v. Administrators of Tulane Educational Fund* (1991) by allowing federal agencies to
remove lawsuits against them from state to federal court.

Small Business Job Protection Act of 1996
Partially overturned *John Hancock Mutual Life Insurance v. Harris Trust* (1993) by giving life
insurance companies an exemption from federal pension regulations for certain funds
until 1999.

---

for those bills are not always aware that they are overriding a Supreme
Court decision.

Congress does not always have the last word when it overrides a statute,
because the new statute is subject to judicial interpretation. In *Westfall v.
Erwin* (1988), the Court held that federal officials could be sued for personal
injuries under some circumstances. A few months later Congress overrode
Westfall by allowing the attorney general to certify that an employee who
had been sued was acting as a federal official and thereby substituting the
federal government for the employee as a defendant. But in *Gutierrez de Martinez v. Lamagno* (1995), the Court weakened the override by holding that the
attorney general's certification could be challenged in court. The Court
sometimes goes even further. In *Plaut v. Spendthrift Farm* (1995), it held that a
congressional override of a 1991 decision on the statute of limitations in securities fraud cases was unconstitutional because it violated the constitutional separation of powers between the legislative and judicial branches.

Constitutional Interpretation. When the Court interprets the Constitution,
the most direct and decisive way to overturn its decision is through a constitutional amendment. But that is a very difficult route, because the

amending process is arduous and there is a widespread reluctance to tamper with the Constitution. It is far easier to adopt a new statute, but a constitutional decision cannot be overturned directly by a statute. Under some circumstances, however, a statute can negate or limit the effects of a constitutional decision.

If the Court has nullified or limited a statute on constitutional grounds, Congress can enact a second statute to try to meet the Court's objections. In *United States v. Harriss* (1954), the Court gave a narrow reading to the coverage of the Federal Regulation of Lobbying Act. The Court did so in order to avoid holding that the act's criminal penalties for failure by lobbyists to register with Congress were unconstitutional because of vagueness about who was required to register. But the Court's narrow interpretation greatly weakened the act, because under that interpretation most people who acted as lobbyists did not have to register. More than forty years later, Congress addressed that problem by enacting the Lobbying Disclosure Act of 1995. The new act required a broad range of people to register as lobbyists, but its description of those people was far more precise than the description in the original act.

When the Court holds that a right is not protected by the Constitution, Congress often can protect that right by enacting a statute. Congress has taken that action on issues such as the use of search warrants to gather information from newsrooms. In one recent instance, however, the Court ruled that such congressional action was invalid. In *Employment Division v. Smith* (1990), the Court gave a narrow interpretation to the protections of freedom of religion in the First and Fourteenth Amendments, making it easier for governments to justify rules that treat religion neutrally but that have the effect of putting a burden on a particular religious practice. A broad set of religious groups attacked the decision. In response, Congress enacted the Religious Freedom Restoration Act in 1993 to restore the broader pre-*Smith* standard of protection for religion. But in *City of Boerne v. Flores* (1997), the Court held that the 1993 act was unconstitutional as applied to state and local governments because it went beyond congressional power to enforce the Fourteenth Amendment.

In situations where constitutional decisions cannot be negated by statute, members of Congress often introduce resolutions to overturn them with constitutional amendments. In recent years, resolutions have been submitted on a variety of issues. The range of these issues is suggested by a sampling of resolutions introduced in 1997, shown in Table 2.

Table 2. Selected Resolutions Introduced in Congress for
Constitutional Amendments to Overturn Supreme Court Decisions, 1997

Purpose	Decisions that would be overturned
Giving states power to impose term limits on members of Congress	U.S. Term Limits v. Thornton (1995)
Giving Congress power to limit campaign spending	Buckley v. Valeo (1976), later decisions
Allowing organized prayer in public schools	Engel v. Vitale (1962)
Giving federal and state governments power to prohibit flag desecration	Texas v. Johnson (1989), United States v. Eichman (1990)
Prohibiting abortion under most circumstances	Roe v. Wade (1973), Planned Parenthood v. Casey (1992), other decisions
Allowing states to reduce prisoners' credits toward early release retroactively	Lynce v. Mathis (1997)

Not surprisingly, few of these efforts to propose amendments have achieved the necessary two-thirds votes in both houses. Only five times has Congress proposed an amendment that was aimed directly at Supreme Court decisions. And one of these, proposed in 1924 to give Congress the power to regulate child labor, was not ratified by the states. (A few amendments have indirectly negated Supreme Court decisions.) Since the child labor proposal, the only amendment that Congress has proposed in order to overturn a decision was the Twenty-sixth Amendment, adopted in 1971. In *Oregon v. Mitchell* (1970), the Court had ruled that Congress cannot regulate the voting age in elections to state office; Congress acted quickly to propose an amendment overturning the decision, and the states quickly ratified it.

In contrast with the Twenty-sixth Amendment, the most prominent failed campaigns for amendments in recent years were aimed at decisions that increased legal protections for civil liberties. Even highly unpopular decisions, such as prohibitions of school prayer, stood up against efforts to overturn them. In these instances, the general reluctance to amend the Constitution was compounded by a special reluctance to limit the protections of rights in the Bill of Rights.

That reluctance is illustrated by the effort to propose an anti–flag-desecration amendment. In *Texas v. Johnson* (1989), the Supreme Court struck down a state statute prohibiting flag burning on the ground that it punished people for political expression. Four months later Congress enacted a federal statute against flag burning, written in an effort to meet the Court's objections to the Texas statute. But in *United States v. Eichman* (1990), the Court held that the new statute was also unconstitutional.

Members of Congress then sought a constitutional amendment to allow prohibition of flag desecration. Its passage seemed inevitable, because a member's vote against the amendment might provide an opponent with a powerful issue in the 1990 election. But the House defeated the amendment by thirty-four votes, the Senate by nine. In the more conservative Congress that resulted from the 1994 election, an amendment that passed the House by a 312–120 margin in 1995 failed by only three votes in the Senate; an amendment approved by the House in 1997 with a similar majority might win Senate approval.[9] Even so, the lack of an anti–flag-desecration proposal from Congress by 1996 underlines the difficulty of amending the Constitution.

Affecting the Implementation of Decisions. By passing legislation, Congress can influence the implementation of Supreme Court decisions by other institutions. Its most important tool is budgetary. Congress can provide or fail to provide funds to carry out a decision. It can also help the Court by withholding federal funds from state and local governments that refuse to comply with the Court's decisions. Congressional use of the latter power was critical in achieving school desegregation in the Deep South.

Occasionally a Supreme Court decision requires implementation by Congress itself. In these situations Congress generally has accepted its obligation with little resistance. The legislative veto is an exception.[10] In *Immigration and Naturalization Service v. Chadha* (1983), the Court indicated that any statutes allowing Congress or one of its units to "veto" proposed executive branch actions are invalid. After the decision, Congress eliminated legislative veto provisions from several statutes. But it maintained others, and since 1983 it has adopted more than two hundred new legislative veto provisions—most requiring that specific congressional committees approve action by administrative agencies. Agency officials are willing to accept these provisions rather than challenging their legality, in order to maintain good relations with congressional committees and to avoid even more stringent congressional controls. Thus political realities have allowed noncompliance with *Chadha* to continue.

Attacks on the Court and Its Members. When members of Congress are dissatisfied with the Supreme Court's behavior, they may attack the Court or the justices directly. The easiest way to do so is verbal, and members of Congress frequently express their disapproval of the Court by denouncing it publicly. More concretely, Congress can take formal legislative action of several types.

One type of action concerns jurisdiction. The Constitution allows Congress to alter the Court's appellate jurisdiction through legislation, though there is some question about whether Congress can narrow the Court's jurisdiction to prevent it from protecting constitutional rights. Congress has used its power over jurisdiction to control the Court only once, in an unusual situation: in 1869 it withdrew the Court's right to hear appeals in habeas corpus actions in order to prevent it from deciding a pending challenge to the post–Civil War Reconstruction legislation. In *Ex parte McCardle* (1869), the Court ruled that this congressional action was constitutionally acceptable.

In recent years, Congress has considered several bills that would have limited the Court's jurisdiction in areas of civil liberties activism. In 1964, the House did pass a bill to eliminate the jurisdiction of all federal courts over the drawing of state legislative districts, and in 1979 the Senate approved a provision to eliminate federal court jurisdiction over cases that concerned school prayer. Both of these bills died in the other house. Since the early 1980s, bills and amendments have been introduced to limit the Court's jurisdiction over such issues as abortion, school busing, and prayer. But none have passed either house.

The most extreme action that Congress can take against individual justices is to remove them through impeachment. One justice was impeached by the House—though not convicted by the Senate—in 1804, and impeachment has been threatened in several other instances. But impeachment based on disagreement over policy is extremely unlikely.

Congress controls the Court budget, limited only by the constitutional prohibition against reducing the justices' salaries. With a few exceptions, Congress has refrained from using its budget power to attack the Court.[11] But in 1964 Congress singled out the justices when it increased their annual salaries by $4,500—$3,000 less than the raises given to other federal judges. That action was motivated by displeasure with the Court's civil liberties policies. A proposal to provide that $3,000 to the justices was defeated in the House the next year, after a debate in which several members attacked the Court, and one—Robert Dole of Kansas—suggested that the pay increase be contingent on the Court's reversing a legislative districting decision that he disliked.[12]

That attack on the justices through their salaries was perhaps the most serious concrete action that Congress has taken against the Court in the twentieth century; Congress has made little use of its enormous powers over the Court. Why has it been hesitant to employ them, even at times when most members were unhappy about the Court's direction?

To begin with, there are always some members of Congress who agree with the Court's policies and lead its defense. Further, serious forms of attack against the Court, such as impeachment and reducing its jurisdiction, seem illegitimate to many people. Finally, when threatened with serious attack, the Court sometimes retreats to reduce the impetus for congressional action. For these reasons, the congressional bark at the Supreme Court has been a good deal worse than its bite.

The President

Influencing Congressional Response. The president can influence congressional responses to the Supreme Court by taking a position on proposals for action. Sometimes it is the president who first proposes anti-Court action. The most dramatic example in the twentieth century is President Roosevelt's Court-packing plan.

Since the 1960s, conservative presidents have encouraged efforts in Congress to limit or overturn some of the Court's liberal rulings on civil liberties. For instance, George Bush led the effort to overturn the Court's flag-burning decisions in 1989 and 1990.

Bill Clinton has also sought action to reverse the effects of some decisions. One effort came after the Court held in 1995 that a federal statute prohibiting guns in and around schools had gone beyond congressional power to regulate interstate commerce. Clinton said in his radio address three days later that "this Supreme Court decision could condemn more of our children to going to schools where there are guns." [13] Clinton then proposed narrower legislation that was tied more directly to interstate commerce. Ultimately, that legislation was enacted as part of an appropriations bill in 1996. It remains to be seen whether the Supreme Court will find the new statute constitutionally acceptable.

Using Executive Power. As chief executive, the president has a number of means to shape the implementation of Supreme Court decisions. For one thing, presidents can decide whether to support the Court with the power of the federal government when its decisions encounter open resistance from officials with the responsibility to carry them out.

The most coercive form of federal power is deployment of the military. When southern states began to defy *Brown v. Board of Education,* President Eisenhower indicated that he would not use troops to enforce the decision. But in 1957, when a combination of state interference and mob action prevented court-ordered desegregation of the schools in Little Rock, Arkansas, Eisenhower abandoned his earlier position and brought in troops. In 1962 President Kennedy used federal troops to enforce desegregation at the University of Mississippi.

Presidents can also use litigation and their control over federal funds. The Johnson administration's vigorous use of both these mechanisms was directly responsible for breaking down segregated school systems in the Deep South. More recent presidents have differed in their readiness to use federal money and initiate lawsuits in conflicts over school desegregation.

President Reagan's use of his executive powers helped to spur a major change in labor-management relations. In *National Labor Relations Board v. Mackay Radio & Telegraph Company* (1938), the Court ruled that under a federal labor law, companies could hire new employees as permanent replacements for workers who were on strike. For several decades companies made little use of the Court's ruling. But after federal air traffic controllers went on strike in 1982, Reagan ordered the strikers replaced. The strike failed, and this episode encouraged employers to take similar action. By doing so, they accelerated a decline in the power of organized labor.

Bill Clinton sought legislation to override *Mackay;* a bill with that purpose passed the House in 1994 but died with a Senate filibuster. The next year Clinton issued an executive order under which companies receiving substantial amounts of money from federal contracts were prohibited from hiring permanent replacement workers. An effort to override the executive order through legislation failed in Congress, but in 1996 a federal court of appeals ruled that the order violated the statute that the Court had interpreted in *Mackay.*[14]

Presidential Compliance. Occasionally a Supreme Court decision requires compliance by the president, either as a party in the case or—more often— as head of the executive branch. Some presidents and commentators have argued that the president need not obey an order of the Supreme Court, which is a coequal body rather than a legal superior. In any case, presidents would seem sufficiently powerful to disobey the Court with impunity.

But in reality their position is not that strong. The president's political power is based largely on the ability to obtain support from other policy makers. This ability, in turn, depends in part on perceptions of the president's legitimacy. Because disobedience of the Court would threaten this legitimacy, Samuel Krislov argued, presidents "cannot afford to defy the Court." [15]

That conclusion is supported by presidential responses to two highly visible Court orders. In *Youngstown Sheet and Tube Co. v. Sawyer* (1952), the Court ruled that President Truman had acted illegally in seizing steel mills to keep them operating during a wartime strike and ordered that they be released. Truman immediately complied.

Even more striking is *United States v. Nixon* (1974). During investigation of the Watergate scandal, President Nixon withheld recordings of certain conversations in his offices that were sought by special prosecutor Leon Jaworski. In July 1974, the Supreme Court ruled unanimously that Nixon must yield the tapes.

In oral argument before the Court, the president's lawyer had indicated that Nixon might not comply with an adverse decision. Immediately after the decision was handed down, Nixon apparently considered noncompliance. By the end of that day, however, Nixon released a statement indicating that he would comply. At the least, this compliance speeded Nixon's departure from office: he released transcripts of some of the tapes, whose content provided strong evidence of presidential misdeeds, and opposition to impeachment evaporated. Fifteen days after the Court's ruling, Nixon announced his resignation.

In light of that result, why did President Nixon comply with the Court order? He apparently did not realize how damaging the evidence in the tapes actually was. Perhaps more important, noncompliance would have damaged his remaining legitimacy fatally. For many members of Congress noncompliance in itself would have constituted an impeachable offense, one on which there would be no dispute about the evidence. Under the circumstances compliance may have been the better of two unattractive choices.

State Legislatures and Governors

State governments have no direct power over the Supreme Court as an institution. But state legislatures and governors can influence the implementation of the Court's decisions. Most noteworthy are the instances when they seek to limit or overturn such decisions.

Like Congress, state legislatures can rewrite statutes to try to meet the Court's constitutional objections. The Supreme Court struck down the existing death penalty statutes in *Furman v. Georgia* (1972), with some members of the five-justice majority emphasizing the arbitrary element in the use of the penalty. In the next few years, thirty-five states adopted new capital punishment laws that were designed to avoid arbitrary sentencing. In a series of decisions from 1976 on, the Court upheld some of the new statutes and overturned others. States whose laws were rejected by the Court then adopted the forms that the Court had found acceptable. As a result, the impact of *Furman* has nearly been nullified.

Legislatures sometimes adopt statutes that seem clearly to violate the Court's decisions, in order to limit the Court's impact and to express opposition to its rulings. In the decade after *Brown v. Board of Education,* southern states passed a large number of statutes to prevent school desegregation, and some states have enacted laws to restore school religious observances that the Supreme Court invalidated. Often, such statutes are overturned quickly by the federal courts.

In eighteen states the voters can amend the state constitution by adopting initiative measures. After the Supreme Court held in 1995 that the states could not impose term limits on members of Congress, voters in nine states adopted initiatives that would punish any federal or state legislator who did not support specified term limits by putting on the ballot next to that member's name, "DISREGARDED VOTER INSTRUCTION ON TERM LIMITS." The Arkansas Supreme Court ruled that its state's initiative was unconstitutional; in 1997 the U.S. Supreme Court chose not to hear the case.[16]

The states can play two roles in amending the Constitution. When Congress proposes amendments, they must be ratified by three-quarters of the states. In an alternative procedure, the Constitution also allows the states a role in the proposal stage. By submitting petitions, two-thirds of the state legislatures can require Congress to convene a convention to consider proposing amendments. This procedure has never been used successfully, but in the 1960s thirty-three of the necessary thirty-four states petitioned for a convention to consider overturning the Court's decisions on legislative districting.

Like presidents, governors can influence both legislative responses to the Court's decisions and their implementation. Southern governors helped to block school desegregation in the 1950s and 1960s through their efforts to stir up resistance. More recently, governors have been prominent in state controversies over issues such as school prayer and criminal procedure, sometimes supporting and sometimes opposing the Court's decisions.

Legislatures and governors must act to put some Supreme Court decisions into effect. In 1989 the Court ruled that it was illegal for states to tax retirement benefits for federal workers while exempting similar benefits for state and local workers, as twenty-three states did. Several state governments balked at refunding tax money to federal retirees, and the Court had to decide cases from Virginia in 1993 and Georgia in 1994 to make clear that refunds were necessary. Even so, federal retirees in Virginia who refused to settle for partial payments did not receive refunds until the state supreme court ruled that the state government had no choice but to pay the money it owed them.[17]

Gideon v. Wainwright (1963) and later decisions required state and local governments to fund legal services for indigent criminal defendants. The response has been mixed. Government now spends well over $1 billion each year for legal defense of the poor,[18] and low-income defendants are in far better position than they were prior to *Gideon*. But funding of counsel has never been fully adequate, and it has become less adequate with growth in the number of criminal cases. As a result, according to one federal judge, "perfunctory representation of indigent criminal defendants is the order of the day in American courts." [19]

State legislatures and governors engage in direct defiance of the Court's decisions more often than do Congress and the president. This difference may result chiefly from the sheer number of states rather than from differences in the behavior of state and federal officials. Still, it suggests that the Court may face special difficulties when it seeks to bring about fundamental changes in state policies.

Yet resistance to the Court by state governments should not be exaggerated. Undoubtedly, their most frequent response to the Court's decisions is compliance. And much of what governors and legislatures do to limit the Court's impact, such as their reinstatement of the death penalty, is an effort to maintain the policies they want within the constraints of the Court's rulings.

Two Policy Areas

Patterns of response to the Court's decisions by the other two branches of government can be examined more closely with a look at two areas in which there has been a good deal of interaction between the Court and other policy makers.

Civil Rights Statutes. Beginning in 1957, Congress adopted a series of statutes that prohibited discrimination along racial and other lines; the two most important were the Civil Rights Act of 1964 and the Voting Rights Act of 1965, both amended to broaden their impact since then. Thousands of cases are brought under the civil rights statutes each year, and the Supreme Court has issued several major decisions and many minor ones interpreting them.

In some decisions the Burger and Rehnquist Courts have interpreted these statutes broadly, giving them greater impact. But other decisions— particularly in the late 1980s and early 1990s—have narrowed the meaning of these statutes, sometimes in important ways. Meanwhile, Congress maintained a relatively liberal position on civil rights issues until the mid-1990s, in part because of effective lobbying by civil rights groups. As a result, at least ten statutes have been adopted to overturn the Court's narrow interpretations.[20]

The Reagan and Bush administrations were more favorable than Congress to the Court's narrow interpretations of the civil rights laws. One bill intended to overturn a Court decision became law only after Congress overrode President Reagan's veto in 1988. The sweeping Civil Rights Act of 1991, which overturned nine Court decisions, became law only after an earlier version had been vetoed by President Bush.

In 1994 the Court ruled that the Civil Rights Act of 1991 does not apply to cases that were pending when it was enacted.[21] Efforts immediately began in Congress to overturn that decision, but they were unsuccessful. With Congress and the Court now closer to each other ideologically than they were up to the early 1990s, overrides of the Court's civil rights decisions are less likely.

Abortion. After the Supreme Court struck down state prohibitions of abortion in *Roe v. Wade* (1973), most states enacted laws to regulate abortion.[22] Many of these laws were neutral regulations that would clearly be acceptable to the Court, such as a requirement that abortions be performed by licensed physicians. But many other state laws were motivated by the goal of limiting the Court's impact by making abortions more difficult to obtain. Some states adopted several different statutes of this type. Rhode Island sought to nullify the Court's decision altogether with a new statute.

Groups that opposed legal restrictions on abortion regularly challenged restrictive state laws. In a series of decisions from 1976 to 1986, the Court struck down a number of these laws as inconsistent with *Roe*. But the Court did uphold federal and state restrictions on the funding of abortion in the Medicaid program for low income people. (Several state courts, however, struck down state funding restrictions on the basis of provisions in state constitutions.)

As new appointments made the Court more conservative, its support for the principles of the *Roe* decision weakened. Many people interpreted the Court's decision in *Webster v. Reproductive Health Services* (1989) to mean that the Court would now allow substantial restrictions on abortion or even overturn *Roe* in an appropriate case. Consequently, legislators and interest groups in nearly every state sought new legislation that heavily restricted abortion. In the two years after *Webster*, the great majority of these efforts failed, but Pennsylvania enacted major restrictions on abortion, and Utah, Louisiana, and Guam prohibited abortions under most circumstances. In contrast, Connecticut and Maryland passed statutes protecting the right to abortion under state law.

The Court's decision in *Planned Parenthood v. Casey* (1992), which reaffirmed *Roe* for the most part, made it clear that the Court would strike down state prohibitions of abortion. But the decision also encouraged states to adopt restrictions that might be consistent with the Court's new rules for regulation of abortion. Since 1992 some states have adopted statutes requiring parental consent or notification for young women unless a judge allows a waiver of that requirement, some have mandated a waiting period between a woman's receiving certain information and obtaining an abortion, and Mississippi in 1996 enacted a substantial set of regulations on abortion. In *Lambert v. Wicklund* (1997) the Court unanimously upheld a parental notification law similar to statutes it had accepted in the past. With that exception, it has said little about what kinds of regulations are acceptable under *Casey*.

At the federal level, the Reagan and Bush administrations established restrictions on the availability of abortion in some areas of federal activity, such as the military. In the early 1990s, Congress took steps to overturn some of these restrictions, but President Bush used the veto power to block these initiatives. One example involved the "gag rule," a set of regulations by the Department of Health and Human Services that broadly prohibited family planning clinics funded by the federal government from engaging in activities that encouraged or facilitated abortion. The Court upheld these regulations in *Rust v. Sullivan* (1991). Later that year Congress passed a bill intended to overturn the regulations, but President Bush vetoed it; he vetoed similar legislation in 1992.

Two days after he became president, Bill Clinton eliminated the regulations of family planning clinics along with several other restrictions on abortion. When the Court ruled in 1993 that abortion clinics could not use a civil rights law to sue those engaged in protests that obstruct access to the clinics, the Clinton administration encouraged Congress to pass a statute aimed at curbing those protests.[23] Congress did so in 1994, allowing criminal prosecutions and civil lawsuits against those engaged in such activities as blockading abortion clinics.

The abortion issue illustrates the importance of legislative responses to the Court's decisions. Even a seemingly definitive ruling in *Roe v. Wade* did not prevent Congress and state legislatures from enacting laws limiting access to abortion, and legislatures have done a great deal to shape the law of abortion within the constraints of the Court's decisions. The issue also underlines the role of chief executives. Governors in some states have encouraged restrictions on abortion, while other governors have prevented their enactment. The difference in the actions of the Bush and Clinton administrations underlines the president's importance in influencing federal responses to the Court's abortion decisions.

Impact on Society

Supreme Court decisions are directed at other public policy makers, establishing legal rules to govern policy decisions within government. But the ultimate significance of those decisions depends primarily on their impact outside government, on American society as a whole. The Court's rulings in labor law are important chiefly because of their potential effects on the relationship between employees and employers. Its decisions on sex discrimination are significant to the extent that they affect the status of women.

People who disapprove of the Supreme Court's policies often depict the Court as a very powerful force in American society. Republican presidential candidate Pat Buchanan said in 1996 that "by redefining individual rights as it wished, the court has centralized control over virtually every moral, political, social and economic issue in this country."[24] One scholar concluded that "clearance rates for violent crime would be several percentage points higher without *Miranda,* with the result that each year police would solve an additional 100,000-plus violent crimes."[25] And the Court's decisions on school religious observances are viewed by many people as having fundamental and highly unfortunate effects. North Carolina senator Jesse Helms said that "I think it is possible to pinpoint when the decline of this country really began"—with "the lawsuit that resulted in the first Supreme Court decision banning prayer. Since that time, America has been on the slippery slope. Morality has been all but forgotten."[26]

By no means does everyone see the Court as holding such enormous power; some commentators argue that it has little capacity to produce significant change in society. In 1991 one scholar advised liberals not to expend energy and resources opposing the confirmation of Clarence Thomas to the Court, because the Court does not have a major effect on achievement of liberal social reform.[27] But interest groups do devote considerable energy to the Court, and the mass media give considerable attention to it. These choices reflect a widely shared belief that the Court's decisions *are* important to American society. To what extent is this belief accurate?

A General View

Any government policy can have a wide range of effects on society, including some that are indirect and quite unexpected. Certainly this is true of Supreme Court decisions. Often it is difficult to distinguish between the Court's impact and that of other forces contributing to the same result. For this reason it is seldom possible to make firm judgments about the effects of the Supreme Court on society.

Still, there is reason to be skeptical about judgments that the Court has a fundamental impact on American society. In reality, the effects of Supreme Court policies on society are constrained a great deal by the context in which those policies operate.

Part of that context is governmental. As we have seen, the impact of decisions is often narrowed by other policy makers who fail to implement them fully or who take other action to limit them. For example, Senator Helms's statement appears to reflect an assumption that public schools ended prayer and Bible-reading exercises after the Supreme Court prohibited those practices, but in fact they remained widespread.

More broadly, the Court is seldom the only government agency that deals with a particular set of issues. Rather, in most areas the Court is one policy maker among many that render decisions and undertake initiatives. In environmental policy, for instance, Congress sets the basic legal rules, administrative agencies elaborate on these rules and apply them to specific cases, and lower courts resolve most disagreements over agency decisions. The Court's participation is limited to resolving a few of the legal questions that arise in the lower courts. The Court can still have considerable impact, but it can hardly determine the character of environmental policy by itself.

The Court's policies also operate within a context of nongovernmental action. Even the direct impact of most decisions depends largely on the responses of people outside government. Especially important are the actions of people and institutions that the Court gives greater freedom. These beneficiaries of the Court's policies may not take full advantage of the freedom that the Court provides them. One reason is that they may not be aware of favorable decisions. But even those who know about such decisions do not always act on them. For example, welfare recipients may not insist on their procedural rights because they do not want to alienate officials who hold power over them. A 1996 decision struck down state prohibitions on advertising of liquor prices,[28] but some store owners may decide against advertising prices because it does not seem profitable to compete on the basis of price.

The broad impact of Supreme Court decisions on society is also limited by nongovernmental forces. Phenomena such as the crime rate and the quality of education are affected by family socialization, the mass media, and the economy. Those forces are likely to exert a much stronger impact on the propensity to commit crimes or the performance of students than does a Supreme Court policy. Moreover, any effects that the Court does have operate within the context of these forces. This limitation is common to all public policies, no matter which branch issues them. But the Supreme Court is in an especially weak position, because it has little control over the behavior of the private sector and because it seldom makes comprehensive policy in a particular area.

Despite all these limitations, Supreme Court decisions can and do have a significant effect on society. Frequently their direct impact is considerable, because they help to determine the scope and content of government action on an issue. The Court plays a part in shaping federal policy on matters ranging from mergers of businesses to criminal justice. By doing so, the Court may have a hand in shaping important social phenomena. To take two examples that were discussed earlier, the effects of the Court's decisions on the hiring of replacement workers for strikers and on government regulation of campaign finance have been quite substantial. The Court's 1995 invalidation of state-imposed term limits for members of Congress will affect the course of national government unless and until term limits are adopted in another fashion, and its 1997 decisions upholding state prohibitions of doctor-assisted suicide are likely to have a fundamental impact on some people's lives. While it would be a mistake to regard the Court as all-important, it would also be a mistake to accept Dr. Jack Kevorkian's judgment that "what the Supreme Court does is irrelevant." [29]

Some Areas of Court Activity

We can gain a better sense of the Court's impact on society and the forces that determine that impact by looking at a few areas of the Court's activity. These examples demonstrate that the Court's impact is complex, highly variable, and sometimes quite difficult to measure.

Abortion. Prior to the Court's 1973 decisions in *Roe v. Wade* and *Doe v. Bolton,* two-thirds of the states allowed abortion only under quite limited circumstances, and all but four states had very substantial restrictions. With its decisions the Court disallowed nearly all significant legal restrictions on abortion. By the best estimates, there are now about 1.5 million legal abortions each year. In light of the sequence of events, it seems reasonable to conclude that the Court is responsible for the performance of large numbers of legal abortions. But the reality is more complicated, and it is impossible to assess the Court's impact with any precision. [30]

As Figure 1 shows, the number of legal abortions increased by about 150 percent between 1972 and 1979. This massive change suggests that the Court made a great deal of difference. But the rate of increase was actually greater between 1969 and 1972. That increase reflected changes in state laws before and during that period, as some states relaxed their general prohibitions of abortion and a few eliminated most restrictions. If the Court had never handed down *Roe v. Wade,* it is likely that the abortion rate would have grown further as a result of increasing numbers of abortions in the states that already allowed it and continuing change in state laws. But it is

Figure 1. Estimated Number of Legal Abortions and Related Government Policy Actions, 1966–1992

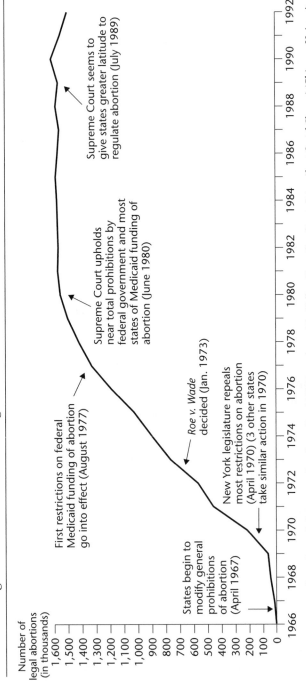

Sources: Estimated numbers of abortions taken from Gerald N. Rosenberg, *The Hollow Hope: Can Courts Bring About Social Change?* (Chicago: University of Chicago Press, 1991), 180 (for 1968–1985); and Stanley K. Henshaw and Jennifer Van Vort, "Abortion Services in the United States, 1991 and 1992," *Family Planning Perspectives* 26 (May–June 1994): 101 (for 1986–1992).

impossible to know how state laws would have evolved if the Court had not intervened. For that reason, there is need for considerable caution in assessing the Court's effects on the abortion rate.

In this area, as in others, the extent of the Court's impact reflects action by other individuals and institutions. Of course, the number of abortions depends largely on women's choices whether to seek them. But also important is the ability of women who want abortions to obtain them.[31] About two-thirds of all abortions occur in clinics, in part because most hospitals do not perform abortions. Urban areas generally have clinics that perform abortions, but many rural areas lack such clinics. The limited number of facilities that perform abortions in some areas and some states reflects personal beliefs about abortion on the part of potential providers as well as restrictive laws and pressures against providing abortions, ranging from disapproval in the local community to threatened and actual violence. Decisions by the federal government and most states not to fund abortions through Medicaid under most circumstances have affected the availability of abortions to low-income women. These conditions help to explain interstate variation in abortion rates and the absence of further increases in the number of legal abortions since 1979, as indicated in Figure 1.

In the 1980s and early 1990s, Presidents Reagan and Bush adopted some new restrictions on abortion and the Court indicated that it was more willing to accept restrictions. Yet the abortion rate remained stable. Actions by the president and Court may have had an effect, but if so that effect was small or counterbalanced by other developments.

Roe v. Wade has had an unexpected and important political impact. The decision greatly strengthened the developing movement against legalized abortion by creating a perceived need for action and a target to attack. By the same token, the groups that had sought legalization of abortion found it difficult to maintain their strength after their major goal had been accomplished. As a result, opponents of legalized abortion had an advantage for several years in influencing elections and legislation. This advantage helped to bring about the array of federal and state restrictions on abortion that followed *Roe*. And the Court at least accelerated the development of a situation in which abortion is a major issue in national politics, one that affects government action on a variety of other issues.

Political Dissent. The Supreme Court often reviews government actions that punish people for making unpopular political statements. The Court has a mixed record in these cases, but over the last four decades it has done much to protect political dissenters from censorship and punishment. In the 1960s it struck down a number of government policies aimed at people with Communist associations. During the Vietnam War it issued several decisions that shielded opponents of official U.S. policy from punishment for their activities. In the past decade it has ruled that people cannot be denied government contracts because they criticized government officials and that they cannot be given criminal penalties for burning the flag as a political statement.

The impact of these decisions is difficult to measure, but undoubtedly the Court has made some difference. For instance, its protection of opponents of the war in Vietnam—particularly its decisions disallowing retaliation by the Selective Service System against antiwar protesters[32]—probably encouraged the open expression of dissent.

Yet there is no evidence that the Court has brought about a massive increase in the level of political dissent in the United States. One reason is the Court's own mixed and incomplete support for political dissent. But also important are conditions that lie primarily in the private sector. For one thing, most people simply do not hold highly unpopular views about political matters that they wish to express; for that reason, their freedom to express such views makes no difference to them.

Further, people realize that the Court cannot prevent all the negative consequences of political dissent. People may refrain from saying what they think because they fear that friends and neighbors will ostracize them, community groups will attack them, customers will withdraw their patronage, or employers will fire them. A player in the National Basketball Association who decided on religious grounds not to stand for the national anthem was suspended by the league until he backed down.[33] Even worse consequences may befall those who express unpopular views. Opponents of government-sponsored religious activities frequently experience property damage, harassment, and death threats. The black parents and local leaders who fought against inadequate and segregated schools in the South often had to deal with severe economic pressures and violence. It is not surprising that people often choose to remain silent rather than face such consequences. This result underlines the limits on the Court's ability to change basic social realities.

Racial Equality

In debates over the Supreme Court's efficacy, considerable emphasis is given to its impact on racial equality. That emphasis is appropriate in light of the Court's heavy involvement in this field and the central importance of racial equality as an issue in American society.

The Court gave strong and increasing support to racial equality between the 1940s and 1960s. It attacked discrimination in areas such as education and voting, and it also sought to protect the civil rights movement from legal attack in the South. The Court took a more mixed position in the 1970s, but in that decade it endorsed strong remedies for school segregation and upheld the use of affirmative action programs in education and employment.

The implicit goal of these decisions was improvement in the status of black Americans. To what extent have the Court's policies achieved that goal?

Change in Status. The process of effecting change in the situation of black Americans has been complex and ambiguous. Understandably, there is considerable disagreement about how much change has actually occurred. Perhaps the best generalization is that progress has varied among the major areas of racial inequality.

Politically, racial barriers to black voting in the South were overcome. The growth in black voting and changes in racial attitudes have led to large increases in the number of black elected officials—from about 300 in 1965 to 8,000 in 1993.[34] Growth in black political power is also reflected in the growing willingness of white officials to respond to black concerns.

Socially, the segregation of American life has broken down to a limited degree. Segregation of hotels and restaurants, once standard practice in much of the country, is now unusual. Legally segregated school systems no longer exist in the Deep South and the border states, but the level of actual segregation remains substantial and has increased somewhat since the 1970s.[35] Continuing racial segregation in schools reflects the high level of housing segregation, which has declined little since 1970.[36]

Economically, the overall status of black citizens has improved significantly, but there remains considerable inequality. In 1994 the median annual income for black families was 62 percent of the median for whites. In the same year 43 percent of black children lived in poverty, compared with 16 percent for whites.[37] Employment discrimination has declined, probably a great deal, but a 1991 study in Chicago and Washington, D.C., demonstrated vividly that it has not disappeared.[38]

The Court's Role. Because progress toward racial equality has been limited, it is clear that the most optimistic expectations of the Supreme Court have not been realized. Federal judge Robert Carter, who was a lawyer with the NAACP Legal Defense Fund in 1954, recalled that when the Court decided *Brown v. Board of Education,* "I really thought that was it, the end of the civil rights struggle." It did not take long for him to realize that he had been wrong.[39]

Of the progress toward racial equality that *has* occurred, how much can be ascribed to the Supreme Court? Certainly there have been other important sources for the change that has occurred. Particularly during the 1960s, Congress and the federal executive branch made significant contributions to the achievement of equal rights; so have many state and local governments. Nongovernmental forces for change include the mass media and, more important, the civil rights movement itself.

The limits of the Court's own impact are clear in education and voting, the areas in which it has been most active. Despite *Brown v. Board of Education* (1954), school segregation in the Deep South did not break down until the Civil Rights Act of 1964 provided financial inducements for desegregation. The Court's decisions eliminated some barriers to black voting, but those decisions did not bring about full access to the ballot box in the South. That access came after the Voting Rights Act of 1965 created administrative mechanisms for effective enforcement of the right to vote. In both areas the Johnson administration's vigorous use of its enforcement powers under these laws was also important.

Because constitutional protections do not apply directly to private discrimination, the Court could do little by itself to attack discrimination in employment and housing. Instead, the initiative has come primarily from the other branches: Congress passed statutes mandating equal treatment, and the executive branch has enforced them. But the Court has given important interpretations to these laws; until the late 1980s it generally gave them expansive interpretations that enhanced their potential impact. There is evidence that the federal laws against employment discrimination have had a significant impact on the economic status of black citizens; this impact can be ascribed primarily to the executive and legislative branches, but the Court might be given a small degree of responsibility for it.

It is difficult to ascertain whether the Court's early civil rights decisions helped to spur passage of federal legislation in this area and strengthened the civil rights movement. In his careful analysis of this issue, Gerald Rosenberg concluded that the Court's impact in both respects was minimal,[40] but a case can be made that the Court actually had significant impact.

The development of a mass civil rights movement in the South was probably inevitable, and the Supreme Court was hardly the major force contributing to its development. But the Court may have speeded the movement's growth. Its decisions in education and other areas created hope for change and established rights to be vindicated by political action. This is particularly true of the *Brown* decision, which had considerable symbolic importance for some people.[41] The Court's protection of the civil rights movement itself did not eliminate the harassment of civil rights groups in the South or the violence against their members, but the Court helped to ensure that the movement would be able to withstand the pressures placed on it.

The series of civil rights laws adopted from 1957 on also may owe something to the Court. In education and voting, the Court initiated government action against discrimination and helped to create expectations that Congress and the executive branch were pressed to fulfill. It is true that congressional action was most directly responsible for bringing about school desegregation in the Deep South. But if the Court had not issued the *Brown* decision, Congress might have had less impetus to act against segregation at all.

In the last decade, a more conservative Court has been less favorable to the goals of civil rights groups. In a series of decisions it gave narrow interpretations to statutes prohibiting employment discrimination. It has set very high standards for governments that seek to justify affirmative action programs for minority-owned businesses or the design of legislative districts to facilitate the election of black candidates.

It is possible that this new wave of decisions will have a significant impact on the status of black citizens, but such an impact seems unlikely. Congress has overturned many of the Court's narrow interpretations of civil rights statutes. It is uncertain whether legislative districting has much impact on the political power of black citizens. If extended to other areas, the Court's limiting of affirmative action ultimately might have a marked effect, but such an impact is not guaranteed.

An Assessment. The issue of racial equality illustrates both the strengths and limitations of government in achieving societal change. Public policy has helped to bring about significant reductions in the disadvantages of black Americans. But these disadvantages have hardly disappeared, and even a stronger government commitment to equality could not have eliminated them altogether.

For the Supreme Court specifically, the assessment is also mixed. The Court has had little direct impact on discrimination in the private sector. Even in the public sector, it has been weak in the enforcement of rights. But it has helped to initiate and support processes of change, and its members probably can take some credit for progress toward racial equality. If the Court's effects have been far more limited than many people had hoped, the Court has contributed to significant social change.

Conclusion: The Court, Public Policy, and Society

It is now possible to reach some general conclusions about the role of the Supreme Court as a public policy maker. As this [essay suggests], that role is fundamentally limited in some respects but still quite important.

The most obvious limitation on the Court's role is that it addresses only a small number of issues. In many policy areas, the Court rarely makes decisions. To take the most important example, the Court is a minor participant in the making of foreign policy. And it plays only a small part in many fields of significant judicial activity, such as contract law and family relations.

Even in its areas of specialization, the Court intervenes in the policy-making process only in limited ways. It makes decisions on a small sample of the issues that affect the rights of criminal defendants or freedom of expression. And the Court has been cautious about substituting its judgment for that of Congress and the president.

When the Court does intervene, its impact is often reduced by the actions of other institutions and individuals. A ruling that public schools must eliminate organized prayers does not guarantee that those observances will disappear. Efforts to broaden freedom of expression may be stymied by conditions in society that the Court cannot influence.

These limitations must be balanced against the Court's considerable strengths. Certainly a great many Supreme Court decisions have significant direct effects. Antitrust decisions determine whether companies can merge. School desegregation decisions determine the schools that students attend. Interpretations of the Voting Rights Act shape the course of local politics. The effects of capital punishment decisions are literally matters of life and death for some people.

The Court also helps to shape political and social change. Its partial opposition to government regulation of private business was ultimately overcome, but the Court slowed a fundamental change in the role of government. If *Roe v. Wade* was not as consequential as most people think, it *has* been the focus of a major national debate and struggle for more than two decades. The Court's decisions have not brought about racial equality, even in conjunction with other forces, but they have helped to spur changes in race relations.

As the examples of abortion and civil rights suggest, the Court is perhaps most important in creating conditions for action by others. Its decisions put issues on the national agenda so that other policy makers and the general public consider them. The Court is not highly effective in enforcing rights, but it often legitimates efforts to achieve them and thus provides the impetus for people to take legal and political action. Its decisions affect the positions of interest groups and social movements, strengthening some and weakening others.

The Supreme Court, then, is neither all-powerful nor insignificant. Rather, it is one of many public and private institutions that shape American society in significant ways. That is a more limited role than some have claimed for the Court. But the role that the Court does play is an extraordinary one for a single small body that possesses little tangible power. In this sense, perhaps more than any other, the Supreme Court is a remarkable institution.

NOTES

1. *Engel v. Vitale* (1962); *Abington School District v. Schempp* (1963).

2. *Jaffree v. Board of School Commissioners*, 554 F. Supp. 1104, 1128 (S.D. Alab. 1983).

3. Edward Keynes, with Randall K. Miller, *The Court vs. Congress: Prayer, Busing, and Abortion* (Durham, N.C.: Duke University Press, 1989), 174–205.

4. William Booth, "Crusade for Prayer in School Wins Converts," *Washington Post*, April 1, 1994, A1, A4; Pamela Coyle, "Prayer Pendulum," *American Bar Association Journal*, January 1995, 62–66.

5. Katharine Q. Seelye, "Religion Amendment Is Introduced," *New York Times*, May 9, 1997, A14.

6. William N. Eskridge, Jr., "Overriding Supreme Court Statutory Interpretation Decisions," *Yale Law Journal* 101 (November 1991): 338; updating through 1996 is from Lori Hausegger and Lawrence Baum, "Behind the Scenes: The Supreme Court and Congress in Statutory Interpretation," in *Great Theater: The American Congress in the 1990s*, ed. Herbert F. Weisberg and Samuel C. Patterson (New York: Cambridge University Press, 1998).

7. Beth M. Henschen and Edward I. Sidlow, "The Supreme Court and the Congressional Agenda-Setting Process" (Paper presented at the annual meeting of the Midwest Political Science Association, Chicago, April 1988); Michael E. Solimine and James L. Walker, "The Next Word: Congressional Response to Supreme Court Statutory Decisions," *Temple Law Review* 65 (1992): 425–458; R. Shep Melnick, *Between the Lines: Interpreting Welfare Rights* (Washington, D.C.: Brookings Institution, 1994), 261–264.

8. Eskridge, "Overriding Statutory Decisions," 348, 351, 359–367.

9. Sam Fulwood III, "House Again Approves Ban on Burning American Flag," *Los Angeles Times,* June 13, 1997, A27.

10. Louis Fisher, "The Legislative Veto: Invalidated, It Survives," *Law and Contemporary Problems* 56 (Autumn 1993): 273–292.

11. Dean L. Yarwood and Bradley C. Canon, "On the Supreme Court's Annual Trek to the Capitol," *Judicature* 63 (February 1980): 324.

12. U.S. Congress, House, *Congressional Record,* 89th Cong., 1st sess., 1965, 111, pt. 4, 5275. See John R. Schmidhauser and Larry L. Berg, *The Supreme Court and Congress: Conflict and Interaction, 1945–1968* (New York: Free Press, 1972), 8–12.

13. "The President's Radio Address," *Weekly Compilation of Presidential Documents* 31 (May 8, 1995): 735.

14. *Chamber of Commerce of the United States v. Reich* (D.C. Cir. 1996).

15. Samuel Krislov, *The Supreme Court in the Political Process* (New York: Macmillan, 1965), 140.

16. *Arkansas Term Limits v. Donovan* (1996, 1997).

17. The decisions were, respectively, *Davis v. Michigan Department of Treasury* (1989); *Harper v. Virginia Department of Taxation* (1993); *Reich v. Collins* (1994); and *Harper v. Virginia Department of Taxation* (Va. Sup. Ct. 1995).

18. Bureau of Justice Statistics, *Justice Expenditure and Employment, 1990* (Washington, D.C.: U.S. Department of Justice, 1992), 3.

19. Richard A. Posner, *The Federal Courts: Challenge and Reform* (Cambridge, Mass.: Harvard University Press, 1996), 326.

20. See William N. Eskridge, Jr., "Reneging on History? Playing the Court/Congress/President Civil Rights Game," *California Law Review* 79 (May 1991): 613–684.

21. *Landgraf v. USI Film Products* (1994); *Rivers v. Roadway Express* (1994).

22. Glen A. Halva-Neubauer, "The States after *Roe:* No 'Paper Tigers,' " in *Understanding the New Politics of Abortion,* ed. Malcolm L. Goggin (Newbury Park, Calif.: Sage Publications, 1993), 167–189.

23. The decision was *Bray v. Alexandria Women's Health Clinic* (1993).

24. From remarks at the Heritage Foundation, Washington, D.C., January 29, 1996 (transcript from Federal Document Clearing House).

25. Paul G. Cassell, "True Confessions About *Miranda's* Legacy," *Legal Times,* July 22, 1996, 21.

26. U.S. Congress, Senate, *Congressional Record,* daily ed., 103d Congress, 2d session, February 3, 1994, S725.

27. Gerald N. Rosenberg, "What the Court Can't Do," *New York Times,* September 22, 1991, 17. See also Rosenberg, *The Hollow Hope: Can Courts Bring about Social Change?* (Chicago: University of Chicago Press, 1991); and Posner, *The Federal Courts,* 325–327.

28. *44 Liquormart, Inc. v. Rhode Island* (1996).

29. "Kevorkian Wants No Part of Supreme Court 'Kooks,'" *Washington Post,* January 6, 1997, A6.

30. This discussion of abortion is based in part on Rosenberg, *The Hollow Hope,* 175–201; and Matthew E. Wetstein, "The Abortion Rate Paradox: The Impact of National Policy Change on Abortion Rates," *Social Science Quarterly* 76 (September 1995): 607–618.

31. Information on facilities performing abortions is from Stanley K. Henshaw, "Factors Hindering Access to Abortion Services," *Family Planning Perspectives* 27 (March 1995): 54–59, 87.

32. *Oestereich v. Selective Service System* (1968); *Gutknecht v. United States* (1970).

33. Jack McCallum, "Oh Say Should We Sing?" *Sports Illustrated,* March 25, 1996, 51–52, 54.

34. Gerald David Jaynes and Robin M. Williams, Jr., *A Common Destiny: Blacks and American Society* (Washington, D.C.: National Academy Press, 1989), 238; U.S. Bureau of the Census, *Statistical Abstract of the United States, 1996* (Washington, D.C.: Government Printing Office, 1996), 284.

35. Peter Applebome, "Schools See Re-Emergence of 'Separate but Equal,'" *New York Times,* April 8, 1997, A8. See also Gary Orfield, Susan E. Eaton, and the Harvard Project on School Desegregation, *Dismantling Desegregation: The Quiet Reversal of* Brown v. Board of Education (New York: New Press, 1996).

36. Douglas S. Massey and Nancy A. Denton, *American Apartheid: Segregation and the Making of the Underclass* (Cambridge, Mass.: Harvard University Press, 1993).

37. Bureau of the Census, *Statistical Abstract 1996,* 461, 472.

38. Margery Austin Turner, Michael Fix, and Raymond J. Struyk, *Opportunities Denied, Opportunities Diminished: Discrimination in Hiring* (Washington, D.C.: Urban Institute, 1991).

39. Ron Grossman and Charles Leroux, "Brown vs. Segregation: Landmark Case at 40," *Chicago Tribune,* May 15, 1994, sec. 1, 1.

40. Rosenberg, *The Hollow Hope,* 107–156.

41. Jesse H. Choper, *Judicial Review and the National Political Process* (Chicago: University of Chicago Press, 1980), 93–94; and Bradley C. Canon, "The Supreme Court as a Cheerleader in Politico-Moral Disputes," *Journal of Politics* 54 (August 1992): 637–653.

9-3

Why It's Getting Harder to Appoint Judges

Stuart Taylor Jr.

Article III of the Constitution provides that judges are nominated by the president and confirmed by the Senate. By assigning the two branches a role in appointing judges, the Constitution attached the federal judiciary to the policy preferences of both—and thus opened up the potential for conflict. During the era of divided party control of these political institutions, judicial appointments have emerged as among the most hard-fought issues. Few political observers can recall the judicial appointment process being so caught up in partisan warfare as have recent dealings between Bill Clinton and the Republican Senate. The result, court observer Stuart Taylor explains below, is record-high vacancy rates throughout the federal judiciary.

IT'S TAKING longer and longer—and getting harder and harder—to fill vacancies on the federal courts. Some new numbers tell part of the story: The average time for Senate action on judicial nominations rose from 38 days in 1977–78 (when both the presidency and the Senate majority were Democratic) to 144 days in 1987–88 (when a Republican President faced a Democratic Senate) and 201 days in 1997–98 (when a Democratic President faced a Republican Senate), according to a bipartisan group called Citizens for Independent Courts.

The creeping partisan paralysis was illustrated on Sept. 21 by the strange spectacle of Senate Democrats filibustering one of President Clinton's judicial nominees—Ted Stewart, a conservative Republican from Utah. Senate Judiciary Committee Chairman Orrin G. Hatch, R-Utah, had forced Clinton to nominate Stewart by putting a virtual freeze on all other nominees for months. The filibuster was provoked by the efforts of Republican leaders to push Stewart ahead of long-languishing nominees favored by Democrats.

Republicans have carried the partisan stalling of judicial confirmations to new lengths, approving only 17 nominees so far this year, while refusing to allow up-or-down votes on liberal Clinton nominees—such as Richard A. Paez, who has been waiting since January 1996.

But Democrats also share the blame. In demonizing Robert H. Bork, Clarence Thomas, and other conservative Republican nominees, they triggered the downward spiral of partisanship and payback that have plagued the nomination process.

No matter who is President, the next vacancy on the Supreme Court seems likely to provoke a partisan donnybrook. With the court split 5-to-4 on such major issues as racial preferences, states' rights, and state aid to religious schools, neither Republicans nor Democrats in the Senate are likely to unilaterally disarm.

Gone are the days when the Senate would confirm a Supreme Court Justice within hours of the nomination, as it did in 1922 with George Sutherland, or confirm a Chief Justice without asking the nominee any questions, as it did in 1953 with Earl Warren. Almost unimaginable is the unanimity that the court displayed in 1954—and for years thereafter in politically explosive decisions—when it struck down school segregation.

Alarmed by the descent into rancorous partisan gridlock, Citizens for Independent Courts—co-chaired by prominent Democratic lawyer Lloyd N. Cutler and former Rep. Mickey Edwards, R-Okla.—called upon Senators and Presidents alike on September 22 to restrain their partisanship and expedite both nominations (which have been slower under President Clinton than ever before) and Senate action. The gridlock not only impedes the administration of justice in the courts but also deepens public cynicism about the ability of Congress and the President to work together.

Why shouldn't the public be cynical? Here's what Senate Majority Leader Trent Lott, R-Miss., had to say in the face of pleas from respected figures, including Chief Justice William H. Rehnquist (in 1997), for more federal judges: "There are not a lot of people (in our states) saying: Give us more federal judges. . . . I am trying to move this thing along, but getting more federal judges is not what I came here to do."

The efforts of Cutler, Edwards, and their colleagues may do some good. But until one party wins both the presidency and a filibuster-proof majority in the Senate, they are fighting an uphill battle. The reason is a fact of modern life that will not soon change: Senators not of the President's political party know that it's a good bet that his nominees will rule in ways that they deplore, in a wide range of politically charged cases.

When court-watchers hear the vote count in a big Supreme Court or federal appeals court decision, they can often guess who was on which side. And in the appellate courts, too, the division is often along party lines, or close to it. (On the Supreme Court, two of the four more-liberal Justices—John Paul Stevens and David H. Souter—were named by Republican Presidents; conservatives vow not to let that happen again.)

In March, for example, when the U.S. Court of Appeals for the 4th Circuit (based in Richmond, Va.) struck down the Violence Against Women Act as an unconstitutional invasion by Congress of the states' domain, all seven judges in the majority were Republican appointees; all four dissenters were Democratic appointees. Such divisions reflect the increasing politicization of the law itself. As judges have extended their powers ever deeper into the realm of politics, any semblance of consensus on what were once called neutral principles of law has disintegrated.

Can universities use racial preferences in admissions? Must they, to achieve racial balance? Can states require parental notification before minors have abortions? Can states fund tuition vouchers to help poor families choose religious or secular private schools? Can states that violate federal minimum-wage laws be sued for damages? Can the Boy Scouts of America bar avowed homosexuals from serving as scoutmasters? The answers to such questions depend less on the words of the Constitution than on the political and moral values of the people appointed to the federal bench, including those on the lower courts. And, increasingly, the answers depend on whether the President who picks them is a Democrat or a Republican.

This has been true for a long time. But it seems to be getting truer. The legal opinions of many judges—especially strong liberals and conservatives—line up with striking regularity with the policy positions of the political parties from whence they came.

Some liberal judges, who rhapsodize about the need to protect freedom of speech when the issue is government subsidies for sexually explicit art, embrace the use of "harassment" laws to punish speech offensive to racial minorities or women, and champion governmental discrimination against religious speech. And some conservative judges, who have preached "judicial restraint" and fidelity to the plain text and original meaning of the Constitution, increasingly compromise their principles in an absolutist zeal to strike down all racial preferences or to expand states' rights. . . .

Judicial legislation in the guise of constitutional interpretation used to be mainly a liberal thing. But conservatives—perhaps realizing that judicial restraint is not a winning strategy in an ideological war—have responded in kind. And as precedents that bend the meaning of the Constitution pile up, it becomes harder to tell the difference between constitutional interpretation and judicial legislation.

However one apportions blame, the descent of legal reasoning into the vortex of political bickering is a fact of life. So it's only natural that liberal groups pressure Clinton to nominate liberals, and conservatives pressure Senate Republicans to stop them, or at least stall them. . . . The stalling of judicial appointments threatens to get worse, not better, as long as we have divided government.

What is to be done? Confronted with a hostile Senate, any President who wants his or her judicial nominees confirmed will have to compromise. He or she will have to do what Clinton has done to a limited degree: find nominees without strong political or ideological views. This may, unfortunately, keep some of our best legal minds off the bench. People who have thought long and hard about the biggest legal-political issues have often written or said things offensive either to liberals or to conservatives—sometimes both.

But pressure for Presidents to shun ideological crusaders is not all bad. Given the lack of consensus about where law leaves off and politics begin, we are better off with judges and Justices who are reluctant to impose their own political and moral values on the body politic, deferential to the primacy of elected officials in making broad legislative choices, sensitive to competing arguments, and suspicious of absolutes and extremes. In short, moderate centrists. That may seem boring to those who want judges to have grand dreams, and to do grand things. But we've had enough judicial grandiosity for a while. Your grand dream may be my nightmare, and vice versa.

Not all moderates are muddled, and not all centrists are mediocre. The best are sensitive to the wisdom of Learned Hand, one of our greatest judges, who said in 1944: "The spirit of liberty is the spirit which is not too sure that it is right."

10

Public Opinion

The relationship between public opinion and public policy is a controversial subject, on both normative and empirical grounds. The normative question is, Should public opinion direct public policy? The empirical question is, Does public opinion direct public policy?

James Madison and other Framers of the Constitution were wary of public opinion. In their view, many state legislatures were too susceptible to its influence. Creating a stronger national government, they hoped, would put greater distance between the general public and policymakers. Within the national government, the power of the one institution directly elected by the people—the House of Representatives—would be checked by institutions that were not directly elected—the Senate, the presidency, and the courts. By popular demand, the Senate eventually became subject to direct election, as did the president for all practical purposes. Today, it is generally assumed that public opinion ought to influence government officials.

Even if one accepts that public opinion should shape public policy, the nature and extent of its influence remains in question. Public opinion on a particular policy issue may not exist. Relatively few issues are subject to coverage and debate in campaigns and in the media, so only a few issues generate real opinions among the general public. Other issues create deeply divided opinions that provide mixed signals to policy makers. Still other issues generate intense opinion among a few interested groups but leave others indifferent, creating strong signals that are deeply biased. Thus in practice the relationship between public opinion and public policy varies across issues and over time. These complexities of democracy are demonstrated in the following essays.

10-1

Analyzing and Interpreting Polls

Herbert Asher

Public opinion polls have gained a prominent place in modern American politics. Polls themselves often are newsworthy, particularly during campaigns and times of political crisis. Unfortunately, as Herbert Asher shows in the following essay, polls are open to misinterpretation and misuse. The wording of questions, the construction of a sample, the choice of items to analyze and report, the use of surveys to measure trends, and the examination of subsets of respondents all pose problems of interpretation. Every consumer of polling information must understand these issues to properly use the information polls provide.

. . . INTERPRETING A POLL is more an art than a science, even though statistical analysis of poll data is central to the enterprise. An investigator examining poll results has tremendous leeway in deciding which items to analyze, which sample subsets or breakdowns to present, and how to interpret the statistical results. Take as an example a poll with three items that measure attitudes toward arms control negotiations. The investigator may construct an index from these three items. . . . Or the investigator may emphasize the results from one question, perhaps because of space and time constraints and the desire to keep matters simple, or because those particular results best support the analyst's own policy preferences. The investigator may examine results from the entire sample and ignore subgroups whose responses deviate from the overall pattern. Again time and space limitations or the investigator's own preferences may influence these choices. Finally, two investigators may interpret identical poll results in sharply different ways depending on the perspectives and values they bring to their data analysis; the glass may indeed be half full or half empty.

As the preceding example suggests, the analysis and interpretation of data entail a high degree of subjectivity and judgment. Subjectivity in this

Originally published in Herbert Asher, *Polling and the Public: What Every Citizen Should Know,* 4th edition (Washington, D.C.: CQ Press, 1998), pp. 141–169.

context does not mean deliberate bias or distortion, but simply professional judgments about the importance and relevance of information. Certainly, news organizations' interpretations of their polls are generally done in the least subjective and unbiased fashion. But biases can slip in—sometimes unintentionally, sometimes deliberately—when, for example, an organization has sponsored a poll to promote a particular position. Because this final phase of polling is likely to have the most direct influence on public opinion, this chapter includes several case studies to illustrate the judgmental aspects of analyzing and interpreting poll results.

Choosing Items to Analyze

Many public opinion surveys deal with multifaceted, complex issues. For example, a researcher querying Americans about their attitudes toward tax reform might find initially that they overwhelmingly favor a fairer tax system. But if respondents are asked about specific aspects of tax reform, their answers may reflect high levels of confusion, indifference, or opposition. And depending upon which items the researcher chooses to emphasize, the report might convey support, indifference, or opposition toward tax reform. American foreign policy in the Middle East is another highly complex subject that can elicit divergent reactions from Americans depending on which aspects of the policy they are questioned about.

Some surveys go into great depth on a topic through multiple items constructed to measure its various facets. The problem for an investigator in this case becomes one of deciding which results to report. Moreover, even though an extensive analysis is conducted, the media might publicize only an abbreviated version of it. In such a case the consumer of the poll results is at the mercy of the media to portray accurately the overall study. Groups or organizations that sponsor polls to demonstrate support for a particular position or policy option often disseminate results in a selective fashion which enables them to put the organization and its policies in a favorable light.

In contrast with in-depth surveys on a topic, *omnibus surveys* are superficial in their treatment of particular topics because of the need to cover many subjects in the same survey. Here the problem for an investigator becomes one of ensuring that the few questions employed to study a specific topic really do justice to the substance and complexity of that topic. It is left to the consumer of both kinds of polls to judge whether they receive the central information on a topic or whether other items might legitimately yield different substantive results.

The issue of prayer in public schools is a good example of how public opinion polling on a topic can be incomplete and potentially misleading. Typically, pollsters ask Americans whether they support a constitutional amendment that would permit voluntary prayer in public schools, and more than three-fourths of Americans respond that they would favor such an amendment. This question misses the mark. Voluntary prayer by individuals is in no way prohibited; the real issue is whether there will be *organized* voluntary prayer. But many pollsters do not include items that tap this aspect of the voluntary prayer issue. Will there be a common prayer? If so, who will compose it? Will someone lead the class in prayer? If so, who? Under what circumstances and when will the prayer be uttered? What about students who do not wish to participate or who prefer a different prayer?

The difficulty with both the in-depth poll and the omnibus survey is that the full set of items used to study a particular topic is usually not reported and thus the consumer cannot make informed judgments about whether the conclusions of the survey are valid. Recognizing this, individuals should take a skeptical view of claims by a corporate executive or an elected officeholder or even a friend that the polls demonstrate public support for or opposition to a particular position. The first question to ask is: What is the evidence cited to support the claim? From there one might examine the question wording, the response alternatives, the screening for nonattitudes, and the treatment of "don't know" responses. Then one might attempt the more difficult task of assessing whether the questions used to study the topic at hand were really optimal. Might other questions have been used? What aspects of the topic were not addressed? Finally, one might ponder whether different interpretations could be imposed on the data and whether alternative explanations could account for the reported patterns.

In evaluating poll results, there is always the temptation to seize upon those that support one's position and ignore those that do not. The problem is that one or two items cannot capture the full complexity of most issues. For example, a *Newsweek* poll conducted by the Gallup Organization in July 1986 asked a number of questions about sex laws and lifestyles. The poll included the following three items (Alpern 1986, 38):

> Do you approve or disapprove of the Supreme Court decision upholding a state law against certain sexual practices engaged in privately by con-

senting adult homosexuals? [This question was asked of the 73 percent who knew about the Supreme Court decision.]

Disapprove	47%
Approve	41%

In general, do you think that states should have the right to prohibit particular sexual practices conducted in private between consenting adult homosexuals?

No	57%
Yes	34%

Do you think homosexuality has become an accepted alternative lifestyle or not?

Yes	32%
No	61%
Don't know	7%

Note that the first two items tap citizens' attitudes toward the legal treatment of homosexuals, while the third addresses citizens' views of homosexuality as a lifestyle. Although differently focused, all three questions deal with aspects of gay life. It would not be surprising to see gay rights advocates cite the results of the first two questions as indicating support for their position. Opponents of gay rights would emphasize the results of the third question.

An Eyewitness News/*Daily News* poll of New York City residents conducted in February 1986 further illustrates how the selective use and analysis of survey questions can generate very different impressions of popular opinion on an issue. This poll asked a number of gay rights questions:

On another matter, would you say that New York City needs a gay rights law or not?

Yes, need gay rights law	39%
No, do not need gay rights law	54%
Don't know/no opinion	8%

On another matter, do you think it should be against the law for landlords or private employers to deny housing or a job to someone because that person is homosexual or do you think landlords and employers should be allowed to do that if they want to?

Yes, should be against law	49%
No, should not be against law	47%
Volunteered responses	
Should be law only for landlord	1%
Should be law only for employers	8%
Don't know/no opinion	3%

Although a definite majority of the respondents oppose a gay rights law in response to the first question, a plurality also believe that it should be illegal for landlords and employers to deny housing and jobs to persons because they are homosexual. Here the two questions both address the legal status of homosexuals, and it is clear which question gay rights activists and gay rights opponents would cite in support of their respective policy positions. It is not clear, however, which question is the better measure of public opinion. The first question is unsatisfactory because one does not know how respondents interpreted the scope of a gay rights law. Did they think it referred only to housing and job discrimination, or did they think it would go substantially beyond that? The second question is inadequate if it is viewed as equivalent to a gay rights law. Lumping housing and jobs together constitutes another flaw since citizens might have divergent views on these two aspects of gay rights.

Additional examples of the importance of item selection are based on polls of Americans' attitudes about the Iraqi invasion of Kuwait in 1990. Early in the Persian Gulf crisis, various survey organizations asked Americans, using different questions, how they felt about taking military action against Iraq. Not surprisingly, the organizations obtained different results.

Do you favor or oppose direct U.S. military action against Iraq at this time? (Gallup, August 3–4, 1990)

Favor	23%
Oppose	68%
Don't know/refused	9%

Do you agree or disagree that the U.S. should take all actions necessary, including the use of military force, to make sure that Iraq withdraws its forces from Kuwait? (ABC News/*Washington Post*, August 8, 1990)

Agree	66%
Disagree	33%
Don't know	1%

Would you approve or disapprove of using U.S. troops to force the Iraqis to leave Kuwait? (Gallup, August 9–12, 1990, taken from *Public Perspective*, September/October 1990, 13)

Approve	64%
Disapprove	36%

(I'm going to mention some things that may or may not happen in the Middle East and for each one, please tell me whether the U.S. should or should not take military action in connection with it). . . . If Iraq refuses to withdraw from Kuwait? (NBC News/ *Wall Street Journal*, August 18–19, 1990, taken from *Public Perspective*, September/October 1990, 13)

No military action	51%
Military action	49%

Note that the responses to these questions indicate varying levels of support for military action even though most of the questions were asked within two weeks of each other. The first question shows the most opposition to military action. This is easily explained: the question concerns military action *at this time*, an alternative that many Americans may have seen as premature until other means had been tried. The other three questions all indicate majority support for military action, although that support ranges from a bare majority to about two-thirds of all Americans. It is clear which question proponents and opponents of military action would cite to support their arguments.

Throughout the Persian Gulf crisis, public opinion was highly supportive of President Bush's policies; only in the period between October and December 1990 did support for the president's handling of the situation drop below 60 percent. For example, a November 1990 CBS News/*New York Times* poll showed the following patterns of response:

Do you approve or disapprove of the way George Bush is handling Iraq's invasion of Kuwait?

Approve	50%
Disapprove	41%
Don't know/NA	8%

Likewise, an ABC News/*Washington Post* poll in mid-November reported:

Do you approve or disapprove of the way George Bush is handling the situation caused by Iraq's invasion of Kuwait?

Approve	59%
Disapprove	36%
Don't know/NA	5%

Some opponents of the military buildup tried to use these and similar polls to demonstrate that support for the president's policies was decreasing, since earlier polls had indicated support levels in the 60–70 percent range. Fortunately, the *Washington Post* poll cited above asked respondents who disapproved of Bush's policy whether the president was moving too slowly or too quickly. It turned out that 44 percent of the disapprovers said "too slowly" and 37 percent "too quickly." Thus, a plurality of the disapprovers preferred more rapid action against Iraq—a result that provided little support for those critics of the president's policies who were arguing against a military solution.

Shortly before the outbreak of the war, the *Washington Post* conducted a survey of American attitudes about going to war with Iraq. To assess the effects of question wording, the *Post* split its sample in half and used two different versions of the same question followed by the identical follow-up question to each item.

Version 1

As you may know, the U.N. Security Council has authorized the use of force against Iraq if it doesn't withdraw from Kuwait by January 15. If Iraq does not withdraw from Kuwait, should the United States go to war against Iraq to force it out of Kuwait at some point after January 15 or not?

Go to war sometime after January 15	62%
No, do not go to war	32%

How long after January 15 should the United States wait for Iraq to withdraw from Kuwait before going to war to force it out?

Do not favor war at any point	32%
Immediately	18%
Less than one month	28%
1–3 months	8%
4 months or longer	2%

Version 2

The United Nations has passed a resolution authorizing the use of military force against Iraq if they do not withdraw their troops from Kuwait by January 15. If Iraq does not withdraw from Kuwait by then, do you think the United States should start military actions against Iraq, or should the United States wait longer to see if the trade embargo and economic sanctions work?

U.S. should start military actions	49%
U.S. should wait longer to see if sanctions work	47%

How long after January 15 should the United States wait for Iraq to withdraw from Kuwait before going to war to force it out?

U.S. should start military actions	49%

For those who would wait:

Less than a month	15%
1–3 months	17%
4 months or longer	9%

Morin (1991) points out how very different portraits of the American public can be painted by examining the two versions with and without the follow-up question. For example, version 1 shows 62 percent of Americans supporting war against Iraq, while version 2 shows only 49 percent. These different results stem from inclusion of the embargo and sanctions option in the second version. Thus it appears that version 2 gives a less militaristic depiction of the American public. Responses to the follow-up question, however, provide a different picture of the public. For example, the first version shows that 54 percent of Americans (18 + 28 + 8) favor going to war within three months. But the second version shows that 81 percent of Americans (49 + 15 + 17) favor war within three months. The point, of course, is that the availability of different items on a survey can generate differing descriptions of the public's preferences.

The importance of item selection is illustrated in a final example on the Gulf War from an April 3, 1991, ABC News/ *Washington Post* poll conducted just after the conflict. It included the following three questions:

> Do you approve or disapprove of the way that George Bush is handling the situation involving Iraqi rebels who are trying to overthrow Saddam Hussein?
>
> | | |
> |---|---|
> | Approve | 69% |
> | Disapprove | 24% |
> | Don't know | 7% |
>
> Please tell me if you agree or disagree with this statement: The United States should not have ended the war with Iraqi President Saddam Hussein still in power.
>
> | | |
> |---|---|
> | Agree | 55% |
> | Disagree | 40% |
> | Don't know | 5% |
>
> Do you think the United States should try to help rebels overthrow Hussein or not?
>
> | | |
> |---|---|
> | Yes | 45% |
> | No | 51% |
> | Don't know | 4% |

Note that the responses to the first item indicate overwhelming approval for the president. But if one analyzed the second question in isolation, one might conclude that a majority of Americans did not support the president and indeed wanted to restart the war against Saddam Hussein. But the third item shows that a majority of Americans oppose helping the rebels. The lesson of this and the previous examples is clear. Constructing an interpretation around any single survey item can generate a very inaccurate description of public opinion. Unfortunately, advocates of particular positions have many opportunities to use survey results selectively and misleadingly to advance their cause.

The health care debate in 1993 and 1994 also provides examples of how the selection of items for analysis can influence one's view of American public opinion. *Washington Post* polls asked Americans whether they thought the Clinton health plan was better or worse than the present system (Morin 1994). In one version of the question, the sample was given the response options "better" or "worse," while in the other version respondents could choose among "better," "worse," or "don't know enough about the plan to say." The following responses were obtained:

Version 1		*Version 2*	
better	52%	better	21%
worse	34%	worse	27%
don't know (volunteered)	14%	don't know enough	52%

Clearly, very different portrayals of American public opinion are presented by the two versions of the question. The first version suggests that a majority of Americans believed that the Clinton plan was better than the status quo, while the second version suggests that a plurality of citizens with opinions on the issue felt that the Clinton plan was worse. It is obvious which version of the question supporters and opponents of the Clinton health plan would be more likely to cite.

Another example from the health care reform area deals with Americans' feelings about the seriousness of the health care problem. Certainly, the more seriously the problem was viewed, the greater the impetus for changing the health care system. Different polling organizations asked a variety of questions designed to tap the importance of the health care issue (questions taken from the September/October 1994 issue of *Public Perspective*, 23, 26):

> Louis Harris and Associates (April 1994): Which of the following statements comes closest to expressing your overall view of the health care system in this country? . . . There are some good things in our health care system, but fundamental changes are needed to make it better. . . . Our health care system has so much wrong with it that we need to completely rebuild it. . . . On the whole, the health care system works pretty well and only minor changes are necessary to make it work.
>
> | | |
> |---|---|
> | Fundamental changes needed | 54% |
> | Completely rebuild it | 31% |
> | Only minor changes needed | 14% |

NBC/*Wall Street Journal* (March 1994): Which of the following comes closest to your belief about the American health care system—the system is in crisis; the system has major problems, but is not in crisis; the system has problems, but they are not major; or the system has no problems?

Crisis	22%
Major problems	50%
Minor problems	26%

Gallup (June 1994): Which of these statements do you agree with more: The country has health care problems, but no health care crisis, or, the country has a health care crisis?

Crisis	55%
Problems but no crisis	41%
Don't know	4%

Gallup (June 1994): Which of these statements do you agree with more: The country has a health care crisis, or the country has health care problems, but no health care crisis?

Crisis	35%
Problems but no crisis	61%
Don't know	4%

Certainly if one were trying to make the case that health care reform was an absolute priority, one would cite the first version of the Gallup question in which 55 percent of the respondents labeled health care a crisis. But if one wanted to move more slowly and incrementally on the health care issue, one would likely cite the NBC News/*Wall Street Journal* poll in which only 22 percent of Americans said there was a crisis. Health care reform is the kind of controversial public policy issue that invites political leaders to seize upon those poll results to advance their positions. In such situations, citizens should be sensitive to how politicians are selectively using the polls.

Schneider (1996) has provided an excellent example of how examination of a single trial heat question may give a misleading impression of the electoral strength of presidential candidates. A better sense of the candidates' true electoral strength is achieved by adding to the analysis information about the incumbent's job approval rating. For example, in a trial heat question in May 1980 incumbent president Jimmy Carter led challenger Ronald Reagan by 40 to 32 percent, yet at the time Carter's job rating was quite negative: 38 percent approval and 51 percent disapproval. Thus Carter's lead in the trial heat item was much more fragile than it appeared; indeed, Reagan went on to win the election. Four years later, in May of 1984, President

Reagan led challenger Walter Mondale by 10 percentage points in the trial heat question. But Reagan's job rating was very positive: 54 percent approval compared with 38 percent disapproval. Thus Reagan's 10-point lead looked quite solid in view of his strong job ratings, and he won overwhelmingly in November. Finally, in April 1992, incumbent president George Bush led challenger Bill Clinton by 50 to 34 percent in the trial heat question, a huge margin. But Bush's overall job rating was negative—42 percent approval versus 48 percent disapproval. Bush's lead over Clinton, then, was not as strong as it appeared, and Clinton ultimately won the election.

By collecting information on multiple aspects of a topic, pollsters are better able to understand citizens' attitudes (Morin and Berry 1996). One of the anomalies of 1996 was the substantial number of Americans who were worried about the health of the economy at a time when by most objective indicators the economy was performing very well. Part of the answer to this puzzle was Americans' ignorance and misinformation about the country's economic health. For example, even though unemployment was substantially lower in 1996 than in 1991, 33 percent of Americans said it was higher in 1996 and 28 percent said the same. The average estimate of the unemployment rate was 20.6 percent when in reality it was just over 5 percent. Americans' perceptions of inflation and the deficit were similar; in both cases Americans thought that the reality was much worse than it actually was. It is no wonder that many Americans expressed economic insecurity during good economic times; they were not aware of how strongly the economy was performing.

The final example in this section focuses on how the media selects what we learn about a poll even when the complete poll and analyses are available to the citizenry. The example concerns a book entitled *Sex in America: A Definitive Survey* by Robert T. Michael et al., published in 1994, along with a more specialized and comprehensive volume, *The Social Organization of Sexuality: Sexual Practices in the United States* by Edward O. Laumann et al. Both books are based on an extensive questionnaire administered by the National Opinion Research Center to 3,432 scientifically selected respondents. . . .

Because of the importance of the subject matter and because sex sells, media coverage of the survey was widespread. How various media reported the story indicates how much leeway the media have and how influential they are in determining what citizens learn about a given topic. For example, the *New York Times* ran a front-page story on October 7, 1994, entitled "Sex in America: Faithfulness in Marriage Thrives After All." Less prominent stories appeared in subsequent issues, including one on October 18, 1994, inaccurately entitled "Gay Survey Raises a New Question."

Two of the three major news magazines featured the sex survey on the covers of their October 17, 1994, issues. The *Time* cover simply read "Sex in America: Surprising News from the Most Important Survey since the Kinsey Report." The *U.S. News & World Report* cover was more risqué, showing a partially clad man and woman in bed; it read "Sex in America: A Massive New Survey, the Most Authoritative Ever, Reveals What We Do Behind the Bedroom Door." In contrast, *Newsweek* simply ran a two-page story with the lead "Not Frenzied, But Fulfilled. Sex: Relax. If you do it—with your mate—around twice a week, according to a major new study, you basically wrote the book of love."

Other magazines and newspapers also reported on the survey in ways geared to their readership. The November issue of *Glamour* featured the survey on its cover with the teaser "Who's doing it? And how? MAJOR U.S. SEX SURVEY." The story that followed was written by the authors of the book. While the cover of the November 15, 1994, *Advocate* read "What That Sex Survey Really Means," the story focused largely on what the survey had to say about the number of gays and lesbians in the population. The lead stated "10%: Reality or Myth? There's little authoritative information about gays and lesbians in the landmark study *Sex in America*—but what there is will cause big trouble." Finally, the *Chronicle of Higher Education*, a weekly newspaper geared to college and university personnel, in its October 17, 1994, issue headlined its story "The Sex Lives of Americans. Survey that had been target of conservative attacks produces few startling results."

Both books about the survey contain a vast amount of information and a large number of results and findings. But most of the media reported on such topics as marital fidelity, how often Americans have sex, how many sex partners people have, how often people experience orgasm, what percentages of the population are gay and lesbian, how long sex takes, and the time elapsed between a couple's first meeting and their first sexual involvement. Many of the reports also presented results for married vs. singles, men vs. women, and other analytical groupings. While most of the media coverage cited above was accurate in reporting the actual survey results, it also was selective in focusing on the more titillating parts of the survey, an unsurprising outcome given the need to satisfy their readerships.

Examining Trends with Polling Data

Researchers often use polling data to describe and analyze trends. To isolate trend data, a researcher must ensure that items relating to the topic under investigation are included in multiple surveys conducted at different points in time. Ideally, the items should be identically worded. But even when they are, serious problems of comparability can make trend analysis difficult. Identically worded items may not mean the same thing or provide the same stimulus to respondents over time because social and political changes in society have altered the meaning of the questions. For example, consider this question:

> Some say that the civil rights people have been trying to push too fast. Others feel they haven't pushed fast enough. How about you? Do you think that civil rights leaders are trying to push too fast, are going too slowly, or are they moving at about the right speed?

The responses to this item can be greatly influenced by the goals and agenda of the civil rights leadership at the time of the survey. A finding that more Americans think that the civil rights leaders are moving too fast or too slowly may reflect not a change in attitude from past views about civil rights activism but a change in the civil rights agenda itself. In this case, follow-up questions designed to measure specific components of the civil rights agenda are needed to help define the trend.

There are other difficulties in achieving comparability over time. For example, even if the wording of an item were to remain the same, its placement within the questionnaire could change, which in turn could alter the meaning of a question. Likewise, the definition of the sampling frame and the procedures used to achieve completed interviews could change. In short, comparability entails much more than simply wording questions identically. Unfortunately, consumers of poll results seldom receive the information that enables them to judge whether items are truly comparable over time.

Two studies demonstrate the advantages and disadvantages of using identical items over time. Abramson (1990) complained that the biennial National Election Studies (NES) conducted by the Survey Research Center at the University of Michigan, Ann Arbor, were losing their longitudinal comparability as new questions were added to the surveys and old ones removed. Baumgartner and Walker (1988), in contrast, complained that the use of the same standard question over time to assess the level of group membership in the United States had systematically underestimated the extent of such activity. They argued that new measures of group membership should be employed, which, of course, would make comparisons between past and present surveys more problematic. Although both the old and the new measures can be included in a survey, this becomes very costly if the survey must cover many other topics.

Two other studies show how variations in question wording can make the assessment of attitude change over time difficult. Borrelli and colleagues (1987) found that polls measuring Americans' political party loyalties in 1980 and in 1984 varied widely in their results. They attributed the different results in these polls to three factors: whether the poll sampled voters only; whether the poll emphasized "today" or the present in inquiring about citizens' partisanship; and whether the poll was conducted close to election day, which would tend to give the advantage to the party ahead in the presidential contest. The implications of this research for assessing change in party identification over time are evident—that is, to conclude that genuine partisan change occurred in either of the two polls, other possible sources of observed differences, such as modifications in the wording of questions, must be ruled out. In a study of support for aid to the Nicaraguan contras between 1983 and 1986, Lockerbie and Borrelli (1990) argue that much of the observed change in American public opinion was not genuine. Instead, it was attributable to changes in the wording of the questions used to measure support for the contras. Again, the point is that one must be able to eliminate other potential explanations for observed change before one can conclude that observed change is genuine change.

Smith's (1993) critique of three major national studies of anti-Semitism conducted in 1964, 1981, and 1992 is an informative case study of how longitudinal comparisons may be undermined by methodological differences across surveys. The 1981 and 1992 studies were ostensibly designed to build upon the 1964 effort, thereby facilitating an analysis of trends in anti-Semitism. But, as Smith notes, longitudinal comparisons among the three studies were problematic because of differences in sample definition and interview mode, changes in question order and question wording, and insufficient information to evaluate the quality of the sample and the design execution. In examining an eleven-item anti-Semitism scale, he did find six items highly comparable over time that indicated a decline in anti-Semitic attitudes.

Despite the problems of sorting out true opinion change from change attributable to methodological factors, there are times when public opinion changes markedly and suddenly in response to a dramatic occurrence and the observed change is indeed genuine. Two examples from CBS News/ *New York Times* polls in 1991 about the Persian Gulf war illustrate dramatic and extensive attitude change. The first example concerns military action against Iraq. Just before the January 15 deadline imposed by the UN for the withdrawal of Iraq from Kuwait, a poll found that 47 percent of Americans favored beginning military action against Iraq if it did not withdraw; 46 percent were opposed. Two days after the deadline and after the beginning of the allied air campaign against Iraq, a poll found 79 percent of Americans saying the United States had done the right thing in beginning military action against Iraq. The second example focuses on people's attitudes toward a ground war in the Middle East. Before the allied ground offensive began, only 11 percent of Americans said the United States should begin fighting the ground war soon; 79 percent said bombing from the air should continue. But after the ground war began, the numbers shifted dramatically: 75 percent of Americans said the United States was right to begin the ground war, and only 19 percent said the nation should have waited longer. Clearly, the Persian Gulf crisis was a case in which American public opinion moved dramatically in the direction of supporting the president at each new stage.

Examining Subsets of Respondents

Although it is natural to want to know the results from an entire sample, often the most interesting information in a poll comes from examining the response patterns of subsets of respondents defined according to certain theoretically or substantively relevant characteristics. For example, a January 1986 CBS News/*New York Times* poll showed President Reagan enjoying unprecedented popularity for a six-year incumbent: 65 percent approved of the president's performance, and only 24 percent disapproved. But these overall figures mask some analytically interesting variations. For example, among blacks only 37 percent approved of the president's performance; 49 percent disapproved. The sexes also differed in their views of the president, with men expressing a 72 percent approval rate compared with 58 percent for women. (As expected among categories of party loyalists, 89 percent of the Republicans, 66 percent of the independents, and only 47 percent of the

Democrats approved of the president's performance.) Why did blacks and whites—and men and women—differ in their views of the president?

There is no necessary reason for public opinion on an issue to be uniform across subgroups. Indeed, on many issues there are reasons to expect just the opposite. That is why a fuller understanding of American public opinion is gained by taking a closer look at the views of relevant subgroups of the sample. In doing so, however, one should note that dividing the sample into subsets increases the sampling error and lowers the reliability of the sample estimates. For example, a sample of 1,600 Americans might be queried about their attitudes on abortion. After the overall pattern is observed, the researcher might wish to break down the sample by religion— yielding 1,150 Protestant, 400 Catholic, and 50 Jewish respondents—to determine whether religious affiliation is associated with specific attitudes toward abortion. The analyst might observe that Catholics on the whole are the most opposed to abortion. To find out which Catholics are most likely to oppose abortion, she might further divide the 400 Catholics into young and old Catholics or regular church attenders and nonregular attenders, or into four categories of young Catholic churchgoers, old Catholic churchgoers, young Catholic nonattenders, and old Catholic nonattenders. The more breakdowns done at the same time, the quicker the sample size in any particular category plummets, perhaps leaving insufficient cases in some categories to make solid conclusions.

Innumerable examples can be cited to demonstrate the advantages of delving more deeply into poll data on subsets of respondents. An ABC News/*Washington Post* poll conducted in February 1986 showed major differences in the attitudes of men and women toward pornography; an examination of only the total sample would have missed these important divergences. For example, in response to the question "Do you think laws against pornography in this country are too strict, not strict enough, or just about right?" 10 percent of the men said the laws were too strict, 41 percent said not strict enough, and 47 percent said about right. Among women, only 2 percent said the laws were too strict, a sizable 72 percent said they were not strict enough, and 23 percent thought they were about right (Sussman 1986b, 37).

A CBS News/*New York Times* poll of Americans conducted in April 1986 found widespread approval of the American bombing of Libya; 77 percent of the sample approved of the action, and only 14 percent disapproved. Despite the overall approval, differences among various subgroups are noteworthy. For example, 83 percent of the men approved of the bombing compared with 71 percent of the women. Of the white respondents, 80 percent approved in contrast to only 53 percent of the blacks (Clymer 1986). Even though all of these demographically defined groups gave at least majority support to the bombing, the differences in levels of support are both statistically and substantively significant.

Polls showed dramatic differences by race in the O. J. Simpson case, with blacks more convinced of Simpson's innocence and more likely to believe that he could not get a fair trial. For example, a field poll of Californians (*U.S. News & World Report*, August 1, 1994) showed that only 35 percent of blacks believed that Simpson could get a fair trial compared with 55 percent of whites. Also, 62 percent of whites thought Simpson was "very likely or somewhat likely" to be guilty of murder compared with only 38 percent for blacks. Comparable results were found in a national *Time*/CNN poll (*Time*, August 1, 1994): 66 percent of whites thought Simpson got a fair preliminary hearing compared with only 31 percent of black respondents, while 77 percent of the white respondents thought the case against Simpson was "very strong" or "fairly strong" compared with 45 percent for blacks. A *Newsweek* poll (August 1, 1994) revealed that 60 percent of blacks believed that Simpson was set up (20 percent attributing the setup to the police); only 23 percent of whites believed in a setup conspiracy. When asked whether Simpson had been treated better or worse than the average white murder suspect, whites said better by an overwhelming 52 to 5 percent margin, while blacks said worse by a 30 to 19 percent margin. These reactions to the Simpson case startled many Americans who could not understand how their compatriots of another race could see the situation so differently.

School busing to achieve racial integration has consistently been opposed by substantial majorities in national public opinion polls. A Harris poll commissioned by *Newsweek* in 1978 found that 85 percent of whites opposed busing (Williams 1979, 48). An ABC News/*Washington Post* poll conducted in February 1986 showed 60 percent of whites against busing (Sussman 1986a). The difference between the two polls might reflect genuine attitude change about busing in that eight-year period, or it might be a function of different question wording or different placement within the questionnaire. Whatever the reason, additional analysis of both these polls shows that whites are not monolithic in their opposition to busing. For example, the 1978 poll showed that 56 percent of white parents whose children had been bused viewed the experience as "very satisfactory." The 1986 poll revealed sharp differences in busing attitudes among younger and older whites. Among whites age thirty and under, 47 percent supported busing and 50 percent opposed it, while among whites over age thirty, 32 percent supported busing and 65 percent opposed it. Moreover, among younger whites whose families had experienced busing firsthand, 54 percent approved of busing and 46 percent opposed it. (Of course, staunch opponents of busing may have moved to escape busing, thereby guaranteeing that the remaining population would be relatively more supportive of busing.)

Another example of the usefulness of examining poll results within age categories is provided by an ABC News/*Washington Post* poll conducted in May 1985 on citizens' views of how the federal budget deficit might be cut. One item read, "Do you think the government should give people a smaller Social Security cost-of-living increase than they are now scheduled to get as a way of reducing the budget deficit, or not?" Among the overall sample, 19 percent favored granting a smaller cost-of-living increase and 78 percent opposed. To test the widespread view that young workers lack confidence in the Social Security system and doubt they will ever get out of the system what they paid in, Sussman (1985c) investigated how different age groups responded to the preceding question. Basically, he found that all age groups strongly opposed a reduction in cost-of-living increases. Unlike the busing issue, this question showed no difference among age groups—an important substantive finding, particularly in light of the expectation that there would be divergent views among the old and young. Too often people mistakenly dismiss null (no difference) results as uninteresting and unexciting; a finding of no difference can be just as substantively significant as a finding of a major difference.

An example where age does make a difference in people's opinions is the topic of physician-assisted suicide. A *Washington Post* poll conducted in 1996 asked a national sample of Americans, "Should it be legal or illegal for a doctor to help a terminally ill patient commit suicide?" (Rosenbaum 1997). The attitudes of older citizens and younger citizens were markedly different on this question—the older the age group, the greater the opposition to doctor-assisted suicide. For example, 52 percent of respondents between ages eighteen and twenty-nine thought doctor-assisted suicide should be legal; 41 percent said it should be illegal. But for citizens over age seventy, the comparable figures were 35 and 58 percent. Even more striking were some of the racial and income differences on this question. Whites thought physician involvement in suicide should be legal by a 55 to 35 percent margin; blacks opposed it 70 to 20 percent. At the lowest income levels, doctor-assisted suicide was opposed by a 54 to 37 percent margin; at the highest income level it was supported by a 58 to 30 percent margin.

In many instances the categories used for creating subgroups are already established or self-evident. For example, if one is interested in gender or racial differences, the categories of male and female or white and black are straightforward candidates for investigation. Other breakdowns require more thought. For example, what divisions might one use to examine the effects of age? Should they be young, middle-aged, and old? If so, what actual ages correspond to these categories? Is middle age thirty-five to sixty-five, forty to sixty, or what? Or should more than three categories of age be defined? In samples selected to study the effects of religion, the typical breakdown is Protestant, Catholic, and Jewish. But this simple threefold division might overlook some interesting variations; that is, some Protestants are evangelical, some are fundamentalist, and others are considered mainline denominations. Moreover, since most blacks are Protestants, comparisons of Catholics and Protestants that do not also control for race may be misleading.

Establishing categories is much more subjective and judgmental in other situations. For example, religious categories can be defined relatively easily by denominational affiliation, as mentioned earlier, but classifying respondents as evangelicals or fundamentalists is more complicated. Those who actually belong to denominations normally characterized as evangelical or fundamentalist could be so categorized. Or an investigator might identify some evangelical or fundamentalist beliefs, construct some polling questions around them, and then classify respondents according to their responses to the questions. Obviously, this would require some common core of agreement about the definition of an evangelical or fundamentalist. Wilcox (1984, 6) argues:

> Fundamentalists and evangelicals have a very similar set of religious beliefs, including the literal interpretation of the Bible, the need for a religious conversion known as being "born-again," and the need to convert sinners to the faith. The evangelicals, however, are less anti-intellectual and more involved in the secular world, while the fundamentalists criticize the evangelicals for failing to keep themselves "pure from the world."

Creating subsets by ideology is another common approach to analyzing public opinion. The most-often-used categories of ideology are liberal, moderate, and conservative, and the typical way of obtaining this information is to ask respondents a question in the following form: "Generally speaking, do you think of yourself as a liberal, moderate, or conservative?" However, one can raise many objections to this procedure, including whether people really assign common meanings to these terms. Indeed, the levels of ideological sophistication and awareness have been an ongoing topic of research in political science.

Journalist Kevin Phillips (1981) has cited the work of political scientists Stuart A. Lilie and William S. Maddox, who argue that the traditional liberal-moderate-conservative breakdown is inadequate for analytical purposes. Instead, they propose a fourfold classification of liberal, conservative, populist, and libertarian, based on two underlying dimensions: whether one supports or opposes governmental intervention in the economy and whether one supports or opposes expansion of individual behavioral liberties and sexual equality. They define liberals as those who support both governmental intervention in the economy and expansion of personal liberties, conservatives as those who oppose both, libertarians as citizens who favor expanding personal liberties but oppose governmental intervention in the economy, and populists as persons who favor governmental economic intervention but oppose the expansion of personal liberties. According to one poll, populists made up 24 percent of the electorate, conservatives 18 percent, liberals 16 percent, and libertarians 13 percent, with the rest of the electorate not readily classifiable or unfamiliar with ideological terminology.

This more elaborate breakdown of ideology may help us to better understand public opinion, but the traditional categories still dominate political discourse. Thus, when one encounters citizens who oppose government programs that affect the marketplace but support pro-choice court decisions on abortion, proposed gay rights statutes, and the Equal Rights Amendment, one feels uncomfortable calling them liberals or conservatives since they appear to be conservative on economic issues and liberal on lifestyle issues. One might feel more confident in classifying them as libertarians.

Additional examples of how an examination of subsets of respondents can provide useful insights into the public's attitudes are provided by two CBS News/*New York Times* surveys conducted in 1991, one dealing with the Persian Gulf crisis and the other with attitudes toward police. Although the rapid and successful conclusion of the ground war against Iraq resulted in widespread approval of the enterprise, before the land assault began there were differences of opinion among Americans about a ground war. For example, in the February 12–13 CBS News/*New York Times* poll, Americans were asked: "Suppose several thousand American troops would lose their lives in a ground war against Iraq. Do you think a ground war against Iraq would be worth the cost or not?" By examining the percentage saying it would be worth the cost, one finds the following results for different groups of Americans:

All respondents	45%	Independents	46%
Men	56%	Republicans	54%
Women	35%	Eighteen to twenty-nine year-olds	50%
Whites	47%	Thirty to forty-four year-olds	44%
Blacks	30%	Forty-five to sixty-four year-olds	51%
Democrats	36%	Sixty-five years and older	26%

Note that the youngest age group, the one most likely to suffer the casualties, is among the most supportive of a ground war. Note also the sizable differences between men and women, whites and blacks, and Democrats and Republicans.

Substantial racial differences in opinion also were expressed in an April 1–3, 1991, CBS News/*New York Times* poll on attitudes toward local police. Overall, 55 percent of the sample said they had substantial confidence in the local police, and 44 percent said little confidence. But among whites the comparable percentages were 59 percent and 39 percent, while for blacks only 30 percent had substantial confidence and fully 70 percent expressed little confidence in the police. Even on issues in which the direction of white and black opinion was the same, there were still substantial racial differences in the responses. For example, 69 percent of whites said that the police in their own community treat blacks and whites the same, and only 16 percent said the police were tougher on blacks than on whites. Although a plurality—45 percent—of blacks agreed that the police treat blacks and whites equally, fully 42 percent of black respondents felt that the police were tougher on blacks. Certainly if one were conducting a study to ascertain citizens' attitudes about police performance, it would be foolish not to examine the opinions of relevant subgroups.

Another example of the importance of examining subsets of respondents is provided by a January 1985 ABC News/*Washington Post* poll that queried Americans about their attitudes on a variety of issues and presented results not only for the entire sample but also for subsets of respondents defined by their attentiveness to public affairs (Sussman 1985b).

Attentiveness to public affairs was measured by whether the respondents were aware of four news events: the subway shooting in New York City of four alleged assailants by their intended victim; the switch in jobs by two key Reagan administration officials, Donald Regan and James Baker; the Treasury Department's proposal to simplify the tax system; and protests against South African apartheid held in the United States. Respondents then were divided into four levels of awareness, with 27 percent in the highest category, 26 percent in the next highest, 25 percent in the next category, and 22 percent falling in the lowest. The next step in the analysis was to compare the policy preferences of the highest and lowest awareness subsets.

There were some marked differences between these two groups. For example, on the issue of support for the president's military buildup, 59 percent of the lowest awareness respondents opposed any major cuts in military spending to lessen the budget deficit. In contrast, 57 percent of the highest awareness group said that military spending should be limited to help with the budget deficit. On the issue of tax rates, a majority of both groups agreed with the president that taxes were too high, but there was a difference in the size of the majority. Among the lowest awareness respondents, 72 percent said taxes were too high and 24 percent said they were not, while among the highest awareness respondents, 52 percent said taxes were too high and 45 percent said they were not (Sussman 1985b).

Opinions about the future of Social Security and Medicare also are affected by citizens' knowledge about the two programs (Pianin and Brossard 1997). In one poll, the more people knew about Social Security and Medicare, the more likely they were to believe that these programs were in crisis and that major governmental action was needed. For example, among highly knowledgeable respondents, 88 percent believed that Social Security either was in crisis or had major problems; only 70 percent of respondents with little knowledge agreed. Likewise, 89 percent of the highly knowledgeable respondents believed Social Security would go bankrupt if Congress did nothing compared to only 61 percent for the less-informed respondents.

All these findings raise some interesting normative issues about public opinion polls. . . . [T]he methodology of public opinion polls is very democratic. All citizens have a nearly equal chance to be selected in a sample and have their views counted; all respondents are weighted equally (or nearly so) in the typical data analysis. Yet except at the polls all citizens do not have equal influence in shaping public policy. The distribution of political resources, whether financial or informational, is not uniform across the population. Polls themselves become a means to influence public policy, as various decision makers cite poll results to legitimize their policies. But should the views of all poll respondents be counted equally? An elitist critic would argue that the most informed segments of the population should be given the greatest weight. Therefore, in the preceding example of defense spending, more attention should be given to the views of the highest awareness subset (assuming the validity of the levels of awareness), which was more supportive of reducing military spending. An egalitarian argument would assert that all respondents should be counted equally. . . .

Interpreting Poll Results

An August 1986 Gallup poll on education showed that 67 percent of Americans would allow their children to attend class with a child suffering from AIDS, while 24 percent would not. What reaction might there be to this finding? Some people might be shocked and depressed to discover that almost one-fourth of Americans could be so mean-spirited toward AIDS victims when the scientific evidence shows that AIDS is not a disease transmitted by casual contact. Others might be reassured and relieved that two-thirds of Americans are sufficiently enlightened or tolerant to allow their children to attend school with children who have AIDS. Some people might feel dismay: How could 67 percent of Americans foolishly allow their children to go to school with a child who has AIDS when there is no absolute guarantee that AIDS cannot be transmitted casually?

Consider this example from a 1983 poll by the National Opinion Research Center (NORC): "If your party nominated a black for President, would you vote for him if he were qualified for the job?" Eighty-five percent of the white respondents said yes. How might this response be interpreted? One might feel positive about how much racial attitudes have changed in the United States. A different perspective would decry the fact that in this supposedly tolerant and enlightened era, 15 percent of white survey respondents could not bring themselves to say they would vote for a qualified black candidate.

In neither example can we assign a single correct meaning to the data. Instead, the interpretation one chooses will be a function of individual values and beliefs, and purposes in analyzing the survey. This is demonstrated in an analysis of two national surveys on gun control, one sponsored by the National Rifle Association (NRA) and conducted by Decision/Making/Information, Inc., and the other sponsored by the Center for the Study and Prevention of Handgun Violence and conducted by Cambridge Reports, Inc. (pollster Patrick Caddell's firm). Although the statistical results from both surveys were comparable, the two reports arrived at substantially different conclusions. The NRA's analysis concluded:

> Majorities of American voters believe that we do *not* need more laws governing the possession and use of firearms and that more firearms laws would *not* result in a decrease in the crime rate. (Wright 1981, 25)

In contrast, the center's report stated:

> It is clear that the vast majority of the public (both those who live with handguns and those who do not) want handgun licensing and registration. . . . The American public wants some form of handgun control legislation. (Wright 1981, 25)

Wright carefully analyzed the evidence cited in support of each conclusion and found that

> the major difference between the two reports is not in the findings, but in what is said about or concluded about the findings: what aspects of the evidence are emphasized or de-emphasized, what interpretation is given to a finding, and what implications are drawn from the findings about the need, or lack thereof, for stricter weapons controls. (Wright 1981, 38)

In essence, it was the interpretation of the data that generated the difference in the recommendations.

Two polls on tax reform provide another example of how poll data can be selectively interpreted and reported (Sussman 1985a). The first poll, sponsored by the insurance industry, was conducted by pollster Burns Roper. Its main conclusion, reported in a press conference announcing the poll results, was that 77 percent of the American public "said that workers should not be taxed on employee benefits" and that only 15 percent supported such a tax, a conclusion very reassuring to the insurance industry. However, Roper included other items in the poll that the insurance industry chose not to emphasize. As Sussman points out, the 77 percent opposed to the taxing of fringe benefits were then asked, "Would you still oppose counting the value of employee benefits as taxable income for employees if the additional tax revenues went directly to the reduction of federal budget deficits and not into new spending?" Twenty-six percent were no longer opposed to taxing fringe benefits under this condition, bringing the overall opposition down to 51 percent of the sample.

A second follow-up question asked, "Would you still oppose counting the value of employee benefits as taxable income for employees if the additional tax revenues permitted an overall reduction of tax rates for individuals?" (a feature that was part of the Treasury Department's initial tax proposals). Now only 33 percent of the sample was opposed to taxing fringes, 50 percent supported it, and 17 percent were undecided. Thus, depending upon which results one used, one could show a majority of citizens supportive of or opposed to taxing fringe benefits.

The other poll that Sussman analyzed also tapped people's reactions to the Treasury Department's tax proposal. A number of questions in the survey demonstrated public hostility to the Treasury proposal. One item read:

> The Treasury Department has proposed changing the tax system. Three tax brackets would be created, but most current deductions from income would be eliminated. Non-federal income taxes and property taxes would not be deductible, and many deductions would be limited. Do you favor or oppose this proposal? (Sussman 1985a)

Not surprisingly, 57 percent opposed the Treasury plan, and only 27 percent supported it. But as Sussman points out, the question is highly selective and leading since it focuses on changes in the tax system that hurt the taxpayer. For example, nowhere does it inform the respondent that a key part of the Treasury plan was to reduce existing tax rates so that 80 percent of Americans would be paying either the same amount or less in taxes than they were paying before. Clearly, this survey was designed to obtain a set of results compatible with the sponsor's policy objectives.

Morin (1995) describes a situation in which polling data were misinterpreted and misreported in the *Washington Post* because of faulty communication between a *Post* reporter and a local polling firm that was conducting an omnibus survey in the Washington, D.C., area. Interested in how worried federal employees were about their jobs given the budgetary battles between the Clinton White House and the Republican Congress in 1995, the reporter commissioned the polling firm to include the following questions in its survey: "Do you think your agency or company will probably be affected by federal budget cutbacks? Do you think your own job will be affected?" The poll discovered that 40 percent of the federal workers interviewed believed their own jobs might be affected. Unfortunately, when the polling outfit prepared a report for its client, the reporter, the report concluded that these federal workers felt their jobs were jeopardized. And then the reporter's story stated, "Four out of every 10 federal employees fear losing their jobs because of budget reductions." As Morin points out, this conclusion does not follow from the polling questions asked. The belief that one's job will likely be affected is not equivalent to the fear of losing one's job. Instead, the effects might be lower salary increases, decreased job mobility, increased job responsibilities, and the like. A correction quickly appeared in the *Post* clarifying what the polling data actually had said. One lesson of this example is the responsibility that pollsters have to clients to communicate carefully and accurately what poll results mean. Another lesson is that one should not try to read too much into the responses to any single survey item. In this case, if the reporter wanted to know exactly how federal workers thought their jobs would be affected, a specific question eliciting this information should have been included in the survey.

Weighting the Sample

Samples are selected to be representative of the population from which they are drawn. Sometimes adjustments must be made to a sample before analyzing and reporting results. These adjustments may be made for substantive reasons or because of biases in the characteristics of the selected sample. An example of adjustments made for substantive reasons is pollsters' attempts to determine who the likely voters will be and to base their election predictions not on the entire sample but on a subset of likely voters.

To correct for biases, weights can be used so that the sample's demographic characteristics more accurately reflect the population's overall properties. Because sampling and interviewing involve statistics and probability theory as well as logistical problems of contacting respondents, the sample may contain too few blacks, or too few men, or too few people in the youngest age category. Assuming that one knows the true population proportions for sex, race, and age, one can adjust the sample by the use of weights to bring its numbers into line with the overall population values. For example, if females constitute 60 percent of the sample but 50 percent of the overall population, one might weight each female respondent by five-sixths, thereby reducing the percentage of females in the sample to 50 percent (five-sixths times 60 percent).

A 1986 *Columbus Dispatch* preelection poll on the gubernatorial preferences of Ohioans illustrates the consequences of weighting. In August 1986 the *Dispatch* sent a mail questionnaire to a sample of Ohioans selected from the statewide list of registered voters. The poll showed that incumbent Democratic governor Richard Celeste was leading former GOP governor James Rhodes, 48 percent to 43 percent, with Independent candidate and former Democratic mayor of Cleveland Dennis Kucinich receiving 9 percent; an undecided alternative was not provided to respondents (Curtin 1986a). Fortunately, the *Dispatch* report of its poll included the sample size for each category (unlike the practice of the national media). One table presented to the reader showed the following relationship between political party affiliation and gubernatorial vote preference (Curtin 1986b):

Gubernatorial preference	Democrat	Republican	Independent
Celeste	82%	14%	33%
Rhodes	9	81	50
Kucinich	9	5	17
Total %	100	100	100
(N)	(253)	(245)	(138)

Given the thrust of the news story that Celeste was ahead, 48 to 43 percent, the numbers in the table were surprising because Rhodes was running almost as well among Republicans as Celeste was among Democrats, and Rhodes had a substantial lead among Independents. Because the *N*'s were provided, one could calculate the actual number of Celeste, Rhodes, and Kucinich votes in the sample as follows:

Celeste votes = .82(253) + .14(245) + .33(138) = 287
Rhodes votes = .09(253) + .81(245) + .50(138) = 291
Kucinich votes = .09(253) + .05(245) + .17(138) = 58

The percentages calculated from these totals show Rhodes slightly *ahead*, 46 to 45 percent, rather than trailing. At first I thought there was a mistake in the poll or in the party affiliation and gubernatorial vote preference. In rereading the news story, however, I learned that the sample had been weighted. The reporter wrote, "Results were adjusted, or weighted, slightly to compensate for demographic differences between poll respondents and the Ohio electorate as a whole" (Curtin 1986b). The reporter did inform the reader that the data were weighted, but nowhere did he say that the adjustment affected who was ahead in the poll.

The adjustment probably was statistically valid since the poll respondents did not seem to include sufficient numbers of women and blacks, two groups that were more supportive of the Democratic gubernatorial candidate. However, nowhere in the news story was any specific information provided on how the weighting was done. This example illustrates that weighting can be consequential, and it is probably typical in terms of the scant information provided to citizens about weighting procedures.

When Polls Conflict: A Concluding Example

A variety of factors can influence poll results and their subsequent interpretation. Useful vehicles for a review of these factors are the polls that led up to the 1980, 1984, 1988, 1992, and 1996 presidential elections—polls that were often highly inconsistent. For example, in the 1984 election, polls conducted at comparable times yielded highly dissimilar results. A Harris poll had Reagan leading Mondale by 9 percentage points, an ABC News/*Washington Post* poll had Reagan ahead by 12 points, a CBS News/*New York Times* survey had Reagan leading by 13 points, a *Los Angeles Times* poll gave Reagan a 17-point lead, and an NBC News poll had the president ahead by 25 points (Oreskes 1984). In September 1988 seven different polls on presidential preference were released within a three-day period with results ranging from Bush ahead by 8 points to a Dukakis lead of 6 points (Morin 1988). In 1992 ten national polls conducted in the latter part of August showed Clinton with leads over Bush ranging from 5 to 19 percentage points (Elving 1992). And in 1996, the final preelection polls showed Clinton leading Dole by margins ranging from 7 to 18 percentage points. How can polls on an ostensibly straightforward topic such as presidential vote preference differ so widely? Many reasons can be cited, some obvious and others more subtle in their effects.

Among the more subtle reasons are the method of interviewing and the number of callbacks that a pollster uses to contact respondents who initially were unavailable. According to Lewis and Schneider (1982, 43), Patrick Caddell and George Gallup in their 1980 polls found that President Reagan received less support from respondents interviewed personally than from those queried over the telephone. Their speculation about this finding was that weak Democrats who were going to desert Carter found it easier to admit this in a telephone interview than in a face-to-face situation.

With respect to callbacks, Dolnick (1984) reports that one reason a Harris poll was closer than others in predicting Reagan's sizable victory in 1980 was that it made repeated callbacks, which at each stage "turned up increasing numbers of well-paid, well-educated Republican-leaning voters." A similar situation occurred in 1984. Traugott (1987) found that persistence in callbacks resulted in a more Republican sample, speculating that Republicans were less likely to have been at home or available initially.

Some of the more obvious factors that help account for differences among compared polls are question wording and question placement. Some survey items mention the presidential and vice-presidential candidates, while others mention only the presidential challengers. Some pollsters ask follow-up questions of undecided voters to ascertain whether they lean toward one candidate or another; others do not. Question order can influence responses. Normally, incumbents and better known candidates do better when the question on vote intention is asked at the beginning of the survey rather than later. If vote intention is measured after a series of issue and problem questions have been asked, respondents may have been reminded of shortcomings in the incumbent's record and may therefore be less willing to express support for the incumbent.

Comparable polls also can differ in how the sample is selected and how it is treated for analytical purposes. Some polls sample registered voters; others query adult Americans. There are differences as well in the methods used to identify likely voters. As Lipset (1980) points out, the greater the number of respondents who are screened out of the sample because they do not seem to be likely voters, the more probable it is that the remaining respondents will be relatively more Republican in their vote preferences. Some samples are weighted to guarantee demographic representativeness; others are not.

It is also possible that discrepancies among polls are not due to any of the above factors, but may simply reflect statistical fluctuations. For example, if one poll with a 4 percent sampling error shows Clinton ahead of Dole, 52 to 43 percent, this result is statistically congruent with other polls that might have a very narrow Clinton lead of 48 to 47 percent or other polls that show a landslide Clinton lead of 56 to 39 percent.

Voss et al. (1995) summarized and compared many of the methodological differences among polls conducted by eight polling organizations for the 1988 and 1992 presidential elections. Even though all eight organizations were studying the same phenomenon, there were enough differences in their approaches that polls conducted at the same time using identical questions might still get somewhat different results for reasons beyond sampling error. One feature Voss et al. examined was the sampling method—how each organization generated a list of telephone numbers from which to sample. Once the sample was selected, polling organizations conducting telephone interviews still had to make choices about how to handle "busy signals, refusals, and calls answered by electronic devices, how to decide which household members are eligible to be interviewed, and how to select the respondent from among those eligible" (Voss et al. 1995). The investigators also examined the various weighting schemes used by each survey operation to ensure a representative sample. Much of this methodological information is not readily available to the consumer of public opinion polls, and if it were many consumers would be overwhelmed by the volume of methodological detail. Yet these factors can make a difference. For example, the eight polling organizations analyzed by Voss et al. treated refusals quite differently. Some of the outfits did not call back after receiving a refusal from a potential respondent; other organizations did make callbacks. One organization generally tried to call back but with a different interviewer, but then gave up if a second refusal was obtained.

Just as different methodological features can affect election polls, they also can influence other surveys. One prominent example dealt with the widely divergent estimates of rape obtained from two different national surveys. Much of this discrepancy stemmed from the methodological differences between the two surveys (Lynch 1996). Because the poll consumer is unaware of many of the design features of a survey, he or she must assume the survey design was appropriate for the topic at hand. Then the consumer can ask whether the information collected by the survey was analyzed and interpreted correctly.

REFERENCES

Abramson, Paul R., Brian Silver, and Barbara Anderson. 1990. "The Decline of Over-time Comparability in the National Election Studies." *Public Opinion Quarterly* 54 (summer): 177–190.

Alpern, David M. 1986. "A *Newsweek* Poll: Sex Laws." *Newsweek,* 14 July, 38.

Baumgartner, Frank R., and Jack L. Walker. 1988. "Survey Research and Membership in Voluntary Associations." *American Journal of Political Science* 32 (November): 908–928.

Borrelli, Stephen, Brad Lockerbie, and Richard G. Niemi. 1987. "Why the Democrat-Republic Partisan Gap Varies from Poll to Poll." *Public Opinion Quarterly* 51 (spring): 115–119.

Clymer, Adam. 1986. "A Poll Finds 77% in U.S. Approve Raid on Libya." *New York Times,* 17 April, A-23.

Curtin, Michael. 1986a. "Celeste Leading Rhodes 48% to 43%, with Kucinich Trailing." *Columbus Dispatch,* 10 August, 1-A.

———. 1986b. "Here Is How Poll Was Taken." *Columbus Dispatch,* 10 August, 8-E.

Dolnick, Edward. 1984. "Pollsters Are Asking: What's Wrong." *Columbus Dispatch,* 19 August, C-1.

Elving, Ronald D. 1992. "Polls Confound and Confuse in This Topsy-Turvy Year." *Congressional Quarterly Weekly Report,* 12 September, 2725–2727.

Laumann, Edward O., et al. 1994. *The Social Organization of Sexuality.* Chicago: University of Chicago Press.

Lewis, I. A., and William Schneider. 1982. "Is the Public Lying to the Pollsters?" *Public Opinion* 5 (April/May): 42–47.

Lipset, Seymour Martin. 1980. "Different Polls, Different Results in 1980 Politics." *Public Opinion* 3 (August/September): 19–20, 60.

Lockerbie, Brad, and Stephen A. Borrelli. 1990. "Question Wording and Public Support for Contra Aid, 1983–1986." *Public Opinion Quarterly* 54 (summer): 195–208.

Lynch, James P. 1996. "Clarifying Divergent Estimates of Rape from Two National Surveys." *Public Opinion Quarterly* 60 (winter): 558–619.

Michael, Robert T., John H. Gagnon, Edward O. Laumann, and Gina Kolata. 1994. *Sex in America: A Definitive Survey.* Boston: Little, Brown.

Morin, Richard. 1988. "Behind the Numbers: Confessions of a Pollster." *Washington Post,* 16 October, C-1, C-4.

———. 1991. "2 Ways of Reading the Public's Lips on Gulf Policy." *Washington Post,* 14 January, A-9.

———. 1994. "Don't Know Much About Health Care Reform." *Washington Post* National Weekly Edition, 14–20 March, 37.

———. 1995. "Reading between the Numbers." *Washington Post* National Weekly Edition, 4–10 September, 30.

Morin, Richard, and John M. Berry. 1996. "Economic Anxieties." *Washington Post* National Weekly Edition, 4–10 November, 6–7.

Oreskes, Michael. 1984. "Pollsters Offer Reasons for Disparity in Results." *New York Times,* 20 October, A-8.

Phillips, Kevin P. 1981. "Polls Are Too Broad in Analysis Divisions." *Columbus Dispatch,* 8 September, B-3.

Pianin, Eric, and Mario Brossard. 1997. "Hands Off Social Security and Medicare." *Washington Post* National Weekly Edition, 7 April, 35.

Rosenbaum, David E. 1997. "Americans Want a Right to Die. Or So They Think." *New York Times,* 8 June, E3.

Schneider, William. 1996. How to Read a Trial Heat Poll." Transcript, CNN "Inside Politics Extra," 12 May (see AllPolitics Web site).

Smith, Tom W. 1993. "Actual Trends or Measurement Artifacts? A Review of Three Studies of Anti-Semitism." *Public Opinion Quarterly* 57 (fall): 380–393.

Sussman, Barry. 1985a. "To Understand These Polls, You Have to Read the Fine Print." *Washington Post* National Weekly Edition, 4 March, 37.

_____. 1985b. "Reagan's Support on Issues Relies Heavily on the Uninformed." *Washington Post* National Weekly Edition, 1 April, 37.

_____. 1985c. "Social Security and the Young." *Washington Post* National Weekly Edition, 27 May, 37.

_____. 1986a. "It's Wrong to Assume that School Busing Is Wildly Unpopular." *Washington Post* National Weekly Edition, 10 March, 37.

_____. 1986b. "With Pornography, It All Depends on Who's Doing the Looking." *Washington Post* National Weekly Edition, 24 March, 37.

Traugott, Michael W. 1987. "The Importance of Persistence in Respondent Selection for Preelection Surveys." *Public Opinion Quarterly* 51 (spring): 48–57.

Voss, D. Stephen, Andrew Gelman, and Gary King. 1995. "Preelection Survey Methodology: Details from Eight Polling Organizations, 1988 and 1992." *Public Opinion Quarterly* 59 (spring): 98–132.

Wilcox, William Clyde. 1984. "The New Christian Right and the White Fundamentalists: An Analysis of a Potential Political Movement." Ph.D. diss., Ohio State University.

Williams, Dennis A. 1979. "A New Racial Poll." *Newsweek,* 26 February, 48, 53.

Wright, James D. 1981. "Public Opinion and Gun Control: A Comparison of Results from Two Recent National Surveys." *Annals of the American Academy of Political and Social Science* 455 (May): 24–39.

10-2

Gender and Public Opinion

Kristi Andersen

Few developments in public opinion and voting in recent decades have been as widely discussed as the "gender gap"—the tendency for women to be more supportive than men of liberal policies and Democrat candidates. In the essay that follows, Kristi Andersen reviews the recent history of gender differences in political opinion and behavior. In addition, she describes how women's groups exploited early polling results to identify issues that had popular appeal and find supportive segments of the public. The results, as Andersen demonstrates, began to shape their thinking about campaigns and election outcomes.

IN THE LAST decade of the twentieth century, women's and men's political differences [occupied] center stage in popular and academic debates. The Year of the Woman in 1992 saw the number of female members of the U.S. House of Representatives increase by two-thirds and the number of female senators double; those numbers remained constant during the Republican takeover of Congress in 1994. Pollsters and politicians attend to the gender gap in voting, for women constitute a majority of the electorate and are more likely than men to support Democratic candidates. With all the recent attention to gender politics, it may seem odd that gender distinctions were barely studied until the 1970s.

Discovering the Difference

For the most part, social scientists, at least until the mid-1970s, denied that men and women held significantly different political beliefs. The prevalent thinking could be described as a convergence model, in which men and women were seen as being subject to similar economic and social forces

Excerpted from Barbara Norrander and Clyde Wilcox, eds., *Understanding Public Opinion* (Washington, D.C.: CQ Press, 1997), pp. 19–36.

and thus unlikely to differ significantly in politics. Typically, studies written in the 1950s and 1960s either omitted sex altogether as a classification worth considering or mentioned the comparison only in passing. As one among many examples, James Sundquist in *Dynamics of the Party System* includes a table that delineates "changes in political affiliation of various population groups" between 1960 and 1970. He lists race, region, social class, education, place of residence (urban or rural), religion, and age—but not sex (1973, 348–349).

Later, when sex differences in public opinion and political behavior surfaced, researchers tried to explain them. These difference models can be classified as either essentialist or constructionist. Essentialist arguments assume that biological differences between men and women are the basis of most—if not all—observable differences on political attributes. Within an essentialist approach we can distinguish between arguments that see women as inferior (for example, those made in the nineteenth and early twentieth century opposing women's suffrage) and those that view women as essentially superior to men (such as the recent "woman-centered" brand of feminism). The alternative to essentialism is a constructionist position, which assumes that differences in how women and men perceive and act on their environment are social constructions. That is, there is no such thing as an essential male or female nature; rather, each culture develops assumptions and expectations about the ways men and women think, talk, and act.

While most American political scientists in the 1950s and 1960s used an unstated convergence model, a few scholars did seriously look at the way women's political thinking and behavior differed from men's. These researchers found small gender differences and attributed them to the essential or natural character of the sexes. For example, whenever women's opinions or preferences seemed to differ from men's, the difference was explained by women's "moralistic" or "apolitical" nature. Thus Robert Hess and Judith Torney (1967, 186) in their study of children's political development remark that "there was some tendency for girls to make a higher assessment [than boys] of the influence of rich people and labor unions in determining laws." Rather than interpreting these views of girls as realistic cynicism or political sophistication, the authors attributed such attitudes to "the tendency of girls to personalize governmental processes." The source of this personalization, Hess and Torney suggest, lies in the fact that girls' "experience with their major role model (mother) is a more

Table 1. Mentions of Gender and Race in Public Opinion Textbooks

Years of publication	*Number of books*	*Index references to sex, gender, or women*	*Index references to race or blacks*
1964–1981	10	9 (in 4 books)	110 (in 6 books)
1982–1995	10	147 (in 8 books)	226 (in 8 books)

personal one and [that] authority figures deal with them in more expressive and personalized ways" (Hess and Torney 1967, 193). . . .

In recent years, social scientists and historians have adopted gender as an important category of analysis.[1] Gender analysis, which now takes a generally social constructionist stance, looks not only at men and women but also at the way language, social interactions, and politics are shaped by assumptions and expectations about feminine and masculine attributes. This research has fundamentally reshaped our understanding of American history, political theory, power, and leadership—just to name a few areas.[2] In studying public opinion, researchers might use the social construction approach to account for observable sex differences in political attitudes by examining the different kinds of familial or work situations in which men and women find themselves. People who study public opinion have, like other scholars, paid more attention recently to the thinking of women and have shifted, in general, from convergence and essentialist models to more social constructionist models.

To get a better sense of the analytical role played by "sex" or—in later years—"gender" in the field of public opinion, I examined twenty public opinion textbooks written between 1964 and 1995, as well as the content of articles appearing in *Public Opinion Quarterly* between 1944 and 1993. For each textbook, I counted references in the index under "sex," "gender," "women," and—for purposes of comparison—"blacks" and "race." Table 1 summarizes the findings. Between 1964 and 1981, six out of ten books made no reference to sex, gender, or women in the index. The fact that only nine references were made to gender in the ten books demonstrates the dominance of the convergence model in this time period. Between 1982 and 1995, only two out of ten books failed to include index entries under gender, sex, or women, and the number of total references to gender increased dramatically. Nevertheless, race was more frequently cited than gender in public opinion textbooks in both eras. In the earlier period, race was mentioned about twelve times as frequently as gender. In the latter period, race received one and a half times as many references as sex.

In *Public Opinion Quarterly*, the major journal of the public opinion and survey research community, only four articles dealt with women, sex differences, sex roles, or gender before 1964 (about 0.5 percent of the total number of articles and research notes). Between 1964 and 1981, nine articles, or approximately 1.4 percent, referred to gender, and between 1982 and 1993 the journal contained sixteen articles about women or gender, or about 3.8 percent.

Even when sex differences in public opinion are examined, however, it is often on a limited number of women's or moral issues. In Richard Niemi, John Mueller, and Tom Smith's (1989) useful collection of survey data, the issues on which opinions are broken down by sex are the following: abortion, child care and work, divorce, drinking, euthanasia, extramarital sex, homosexuality, marijuana, nudity, women as politicians, premarital sex, sex education, smoking, suicide, and working. This is an interesting commentary on the extent to which women are still seen as primarily defined by family and by their sexuality—only on these kinds of "family," social, or sexual issues is sex or gender considered a significant category of analysis.

In examining textbooks and journal articles, I counted references to both "sex" and "gender" (as well as to "women"). In fact, often the word *gender* is used interchangeably with the word *sex*. I try in this chapter to use the two terms in distinct and—I believe—appropriate ways. According to our biological differences, we are categorized by sex as either male or female. But gender is a socially constructed set of assumptions and expectations about how these biological differences play out in people's interactions, including political interactions. Unfortunately, the current intellectual fashion to substitute *gender* for *sex* can blind us to the implications of the distinctions between the two.[3] As Sue Tolleson-Rinehart and Jeannie Stanley argue in a recent book (1994, 155–156), in politics we are interested in both sex and gender. For example, we ask questions about how many women senators there are, and also about whether women, because of their particular experiences, bring different perspectives to the policy process. In the first case, we are asking questions that can be answered by categorizing the population in terms of biological sex. In the second case, an answer would need to be shaped by an understanding of gender differences, which we might or might not find among senators.

Should we be interested in questions of sex or questions of gender when we approach the topic of gender and public opinion? I believe the answer is both. When we find differences between men's and women's policy preferences, candidate choices, or party identifications, we will be able to understand those differences if we cast them in the framework of gender. We account for such differences by discovering how men's and women's socialization, structural positions in society, or family relationships affect their politics. But it is also important to understand the political impact of gender differences. Have these differences resulted in the election of more women, changed the policy agenda to be more sensitive to women's issues, meant defeat for some candidates and victory for others, or forced the parties to craft new sorts of appeals? When we ask these questions, we are bringing to the foreground questions about sex differences, that is, women's political behavior and women's representation; questions about gender, though related, recede into the background.

Opinion Differences over Time

Sex differences in public opinion vary by region and over time. The ways that gender affects public opinion (and political behavior) are historically and politically contextual. This chapter focuses on the United States in the 1990s, but we should not lose sight of the fact that the differences we observe now reflect a particular place and time. In this section I examine some of the vast array of data comparing men's and women's opinions on a variety of public issues. . . .

Two trends converged in the 1970s to increase women's visibility and to focus new attention on possible sex differences in public opinion. First, women's rates of participation in electoral politics increased. Although as late as the 1968 elections men outpaced women in voting turnout by 4 to 5 percentage points, by 1980 the relationship was reversed. For the first time women turned out to vote at a higher rate than men. Because women outnumber men in the population, women voters now constitute a clear majority of voters everywhere in the country. Women constituted about 54 percent of the presidential electorate in 1992.

The second trend was the rise of the feminist movement and the dramatic increase in the size and visibility of women's organizations. These organizations worked to move the national political agenda toward concerns for "women's issues," such as reproductive rights, equal opportunity in employment and education, the Equal Rights Amendment, and electing more women to high political office. Suddenly, possible differences between men's and women's opinions took on political meaning. By the end of the decade, pollsters were discovering a gender gap in candidate preference. Gallup polls found that 38 percent of men supported Carter in 1980, compared with 44 percent of women. The discovery of the gender gap in 1980 led to a systematic exploration of gender differences in policy preferences.

Gender Differences on Women's Issues

On most of the issues directly related to women or to women's interests, sex differences have recently been small to nonexistent, but this has not always been the case. Hazel Erskine's 1971 study examined sex differences in opinions about women's roles in politics and society. Until the 1960s, women were much more likely than men to support such things as equal employment opportunities for women or the idea of women in public office. As one example among many, Gallup asked in 1952: "Some people say that if there were more women in Congress and holding important government positions, the country would be better governed. Do you agree or disagree?" Only 31 percent of men agreed, but 47 percent of women did (Erskine 1971, 282). During and after the 1960s, however, such differences were erased or reversed, primarily because men increased their support for sex equality. For example, Gallup poll questions about support of the Equal Rights Amendment, asked seven times between 1975 and 1982, found that an average of 57 percent of the women respondents and 61 percent of the men respondents supported the ERA (Simon and Landis 1989, 275). Similarly, Robert Shapiro and Harpreet Mahajan (1986, 53) found that "on other women's issues [other than abortion, that is] there are few clear and consistent differences." It is worth noting here that black women were more supportive than white women of the ERA in the 1970s, and they were also more supportive of collective and legal action to improve women's status (Wilcox 1990).

When men and women were asked about their thinking on the issue of abortion, in the aggregate their responses looked similar. For example, over a twenty-two-year period (1972–1994), the General Social Survey (GSS) asked this question: "Please tell me whether or not you think it should be possible for a pregnant woman to obtain a legal abortion if there is a strong chance of serious defect in the baby." The approval averaged just over 79

Table 2. Abortion Opinions in 1990 (in percentages)

	Men	Women	Difference: women–men	Men aged 18–29	Women aged 18–29	Difference: women–men
Favor leaving decision . . . to woman and her physician	69	72	+3	65	80	+15
Should be able to get abortion . . . no matter what the reason	40	45	+5	40	48	+8
Abortion should be legal only in certain circumstances	50	41	−9	52	42	−10
Personally believe having an abortion is wrong	44	50	+6	—	—	—
Abortion should be illegal in all circumstances	18	12	−6	6	10	+4

Source: 1990 General Social Survey.

percent for the whole sample, and there was never more than a 4 percent-age point difference between the positive responses of men and women (the difference averaged 1.9 points). This pattern is the norm on the so-called traumatic reasons for approving of abortion: the chance of a serious defect in the baby, or pregnancy as a result of rape or incest. To the extent that there is a difference, men are slightly more favorable to abortion in these circumstances than women.

It is possible that men and women reach similar issue positions through very different routes. Women, not men, confront the possibility of pregnancy because of rape or incest and have to deal most immediately with the reality or the possibility of a severely ill or handicapped child. Furthermore, virtually all women of childbearing age have had to deal intimately with the implications of having a child at a particular moment in their lives—with all the economic, emotional, educational, and career implications associated with such a decision.[4] Consequently, women may tend to have more intensely held views on abortion, to have views based on their own experiences with pregnancy and child rearing, and to make more use of the abortion issue in deciding how to vote.

Opinion polls on abortion, as illustrated by Table 2, show that women place themselves at the extremes more often than do men. That is, while

Table 3. Abortion and Voting in 1992 by Age Group (Percentage Saying Abortion Was Important to Their Vote)

	18–29	30–44	45–59	60+
Men	10	9	8	6
Women	21	18	12	8

Source: *American Enterprise*, January/February 1993, 102.

women are more likely than men to endorse free access to abortion or to view abortion as a private matter best left to the woman and her physician (the first two questions in Table 2), more women than men also believe that having an abortion is wrong. Among eighteen- to twenty-nine-year-olds, more women than men believe that abortion should be illegal in all circumstances. These sex differences appear to be accentuated among people ages eighteen to twenty-nine, the ages when women are feeling the full force of the choices and constraints represented by their childbearing capabilities.

In the GSS time series (1972–1994) there are few sex differences in responses to questions on abortion, and when they do occur, men are likely to be more liberal than women. But in thirteen of the sixteen surveys, women aged eighteen to twenty-nine are more likely than men in that age group to endorse abortion in the case of a serious defect in the baby. Furthermore, women are more likely to see candidates' stands on abortion issues as an important component of their voting decisions. In 1992, women in all age groups were more likely than men to say that abortion was important to their vote. Women of childbearing age were twice as likely as men to have used abortion as a factor, as illustrated by Table 3.

Gender Differences on Use-of-Force Issues

Polls have found the clearest differences between men and women in the area of force and violence. During the 1970s and 1980s there were consistent differences between the sexes in their responses to questions from all major survey organizations on gun control, capital punishment, military and defense spending, and withdrawal from Vietnam. Men consistently chose the more violent options (such as supporting capital punishment, higher military spending, and less regulation of handguns).

The preferences of both men and women on the appropriate level of defense spending have fluctuated over the years. Both sexes initially approved

Figure 1. Support of U.S. Presence in Gulf and for Possibility
of War in January 1991

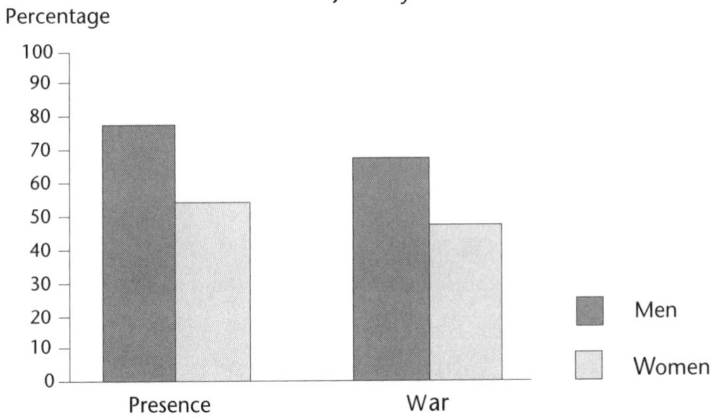

Source: Gallup Poll Monthly, January 1991, 14.

of Ronald Reagan's plea for the strengthening of American military capabilities. However, over the last twenty-one years, men generally have been more willing than women to have the government spend more on the military, armaments, and defense.

Fairly dramatic differences between men and women were characteristic of public opinion during the Gulf War. For instance, consider two questions asked by Gallup in January 1991. One asked for approval or disapproval of the decision to send U.S. troops to Saudi Arabia, and the other asked, "If the current situation in the Middle East involving Iraq and Kuwait does not change by January 15, would you favor or oppose the U.S. going to war with Iraq in order to drive the Iraqis out of Kuwait?" Figure 1 shows clear differences between men's and women's responses, with women showing less support for resorting to war.

Even clearer is the tendency for women to oppose the use of force in situations that arise in the United States. Women are much more likely to endorse stricter controls on firearms. For example, in 1994, 84 percent of female General Social Survey respondents versus 70 percent of male respondents endorsed the idea of requiring a police permit to own a handgun. Women have been consistently less likely to support the death penalty than men, as shown in Figure 2. It is also worth noting that more women than men disagreed with the statement on the General Social Survey that "it is sometimes necessary to discipline a child with a good hard spanking."

Figure 2. Percentage Favoring the Death Penalty, 1974–1994

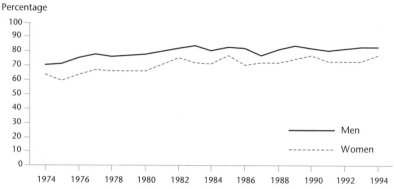

Note: Question wording is: "Do you favor or oppose the death penalty for persons convicted of murder?"

Source: 1974–1994 General Social Surveys.

Gender Differences on Compassion Issues

Compassion issues, such as welfare, care for the elderly, and environmentalism, make up the second area to show consistent gender differences in public opinion. These distinctions, however, tend to be slightly smaller than those found for use-of-force issues. While Shapiro and Mahajan (1986) found an average of 6 percentage points difference between men's and women's responses on force and violence issues, they found an average 3-point difference on compassion issues. Women in the 1970s and 1980s were "more supportive of a guaranteed annual income, wage-price controls, equalizing wealth, guaranteeing jobs, government-provided health care, student loans, and rationing to deal with scarce goods" (Shapiro and Mahajan 1986, 51). They found larger differences in opinion on policies which "regulate and protect consumers, citizens, and the environment." More women than men, in a number of different surveys, opposed cigarette advertising and nuclear power plants. Women were more likely than men to support stiffer penalties for those who drive drunk or fail to wear seatbelts, and to support highway speed limits. Women's greater support for environmental regulation appears to be a product of the 1980s (Shapiro and Mahajan 1986, 51–52). In Figure 3 men and women are compared on the GSS time series asking about government spending on health care, welfare, and the problems of big cities. Differences are consistent and minor, and they generally appear to be larger now than in the 1970s.

Figure 3. Gender Gaps in Spending on Social Services, 1973–1994

Percentage

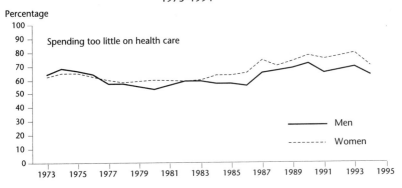

Spending too little on health care

Men

------- Women

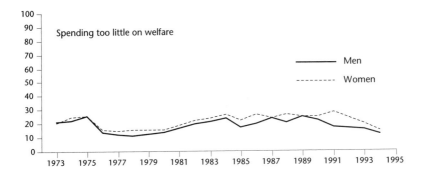

Spending too little on welfare

Men

------- Women

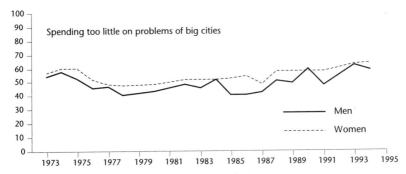

Spending too little on problems of big cities

Men

------- Women

Note: Question wording is: "We are faced with many problems in this country, none of which can be solved easily and inexpensively. I'm going to name some of these problems, and for each one I'd like you to tell me whether you think we are spending too little money, too much money, or about the right amount. Improving and protecting the nation's health./Welfare./Solving the problems of big cities." Entries are proportion saying too little is spent.

Source: 1973–1994 General Social Surveys.

Gender differences on issue opinions become politically important as they are linked to policy and candidate preferences. Women's more liberal opinions since 1980 have been associated with less positive evaluations of Republican presidents, more positive evaluations of Bill Clinton, and (relative to men) a preference for the Democratic Party. The "gender gap" began when analysts discovered that women's evaluations of Ronald Reagan were significantly less positive than men's. Gallup and other polls during Reagan's first administration found a consistent difference of about 8 percentage points (and sometimes as much as 12 to 14 points) between men and women. Analysis of forty-one Gallup polls through 1983 found that "gender differences existed not only on the national level, but in every major population subgroup as well," including both groups that had many Reagan supporters (for example, Republicans) and groups that were generally less supportive (blue-collar workers, blacks).[5] George Bush also received a lower approval rating from women than from men during his four years in office, by an average of about 6 points on the Gallup polls. Correspondingly, Clinton's ratings have been higher among women (by about 4 percentage points in 1993) than among men.

Bases of Opinion Differences

Just how does gender shape citizens' thinking about politics? Why should the fact that one is male or female, and thus brought up in certain ways and confronted with particular life choices, affect the way one thinks about capital punishment or welfare? Thinking about this question is an important next step beyond identifying gender differences.

Age or generational differences—in addition to work status, education, and race—almost certainly supply different conditions in which gender expectations and ideologies work themselves out for individuals. Political scientists mostly have sought to understand how gender influences opinion as part of a larger effort to explain the gender gap in political opinions. In general, the dependent variables in these analyses have been gender differences in presidential vote or presidential approval, but others have examined differences in issue positions and in basic values. Virginia Sapiro and Pamela Johnston Conover (1993) tested alternative explanations of gender differences in attitudes toward militarism and war, and particularly toward the

Gulf War. One primarily journalistic explanation—that the gender gap in the 1980s was simply a reaction on the part of women to Ronald Reagan's particular "macho" rhetoric and political style—has been disproved by time. As we have seen, the pro-Democratic, liberal bias among women, though not dramatic, has persisted in the post-Reagan era.

When social scientists attempt to explain the gender gap in voting or presidential approval, they have generally sought to identify other demographic factors that might cause men and women to think differently. For example, many studies focus on structural or economic explanations, and attempt to compare men and women with similar levels of income. Although women make less money than men, are economically more vulnerable, and are more dependent on government benefits, these economic differences do not explain voting patterns in 1980 and 1984 (Miller 1988, 261–264; Frankovic 1982, 443–444). Susan Carroll has suggested a more sophisticated theory which uses psychological as well as economic independence from men to construct a successful explanation of gender differences in voting and Reagan approval in 1980.

A second set of explanations has to do with the women's movement or with feminist ideology. Arthur Miller (1988) found that correlations between feminism and the vote in 1984 were weak and similar for men and women. Kathleen Frankovic (1982) agreed: opinions on ERA or abortion did not predict opinions about Reagan. Conover (1988) finds that feminist identity provides a robust explanation of differences. She writes, "There is not so much a gap between men and women [but] a gap between men and feminist women" (p. 1005). But Elizabeth Adell Cook and Clyde Wilcox (1991) argue persuasively that feminist identity cannot "explain" the gender gap because feminism has a reciprocal relationship with liberal opinions and egalitarian values. When feminism is seen as an ideology that can characterize men as well as women, they show, there remain gender gaps between feminist men and women and nonfeminist men and women. Without some long-term panel data or alternative kinds of research into people's political life histories, our view of causal relationships between feminist attitudes and other political values and opinions remains cloudy.

In searching for an explanation for the gender gap as it manifests itself in vote choice, scholars have focused on issues of war and peace and compassion, arguing that women's typical positions on these issues predisposed them to vote less Republican in 1980 and 1984 (see Frankovic 1982, 444–446; Miller 1988, 272–277). Such issue differences have persisted, widening in some cases, and it may be that women and men construct different political agendas in making up their minds about how to vote (see Miller 1988).

Explaining voting differences in terms of issue differences begs the question of why men's and women's opinion distributions are distinct in the first place. While the structural and feminist mobilization arguments may have some explanatory power here, Conover and Sapiro (1993) address the question of issue differences (in the area of war and violence) directly, offering the contending explanations of "maternalism," feminism, and gender. Maternalism introduces a version of a socialization explanation which others (notably Miller 1988) have rejected. The maternalist hypothesis posits that the practices and experience of mothering foster antimilitaristic attitudes. Though this hypothesis has not been thoroughly tested—there are problems measuring "motherhood"—Conover and Sapiro's (1993) analysis suggests that the maternal model does not explain gender difference. The feminist consciousness hypothesis, according to Conover and Sapiro (1993), is only partially supported. In particular, feminist consciousness led to greater emotional distress over the Gulf War but not to a more negative overall evaluation of the war. The best explanation, in their view, is the "gender hypothesis." In the context of the Gulf War, women were more fearful and concerned about the war than men and more strongly opposed to bombing civilians (though not less supportive of the war in general). The fact that these differences "cannot be eliminated by controlling for the effects of a wide-range of other explanatory elements points to a pervasive, gendered pattern of *early* learning of cognitive and especially affective orientations toward the use of violence" (Conover and Sapiro 1993, 1096). In a nutshell, women are simply different from men and this difference is, though "socially constructed," virtually innate. It seems that we are back to square one.

The Political Impact of Differences: From Gender Gap to Gender Wars?

Gender is socially constructed. It is socially contextual—constructed differently for different generations and races—and it is a complex phenomenon. Over the past fifteen years the differences between men's and women's political attitudes and opinions have received new and vigorous attention. I think it is fair to say that the differences we find are persistent (if still time-bound) and that research into their correlates and antecedents has contributed to our (still partial) understanding of how gender affects politics. Perhaps the questions that now deserve more thought have to do with the political implications of these differences.

When the gender gap became apparent after the 1980 election and was publicized by women's organizations such as the National Organization for Women as a way to drum up support for the Equal Rights Amendment and for the Democrats' nomination of a woman for vice president, it marked an important turning point in the long struggle to reshape the policy agenda to incorporate issues of particular concern to women (Mueller 1988). Today the perception that women have a distinct agenda—or even that citizens as a whole are increasingly embracing aspects of what might be termed a women's agenda—continues to shape candidacies and campaigns. Candidates like one of Barbara Boxer's opponents in her 1992 Senate primary, who declared breast cancer "a state emergency," try to stake out advantageous positions on what have been conventionally described as women's issues. Of course how such issues translate into votes and eventually into policy depends critically on the parties and political leaders who are mobilizing support for them.

The often small differences between men's and women's opinions, as well as the dramatic variance among women, means that women voters are far from a monolithic bloc, despite media oversimplifications to that effect. Karen Paget (1993) argues that "if the pitfall in the past was to assume that women's interests were identical to men's, it is equally misleading today to equate the gender gap with an emergent female voting bloc, let alone a monolithic one" (p. 101). Nonetheless, women's votes are more important than ever, and over time they have had the effect of electing more women to office, increasing the electoral salience of issues that interest women voters, and reshaping the policy agenda. Small differences can be politically significant depending on the media interpretation of the differences, public perceptions of these interpretations, and the actions and goals of the political leaders who make use of them to mobilize resources and supporters.

In this context, the 1990s might be characterized as the era of gender wars rather than of the gender gap. Susan Faludi's 1991 bestseller *Backlash* described a variety of vocal and belligerent antifeminist reactions. What we might consider as opinion differences seem frequently to have escalated

Table 4. Group Differences in Percentage Approving of Hillary Clinton

Age and party groups	Men	Women	Difference: women–men
Overall	40	60	+20
Republicans	23	39	+16
Independents	35	60	+25
Democrats	69	75	+6
18–29 years old	32	55	+23
30–44 years old	41	67	+26
45 and over	43	57	+14

Source: Gallup poll, June 1993.

into bitter conflicts: violence and killing at abortion clinics, record numbers of sexual harassment grievances, including men's claims against women,[6] an intense focus on domestic violence, and Rush Limbaugh's derogatory term "femi-Nazis" applied to feminists.

Since the 1992 presidential election, Hillary Rodham Clinton has been a focal point of the gender wars. One of the more interesting public opinion phenomena during the Clinton administration has been the over-time and across-group variation in approval of the First Lady. Over the course of 1992 and the first half of 1993, for example, the proportion of respondents expressing "generally favorable" opinions of Hillary Clinton ranged from a low of 25 percent to a high of 61 percent (Yankelovich/Time/CNN polls). In the Gallup poll conducted in June 1993, the overall gender gap (that is, the difference between male and female respondents' favorable opinions) was a substantial 20 points, with 60 percent of women but only 40 percent of men expressing a favorable opinion. Table 4 shows how this male/female difference is exacerbated among certain groups. Party and age are important determinants of favorability also. Those women who, we might expect intuitively, would identify most strongly with Hillary Clinton— those who are thirty to forty-four years old and Democrats—are most positive toward her.

The data in Table 4, which show a remarkable difference between men and women in the thirty- to forty-four-year-old group of 26 percentage points, suggest that the gender wars are being fought among people in similar situations or close proximity. A few more examples of these striking differences follow. The *Los Angeles Times* surveyed 2,346 enlisted men and women on active duty in February 1993. When asked, "How do you feel about allowing women to take combat roles in the U.S. Armed Forces?" 55 percent of the men and fully 79 percent of the women approved.[7] In 1992, exit polls in four states asked whether the nomination of Clarence Thomas to the Supreme Court should have been confirmed. In all four states men essentially said yes and women said no. This was true in every age group and particularly for younger people. For example, in Pennsylvania, 52 percent of eighteen- to twenty-nine-year-old men backed Thomas, whereas only 31 percent of women in that group did.[8] A Gallup poll in May of 1992 asked registered voters their opinion of Clarence Thomas. Among the college-educated, 55 percent of the men but only 37 percent of the women had a favorable opinion. Perhaps picking up on this conflictual atmosphere, Gallup asked a national sample in August 1993, "How often would you say that you feel resentful specifically toward men/women because of something they do, or perhaps something they don't do, that you find irritating and just typically male/female?" Twenty percent of men and a substantial 40 percent of women replied "very often" or "often"—virtually no one said "never."

In the 1992 election, the Perot candidacy seemed to bring out gender conflict. Among his strongest supporters in June, according to a Gallup poll for *USA Today*/CNN, were men aged thirty to forty-four (43 percent "considered themselves a supporter"). Women in this age group were much more negative (only 21 percent were supporters). While Democratic men and women were similar to one another in their preferences for Perot, a gender gap of 19 points existed among Republicans, with men much more supportive of Perot than women.[9]

One thing that most all of the explanations of the gender gap have had in common is that they seek understanding by looking at women—that is, they try to explain why women think or behave as they do. Male behavior or opinion is, implicitly, the norm. Why are women more supportive of welfare spending? It must be women's socialization, women's mothering experiences, women's dependence on government benefits. Why are women more opposed to war? It must be women's nurturing, compassionate nature. Why were women less supportive of Reagan? It was something about his message or style of presentation to which women did not respond. Much of the time when journalists and even social scientists say something has to do with gender, they really mean that it has to do with women. This is even more strongly the case with politics, where a deep and

Figure 4. Percentage Shift to Republicans (between 1992 and 1994
House Votes) for Age/Sex Groups

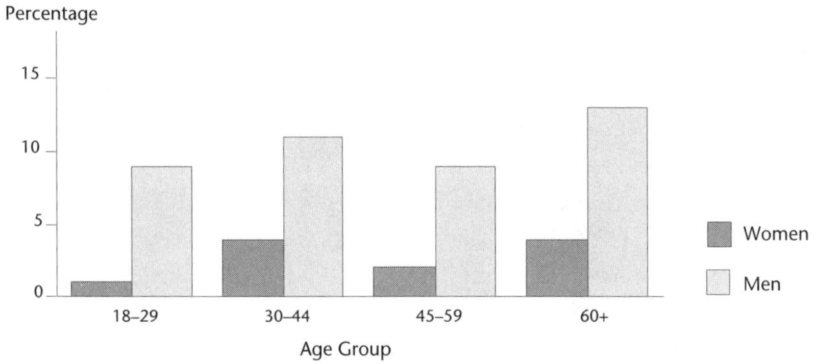

Source: Everett Carll Ladd, "1994 Vote: Against the Background of Continuing Realignment," in America at the Polls, 1994, ed. Everett Carll Ladd (Storrs, Conn.: Roper Center, 1995), 48.

hard-to-shake assumption that politics is a male domain means that it is women's behavior that demands explanation.

Looking at the party identification measure in the American National Election Studies from 1952 to 1992, women's preferences have remained quite a bit more stable than men's. Averaging the first four and the last four surveys in the series, the level of Democratic identification among men fell 12 points (from 48 percent to 36 percent) while women's dropped only 5 points (47 percent to 42 percent). Certainly the change in voting behavior from 1992 to 1994 was far greater for men than for women, as illustrated in Figure 4. Here we see that men's shift toward the Republicans was about three times the magnitude of women's.

These data suggest that perhaps men's behavior or thinking is just as deserving of explanation as women's, that gender is not just about women. Political discourse should ask how (or whether) men should fulfill their traditional "breadwinner" role; where assertiveness, independence, and other traditionally male attributes fit into an effective leadership style; how men can balance the demands of family with the demands of careers; whether, and in what ways, men or women are better off in present-day American society. The expectations and conflicts of modern American society affect men as well as women.

In the 1992 election cycle, the media seemed quite taken with the number of women running for and winning office. In 1994, the spotlight shifted away from women candidates (as the *New York Times* announced in October, "In 1994, 'Vote for Woman' Does Not Play so Well") and toward the angry male electorate. In the 1994 elections, fifty-one of sixty-three races covered by Voter News Service exit polls (twenty-four of thirty gubernatorial races, twenty-one of twenty-seven senatorial races, all four of the state attorney general races covered, and both of the at-large House races) were characterized by a gender gap of 4 points or more. In virtually all these situations (forty-nine of fifty-one) women were more supportive of the Democratic candidate.

One of the most striking things about coverage of the 1994 election was that the media began to broaden its understanding of gender. Rather than continuing to try and explain why women again voted more Democratic than men, we saw attempts to explain why men (particularly young white men) voted so heavily for Republicans. *USA Today*'s front page story in the weekend edition of November 11–13, 1994, headlined "Angry White Men: Their Votes Turn the Tide for GOP." As Celinda Lake described it when interviewed for that article, "Women want to change Washington. Men want to torch it." Another pollster suggested that working-class white men are "increasingly convinced society and government aren't making room for them. They feel they are the butt of jokes, condescended to." These men opposed Clinton's attempt to allow openly gay people to remain in or join the military, distrusted and disliked Hillary Clinton and her role, and objected to high taxes and spending on social programs. The gender wars—real conflict over sex roles, rules of discourse, and expectations—combined with the economic insecurity increasingly felt by those in traditionally male jobs (such as assembly-line, heavy industry workers as well as the middle management ranks which many companies are shrinking) to produce a distinctive outlook which can be usefully approached via a gender analysis.

The relationship between gender and public opinion over the past thirty years has been a complicated one. Through the 1970s, women were presumed to be identical to men on one level and different from men on another—a combination that reduced sex to a politically uninteresting distinction. That is, women were seen as essentially and uniquely conservative and apolitical—but to the extent that they did think about politics or vote, their interests were assumed to be identical to men's. When empirical sex differences suggested in the 1980s that the essential attributes of women were perhaps not so fixed, women's organizations took advantage of this change in perception to construct a new picture of women as having distinct political interests. At the same time, the emergence of gender analysis as a way of achieving a deeper understanding of men's and women's political thinking and behavior allowed social scientists and historians to suggest reasons for the observed sex differences. From these perspectives, differences in the opinions held by males and females became both intellectually interesting and politically important. As the 1980s waned, gender itself and gender issues became a focus of political contestation; now, in the 1990s, gender may become a useful tool of analysis to understand both men and women, just as women's issues and women candidates assume an ever more central role in American politics.

NOTES

1. Joan Scott's 1986 article, "Gender: A Useful Category of Historical Analysis," is particularly relevant in this context.

2. A few of the books which have had an impact on historians' thinking about various periods in American history include Kerber (1980), Muncy (1991), and Skocpol (1992); on political theory, Susan Muller Okin's two books (1979 and 1991); and on power see Hartsock (1983).

3. If you order clothing from Lands End, for example, the shipping label will be marked with color, size, and "gender." I would argue that Lands End is really talking about biological sex but is (incorrectly) substituting what seems to be a more current term.

4. Klein (1984) also discusses the possibility that while men may come to their stands on abortion through general principles based on rights or liberalism, the issue for women may be more strongly shaped by their personal experience.

5. *Gallup Report* 1983, cited by Kenski 1988, 47–49.

6. The press in February 1995 reported a suit by eight men who had worked for Jenny Craig Inc., a corporation dominated by women, who claimed they had been the target of sexual remarks, been asked to perform demeaning jobs, and denied promotions because of their sex.

7. Data from *American Enterprise,* July / August 1993, 102.

8. Data from *American Enterprise,* January / February 1993, 104.

9. Data from *American Enterprise,* July / August 1993, 98.

REFERENCES

Conover, Pamela Johnston. 1988. "Feminists and the Gender Gap." *Journal of Politics* 50:985–1010.

Conover, Pamela Johnston, and Virginia Sapiro. 1993. "Gender, Feminist Consciousness and War." *American Journal of Political Science* 37:1079–1099.

Cook, Elizabeth Adell, and Clyde Wilcox. 1991. "Feminism and the Gender Gap: A Second Look." *Journal of Politics* 53:1111–1122.

Erskine, Hazel. 1971. "The Polls: Women's Role." *Public Opinion Quarterly* 35:275–290.

Faludi, Susan. 1991. *Backlash: The Undeclared War Against American Women.* New York: Crown.

Frankovic, Kathleen A. 1982. "Sex and Politics: New Alignments, Old Issues." *PS: Political Science and Politics* 15:439–448.

Hartsock, Nancy. 1983. *Money, Sex and Power: Toward a Feminist Historical Materialism.* New York: Longman.

Hess, Robert, and Judith Torney. 1967. *The Development of Political Attitudes in Children.* Garden City, N.Y.: Doubleday.

Kenski, Henry C. 1988. "The Gender Factor in a Changing Electorate." In *The Politics of the Gender Gap,* ed. Carol M. Mueller. Newbury Park, Calif.: Sage Publications.

Kerber, Linda K. 1980. *Women of the Republic: Intellect and Ideology in the Revolutionary America.* Chapel Hill: University of North Carolina Press.

Klein, Ethel. 1984. *Gender Politics: From Consciousness to Mass Politics.* Cambridge: Harvard University Press.

Miller, Arthur. 1988. "Gender and the Vote: 1984." In *The Politics of the Gender Gap,* ed. Carol M. Mueller. Newbury Park, Calif.: Sage Publications.

Mueller, Carol M. 1988. "The Empowerment of Women: Polling and the Women's Voting Bloc." In *The Politics of the Gender Gap,* ed. Carol M. Mueller, Newbury Park, Calif.: Sage Publications.

Muncy, Robyn. 1991. *Creating a Female Dominion in American Reform 1890–1935.* New York: Oxford University Press.

Niemi, Richard G., John Mueller, and Tom W. Smith. 1989. *Trends in Public Opinion: A Compendium of Survey Data.* New York: Greenwood Press.

Okin, Susan Moller. 1979. *Women in Western Political Thought.* Princeton, N.J.: Princeton University Press.

_____. 1991. *Justice, Gender, and the Family.* New York: Basic Books.

Paget, Karen M. 1993. "The Gender Gap Mystique." *The American Prospect* 15 (Fall): 93–101.

Sapiro, Virginia, and Pamela Johnston Conover. 1993. "Gender in the 1992 Electorate." Presented at the Annual Meeting of the American Political Science Association, Washington, D.C.

Scott, Joan. 1986. "Gender: A Useful Category of Historical Analysis." *American Historical Review* 91:1053–1075.

Shapiro, Robert, and Harpreet Mahajan. 1986. "Gender Differences in Policy Preferences: A Summary of Trends from the 1960s to the 1980s." *Public Opinion Quarterly* 50:42–61.

Simon, Rita J., and Jean M. Landis. 1989. "The Polls—A Report: Women's and Men's Attitudes About a Woman's Place and Role." *Public Opinion Quarterly* 53:265–276.

Skocpol, Theda. 1992. *Protecting Soldiers and Mothers: The Political Origins of Social Policy in the United States.* Cambridge: Harvard University Press.

Sundquist, James L. 1973. *Dynamics of the Party System.* Washington, D.C.: Brookings Institution.

Tolleson-Rinehart, Sue, and Jeannie Stanley. 1994. *Claytie and the Lady: Ann Richards, Gender, and Politics in Texas.* Austin: University of Texas Press.

Wilcox, Clyde. 1990. "Race, Gender Role Attitudes and Support for Feminism." *Western Political Quarterly* 43:113–121.

10-3

Disconnected Politics

Lyn Ragsdale

In the following essay, we revisit the subject of public opinion polls and presidents. Lyn Ragsdale observes that polls represent a new and important technology and notes the similarities and differences among presidents in their relations with the public and in their use of polls. She concludes that, because of the influence of polls, presidents have found public opinion more important and, at the same time, less manageable. In response, presidents have been forced to simplify and dramatize their messages and policies.

"PEOPLE USED TO SAY of me that I . . . divined what the people were going to think. I did not 'divine.' I simply made up my mind what they ought to think, and then did my best to get them to think it." Theodore Roosevelt, speaking at the turn of the twentieth century, made clear that his strategy was to create rather than to follow public opinion (1926, vol. 20, 414). Near the end of the century, Ronald Reagan modified speeches according to what internal White House polls and focus groups showed public opinion to support. George Bush received daily poll reports on American attitudes toward Iraq months before the start of the Gulf War. These polls helped administration officials to establish the ultimate direction of American involvement in the war and to frame their justification for the war. In the aftermath of a Republican sweep of the House and Senate in the 1994 elections, Bill Clinton's specially prepared White House polls showed that the public felt the president should be more faithful to his centrist campaign promises. In the ensuing days, Clinton made announcements backing a middle-class tax cut, denouncing the size of the federal government, and calling for a line-item veto. Unlike Roosevelt, three presidents at the end of the century followed, rather than created, public opinion.

Excerpted from Barbara Norrander and Clyde Wilcox, eds., *Understanding Public Opinion* (Washington, D.C.: CQ Press, 1997), pp. 229–251.

The nature of presidents' relations with the public has changed technologically, philosophically, and politically in the twentieth century. Technological changes have affected how presidents present themselves to the public, how the public responds, and how the public's responses are measured. Presidents no longer have the luxury afforded Theodore Roosevelt to divine public opinion. Instead, monthly (sometimes even weekly) public opinion polls, taken by various polling organizations and inside the White House, monitor public opinion. These polls began in 1938 when the Gallup Organization first asked a random sample of Americans the question, "Do you approve or disapprove of the way [the incumbent] is handling his job as president?" Since that initial poll—in which 60 percent of Americans approved of Franklin D. Roosevelt's job performance—presidential popularity, or presidential approval, has become a part of the body politic. The question was asked about Harry S. Truman during his first term (1945–1948) just fifteen times. But the advent of computer-assisted telephone polling has made these surveys far more numerous. Polls measured George Bush's approval 110 times during his four years in office. The polls do not merely inquire about a president's overall job performance; they capture public opinion on specific presidential decisions and White House problems. It is not uncommon to see poll results on whether the Senate should confirm a controversial presidential nominee, whether the president should fire a wayward aide, or whether the president has taken an appropriate stance on a factious issue, such as the pardon of Richard Nixon, the American hostage crisis in Iran, or allowing homosexuals to serve in the military.

Other technological changes grant the public greater access to more information about the president from more varied sources than ever before. Theodore Roosevelt counted on newspaper and wire service reports as the primary outlets for presidential news. Today, presidential news may appear through live coverage, network and local television and radio news broadcasts, news talk shows, entertainment talk shows, news magazines, newspapers, radio call-in shows, and on-line computer services.

These technological changes have worked in tandem with and accentuated philosophical changes. Philosophically, Theodore Roosevelt and his successor, Woodrow Wilson, made the presidency a public office and the president a public representative in new ways. The prevailing notion in the nineteenth century was that presidents might be seen, but they were rarely heard on policy issues before the nation. Presidents typically did not advance their own policy views or take positions on matters before Congress. Roosevelt changed that by insisting that the president could offer policy reforms as the "steward of the people" who was "bound actively and affirmatively to do all he could for the people. . . . My belief was that it was not only his right but his duty to do anything that the needs of the nation demanded unless such action was forbidden by the Constitution or by the laws" (Roosevelt 1913, 389). In Roosevelt's view, the public provided the president with a mandate for policy activism.

Roosevelt also saw the president as a particular kind of representative. Two views have long been associated with the idea of representation: that a representative may act as a delegate on behalf of the expressed desires of the public or as a trustee in the best interests of the public (as the representative construes those interests). Roosevelt, as the only nationally elected official, believed that presidents should act as trustees to do what was best for the country, even if their actions were controversial.

Today's philosophy is different. Presidential stewardship and the accompanying policy activism are bolder and broader than Roosevelt could have imagined. Furthermore, today's presidents must take into account the omnipresence of public opinion polls, which present an immediate and continuous plebiscite on their performance. The frequency and visibility of public opinion surveys put pressure on presidents to conform with the known preferences of the public as documented in the polls. Consequently, presidents are more likely to behave as delegates who react to public opinion than as trustees who may shape it. This is not to say that presidents do not attempt to act as trustees, but that they will have greater difficulty doing so.

These technological and philosophical changes have fundamentally changed the politics of the presidency. Politically, the omnipresence of the president as national representative and the ongoing popular plebiscite change the way presidents do their public business. Both place considerable pressure on the chief executives to take their case directly to the American people all of the time. To be sure, Theodore Roosevelt's voice captured the public's attention "noisily, clamorously; while he is in the neighborhood the public can no more look the other way than the small boy can turn his head away from a circus parade followed by a steam calliope" (quoted in Cornwell 1965, 15). But it was a voice that was heard only sporadically and only in direct appeals at public rallies. The president's voice was not heard live across the nation or in daily news broadcasts, subject to an immediate critique by officials of the other party, momentary media analysis, and overnight public evaluation. Contemporary presidents are seen and heard daily on all major and minor issues facing the nation. Their messages may actually have less impact on public opinion than those of their predecessors did, because the communication takes on the quality of background noise.

In addition, with so many polls available, a president's job performance is overevaluated. The poll results become "political facts" about the president that people in Washington cite, regularly update, and, most important, use to construct political strategies. Consequently, the opening for presidential success may not extend beyond the next poll. It is increasingly difficult for presidents to get ahead of Americans' opinions on various issues. Instead, presidents often choose courses of action that are, in the vernacular of the Reagan administration's pollsters, "resonators"—positions and issues that people generally like or do not find controversial (Brace and Hinckley 1992, 3). The more presidents do or say counter to these resonators, the less likely they will be to be able to follow public opinion satisfactorily. Activist presidents have difficulty faring well amidst these political changes.

This essay addresses the changing relationship between presidents and the public by highlighting three dimensions to public opinion toward presidents: personal, historical, and institutional. The personal dimension defines the individual differences that occur among presidents in their relations with the public. The historical dimension marks different periods in the relationship between presidents and the public; within these periods, presidents share similar problems and resources in dealing with the public. The institutional dimension identifies regularly occurring patterns of behavior which all presidents follow: every president engages in certain policy activities and public activities that are expected of the occupant of the White House. The chapter concludes with an assessment of how the three dimensions together affect the way the public approves of presidents' performance in office. The interweaving of the three dimensions makes presidents less important to the public at the same time as the public becomes more important to, but less manageable by, presidents.

Personal Differences among Presidents

People in and out of the Clinton administration commented on the low approval ratings of President Clinton during his first year. Clinton's approval peaked in his second month in office, February 1993, at 59 percent and dropped to its lowest point, 38 percent, just four months later. Most of the explanations for these low marks centered on Clinton himself—as a novice in Washington; someone ill at ease in foreign affairs; an advocate of an aggressive, but not well thought out, domestic agenda; and a figure plagued by charges of sexual harassment and financial misdealings.

Of the three dimensions of public opinion toward presidents, the personal dimension is the most vivid and easiest to grasp. It points to unique decisions and mistakes that presidents make in office and the unique circumstances that confront them. These individual differences also lead sometimes to exceptional ebbs and flows of popularity. Bill Clinton was not alone in facing large swings in presidential approval ratings. Gerald Ford's popularity plummeted 21 points when he pardoned Richard Nixon. Jimmy Carter enjoyed a 14-point increase in approval after the Iranian seizure of American hostages. George Bush's approval ratings shot up 25 percentage points in just twenty days in January 1991 as the nation sat transfixed by the nightly television war in the Persian Gulf. He gained 6 more points by the end of February to reach an 89 percent approval rating, the highest approval ever recorded for any president. During the next year, Bush's popularity was in free fall; it dropped 51 percentage points from February 1991 to February 1992.

Table 1 provides a more systematic look at the approval ratings of individual presidents from Franklin Roosevelt to Clinton. The table shows a wide variation in popularity among the eleven presidents. Presidents Truman and Nixon (in their second terms) shared the lowest average popularity for a term, at 36 percent approval and 35 percent approval, respectively. President Roosevelt achieved the highest average popularity rating during his third term: 74 percent approval. The standard deviation column in the table also reveals the volatility of several presidents' popularity. In particular, Truman, Johnson, Nixon (in his second term), Carter, and Bush had wide swings in approval ratings during their terms, as shown in the "difference" column in the table, which subtracts the lowest approval rating from the highest approval rating. Presidents Truman and Bush experienced the largest shifts in their approval—a 55 percentage point difference for Truman in his first term and the 51 percentage point gap noted for Bush.

The personal dimension seems to provide analysts with reassurance that what they see is what they get. A drop or rise in approval can be matched with a specific event, decision, or activity during a president's term. Seemingly, these events, conditions, and decisions are unique to a given president. People assume that Vietnam could have happened only on Johnson's watch. No one but Nixon would have let Watergate get out of hand. Other

Table 1. The Personal Dimension: Approval of Individual Presidents,
Franklin Roosevelt to Bill Clinton

President	Average	Standard deviation	High	Low	Difference	Number of polls
Roosevelt						
2d term (1938–1940)	59%	3.2	65%	54%	11%	19
3d term (1941–1943)	74	3.9	84	66	18	24
Total (1938–1943)	67	8.3	84	54	30	43
Truman						
1st term (1945–1948)	52	16.9	87	32	55	15
2d term (1949–1952)	36	11.3	69	23	46	29
Total (1945–1952)	42	16.0	87	23	64	44
Eisenhower						
1st term (1953–1956)	69	5.4	79	57	22	52
2d term (1957–1960)	60	5.8	73	49	24	55
Total (1953–1960)	65	7.2	79	49	30	107
Kennedy (1961–1963)	71	6.9	83	58	25	40
Johnson (1964–1968)	56	13.4	80	36	44	81
Nixon						
1st term (1969–1972)	57	5.3	65	48	17	60
2d term (1973–1974)	35	12.4	67	23	44	34
Total (1969–1974)	49	13.2	67	23	44	94
Ford (1974–1976)	47	7.0	71	37	34	35
Carter (1977–1980)	47	12.0	75	28	47	88
Reagan						
1st term (1981–1984)	50	7.6	68	35	33	76
2d term (1985–1988)	56	6.9	65	40	25	46
Total (1981–1988)	52	8.0	68	35	33	122
Bush (1989–1992)	61	14.8	83	32	51	110
Clinton (1993–1994 only)	48	5.5	59	38	21	56

Sources: Roosevelt to Ford calculated from *Gallup Opinion Index,* October–November 1980, 13–59. Polls on Roosevelt began in 1938; no polls were conducted in 1944. Carter to Clinton calculated from successive volumes of *Gallup Poll Monthly.*

presidents would not have handled the Iranian hostage crisis the way Carter did. Thus, the personal dimension allows presidency watchers to focus on differences among presidents as individuals: Johnson is not Nixon who is not Carter. And these differences are confirmed in their approval ratings.

Yet, although the personal dimension is the simplest aspect of presidential popularity to understand, it is surely the most misleading. The personal dimension reveals that there are variations in presidents' approval ratings. Those variations, however, may not be wholly attributable to the uniqueness of individual chief executives. Bill Clinton's early-term popularity problems may have been only partly his own doing. Forgotten in the simplicity of the personal dimension are systematic comparisons across presidents. Without such comparisons, students of public opinion do not really know how much of the variations across presidents are actually the result of personal differences. With such comparisons, the importance of personal differences is not denied but is placed in a more appropriate context.

Historical Trends

One type of comparison that can be made is to examine differences across time periods. The historical dimension denotes whether technological, philosophical, and political shifts over time have altered the way people view presidents. If such historical trends exist, then presidents of one time period will have approval ratings that look distinctly unlike those of another era regardless of who the presidents are, what they do, or what they encounter during their terms. For instance, people often commented on the personal popularity of Ronald Reagan. Early in his first term, the press dubbed Reagan the "Teflon president." Problems encountered by his administration never seemed to stick to him, and his honeymoon never completely ended. Many likened Reagan's personal popularity to that of Dwight Eisenhower, a spectacularly successful general of World War II turned highly popular president of the 1950s. Others suggested that Reagan had revitalized public impressions of the presidency after the disappointments of Jimmy Carter.

Despite these characterizations, each of which stresses the unique personal nature of Reagan's approval, a comparison of Eisenhower's and Reagan's popularity from Table 1 reveals marked differences. And a comparison of Reagan's, Carter's, and Clinton's approval ratings shows stunning similarities. Eisenhower's average popularity for his first term was 69 percent; his highest popularity point was 79 percent approval and his lowest popularity point was only 57 percent approval. In contrast, Reagan's average popularity for his first term was just 50 percent; his highest approval was 68 percent and his lowest rating was 35 percent. Reagan's average ratings were higher in his second term, but they still did not match those of

Eisenhower in either term. Eisenhower's popularity was more like that of his immediate successor, Kennedy, whose popularity rating averaged 71 percent.

Reagan's approval was more like the ratings of two Democratic presidents—his predecessor, Carter, whose average popularity was 47 percent, and Clinton, whose midterm popularity averaged 48 percent.[1] Indeed, the levels of public approval that Carter and Reagan received during their first two years in office were nearly identical, and they were quite similar during their third years (see Ragsdale 1993, 148). Only in the fourth year of their terms did their approval ratings drastically diverge. Both Carter and Reagan saw their honeymoons fade toward the end of their first year in office; both faced growing disillusionment over the next two years, as economic problems worsened—Carter's primarily inflation, Reagan's primarily unemployment. Although Reagan may have projected a more comfortable image than Carter, he was no more a Teflon president than his predecessor had been. In addition, his midterm average approval rating was 50 percent, only slightly better than Clinton's 48 percent approval. This pattern suggests that there are similarities in public opinion from one president to another relevant to the period of presidential politics in which they served. The supposed personal difficulties of Clinton and the supposed personal fortunes of Reagan can be placed in clearer perspective by considering political similarities within time periods of the presidency.

Historical eras are examined more closely in Table 2, which provides a breakdown of approval and disapproval during two periods of the presidency—from Franklin Roosevelt to Lyndon Johnson (1938–1968) and from Richard Nixon to Bill Clinton (1969–1994). Presidents from Roosevelt to Johnson received notably higher approval ratings during their terms than presidents since Nixon have. President Johnson's average popularity, which significantly eroded with worsening problems in Vietnam, still was higher than that of any of the presidents since Nixon, except Bush. Johnson's annual approval ratings for the years 1964 through 1966 were above 50 percent. It was only in 1967 and 1968 that Johnson's approval ratings dipped below that mark. In this vein, Johnson's popularity fits better with the earlier pattern than with the later one.

The differences between the two periods in average approval and in annual approval for each year of the term are striking. Average approval during the early period is 61 percent, while average approval during the later period is 52 percent. The large gap between the periods holds for both the

Table 2. The Historical Dimension: Average Approval for Year in Term,
Comparing Roosevelt through Johnson (1938–1968)
with Nixon through Clinton (1969–1994)

	1938–1968 Approval	1969–1994 Approval	Difference
Average	61%	52%	−9%
Average first term	63	53	−10
Average second term	57	48	−9
First Term			
First year	72	56	−16
Second year	61	52	−9
Third year	58	54	−4
Fourth year	53	46	−7
Second term			
Fifth year	67	50	−17
Sixth year	58	44	−14
Seventh year	54	48	−6
Eighth year	52	53	1

Sources: Calculated from all available Gallup polls from 1938 to 1994. For 1938 to 1976, poll results found in *Gallup Opinion Index,* October–November 1980, 13–59. For Carter to Clinton, poll results found in successive volumes of *Gallup Poll Monthly.*

first term and the second term. The table also reveals how the average approval ratings per year were lower in every year of the later period except the eighth. Presidential honeymoons are decidedly less happy affairs in the later period, when presidents received an average of only 56 percent approval for their first year in office; 72 percent approval was the average for presidents in the earlier period. The gap is no less pronounced in the second term. The later presidents start their second terms with an average 50 percent approval rating, whereas the earlier presidents had received a 67 percent approval rating.

The long-term downward shift in popularity may point to certain systematic changes in the environment within which presidents perform and within which the public evaluates their performance. Three such changes are discussed here: changes in media coverage of presidents, changes in presidents' luck in facing unfolding political events, and changes in economic conditions in the country.

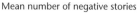

Figure 1. The Rise of Bad Press for Presidents, 1949–1994

Mean number of negative stories

Note: Negative stories are coded and counted from the *New York Times.*

Bad Press

One fundamental historical change involves press coverage of presidents. Figure 1 charts negative coverage of presidents from Truman (in his second term) to Clinton, as displayed in the *New York Times.*[2] It is immediately clear from the figure that negative press coverage soared, as one would expect, during Watergate, soon returned to levels relatively like those from before the scandal, and then since 1985 has slowly increased. During the earlier period (1949–1968) 14 percent of stories (twenty-six stories per quarter) in the *New York Times* were negative. The bad press more than doubled, to 30 percent of presidential news stories, in the period since 1969, amounting to seventy-seven negative stories per quarter. Even excluding the Watergate years 1973 and 1974, negative stories amounted to 28 percent of total coverage in the later period. The negative coverage during the 1990s is especially striking. Fully 36 percent of coverage was negative during the first half of the decade. Even during 1991, as the Persian Gulf War unfolded, negative news climbed, accounting for 37 percent of the coverage. Bad news continued for Bill Clinton: 35 percent of news coverage was negative in 1993 and 43 percent was negative in 1994.[3]

To understand this rise in bad press, one must first consider the more general increase in media coverage of presidents. As illuminated in Figure 2, the beginnings of this overall increase in presidential news coverage occurred in 1963 and can be traced in part to the Kennedy assassination. Jour-

Figure 2.   Media Coverage of Presidents, 1949–1994

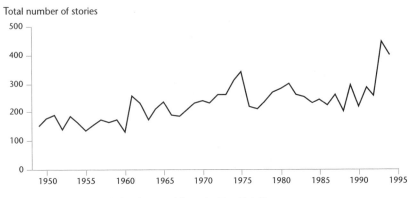

Note: Stories are coded and counted from the New York Times.

nalists were distressed about their inability to provide immediate coverage of the assassination, in part because of the growing size of the White House press corps. There were so many press vans in the Dallas motorcade and they were so far behind the presidential limousine that no reporter or camera operator witnessed the assassination or even knew it had taken place. The press vans merely followed the chase to Parkland Memorial Hospital, where the president was taken. The last van pulled up to the hospital well after all members of the presidential and vice presidential entourages were inside. From this event, the "body watch" in presidential news evolved.

The body watch dictates that members of the press cover presidents' every public move just in case, in Ronald Reagan's words, "the awful, awful" happens—the president is shot, becomes ill, has an accident, or dies. A Washington bureau chief for Newsweek elaborated: "The worst thing in the world that could happen to you [as a journalist] is for the President of the United States to choke on a piece of meat, and for you not to be there" (Grossman and Kumar 1981, 43). The body watch expanded further in the 1960s as technological advances in satellites created more opportunities for live coverage. The body watch also intensified as nightly network news shows enlarged their formats from fifteen minutes to thirty minutes in the early 1960s and had more time for presidential news.

The consequence of the body watch is total coverage of presidents, from their most trivial and mundane public actions to their sometimes dramatic official announcements. Total coverage means that many more personal and official mistakes are captured and critiqued than would have been with less comprehensive coverage. As one example, Lyndon Johnson enjoyed playing with his two beagles, pulling them up by their long floppy ears. One day photographers recorded Johnson's play session on the White House lawn. The next day newspapers across the country ran the picture of the president smiling broadly and holding one of the dogs up by its ears. Dog owners were enraged. The White House swiftly announced that Johnson would abandon the practice. In earlier times the event would not have been recorded and no controversy would have occurred.

In recent years the body watch has focused attention on the personal foibles and past liaisons of presidents and presidential candidates. For example, during the 1988 presidential campaign, rumor had it that Sen. Gary Hart, a contender for the Democratic nomination, was having an affair. Hart denied the rumors and cavalierly challenged reporters to follow him. They did. Reporters watched as he left the woman's home early one morning. Since then, what might be called the "Gary Hart rule" has been invoked on all candidates and chief executives. Reporters question all details— whether recent or from the distant past—of the politicians' personal lives. This replaces a starkly different "Franklin Roosevelt rule" previously followed by reporters: never disclose details of presidents' or presidential candidates' personal lives. This earlier practice began as an informal agreement among reporters and camera operators that they would never mention or photograph Franklin Roosevelt in his wheelchair. The practice was later extended to not covering Roosevelt's problematic marriage. Under the Gary Hart rule invoked during the 1992 presidential campaign, it was not surprising to see NBC News correspondent Stone Phillips ask George Bush about an affair the president was rumored to have had with a state department official. Bush's brusque retort—"You don't ask questions like that in the White House"—did little to dampen the controversy. Nor, given the new scope of the body watch, did it seem shocking to see Bill and Hillary Clinton discuss their marriage on the news show *60 Minutes*.

Coupled with the body watch has been a notable rise in skepticism, if not outright cynicism, among the White House press corps about presidents' actions and, in particular, about presidential accounts of those actions. Reporters witnessed the so-called credibility gap of the Johnson administration during the Vietnam War. The gap was identified when the troop levels and casualty figures announced by the administration were lower than figures found independently by reporters. Reporters helped to expose the outright lies of President Nixon during the Watergate cover-up and the web of deception and illegality in the Iran-contra affair in the Reagan administration. The melodrama of these episodes was deepened by the lack of candor from presidents in several other less divisive actions, including the U-2 incident in 1960, the Bay of Pigs invasion in 1961, and troops sent to the Dominican Republic in 1965. Consequently, as the columnist Max Frankel observed, White House reporters increasingly treat "virtually every official utterance as a carefully contrived rendering that needs to be examined for the missing word or phrase, the sly use of statistics, the slippery syntax or semantics" (1971, 16).

The now total coverage of presidents partially reflects technological advances in broadcasting which make it feasible for reporters to cover every move a president makes. But the body watch has prompted a not so subtle shift in the philosophical tenets of the office as well. Theodore Roosevelt's public representative faces assessments of moral and ethical conduct that were not undertaken before. Moreover, distinctions among official public activities, personal activities done in public, and personal activities have collapsed. There is an ever widening domain of what is considered an acceptable, if not highly sought after, topic for a presidential news story. Evolutions of this kind are not easily stopped or even slowed. An uneasy shift in presidential politics has accompanied this philosophical change. The body watch draws up new definitions of success and failure for presidents, which include how adept they are at handling past or present personal problems, how they face political battles which may erupt from any and all activities covered in the watch, and how well they handle the media.

Bad Luck and a Bad Economy

Beyond the bad press presidents received in the later period, they also encountered more bad luck and worse economic times than their predecessors. Table 3 provides a summary comparison for the two periods on a number of political and economic measures. Presidents in the later period encountered five times more negative events than presidents in the earlier period had.[4] These events are relatively long-lived and prominent; they are national or international in scope; they specifically involve some form of presidential action; and they have a directly adverse consequence for the president. Some of these events presidents bring on themselves, but others

Table 3. Political and Economic Differences between 1949–1968
and 1969–1994 (Quarterly Averages)

	1949–1968	*1969–1994*	*Difference*
Media coverage (number of stories)	180	255	75
Negative coverage (percentage of stories)	14.30	30.10	15.80
Positive coverage (percentage of stories)	48.30	36.00	−12.30
Negative events (number)	0.13	0.63	0.50
Unemployment (percentage)	6.85	6.57	−0.28
Consumer price index (total change)	1.91	31.52	29.61

Sources: Data on media coverage are from Michael Grossman and Martha Kumar, *Portraying the President* (Baltimore: Johns Hopkins University Press, 1981), as updated by the author. Data on negative events as described in the text were coded and calculated by the author. Data on unemployment and consumer prices are taken from successive volumes of the U.S. Department of Commerce, *Survey of Current Business.*

are out of their control. They include negative international events (the communist victory in Vietnam in September 1974), massive political protests and riots (the Los Angeles riots in 1991), the failure of major legislation or a key nomination actively sought by a president before Congress (the demise of health care reform in 1994, the defeat of Robert Bork's nomination to the Supreme Court in 1987), and highly unpopular executive actions, staff misdealings, or personal problems (such as Ford's pardon of Nixon in 1974). While presidents encountered only ten such negative events in the early period, they were plagued by forty-six negative events in the later period. The economy was also much more problem-filled in the later period. Unemployment rates during the two periods are quite similar (an average of 6.9 percent for the early period as compared with 6.6 percent for the later period). But consumer price increases were fifteen times greater in the later period than in the earlier era.

Thus, later presidents coped with a much more rough-and-tumble political and economic environment than their earlier counterparts. The historical increase in negative events included terrorist campaigns, civil wars in newly organized countries, and presidents' own political scandals in the Watergate and the Iran-contra affairs. Economic woes of the later period also were more complicated and difficult to handle—problems of stagflation (a combination of slow growth and high inflation) and oil-price shocks in the 1970s, the rising budget deficit in the 1980s, and severe budget cuts in the 1980s and 1990s to cope with the deficit. Press coverage devoted attention to these big problems and bad economic times, thereby amplifying the negative environment within which presidents worked and within which the public evaluated their work.

Institutional Behavior

This [essay] has examined the ways presidents are affected by factors outside the institution. But one can also look at the presidency itself in different eras. An institution has a life of its own, independent of the people who participate in it. The institution establishes a set of regular patterns of behavior that individuals within it follow, whatever they do at other times in their life. Institutional behavior thus involves the extent to which different individuals faced with similar circumstances respond in much the same way. This is not to say that institutional behavior remains static—it may change with the times. But presidents abandon established patterns of behavior at their peril. If they do so, they violate expectations people have of someone who holds the chief executive's job. The institution of the presidency thus guides the behavior of presidents. This means that presidents with very different backgrounds, political skills, and policy agendas nonetheless behave in certain similar ways. Two types of institutional behavior exist for presidents: policy activism and public appearances.

Policy Activism

Theodore Roosevelt originated presidential policy activism with his shift in the philosophical tenets of the office. According to the principle of activism, presidents, as Roosevelt's stewards of the people, make independent policy actions and are fully involved in the legislative policy debate in Congress. Contemporary presidents, regardless of individual differences, are all but required to engage in policy activity; it comes with the job. For example, many people typecast Bill Clinton as a "policy wonk," someone who immersed himself in the details of policy and offered many, perhaps too many, policy items for the national agenda. Yet Clinton's personal interests had seemingly less to do with his policy activity than institutional requirements at hand. His first-year policy activism was no greater than Truman's,

Table 4. Presidents' Institutional Behavior Differences between 1949–1968
and 1969–1994 (Quarterly Average Number)

	1949–1968	1969–1994	Difference
Total policy activity	60	51	−9
Legislative requests	22	15	−7
Policy positions (taken on roll calls)	20	22	2
Executive orders	18	14	−4
Total public appearances	41	61	20
Major addresses	1	1	0
News conferences	7	4	−3
Minor policy speeches	2	3	1
Ceremonial appearances	31	53	22

Source: Data from Lyn Ragsdale, *Vital Statistics on the American Presidency* (Washington, D.C.: Congressional Quarterly, 1996).

nearly fifty years before—both made 159 policy requests to Congress.

In the contemporary period, Roosevelt's legacy has taken three key forms. First, presidents since Truman have submitted annual legislative programs to Congress, in an effort to influence, if not define, the congressional agenda. Second, presidents take positions on numerous matters before Congress, beyond their own legislative proposals. Finally, presidents since Franklin Roosevelt have used executive orders as a device to fashion substantive policy decisions bypassing the legislative process. Executive orders are documents signed by presidents which carry the same weight in law as a statute but do not require passage by Congress. Presidents have signed executive orders to accomplish such things as the desegregation of the military, implementation of affirmative action guidelines, and enacting restrictions on abortion counseling. Policy activism, then, is a key form of institutional behavior in the presidency. Combining the three types of activities, presidents have made about fifty-five policy actions per quarter during the period from 1949 to 1994. As shown in Table 4, there has been a slight drop in policy activism between the two historical periods discussed here. Presidents in the early period took an average of sixty policy actions per quarter, while presidents in the later period took fifty-one quarterly policy actions. Much of the drop can be attributed to Ronald Reagan, who made a limited number of legislative requests to Congress in his terms.[5]

Public Appearances

Theodore Roosevelt also enlarged the public face of the presidency. Roosevelt's philosophical view of the president as key public representative instructed chief executives to take their case directly to the public. In Roosevelt's words, "I achieved results only by appealing over the heads of the Senate and House leaders to the people, who were the masters of both of us" (1926, vol. 20, 342). This philosophical perspective coupled with technological advances in broadcasting and air travel invite current presidents to go to the public often.

In considering presidents' public appearances, it is important to distinguish among four types of appearances: major national addresses, news conferences, minor policy speeches, and ceremonial appearances. The appearances target different audiences and contain varying degrees of policy content. Major national addresses are prime-time speeches before the nation which include State of the Union messages, other speeches to joint sessions of Congress, and special addresses from the White House. The major addresses typically contain substantive policy remarks, but, more than any other forum, they also depict the president as the nation's symbolic leader. News conferences contain policy content and attract national audiences but the give-and-take between reporters and the president offers a far different format from that of major addresses. Minor policy speeches are made before a specific audience, often at a university commencement or business or labor convention. In the speech, the president may outline a significant policy proposal, but the forum is less visible than a major national address or news conference. Ceremonial appearances involve presidents' greeting specific groups at the White House or being welcomed to various communities in rallies and motorcades across the country. As shown in Table 4, major addresses and minor policy speeches have remained relatively constant over the total forty-five-year period. There has been a small drop in the number of news conferences but a distinct rise in the number of ceremonial appearances. Although ceremonial appearances were certainly an important form of institutional behavior in the earlier period, they have become decidedly more a part of presidents' activities in the later period. Combining the appearances, presidents in the later period made sixty-one public appearances per quarter, while presidents in the earlier period made only forty-one appearances; the increase is almost completely accounted for by the rise in ceremonial appearances.

Table 5. Effects of Policy Activism and Public Appearances on Popularity, 1949–1968 and 1969–1994

	1949–1968		1969–1994	
	Percentage	(n)	Percentage	(n)
Low policy activism	61	(36)	54	(53)
High policy activism	54	(34)	49	(52)
Low public appearances	59	(49)	52	(54)
High public appearances	57	(31)	51	(51)

Notes: The low and high categories are broken at the mean. The numbers of cases are in parentheses. Policy activism combines legislative requests, policy positions on roll calls, and executive orders. Public appearances combine major addresses, news conferences, minor policy speeches, and ceremonial appearances.

With these appearances, presidents have adopted a fundamental political strategy. They engage in a perpetual campaign of public appearances which continues long after the election is over. Driving this perpetual campaign is the assumption that maximum public exposure leads to maximum popular benefit. Campaigners typically assume that they should make as many appearances in as many forums as they have time, energy, and money to make. The rationale is that appearances can only help the campaign. Presidents have applied this assumption to their appearances in office, especially the ceremonial ones, believing that public exposure can only help in their efforts to maintain or build a favorable public image and gain public support for particular policy decisions. The assumption holds a kind of self-generating quality which pushes presidents to make ever more public appearances, thus helping to account for their increase from the earlier period to the later period. This cycle makes public appearances as a form of institutional behavior all the more entrenched.

Institutional Behavior and the Public

The problem for presidents is that neither policy activism nor public appearances pay off much in their popularity ratings. Table 5 examines the average popularity obtained by presidents when they engaged in low and high levels of policy activism and public appearances during the two periods of presidential politics (1949–1968 and 1969–1994). In both eras, more active presidents have lower approval ratings. In the early period, more active presidents average 54 percent approval, while less active presidents earn 61 percent approval. In the later period, more active presidents receive 49 percent approval; again less active presidents have higher approval, with 54 percent. Above average numbers of public appearances likewise do not guarantee higher approval ratings. In fact, there is not much difference in either period in approval ratings between presidents who make above average numbers of appearances and those who make below average numbers of appearances. Perhaps the perpetual campaign does not help a president govern. . . .

Conclusion: Presidential Disconnections

Theodore Roosevelt died in 1919, before radio broadcasts had begun. In 1924, Calvin Coolidge made the first nationally broadcast address to the nation from the back platform of a railroad car. Two decades later, public opinion polls began to capture popular reactions to these addresses and presidents' other actions. And only ten years after that, presidents began to appear on live television; meanwhile, poll results, as ingredients to make or break a presidential decision, were increasingly commonplace. Roosevelt would have been pleased that since the 1930s presidents have ardently expanded the philosophical tenets of policy activism and public representation which he espoused. He would be dismayed that those tenets coupled with around-the-clock media coverage and continual public opinion polls have made the philosophical requirements no longer politically feasible.

Presidents face a bitter irony. The current philosophy of the presidency requires that they be policy stewards and public representatives. Presidents have adopted political strategies to fit these philosophical requirements. They have taken numerous policy actions and have spent a considerable time in office making public appearances in Washington and around the country. But these activities confront the ever present public opinion polls within which presidents are punished for policy activism and get no credit for their public appearances, except major addresses (and only in the recent period). Although Americans may say that they prefer activist presidents who get the job done, evidence belies such statements. The more active presidents are, the more unpopular they are. Media coverage has made the president a public figure with little, if any, private space. This coverage has so enlarged the requirements of presidents' public representation that people may become distrustful of presidents about whom they know so much. Presidents make ever more varied national appearances, but their messages are buried in their own avalanche.

With the ability to measure minute shifts in public opinion on literally everything that occurs during a presidency, presidents have lost much, although not all, of their ability to shape and focus public opinion, as either policy activists or public representatives. Thus, the combination of public representation, policy activism, media coverage, and public opinion polls fundamentally recalibrates the metric by which presidents' success in office is measured. Success is equated with popularity, failure with disapproval.

To accommodate this new equation, presidents must offer grand simplifications in their policy actions and public appearances. They must offer bold, clear-cut solutions to complex problems which can be portrayed in media coverage as major administration victories. Two Carter administration officials asked "whether any president can be perceived as successful today unless his governing victories are overwhelming" or are depicted as overwhelming (Heineman and Hessler 1980, 108). Reagan's early budget- and tax-cutting victories and Bush's Persian Gulf War victory stand as elegant examples of the inelegant new requirements of the office. Too, presidents are judged harshly when their defeats appear overwhelming, as Clinton's health care reform defeat did. Far more ordinary achievements such as trade agreements, budget deals, and executive reorganizations do not provide items for the clear-cut ledger of success and failure. Similarly, presidents' public appearances must be dramatic rather than routine and less frequent rather than more frequent.

Thus, the rationales behind policy activism and the perpetual campaign are in need of reexamination. Although successive presidents have offered numerous policy proposals and maintained a breakneck pace of appearances, the evidence here suggests they would be better off making policy suggestions and public appearances less often and more strategically. Presidents run the risk of overexposure from both forms of institutional behavior and a devaluation of the political import of the presidency in the process.

While one might believe that technological, philosophical, and political changes have brought presidents and the public closer together, in some ways the changes have actually forced them further apart. The very polls and media used to establish the connection between presidents' performances in office and the public's evaluations of them are responsible for the disconnection between president and public. The disconnection occurs because the public is not persuaded by most presidential public appearances and dislikes policy activism. They continue to hold presidents responsible for economic conditions that are becoming increasingly international, complex, and out of presidents' hands. Presidents attempt to make economic and other decisions with public opinion in mind, but the public is much less persuaded by the merits of the actions. Presidents do not get credit for acting as delegates, even when the web of public opinion prevents them from acting as trustees. This disconnection between presidents and the public is one that Theodore Roosevelt would neither have envisioned nor praised.

NOTES

1. Reagan's midterm popularity (1981–1982) averaged 50 percent.

2. Newspaper coverage data have not yet been gathered for Roosevelt or Truman in his first term. So the remainder of the discussion is based on quarterly data from Truman (1949) to Clinton (1994). The news data come from a content analysis of the *New York Times* in which all stories on the presidency are coded as having positive, negative, or neutral tone. The original content analysis from 1953 to 1978 was conducted by Michael Grossman and Martha Kumar (1981, 253–272). Their time series has been extended and updated by the author. Ideally, data on television coverage would also be useful in ascertaining the nature of good and bad press, since the presidency has become such a television-oriented office during the period since Truman. Television news data for this time period, however, are not fully available. The Grossman and Kumar study does include an analysis of CBS News coverage of the presidency; it shows great similarity between CBS News and the *New York Times*, which is recognized as a national newspaper with extensive, often leading, coverage of the presidency.

3. Others also have observed this increase in negative coverage in television news (see Lichter and Noyes 1991; Smoller 1986).

4. Identification of these negative events for the period 1949 to 1994 was based on matching of material presented in weekly issues of *Facts on File* and monthly breakdowns of the *World Almanac*. An event had to be consistently mentioned for at least four consecutive weeks in the *File*. In addition, the event had to be discussed in the almanac's monthly chronology of major world occurrences. Both sources also had to note specifically the presence of presidential involvement in the event: Did the president take some action? The two sources were evaluated to establish the negative impact of an event on a president's administration.

5. The policy measure discussed is an additive index of the following three measures: (1) the annual number of legislative requests presidents make to Congress in their State of the Union messages, as first determined by Light (1991, 42) and extended and updated by the author; (2) the quarterly number of policy positions presidents take on legislation being voted on before Congress, as calculated in successive volumes of the

Congressional Quarterly Almanac; and (3) the quarterly number of executive orders signed by a president. These data are all found in Ragsdale (1996).

REFERENCES

Brace, Paul, and Barbara Hinckley. 1992. *Follow the Leader.* Chicago: University of Chicago Press.

Cornwell, Elmer. 1965. *Presidential Leadership of Public Opinion.* Bloomington: Indiana University Press.

Frankel, Max. 1971. "The Press and the President." Letter to *Commentary,* July 16, 16.

Grossman, Michael, and Martha Kumar. 1981. *Portraying the President.* Baltimore: Johns Hopkins University Press.

Heineman, Ben, and Curtis Hessler. 1980. *Memorandum for the President: A Strategic Approach to Domestic Affairs in the 1980s.* New York: Random House.

Lichter, Robert, and Richard E. Noyes. 1991. "In the Media Spotlight: Bush at Midpoint." *The American Enterprise* 2:50.

Light, Paul. 1991. *The President's Agenda,* rev. ed. Baltimore: Johns Hopkins University Press.

Okin, Susan Moller. 1991. *Justice, Gender and the Family.* New York: Basic Books.

Ragsdale, Lyn. 1993. *Presidential Politics.* Boston: Houghton Mifflin.

_____. 1996. *Vital Statistics on the American Presidency: Washington to Clinton.* Washington, D.C: Congressional Quarterly.

Roosevelt, Theodore. 1913. *Theodore Roosevelt: An Autobiography.* New York: Macmillan.

_____. 1926. *The Works of Theodore Roosevelt.* New York: Scribner.

Smoller, Fred. 1986. "The Six O'Clock President: Patterns of Network News Coverage of the Presidents." *Presidential Studies Quarterly* 16:40–42.

10-4

Dynamic Representation

James A. Stimson, Michael B. MacKuen, and Robert S. Erikson

The relationship between public opinion and government action is complex. In the United States, with single-member congressional districts, we often consider relationship at the "micro" level—that is, whether individual elected officials are following the wishes of their home constituencies. But the overall relationship between public preferences and government behavior, the "macro" level, is more difficult to assess. In the following essay, James Stimson, Michael MacKuen, and Robert Erikson provide a look at this relationship with the help of a creative invention. These scholars use a statistical technique to build an aggregate measure of public opinion from dozens of polls. The technique allows them to measure change in the liberalism of views expressed in the polls over several decades. Then, using similarly aggregated measures of the behavior of Congress, the president, and the Supreme Court, they evaluate the relationship between the liberalism of public opinion and the behavior of the institutions. Government as a whole proves responsive to public opinion, and Congress and the presidency prove more responsive to public opinion than the Supreme Court.

. . . WHAT DOES IT mean that a government represents public feelings? Responsiveness must be a central part of any satisfactory answer. Representative governments respond to—meaning act as a consequence of—changes in public sentiment. To "act as a consequence of" changes in public sentiment implies a sequence, inherently structured in time. We may say that if, by knowing about earlier changes in public sentiment, we can improve the prediction of public policy over what we could have done from knowing only the history of public policy itself, then opinion causes policy, and this is dynamic representation. . . .

Excerpted from article originally published in *American Political Science Review* 89, no. 3 (September 1995): 543–64. Reprinted by permission. Notes appearing in the original have been cut.

The *dynamic* character of representation has a second aspect. Most political decisions are about change or the prevention of change. Governments decide to change health care systems, to reduce environmental regulations, to develop new weapons systems, or to increase subsidies for long staple cotton growers. Or not. Thus, political decisions have a directional force to them, and their incremental character is inherently dynamic. Further, most public opinion judgments concern change as well. The public expresses preferences for "more" or "less" governmental action across different spheres: "faster school integration," "cuts in welfare spending," "getting tougher on crime," and so on. The main difference is that public sentiment is generally more vague, diffuse, than the more concrete government action.

This understanding suggests something akin to the familiar "thermostat" analogy. The public makes judgements about current public policy—most easily that government's actions need to be enhanced or trimmed back. These judgements will change as policy changes, as real-world conditions change, or as "politically colored" perceptions of policy and conditions change. And as the simple model indicates, politicians and government officials sense these changes in public judgment and act accordingly. Thus, when public policy drifts away from the public's demands for policy, the representation system acts as a control mechanism to keep policy on course.

The question now is how. If public opinion governs, how does it find its way into the aggregation of acts that come to be called public policy.

The Mechanisms of Dynamic Representation

Start with a politician facing a policy choice. With both preferences over policy options and a continuing need to protect the electoral career from unwanted termination, the elected official will typically need to balance personal preference against electoral expediency. We presume that politicians have personal preferences for and against particular policies and also that they value reelection. Then for each choice, we can define (1) a personal ideal point in the space of policy options and (2) an *expediency point* (that position most likely to optimize future reelection changes). The expediency point might be the median voter of the relevant constituency or some similar construct. We are not concerned here about particular rules. All that matters is that the politician have a *perception* of the most expedient position.

. . . Politicians create an appropriate margin of safety: those who highly value policy formulation or who feel safe at home choose policy over security; those who face competitive challenge in the next election lean toward "expediency" and security. . . .

. . . [E]lectoral turnover stems from events that overwhelm the margin of safety that the politicians select. Campaign finance, personal scandals, challenger tactics, the framing of electoral choice—all affect outcomes. The victims come both from those who take electoral risk by pursuing policy and also from those who ignore personal preference and concentrate solely on reelection: what matters is the force of electoral events relative to the politician's expectations. . . .

To breathe life into this system, let us put it into motion to see its aggregate and dynamic implications. Assume that public opinion—global attitudes toward the role of government in society—moves over time. Immediately we can expect greater turnover as the force of public opinion augments the normal electoral shocks to upset incumbent politicians' standard calculus. Now, the changes in personnel will prove systematic: rightward shifts in public opinion will replace Democrats with Republicans, and leftward shifts Republicans with Democrats. . . .

Rational Anticipation, Turnover, and Policy Consequence

Turnover from elections works most transparently with politicians who are neither well informed (until hit on the head by the club of election results) nor strategic. But that does not look at all like the politicians we observe. The oft-painted picture of members of Congress, for example, as people who read five or six daily newspapers, work 18-hour days, and leave no stone unturned in anticipating the electoral problems that might arise from policy choices does not suggest either limited information or naïveté.

We explicitly postulate the reverse of the dumb and naïve politician: (1) elected politicians are rational actors; (2) they are well informed about movements in public opinion; and (3) they agree with one another about the nature of those movements. This was well said by John Kingdon: "People in and around government sense a national mood. They are comfortable discussing its content, and believe they know when the mood shifts. The idea goes by different names. . . . But common to all . . . is the notion that a rather large number of people out in the country are thinking along certain common lines, that this national mood changes from one time to another in discernible ways, and that these changes in mood or climate have important impacts on policy agendas and policy outcomes" (1984, 153). . . .

Elected politicians, we believe, sense the mood of the moment, assess its trend, and anticipate its consequence for future elections. Changes in opinion, correctly perceived, will lead politicians to revise their beliefs about future election opportunities and hazards. Revised beliefs imply also revised expedient positions. Such strategic adjustment will have two effects: (1) it will dampen turnover, the conventional path of electoral influence; and (2) it will drive policy through rational anticipation.

When politicians perceive public opinion change, they adapt their behavior to please their constituency and, accordingly, enhance their chances of reelection. Public opinion will still work through elections, however. When they are surprised by the suddenness or the magnitude of opinion change or when they are unable credibly to alter their policies, politicians, despite their best efforts, will occasionally face defeat at the polls. Rather more fitfully than was the case with dumb politicians, public preferences will operate on electoral institutions by changing the personnel and thus the aggregated preferences of elected officials.

But that is not the only public opinion effect. Changing policy from shifting perceptions of what is electorally expedient we will refer to as *rational anticipation*. In a world of savvy politicians, rational anticipation produces dynamic representation without need for actual electoral defeats.

Politicians modify their behavior at the margin. Liberals and conservatives do not change their stripes, but they do engage in strategic behavior either to minimize risk from movements adverse to their positions or to maximize electoral payoff from movements supportive of their positions. For example, in a conservative era, such as the early 1980s, conservative Democrats found it easier to break with their party and did it more often, while liberal Republicans found it more difficult and dangerous and did it less often. The result of such conditions can be substantial shifts in winning and losing coalitions without any change of personnel.

Moreover, such direct anticipation of the electoral future does not exhaust the possibilities. For other actors also anticipate the effects of future elections on the current behavior of elected officials. Those who advance policy proposals—bureaucrats, lobbyists, judges, and citizens—are concerned with what can be done successfully, be it administrative act, judicial decision, or legislative proposal. And other politicians—those who pursue a leadership role or advocate particular policies—may choose to push ahead of the curve, to multiply the effects of even marginal shifts in opinion by anticipating others' anticipated reactions.

The impact of rational anticipation is thus a net shift in policy outputs from the aggregation of all these smallish strategic decisions, which (responding to the same signal) tend to move all in the same direction. It should be observable as the direct response of policy to opinion change, when election turnover effects are controlled.

A Design for Assessing Representation

This two-part setup permits three possible empirical outcomes: (1) two-stage representation may occur through the mechanism of electoral turnover, where candidate success depends upon the public opinion of the moment, which is then reflected in policy behavior; (2) movements in policy acts may reflect opinion without changes in elite personnel, the rational anticipation scheme; and (3) no representation might occur if both schemes fail. The alternatives are laid out in Figure 1. There we can see three testable linkages. The first, A, is the first stage of the electoral sequence. The question to be answered is, Does public opinion affect election outcomes? The second stage, B, is not much in doubt. Its question is no cliff-hanger: Is there a difference in policy behavior between liberals and conservatives? The third linkage, C, is rational anticipation. Its question is, Does public policy move with public opinion independently of the effects of (past) elections? . . .

. . . The scheme of Figure 1 takes account of reality by positing other sets of causes of all phenomena as disturbances. The first, u_o, is the exogenous factors that account for changes in opinion. Not a focus of attention here (but see Durr 1993), they are such plausible forces as national optimism or pessimism arising from economic performance and reactions to past policies as experienced in daily life.

Elections are influenced by factors such as incumbent party performance, incumbency, macropartisanship, and so forth. Those factors appear as u_e on Figure 1. And finally, u_p captures sets of causes of public policy other than representation—such things as the events and problems to which policy is response or solution. Some of these "disturbances" are amenable to modeling, and will be. Some are irreducible, and must remain unobserved. . . .

Figure 1. The Pathways to Dynamic Representation

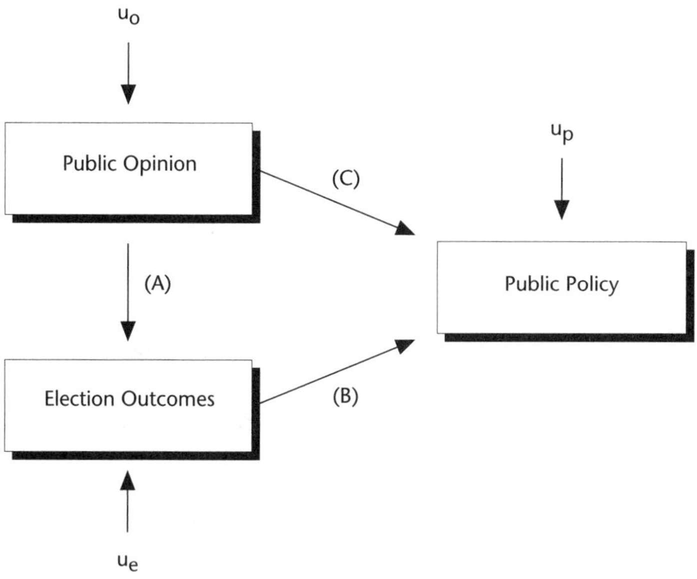

Measurement

The raw materials of dynamic representation are familiar stuff: public opinion, elections, and public policy together form the focus of a major proportion of our scholarly activity. But familiar as these concepts are, longitudinal measures of them are (excepting elections) ad hoc at best and more often nonexistent. It is easy to think of movements of public opinion over time and public policy over time. It is not easy to quantify them. The situation—familiar concepts but novel measures—requires more than the usual cursory attention to measurement concerns. We begin with public opinion.

The Measures: Public Opinion and Elections

To tap public opinion over time we have the measure *domestic policy mood* (Stimson 1991). Mood is the major dimension underlying expressed preferences over policy alternatives in the survey research record. It is properly interpreted as left versus right—more specifically, as global preferences for a larger, more active federal government as opposed to a smaller, more passive one across the sphere of all domestic policy controversies. Thus our public opinion measure represents the public's sense of whether the political "temperature" is too hot or too cold, whether government is too active or not active enough. The policy status quo is the baseline, either explicit or implicit, in most survey questions. What the questions (and the mood measure) tap then is relative preference—the preferred direction of policy change.

Displayed in Figure 2, the *policy mood* series portrays an American public opinion that moves slowly back and forth from left (up on the scale) to right (down) over time and is roughly in accord with popular depictions of the eras of modern American politics. It reaches a liberal high point in the early 1960s, meanders mainly in the liberal end of its range through the middle 1970s, moves quite dramatically toward conservatism approaching 1980, and then begins a gradual return to liberalism over the 1980s. Note as well that the neutral point (50% liberal, 50% conservative) means something: points above 50 mean that the public wants more conservative policy. Thus, while the public's conservatism peaked in 1980, the public continued to demand more conservative policy (though by smaller margins) until 1984. (Thus we may think of our mood measure as a signal to politicians about the intensity and the direction of political pressure. It represents a demand for change.) . . .

The Measures: Policy Change

What is policy liberalism, and how can we measure it? What we observe is decisions such as congressional votes—not quite "policy." Our view is that each involves policy *change* at the margin. The issue as it is typically confronted is, Should we move current government policy in more liberal (expansive) directions or in more conservative ones? What we observe is who votes how. We see, for example, a particular vote in which the liberal forces triumph over conservative opponents. We take such a vote to mean that in fact the (unobserved) content of the vote moves policy in a liberal direction—or resists movement in the conservative direction.

This is a direct analogy to public opinion as we measure it. We ask the public whether government should "do more" or "spend more" toward some particular purpose. We take the response, "do more," "do less," "do about the same" to indicate the preferred direction of policy *change*. In both cases direction of change from the status quo is the issue.

Figure 2. Public Opinion over Time: Domestic Policy Mood, 1956–1993

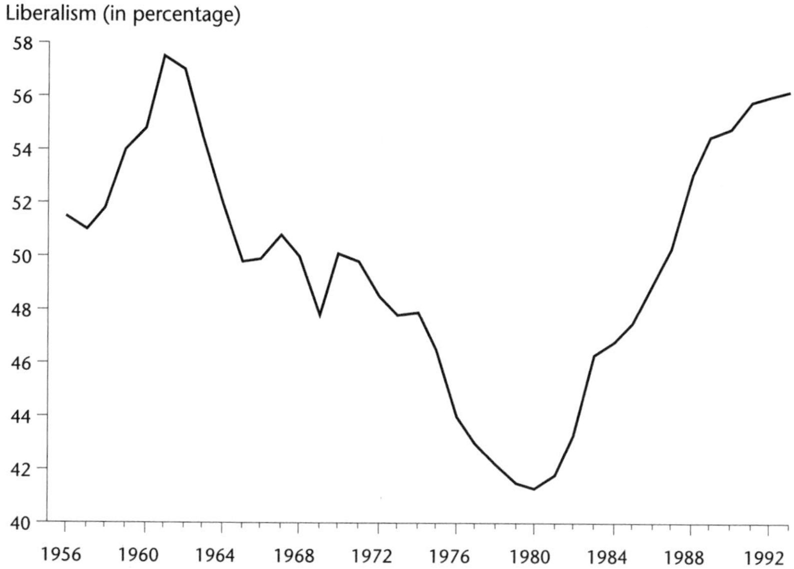

Liberalism (in percentage)

Measuring this net liberalism or conservatism of global policy output seems easy enough in concept. We talk about some Congresses being more or less liberal than others as if we knew what that meant. But if we ask how we know, where those intuitions come from, the answer is likely to be non-specific. The intuitions probably arise from fuzzy processing of multiple indicators of, for example, congressional action. And if none of them by itself is probably "the" defensible measure, our intuitions are probably correct in netting out the sum of many of them, all moving in the same direction. That, at least, is our strategy here. We will exploit several indicators of annual congressional policy output, each by itself dubious. But when they run in tandem with one another, the set will seem much more secure than its members.

Congressional Rating Scales. Rating scales are a starting point. Intended to tap the policy behaviors of individual House members and Senators, scales produced by groups such as Americans for Democratic Action (ADA) and Americans for Constitutional Action (ACA), later American Conservative Union (ACU), are now available for most of the period in question. Neither of these is intended to be a longitudinal measure of congressional action;

and from a priori consideration of the properties such a measure would want, this is not how we would derive one. But if scales move similarly across chambers and scales from different organizations move in common over time, then we begin to believe that whatever it is they are measuring is probably global liberalism or conservatism of roll-call voting. Thus, as a measure of *net group rating*, we take the yearly average of the House's (or Senate's) ADA score and (100 minus) the ACA/ACU score.

Congressional Roll-Call Outcomes. The strength of the rating scales is their cross-sectional validity: they discriminate liberals from moderates from conservatives in any given year. Their weakness is longitudinal validity: we are less confident that they discriminate liberal from moderate from conservative Congresses. For greater face validity, we turn to the roll calls themselves as measures of policymaking. A quite direct measure is the answer to the questions, On ideological votes, who wins? and By how much do they win? Provided that we can isolate a set of roll calls that polarize votes along the left-versus-right main dimension of American domestic politics, measuring the degree of, say, liberalism is as easy as counting the votes. If we know which position on the vote is liberal and which conservative, then all that remains is to observe who won and by how much (and then aggregate that roll-call information to the session).

We exploit the cross-sectional strength of the rating scales (specifically, ADA) to classify roll calls. For each of the 25,492 roll-call votes in both houses for 1956–90, we classify the vote as left-right polarized or not (and then in which direction). The criterion for the classification as polarized is that the vote must show a greater association with member ADA scores than a hypothetical party-line vote for the particular members of each Congress. The intuition of this criterion is that we know we are observing a left-right cleavage when defection from party lines is itself along left–right lines—conservative Democrats voting with Republicans, liberal Republicans voting with Democrats. Although the party vote itself might be ideological, we cannot know that it is. One measure of the net liberalism of the session (for each house separately) is then simply the median size of the liberal coalition (on votes where the liberal and conservative sides are defined). A second approach to the same raw data is to focus on winning and losing, rather than coalition size. In this set of measures we simply count the percentage of liberal wins. We are observing quite directly then who wins, who loses, and by how much.

The Dramatic Acts of Congress: Key Votes. Scales of roll-call votes tell us about the overall tenor of public policy. Probably an excellent basis for inference about the net direction of policy movement, they do not distinguish between minor matters and those of enormous public consequence and visibility. Getting a good measure of "importance" presents a formidable challenge, requiring great numbers of subtle judgments about content and context. It is nonetheless desirable to have some indication of whether legislative activity produces something of import. A particular subset of legislation, the *Congressional Quarterly* "key votes" for each session of Congress, does attempt to distinguish the crucial from the trivial. The virtues of this set of votes are that it reflects the wisdom of expert observers of Congress at the time about what was important, and the measures are readily coded into liberal or conservative actions (and some that are neither).

We quantify the key votes as a combination of who wins and by how much. Accordingly, we average (1) the percentage of liberal wins and (2) the size of the liberal winning coalition. Crude, the measures nonetheless tap the issue in question, the direction of highly visible outcomes. The resulting time series are noisy (as would be expected from the small numbers of votes for each year), evincing a good deal of year-to-year fluctuation that seems meaningless. But they also show a picture of episodes of major policy change occurring exactly when expected for the Great Society (liberalism, peaking in 1965) and the Reagan Revolution (conservatism, peaking in 1981) periods respectively.

To get a sense of how legislative policy has moved over the years, look at Figure 3. (Figure 3a) presents our four measures for the House of Representatives. (To keep the eye on systematic movement, we have smoothed the graphs by taking a centered three-year moving average for each series. Note that we smooth only in this graph: we use the measured data for the statistical analysis.) It is clear that each indicator (wins, coalition size, ADA–ACA ratings, and key votes) contains both a common component and an idiosyncratic component. The lines move together, with a bit of zig and zag around the main flow. The panel for the Senate (Figure 3b) carries a similar message. Peaks of liberalism came during the early 1960s and the late 1980s, with conservatism at its height around 1980. While thus similar in outline, the patterns are not quite identical.

Presidential Policy Liberalism. The beginning point of dealing with the presidency is noting the near impossibility of direct measures of presiden-

Figure 3. Indicators of Public Policy Change in Four Parts of American Government (Three Year Moving Averages)

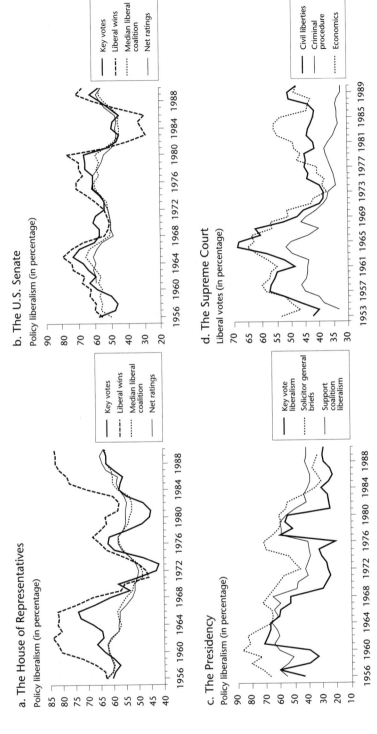

tial liberalism from what presidents say and do. While we have an intuition about various acts and speeches, any attempt to quantify that intuition, to extract acts from the context of actions, quickly becomes hopelessly subjective. The alternative is to look instead at presidents through their quantifiable records of interacting with the legislature and judiciary.

We know how often particular members of Congress support and oppose the president. And we can measure the liberalism of individual members in several ways. The most convenient of these is ADA scores, which are present for the entire period, as other comparable indicators are not. And we know that ADA ratings are very highly correlated with other ratings when available—positively or negatively—so that they can serve as a useful instrument of the underlying concept.

How then to combine these different pieces of information? A first approach is to ask the question, How liberal are the regular supporters of the president each year?, and then adopt that standard as a reflection of what the president wanted from Congress. That, however, is confounded by shared partisanship between president and member. We expect members of the president's party to be more likely to be regular supporters—independent of ideological agreement with the president's program. To deal with shared party ties as a confounding factor in presidential support, we opt instead to focus on presidential support within party. The strategy is first to divide each party into support and opposition groups based upon whether member presidential support is above or below the average for the party. The mean ADA rating of each party's "support" group is then an estimate of the president's ideological position. The opposition groups similarly measure the reverse. The measurement question then may be reduced to how such separate estimates are to be combined. For a summary measure of presidential position we perform a principal components analysis of the eight indicators (*support* vs. *oppose,* by party, by house). That analysis shows decisively that each of the eight taps a single underlying dimension. Such a dimension is estimated with a factor score and rescaled . . . to approximate the ADA scales from which it was derived.

For a second legislative presidential position measure we simply take the recorded presidential position for the key votes and compute the percentage of presidential stands each year that are liberal, where again the votes are classified by polarization with individual ADA ratings.

Presidential Interaction with the Court. With less regularity and on a quite different set of issues, presidents make their policy views known to the U.S.

Supreme Court. The mechanism for doing so formally is the amicus curiae brief filed by the presidency's designated agent to the courts, the solicitor general. On over 700 occasions in the 1953–89 terms, the solicitor general went on record with the Court, arguing that the holdings of particular judicial decisions ought to be affirmed or reversed. About 90% of these briefs take positions on cases that are themselves classifiably liberal or conservative.

We employ the solicitor general briefs data as leverage to measure presumed presidential position on judicial issues. Using the direction coding from the Spaeth Supreme Court data base for the case and our knowledge of whether the solicitor general argued to affirm or reverse, we code each of the briefs as to direction—liberal, conservative, or nonideological. It is then an easy matter to produce aggregated annual scales as percentage liberal of the ideological positions taken.

A quick comparison of the presidential series with the legislative series (in Figure 3) suggests less coherence in the presidential measures. Much of the discord comes from the *Solicitor General* series (which we retain, nevertheless, for its substantive value). Note also that the presidential series is typically more conservative than the two congressional series, as we might reasonably expect from the historical party control of the two institutions.

Supreme Court Liberalism. For data we have the Supreme Court data base for the period 1953–90. From that, we can content-classify the majority position in individual cases as liberal, conservative, or neither; and from that, the lifetime liberalism or conservatism of individual justices is readily derived. Then we return to the individual cases and scale the majority and dissenting votes by the justices who cast them. This allows a content-free second classification of the majority position as liberal, conservative, or not ideological. From this we build annual measures of the major-case content categories. We have chosen four such categories—*civil rights and liberties, criminal procedure, economics,* and *other*—the number a compromise between separating matters which might in principle produce different alignments and grouping broadly enough to have sufficient cases in each for reliable annual measures.

For each measure we construct a time series consisting of the percentage of all votes cast by the justices on the liberal side of the issue, whichever that is, for the year. This focus on justice decisions, rather than aggregate outcomes of the Court, appears to produce a more moderate measure over time than the alternative. . . .

We examine the first three domains in Figure 3. There we see that the issue domains move pretty much in tandem. All domains show the famous liberalism of the Warren Court in the mid-1960s and the conservative reaction of the Burger Court. Most show a modest rebound of liberalism in the early 1980s, which then reverses from the influence of new Reagan justices.

The pattern of more substantive notice is that the *"criminal procedure"* cases produce no liberal rebound in the 1980s. This is an interesting exception, for public attitudes toward crime and criminals are themselves an exception to the growing liberalism of the 1980s (Stimson 1991). This is a case where the conservative message ("The solution is more punitive law enforcement") is still dominant. . . .

A Summary Analysis of Governmental Responsiveness

For a summation of dynamic representation we slice across the institutional structure of American politics, returning to the familiar questions, Does public opinion influence public policy? and By what process? Our combining the policy output of the four institutions is, of course, a fiction: a single national public policy is not the average of independent branches. We "average" across different branches to provide a rough answer to a rough question. Here we select two indicators from each of the four prior analyses (president, House, Senate, and Supreme Court) and then estimate representation as it works on the American national government as a whole. . . .

We get a better sense of the historical dynamic by examining Figure 4. Plotted here are measures of public opinion, public policy and predicted policy. The first (in the light, solid line) is public opinion, with its liberal peaks during the early 1960s and late 1980s and its conservative peak around 1980. The dark, solid line represents policy, a simple average of our eight policy indicators. Without much work, it is clear that the two series are basically similar: policy reflects the timing and range of public opinion change.

Yet the two paths are not identical. Policy turned much more conservative during the late 1960s and early 1970s than the public demanded. Then, contrary to the continuing turn to the right, policy temporarily shifted leftward under Carter's leadership. Now look at the small dots that show predicted policy. . . . The exceptionally good fit is apparent. More important, the model is now able to account for the otherwise surprising conservatism just before 1972 and the liberalism of the late 1970s by including the Vietnam War and the composition variables. Thus, while the main part of

Figure 4. Global Public Opinion and Global Public Policy:
Predicted and Actual Policy

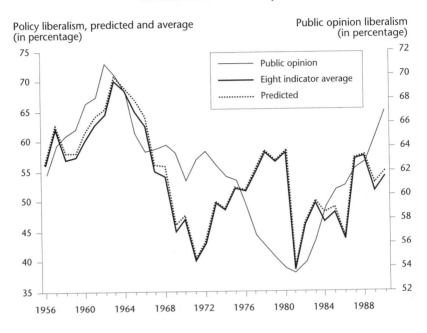

policy moves in accord with public preferences, significant deviations can and do occur. Those deviations seem explicable but not by public preferences. Public opinion is powerful but not all-powerful.

Figure 4 takes us back to where we started, public policy preferences, and forward to the end of the story, the policy liberalism of American government, 1956–90. The point is that the two are a lot alike. . . .

Some Reflections on American Politics

The past four decades of United States history show that politicians translate changes in public opinion into policy change. Further, the evidence suggests that this translation varies by institution, both in the mechanisms that produce the link and in the nature of the dynamics.

Most important, dynamic representation finds strong support. Our work indicates that when the public asks for a more activist or a more conservative government, politicians oblige. The early peak of public opinion liberalism during the early 1960s produced liberal policy; the turn away from activism and the steady move toward conservatism was similarly reflected in national policy; and the recent 1980s upsurge of public demand for action was also effective (with the exception of the Court). To be sure, other things matter too. We have modeled a late 1960s shift rightward in policy (beyond that driven by public opinion) as a function of the Vietnam War's dominance over domestic political agendas. In addition, we modeled the shift leftward during the years of the Carter presidency (a shift contrary to the prevailing movement in public opinion) as a coincidence of compositional factors.

While we are confident that the basic result holds, we know that we do not yet fully understand movement in public policy. Nevertheless, the main story is that large-scale shifts in public opinion yield corresponding large-scale shifts in government action.

The link between opinion and policy is undoubtedly more complicated. While concentrating on policy response to opinion, we have seen little evidence of opinion reaction to policy. Elementary analyses generate contradictory inferences: the matter is subtle, the timing probably complex. We do know enough to assert that opinion reaction cannot explain the structural associations we uncover. We do not know enough to characterize the fuller relationship. This, of course, is a compelling subject for hard work.

Beyond the basic result, we can say that American national institutions vary in the mechanisms that produce responsiveness. It is the Senate, not the House of Representatives, that most clearly mimics the eighteenth-century clockwork meant to produce electoral accountability. When comparing the effectiveness of turnover and rational anticipation, we find that for the Senate (and also for the presidency), the most important channel for governmental representation is electoral replacement. Equally responsive, however, is the House of Representatives. Its members employ rational anticipation to produce a similarly effective public policy response, without the overt evidence of personnel change. The Supreme Court appears to reflect public opinion far more than constitutionally expected; but, in comparison, it is the institution that responds least.

Finally, the dynamics prove interesting. Each of the electoral institutions translates immediately public opinion into public policy. That is to say, when electoral politicians sense a shift in public preferences, they act directly and effectively to shift the direction of public policy. We find no evidence of delay or hesitation. The Court, not surprisingly, moves at a more deliberate speed. But equally important, rational anticipation is based not only on the long-term trends in public opinion but also on year-to-year shifts. That is to say, politicians constantly and immediately process public opinion changes in order to stay ahead of the political curve. Understanding politics well, the constitutional framers were correct in expecting short-term politics to be a fundamental part of dynamic representation.

The United States government, as it has evolved over the years, produces a complex response to public demands. The original constitutional design mixed different political calculations into different institutions so that no personal ambition, no political faction, no single political interest, or no transient passion could dominate. We now see the founders' expectations about complexity manifest in contemporary policymaking. Constitutional mechanisms harness politicians' strategies to the public's demands. In the end, the government combines both short- and long-term considerations through both rational anticipation and compositional change to produce a strong and resilient link between public and policy. . . .

REFERENCES

Durr, Robert H. 1993. "What Moves Policy Sentiment?" *American Political Science Review* 87:158–70.

Kingdon, John W. 1984. *Agendas, Alternatives, and Public Policies*. Boston: Little, Brown.

Stimson, James A. 1991. *Public Opinion in America: Moods, Cycles, and Swings*. Boulder: Westview.

10-5

Poll Positions

LEADERS' OVER-DEPENDENCE ON PUBLIC OPINION

Jean Bethke Elshtain

In the following essay, Jean Bethke Elshtain addresses a difficult issue for modern democracies: Are leaders too responsive to public opinion polls? This issue is an old one. In Federalist No. 10, *for example, James Madison argued in favor of a republic rather than a direct democracy. In a republic we seek "to refine and enlarge the public views, by passing them through the medium of a chosen body of citizens, whose wisdom may best discern the true interest of their country." For Madison, the public interest should not be equated with public opinion. Elshtain shares Madison's view, and argues that modern leaders have become overly dependent on polls.*

IT'S HARDLY NEWS that polls are looming ever larger in our civic life, threatening, at this critical juncture, to overwhelm our capacity for reason, discernment, and judgment. After all, we know that polls have already played a key role in the unfolding scandal—most memorably when President Clinton first asked his consultant, Dick Morris, to test whether the public would forgive a president for lying under oath about sex. (The answer, a qualified "yes," helped set in motion all the shenanigans, rhetorical contortions, legalistic hairsplitting, and "I have sinned" confessionals of the past eight months.)

What is a little surprising, however, is that many close observers of the American scene argue that the vast influence of polling, whether in this scandal or in general, is a good thing. I mention this because just such an argument appeared on the op-ed page of the *New York Times* last week. Under the headline "power to the polls," Frank Newport, an editor-in-chief of the Gallup Poll and thus hardly a disinterested observer, could scarcely contain his enthusiasm for the truth of polls: *vox populi, vox dei.* He took issue with any and all naysayers, including Congressman Henry Hyde, who

Originally published in the *New Republic,* October 19, 1998, p. 13. Reprinted by permission of The New Republic. Copyright © 1998, The New Republic, Inc.

had said, "Poll-taking is an art, not a science." In Newport's opinion, those who suggest we take polls with a grain of salt, or even ignore them altogether from time to time, are arrogant: "Why should we assume that pundits and elected officials know more than the average American or that careful scientific polls don't accurately measure public sentiment?"

Although few others put the argument in such stark terms, many commentators and public officials have argued against impeachment, resignation, or even censure for the president merely on the grounds that the people don't want it that way—again, according to the polls. Members of both parties are said to be calibrating their strategy based on survey results and not so much on their own ideas of right and wrong. Is this a good thing? According to poll-populists, the answer is a resounding "yes."

This is, in a sense, a familiar argument. Those impatient with the compromises and mediations of democratic civil society have long believed that direct democracy would be preferable. Some have even proposed bringing technology to our rescue by holding instant plebiscites via interactive television and telepolling. Think what it would do for the scandal: Should we impeach the president, force him to resign, or embrace him as a sincere man who feels our pain and now feels his own as well? Press the button of your choice. Should we sally forth on yet another bombing mission or not? Just let us know.

But direct-democracy advocates fail to realize that the point of American democracy is not simply to express the people's will or even to assume that such a thing exists or could be articulated in a way that would protect individual rights and minority viewpoints. The point of our system is to put some distance between the people and their leaders, to temper the whims of the majority, and to allow officials to make independent judgments— even though it means explaining such decisions later.

The Clinton scandal, far from undermining this argument, shows why it makes sense now more than ever. Consider Newport's most revealing sentence: "In a Gallup survey conducted this month, 63 percent of those surveyed said that, on the question of the possible impeachment of President Clinton, members of Congress should stick closely to public opinion, rather than doing what they themselves think is best." In other words, Congress should do what the polls say the public wants because a poll said that is what the public wants. Isn't this what used to be called a tautology? If anything, following this strategy would be profoundly anti-democratic, if democracy is the making of political decisions following a period of airing of alternatives and extensive, careful deliberations of the possible effects of one action or another.

It is true that many people feel powerless. As Stephen Carter writes in his recent book, *The Dissent of the Governed,* citizens increasingly believe that "their petitions to their government go unanswered, and, as a result, [they] have lost a degree of faith in that government." But polls simply highlight powerlessness. To participate meaningfully as citizens, not as ciphers voicing a passing "sentiment," citizens must be part of institutions that enable them to express complex opinions. Responding to simplistic yes-or-no questions and then demanding that politicians obey is a political form of cheap grace. We cannot restore faith in our political system by treating elected representatives like marionettes.

In the context of the Clinton scandal, that means elected representatives should do what they are supposed to do: investigate, gather the facts, and then deliberate about what course of action to follow. While the public should be consulted, no lawmaker should act simply because a Gallup poll he read in today's newspaper gave him his marching orders. The American people surely want their elected officials to do what they—the officials, that is—think is best, hopefully after listening to the informed petitions of politically engaged citizens. If this is not in fact the case, we are in even more trouble than we realize.

11

Voting, Campaigns, and Elections

In recent decades, new concerns have arisen about the condition of American democracy. Voting turnout has declined. Campaigns have become more expensive and more negative. Presidential primaries are now bunched in the winter, many months before the summer nominating conventions—greatly extending the length and increasing the costs of presidential campaigns. In the view of some observers, the quality and even the legitimacy of American democracy have deteriorated. A wide variety of reforms have been proposed, but the obstacles are many.

The essays in this chapter investigate several facets of elections. The first essay, by Samuel Popkin, considers the problems voters face in making decisions with far from perfect information. Intuitively, we believe that voting on the basis of little information would undermine democracy. Popkin's depiction of voters' decision-making processes suggests that the story may be more complicated than that. In the second essay James Barnes discusses the implications of recent trends in the processes the major parties use to nominate presidential candidates. States that have instituted changes in the nomination process, in order to enhance their own voters' voices in the selection of presidential candidates, may have weakened the quality of choices in the November election. The third essay, by Martin Wattenberg, evaluates a proposal to encourage higher turnout on election day by making the day a holiday. Such a reform might make voting more convenient for many people, but it would not necessarily address the root causes of low turnout. In each of these essays, the author attempts to deepen our diagnosis of the problem at hand, to consider the political implications of recent developments, and, in discussions of the nomination process and voter turnout, to offer directions for reform.

11-1

from *The Reasoning Voter*

Samuel L. Popkin

Voters confront difficult choices with incomplete and usually biased information. Many voters are not strongly motivated to learn more. Even if they want to learn more, the information they need is often not available in a convenient form. In the following essay, Samuel Popkin argues that this predicament does not necessarily lead voters to make irrational decisions. Voters instead rely on low-cost shortcuts to obtain information and make decisions. Popkin's analysis can help us better understand the role of campaigns in voters' decision-making processes, and other features of American politics as well.

In recent decades, journalists and reformers have complained with increasing force about the lack of content in voting and the consequent opportunities for manipulating the electorate. And yet over the same period academic studies of voting have begun to expose more and more about the substance of voting decisions and the limits to manipulation of voters. The more we learn about what voters know, the more we see how campaigns matter in a democracy. And the more we see, the clearer it becomes that we must change both our critiques of campaigns and our suggestions for reforming them.

In this [essay] I summarize my findings about how voters reason and show how some modest changes which follow from my theory could ameliorate some defects of the campaign process.

I have argued . . . that the term *low-information rationality*, or "gut" rationality, best describes the kind of practical reasoning about government and politics in which people actually engage. . . . [L]ow-information reasoning is by no means devoid of substantive content, and is instead a process that economically incorporates learning and information from past experiences, daily life, the media, and political campaigns. . . .

Excerpted from Samuel L. Popkin, *The Reasoning Voter: Communication and Persuasion in Presidential Campaigns*, 2d edition (University of Chicago Press, 1994), pp. 212–219. Coypright © 1991, 1994 by The University of Chicago. All rights reserved. Reprinted by permission. Notes appearing in the original have been cut.

Gut rationality draws on the information shortcuts and rules of thumb that voters use to obtain and evaluate information and to choose among candidates. These information shortcuts and rules of thumb must be considered when evaluating an electorate and considering changes in the electoral system.

How Voters Reason

It is easy to demonstrate that Americans have limited knowledge of basic textbook facts about their government and the political debates of the day. But evaluating citizens only in terms of such factual knowledge is a misleading way to assess their competence as voters.

Because voters use shortcuts to obtain and evaluate information, they are able to store far more data about politics than measurements of their textbook knowledge would suggest. Shortcuts for obtaining information at low cost are numerous. People learn about specific government programs as a by-product of ordinary activities, such as planning for retirement, managing a business, or choosing a college. They obtain economic information from their activities as consumers, from their workplace, and from their friends. They also obtain all sorts of information from the media. Thus they do not need to know which party controls Congress, or the names of their senators, in order to know something about the state of the economy or proposed cuts in Social Security or the controversies over abortion. And they do not need to know where Nicaragua is, or how to describe the Politburo, in order to get information about changes in international tensions which they can relate to proposals for cutting the defense budget.

When direct information is hard to obtain, people will find a proxy for it. They will use a candidate's past political positions to estimate his or her future positions. When they are uncertain about those past positions, they will accept as a proxy information about the candidate's personal demographic characteristics and the groups with which he or she has associated. And since voters find it difficult to gather information about the past competence of politicians who have performed outside their district or state, they will accept campaign competence as a proxy for competence in elected office—as an indication of the political skills needed to handle the issues and problems confronting the government.

Voters use evaluations of personal character as a substitute for information about past demonstrations of political character. They are concerned about personal character and integrity because they generally cannot infer the candidate's true commitments from his past votes, most of which are based on a hard-to-decipher mixture of compromises between ideal positions and practical realities. Evaluating any sort of information for its relevance to politics is a reasoning process, not a reflex projection directly from pocketbook or personal problems to votes. But in making such evaluations, voters use the shortcut of relying on the opinions of others whom they trust and with whom they discuss the news. These opinions can serve as fire alarms that alert them to news deserving more than their minimal attention. As media communities have developed, voters have the additional shortcut of validating their opinions by comparing them with the opinions of political leaders whose positions and reputations people grow to know over time.

People will use simplifying assumptions to evaluate complex information. A common simplifying assumption is that a politician had significant control over an observable result, such as a loss of jobs in the auto industry. This saves people the trouble of finding out which specific actions really caused the result. Another example of a simplifying assumption is the notion that "My enemy's enemy is my friend."

People use party identification as running tallies of past information and shortcuts to storing and encoding their past experiences with political parties. They are able to encode information about social groups prominent in the party, the priorities of the party, and the performance of the party and its president in various policy areas. This generalized information about parties provides "default values" from which voters can assess candidates about whom they have no other information. In keeping generalized tallies by issue area, they avoid the need to know the specifics of every legislative bill.

As a shortcut in assessing a candidate's future performance, without collecting more data, people assemble what data they have about the candidate into a causal narrative or story. Because a story needs a main character, they can create one from their knowledge of people who have traits or characteristics like those of the candidate. This allows them to go beyond the incomplete information they have about a candidate, and to hold together and remember more information than they otherwise could. Because these stories are causal narratives, they allow voters to think about government in causal terms and to evaluate what it will do. Narratives thus help people incorporate their reasoning about government into their projections about candidates; their assumptions "confer political significance on some facts and withhold it from others." They offer people a way to connect personal and political information, to project that information into the future, and to make a complete picture from limited information.

Finally, people use shortcuts when choosing between candidates. When faced with an array of candidates in which some are known well and some are known poorly, and all are known in different and incomparable ways, voters will seek a clear and accessible criterion for comparing them. This usually means looking for the sharpest differences between the candidates which can be related to government performance. Incorporating these differences into narratives allows them to compare the candidates without spending the calculation time and the energy needed to make independent evaluations of each candidate.

Working Attitudes

People do not and cannot use all the information they have at one time. What they use will depend in part on the point of view or frame with which they view the world; attitudes and information are brought to bear if they fit the frame. Of the attitudes and bits of information available, people tend to use those they consider important or those they have used recently. As the changes in voter attitudes entailed by the emergence of new candidates in primaries suggests, attitudes and information will also be brought to the foreground when they fit with what is *expected* in a situation. Our realizations, the thoughts that come clearly to mind, depend in part on what others say about their own thoughts and perceptions.

Thus, as options change, expectations change. If a Democrat were asked in early 1984 what he or she thought of Walter Mondale as a presidential candidate, and the reply was "He'll be all right," that response could be interpreted as coming from a nonthinking voter who was passively following a media report about the thinking of others. But the same response could also be interpreted as an indication of a complex ability to come to grips with the available choices, with issue concerns that cannot be satisfied simultaneously, and with the compromises considered necessary to reach consensus with other people. Similarly, if the same voter were asked a few weeks later what he or she thought about Gary Hart and the reply was "He's just what we need," the response could be interpreted to mean that this voter was simply following the media-reported bandwagon. On the other hand, it could be interpreted to mean that reported changes in public expectations had brought other attitudes and concerns forward in the voter's mind. As this example suggests, the information voters use depends on the reasoning they do, and the reasoning they do depends in part on their expectations. It also indicates that the way in which the content of a voter's response is interpreted depends on a theory about how voters use information and make choices. And I am convinced that any such theory must account for the "working attitudes" of voters—the combinations of feeling, thought, and information they bring to bear when they make their choices at the polls.

Why Campaigns Matter

Changes in government, in society, and in the role of the mass media in politics have made campaigns more important today than they were fifty years ago, when modern studies of them began. Campaign communications make connections between politics and benefits that are of concern to the voter; they offer cognitive focal points, symbolic "smoking guns," and thus make voters more aware of the costs of misperception. Campaigns attempt to achieve a common focus, to make one question and one cleavage paramount in voters' minds. They try to develop a message for a general audience, a call that will reach beyond the "disinterested interest" of the highly attentive, on one hand, and the narrow interests of issue publics, on the other. Each campaign attempts to organize the many cleavages within the electorate by setting the political agenda in the way most favorable to its own candidates. . . .

The spread of education has both broadened and segmented the electorate. Educated voters pay more attention to national and international issues and they are now connected in many more electronic communities—groups of people who have important identifications maintained through media rather than direct, personal contact. There are also today more government programs—Medicare, Social Security, welfare, and farm supports are obvious examples—that have a direct impact on certain groups, which become issue publics. Other issue publics include coalitions organized around policies toward specific countries, such as Israel or Cuba; various conservation and environmental groups; and groups concerned with social issues, such as abortion and gun control. Furthermore, there are now a great many more communications channels with which these people can keep in touch with those outside their immediate neighborhoods or communities. Such extended groups are not new, and modern communications technology is not necessary to mobilize them, as the abolitionist and temperance movements remind us; but the channels to mobilize such groups are more available today, and I believe that the groups they have nurtured are more numerous. When the national political conventions were first telecast in 1952, all three networks showed the same picture at the same time because there was only one national microwave relay; today, with the proliferation of cable systems and satellite relays, television and VCRs can now show over a hundred channels. Furthermore, as channels and options have proliferated, and as commuting time has increased and two-career families become more common, the proportion of people watching mainstream networks and network news is also dropping.

Over the past fifty years, as surveys have become increasingly available to study public opinion, there have been many gains in knowledge about voting and elections. There have also been losses, as national surveys have replaced the detailed community orientation of the original Columbia studies. We know much more about individuals and much less about extended networks, and we have not adequately examined the implications for society and campaigning of the transitions from face-to-face to electronic communities.

Both primaries and the growth of media communication have increased the amount of exposure people get to individual candidates, particularly the quantity of personal information they get about the candidates. This increases the importance of campaigns because it gives voters more opportunities to abandon views based on party default values in favor of views based on candidate information, and also more opportunities to shift from views based on a candidate's record to views based on his or her campaign image. Moreover, as primaries have expanded, parties have had to deal with the additional task of closing ranks after the campaign has pitted factions within the party against each other. Primaries have also changed the meaning of political party conventions. Conventions no longer deliberate and choose candidates; instead, they present the electorate with important cues about the social composition of the candidate's coalition and about the candidate's political history and relations with the rest of the party. The more primaries divide parties, the more cues are needed to reunite parties and remind supporters of losing candidates about their differences with the other party.

The Implications of Shortcuts

Recognizing the role of low-information rationality in voting behavior has important implications for how we measure and study attitudes, how we evaluate the effects of education, and how we evaluate electoral reforms. To begin with, we must acknowledge that the ambivalence, inconsistency, and changes in preference that can be observed among voters are not the result of limited information. They exist because as human beings we can never use all of what we know at any one time. We can be as ambivalent when we have a lot of information and concern as when we have little information and limited concern. Nor do inconsistency, ambivalence, and change result from a lack of education (especially civic education) or a lack of political interest. Ambivalence is simply an immutable fact of life. Economists and psychologists have had to deal with the inconsistencies people demonstrate in cognitive experiments on framing and choice: preference reversals and attitude changes can no longer be attributed to a lack of information, a lack of concern, a lack of attention, low stakes, or the existence of "non-attitudes."

The use of information shortcuts is likewise an inescapable fact of life, and will occur no matter how educated we are, how much information we have, and how much thinking we do. Professionals weighing résumés and past accomplishments against personal interviews, or choosing from an array of diverse objects, have the same problems and use the same shortcuts as voters choosing presidents. What we have called Gresham's law of information—that new and personal information, being easier to use, tends to drive old and impersonal political information out of circulation—applies not only to the inattentive and the uneducated but to all of us. We must therefore stop considering shortcuts pejoratively, as the last refuge of citizens who are uneducated, lacking in the political experience and expertise of their "betters," or cynically content to be freeloaders in our democracy.

Drunkard's Searches and information shortcuts provide an invaluable part of our knowledge and must therefore be considered along with textbook knowledge in evaluating any decision-making process. As Abraham Kaplan has noted, the Drunkard's Search—metaphorically, looking for the lost keys under the nearest streetlight—seems bothersome because of the assumption that we should begin any search rationally, in the most likely places rather than in those that are the best lit and nearest to hand. He adds, "But the joke may be on us. It may be sensible to look first in an unlikely place just *because* 'it's lighter there.'. . . . The optimal pattern of search does not simply mirror the pattern of probability density of what we seek. We accept the hypothesis that a thing sought is in a certain place because we remember having seen it there, or because it is usually in places of that kind, or for like reasons. But . . . we look in a certain place for additional reasons: we happen to be in the place already, others are looking elsewhere." At least when people look under the streetlight, they will almost certainly find their keys if they are there; if they look by the car, in the dark, they are far less likely to find them even if they are there.

. . . [W]e should keep in mind the main features about how voters obtain information and reason about their political choices. The Drunkard's Search is an aid to calculation as well as an information shortcut. By telling us where to look, it also tells us how to choose, how to use easily obtained information in making comparisons and choices. As long as this is how we search and choose, people will neither have nor desire all the information about their government that theorists and reformers want them to have.

The faith that increased education would lead to higher levels of textbook knowledge about government, and that this knowledge in turn would enable the electorate to measure up to its role in democratic theory, was misplaced. Education doesn't change *how* we think. Education broadens the voter, because educated voters pay attention to more problems and are more sensitive to connections between their lives and national and international events. However, educated voters still *sample* the news, and they still rely on shortcuts and calculation aids in assessing information, assembling scenarios, and making their choices. Further, an educated, broadened electorate is a more diffuse electorate, an electorate segmented by the very abundance of its concerns. Such an electorate will be harder to form into coalitions. The more divided an electorate, the more time and communication it takes to assemble people around a single cleavage.

Since all citizens sample the news and use shortcuts, they must be judged in part by the quality of the "fire alarms" to which they respond. They must be judged in part by *who* they know and respond to, not simply by *what* they know. Furthermore, this use of fire alarms has an important implication. Since people can only respond to the fire alarms they hear, it matters how the fire alarms to which they are exposed are chosen. If it matters whether the responses to a policy or crisis are mediated electronically by Jesse Jackson and Jesse Helms, or by Bill Bradley and Robert Dole, then attention must be given to how the mediators are chosen by the networks.

11-2

Rules of the Game

James A. Barnes

The presidential campaign of 2000 illustrates a remarkable change in the process of nominating presidential candidates. Whereas in previous elections primaries had been scheduled throughout the season, most delegates to the 2000 national nominating conventions, which occur in late July and August, were chosen by the end of March. The shift forward, or "frontloading," of the presidential primary schedule has forced candidates to start their campaigns much earlier and has moved the effective selection of candidates far ahead of the party conventions and the November general election. In the following essay, James Barnes outlines the causes and consequences of these developments.

Consider, for a moment, this bit of campaign 2000 trivia: Barring a last-minute entry into the Republican presidential race, more GOP candidates (six) will have dropped out of contention for their party's nomination before any votes are cast than afterward (five). On the roster of the vanquished so far are a former Vice President (Dan Quayle), a former Governor (Lamar Alexander), a former Cabinet Secretary (Elizabeth Dole), a House member (John Kasich), a Senator (Bob Smith), and a former television commentator (Pat Buchanan) who has bolted the GOP for the Reform Party.

To understand what's happened, it's not enough to look at Texas Gov. George W. Bush's big lead in the polls and huge advantage in fund raising. It's also important to remember a bit of history from two decades ago—in particular, from the 1980 race for the Democratic nomination. Facing a serious challenge from Sen. Edward Kennedy, D-Mass., then-President Jimmy Carter and his strategists took a look at the primary calendar and did not like what they saw. After the January 21 Iowa caucuses, three New England states were holding their presidential primaries—New Hampshire on February 26, followed by Massachusetts and Vermont on March 4.

To offset what might turn out to be an early regional advantage for Kennedy, the Carter White House cajoled allies in several Southern states to move their primaries and caucuses up to mid-March. Alabama and Georgia selected March 11 to hold their primaries, and Oklahoma Democrats moved their caucuses up to that day as well. Party leaders in Mississippi and South Carolina set their caucuses for March 15.

As events played out, Carter beat Kennedy in New Hampshire and didn't need the fire wall his operatives had erected for him in the South. The candidate whom the Democrats really helped, unintentionally, by this acceleration was the eventual Republican nominee, three-time White House hopeful Ronald Reagan. He captured the two GOP Dixie primaries handily.

Nearly 20 years later, Bush is also benefiting from what the Carter operatives started. As in 1980, Iowa and New Hampshire represent the first stage of the process, but early March has been front-loaded with so many primaries that an extraordinary premium has been placed on raising the necessary money to compete before then. Between 1980 and 2000, the percentage of the Republican convention delegates allocated on or before the second Tuesday in March has tripled. For Democrats, the figure has quadrupled.

This process favors well-known candidates with wide backing from the party establishment, such as Bush and Vice President Al Gore, the respective front-runners for the 2000 Republican and Democratic presidential nominations. The winnowing process formerly done by the Iowa caucuses and the New Hampshire primary is now happening during what used to be called the "invisible primary"—the activities of the year before the election year, when White House hopefuls assembled their staffs, raised money, and visited the early-primary and early-caucus states. Here's a look at some of the ways the nominating rules are affecting campaign 2000.

Front-Loading

Jimmy Carter's campaign operatives could not possibly have foreseen the effects of the forces they unleashed in 1980. In 1984, even more states took the leap forward. Some wanted a share of the candidate and media attention that came with early primaries and caucuses. Others moved up their voting dates because their Democratic establishments were backing former Vice President Walter F. Mondale for the presidential nomination. The thought in the Mondale camp was that the more states that went early, the easier it would be for the front-runner to build up an insurmountable delegate lead.

As a result, the percentage of Democratic convention delegates allocated by the second Tuesday in March rose from roughly 18 percent of the total in 1980 to about 23 percent in 1984. But, as usual, the political dynamics that year upset the perceived logic of the Democratic calendar, when a little-known Democratic Senator from Colorado named Gary Hart managed to upset Mondale in the February 28 New Hampshire primary.

Hart's momentum from that victory built as he defeated the former Vice President in the March 4 Maine caucuses, the March 6 Vermont primary, and the March 10 Wyoming caucuses. And then Hart won three of the five primaries held on March 13—Florida, Massachusetts, and Rhode Island—and three of the four caucuses—Nevada, Oklahoma, and Washington. Mondale, who won the Alabama and Georgia primaries, barely hung on against the Hart surge. An uncommitted slate captured the Hawaii caucuses.

Mondale ultimately won the Democratic nomination, in no small part because of the support he had from the new category of "superdelegates." A new provision in the party's rules for 1984 gave two-thirds of the Democratic members of Congress automatic status as unpledged convention delegates, as well as some 350 state and local party leaders and elected officials. Better than four out of every five of these superdelegates supported Mondale.

After Reagan trounced Mondale in the 1984 general election, Democratic leaders in the South looked for a way to exert more influence over the party's presidential nominating process in hopes of gaining a more-moderate standard-bearer who would sell better in their region. The solution they hit upon was Super Tuesday. Democratic officials in 14 Southern and border states agreed to hold an early regional presidential primary on March 8. The result would boost the proportion of the 1988 Democratic delegates who would now be allocated by the second Tuesday in March to 45 percent.

But once again, in 1988, political dynamics undid the political calculus that went into the calendar. Massachusetts Gov. Michael S. Dukakis won three of these Super Tuesday Southern primaries, including the two largest, Florida and Texas; civil rights leader Jesse Jackson captured five. Dukakis' success in Dixie established him as the front-runner for the nomination he eventually captured.

Because Democrats controlled the Southern statehouses, Republicans were largely forced to go along with the Super Tuesday primary system. Thus, the percentage of GOP convention delegates allocated by the second

Tuesday in March soared from almost 21 percent in 1980 to more than 48 percent in 1988.

In 1992, the Democratic Party moved the official launch date of its nominating calendar up a week, from the second Tuesday to the first Tuesday in March. (Party organizations in Iowa and New Hampshire and a handful of other states had been granted exemptions from this guideline.)

A few states—Colorado, Georgia, and Maryland—took advantage of this change and set their primaries on that day. But the front-loading in 1992 was minimal, and a few Super Tuesday states moved their primaries backward. The proportion of Democratic convention delegates allocated by the second Tuesday in March rose to 49 percent, while the Republican percentage actually fell to about 40 percent.

In 1996, more states sought to garner the attention that came with an early nominating contest. The five New England states besides New Hampshire set up a regional primary on March 5. New York also moved its primary to that date, but postponed it for two days so as not to conflict with a Jewish holiday that year. With President Clinton unchallenged for renomination, the changes had the most impact on the Republican race. About half of the GOP convention delegates were allocated by the second Tuesday in March.

In 2000, the front-loading phenomenon will be all the more apparent because of the participation of three large states: New York, Ohio, and delegate-rich California, which traditionally held its vote in June. And 11 other states are scheduled to conduct a Republican presidential primary or caucus on that day, while a total of 13 states will hold a Democratic primary or caucus. The impact is huge. By March 7, the primaries and caucuses will have allocated more than 66 percent of both the Democratic and GOP pledged convention delegates. If you factor into the equation the Democrats' unpledged superdelegates who will be certified no later than March 1, some 70 percent of that party's delegates will be allocated by the second Tuesday in March.

The Democrats

The Democratic race today is where you'd expect it to be on the morning after the New Hampshire primary—down to the two finalists. Both Gore and former Sen. Bill Bradley of New Jersey are claiming the role of underdog, tamping down expectations for the Iowa caucuses and the New Hampshire primary.

Bradley likes to say he is up against the "entrenched power" of the party in his bid for the Democratic nomination at the Los Angeles convention next August—and that isn't just rhetoric. Every member of Congress, every member of the Democratic National Committee, scores of important figures and fund-raisers in the state parties, and even former congressional leaders are automatic unpledged delegates to the national convention. They account for 799 delegate votes out of a total of 4,336, or 18.4 percent. And that figure represents the highest level of superdelegates since their status was established in 1984, when 568 attended the convention in San Francisco and constituted 14.2 percent of the party conclave.

Over the years, their ranks have been expanded in different ways. Originally, superdelegate slots were set aside for only 60 percent of the Democratic members of Congress; now all attend. And as the overall size of the Democratic National Committee grew, so did the number of superdelegates.

Ironically, the superdelegates' clout in next year's Democratic contest is even greater than the percentage of convention seats they'll take up, thanks to the demands made 11 years ago in Atlanta by the ultimate anti-establishment candidate, Jesse Jackson.

Michael Dukakis—in an effort to placate Jackson, his last remaining Democratic rival for the nomination—agreed to eliminate direct-election primaries. These were contests in which voters elected slates of delegates directly, instead of having candidates gain delegates in rough proportion to the percentage of votes the candidates receive. In direct-election primaries, a slate with just a slender plurality of votes would get all of the convention delegates allocated to a congressional district. Jackson correctly believed that this scheme, along with others that went against proportional representation, had cost him at least 100 delegates in Atlanta.

But the change to ban those so-called loophole primaries has made the superdelegates more important in determining the Democratic nominee. In 1984 and 1988, candidates had opportunities to make up big ground in the delegate count by capturing key states that awarded all their delegates to the winner, instead of allocating delegates by proportional representation. Under rules of proportional representation, if Bradley beats the Vice President in primaries, but wins by something less than a landslide, he might come away with only a handful of extra delegates. That makes Gore's advantage among superdelegates, which his camp estimates will be 500 by next year, a hard one to overcome.

"On our side, you must win broad support within the ranks of the superdelegates or you will not win," said Tad Devine, a Gore consultant and veteran Democratic delegate strategist. "You must reinforce that support by demonstrating strength with voters. You don't need to demonstrate ubiquitous strength all the time."

Bradley campaign Chairman Doug Berman disputed the notion that superdelegates would drive the dynamics of the Democratic nominating contest. "We start behind in superdelegates, but we believe that the nomination will be decided by Democrats across the country in the primaries and the caucuses," he said. Berman reasons either that Bradley would convincingly win enough states to offset Gore's superdelegate advantage, or that a "clear consensus" would emerge for his candidacy, and the party would coalesce around him.

In Iowa, Gore continues to lead Bradley in the polls and in intangibles, with the Vice President receiving the endorsements of such party leaders as Sen. Tom Harkin, as well as the AFL-CIO. Bradley's hopes are clearly pinned to winning the primary in New Hampshire, a state where a highly educated Democratic primary electorate appreciates his high-brow approach to campaigning. He's already ahead in most polls there, so it would be hard for his aides to spin a second-place showing, no matter how strong, as a better-than-expected performance.

If the Vice President were to prevail in both Iowa and New Hampshire, Bradley would inevitably face questions about his viability, and pressure would mount within the party to consolidate behind the Vice President. Unfortunately for Bradley, that period of scrutiny would come during the five-week limbo between New Hampshire and the first Tuesday in March, when Democratic Party rules prevent any primary or caucus from being held. Thus, Bradley wouldn't have a chance to bounce back quickly by demonstrating electoral viability at the polls.

If Gore loses in New Hampshire, his campaign could be bolstered during that five-week period by the support he has within the party establishment. Then, the plan would be to target states he needs to win on March 7, and hope that the round of Southern primaries one week later would at least put him on a par with Bradley in terms of pledged delegates.

At that point, with only about a third of the convention delegates still up for grabs, Gore's superdelegate advantage would become decisive, according to his strategists. The only hitch in that scenario is that these delegates, unlike the regular delegates who are selected in primaries, are not bound by anything stronger than their personal word to support a particular candidate when they arrive at the convention. In the past, superdelegates haven't defected from a front-running candidate they've publicly pledged to support. But since 1984, the putative nominee has had a clear advantage among the pledged delegates selected in primaries and caucuses.

"I understand why I'd make that argument, but if it's tight going into the convention on pledged delegates, I think you might see some superdelegates shift," said veteran party strategist Harold M. Ickes, who ran Bill Clinton's 1992 convention in New York City. "The superdelegates are thin reeds. They blow with the wind."

The Republicans

Republicans have a much-less-regulated nominating contest than Democrats do. Their party rules and traditions have given state organizations more flexibility about when they hold their presidential caucus or primary. That has produced a system that is still dominated by Iowa and New Hampshire early on, and a crush of primaries in the second and third weeks in March. . . .

Although Bush also maintains a lead in New Hampshire [in November 1999], some of his advisers have always worried that he could lose there. McCain's recent jump in the Granite State polls has gotten their attention. "I felt all along we could lose New Hampshire because of a cultural schism—New Englanders not taking to a Texan," said Bush pollster Frederick T. Steeper. Indeed, Texas politicians such as the late former Gov. John B. Connally, who sought the Republican nomination in 1980, and Sen. Phil Gramm, who ran in 1996, never demonstrated significant support in the region.

Another McCain advantage in New Hampshire is that independents, who could be attracted by his maverick nature and strong advocacy for campaign finance reform, are permitted to vote in the primary. But his campaign's strategic decision to bypass the upcoming Iowa caucuses could come back to haunt him in New Hampshire. No candidate has skipped a contested caucus in Iowa and then done well in the New Hampshire primary. The challenge for McCain is to keep himself and his message in the media limelight before and after the caucuses—at a time when another candidate could steal the media bounce by doing unexpectedly well in Iowa.

Unlike the Democratic nominating calendar, which has a five-week hiatus between the February 1 New Hampshire primary and the mega-primary on March 7, the Republican schedule is filled with key primaries between those two dates. This has both advantages and disadvantages for a candidate who is able to upset Bush or score a near victory in New Hampshire.

Although the Delaware primary and the Hawaii caucuses are the next two contests, neither one is shaping up to be a key battleground on the GOP schedule. But the South Carolina primary on February 19 is. Its winner has traditionally gone on to victories in other states and, eventually, to the nomination: Ronald Reagan in 1980, George Bush in 1988, and Bob Dole in 1996. All three captured the Palmetto State primary and scored subsequent victories in the South that were critical to their nomination victories.

Next to Bush, McCain appears to be the best-organized in South Carolina. He has the backing of GOP Reps. Lindsey Graham and Mark Sanford and a sizable population of military retirees. The primary comes two and a half weeks after New Hampshire's, which might be enough time for McCain to raise campaign contributions on the strength of a victory there.

Forbes can't be dismissed as a contender in any of the early states because his personal wealth allows him to finance his campaign as long as he desires. But there's a limit to what money can do. Forbes won the Delaware and Arizona primaries in 1996, after he paid for television-ad blitzes in both states. Yet five days after his victory in Arizona, he won only 12.7 percent of the vote in South Carolina, finishing a distant third to Dole and Pat Buchanan.

The problem for McCain—or any other candidate—is that you can't sock away much post–New Hampshire money for the March 7 round of primaries. Right on the heels of South Carolina come three likely battlegrounds—the Arizona and Michigan primaries on February 22, and the Virginia primary on February 29. Along with South Carolina, these three states should soon start seeing the latest Bush campaign television spots, which are expected to run almost nonstop until the primaries are held.

Those are all contests that would drain dollars, and McCain, if he bested Bush in New Hampshire or South Carolina, yet couldn't afford to skip Michigan and Virginia. Many Republican observers presume that Michigan GOP Gov. John Engler and Virginia GOP Gov. James S. Gilmore III shoehorned their respective states' primaries ahead of the March 7 round in order to give Bush, who has plenty of money, a chance to rebound from potential losses in earlier states.

"Look at those states, run by strong chief executives who are big Bush supporters," said Scott Reed, Dole's 1996 presidential campaign manager. "It didn't just happen that way. Nothing just happens in national politics."

Bush's huge advantage in money and support from GOP elected officials becomes even more pronounced on March 7, when 13 states hold primaries or caucuses, and a week later, when Republicans in six Southern states go the polls. States holding votes on March 14 include Texas, Bush's own state, and Florida, where his brother, Jeb, is Governor. Right now, the most probable scenario is that Bush will wrap up the nomination on one of those two days.

Many people have concerns about this front-loaded system, and these worries are not limited to the tremendous emphasis the calendar puts on early fund raising. Some also fear that the quality of the campaign and voter participation will be shortchanged, particularly if one candidate blows away the competition. Others worry that a badly flawed candidate could amass a huge delegate lead before his defects were discovered or understood.

"Will there be a good debate among our candidates in Ohio and California, key states we have to carry in November? Absolutely not," said former Dole manager Reed. "This system makes sense if you're the front-runner and you have practical control of most of the states."

Which is why there aren't many complaints coming from the Bush or Gore headquarters.

11-3

Should Election Day Be a Holiday?

Martin P. Wattenberg

Declining turnout in American elections appears to have multiple causes and few easy solutions. In many other countries, voting is mandatory. In some, elections are held on weekends to reduce conflicts with work and school. In the following essay, Martin Wattenberg considers one proposal for increasing turnout—to make election day a holiday. Wattenberg's analysis of this proposal provides a useful introduction to the problem of low turnout and its possible causes.

THERE IS ONLY one practical way to increase voter turnout. Regardless of who wins in next month's midterm elections, a sure bet is that less than half of the voting-age population will actually participate. The percentage of the electorate casting ballots for the House of Representatives has fluctuated between 33 and 45 percent over the past sixteen midterm elections. Recent turnout rates suggest that the percentage in 1998 will probably be near the bottom of this range, and quite possibly even lower. In 1996 the presidential-election turnout fell below 50 percent for the first time since the early 1920s—when women had just received the franchise and had not yet begun to use it as frequently as men. Last year not a single one of the eleven states that called their citizens to the polls managed to get a majority to vote. The best turnout occurred in Oregon, where a heated campaign debate had taken place on the question of whether to repeal the state's "right to die" law. The worst turnout last year was a shockingly low five percent, for a special election in Texas. This occurred even though Governor George W. Bush stumped the state for a week, urging people to participate and promising that a "yes" vote would result in a major tax cut.

Universal suffrage means that everyone should have an equal opportunity to vote, regardless of social background. But over the past three decades studies have found increasing biases in turnout. In particular,

Originally published in *Atlantic Monthly*, October 1, 1998, p. 42. Reprinted by permission.

people without college degrees have become less likely to go to the polls. Statistics from the Census Bureau on turnout by educational achievement make the point. Respondents were asked if they had taken part in the most recent national election.

	1966	1994
No high school diploma	47%	26%
High school diploma	60%	41%
Some college	65%	50%
College degree	71%	64%

[Figures represent percentage of "yes" respondents.]

Since 1966 turnout rates have declined most sharply among people at the lower levels of education. In 1994 people with no college education made up 53 percent of the adult population but only 42 percent of the voters.

Turnout is now also greatly related to experience in life. Turnout rates have always been lowest among young people; perhaps this is why there was relatively little opposition in the early 1970s to lowering the voting age to eighteen. But not even the most pessimistic analysts could have foreseen the record-low participation rates of Generation X, as shown in the following census findings on age and turnout:

	1966	1994
18–20	—	17%
21–24	32%	22%
25–44	53%	39%
45–64	65%	57%
over 65	56%	61%

The low turnout among young voters today is paradoxical given that they are one of the best-educated generations in American history. Even those who have made it to college are expressing remarkably little concern for politics. Chelsea Clinton's class of 2001 recently set a new record for political apathy among college freshmen: only 27 percent said that keeping up with politics was an important priority for them, as opposed to 58 percent of the class of 1970, with whom Bill and Hillary Clinton attended college.

Of course, Chelsea's classmates have not seen government encroach on their lives as it did on the lives of their parents—through the Vietnam War and the draft. Nor has any policy affected them as directly as Medicare has affected their grandparents. It is noteworthy that senior citizens are actually voting at higher rates today than when Medicare was first starting up. Political scientists used to write that the frailties of old age led to a decline in turnout after age sixty; now such a decline occurs only after eighty. The greater access of today's seniors to medical care must surely be given some credit for this change. Who says that politics doesn't make a difference?

Yet it is difficult to persuade people who have channel surfed all their lives that politics really does matter. Chelsea's generation is the first in the age of television to grow up with narrowcasting rather than broadcasting. When CBS, NBC, and ABC dominated the airwaves, their blanket coverage of presidential speeches, political conventions, and presidential debates sometimes left little else to watch on TV. But as channels have proliferated, it has become much easier to avoid exposure to politics altogether. Whereas President Richard Nixon got an average rating of 50 for his televised addresses to the nation, President Clinton averaged only about 30 in his first term. Political conventions, which once received more TV coverage than the Summer Olympics, have been relegated to an hour per night and draw abysmal ratings. In sum, young people today have never known a time when most citizens paid attention to major political events. As a result, most of them have yet to get into the habit of voting.

The revolutionary expansion of channels and Web sites anticipated in the near future is likely to worsen this state of affairs, especially for today's youth. Political junkies will certainly find more political information available than ever before, but with so many outlets for so many specific interests, it will also be extraordinarily easy to avoid public-affairs news altogether. The result could well be further inequality of political information, with avid followers of politics becoming ever more knowledgeable while the rest of the public slips deeper into political apathy. This year's expected low turnout may not be the bottom of the barrel.

Some commentators welcome, rather than fear, the decline in turnout rates in America. If people do not vote, they say, citizens must be satisfied with the government. There is a certain logic to this view, because if nonvoters were extremely disgruntled with our leaders, they would undoubtedly take some political action. However, to argue that nonvoters are content with government just because they aren't actively opposing it stretches the logic too far. When the 1996 National Election Study asked people to rate their satisfaction with how democracy works in the United States, nonvoters were less positive than voters. Furthermore, young people were more than twice as likely as senior citizens to be dissatisfied with American democracy.

Why should young adults be satisfied with government, given how few benefits they receive from it in comparison with their grandparents? But until they start showing up in greater numbers at the polls, there will be little incentive for politicians to focus on programs that will help the young. Why should politicians worry about nonvoters any more than the makers of denture cream worry about people with healthy teeth? It is probably more than coincidental that Clinton's two most visible policy failures—the 1993 economic-stimulus package and the 1994 effort to establish universal health care—had their strongest backing from people who were not even registered to vote. Congressional Republicans may rationally have anticipated that many of these proposals' supporters were unlikely to be judging them in the 1994 elections.

After the Republican takeover of Congress in 1994, I saw a bumper sticker that read NEWT HAPPENS WHEN ONLY 37 PERCENT OF AMERICANS VOTE. Although I don't usually let bumper stickers determine my research agenda, this one piqued my interest. Would the Republicans have won the majority of House seats if turnout had been greater? A simple way to address this question is to assess how much difference it would have made if voters had mirrored the adult population in terms of education. According to the 1994 National Election Study, 30 percent of voters who lacked a high school diploma and 62 percent of voters with college degrees voted for Republican candidates for the House. Increasing turnout among the least educated citizens would thus have made some difference. If turnout rates had been equal in all education categories, the Republican share of the vote would have fallen from 52.0 to 49.2 percent.

Although it is unlikely that people of differing education levels would ever vote at exactly the same rate, this is only one of many biases in electoral participation. A more comprehensive method of estimating the impact of higher turnout is to gauge the attitudes of nonvoters toward those factors that influenced voters in 1994: party identification, approval of Clinton, stands on issues, and incumbency. Examining only survey respondents who were registered but did not vote, I found that these nonvoters would have favored Democratic candidates by an even greater margin than that by which actual voters supported the Republicans. Had all registered citizens gone to the polls, the Republicans' share of the vote would have been reduced by 2.8 percent—exactly the same estimate as arrived at above. If this loss occurred in all districts, the Republicans would have won only 206 seats—twenty-four fewer than they actually won, and twelve short of a majority.

Such findings, regrettably, suggest that nothing will be done to increase turnout in America. Few Republicans will want to correct a situation that has benefited them in the past. Yet until something is done, the House of Representatives will be representative not of the electorate but only of the minority that actually votes.

What can be done to reverse the decline in turnout? At his first press conference after the 1996 election Bill Clinton was asked about the poor turnout and how to increase participation in the future. The President stumbled over this question—he didn't really have an opinion on what could be done, and he concluded by asking the members of the press corps whether they had any ideas. Clinton's apparent frustration in addressing the question probably stems from his involvement in passing the 1993 Motor Voter Act. He and many others believed that its voter-registration reforms would increase turnout. But although the registration rolls swelled in state after state prior to the 1996 election, the turnout rate fell dramatically on Election Day. (The Census Bureau, paradoxically, found fewer people in 1996 than in 1992 who said they were registered. Apparently, the Motor Voter procedures made registering so easy that many forgot they had placed their names on the voting ledgers.)

Had Clinton been better advised on this subject, he would not have expected turnout to increase simply because registering to vote had become easier. North Dakota has since 1951 not required people to register in order to vote, yet it has seen turnout in presidential elections decline by 22 percent since 1960. Minnesota and Wisconsin have allowed citizens to register on Election Day since the mid-1970s, but they have lower turnout rates today than when they had tighter registration laws. In short, not even the most lenient voter-registration procedures are the answer to the problem of low turnout.

Clinton is said occasionally to remark that solutions to most public-policy problems have already been found somewhere—we just have to scan the horizons for them. This certainly applies to increasing turnout. Three possible changes stand out as particularly likely to get Americans to the polls—though, unfortunately, their probable effectiveness is inversely related to the plausibility of their ever being enacted in the United States.

If in an ideal democracy everyone votes, people could simply be required to participate. This is how Australians reasoned when they instituted compulsory voting after their turnout rate fell to 58 percent in 1922. Since then the turnout in Australia has never fallen below 90 percent, even though the maximum fine for not voting is only about $30, and judges readily accept any reasonable excuse. However, American political culture is based on John Locke's views on individual rights, whereas Australian culture was shaped by Jeremy Bentham's concept of the greatest good for the greatest number. Most Americans would probably assert that they have an inviolable right not to vote.

Beyond that, it is debatable whether we really want to force turnout rates in America up to 90 percent. People with limited political knowledge might deal with being compelled to vote by making dozens of decisions in the same way they choose lottery numbers. In Australia this is known as the "donkey vote," for people who approach voting as if they were playing the old children's game. Given Australia's relatively simple electoral process, the donkey vote is a small proportion; in America it would probably be greater.

Evidence from around the world indicates that our turnout rates could be increased if we adopted some form of proportional representation. In our winner-take-all system many Americans rightly perceive that their votes are unlikely to affect election outcomes. Proportional representation changes this perception by awarding seats to small voting blocs. The threshold for representation varies by country, but typically any party that receives more than five percent of the national vote earns seats in the legislature. Almost inevitably when proportional representation is instituted, the number of political parties grows. And with a range of viable parties to choose from, people tend to feel that their choice truly embodies their specific interests. Hence they are more likely to vote.

If we were to adopt proportional representation, new parties would be likely to spring up to represent the interests of groups such as African Americans, Latinos, and the new Christian right. Although this would give members of these groups more incentive to vote, and thus would raise the low turnout rates of minority groups, a price would be paid for this benefit. The current system brings diverse groups together under the umbrellas of two heterogeneous parties; a multi-party system would set America's social groups apart from one another. Proportional representation therefore seems no more practical on the American scene than compulsory voting.

A simple but effective change, however, could be made in election timing. An ordinary act of Congress could move Election Day to a Saturday or make it a holiday, thereby giving more people more time to vote. An 1872 law established the first Tuesday after the first Monday in November as Election Day. At that point in history it made little difference whether elections were on Saturday or Tuesday, because most people worked on Saturday. Only Sunday would have been a day free of work, but with elections in the late nineteenth century being occasions for drinking and gambling, that option was out of the question in such a religious country.

Americans have become quite accustomed to Tuesday elections, just as they have to the nonmetric system for weights and measures and other artifacts of another time. State after state has set primary-election dates on Tuesdays—all twentieth-century decisions, some of them quite recent. It would be difficult to change this custom. Furthermore, there would probably be some resistance from Orthodox Jews and Mormons to putting Election Day on their sabbath.

An alternative would be to declare Election Day a national holiday. This would probably be resisted on the basis of cost. A solution would be to move Election Day to the second Tuesday of November and combine it with Veterans' Day, traditionally celebrated on November 11. This would send a strong signal about the importance our country attaches to voting. And what better way could there be to honor those who fought for democratic rights than for Americans to vote on what could become known as Veterans' Democracy Day?

12

Political Parties

Political parties are an essential feature of modern democracies. Some analysts define democracies as political systems with competitive elections—that is, systems in which a peaceful change in the control of government from one party to another occurs with some frequency. Parties are the means for aggregating interests in a society. Parties recruit individuals for public service and help to define a limited number of options at election time.

In spite of its great size and diversity, the United States has had only two major parties during most of its history, whereas most other democracies have had more. The electoral system used most frequently in the United States—in which a single winner is chosen by plurality voting, with only one winner per district or state—encourages serious competitors to coalesce into two camps or parties. New parties usually find their messages usurped by candidates of the two major parties. And office seekers, recognizing that voters consider the candidates of the two major parties as the most likely to win, usually join one of the two major parties.

American political parties have evolved in many ways since the first days of the republic. In recent decades, candidates have become more independent of parties. By organizing their own campaigns, using the techniques of mass media, and raising their own money, candidates have come to rely less on party activists and leaders for assistance. As the essays in this chapter demonstrate, parties have changed in response. To maintain an influence on the political process, the parties have assumed a more active role in recruiting candidates, raising and spending money, and providing a variety of services to candidates' campaign organizations.

12-1

from *Why Parties?*

John H. Aldrich

*American political parties were created by politicians and committed
citizens who sought to win elections and control legislatures, executives,
and even the courts. They exist at local, state, and national levels—
wherever elections are held for coveted offices. The system of political
parties that has evolved over time is fragmented and multilayered. In the
following essay, John Aldrich describes the nature of the political problems that parties solve for candidates and voters. As much as we may
dislike partisanship, modern democracies could not, Aldrich explains,
function without it.*

Is the Contemporary Political Party Strong or in Decline?

The Case for the Importance of Political Parties

THE PATH TO OFFICE for nearly every major politician begins today, as it has for
over 150 years, with the party. Many candidates emerge initially from the
ranks of party activists, all serious candidates seek their party's nomination,
and they become serious candidates in the general election only because they
have won their party's endorsement. Today most partisan nominations are
decided in primary elections—that is, based on votes cast by self-designated
partisans in the mass electorate. Successful nominees count on the continued support of these partisans in the general election, and for good reason.
At least since surveys have provided firm evidence, all presidential nominees
have won the support of no less than a majority of their party in the electorate, no matter how overwhelming their defeat may have been.

This is an age of so-called partisan dealignment in the electorate. Even so, a substantial majority today consider themselves partisans. The lowest percentage of self-professed (i.e., "strong" and "weak") partisans yet recorded in National Election Studies (NES) surveys was 61 percent in 1974, and another 22 percent expressed partisan leanings that year. Evidence from panel surveys demonstrates that partisanship has remained as stable and enduring for most adults after dealignment as it did before it, and it is often the single strongest predictor of candidate choice in the public.

If parties have declined recently, the decline has not occurred in their formal organizations. Party organizations are if anything stronger, better financed, and more professional at all levels now. Although its importance to candidates may be less than in the past, the party provides more support—more money, workers, and resources of all kinds—than any other organization for all but a very few candidates for national and state offices.

Once elected, officeholders remain partisans. Congress is organized by parties. Party-line votes elect its leadership, determine what its committees will be, assign members to them, and select their chairs. Party caucuses remain a staple of congressional life, and they and other forms of party organizations in Congress have become stronger in recent years. Party voting in committee and on the floor of both houses, though far less common in the United States than in many democracies, nonetheless remains the first and most important standard for understanding congressional voting behavior, and it too has grown stronger, in this case much stronger, in recent years.

Relationships among the elected branches of government are also heavily partisan. Conference committees to resolve discrepancies between House and Senate versions of legislation reflect partisan as well as interchamber rivalries. The president is the party's leader, and his agenda is introduced, fought for, and supported on the floor by his congressional party. His agenda becomes his party's congressional agenda, and much of it finds its way into law.

The Case for Weak and Weakening Parties

As impressive as the scenario above may be, not all agree that parties lie at the heart of American politics, at least not anymore. The literature on parties over the past two decades is replete with accounts of the decline of the political party. Even the choice of titles clearly reflects the arguments.

David Broder perhaps began this stream of literature with *The Party's Over* (1972). Since then, political scientists have written extensively on this theme: for example, Crotty's *American Political Parties in Decline* (1984), Kirkpatrick's *Dismantling the Parties* (1978), Polsby's *Consequences of Party Reform* (1983) . . . , Ranney's thoughtful *Curing the Mischiefs of Faction* (1975), and Wattenberg's *The Decline of American Political Parties* (1990).

Those who see larger ills in the contemporary political scene often attribute them to the failure of parties to be stronger and more effective. In "The Decline of Collective Responsibility" (1980), Fiorina argued that such responsibility was possible only through the agency of the political party. Jacobson concluded his study of congressional elections (1992) by arguing that contemporary elections induce "responsiveness" of individual incumbents to their districts but do so "without [inducing] responsibility" in incumbents for what Congress does. As a result, the electorate can find no one to hold accountable for congressional failings. He too looked to a revitalized party for redress. These themes reflect the responsible party thesis, if not in being a call for such parties, at least in using that as the standard for measuring how short the contemporary party falls.

The literature on the presidency is not immune to this concern for decaying parties. Kernell's account of the strategy of "going public" (1986)—that is, generating power by marshaling public opinion—is that it became more common as the older strategy of striking bargains with a small set of congressional (and partisan) power brokers grew increasingly futile. The earlier use of the president's power to persuade (Neustadt 1960, 1990) failed as power centers became more diverse and fragmented and brokers could no longer deliver. Lowi argued this case even more strongly in *The Personal President* (1985). America, he claimed, has come to invest too much power in the office of the president, with the result that the promise of the presidency and the promises of individual presidents go unfulfilled. Why? Because the rest of government has become too unwieldy, complicated, and fragmented for the president to use that power effectively. His solution? Revitalize political parties.

Divided partisan control over government, once an occasional aberration, has become the ordinary course of affairs. Many of the same themes in this literature are those sounded above—fragmented, decentralized power, lack of coordination and control over what the government does, and absence of collective responsibility. Strong political parties are, among other things, those that can deliver the vote for most or all of their candidates. Thus another symptom of weakened parties is regularized divided government, in the states as well as in the nation.

If divided government is due to weakened parties, that condition must be due in turn to weakened partisan loyalties in the electorate. Here the evidence is clear. The proportions and strength of party attachments in the electorate declined in the mid-1960s. There was a resurgence in affiliation twenty years later, but to a lower level than before 1966. The behavioral consequences of these changes are if anything even clearer. Defection from party lines and split-ticket voting are far more common for all major offices at national, state, and local levels today than before the mid-1960s. Elections are more candidate centered and less party centered, and those who come to office have played a greater role in shaping their own more highly personalized electoral coalitions. Incumbents, less dependent on the party for winning office, are less disposed to vote the party line in Congress or to follow the wishes of their party's president. Power becomes decentralized toward the individual incumbent and, as Jacobson argues, individual incumbents respond to their constituents. If that means defecting from the party, so be it.

Is the Debate Genuine?

Some believe that parties have actually grown stronger over the past few decades. This position has been put most starkly by Schlesinger: "It should be clear by now that the grab bag of assumptions, inferences, and half-truths that have fed the decline-of-parties thesis is simply wrong" (1985, p. 1152). Rather, he maintains, "Thanks to increasing levels of competition between the parties, then, American political parties are stronger than before" (p. 1168). More common is the claim that parties were weakened in the 1960s but have been revitalized since then. Rohde pointed out that "in the last decade, however, the decline of partisanship in the House has been reversed. Party voting, which had been as low as 27 percent in 1972, peaked at 64 percent in 1987" (1989, p. 1). Changes in party voting in the Senate have been only slightly less dramatic, and Rohde has also demonstrated that party institutions in the House strengthened substantially in the same period (1991). If, as Rohde says, parties in the government are stronger, and if . . . others are correct that party organizations are stronger, a thesis of decline with resurgence must be taken seriously. The electorate's partisan affiliations may be a lagging rather than a leading indicator, and even they have rebounded slightly.

A Theory of Political Parties

As diverse as are the conclusions reached by these and other astute observers, all agree that the political party is—or should be—central to the American political system. Parties are—or should be—integral parts of all political life, from structuring the reasoning and choice of the electorate, through all facets of campaigns and seemingly all facets of the government, to the very possibility of effective governance in a democracy.

How is it that such astute observers of American politics and parties, writing at virtually the same time and looking at much the same evidence, come to such diametrically opposed conclusions about the strength of parties? Eldersveld . . . wrote that "political parties are complex institutions and processes, and as such they are difficult to understand and evaluate" (1982, p. 407). As proof, he went on to consider the decline of parties thesis. At one point he wrote, "The decline in our parties, therefore, is difficult to demonstrate, empirically or in terms of historical perspective" (p. 417). And yet he then turned to signs of party decline and concluded his book with the statement: "Despite their defects they continue today to be the major instruments for democratic government in this nation. With necessary reforms we can make them even more central to the governmental process and to the lives of American citizens. Eighty years ago, Lord James Bryce, after studying our party system, said, 'In America the great moving forces are the parties. The government counts for less than in Europe, the parties count for more. . . .' If our citizens and their leaders wish it, American parties will still be the 'great moving forces' of our system" (1982, pp. 432–33).

The "Fundamental Equation" of the
New Institutionalism Applied to Parties

That parties are complex does not mean they are incomprehensible. Indeed complexity is, if not an intentional outcome, at least an anticipated result of those who shape the political parties. Moreover, they are so deeply woven into the fabric of American politics that they cannot be understood apart from either their own historical context and dynamics or those of the political system as a whole. Parties, that is, can be understood only in relation to the polity, to the government and its institutions, and to the historical context of the times.

The study of political parties, second, is necessarily a study of a major pair of political *institutions*. Indeed, the institutions that define the political party are unique, and as it happens they are unique in ways that make an institutional account especially useful. Their establishment and nature are fundamentally extralegal; they are nongovernmental political institutions. Instead of statute, their basis lies in the actions of ambitious politicians that created and maintain them. They are, in the parlance of the new institutionalism, *endogenous institutions*—in fact, the most highly endogenous institutions of any substantial and sustained political importance in American history.

By endogenous, I mean it was the actions of political actors that created political parties in the first place, and it is the actions of political actors that have shaped and altered them over time. And political actors have chosen to alter their parties dramatically at several times in our history, reformed them often, and tinkered with them constantly. Of all major political bodies in the United States, the political party is the most variable in its rules, regulations, and procedures—that is to say, in its formal organization—and in its informal methods and traditions. It is often the same set of actors who write the party's rules and then choose the party's outcomes, sometimes at nearly the same time and by the same method. Thus, for example, one night national party conventions debate, consider any proposed amendments, and then adopt their rules by a majority vote of credentialed delegates. The next night these same delegates debate, consider any proposed amendments, and then adopt their platform by majority vote, and they choose their presidential nominee by majority vote the following night.

Who, then, are these critical political actors? Many see the party-in-the-electorate as comprising major actors. To be sure, mobilizing the electorate to capture office is a central task of the political party. But America is a republican democracy. All power flows directly or indirectly from the great body of the people, to paraphrase Madison's definition. The public elects its political leaders, but it is that leadership that legislates, executes, and adjudicates policy. The parties are defined in relation to this republican democracy. Thus it is political leaders, those Schlesinger (1975) has called "office-seekers"—*those who seek and those who hold elective office*—who are the central actors in the party.

Ambitious office seekers and holders are thus the first and most important actors in the political party. A second set of important figures in party politics comprises those who hold, or have access to, critical resources that office seekers need to realize their ambitions. It is expensive to build and maintain the party and campaign organizations necessary to compete effectively in the electoral arena. Thomas Ferguson, for example, has made an extended argument for the "primary and constitutive role large investors play in American politics" (1983, p. 3). Much of his research emphasizes this primary and constitutive role in party politics in particular, such as in partisan realignments. The study of the role of money in congressional elections has also focused in part on concentrations of such sources of funding, such as from political action committees which political parties are coming to take advantage of. Elections are also fought over the flow of information to the public. The electoral arm of political parties in the eighteenth century was made up of "committees of correspondence," which were primarily lines of communication among political elites and between them and potential voters, and one of the first signs of organizing of the Jeffersonian Republican party was the hiring of a newspaper editor. The press was first a partisan press, and editors and publishers from Thomas Ritchie to Horace Greeley long were critical players in party politics. Today those with specialized knowledge relevant to communication, such as pollsters, media and advertising experts, and computerized fund-raising specialists, enjoy influence in party, campaign, and even government councils that greatly exceeds their mere technical expertise.

In more theoretical terms, this second set of party actors include those Schlesinger (1975) has called "benefit seekers," those for whom realization of their goals depends on the party's success in capturing office. Party activists shade from those powerful figures with concentrations of, or access to, money and information described above to the legions of volunteer campaign activists who ring doorbells and stuff envelopes and are, individually and collectively, critical to the first level of the party—its office seekers. All are critical because they command the resources, whether money, expertise, and information or merely time and labor, that office seekers need to realize their ambitions. As a result, activists' motivations shape and constrain the behavior of office seekers, as their own roles are, in turn, shaped and constrained by the office seekers. The changed incentives of party activists have played a significant role in the fundamentally altered nature of the contemporary party, but the impact of benefit seekers will be seen scattered throughout this account.

Voters, however, are neither office seekers nor benefit seekers and thus are not a part of the political party at all, even if they identify strongly with a party and consistently support its candidates. Voters are indeed critical, but they are critical as the targets of party activities. Parties "produce" candidates, platforms, and policies. Voters "consume" by exchanging their votes for the party's product (see Popkin et al. 1976). Some voters, of course, become partisans by becoming activists, whether as occasional volunteers, as sustained contributors, or even as candidates. But until they do so, they may be faithful consumers, "brand name" loyalists as it were, but they are still only the targets of partisans' efforts to sell their wares in the political marketplace.

Why, then, do politicians create and recreate the party, exploit its features, or ignore its dictates? The simple answer is that it has been in their interests to do so. That is, this is a *rational choice* account of the party, an account that presumes that rational, elective office seekers and holders use the party to achieve their ends.

I do not assume that politicians are invariably self-interested in a narrow sense. This is not a theory in which elective office seekers simply maximize their chances of election or reelection, at least not for its own sake. They may well have fundamental values and principles, and they may have preferences over policies as means to those ends. They also care about office, both for its own sake and for the opportunities to achieve other ends that election and reelection make possible. . . . Just as winning elections is a means to other ends for politicians (whether career or policy ends), so too is the political party a means to these other ends.

Why, then, do politicians turn to create or reform, to use or abuse, partisan institutions? The answer is that parties are designed as attempts to solve problems that current institutional arrangements do not solve and that politicians have come to believe they cannot solve. These problems fall into three general and recurring categories.

The Problem of Ambition and Elective Office Seeking

Elective office seekers, as that label says, want to win election to office. Parties regulate access to those offices. If elective office is indeed valuable, there will be more aspirants than offices, and the political party and the two-party system are means of regulating that competition and channeling those ambitions. Major party nomination is necessary for election, and partisan institutions have been developed—and have been reformed and re-reformed—for regulating competition. Intra-institutional leadership positions are also highly valued and therefore potentially competitive. There is, for example, a fairly well institutionalized path to the office of Speaker of the House. It is, however, a Democratic party institution. Elective politicians, of course, ordinarily desire election more than once. They are typically careerists who want a long and productive career in politics. Schlesinger's ambition theory (1966) . . . is precisely about this general problem. Underlying this theory, though typically not fully developed, is a problem. The problem is that if office is desirable, there will be more, usually many more, aspirants than there are offices to go around. When stated in rigorous form, it can be proved that in fact there is no permanent solution to this problem. And it is a problem that can adversely affect the fortunes of a party. In 1912 the Republican vote was split between William Howard Taft and Theodore Roosevelt. This split enabled Woodrow Wilson to win with 42 percent of the popular vote. Not only was Wilson the only break in Republican hegemony of the White House in this period, but in that year Democrats increased their House majority by sixty-five additional seats and captured majority control of the Senate. Thus failure to regulate intraparty competition cost Republicans dearly.

For elective office seekers, regulating conflict over who holds those offices is clearly of major concern. It is ever present. And it is not just a problem of access to government offices but is also a problem internal to each party as soon as the party becomes an important gateway to office.

The Problem of Making Decisions for the Party and for the Polity

Once in office, partisans determine outcomes for the polity. They propose alternatives, shape the agenda, pass (or reject) legislation, and implement what they enact. The policy formation and execution process, that is, is highly partisan. The parties-in-government are more than mere coalitions of like-minded individuals, however; they are enduring institutions. Very few incumbents change their partisan affiliations. Most retain their partisanship throughout their career, even though they often disagree (i.e., are not uniformly like-minded) with some of their partisan peers. When the rare incumbent does change parties, it is invariably to join the party more consonant with that switcher's policy interests. This implies that there are differences between the two parties at some fundamental and enduring level on policy positions, values, and beliefs. Thus, parties are institutions designed to promote the achievement of collective choices—choices on which the parties differ and choices reached by majority rule. As with access to office and ambition theory, there is a well-developed theory for this problem: *social choice theory*. Underlying this theory is the well-known problem that no method of choice can solve the elective officeholders' problem of combining the interests, concerns, or values of a polity that remains faithful to democratic values, as shown by the consequences flowing from Arrow's theorem (Arrow 1951). Thus, in a republican democracy politicians may turn to partisan institutions to solve the problem of collective choice. In the language of politics, parties may help achieve the goal of attaining policy majorities in the first place, as well as the often more difficult goal of maintaining such majorities.

The Problem of Collective Action

The third problem is the most pervasive and thus the furthest-ranging in substantive content. The clearest example, however, is also the most important. To win office, candidates need more than a party's nomination. Election requires persuading members of the public to support that candidacy and mobilizing as many of those supporters as possible. This is a problem of collective action. How do candidates get supporters to vote for them—at least in greater numbers than vote for the opposition—as well as get them to provide the cadre of workers and contribute the resources needed to win election? The political party has long been the solution.

As important as wooing and mobilizing supporters are, collective action problems arise in a wide range of circumstances facing elective office seekers. Party action invariably requires the concerted action of many partisans to achieve collectively desirable outcomes. Jimmy Carter was the only president in the 1970s and 1980s to enjoy unified party control of government. Democrats in Congress, it might well be argued, shared an interest in achieving policy outcomes. And yet Carter was all too often unable to get them to act in their shared collective interests. In 1980 not only he but the Democratic congressional parties paid a heavy price for failed cooperation. The theory here, of course, is the *theory of public goods* and its consequence, the *theory of collective action*.

The Elective Office Seekers' and Holders' Interests Are to Win

Why should this crucial set of actors, the elective office seekers and officeholders, care about these three classes of problems? The short answer is that these concerns become practical problems to politicians when they adversely affect their chances of winning. Put differently, politicians turn to their political party—that is, use its powers, resources, and institutional forms—when they believe doing so increases their prospects for winning desired outcomes, and they turn from it if it does not.

Ambition theory is about winning per se. The breakdown of orderly access to office risks unfettered and unregulated competition. The inability of a party to develop effective means of nomination and support for election therefore directly influences the chances of victory for the candidates and thus for their parties. The standard example of the problem of social choice theory, the "paradox of voting," is paradoxical precisely because all are voting to win desired outcomes, and yet there is no majority-preferred outcome. Even if there happens to be a majority-preferred policy, the conditions under which it is truly a stable equilibrium are extremely fragile and thus all too amenable to defeat. In other words, majorities in Congress are hard to attain and at least as hard to maintain. And the only reason to employ scarce campaign resources to mobilize supporters is that such mobilization increases the odds of victory. Its opposite, the failure to act when there are broadly shared interests—the problem of collective action—reduces the prospects of victory, whether at the ballot box or in government. Scholars may recognize these as manifestations of theoretical problems and call them "impossibility results" to emphasize their generic importance. Politicians recognize the consequences of these impossibility results by their adverse effects on their chances of winning—of securing what it is in their interests to secure.

So why have politicians so often turned to political parties for solutions to these problems? Their existence creates incentives for their use. It is, for example, incredibly difficult to win election to major office without the backing of a major party. It is only a little less certain that legislators who seek to lead a policy proposal through the congressional labyrinth will first turn to their party for assistance. But such incentives tell us only that an ongoing political institution is used when it is useful. Why form political parties in the first place? . . .

First, parties are institutions. This means, among other things, that they have some durability. They may be endogenous institutions, yet party reforms are meant not as short-term fixes but as alterations to last for years, even decades. Thus, for example, legislators might create a party rather than a temporary majority coalition to increase their chances of winning not just today but into the future. Similarly, a long and successful political career means winning office today, but it also requires winning elections throughout that career. A standing, enduring organization makes that goal more likely.

Second, American democracy chooses by plurality or majority rule. Election to office therefore requires broad-based support wherever and from whomever it can be found. So strong are the resulting incentives for a two-party system to emerge that the effect is called Duverger's law (Duverger 1954). It is in part the need to win vast and diverse support that has led politicians to create political parties.

Third, parties may help officeholders win more, and more often, than alternatives. Consider the usual stylized model of pork barrel politics. All winners get a piece of the pork for their districts. All funded projects are paid for by tax revenues, so each district pays an equal share of the costs of each project adopted, whether or not that district receives a project. Several writers have argued that this kind of legislation leads to "universalism," that is, adoption of a "norm" that every such bill yields a project to every district and thus passes with a "universal" or unanimous coalition. Thus everyone "wins." . . . As a result, expecting to win only a bit more than half the time and lose the rest of the time, all legislators prefer consistent use of the norm of universalism. But consider an alternative. Suppose some majority agree to form a more permanent coalition, to control outcomes now and into the future, and develop institutional means to encourage fealty to this agreement. If they successfully accomplish this, they will win regularly. Members of this institutionalized coalition would prefer it to universalism, since they always win a project in either case, but they get their projects at lower cost under the institutionalized majority coalition, which passes fewer projects. Thus, even in this case with no shared substantive interests at all, there are nonetheless incentives to form an enduring voting coalition—to form a political party. And those in the excluded minority have incentives to counterorganize. United, they may be more able to woo defectors to their side. If not, they can campaign to throw those rascals in the majority party out of office.

In sum, these theoretical problems affect elective office seekers and officeholders by reducing their chances of winning. Politicians therefore may turn to political parties as institutions designed to ameliorate them. In solving these theoretical problems, however, from the politicians' perspective parties are affecting who wins and loses and what is won or lost. And it is to parties that politicians often turn, because of their durability as institution-alized solutions, because of the need to orchestrate large and diverse groups of people to form winning majorities, and because often more can be won through parties. Note that this argument rests on the implicit as-sumption that winning and losing hang in the balance. Politicians may be expected to give up some of their personal autonomy only when they face an imminent threat of defeat without doing so or only when doing so can block opponents' ability to build the strength necessary to win.

This is, of course, the positive case for parties, for it specifies conditions under which politicians find them useful. Not all problems are best solved, perhaps even solved at all, by political parties. Other arrangements, perhaps interest groups, issue networks, or personal electoral coalitions, may be su-perior at different times and under different conditions. The party may even be part of the problem. In such cases politicians turn elsewhere to seek the means to win. Thus this theory is at base a theory of ambitious politicians seeking to achieve their goals. Often they have done so through the agency of the party, but sometimes, this theory implies, they will seek to realize their goals in other ways.

The political party has regularly proved useful. Their permanence sug-gests that the appropriate question is not When parties? but How much par-ties and how much other means? That parties are endogenous implies that there is no single, consistent account of the political party—nor should we expect one. Instead, parties are but a (major) part of the institutional con-text in which current historical conditions—the problems—are set, and so-lutions are sought with permanence only by changing that web of institutional arrangements. Of these the political party is by design the most malleable, and thus it is intended to change in important ways and with relatively great frequency. But it changes in ways that have, for most of American history, retained major political parties and, indeed, retained two major parties.

REFERENCES

Arrow, Kenneth J. 1951. *Social choice and individual values*. New York: Wiley.

Broder, David S. 1972. *The party's over: The failure of politics in America*. New York: Harper and Row.

Crotty, William. 1984. *American political parties in decline*. 2d ed. Boston: Little, Brown.

Duverger, Maurice. 1954. *Political parties: Their organization and activities in the modern state.* New York: Wiley.

Eldersveld, Samuel J. 1982. *Political parties in American society.* New York: Basic Books.

Ferguson, Thomas. 1983. Party realignment and American industrial structures: The investment theory of political parties in historical perspective. In *Research in political economy,* vol. 6, ed. Paul Zarembka, pp. 1–82. Greenwich, Conn.: JAI Press.

Fiorina, Morris P. 1980. The decline of collective responsibility in American politics. *Daedalus* 109 (summer): 25–45.

Jacobson, Gary C. 1992. *The politics of congressional elections.* 3d ed. New York: Harper-Collins.

Kernell, Samuel. 1986. *Going public: New strategies of presidential leadership.* Washington, D.C.: CQ Press.

Kirkpatrick, Jeane J. 1978. *Dismantling the parties: Reflections on party reform and party decomposition.* Washington, D.C.: American Enterprise Institute of Public Policy Research.

Lowi, Theodore. 1985. *The personal president: Power invested, promise unfulfilled.* Ithaca, N.Y.: Cornell University Press.

Neustadt, Richard E. 1960. *Presidential power: The politics of leadership.* New York: Wiley.

———. 1990. *Presidential power and the modern presidents: The politics of leadership from Roosevelt to Reagan.* New York: Free Press.

Polsby, Nelson W. 1983. *Consequences of party reform.* Oxford: Oxford University Press.

Popkin, Samuel, John W. Gorman, Charles Phillips, and Jeffrey A. Smith. 1976. Comment: What have you done for me lately? Toward an investment theory of voting. *American Political Science Review* 70 (September): 779–805.

Ranney, Austin. 1975. *Curing the mischiefs of faction: Party reform in America.* Berkeley and Los Angeles: University of California Press.

Rohde, David W. 1989. "Something's happening here: What it is ain't exactly clear": Southern Democrats in the House of Representatives. In *Home style and Washington work: Studies of congressional politics,* ed. Morris P. Fiorina and David W. Rohde, pp. 137–163. Ann Arbor: University of Michigan Press.

———. 1991. *Parties and leaders in the postreform House.* Chicago: University of Chicago Press.

Schlesinger, Joseph A. 1966. *Ambition and politics: Political careers in the United States.* Chicago: Rand McNally.

———. 1975. The primary goals of political parties: A clarification of positive theory. *American Political Science Review* 69 (September): 840–49.

———. 1985. The new American political party. *American Political Science Review* 79 (December): 1152–69.

Wattenberg, Martin P. 1990. *The decline of American political parties: 1952–1988.* Cambridge: Harvard University Press.

12-2

National Party Organizations at the Century's End

Paul S. Herrnson

*In the 1970s, many keen political observers declared American political
parties nearly dead. Parties lost their significance in campaigns as candidates raised their own money, created their own organizations, and
hired their own campaign managers, pollsters, and advertising specialists. Many analysts have decried the weakness of the parties—sometimes attributing policy stalemate to the inability of the parties to
devise coherent programs. In fact, parties have evolved to play new roles
in American politics. In the following essay, Paul Herrnson describes the
emerging strategies and resources of the national Democratic and Republican party organizations.*

ONCE CHARACTERIZED as poor, unstable, and powerless, national party organizations in the United States ended the twentieth century as financially secure, institutionally stable, and highly influential in election campaigns and
in their relations with state and local party committees. The national party
organizations—the Democratic and Republican national, congressional,
and senatorial campaign committees—have adapted to the candidate-centered, money-driven, "high-tech" style of modern campaign politics. This
[essay] examines the development of the national party organizations, their
evolving relations with other party committees, and their role in contemporary elections.

Party Organizational Development

Origins of the National Parties

The birth and subsequent development of the national party organizations
were the outgrowth of forces impinging on the parties from the broader

From *The Parties Respond: Changes in American Politics*, 2d edition, ed. by L. Sandy Maisel. Copyright
© 1990, 1994 by Westview Press. Reprinted by permission of Westview Press, a member of Perseus
Books, L.L.C. Notes and bibliographic references appearing in the original have been cut.

political environment and of pressures emanating from within the parties themselves. The Democratic National Committee was formed during the Democratic national convention of 1848 for the purpose of organizing and directing the presidential campaign, promulgating the call for the next convention, and tending to the details associated with setting up future conventions. The Republican National Committee was created in 1856 at an ad hoc meeting of future Republicans for the purposes of bringing the Republican Party into existence and conducting election-related activities similar to those performed by its Democratic counterpart. The creation of the national committees was an important step in a process that transformed the parties' organizational apparatuses from loosely confederative structures to more centralized, federal organizations.

The congressional campaign committees were created in response to electoral insecurities that were heightened as a result of factional conflicts that developed within the two parties following the Civil War. The National Republican Congressional Committee (NRCC) was formed in 1866 by radical Republican members of the House who were feuding with President Andrew Johnson. The House members believed they could not rely on the president or the RNC for assistance, so they created their own campaign committee to assist with their elections and to distance themselves from the president. As is often the case in politics, organization begot counterorganization. Following the Republican example, pro-Johnson Democrats formed their own election committee—the Democratic Congressional Campaign Committee (DCCC).

Senate leaders created the senatorial campaign committees in 1916, after the Seventeenth Amendment transformed the upper chamber into a popularly elected body. The Democratic Senatorial Campaign Committee (DSCC) and the National Republican Senatorial Committee (NRSC) were founded to assist incumbent senators with their reelection campaigns. Like their counterparts in the House, the Senate campaign committees were established during a period of political upheaval—the Progressive movement—to assuage members' electoral insecurities during an era of exceptionally high partisan disunity and political instability.

The six national party organizations have not possessed abundant power during most of their existence. Flow charts of the party organizations are generally pyramid-like, with the national conventions at the apex, the national committees directly below them, the congressional and senatorial campaign committees (also known as the Hill committees) branching off the national committees, and the state and local party apparatus placed below the national party apparatus. However, power is not, and has never been, distributed hierarchically. Throughout most of the parties' history, and during the height of their strength (circa the late nineteenth and early twentieth centuries), power was concentrated at the local level, usually in countywide political machines. Power mainly flowed up from county organizations to state party committees and conventions, and then on to the national convention. The national, congressional, and senatorial campaign committees had little, if any, power over state and local party leaders.

Local party organizations are reputed to have possessed tremendous influence during the golden age of political parties. Old-fashioned political machines had the ability to unify the legislative and executive branches of local and state governments. The machines also had a great deal of influence in national politics and with the courts. The machines' power was principally rooted in their virtual monopoly over the tools needed to run a successful campaign. Party bosses had the power to award the party nominations to potential candidates. Local party committees also possessed the resources needed to communicate with the electorate and mobilize voters.

Nevertheless, party campaigning was a cooperative endeavor during the golden age, especially during presidential election years. Although individual branches of the party organization were primarily concerned with electing candidates within their immediate jurisdictions, party leaders at different levels of the organization had a number of reasons to work together. They recognized that ballot structures and voter partisanship linked the electoral prospects of their candidates. Party leaders further understood that electing candidates to federal, state, and local governments would enable them to maximize the patronage and preferments they could exact for themselves and their supporters. Party leaders were also conscious of the different resources and capabilities possessed by different branches of the party organization. The national party organizations, and especially the national committees, had the financial, administrative, and communications resources needed to coordinate and set the tone of a nationwide campaign. Local party committees had the proximity to voters needed to collect electoral information, conduct voter registration and get-out-the-vote drives, and perform other grassroots campaign activities. State party committees had relatively modest resources, but they occupied an important intermediate position between the other two strata of the party organization. State party leaders channeled electoral information up to the national party organizations and arranged for candidates and other prominent party leaders to speak at local rallies and events. Relations between the national party organizations and other branches of the party apparatus were characterized by negotiations and compromise rather than command. Party organizations in Washington, D.C., did not dominate party politics during the golden age. They did, however, play an important role in what were essentially party-centered election campaigns.

Party Decline

The transition from a party-dominated system of campaign politics to a candidate-centered system was brought about by legal, demographic, and technological changes in American society and by reforms instituted by the parties themselves. The direct primary and civil service regulations instituted during the Progressive Era deprived party bosses of their ability to handpick nominees and reward party workers with government jobs and contracts. The reforms weakened the bosses' hold over candidates and political activists and encouraged candidates to build their own campaign organizations.

Demographic and cultural changes reinforced this pattern. Increased education and social mobility, declining immigration, and a growing national identity contributed to the erosion of the close-knit, traditional ethnic neighborhoods that formed the core of the old-fashioned political machine's constituency. Voters began to turn toward nationally focused mass media and away from local party committees for their political information. Growing preferences for movies, radio, and televised entertainment underscored this phenomenon by reducing the popularity of rallies, barbecues, and other types of interpersonal communication at which old-fashioned political machines excelled. These changes combined to deprive the machines of their political bases and to render many of their communications and mobilization techniques obsolete.

The adaptation to the electoral arena of technological innovations developed in the public relations field further eroded candidates' dependence on party organizations. Advancements in survey research, computerized data processing, and mass media advertising provided candidates with new tools for gathering information about voters and communicating messages to them. The emergence of a new corps of campaigners—the political consultants—enabled candidates to hire nonparty professionals to run their campaigns. Direct-mail fund-raising techniques helped candidates raise the money needed to pay their campaign staffs and outside consultants. These developments helped to transform election campaigns from party-focused, party-conducted affairs to events that revolved around individual candidates and their campaign organizations.

Two recent developments that initially appeared to weaken party organizations and reinforce the candidate-centeredness of American elections were party reforms introduced by the Democrats' McGovern-Fraser Commission and the Federal Election Campaign Act of 1971 and its amendments. The McGovern-Fraser reforms, and reforms instituted by later Democratic reform commissions, were designed to make the presidential nominating process more open and more representative. Their side effects included making it more difficult for longtime party "regulars" to attend national party conventions or play a significant role in other party activities. They also made it easier for issue and candidate activists who had little history of party service (frequently labeled "purists" or "amateurs") to play a larger role in party politics. The rise of the "purists" also led to tensions over fundamental issues such as whether winning elections or advancing particular policies should have priority. Heightened tensions made coalition building among party activists and supporters more difficult. Intraparty conflicts between purists and professionals, and the purists' heavy focus on the agendas of specific candidates and special interests, also resulted in the organizational needs of the parties being neglected. The reforms were debilitating to both parties, but they were more harmful to the Democratic Party, which had introduced them.

The FECA also had some negative effects on the parties. The FECA's contribution and expenditure limits, disclosure provisions, and other regulatory requirements forced party committees to keep separate bank accounts for state and federal election activity. The reforms had the immediate effect of discouraging state and local party organizations from fully participating in federal elections. The FECA also set the stage for the tremendous proliferation of PACs that began in the late 1970s. The Federal Election Commission's SunPAC Advisory in 1976 opened the gateway for PACs to become the major organized financiers of congressional elections.

The progressive reforms, demographic and cultural transformations, new campaign technology, recent party reforms, and campaign finance legislation combined to reduce the roles that party organizations played in elections and to foster the evolution of a candidate-centered election system. Under this system, candidates typically assembled their own campaign organizations, initially to compete for their party's nomination and then to contest the general election. In the case of presidential elections, a candidate who succeeded in securing the party's nomination also won control of the national committee. The candidate's campaign organization directed most national committee election activity. In congressional elections, most campaign activities were carried out by the candidate's own organization, both before and after the primary. The parties' seeming inability to adapt to the new "high-tech," money-driven style of campaign politics resulted in their being pushed to the periphery of the elections process. These trends were accompanied by a general decline in the parties' ability to structure political choice, to furnish symbolic referents and decision-making cues for voters, and to foster party unity among elected officials.

National Party Reemergence

Although the party decline was a gradual process that took its greatest toll on party organizations at the local level, party renewal occurred over a relatively short period and was focused primarily in Washington, D.C. The dynamics of recent national party organizational development bear parallels to changes occurring during earlier periods. The content of recent national party organizational renewal was shaped by the changing needs of candidates. The new-style campaigning that became prevalent during the 1960s places a premium on campaign activities requiring technical expertise and in-depth research. Some candidates were able to run a viable campaign using their own funds or talent. Others turned to political consultants, PACs, and special interests for help. However, many candidates found it difficult to assemble the money and expertise needed to compete in a modern election. The increased needs of candidates for greater access to technical expertise, political information, and money created an opportunity for national and some state party organizations to become the repositories of these electoral resources.

Nevertheless, national party organizations did not respond to changes in the political environment until electoral crises forced party leaders to recognize the institutional and electoral weaknesses of the national party organizations. As was the case during earlier eras of party transformation, crises that heightened officeholders' electoral anxieties furnished party leaders with the opportunities and incentives to augment the parties' organizational apparatuses. Entrepreneurial party leaders recognized that they might receive payoffs for restructuring the national party organizations so that they could better assist candidates and state and local party committees with their election efforts.

The Watergate scandal and the trouncing Republican candidates experienced in the 1974 and 1976 elections provided a crisis of competition that was the catalyst for change at the Republican national party organizations. The Republicans lost forty-nine seats in the House in 1974, had an incumbent president defeated two years later, and controlled only twelve governorships and four state legislatures by 1977. Moreover, voter identification with the Republican Party, which had previously been climbing, dropped precipitously, especially among voters under thirty-five.

The crisis of competition drew party leaders' attention to the weaknesses of the Republican national, congressional, and senatorial campaign committees. After a struggle that became entwined with the politics surrounding the race for the RNC chair, William Brock, an advocate of party organizational development, was selected to head the RNC. Other party-building entrepreneurs were selected to chair the parties' other two national organizations: Representative Guy Vander Jagt of Michigan took the helm of the NRCC in 1974 and Senator Robert Packwood of Oregon was selected to chair the NRSC in 1976. The three party leaders initiated a variety of programs aimed at promoting the institutional development of their committees, increasing the committees' electoral presence, and providing candidates with campaign money and services. All three leaders played a major role in reshaping the missions of the national parties and in placing them on a path that would result in their organizational transformation.

The transformation of the Democratic national party organizations is more complicated than that of their Republican counterparts because DNC institutionalization occurred in two distinct phases. The first phase of DNC development, which is often referred to as party reform and associated with party decline, was concerned with enhancing the representativeness and openness of the national committee and the presidential nominating convention. The second phase, which resembles the institutionalization of the Republican party organizations and is frequently referred to as party renewal, focused on the committee's institutional and electoral capabilities.

Democratic party reform followed the tumultuous 1968 Democratic National Convention. Protests on the floor of the convention and in the streets of Chicago constituted a factional crisis that underscored the deep rift between liberal reform-minded "purists" and party "regulars." The crisis and the party's defeat in November created an opportunity for major party organizational change. The McGovern-Fraser Commission, and later reform commissions, introduced rules that made the delegate selection process more participatory and led to the unexpected proliferation of presidential primaries, increased the size and demographic representativeness of the DNC and the national convention, instituted midterm issue conferences (which were discontinued by Paul Kirk after his selection as DNC chair in 1984), and resulted in the party adopting a written charter. Some of these changes are believed to have been a major cause of party decline.

Other changes may have been more positive. Upon adopting the decisions of the McGovern-Fraser Commission, the DNC took on a new set of responsibilities that concern state party compliance with national party rules governing participation in the delegate selection process. The expansion of DNC rule making and enforcement authority has resulted in the committee usurping the power to overrule state party activities connected with the process that are not in compliance with national party rules. This represents a fundamental shift in the distribution of power between the national committee and state party organizations. Democratic party reform transformed the DNC into an important agency of intraparty regulation and increased committee influence in both party and presidential politics.

The second phase of Democratic national party institutionalization followed the party's massive defeat in the 1980 election. The defeat of incumbent President Jimmy Carter, the loss of thirty-four House seats (half of the party's margin), and loss of control of the Senate constituted a crisis of competition that was the catalyst for change at the Democratic national party organizations. Unlike the previous phase of national party development, Democratic party renewal was preceded by widespread agreement among DNC members, Democrats in Congress, and party activists that the party should increase its competitiveness by imitating the GOP's party-building and campaign service programs.

The issue of party renewal was an important factor in the selection of Charles Manatt as DNC chair and Representative Tony Coelho as DCCC chair in 1980. It also influenced Democratic senators' choice of Lloyd Bentsen of Texas to chair the DSCC in 1982. All three party leaders were committed to building the national party organizations' fund-raising capabilities, improving their professional staffs and organizational structures, and augmenting the Republican party-building model to suit the specific needs of Democratic candidates and state and local committees. Like their

Republican counterparts, all three Democratic leaders played a critical role in promoting the institutionalization of the Democratic national party organizations.

Institutionalized National Parties

The institutionalization of the national party organizations refers to their becoming fiscally solvent, organizationally stable, larger and more diversified in their staffing, and adopting professional-bureaucratic decision-making procedures. These changes were necessary for the national parties to develop their election-related and party-building functions.

Finances

National party fund-raising improved greatly from the 1970s through the 1990s. During this period, the national parties set several fund-raising records, using a variety of approaches to raise money from a diverse group of contributors. The Republican committees raised more "hard" money, which could be spent to directly promote the elections of federal candidates, than their Democratic rivals throughout this period (see Table 1). However, following the 1980 election the Democrats began to narrow the gap in fund-raising.

The GOP's financial advantage reflects a number of factors. The Republican committees began developing their direct-mail solicitation programs earlier and adopted a more businesslike approach to fund-raising. The greater wealth and homogeneity of their supporters also makes it easier for the Republican committees to raise money. Finally, the Republicans' minority status in Congress provided them with a powerful fund-raising weapon prior to the 1994 elections, as did Bill Clinton's occupancy of the White House after 1992. Negative appeals, featuring attacks on those in power, are generally more successful in fund-raising than are appeals advocating the maintenance of the status quo. The competitiveness over control of the House and Senate and the excitement generated by the presidential election enabled the national organizations of both parties to set new fund-raising records in 1996, with the Democrats' three Washington committees raising nearly $165 million over the course of the 1996 elections, an increase of 94 percent over the amount they had collected during the 1994 midterm

Table 1. National Party Receipts, 1976–1996 (in millions of dollars)

Party	1976	1978	1980	1982	1984	1986	1988	1990	1992	1994	1996
Democrats											
DNC	13.1	11.3	15.4	16.5	46.6	17.2	52.3	14.5	65.8	41.8	103.1
DCCC	.9	2.8	2.9	6.5	10.4	12.3	12.5	9.1	12.8	19.4	26.3
DSCC	1.0	.3	1.7	5.6	8.9	13.4	16.3	17.5	25.5	26.4	30.5
Total	15.0	14.4	20.0	28.6	65.9	42.9	81.1	41.1	104.1	87.6	159.9
Republicans											
RNC	29.1	34.2	77.8	84.1	105.9	83.8	91.0	68.7	85.4	87.4	187.2
NRCC	12.1	14.1	20.3	58.0	58.3	39.8	34.5	33.8	34.4	28.7	76.6
NRSC	1.8	10.9	22.3	48.9	81.7	86.1	65.9	65.1	72.3	65.4	62.4
Total	43.0	59.2	120.4	191.0	245.9	209.7	191.4	167.6	192.1	181.5	326.2

Source: Federal Election Commission press releases. The 1996 figures are incomplete and only include funds raised from January 1, 1995, through November 25, 1996. All other figures include funds raised from January 1 of the year preceding the election through December 31 of the election year. All figures include only "hard" money.

elections and an increase of 60 percent over the amount they had collected during the 1992 presidential election year contests. The three Republican committees raised $321 million during the 1996 elections, nearly 88 percent more than they had collected during the 1994 midterms and 72 percent more than they had raised during the 1992 presidential contest. Although the Democrats have made strides in improving their fund-raising programs, whether they can catch up to the GOP committees remains questionable.

The national parties raise most of their hard money in the form of direct-mail contributions of under $100. Telephone solicitations are also used to raise both small and large contributions. Traditional fund-raising dinners, parties, and other events experienced a revival as important vehicles for collecting large contributions from individual donors during the 1988 election.

Sometimes individuals, PACs, corporations, and other groups will contribute to a national party's building fund or some other nonfederal, "soft money" account that the national parties have traditionally used to purchase equipment and other organizational resources, strengthen local party organizations, help pay for national conventions, finance voter registration and get-out-the-vote drives, and broadcast generic television and radio advertisements designed to benefit the entire party ticket. Because soft money resides in a loophole in the FECA—it is mainly subject to the limits imposed by state laws—wealthy individuals, corporations, and other groups give soft money contributions in order to circumvent the FECA's contribution limits. The law requires that national party committees disclose the amounts of soft money they transfer to state and local party committees and places ceilings on the amount of national party soft money that can be spent in those contests, but it places few restrictions on the source of the funding.

During the 1994 elections, the Democratic national party organizations raised more than $49 million in soft money, compared with the nearly $53 million raised by their Republican counterparts. Spurred on by the presidential contest and the struggle for control over the House and Senate, the Democratic and Republican national parties raised soft money at a record-breaking pace during the 1996 election cycle, raising more than $122 million and $141 million, respectively. The 1996 figures represent increases of more than 42 percent (Democrats) and 54 percent (Republicans) over the previous presidential election. Included in these funds are numerous contributions of $100,000 or more that were given by individuals, corporations, and other groups.

In return for their donations, individuals and group representatives become members of the national committees' labor or business councils, the DCCC's Speaker's Club, the DSCC's Leadership Council, the NRCC's Congressional Leadership Council, the NRSC's Senate Trust Club, or some other "club" created by a national party organization for the purpose of raising large contributions. Club members also receive electoral briefings from the committees and other useful "perks." The existence of these clubs is indicative of the symbiotic nature of the relationships that have developed between the national parties, PACs, and other groups.

Infrastructure

Success in fund-raising has enabled the national parties to invest in the development of their organizational infrastructures. Prior to their institutionalization, the national party organizations had no permanent headquarters. For a while, the four Hill committees were quartered in small offices in congressional office buildings. Upon leaving congressional office space they became transient, following the national committees' example of moving at the end of each election cycle in search of cheap office space. The national parties' lack of permanent office space created security problems, made it difficult for them to conduct routine business, and did little to bolster their standing in Washington.

All six national party organizations are now housed in party-owned headquarters buildings located only a few blocks from the Capitol. The headquarters buildings furnish the committees with convenient locations for carrying out fund-raising events and holding meetings with candidates, PACs, journalists, and campaign consultants. They also provide a secure environment for the committees' computers, records, and radio and television studios. The multimillion-dollar studios, each of which is owned by one of the congressional campaign committees, allow the parties to produce professional quality campaign commercials for their candidates.

Staff

Each national party organization has a two-tiered structure consisting of members and professional staff. The members of the Republican and Democratic national committees are selected by state parties, and the members of the Hill committees are selected by their colleagues in Congress. The national parties' staffs have grown tremendously in recent years. Republican committee staff development accelerated following the party's Watergate scandal, whereas the Democratic Party experienced most of its staff growth after the 1980 election. In 1996, the DNC, DCCC, and DSCC employed 264, 64, and 38 full-time staff, respectively, whereas their Republican counterparts had 271, 64, and 150 full-time employees. Committee staffs are divided along functional lines; different divisions are responsible for administration, fund-raising, research, communications, and campaign activities. The staffs have a great deal of autonomy in running the committees and are extremely influential in formulating their campaign strategies. In the case of the NRCC, for example, committee members have adopted a "hands-off" attitude toward committee operations similar to that of a board of directors.

Relationships with Interest Groups and Political Consultants

Although it was first believed that the rise of the political consultants and the proliferation of PACs would hasten the decline of parties, it is now recognized that many political consultants and PACs try to cooperate with the political parties. Few, if any, would seek to destroy the parties. National party organizations, consultants, PACs, and other interest groups frequently work together in pursuit of their common goals. Fund-raising constitutes one area of party-PAC cooperation, the dissemination of information and the backing of particular candidates constitute others. National party organizations handicap races for PACs and arrange "meet-and- greet" sessions for PACs and candidates. The national parties also mail, telephone, and fax large quantities of information to PACs in order to advise them of developments in competitive elections. PAC managers use party information when formulating their contribution strategies.

Another area of party–interest group cooperation involves campaign spending. FECA limitations on the amount of soft money that a national party committee can transfer to individual states have encouraged the RNC to contribute some of its soft money to interest groups. In 1996, the RNC transferred a record $6 million, most of which went to Americans for Tax Reform, a nonpartisan group that shares the GOP's position on tax cuts and is not required to report how it spends its funds. The DNC, by contrast, transferred only a few hundred thousand dollars to allied groups, most of it to the National Coalition for Black Participation, a nonpartisan group that works to mobilize African American voters. National party contributions to allied interest groups enable the parties to help their federal, state, and local candidates without violating federal law.

Relations between the national party organizations and political consultants have also become more cooperative. During election years, the national parties facilitate contacts and agreements between their candidates and political consultants. The parties also hire outside consultants to assist with polling and advertising and to furnish candidates with campaign services. During nonelection years, the parties hire private consultants to assist with long-range planning. These arrangements enable the parties to draw upon the expertise of the industry's premier consulting firms and provide the consultants with steady employment, which is especially important between election cycles.

The symbiotic relationships that have developed between the national parties, political consultants, PACs, and other interest groups can be further appreciated by looking at the career paths of people working in electoral politics. Employment at one of the national party organizations can now serve as a stepping stone or a high point in the career of a political operative. A pattern that has become increasingly common is for consultants to begin their careers working in a low-level position for a small consulting firm, campaign, PAC, or other interest group, then to be hired by one of the national party organizations, and then to leave the party organization to form their own political consulting firm or to accept an executive position with a major consulting firm, PAC, or interest group. Finding employment outside of the national parties rarely results in the severing of relations between consultants and the national party organizations. It is common for the parties to hire past employees and for their firms to conduct research, give strategic or legal advice, or provide campaign services to candidates. The "revolving door" of national party employment provides political professionals with opportunities to gain experience, make connections, establish credentials that can help them move up the hierarchy of political operatives, and maintain profitable relationships with the national parties after they have gained employment elsewhere.

Party Building

The institutionalization of the national party organizations has provided them with the resources to develop a variety of party-building programs. The vast majority of these are conducted by the two national committees. Many current RNC party-building efforts were initiated in 1976 under the leadership of Chairman William Brock. Brock's program for revitalizing state party committees consisted of (1) appointing regional political directors to assist state party leaders in strengthening their organizations and utilizing RNC services; (2) hiring organizational directors to help rebuild state party organizations; (3) appointing regional finance directors to assist state parties with developing fund-raising programs; (4) making computer services available to state parties for accounting, fund-raising, and analyzing survey data; and (5) organizing a task force to assist parties with developing realistic election goals and strategies. Brock also established a Local Elections Campaign Division to assist state parties with creating district profiles and recruiting candidates, to provide candidate training and campaign management seminars, and to furnish candidates for state or local office with on-site campaign assistance.

Frank Fahrenkopf, RNC chair from 1981–1988, expanded many of Brock's party-building programs and introduced some new ones. The national committee continues to give Republican state parties financial assistance and help them with fund-raising. An RNC computerized information network created during the 1984 election cycle furnishes Republican state and local party organizations and candidates with issue and opposition research, newspaper clippings, and other sorts of electoral information. RNC publications, such as *First Monday* and *County Line,* provide Republican candidates, party leaders, and activists with survey results, issue research, and instructions on how to conduct campaign activities ranging from fund-raising to grassroots organizing. Moreover, NRCC and NRSC agency agreements with Republican state party organizations enable these two Washington-based committees to make the state parties' share of campaign contributions and coordinated expenditures in House and Senate elections. This enables the state parties to concentrate their resources, which are often collected in the form of soft money, on party-building functions, generic and issue-oriented advertising, get-out-the-vote drives, and other party-focused campaign activities.

DNC party-building activities lagged slightly behind those of its Republican counterpart and did not become significant until the 1986 election. During that election, Chairman Paul Kirk created a task force of thirty-two professional consultants who were sent to sixteen states to assist Democratic state committees with fund-raising, computerizing voter lists, and other organizational activities. In later elections, task forces were sent to additional states to help modernize and strengthen their Democratic party committees. The task forces are credited with improving Democratic state party fund-raising, computer capacities, voter mobilization programs, and helping Democratic state and local committees reach the stage of organizational development achieved by their Republican rivals in earlier years.

National committee party-building programs have succeeded in strengthening, modernizing, and professionalizing many state and local party organizations. Agency agreements between the Hill committees and state party organizations further contribute to these efforts by encouraging state parties to spend their money on organizational development, state and local elections, and generic party campaigning rather than House and Senate elections. These programs have altered the balance of power within the parties' organizational apparatuses. The national parties' ability to distribute or withhold party-building or campaign assistance gives them some influence over the operations of state and local party committees. The DNC's influence is enhanced by its rule-making and enforcement authority. As a result of these developments, the traditional flow of power upward from state and local party organizations to the national committees has been complemented by a new flow of power downward from the national parties to state and local parties. The institutionalization of the national party organizations has enabled them to become more influential in party politics and has led to a greater federalization of the American party system.

National Party Campaigning

The institutionalization of the national parties has provided them with the wherewithal to play a larger role in elections, and national party campaign activity has increased tremendously since the 1970s. Yet the electoral activities of the national parties, and party organizations in general, remain constricted by electoral law, established custom, and the level of resources in the parties' possession.

Candidate Recruitment and Nominations

Most candidates for elective office in the United States are self-recruited and conduct their own nominating campaigns. The DNC and the RNC have a hand in establishing the basic guidelines under which presidential nominations are contested, but their role is defined by the national conventions and their recommendations are subject to convention approval. The rules governing Democratic presidential nominations are more extensive than are those governing GOP contests, but state committees of both parties have substantial leeway in supplying the details of their delegate selection processes.

Neither the DNC nor the RNC expresses a preference for candidates for its party's presidential nomination. Such activity would be disastrous should a candidate who was backed by a national committee be defeated because the successful, unsupported candidate would become the head of the party's ticket and its titular leader. As a result, candidates for the nomination assemble their own campaign staffs and compete independently of the party apparatus in state-run primaries and caucuses. Successful candidates arrive at the national convention with seasoned campaign organizations composed of experienced political operatives.

The national party organizations, however, may get involved in selected nominating contests for House, Senate, and state-level offices. They actively recruit some candidates to enter primary contests and just as actively discourage others from doing likewise. Most candidate recruitment efforts are concentrated in competitive districts, but sometimes party officials will encourage a candidate to enter a primary in a district that is safe for the opposite party so that the general election will not be uncontested. National party staff in Washington, D.C., and regional coordinators in the field meet with state and local party leaders to identify potential candidates and encourage them to enter primaries. Party leaders and staff use polls, the promise of party campaign money and services, and the persuasive talents of party leaders, members of Congress, and even presidents to influence the decisions of potential candidates.

Once two or more candidates enter a primary, however, they rarely take one candidate's side. In 1984, the RNC enacted a rule prohibiting committee involvement in contested primaries. NRCC policy requires nonincumbent primary candidates to have the support of their state delegation in the House and local party leaders before support can be given. The DCCC's bylaws bar it from becoming involved in contested primaries, and the DNC, RNC, and DSCC rarely get involved in them. Situations where a party member challenges an incumbent are the major exceptions to the rule.

The Democrats' control over most state and local offices has traditionally given them an advantage in candidate recruitment. Prior to the 1990s, the NRCC had only limited success in encouraging candidates who had either held elective office or had significant unelective experience in politics to run for the House. The Republicans' lack of a congressional "farm team," particularly the small numbers of Republican state legislators and municipal officials, was thought by many to be a major contributor to its persistence as the minority party in the House. However, by the 1994 elections the party-building and candidate recruitment and training efforts of the RNC, GOPAC, and Republican state and local party organizations had begun to pay off, significantly increasing the number of Republicans occupying state and local offices.

The NRCC also turned to other talent pools in search of House candidates in 1994. Although previous officeholding experience is thought by many to be the mark of a well-qualified Democratic House challenger, strong Republican candidates have traditionally come from more diverse backgrounds. Political aides, party officeholders, previously unsuccessful candidates, administration officials, and other "unelected politicians" have long been an important source of strong Republican, as well as Democratic, House candidates. Wealthy individuals have often been viewed by GOP and Democratic strategists as good candidates because of their ability to finance significant portions of their own campaigns.

The GOP's party-building and recruitment efforts resulted in its fielding record numbers of challenger and open-seat contestants in 1994, making it the first contest in recent history in which more Republicans than Democrats ran for the House and more Republican-held than Democratic-held House seats went uncontested. Nearly 20 percent of all Republican nonincumbents in two-party contested races had previously held elective office and another 10 percent had some form of unelective political experience. In addition, 54 GOP nonincumbents (more than 20 percent) invested over $50,000 in their own campaigns, and 34 (roughly 13 percent) invested at least $100,000. The 1996 congressional elections also showed the Republicans having a banner recruitment year, fielding 722 House candidates to the Democrats' 704.

National party candidate recruitment and primary activities are not intended to do away with the dominant pattern of self-selected candidates assembling their own campaign organizations to compete for their party's nomination. Nor are these activities designed to restore the turn-of-the-century pattern of local party leaders selecting the party's nominees. Rather, most national party activity is geared toward encouraging or discouraging the candidacies of a small group of politicians who are considering running in competitive districts. Less-focused recruitment efforts attempt to arouse the interests of a broader group of party activists by informing them of the campaign assistance available to candidates who make it to the general election.

National Conventions

The national conventions are technically a part of the nominating process. After the 1968 reforms were instituted, however, the conventions lost control of their nominating function and became more of a public relations event than a decisionmaking one. Conventions still have platform writing and rule-making responsibilities, but these are overshadowed by speeches and other events designed to attract the support of voters.

The public relations component of the national conventions reached new heights during the 1980s and 1990s. Contemporary conventions are known for their technically sophisticated video presentations and choreographed pageantry. Convention activities are designed to be easily dissected into sound bites suited for television news programs. National committee staff formulate strategies to ensure that television newscasters put a desirable "spin" on television news coverage.

Both parties' 1996 national conventions were public relations extravaganzas. The parties' national convention featured dynamic speakers and engaging video clips. Elizabeth Dole's stroll around the convention floor was reminiscent of a scene from a television talk show and was particularly effective at captivating television viewers. Both parties' prime-time speakers stressed popular themes and appealed to important voting groups. The Democrats featured quadriplegic actor Christopher Reeve to emphasize their compassionate side, and Republicans used Jim and Sarah Brady to highlight their support for gun control. The Republicans showcased Representatives Susan Molinari (R–NY), J. C. Watts (R–OK), and Gulf War hero retired General Colin Powell in order to present images of diversity and national strength.

Party leaders whose views had the potential to conflict with this message, such as nomination candidate Pat Buchanan, were not given a place on the podium. The few disputes among convention delegates that arose, such as the Republicans' disagreement over whether to include so-called tolerance language on abortion in their platform, were dealt with in meeting rooms and received relatively little attention. Moreover, protesters at both conventions were directed to special "protest sites" away from the convention halls, where they received virtually no publicity.

Convention organizers have made special efforts to cultivate the media at recent conventions. Both parties have given television stations across the country the opportunity to use live feed from their conventions in their nightly news shows. In 1996, the Republicans set a new precedent when they went so far as to provide their own televised convention coverage. The GOP featured RNC Chairman Haley Barbour and other GOP leaders as narrators and was broadcast over the Family Channel, Pat Robertson's cable TV station. Nevertheless, not all members of the press are happy with the made-for-television aspects of modern conventions. Some have complained that the conventions have been transformed into extended campaign commercials that no longer generate any real news. Ted Koppel, the host of the television news show *Nightline*, became so disenchanted with the "packaged" quality of the Republican convention that he departed early and stayed away from the Democratic convention entirely.

The national parties also conduct less-visible convention activities to help nonpresidential candidates with their bids for office. Congressional and senatorial candidates are given access to television and radio satellite up-links and taping facilities. The Hill committees also sponsor "meet-and-greet" sessions to introduce their most competitive challengers and open-seat candidates to PACs, individual big contributors, party leaders, and the press. The atrophy of the national conventions' nominating function has been partially offset by an increase in their general election-related activities.

The General Election

Presidential Elections. Party activity in presidential elections is restricted by the public-funding provisions of the FECA. Major party candidates who accept public funding are prohibited from accepting contributions from any other sources, including the political parties. The amount that the national parties can spend directly on behalf of their presidential candidates is also limited. In 1996, President Clinton and Republican nominee Bob Dole each received $61.82 million in general election subsidies, and the national committees were each allowed to spend just under $12 million directly advocating the election or defeat of their candidates.

The legal environment reinforces the candidate-centeredness of presidential elections in other ways. Rules requiring candidates for the nomination to compete in primaries and caucuses guarantee that successful candidates will enter the general election with their own sources of technical expertise, in-depth research, and connections with journalists and other Washington elites. These reforms combine with the FECA to create a regulatory framework that limits national party activity and influence in presidential elections.

Nevertheless, the national parties do play an important role in presidential elections. The national committees furnish presidential campaigns with legal and strategic advice and public relations assistance. National committee opposition research and archives serve as important sources of political information. The hard money that the national committees spend directly on behalf of their candidates can boost the total resources under the candidates' control by over 15 percent.

The national committees also assist their candidates' campaigns by distributing both hard and soft money to state parties that they use to finance voter mobilization drives and party-building activities. During the 1996 elections, the DNC transferred more than $76 million, roughly $11 million more than its Republican counterpart. Most of these funds were distributed in accordance with the strategies of their presidential candidates. Soft money enabled the national parties to wage a coordinated campaign that supplemented, and in some cases replaced, the voter mobilization efforts of presidential and other candidates.

Moreover, a Supreme Court ruling handed down in June 1996 enabled party committees and other groups to use soft money to broadcast political advertisements that mention the names of specific federal candidates. The ruling, which allows parties to spend soft money on "issue advocacy" campaigns that do not expressly call for a candidate's election or defeat, has enabled the national parties to get far more involved in their candidates' campaigns. The Democrats began broadcasting issue advocacy ads in October 1995, over a full year before the election, in order to raise the president's standing in the polls and set the political agenda on which the upcoming election would be waged. They spent $42.4 million on the ads over the course of the election. Most of the ads were designed to paint the Republican-controlled Congress as a group of radical extremists who wanted to help large corporations and wealthy individuals at the expense of working people.

The Republicans waited until March, when Senator Robert Dole of Kansas had clinched the nomination, before launching their issue advocacy ad campaign. From late March through the Republican national convention, the RNC spent approximately $20 million on ads designed to boost Dole's image. As RNC Press Secretary Mary Crawford explained, the committee made the expenditures to fill the void in Dole's campaign communications that was created when the Dole campaign had nearly exhausted its primary funds clinching the nomination and had to wait until the convention to receive its federal general election funds. Following the convention, the committee, in conjunction with the NRCC, spent in excess of $20 million more on a coordinated television campaign that was intended to help Dole, Republican House candidates, and other members of the GOP ticket.

Another Supreme Court ruling, which was also handed down in the midst of the 1996 election cycle, allows the parties to make independent expenditures in federal elections. These expenditures, which are to be treated the same as independent expenditures made by PACs, enable the parties to advocate the election or defeat of a federal candidate so long as the expenditure is made without the candidate's knowledge or consent. Nevertheless, because they worked so closely with the presidential campaigns, neither the

DNC nor the RNC was in a position to make independent expenditures on behalf of its presidential contestant. The Court's rulings on issue advocacy campaigns and independent expenditures have created new avenues for party spending in federal elections that, barring reform, will probably be heavily used in future contests.

Congressional Elections. The national party organizations also play a big role in congressional elections. They contribute money and campaign services directly to congressional candidates and provide transactional assistance that helps candidates obtain other resources from political consultants and PACs. Most national party assistance is distributed by the Hill committees to candidates competing in close elections, especially those who are nonincumbents. This reflects the committees' goal of maximizing the number of congressional seats under their control.

As is the case with presidential elections, the FECA limits party activity in congressional races. National, congressional, and state party organizations are each allowed to contribute $5,000 to House candidates. The parties' national and senatorial campaign committees are allowed to give a combined total of $17,500 to Senate candidates; state party organizations can give $5,000. National party organizations and state party committees are also allowed to make coordinated expenditures on behalf of their candidates, giving both the party and the candidate a measure of control over how the money is spent. Originally set at $10,000 per committee, the limits for coordinated expenditures on behalf of House candidates are adjusted for inflation and reached $30,910 in 1996. The limits for coordinated expenditures in Senate elections vary by the size of a state's population and are also indexed to inflation. They ranged from $61,820 per committee in the smallest states to $1.41 million per committee in California during the 1996 election cycle. The national parties made the maximum contribution and coordinated the expenditures in virtually every competitive House or Senate race that year. The Hill committees routinely enter into agency agreements that allow them to make some of their national and state party committees' coordinated expenditures. When they are flush with soft money but short on hard dollars, the Hill committees have transferred soft money to state committees, enabling the state committees to spend corresponding amounts in hard dollars.

Most party money, especially in Senate elections, is distributed as coordinated expenditures, reflecting the higher legal limits imposed by the FECA (see Table 2). Republican party organizations spent more than Democratic

Table 2. Party Contributions and Coordinated Expenditures
in the 1994 Congressional Elections (in dollars)

	House		Senate	
	Contributions	Coordinated expenditures	Contributions	Coordinated expenditures
Democratic				
DNC	58,693	18,755	17,543	160,110
DCCC	974,239	7,730,815	16,750	0
DSCC	10,000	0	525,000	12,295,902
State and local	458,288	705,500	79,344	748,297
Total	1,501,220	8,455,070	638,637	13,204,309
Republican				
RNC	539,069	4,607,337	5,084	128,831
NRCC	705,382	3,926,641	82,559	0
NRSC	122,500	0	498,779	10,905,500
State and local	669,761	317,897	161,589	537,535
Total	2,036,712	8,851,875	748,011	11,571,866

Source: "FEC Reports on Political Party Activity for 1993–94," Federal Election Commission press release, April 13, 1995.

party organizations in 1994, but the gap between the parties has been closing. Most party expenditures originated at the national rather than the state and local levels. Some "crossover spending" from the two senatorial campaign committees to House candidates also occurred. One unusual development is the large amount of RNC spending in House races. Spending by either national committee had rarely reached the $1.5 million mark in previous elections, but in 1994, RNC spending exceeded $5.1 million. The RNC's large investment reflects both the opportunities offered by the heightened competitiveness of the 1994 congressional elections and the fact that the NRCC was unable to spend much of the money that it had raised during the 1994 election cycle because of the large debt it had incurred during the 1992 contest.

Despite the NRCC's financial difficulties, Republican House candidates typically received slightly more financial assistance from party committees than did their Democratic opponents. Republican party committees targeted challenger and open-seat candidates for their largest contributions and coordinated expenditures, reflecting the relative security of GOP incumbents and the heightened prospects of defeating Democratic incumbents and claiming the lion's share of open seats (see Table 3). The

Table 3. Average Party Spending in the 1994 Congressional Elections

	House			Senate		
	Incumbent	Challenger	Open seat	Incumbent	Challenger	Open seat
Democratic Party contributions	3,380	2,328	6,626	15,852	17,300	16,658
Party coordinated expenditures	17,243	17,308	44,027	401,900	92,773	412,036
Candidate expenditures	622,913	155,464	558,873	5,154,597	753,790	2,624,182
Total spending[a]	640,156	172,772	602,900	5,556,497	846,563	3,036,218
Party share[b]	3.2%	11.3%	8.1%	7.5%	13.0%	14.1%
(N)	(211)	(125)	(52)	(16)	(9)	(9)
Republican Party contributions	1,849	5,113	9,168	18,486	18,944	23,784
Party coordinated expenditures	9,764	22,088	47,875	130,397	265,107	409,058
Candidate expenditures	505,099	242,683	602,788	2,982,282	5,708,493	3,377,844
Total spending[a]	514,863	264,771	650,663	3,112,679	5,973,600	3,786,902
Party share[b]	2.0%	10.1%	8.6%	4.7%	4.7%	11.4%
(N)	(125)	(211)	(52)	(9)	(16)	(9)

Note: Includes general election candidates in major-party contested races only.

a. Equals candidate expenditures plus party coordinated expenditures.

b. Denotes the percentage of all campaign money over which the candidates had some direct control (candidate receipts and party coordinated expenditures).

Source: Calculated by the author from Federal Election Commission data.

Democrats, by contrast, responded to the GOP threat by investing significantly larger sums in incumbent campaigns and delivering smaller amounts to nonincumbents.

The percent figures in Table 3 indicate that the importance of party money varies more by incumbency than by party. Party money only accounted for 3 percent of the funds spent by or on behalf of House Democrats and 2 percent of the funds spent by House Republicans in 1994. Yet, it accounted for over 10 percent of the funds spent in connection with House challengers and over 8 percent of the funds spent in connection with House open-seat candidates.

Party spending in the 1994 Senate elections accounted for a greater portion of the money spent in connection with Democratic than Republican campaigns. Because the FECA's coordinated spending limits vary by state, they have a profound impact on the distribution of party money and make it difficult for party committees to pursue either an offensive or a defensive strategy. Nevertheless, it is apparent that the Republican committees played a greater role in their challengers' campaigns and the Democrats were more active in their incumbents' races. Party money was a significant factor in the open-seat campaigns of both parties' candidates, accounting for 14 percent of the money spent in the typical Democratic campaign and over 11 percent of the money spent in the typical Republican campaign.

The national parties target most of their money to candidates in close races. In 1994, for example, the parties spent over $50,000 in connection with each of 239 House candidacies and $1,000 or less in connection with 249 others. Challengers who show little promise and incumbents in safe seats usually receive only token sums, whereas incumbents in jeopardy, competitive challengers, and contestants in open seats typically benefit from large party expenditures.

Party money played a decisive role in at least a few House contests. It accounted for nearly 38 percent of the funds spent in Michael Patrick Flanagan's upset victory over longtime House Ways and Means Chairman Daniel Rostenkowski in Illinois' Fifth District in 1994. Many believe that $50,000 worth of late media buys that were financed by a last-minute infusion of RNC funds were largely responsible for Flanagan's win.

The discrepancies in party spending in Senate elections were even greater, reflecting party strategy and the FECA's contribution and spending limits. At one extreme, neither party spent any money in the one-sided contest between Democratic incumbent Daniel Akaka and Republican challenger Maria Hustace in Hawaii in 1994. At the other, the Democratic Party spent over $2.6 million in order to help incumbent Dianne Feinstein gain a two-point victory over Representative Michael Huffington, who spent nearly $28.4 million of his own money in California's Senate race.

Even though individuals and PACs still furnish candidates with most of their campaign funds, political parties currently compose the largest single source of campaign money for most candidates. Party money comes from one, or at most a few, organizations that are primarily concerned with one goal—the election of their candidates. Individual and PAC contributions, by contrast, come from a multitude of sources that are motivated by a variety of concerns. In addition, it is important to recognize that dollar-for-dollar national party money has greater value than the contributions of other groups. National party contributions and coordinated expenditures often take the form of in-kind campaign services that are worth many times more than their reported value. Moreover, national party money is often accompanied by fund-raising assistance that helps candidates attract additional money from PACs.

The national parties also furnish many congressional candidates with campaign services ranging from legal advice to assistance with campaign advertising. The national parties distribute most of their services to competitive contestants, especially those who are non-incumbents. National party help is more likely to have an impact on the outcomes of these candidates' elections than on those of incumbents holding safe seats or nonincumbents challenging them.

The national parties provide a variety of management-related campaign services. They run training colleges for candidates and campaign managers, introduce candidates and political consultants to each other, and frequently provide candidates with in-kind contributions or coordinated expenditures consisting of campaign services. The national parties also help congressional campaigns file reports with the Federal Election Commission and perform other administrative, clerical, and legal tasks. Most important, the national parties furnish candidates with strategic assistance. Hill committee field-workers visit campaign headquarters to help candidates develop campaign plans, develop and respond to attacks, and perform other crucial campaign activities.

The national party organizations assist congressional candidates with gauging public opinion in three ways. They distribute newsletters that analyze voter attitudes toward party positions and report the mood of the national electorate. The Hill committees also conduct district-level analyses of voting patterns exhibited in previous elections to help congressional candidates locate where their supporters reside. Last, they commission surveys for many of their most competitive candidates. These surveys help the candidates ascertain their levels of name recognition, electoral support, and the impact that their campaign communications are having on voters.

National party assistance in campaign communications takes many forms. All six national party organizations conduct issue and opposition research. DNC and RNC research revolves around traditional party positions and the issue stands of incumbent presidents or presidential candidates. Congressional and senatorial campaign committee research is usually more individualized. The Hill committees send competitive candidates issue packets consisting of hundreds of pages detailing issues that are likely to attract press coverage and win the support of specific voting blocs. The packets also include suggestions for exploiting an opponent's weaknesses. Additional research is disseminated by party leaders in Congress.

In 1994, then–Minority Leader Newt Gingrich (R–GA) and the House Republicans made an unprecedented attempt to nationalize the political agenda when they unveiled their Contract with America. The Contract was a ten-point program that distilled a number of popular ideas into a campaign manifesto. It included GOP positions on congressional reform, the line-item veto, crime control, welfare reform, deregulation, tax reform, national defense, tort reform, child support, a balanced budget, and term limits. The Contract was unveiled and signed by 367 Republican House members and candidates at a formal ceremony that took place in September 1994 on the Capitol steps. Copies of the Contract were sent to Republican candidates and activists along with written and recorded talking points that expounded on the Contract's themes. Even though only one-third of the electorate had ever heard of the Contract and many GOP candidates did not agree with or campaign on every one of its issues, it was important because it gave candidates some substantive policy information to talk about on the stump and it was later treated as a binding platform by House Republicans.

While the Contract furnished GOP candidates with some positive campaign themes, "Under the Clinton Big Top," which was published by then House Republican Conference Chairman Richard Armey (R–TX), provided them with some decidedly negative ones. Armey's document provided a detailed critique of the president's performance on domestic policy, defense policy, foreign affairs, ethics, and leadership. Armey and Representatives Jennifer Dunn (R–WA) and Christopher Shays (R–CT) also published "It's Long Enough: The Decline of Popular Government Under Forty Years of Single Party Control of the U.S. House of Representatives," a "populist/ progressive" critique of the special interest culture that developed in the House under forty years of Democratic control. These publications laid the groundwork for the negative, anti-Clinton and anti-Congress campaigns waged by many GOP congressional candidates.

House Republicans did not sign a new Contract with America in 1996, choosing instead to carry out a communications strategy to defend their performance in the 104th Congress. Congressional Democrats did put forth a party platform. The "Families' First Agenda," which was developed by party members in both chambers, articulated a number of popular themes and policy goals. It was designed to convey the message that once congressional Democrats were back in the majority, they were ready to implement realistic solutions to national problems. Part of the Democrats' strategy was to put forth a modest, centrist platform that voters and journalists would contrast with the "revolutionary" and ideologically driven legislative measures that congressional Republicans sought to enact during the 104th Congress.

The national party organizations also furnish candidates with assistance in mass media advertising. In 1996, both parties' congressional campaign committees made their media centers available to House members and candidates, enabling them to film, edit, and even transmit their ads via satellite to television stations in their districts using top-notch equipment at reduced rates. Seventeen incumbents, two challengers, and two open-seat candidates used the NRCC's media center to produce their television commercials. Another nineteen incumbents, two challengers, and two open-seat candidates used the center to produce their radio spots. The committee also provided eighteen House candidates, including Representatives Jim Bunn (R–KY) and Harris Fawell (R–IL), and open-seat contestant Kevin Brady (R–TX), with more comprehensive media packages. The committee helped nine of its candidates develop advertising themes and scripts and arranged for their advertisements to be aired on local television stations. Eleven candidates received similar amounts of assistance in producing their radio ads. The NRCC had furnished many more candidates with full-service advertising assistance in previous elections; however, following the GOP takeover of the House, committee leaders decided they could better serve more candidates by having them supply their own creative talent. This decision was based on the fact that for the first time in forty years, the majority of Republican House candidates were incumbents, who were in a position to hire their own creative talent.

Like its Republican counterpart, the DCCC made its production and editing facilities available to House candidates. The committee did not provide any of its candidates with full-service advertising assistance, and the vast majority of Democratic House candidates hired their own media consultants to provide the content for their ads. Some nonincumbents who could not afford to hire a high-powered media consultant to create their own ads—mostly uncompetitive House candidates—chose to customize one or more of the twelve generic ads that the committee's Harriman Communications Center had produced for this purpose. The DCCC gave virtually every Democratic House candidate $20,000 in credits that could be redeemed at its Harriman Communications Center, but it recorded neither the number of candidates who used the center's facilities nor the number of ads that were produced. DCCC staff estimate that roughly 70 percent of the party's House candidates used the center.

House candidates received millions of dollars in additional campaign communications assistance in the form of issue advocacy ads. During the 1996 elections, the NRCC hired Sipple Strategic Communications to design a series of six issue advocacy ads that were televised in the districts of Republican candidates involved in competitive races. The party spent $7 million to air the first three ads in thirty districts from the third week in July though Labor Day. These ads were designed to remind voters of GOP accomplishments and positions on welfare reform, congressional reform, and Medicare. The second three ads, which cost roughly $20 million, were broadcast in fifty-eight districts from October 5 through election day. These sought to counter the anti-Republican media campaign waged by organized labor, to remind voters of some of the policy failures of the Clinton administration, and to discourage them from electing a Democratic Congress.

The DCCC also aired several issue advocacy ads. The committee spent $8.5 million to air television and radio commercials in sixty races. The Democrats' ads were produced in-house, at the Harriman Center, and focused on Medicare, health care, education, jobs, and pensions. The DCCC also sent issue advocacy mail to voters in a number of competitive House districts. Neither the DCCC nor the NRCC made any independent expenditures during the 1996 elections.

The DSCC and NRSC have traditionally not become as deeply involved in their candidates' campaign communications, offering advice, criticisms, and occasionally pretesting their candidates' television and radio advertisements. The senatorial campaign committees played only a limited role because Senate candidates typically have enough money and experience to hire premier consultants on their own. The committees' roles changed somewhat in 1996 in response to the Supreme Court's rulings on party spending, which opened the door for the parties to make issue advocacy ads and independent expenditures. The NRSC committees spent approximately $2 million on issue advocacy ads that were broadcast in five states during the 1996 elections; its Democratic counterpart spent an estimated $10 million in fourteen states. The two senatorial committees also set up separate divisions charged with making independent expenditures. The Republicans made more than $9 million in independent expenditures: nearly $4.7 million was spent to help fifteen candidates for the Senate, and another $4.7 million was spent against thirteen Democratic Senate candidates. The Democrats spent approximately $1.4 million against six Republican Senate candidates and another $50,000 to advocate the election of three Democratic candidates.

The national parties help their congressional candidates raise money from individuals and PACs both in Washington, D.C., and in their election districts. Congressional party leaders frequently contribute money from their campaign accounts and leadership PACs to junior members and nonincumbents involved in close contests. The leaders also help these members raise money from wealthy individuals and PACs. During the 1994 elections, House leaders carried out an unprecedented effort to redistribute the wealth to other candidates.

The Hill committees help congressional candidates organize fund-raising events and develop direct-mail lists. The Hill committees' PAC directors help design the PAC kits that many candidates use to introduce themselves to the PAC community, and they mail campaign progress reports, fax messages, and spend countless hours on the telephone with PAC managers. The goals of this activity are to get PAC money flowing to the party's most competitive candidates and away from their candidates' opponents. National party endorsements, communications, contributions, and coordinated expenditures serve as decision-making cues that help PACs decide where to invest their money. National party services and transactional assistance are especially important to nonincumbents running for the House because typically, they do not possess fund-raising lists from previous campaigns, are less skilled at fund-raising than incumbents, have none of the clout with PACs that comes with incumbency, and begin the election cycle virtually unknown to members of the PAC community.

Finally, the congressional and senatorial campaign committees also help their candidates by transferring funds to their respective state parties. During the 1994 elections, the two Republican Hill committees distributed nearly $3.1 million to GOP state party organizations, and the two Democratic committees distributed $758,000 to their Democratic counterparts. The amounts transferred in 1996 were far greater, with the Republicans distributing more than $2.4 million and the Democrats distributing in excess of $20 million.

State and Local Elections. The national parties' state and local election programs bear similarities to those for congressional elections. The DNC and RNC work with state party leaders to recruit candidates, formulate strategy, and distribute campaign money and services. The national committees hold workshops to help state and local candidates learn the ins and outs of modern campaigning. The committees also recommend professional consultants and disseminate strategic and technical information through party magazines and briefing papers.

There are also important differences between national party activity in state and local contests and in congressional elections. First, the parties give less campaign money and services to state and local candidates, reflecting the smaller size of state legislative districts. Second, national committee strategy for distributing campaign money and services to state and local candidates incorporates considerations related to national trends that could influence House, Senate, and presidential elections. The Hill committees, by contrast, focus almost exclusively on factors related to an individual candidate's prospects for success. Last, the national committee staffs go to great lengths to locate state and local candidates worthy of assistance, whereas the Hill committee staffs are inundated with requests for campaign assistance by candidates for Congress.

Party-Focused Campaigning. In addition to the candidate-focused campaign programs discussed earlier, the national parties conduct generic, or party-focused, election activities designed to benefit all candidates on the party ticket. Among these are party-focused television commercials that are designed to convey a message about an entire political party and activate voters nationwide. More traditional forms of party-focused campaigning include rallies, door-to-door get-out-the-vote campaigns, and other grass-roots events. Most of these activities are spearheaded by the national committees and conducted in cooperation with congressional, senatorial, state, and local party committees and candidates. National party organizations often provide the money and targeting information needed to perform these activities effectively, and state and local organizations provide the foot soldiers to carry them out.

Conclusion

American political parties are principally electoral institutions. They focus more on elections and less on initiating policy change than do parties in other Western democracies. American national party organizations were created to perform electoral functions. They developed in response to changes in their environment and the changing needs of their candidates.

National party organizational change occurs sporadically. Electoral instability and political unrest have occasionally given party leaders opportunities to restructure the national parties. The most recent waves of party organizational development followed the turbulent 1968 Democratic National Convention, the Republicans' post-Watergate landslide losses, and the Democrats' traumatic defeat in 1980. These crises provided opportunities and incentives for party entrepreneurs to restructure the roles and missions of the national, congressional, and senatorial campaign committees.

Other opportunities for party change were created as a result of technological advances and changes in the regulatory environment in which the parties operate. The development of direct-mail techniques created new opportunities for party fund-raising, the advent of satellite communications enabled the parties to enhance their communications, and these and other technological advancements enabled the parties to play a greater role in their candidates' campaigns. Recent Supreme Court rulings on issue advocacy campaigns and independent expenditures have had a similar impact.

The result is that the national parties are now stronger, more stable, and more influential in their relations with state and local party committees and candidates than ever. National party programs have led to the modernization of many state and local party committees. National parties also play an important role in contemporary elections. They help presidential candidates by supplementing their campaign communications and voter mobilization efforts with party-sponsored campaign activities. The national parties also give congressional candidates campaign contributions, make coordinated expenditures and campaign communications on their behalf, and provide services in areas of campaigning that require technical expertise, in-depth research, or connections with political consultants, PACs, or other organizations possessing the resources needed to conduct a modern campaign. The national party committees play a smaller and less visible role in state and local candidacies. Although most national party activity is concentrated in competitive elections, party-sponsored television and radio ads and voter mobilization efforts help candidates of varying degrees of competitiveness. The 1980s witnessed the reemergence of national party organizations. By the century's end, these organizations had become very important players in party politics and elections.

12-3

Of Political Parties Great and Small

Everett Carll Ladd

In the following essay Everett Carll Ladd challenges the suggestion that parties are too weak. The call for stronger party organizations and a stronger party apparatus in government, Ladd claims, runs contrary to most Americans' view of good politics. If anything, the two major parties are too strong already, too closely tied with special interests, and too out of touch with popular sentiments. Ladd argues that America needs, and has, a mixed system, in which parties play an important role but do not dictate the behavior of government officials or voters.

FOR MOST OF this century, political science orthodoxy has held that American political parties need strengthening to the end of improving the quality of the nation's democracy. For the last 20 years, the Committee for Party Renewal has carried high the torch for stronger parties with this message embodied in its statement of principles: "Parties are indispensable to the realization of democracy. The stakes are no less than that."

The committee believes that party organization must be revitalized and refurbished, that political parties need to be more coherent and programmatic participators in government, and that the ties of individual voters to parties need to be made deeper and more evidently influential in voting decisions. In this view, a bigger party presence is the *sine qua non* of improving governmental performance and thus of restoring citizen confidence in the political system.

My own dissatisfaction with this view has been rising steadily. Over the years I have come to realize that the argument for stronger parties is at its base an argument for a larger government. It rests on a bundle of normative assumptions about what government should do, not on inherent democratic requirements. It goes hand in hand with arguments that the United States needs more government to solve problems, that the checks and

Excerpted from *The American Enterprise*, November/December 1994, pp. 62–70. Reprinted with permission from *The American Enterprise*, a national magazine of politics, business, and culture.

balances system has been a terrible barrier to getting needed programs enacted, and finally that, in general, the good society requires a big polity. Political science has been making a statement about desired ends with regard to government's role instead of a hard analysis of the kind of party roles an effective democracy requires. This is not to say that parties are unneeded as representative institutions or that their continued weakening is desirable. Parties are needed. However, much of the contemporary unease with politics and government does not result from a diminished party role: indeed, a strengthening of parties might well exacerbate present discontent. . . .

From Great Parties to Strong Parties . . . and Strong Government

It is not by chance that the United States, where political parties are institutionally weaker than in any other industrial democracy, is also the country where the reach of the national government—though it has expanded greatly in recent decades—is still the most restricted. More collectivist, less individualist political outlooks encourage the formation of stronger, more elite-directed parties, and such parties are in turn powerful instruments for state action. Granted, a strong disciplined party may on occasion be used, as it was in part in Margaret Thatcher's Britain, to dismantle programs enacted by earlier governments, Labour and Conservative alike. But on the whole, one wants strong parties in order to advance "positive" government—to enact and enlarge programs. E. E. Schattschneider made the point clearly in his classic *The Struggle for Party Government* in 1948:

> As a nation we have had little opportunity to prepare ourselves for the realization that it is now necessary for the government to act as it has never acted before. . . . The essence of the governmental crisis consists of a deficiency of the power to create, adopt, and execute a comprehensive plan of action in advance of a predictable catastrophe in time to prevent and minimize it. . . . The central difficulty of the whole system—the difficulty which causes all of the difficulties—is the fact the government characteristically suffers from a deficiency of the power to govern.

While the proposition has rarely received systematic empirical examination, some political scientists have at least questioned whether strong parties have in fact been associated with sounder policy. Leon D. Epstein has observed, for instance, that both Don K. Price and Pendleton Herring concluded at the end of the Depression decade that the disciplined party leadership found in the United Kingdom might well have produced far less desirable policy results than America's relatively weak and decentralized parties operating in a system of vastly separated and checked authority. Whether strong parties tend to advance sounder policy is, admittedly, a huge and complex empirical question. But until it is seen as an empirical question, treatment of it cannot advance much beyond the position— "Well, that's what I want anyway!" I find nothing in the canon of American political science that gives more empirical weight to the critics of the present workings of the separation of powers than to the proponents. Evidence seems at least as strong for the argument that America's system of separated power, relatively uncurbed by strong and disciplined parties, has improved public policy by helping to slow the rush of government expansion and lessen the likelihood of ill-considered, precipitant actions.

Questioning the Ideal of "Maximalist Politics"

The idea that "more politics" is more or less automatically desirable is deeply entrenched in contemporary political commentary—in the writings of political scientists, journalists, and other analysts. We see this in the literature on nonvoting. With some notable exceptions, much of the work on voter turnout sees low turnout as a huge problem, as a failure of democracy.

One may advocate efforts to promote vigorous citizenship—including encouraging voting—without subscribing to the argument that the relatively low turnout in the United States—about 56 percent of the adult resident population cast votes for president in 1992, for example—is on its face evidence of a grievous weakness in our democratic life. But many have argued that it does indicate just that. Thus Arthur T. Hadley wrote, "America's present problem . . . is an apathetic, cross-pressured society with strong feelings of political impotence, where more and more people find their lives out of control, believe in luck, and refrain from voting. These growing numbers of refrainers hang over our democratic process like a bomb, ready to explode and change the course of our history. . . . For us, now, an increase in voting is a sign of political health." Gary R. Orren argues that "if the health of a democracy can be measured by the level of popular participation in its electoral system, ours is ailing."

The argument is riddled with flaws. Consider, for example, Hadley's view that America is beset by an increasingly widespread decline of social obligation and participation—a surge in the number of "refrainers." This is simply not true. Voter turnout *has* declined from the 1960 level—the highest in this century. (Even here, it's worth noting that turnout in 1992 was almost exactly the same as it was in 1936—a presidential election in which Franklin Roosevelt and the New Deal had presumably galvanized the population to action.) But outside of voting, the data do not support an argument that participation is in decline. A study done in 1990 under the direction of Sidney Verba, Kay L. Schlozman, Henry R. Brady, and Norman H. Nie showed once again a populace that is highly participatory in most areas of political activity (such as contributing money to political organizations, getting in contact with government officials, and the like) and even more so in nonpolitical public affairs (from a vast variety of organizational memberships to charitable giving and voluntary action).

Similarly, new findings in the United States and in Western Europe show that (1) charitable giving and voluntary action levels are increasing, not decreasing, in the United States and (2) the levels dwarf those in Western Europe.

Returning to the matter of voter turnout as such, many different factors account for the American experience of relatively low participation. Not all of these are cause for concern. Ivor Crewe notes, for example, that while turnout in a given national election in the United States falls below that in Western Europe, Americans go to the polls far more often than the citizens of any other democracy. Not surprisingly, no one election is much of a novelty. The frequency of our elections probably reduces the turnout in any one of them.

Some factors that encourage high turnout are surely undesirable. Extreme fear can be a powerful incentive to vote—so as to prevent the feared outcome. Columnist George F. Will has reminded us that in the two presidential ballots conducted in Germany in 1932, 86 and 84 percent of the electorate cast ballots. In 1933, 89 percent voted in the assembly election in which the Nazis triumphed. Will asked: "Did the high 1933 turnout make the Nazi regime especially legitimate? Were the 1932 turnouts a sign of the health of the Weimar Republic?" His answer is the right one: "The turnouts reflected the unhealthy stakes of politics then: elections determined which mobs ruled the streets and who went to concentration camps." Americans are less inclined to fear massive upheaval or a dramatic discontinuity resulting from any particular election. In this environment, some people who are less interested in politics apparently feel a degree of security sufficient to permit them not to vote.

Raising these points is not a defense of nonvoting, but an argument instead that "more politics" is not automatically a good thing. A condition in which many people feel free to concentrate their energies on other aspects of life—raising families, working in churches, volunteering their time, and giving money to charitable institutions—has much to commend it. If better citizenship education and changes in electoral processes can help more people vote as well, so much the good. But let's not in the process claim that relatively low voter turnout is a sign of an apathetic populace generally abandoning its common and collective responsibilities.

The American ideological tradition has from the country's forming insisted on the need for a large public sector and a relatively small state. Properly construed, "public sector" refers to matters of common concern and action. The public sector hardly need be just governmental. The American idea has been that our common or public concerns as a people require vigorous activity outside the sphere of government. Tocqueville remarked on this at length a century and a half ago. He noted, for example, the extraordinary interest-group activity on behalf of all kinds of issues and objectives. "The political associations that exist in the United States," he wrote, "are only a single feature in the midst of the immense assemblage of associations in that country. . . . The Americans make associations to give entertainments, to found seminaries, to build inns, to construct churches, to diffuse books, to send missionaries to the antipodes: in this manner they found hospitals, prisons, and schools. . . . Wherever at the head of some new undertaking you see the government in France, or a man of rank in England, in the United States you will be sure to find an association.

In the first volume of *Democracy,* Tocqueville had given the classic statement of the fact that—far from holding back collective energy and participation—American individualism was its very source: "In the United States associations are established to promote the public safety, commerce, industry, morality, and religion. There is no end which the human will despairs of attaining through the combined power of individuals united into a society."

Today's Publics Assess Government

Over the last several decades, Americans have been expressing increasingly ambivalent feelings about the scope of government and the quality of governmental performance.

On the one hand, we have remained—despite our complaints about government's record—an optimistic people who believe that problems are something to be solved, not endured. Thus, in an age of considerable national affluence, we have fairly high expectations with regard to action in areas as wide-ranging as the environment, crime, schools, health care, and poverty. We want action in these areas and usually see governmental action as one part of the necessary response.

On the other hand, all kinds of indicators reveal doubts about the wisdom of continuing to expand government's reach. Ever since the passage of Proposition 13 in California in 1978, tax protests have been a common part of the American political experience, and a highly democratic one at that. That is, the strongest insistence that tax hikes be curbed has often come from the lower half of the income spectrum, not from the upper half. In general, at the same time we are endorsing major interventions by government, we are calling government too big, too inefficient, too intrusive. Given the choice between government that does more and costs more, and that which does less and costs less, we are indicating a strong preference for the latter.

Many Americans are evidently angry about the performance of the country's political institutions. Consider, for example, judgments about Congress. Surveys from the 1940s through the 1960s consistently showed the national legislature getting pretty good marks. When Gallup asked in 1958 whether Congress was doing a good or poor job, it found only 12 percent saying poor. In a June 1970 survey, Gallup showed its respondents a card on which there were 10 boxes, numbered from +5 (for institutions "you like very much") down to –5 ("dislike very much"). Only 3 percent assigned Congress to the –4 and –5 boxes, and only 10 percent gave it a negative rating of any kind. Thirty-six percent gave it either a +4 or a +5. Things are surely different now. A number of survey organizations regularly ask their respondents whether they approve or disapprove of the way Congress is doing its job. The proportions bounce around, depending on the overall national mood and the latest headlines on congressional doings. But with a few brief exceptions, one of which was at the onset of the Gulf War, the proportions saying they approve Congress's performance has remained in the range of one-fourth to one-third of the public. In 64 iterations of this question for the period from 1989 through January 1994, only 27 percent of respondents, on average, put themselves in the "approve" column.

Today Americans' complaints about governmental performance are generally sweeping. The expectations of government from this highly ambivalent and conflicted public seems reasonably well heeded by the current system. Looking at the almost $1.5 trillion federal budget enacted for FY '94, it's hard to make the case that governmental action has been throttled. At the same time, a public that is dubious about government's performance and about the wisdom of expanding state action further may be well served by a system that puts substantial checks and limits on the development of new programs.

The founders of the American system sought to establish and sustain a type of government at once energetic and limited. This admixture of seeming opposites is in a sense jarring, but it has received the continuing support of much of the populace. The levels of government today are far higher than they were in the past, but the same admixture pertains. The American system continues to produce government that is extraordinarily energetic and highly constrained.

Knowing What's Best

If Americans are ambivalent about government's proper role and reluctant to issue the call, "Charge!" and if they show no signs of wanting to strengthen political parties, why should we urge upon them steps toward a stronger and "more responsible" party system? The only defensible answer would be: because, though much of the public doesn't know it, the absence of a stronger party system is a major reason why so many people are so dissatisfied with governmental performance. Is that answer valid?

One reason to doubt its validity is the fact that dissatisfaction with government's performance is evident in nearly all of the world's industrial democracies, not just the United States. Indeed, the United States does not rank at all high comparatively on many of these measures. If many countries with strong party systems manifest as much or more dissatisfaction with governmental institutions and performance as the United States does, the idea that strengthening our party system is likely to contribute to increased satisfaction and confidence is dubious. Admittedly, it does not necessarily reject such strengthening, since many other factors can shape confidence levels.

Today, majorities of record or near-record proportions are expressing dissatisfaction with or pessimism about their country's political and economic performance and their own personal prospects. In France, for example, a country with strong and disciplined political parties, economic pessimism is rampant, and the entire political class has come under intense criticism. The ruling Socialists were dealt a massive defeat in the 1993 elections for the National Assembly. With only a couple of exceptions, politicians of all the parties got low marks. In Great Britain, Prime Minister John Major has some of the lowest approval ratings of any British prime minister. Labour fares better, but its showing in the recent local elections where the Liberal Democrats bested it reveals a real lack of enthusiasm for the country's other major party.

The argument on behalf of stronger parties needs to be examined in three distinct arenas—party organization, party in government, and party in the electorate. The case for stronger parties in the first two seems very weak. What's more, the argument runs in precisely the opposite direction from that which the public says it wants. The public's criticism, as seen clearly in survey data, is that politics is too much captured by political insiders—for example, by the elected Democratic and Republican politicians in the national legislature—and in general that "the system" is too insulated from meaningful day-to-day popular control. The call is somehow to check and limit the political class.

The last thing this public wants is stronger party organization and stronger party apparatus in government. Its present discontents push it in a direction similar to that pursued by the Progressive Movement early in this century. The Progressives believed that the principal institutions of American representative democracy—political parties, legislatures, city councils, and the like—had been captured by "the interests," were riddled with corruption, and often had been wrested from popular control. Muckraking journalists, among them Ida M. Tarbell and Lincoln Steffans, graphically portrayed the veniality and unresponsiveness that they saw as all too common in the nation's political life.

Many in the Progressive Movement concluded that the only way to cure these ills was to give individual citizens new authority to override and control representative institutions. They backed and saw enacted a host of "direct democracy" reforms: the direct primary to take nominations away from party "bosses"; initiatives and referenda, to allow the people to make laws directly; the recall, to permit voters to "kick the bums out" when they were performing badly, even before their regular terms were up. The success that the reformers had makes clear that they tapped a deep lode of resentment.

Today public frustrations resemble those of the Progressive Era and probably surpass anything between that era and our own. As in the Progressive Era, dissatisfaction gets expressed in increased backing for direct democracy. The American political culture is strongly individualistic, and we are always sympathetic to the idea of direct citizenry intervention above and beyond elections. But when things are seen going poorly in terms of the institutions' performance, direct democracy's appeal gets a special boost.

Many of the innovations of the Progressive Era, such as referenda and primaries, are in wide use today. And the public would now extend them further. But today's direct democracy agenda finds other expressions. Backing for term limits is one. Support for the Perot movement is another.

Appropriate Individualism

Political science has long favored a strengthening of parties, as opposed to more direct democracy, to deal with governmental unresponsiveness and increase popular control. The public plainly doesn't agree. Some might dismiss its evident disagreement with anything that smacks of augmenting the party apparatus and control as simply the unthinking response of a highly individualist culture. The culture *is* highly individualist. And that's not going to change, so practical politics suggests that improvements be made within its dictates. But beyond this, if Americans are at times excessively obedient to individualist assertions, it's not at all clear that they are wrong on the proper role of party organization and party machinery in government. Party leaders *are* political insiders. As modern government has mushroomed, the political class *has* become more insulated. Finding ways to check it further might permit ordinary voters to intervene more effectively and extensively in setting public policy.

The United States may not be beset by the old-fashioned veniality and corruption that the Progressives faced, but the primary representative institutions often seem worlds apart from the general public, responding to insider agendas. Politics as usual inside the Beltway is highly insulated and in a sense isolated. The interests that dominate "Beltway politics" differ from those that the Progressives battled, but they may be no less insensitive to popular calls for change. The old Progressive answer of extending direct citizen authority and intervention deserves careful reconsideration as a partial answer to present-day insufficiencies and shortcomings in representative democracy.

Appropriate Party Bolstering

The one area where a strong case can be made for modest steps to strengthen the party presence involves the electorate. One of the most unusual features of the contemporary party system is the frequency with which split results are attained—for example, the Republicans winning the presidency pretty regularly, but not controlling both houses of Congress since 1954. This condition seems to have two quite different sources—one involving something that much of the public intends, but the other quite unintentional and indeed fundamentally unwanted.

The intended dimension, what I call cognitive Madisonianism, starts from the fact that Americans have historically been less troubled than their counterparts in other democracies about divided control. It accords with the general thrust and biases of separation of powers. Into this, however, it seems that something new has been added. The high measure of ambivalence that so many citizens have about government's role, and from this the doubts they entertain about both political parties, seems to be well served by electoral outcomes that frequently give each of the major parties a piece of the action.

Today's public wants somewhat contradictory things of the modern state. And it sees the Democrats and Republicans as differing significantly on the issue of government's role. Cognitive Madisonianism insists that the two parties' competing views on government's proper role be pitted one against another, as when a Republican executive pushes one way and a Democratic legislature the other. The empirical work needed to explore cognitive Madisonianism satisfactorily has not been done—despite extensive surveys on related topics. We do know that high degrees of ambivalence concerning government's role have been present over the last 25 years, but survey data show nothing comparable for earlier periods, and large segments of the public express broad approval of divided government.

Those who see evidence of cognitive Madisonianism in two-tier voting must acknowledge nonetheless that more is at work. Even in the face of pronounced voter dissatisfaction with Congress, for example, historically unprecedented majorities of incumbents of both parties have been winning reelection, and House incumbents typically win by big margins. Underlying this development are several notable features of contemporary electioneering: (1) incumbents generally enjoy huge advantages in campaign contributions, and (2) they also enjoy a big advantage in government-provided resources—notably in the very large staffs given members through the "reforms" of the late 1960s and early 1970s. House members' staff was tripled, and many members have put a large bloc of their new assistants to work back in their districts—little electoral machines available to them year round at public expense. Finally, whereas in races for governor and U.S. senator, as well as for president, many voters know something substantial about the candidates' policy stands and records, they usually don't have much information of this kind on House members. They are likely, though, to have some vaguely favorable image of him or her, while having no impression at all of the challenger.

Getting voters to pay a bit more attention to party labels is the one thing that could upset this present dynamic. A voter might not know anything about a member of Congress's voting record, but still vote against him or her in favor of a challenger who is less known because the voter wanted to change party control, to give the "outs" a chance. There is abundant evidence that this is exactly what has happened historically. But over the last quarter-century, as incumbents have gained election resources far greater than ever before, the proportion of voters bound by significant "party awareness" has declined precipitously. "Vote for the person, not the party," is in many ways laudable. It conforms entirely to the American individualist tradition of democratic governance. Nonetheless, it sometimes works poorly, especially when large numbers of voters know little of consequence about the person. What's more, the person in Congress usually votes with his party these days. The pronounced decline of "party thinking" leaves many voters ill-equipped to express effectively the dissatisfaction they clearly feel. Voters don't like important aspects of legislative performance, for example, but voting "for the person" denies them a means of doing much to address their dissatisfaction.

As for a revival of what we have called party thinking, those who believe it is needed ultimately have to make the case. The Republicans, notably, appear to have suffered electorally from the absence of greater party thinking in a broad array of less visible legislative races. If they haven't suffered thus—that is, if much of the electorate on cognitive Madisonian or other grounds wants an essentially permanent Democratic majority in the House of Representatives—the Republicans will undoubtedly be unable to make this case successfully, regardless of the adroitness of their efforts.

A Substantial Party Presence

More than three decades ago, political scientist and historian Clinton Rossiter wrote eloquently on the virtues of a "mixed" party system, one that gives a large role to the institutional parties and at the same time to individual voters. The current assumption in political science, though, is that the mixed system is no more because the party presence has declined so markedly. This is an excessive response to current trends and an unbalanced reading of them. Some developments have reduced the party presence. The media, for example, play a much larger role in political communication generally and in the process of candidate choice than ever before—mostly at the parties' expense.

But at the same time, in other areas we have actually moved toward stronger and in a way more disciplined political parties. The vehicle of the new "discipline" isn't institutional sanctions—party leaders being able to "punish" recalcitrant members—but rather growing ideological homogeneity within each of the two major parties. Thirty years ago when Rossiter wrote *Parties and Politics in America,* the Democratic congressional party was highly irresponsible and undisciplined. It carried within it competing wings or factions, each resting on a firm local base, which could agree upon little about how the country should be governed except that they wanted the Democratic party to organize the Congress. *Congressional Quarterly* introduced in 1957 the concept "conservative coalition" votes in Congress—defining them as ones in which a majority of southern Democrats vote with a majority of Republicans against a majority of northern Democrats. "Conservative coalition voting scores" for individual members were a key CQ tally. The Democratic party was, then, highly irresponsible, in the sense that its southern wing often worked for aims contrary to what the national party proclaimed. As for the Republicans, while they lacked a split as wide and deep as that between the Democrats' northern and southern wings, liberal, moderate, and conservative blocs detracted from the programmatic coherence of congressional Republicanism as well.

In recent years, however, there has been a powerful movement toward greater "discipline," through the vehicle of internal philosophical agreement. Congressional Democrats today are much more coherently a liberal party, and congressional Republicans much more a conservative one than ever before. We can see this from the splendid roll-call analysis done regularly by political scientist William Schneider and his colleagues at *National Journal*. In their January 1991 report, for example, Richard E. Cohen and William Schneider noted that "bipartisanship was a rare commodity on key congressional votes in 1990. And divisions within each party narrowed according to *National Journal*'s annual congressional vote ratings. . . . Southern Democrats and eastern Republicans, the traditional centers of ideological moderation in both the House and Senate, moved further apart in 1990. Their shifts (the southern Democrats to the Left and the eastern Republicans to the Right) were another sign of the increased partisanship [i.e., united parties arrayed against each other] in both chambers." The 1994 report by Cohen and Schneider reiterated similar findings and gave powerful evidence on the newfound responsibility of both congressional parties.

A Final Word

Today's "mixed" system is different from the one Rossiter described. But the present party system contains its own distinctive strengths as well as new elements of weakness. The parties are much more programmatically coherent and internally disciplined by ideological agreement today than in Rossiter's time. They present far clearer choices for all who care to pay attention. Advocates of stronger and more responsible parties have for the most part failed to call attention to the marked party strengthening evident in the data on the new internal coherence of the congressional Republican and Democratic parties.

The United States needs a mixed system, and it has one. Parties have been weakened in some regards but strengthened in others. They remain a substantial presence in American political life. They remain about as much of a presence as the public wants or will abide. And it is far from clear that groups such as the Committee on Party Renewal, which seek a general strengthening of parties in the electorate, as organizations, and in government, address the principal source of voter complaint—partisan unresponsiveness and a politics too dominated by institutions inside the Beltway.

13

Interest Groups

Special interests, particularly moneyed interests, have been the favorite target of political reformers throughout American history. At the end of the nineteenth century and into the twentieth, progressive reformers sought to reduce the influence of money in politics by breaking up the large corporations that wielded so much power and by reducing the power of the party bosses who were their beneficiaries. Contemporary reformers have sought to limit the reliance of candidates on campaign contributions from sources of wealth, ban gifts to office holders, and make public the identity of those who hire lobbyists and contribute to campaigns.

The Constitution limits the ability of the government to regulate campaign contributions and lobbying. The Supreme Court has held that campaign contributions and spending are essential to political speech, and therefore protected by the First Amendment. As a consequence, the government must have strong reasons to set contribution and spending limits. Restrictions that may be placed on lobbying are likewise limited by the First Amendment's protection of the right to petition the government. The result of the conflict between the reformers and the Court is a complex set of laws governing campaign finance and lobbying.

In light of recent arguments that policymakers are too dependent on public opinion polls (reviewed in chapter 10), we should pause to ask whether money in politics is really a problem. Can politicians be too susceptible to influence from both polls and moneyed interests, as many critics charge? In principle, perhaps. Money may help special interests influence both the general public and politicians. Or money may influence policy makers on some issues, whereas the polls drive policy decisions on others. The essays in this chapter examine the complex relationship between public opinion, special interests, and policy.

13-1

The Scope and Bias of the Pressure System

E. E. Schattschneider

In the mid twentieth century, many observers believed that James Madison's vision of America—as a multitude of groups or factions, none of which dominated the government—had been realized. E. E. Schattschneider provided an alternative view. In the following essay, which was originally published in 1960, Schattschneider argues that moneyed interests dominated mid-twentieth-century politics. In his view, the dominance of moneyed interests limited the scope of government action and created a bias in the pressures placed on policymakers. As we enter the twenty-first century, the issues raised by Schattschneider remain relevant to debates over the influence of organized and moneyed interests in American government and politics.

THE SCOPE OF CONFLICT is an aspect of the scale of political organization and the extent of political competition. The size of the constituencies being mobilized, the inclusiveness or exclusiveness of the conflicts people expect to develop leave a bearing on all theories about how politics is or should be organized. In other words, nearly all theories about politics have something to do with the question of who can get into the fight and who is to be excluded. . . .

If we are able . . . to distinguish between public and private interests and between organized and unorganized groups we have marked out the major boundaries of the subject; *we have given the subject shape and scope.* . . . [W]e can now appropriate the piece we want and leave the rest to someone else. For a multitude of reasons *the most likely field of study is that of the organized, special-interest groups.* The advantage of concentrating on organized groups is that they are known, identifiable, and recognizable. The advantage of concentrating on special-interest groups is that they have one important

Excerpted from *The Semisovereign People: A Realist's View of Democracy in America* by E. E. Schattschneider, copyright © 1975 by Holt, Rinehart and Winston, reprinted by permission of the publisher. Some notes appearing in the original have been cut.

characteristic in common; they are all exclusive. This piece of the pie (the organized special-interest groups) we shall call the *pressure system*. The pressure system has boundaries we can define; we can fix its scope and make an attempt to estimate its bias.

It may be assumed at the outset that all organized special-interest groups have some kind of impact on politics. A sample survey of organizations made by the Trade Associations Division of the United States Department of Commerce in 1942 concluded that "From 70 to 100 percent (of these associations) are planning activities in the field of government relations, trade promotion, trade practices, public relations, annual conventions, cooperation with other organizations, and information services."

The subject of our analysis can be reduced to manageable proportions and brought under control if we restrict ourselves to the groups whose interests in politics are sufficient to have led them to unite in formal organizations having memberships, bylaws, and officers. A further advantage of this kind of definition is, we may assume, that the organized special-interest groups are the most self-conscious, best developed, most intense and active groups. Whatever claims can be made for a group theory of politics ought to be sustained by the evidence concerning these groups, if the claims have any validity at all.

The organized groups listed in the various directories (such as *National Associations of the United States,* published at intervals by the United States Department of Commerce) and specialty yearbooks, registers, etc. and the *Lobby Index,* published by the United States House of Representatives, probably include the bulk of the organizations in the pressure system. All compilations are incomplete, but these are extensive enough to provide us with some basis for estimating the scope of the system.

By the time a group has developed the kind of interest that leads it to organize, it may be assumed that it has also developed some kind of political bias because *organization is itself a mobilization of bias in preparation for action.* Since these groups can be identified and since they have memberships (i.e., they include and exclude people), it is possible to think of the *scope* of the system.

When lists of these organizations are examined, the fact that strikes the student most forcibly is that *the system is very small.* The range of organized, identifiable, known groups is amazingly narrow; there is nothing remotely universal about it. There is a tendency on the part of the publishers of directories of associations to place an undue emphasis on business organizations, an emphasis that is almost inevitable because the business community is by a wide margin the most highly organized segment of society. Publishers doubtless tend also to reflect public demand for information. Nevertheless, the dominance of business groups in the pressure system is so marked that it probably cannot be explained away as an accident of the publishing industry.

The business character of the pressure system is shown by almost every list available. *National Associations of the United States* lists 1,860 business associations out of a total of 4,000 in the volume, though it refers without listing to 16,000 organizations of businessmen. One cannot be certain what the total content of the unknown associational universe may be, but, taken with the evidence found in other compilations, it is obvious that business is remarkably well represented. Some evidence of the overall scope of the system is to be seen in the estimate that 15,000 national trade associations have a gross membership of about one million business firms. The data are incomplete, but even if we do not have a detailed map this is the shore dimly seen.

Much more directly related to pressure politics is the *Lobby Index, 1946–1949* (an index of organizations and individuals registering or filing quarterly reports under the Federal Lobbying Act), published as a report of the House Select Committee on Lobbying Activities. In this compilation, 825 out of a total of 1,247 entries (exclusive of individuals and Indian tribes) represented business. A selected list of the most important of the groups listed in the *Index* (the groups spending the largest sums of money on lobbying) published in the *Congressional Quarterly Log* shows 149 business organizations in a total of 265 listed.

The business or upper-class bias of the pressure system shows up everywhere. Businessmen are four or five times as likely to write to their congressmen as manual laborers are. College graduates are far more apt to write to their congressmen than people in the lowest educational category are.

The limited scope of the business pressure system is indicated by all available statistics. Among business organizations, the National Association of Manufacturers (with about 20,000 corporate members) and the Chamber of Commerce of the United States (about as large as the N.A.M.) are giants. Usually business associations are much smaller. Of 421 trade associations in the metal-products industry listed in *National Associations of the United States,* 153 have a membership of less than 20. The median membership was somewhere between 24 and 50. Approximately the same scale of memberships is to be found in the lumber, furniture, and paper industries, where 37.3 percent of the associations listed had a membership of less than 20 and the median membership was in the 25 to 50 range.

The statistics in these cases are representative of nearly all other classifications of industry.

Data drawn from other sources support this thesis. Broadly, the pressure system has an upper-class bias. There is overwhelming evidence that participation in voluntary organizations is related to upper social and economic status; the rate of participation is much higher in the upper strata than it is elsewhere. The general proposition is well stated by [political scientist Paul] Lazarsfeld:

> People on the lower SES levels are less likely to belong to any organizations than the people on high SES (Social and Economic Status) levels. (On an A and B level, we find 72 percent of these respondents who belong to one or more organizations. The proportion of respondents who are members of formal organizations decreases steadily as SES level descends until, on the D level only 35 percent of the respondents belong to any associations).[1]

The bias of the system is shown by the fact that *even non-business organizations reflect an upper-class tendency.*

Lazarsfeld's generalization seems to apply equally well to urban and rural populations. The obverse side of the coin is that large areas of the population appear to be wholly outside the system of private organization. A study made by Ira Reid of a Philadelphia area showed that in a sample of 963 persons, 85 percent belonged to no civic or charitable organization and 74 percent belonged to no occupational, business, or professional associations, while another Philadelphia study of 1,154 women showed that 55 percent belonged to no associations of any kind.[2]

A *Fortune* farm poll taken some years ago found that 70.5 percent of farmers belonged to no agricultural organizations. A similar conclusion was reached by two Gallup polls showing that perhaps no more than one third of the farmers of the country belonged to farm organizations, while another *Fortune* poll showed that 86.8 percent of the low-income farmers belonged to no farm organizations. All available data support the generalization that the farmers who do not participate in rural organizations are largely the poorer ones. . . .

The class bias of associational activity gives meaning to the limited scope of the pressure system, because *scope and bias are aspects of the same tendency.*

The data raise a serious question about the validity of the proposition that special-interest groups are a universal form of political organization reflecting *all* interests. As a matter of fact, to suppose that everyone participates in pressure-group activity and that all interests get themselves organized in the pressure system is to destroy the meaning of this form of politics. The pressure system makes sense only as the political instrument of a segment of the community. It gets results by being selective and biased; *if everybody got into the act, the unique advantages of this form of organization would be destroyed, for it is possible that if all interests could be mobilized the result would be a stalemate.*

Special-interest organizations are most easily formed when they deal with small numbers of individuals who are acutely aware of their exclusive interests. To describe the conditions of pressure-group organization in this way is, however, to say that it is primarily a business phenomenon. Aside from a few very large organizations (the churches, organized labor, farm organizations, and veterans' organizations) the residue is a small segment of the population. *Pressure politics is essentially the politics of small groups.*

The vice of the groupist theory is that it conceals the most significant aspects of the system. The flaw in the pluralist heaven is that the heavenly chorus sings with a strong upper-class accent. Probably about 90 percent of the people cannot get into the pressure system.

The notion that the pressure system is automatically representative of the whole community is a myth fostered by the universalizing tendency of modern group theories. *Pressure politics is a selective process* ill designed to serve diffuse interests. The system is skewed, loaded, and unbalanced in favor of a fraction of a minority.

On the other hand, pressure tactics are not remarkably successful in mobilizing general interests. When pressure-group organizations attempt to represent the interests of large numbers of people, they are usually able to reach only a small segment of their constituencies. Only a chemical trace of the fifteen million Negroes in the United States belong to the National Association for the Advancement of Colored People. Only one five hundredths of 1 percent of American women belong to the League of Women Voters, only one sixteen hundredths of 1 percent of the consumers belong to the National Consumers' League, and only 6 percent of American automobile drivers belong to the American Automobile Association, while about 15 percent of the veterans belong to the American Legion.

The competing claims of pressure groups and political parties for the loyalty of the American public revolve about the difference between the results likely to be achieved by small-scale and large-scale political organization. Inevitably, the outcome of pressure politics and party politics will be vastly different. . . .

. . . Everything we know about politics suggests that a conflict is likely to change profoundly as it becomes political. It is a rare individual who can confront his antagonists without changing his opinions to some degree. Everything changes once a conflict gets into the political arena—*who* is involved, *what* the conflict is about, the resources available, etc. It is extremely difficult to predict the outcome of a fight by watching its beginning because we do not even know who else is going to get into the conflict. The logical consequence of the exclusive emphasis on the determinism of the private origins of conflict is to assign zero value to the political process.

The very expression "pressure politics" invites us to misconceive the role of special-interest groups in politics. The word "pressure" implies the use of some kind of force, a form of intimidation, something other than reason and information, to induce public authorities to act against their own best judgment. [This is reflected in the famous statement by political scientist Earl Latham, in his 1952 book *The Group Basis of Politics,* that] the legislature is a "referee" who "ratifies" and "records" the "balance of power" among the contending groups.[3]

It is hard to imagine a more effective way of saying that Congress has no mind or force of its own or that Congress is unable to invoke new forces that might alter the equation.

Actually the outcome of political conflict is not like the "resultant" of opposing forces in physics. To assume that the forces in a political situation could be diagramed as a physicist might diagram the resultant of opposing physical forces is to wipe the slate clean of all remote, general, and public considerations for the protection of which civil societies have been instituted.

Moreover, the notion of "pressure" distorts the image of the power relations involved. *Private conflicts are taken into the public arena precisely because someone wants to make certain that the power ratio among the private interests most immediately involved shall not prevail.* To treat a conflict as a mere test of the strength of the private interests is to leave out the most significant factors. This is so true that it might indeed be said that the only way to preserve private power ratios is to keep conflicts out of the public arena.

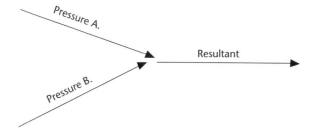

The assumption that it is only the "interested" who count ought to be re-examined in view of the foregoing discussion. The tendency of the literature of pressure politics has been to neglect the low-tension force of large numbers because it *assumes that the equation of forces is fixed at the outset.*

Given the assumptions made by the group theorists, the attack on the idea of the majority is completely logical. The assumption is that conflict is monopolized narrowly by the parties immediately concerned. There is no room for a majority when conflict is defined so narrowly. It is a great deficiency of the group theory that it has found no place in the political system for the majority. The force of the majority is of an entirely different order of magnitude, something not to be measured by pressure-group standards.

Instead of attempting to exterminate all political forms, organizations, and alignments that do not qualify as pressure groups, would it not be better to attempt to make a synthesis, covering the whole political system and finding a place for all kinds of political life?

One possible synthesis of pressure politics and party politics might be produced by *describing politics as the socialization of conflict.* That is to say, the political process is a sequence: conflicts are initiated by highly motivated, high-tension groups so directly and immediately involved that it is difficult for them to see the justice of competing claims. As long as the conflicts of these groups remain *private* (carried on in terms of economic competition, reciprocal denial of goods and services, private negotiations and bargaining, struggles for corporate control or competition for membership), no political process is initiated. Conflicts become political only when an attempt is made to involve the wider public. Pressure politics might be described as a stage in the socialization of conflict. This analysis makes pressure politics an integral part of all politics, including party politics.

One of the characteristic points of origin of pressure politics is a break-down of the discipline of the business community. The flight to government is perpetual. Something like this is likely to happen wherever there is a point of contact between competing power systems. It is the *losers in intrabusiness conflict who seek redress from public authority. The dominant business interests resist appeals to the government.* The role of the government as the patron of the defeated private interest sheds light on its function as the critic of private power relations.

Since the contestants in private conflicts are apt to be unequal in strength, it follows that *the most powerful special interests want private settlements* because they are able to dictate the outcome as long as the conflict remains private. If A is a hundred times as strong as B he does not welcome the intervention of a third party because he expects to impose his own terms on B; he wants to isolate B. He is especially opposed to the intervention of public authority, because public authority represents the most overwhelming form of outside intervention. Thus, if $A/B = 100/1$, it is obviously not to A's advantage to involve a third party a million times as strong as A and B combined. Therefore, it is the weak, not the strong, who appeal to public authority for relief. It is the weak who want to socialize conflict, i.e., to involve more and more people in the conflict until the balance of forces is changed. In the schoolyard it is not the bully but the defenseless smaller boys who "tell the teacher." When the teacher intervenes, the balance of power in the schoolyard is apt to change drastically. It is the function of public authority to *modify private power relations by enlarging the scope of conflict.* Nothing could be more mistaken than to suppose that public authority merely registers the dominance of the strong over the weak. The mere existence of public order has already ruled out a great variety of forms of private pressure. Nothing could be more confusing than to suppose that the refugees from the business community who come to Congress for relief and protection *force* Congress to do their bidding.

Evidence of the truth of this analysis may be seen in the fact that the big private interests do not necessarily win if they are involved in public conflicts with petty interests. The image of the lobbyists as primarily the agents of big business is not easy to support on the face of the record of congressional hearings, for example. The biggest corporations in the country tend to avoid the arena in which pressure groups and lobbyists fight it out before congressional committees. To describe this process exclusively in terms of an effort of business to intimidate congressmen is to misconceive what is actually going on.

It is probably a mistake to assume that pressure politics is the typical or even the most important relation between government and business. The pressure group is by no means the perfect instrument of the business community. What does big business want? The *winners* in intrabusiness strife want (1) to be let alone (they want autonomy) and (2) to preserve the solidarity of the business community. For these purposes pressure politics is not a wholly satisfactory device. The most elementary considerations of strategy call for the business community to develop some kind of common policy more broadly based than any special-interest group is likely to be.

The political influence of business depends on the kind of solidarity that, on the one hand, leads all business to rally to the support of *any* businessman in trouble with the government and, on the other hand, keeps internal business disputes out of the public arena. In this system businessmen resist the impulse to attack each other in public and discourage the efforts of individual members of the business community to take intrabusiness conflicts into politics.

The attempt to mobilize a united front of the whole business community does not resemble the classical concept of pressure politics. The logic of business politics is to keep peace within the business community by supporting as far as possible all claims that business groups make for themselves. The tendency is to support all businessmen who have conflicts with the government and support all businessmen in conflict with labor. In this way *special-interest politics can be converted into party policy.* The search is for a broad base of political mobilization grounded on the strategic need for political organization on a wider scale than is possible in the case of the historical pressure group. Once the business community begins to think in terms of a larger scale of political organization the Republican party looms large in business politics.

It is a great achievement of American democracy that business has been forced to form a political organization designed to win elections, i.e., has been forced to compete for power in the widest arena in the political system. On the other hand, *the power of the Republican party to make terms with business rests on the fact that business cannot afford to be isolated.*

The Republican party has played a major role in *the political organization of the business community,* a far greater role than many students of politics seem to have realized. The influence of business in the Republican party is great, but it is never absolute because business is remarkably dependent on the party. The business community is too small, it arouses too much antagonism, and its aims are too narrow to win the support of a popular majority. The political education of business is a function of the Republican party that can never be done so well by anyone else.

In the management of the political relations of the business community, the Republican party is much more important than any combination of pressure groups ever could be. The success of special interests in Congress is due less to the "pressure" exerted by these groups than it is due to the fact that Republican members of Congress are committed in advance to a general probusiness attitude. The notion that business groups coerce Republican congressmen into voting for their bills underestimates the whole Republican posture in American politics.

It is not easy to manage the political interests of the business community because there is a perpetual stream of losers in intrabusiness conflicts who go to the government for relief and protection. It has not been possible therefore to maintain perfect solidarity, and when solidarity is breached the government is involved almost automatically. The fact that business has not become hopelessly divided and that it has retained great influence in American politics has been due chiefly to the overall mediating role played by the Republican party. There has never been a pressure group or a combination of pressure groups capable of performing this function.

NOTES

1. Paul F. Lazarsfeld, Bernard Berelson, and Hazel Gaudet. *The People's Choice* (New York: Columbia University Press, 1948), p. 145.

2. Reid and Ehle, "Leadership Selection in the Urban Locality Areas," *Public Opinion Quarterly* (1950), 14:262–284. See also Norman Powell, *Anatomy of Public Opinion*, New York, 1951, pp. 180–181.

3. Earl Latham, *The Group Basis of Politics* (Ithaca: Cornell University Press, 1952), pp. 35–36.

13-2

The Evolution of Interest Groups

John R. Wright

In the following essay John Wright provides an overview of the development of interest groups in America. Interest groups form, Wright explains, as a net result of two factors—societal disturbances and collective action problems. Societal disturbances create common interests for groups of individuals, who then join forces to pursue those interests. But all groups face the collective action problem known as free riding—the tendency for group members to benefit from others' contributions to the provision of a public good without contributing themselves. Interest groups must find a way to encourage people to join and contribute in order to achieve their political goals.

THE RAPID ECONOMIC and social development in the United States immediately following the Civil War created a new and uncertain political environment for members of Congress. Congress emerged as the dominant force in national policy making, and members' electoral constituencies became far more heterogeneous and complex than ever before. In this new and uncertain political environment, the informational needs of members of Congress were greater than at any previous time, and it was in this environment that the American interest group system evolved.

Although the evolution of interest groups in the United States did not begin in earnest until after the Civil War, the groundwork for their development was laid much earlier in several key provisions of the U.S. Constitution. These constitutional provisions have had a profound effect on the American political party system, which in turn has had a major impact on the interest group system.

From *Interest Groups & Congress* by John R. Wright, pp. 11–22. Copyright 1996 by Allyn & Bacon. Reprinted by permission of Addison-Wesley Educational Publishers, Inc. Some notes appearing in the original have been cut.

Constitutional Underpinnings

The place of special interests in American politics today is largely a consequence of two competing political values expressed in the U.S. Constitution: a concern for liberty and freedom of political expression on the one hand, and the desire to prevent tyranny on the other. James Madison's *Federalist* No. 10 is the classic justification for the various constitutional checks and balances, which disperse power and make it difficult for any single group of citizens to control the entire government. Madison, whose thinking was strongly influenced by the English philosopher David Hume, believed that it is natural for people to differ, and in differing, to form into factions, or parties. The problem with factions, according to Madison and his contemporaries Jefferson and Hamilton, is their potential for subverting government and the public good. Factions, in Madison's words, are mischievous.

Madison's primary concern in *Federalist* No. 10 was with *majority* factions—typically, but not exclusively, political parties as we know them today—not minority factions such as contemporary interest groups. Although he recognized that minority factions could lead to disorder and conflict, Madison believed that it is the possibility of tyranny by the majority that poses the greatest threat to individual liberties. Madison did not recommend that factions be forbidden or repressed, a practice that would conflict with the fundamental values of liberty and freedom of expression, but instead that their negative tendencies be held in check and controlled through explicit constitutional safeguards.

Formal mechanisms in the U.S. Constitution for controlling majority factions include the requirements that the president be elected separately from members of Congress and that members of Congress reside in the states from which they are elected. These provisions disperse power horizontally—across national institutions of government—and vertically—from national to local political jurisdictions. Separation of the executive and legislative branches eased fears among the smaller states in 1787 that large states, which presumably would control the Congress, would also control the presidency; and geographic representation ensured that control over elected representatives would rest with local rather than national interests, thereby lessening the influence of the national government over state decisions.

These basic constitutional provisions have had a profound effect on the abilities of modern political parties to control and manage American government. Historically, control of the government has frequently been divided between the two major political parties, neither of which has been capable of exerting much discipline over its members. A single party has controlled the presidency and a majority in the U.S. House and Senate in just 43 of the 70 Congresses—61 percent—that have convened from 1855 to 1993. Even in times of single-party control of the government, voting defections within both major parties have been common. Since World War II, a majority of Democrats has voted against a majority of Republicans only 44 percent of the time on average in the U.S. House of Representatives and only 45 percent of the time on average in the U.S. Senate. American legislators have little incentive to toe the party line for the simple reason that a cohesive majority is not required to maintain control of the government or to preclude calling new elections, as is the case in parliamentary regimes. In the absence of party discipline, American legislators look to their geographic constituencies rather than to their parties for voting cues.

Madison and his contemporaries succeeded brilliantly in designing a constitutional system to attenuate the power of majority factions, but in doing so, they also created unanticipated opportunities for minority factions to be influential. When political parties are unable to take clear responsibility for governing, and when they cannot maintain cohesion and discipline among those elected under their labels, special interests have opportunities to gain access to the key points of decision within the government. David Truman explains that when a single party succeeds regularly in electing both an executive and a majority in the legislature, channels of access "will be predominantly those within the party leadership, and the pattern will be relatively stable and orderly."[1] He notes, however, that when "the party is merely an abstract term referring to an aggregation of relatively independent factions," as in the case of the United States, then the channels of access "will be numerous, and the patterns of influence within the legislature will be diverse, constantly shifting, and more openly in conflict."[2]

One important consequence of this "diffusion of access" is that legislators will be much more accessible to interests within their local constituencies, especially *organized* interests. Simply put, interest groups will thrive in an environment in which legislators take their behavioral cues from heterogeneous constituencies rather than from cohesive political parties. E. E. Schattschneider has summed up the situation succinctly:

> If the parties exercised the power to govern effectively, *they would shut out the pressure groups.* The fact that American parties govern only spasmodically and fitfully amid a multitude of lapses of control provides the opportunity for the cheap and easy use of pressure tactics.[3]

Although the constitution makes no specific mention of interest groups, or even political parties for that matter, it has influenced the evolution of both. The weakness of the political parties in their ability to control and manage the government is an intended consequence of the efforts by the founding fathers to inhibit majority factions; the prevalence of special interests, however, is an unintended consequence of weak parties. The U.S. Constitution indirectly laid the groundwork for a strong interest group system, but that system, unlike the political party system, did not evolve right away. It took nearly 70 years from the development of the first party system in 1800 until groups began to form and proliferate at a significant rate.

The Formation and Maintenance of Interest Groups

Although trade unions and associations have historical roots dating to the beginning of the republic, interest groups of regional or national scope as we know them today did not develop significantly until after the Civil War, and even then, pronounced growth did not really begin to take place until the late 1800s. Table 1 lists a few of the early organizations and their founding dates.

In what is known as the "disturbance theory" of interest group formation, David Truman argued that organizations will form when the interests common to unorganized groups of individuals are disturbed by economic, social, political, or technological change.[4] As society becomes increasingly complex and interconnected, Truman argued that individuals have greater difficulty resolving their differences and grievances on their own and instead must seek intervention from the government. It is at this time that political organizations will begin to take shape. Once interest groups begin to form, they will then tend to form in "wavelike" fashion, according to Truman, because policies designed to address one group's needs typically disturb the interests of other unorganized citizens, who then form groups to seek governmental intervention to protect and advance their particular interests.

The period from 1870 to 1900 was rife with disturbances favorable to the formation of interest groups in the United States. The economic, social, and political upheaval following the Civil War destabilized relationships within and between numerous groups of individuals. The completion of the railroads and the introduction of the telegraph dramatically altered communication and transportation patterns; immigration and population growth gave rise to new economic and social relationships; and commercial

Table 1. Selected Organizations and Their Founding Dates

American Medical Association	1847
National Grange	1867
National Rifle Association	1871
American Bankers Association	1875
American Federation of Labor	1886
Sierra Club	1892
National Association of Manufacturers	1895
National Audubon Society	1905
National Association for the Advancement of Colored People	1909
U.S. Chamber of Commerce	1912
American Jewish Congress	1918
American Farm Bureau Federation	1919
National League of Cities	1924

and territorial expansion in the West, combined with the task of maintaining order and rebuilding the infrastructure in the South, increased demands for routine services such as post offices, law enforcement, internal improvements, customs agents, and so forth. The process of industrialization created further economic and political tensions and uncertainties. The period 1870 to 1900 witnessed three economic depressions: a major one from 1873 to 1879, a minor one in the mid-1880s, and the collapse of 1893. Overall, the period from 1870 to 1900 was one when conditions were finally right for the widespread growth of organized interests in the United States.

Margaret Susan Thompson points out that in addition to the unprecedented economic and social upheaval at the end of the Civil War, political conditions in the 1870s were also favorable to the formation of groups and, in particular, the lobbying of Congress.[5] Two factors—the ascendancy of congressional power associated with the impeachment proceedings against Andrew Johnson and the growing heterogeneity of congressional constituencies—were instrumental in the growth of congressional lobbying and interest group activity. Congress, by enacting a comprehensive program on reconstruction in 1865 over the determined opposition of the president, established political preeminence over federal policy making and, as a consequence, became the focal institution for receiving and processing the conflicting demands of many newly recognized interests. Then, as congressional constituencies diversified economically and socially, the presence of multiple and competing interests began to force legislators to develop "representational priorities." [6] Thompson notes that legislators at this time had to determine which were their "meaningful" constituencies, and organization was the critical means by which interests achieved such designation. Thompson refers to the nascent organization of interests during the 1870s as "clienteles" rather than interest groups, for even though numerous subgroups of the population began making significant demands on the government during the 1870s, there was not a great deal of formal organization then as we know it today. Still, even these nascent groups began to provide important information to members of Congress about the interests and priorities of their constituents.

One example of how interest groups formed in response to economic and political disturbances during the post–Civil War period is provided by the organization of postal workers. Even before the Civil War, the volume of mail had grown tremendously in response to the development of railroads and the resulting decrease in the costs of postage. But in 1863, another significant increase in the volume of mail occurred when Congress lowered the long-distance postage rates. This created additional strains for letter carriers and postal clerks who already were greatly overworked. Then, in 1868, the Post Office Department refused to apply the "eight-hour" law—a law enacted that same year by Congress stipulating that eight hours constituted a day's work for laborers, workmen, and mechanics—to letter carriers on the grounds that they were government employees, not laborers, workmen, or mechanics. Finally, implementation of civil service following passage of the Pendleton Act in 1883 eliminated what little political clout the letter carriers had enjoyed. Once the patronage system was eliminated, politicians lost interest in the letter carriers and no longer intervened on their behalf.

In response to these deteriorating circumstances, the letter carriers organized into the National Association of Letter Carriers in 1889. Once organized, the letter carriers had a significant advantage over the unorganized postal clerks in the competition for wages. At the time, wages for all postal workers, letter carriers and clerks alike, were provided through a single congressional appropriation to the Post Office Department, and the letter carriers used their organizational clout to claim a disproportionate share of the annual appropriation. Thus, the postal workers came under pressure to organize as well, and so in predictable "wavelike" fashion, the National Association of Post Office Clerks was established in 1894.

Changing economic, social, and political conditions are necessary but not sufficient circumstances for the formation and development of organized interests. Even when environmental conditions are favorable to the formation of groups, there is still a natural proclivity for individuals *not* to join political interest groups. The reason is that individuals do not always have to belong to political groups in order to enjoy the benefits they provide. Wheat farmers, for example, benefit from the price supports that Congress establishes for wheat even though they do not belong to the National Association of Wheat Growers (NAWG), which lobbies for price supports. Similarly, individuals do not have to belong to environmental groups in order to reap the benefits of a cleaner environment brought about by the lobbying efforts of groups such as the Sierra Club and the National Wildlife Federation. More generally, the lobbying benefits provided by groups such as the wheat growers and the environmentalists are consumed *jointly* by all citizens affected; that is, Congress does not guarantee a higher price for wheat only to farmers who have paid dues to the National Association of Wheat Growers, and it does not and cannot restrict the benefit of a clean environment only to individuals who have paid their dues to environmental groups.

Unlike lobbying benefits, which are available even to those who do not contribute to lobbying efforts, the costs of lobbying are borne only by those who actually pay their dues to political groups or otherwise participate in lobbying activities. This creates a major organizational problem, for when it is possible to get something for nothing, many individuals will rationally choose to free ride on the efforts of others. When there are thousands of wheat farmers, for example, and the annual dues to the National Association of Wheat Growers are $100 or less, individual wheat farmers might very well conclude that their single contributions are not very important, that the NAWG will manage quite nicely without their money because there are so many other wheat farmers paying dues, and that there are much better uses for the $100 in light of the fact that the government will still provide price supports for their crop. The problem for the NAWG is that if every wheat farmer reasoned this way there would be no national association, and thus probably no price supports for wheat.

Given the natural proclivity for individuals to be free riders, all organizations must provide incentives of one sort or another to induce individuals to pay dues and otherwise contribute to the collective efforts of the organization. Generally speaking, individuals do not join interest groups because of benefits that can be consumed jointly; they join because of benefits that can by enjoyed *selectively* only by those individuals who pay dues to political groups. There are three main types of selective benefits. A selective *material* benefit includes such things as insurance and travel discounts and subscriptions to professional journals and other specialized information. A second type of selective benefit is what Peter Clark and James Q. Wilson have labelled *solidary* incentives. These, too, derive only from group membership and involve benefits such as "socializing, congeniality, the sense of group membership and identification, the status resulting from membership, fun and conviviality, the maintenance of social distinctions, and so on."[7] The third basic type of selective benefit is an *expressive* incentive. Expressive incentives are those that individuals attach to the act of expressing ideological or moral values such as free speech, civil rights, economic justice, or political equality. Individuals obtain these benefits when they pay dues or contribute money or time to an organization that espouses these values. What is important in receiving these benefits is the feeling of satisfaction that results from expressing political values, not necessarily the actual achievement of the values themselves.

Most organizations provide a mix of these various benefits, although different kinds of organizations typically rely more heavily on one type of benefit than another. Professional and trade associations, for example, are more likely to offer selective material benefits than purposive benefits, whereas environmental groups and other organizations claiming to lobby for the public interest rely more heavily on expressive benefits. Expressive benefits are also common in organizations relying heavily on mass mailings to attract and maintain members. Many direct mail approaches use negatively worded messages to instill feelings of guilt and fear in individuals, with the hope that people will contribute money to a cause as a means of expressing their support for certain values or else assuaging their guilt and fear.

That individuals are not drawn naturally to interest groups and must instead be enticed to join makes it very difficult for groups to get started. Organizations often need outside support in the form of a patron—perhaps a wealthy individual, a nonprofit foundation, or a government agency—to get over the initial hurdle of organizing collective action. In one of the leading studies on the origins and maintenance of interest groups, Jack Walker discovered that 89 percent of all citizen groups and 60 percent of all nonprofit occupational groups (e.g., the National Association of State Alcohol and Drug Abuse Directors) received financial assistance from an outside source at the time of their founding.[8] Many of these organizations continued to draw heavily from outside sources of support to maintain themselves once they were launched. Walker concluded that "the number of interest groups in operation, the mixture of group types, and the level and direction of political mobilization in the United States at any point in the country's history will be determined by the composition and accessibility of the system's major patrons of political action."[9]

In summary, the proficiency that contemporary interest groups have achieved in attracting and maintaining members has evolved from a combination of factors. Most fundamental to their evolution has been a constitutional arrangement that has not only encouraged their participation but also created unanticipated opportunities for them to exert influence. Changing economic, social, and political circumstances have also played critical roles at various times throughout American history. However, even under conditions favorable to their development, the formation and maintenance of interest groups requires leadership and creative approaches for dealing with the natural inertia that individuals exhibit toward collective activities. The number of groups continues to grow each year, however, as does the diversity of the issues and viewpoints they represent.

NOTES

1. David B. Truman, *The Governmental Process: Political Interests and Public Opinion* (New York: Knopf, 1951), p. 325.

2. Ibid., p. 325.

3. E. E. Schattschneider, *Party Government* (New York: Holt, Rinehart and Winston, 1941), p. 192.

4. David B. Truman, *The Governmental Process,* Chapters 3 and 4.

5. Margaret Susan Thompson, *The Spider Web: Congress and Lobbying in the Age of Grant* (Ithaca, NY: Cornell University Press, 1985).

6. Thompson, *The Spider Web,* pp. 130–131.

7. Peter B. Clark and James Q. Wilson, "Incentive Systems: A Theory of Organizations," *Administrative Science Quarterly* 6 (1961): 134–135.

8. Jack L. Walker, "The Origins and Maintenance of Interest Groups in America," *American Political Science Review* 77 (1983): 390–406.

9. Ibid., p. 406.

13-3

From Big Bird to Bill Gates

ORGANIZED INTERESTS AND
THE EMERGENCE OF HYPERPOLITICS

Allan J. Cigler and Burdett A. Loomis

The community of interest groups has undergone remarkable change in recent decades. Groups have proliferated, and many new groups have moved to Washington; single-issue groups have multiplied; and technological changes have altered the strategies of all groups. In the following essay, Allan Cigler and Burdett Loomis explore the implications of these changes for American national government and politics.

> It was a wonderful lesson in democracy. Here was "evil Newt" trying to kill Big Bird. There was a public outcry and we were inundated with calls from viewers. We told them if they cared about [cutting funds for public broadcasting], they should let their elected representatives know.
>
> —PAULA KERGER, WNET VICE PRESIDENT FOR GOVERNMENTAL RELATIONS

> [PBS] had a letter-writing campaign. They organized grass-roots lobbying.
>
> —LAWRENCE JARVIK, AUTHOR AND PBS CRITIC

IN 1995–1996, after gaining control of Congress, members of the new Republican majority set their sights on cutting all funds for television's Public Broadcasting Service (PBS), which they saw as representing both an inappropriate use of federal funds and a bastion of liberal thought. Given that federal spending on public broadcasting had been declining since the 1980s and that it could not lobby (at least formally) on its own behalf, PBS looked vulnerable, given the House Republicans' early success in 1995 in passing its Contract with America. But PBS did have an important, latent resource: the support of millions of individuals who watched public television, and

Excerpted from Allan J. Cigler and Burdett A. Loomis, eds. *Interest Group Politics*, 5th edition (Washington, D.C.: CQ Press, 1998), pp. 389–403. Some notes appearing in the original have been cut.

especially those whose children had grown up with *Sesame Street*'s endearing characters.

PBS and its member stations were prohibited from lobbying, yet they did find ways to mobilize their viewers and subscribers to communicate with their representatives in Congress. In that PBS supporters are widely distributed across the country and disproportionately well-educated, this group responded quickly and effectively to the congressional threats, as framed by PBS executives such as Paula Kerger of New York's WNET. Once the political conflict was defined in terms of increasingly unpopular Speaker Newt Gingrich (R-Ga.) against the always popular Big Bird, the battle was essentially over—and PBS survived, more or less intact. Indeed, in 1997 the Congress voted to appropriate $300 million for PBS in fiscal year 2000, an increase of $50 million above the 1999 spending level.

In 1988 Microsoft had no meaningful Washington presence, and Democrats controlled both houses of Congress. Ten years later Microsoft was discovered planning a huge (and surreptitious) public relations offensive to counter federal antitrust initiatives, to say nothing of burnishing the image of CEO Bill Gates. And Republicans were seeking to extend their four years of control on Capitol Hill, which might allow them to mount another attack on public broadcasting. Even more important than these major changes to the political landscape, however, has been the broad trend toward the politicization of almost all communication—ranging from television's *Ellen*'s conversion from a situation comedy to an advocacy program for gay rights to the exponential increase in Internet usage. . . .

In this [essay] we will broach the argument that interests—especially moneyed interests—increasingly have come to dominate political communication in the United States. Both on the electoral and policy-making sides of American politics, information is shaped by expensive campaigns that seek to dominate the discourse on the major issues of the day. This does not mean that traditional electoral politics is unimportant, nor that honored lobbying tactics of access and personal relationships are insignificant. Far from it. Still, in a post–Cold War, post–civil rights era, the absence of overarching societal issues (with abortion as something of an exception) means that interests will compete aggressively in selling their version of public policy problems and solutions—solutions that may, as with telecommunications reform, greatly enrich specific private groups.

Politics more than ever has become an offshoot of marketing. In such a context, most information is "interested." That is, the information reflects, sometimes subtley, sometimes not, the underlying views of the interests who sponsor and disseminate it. Even science becomes adversarial, because, it seems, every side on an issue can purchase a study to support its point of view. Indeed, the tobacco discourse of the late 1990s is noteworthy because the industry finally retreated from some of its most ludicrous "scientific" claims that denied the carcinogenic and addictive elements of smoking. Most lessons of the past thirty years have schooled interests to construct a coherent story line and stick to it, on policies ranging from teenage pregnancy to international trade. We will examine the changing roles of organized interests in electoral politics and policy making. . . .

Groups, Parties, and Campaigns: A Blurring of Roles

The long-standing relationship between political parties and interest groups in elections has changed in recent decades. Rather than aggregating various mass interests, parties have developed some of the policy-advocating characteristics typically associated with more narrow interests. At the same time parties have become less important to mobilizing voters and running campaigns. Although the vast majority of interest groups still refrain from direct electoral involvement, more and more of them have assumed some of the activities usually associated with parties, such as recruiting candidates, organizing campaigns, and running advertisements. In some tight races, interest group voices have even drowned out those of the candidates.

The decline of parties in elections represents a long-term trend that began around the turn of the century, but a series of party and campaign reforms in the early 1970s were responsible for drastically altering party–interest group relations in the electoral process. The party reforms broke the state and local organizational control over party business, including the nomination process, and thus created opportunities for organized interest influence. The campaign finance changes of the early 1970s also offered advantages to interest groups. The growth of political action committees (PACs), the limitations on party spending, and the requirements that the individual campaign organization be the legal agent of the candidate all had the effect of decreasing an already diminished party role in providing campaign resources to candidates.

The parties did adapt to the interest group threat. By the mid-1980s the national parties were increasingly becoming service vendors to party candidates, successfully coping with the realities of modern, candidate-centered campaigns. PAC–party relations became less conflictual and more cooperative. Both parties embraced their emerging role as brokers by forming loose fund-raising alliances with many PACs and beginning to offer them regular assistance in directing contributions to particular campaigns, as well as aiding candidates in soliciting funds from potential donor PACs. The fear of some that organized interests (through PACs) would supplant parties in the electoral process never materialized.

The 1990s have witnessed another benchmark in relations between parties and organized interests, one that may presage an even more prominent role for *both* parties and organized interests in the electoral process, perhaps at the expense of candidate domination of campaign agendas. . . . [T]he candidate-centered system that has characterized electoral politics for more than half a century may face its most serious challenge to date.

There are a number of prominent features of the emerging system. Foremost is the huge escalation of organized interest money found in our most recent elections, much of it raised and spent outside of the controlling provisions of the Federal Election Campaign Act (FECA). Although some of the growth has been in PAC and independent spending . . . the most startling development has come in extensive soft money contributions by organized interests to the national political parties—money creatively spent by the parties beyond FECA restrictions. These contributions, in some instances more than $1 million, do not typically come from interest groups per se but most notably from individual corporations. The rise in importance of soft money to the parties may increase organized interest leverage on individual campaigns, as well as on the parties. In 1996, for example, the major parties succeeded in raising $285 million in soft money, but this achievement rendered them highly dependent on large contributions from affluent interests.

The overall number of organized interests offering financial support has expanded as well, with many new groups entering the fray. For example, the American Cancer Society, a venerable nonprofit organization, recently contributed $30,000 to the Democratic and Republican parties in order to gain "the same access" as others, according to its national vice president for federal and state affairs, who said, "We wanted to look like players and be players."[1] Although this action is subject to a court challenge, the tax-exempt society sees such gifts as appropriate because the funds were targeted to party annual conferences and dinners, not campaign activity.

Beyond soft money contributions, the direct campaign efforts mustered by some organized interests in the mid-1990s were of historical proportions. Organized labor spent $35 million in 1996 to reverse the 1994 Democratic loss of Congress; some of these funds went to train union activists to organize targeted congressional districts and to increase voter registration, but the bulk of the funds went to buy air time for 27,000 television commercials in forty congressional districts—almost 800 spots per district. In 1996 the National Rifle Association became active in more than 10,000 political races at local, state, and national levels, despite running a deficit and cutting its staff.

Another distinguishing feature of the emerging system is the blurring of traditional party and interest group roles in campaigns. In 1996, for example, both national parties became *group patrons,* as they used some of their soft money to fund group electoral activity such as registration drives and telephone banks. Republicans contributed to a number of antitax and prolife groups, and Democrats channeled some of their funds to a variety of groups they believed would mobilize minority voters. In a very real sense, the parties were contracting out their voter mobilization function to various organized interests. Both parties, but the Republicans in particular, have also "created a dazzling galaxy of policy institutes, foundations and think tanks, each of which can raise money from private interests and which can aid the party and party candidates in a variety of ways."

A number of organized interests have been increasing the level of their activities in what traditionally has been thought of as party arena. As James Guth and his associates put it, "In an era when party organizations have either atrophied or find it difficult to activate sympathetic voters, religious interest groups are an important new force. . . . Such groups have become significant electoral competitors (and often adjuncts) to party committees, candidate organizations, and other traditional interest groups." Thus, in 1996 religious grassroots contacts of potential voters compared "quite favorably" with voters' contacts by party organizations, political candidates, and business or labor groups. More than 54 million voter guides were distributed using church-based networks in 1996. In a number of states, Christian Right adherents have captured the formal Republican Party organization, and one estimate counted roughly 200,000 movement activists as involved in the 1996 elections at various levels.

Although many of the efforts of organized labor and the Christian Right have been coordinated with party or candidate efforts (most often unofficially, so campaign finance laws would not be violated), a lot of interest group electoral activity in the 1990s has been independent of candidate or party efforts. It is difficult at times to discern which organized interests were involved, because expenditures and disclosure are not regulated by current campaign finance laws. For example, at least $150 million was spent on issue advocacy campaigns in 1996. As long as the ads did not advocate voting for or defeating a specific candidate, interests could express their issue-based concerns in a thinly veiled attempt to support or oppose a given candidate. Well-known groups such as the AFL-CIO, the Sierra Club, the National Education Association, the National Abortion Rights Action League, and the National Federation of Independent Businesses were especially prominent. Some entities operated in the shadows. Triad Management, a political consulting firm, apparently channeled at least $3 million from conservative donors to purchase television ads in support of competitive-seat Republican candidates. Approximately twenty-five groups sponsored $100 million in issue advocacy ads in 1996, and they concentrated their efforts in fifty-four competitive House and Senate races. In some cases the amount spent on issue advocacy in a race has exceeded that spent by the candidates, raising concerns that the candidates themselves had lost control over the discourse of the campaign. That is precisely the point for some interest group leaders. As Paul Jacob, executive director of U.S. Term Limits, observed, "If politicians get to control the campaign, these issues [such as term limits] won't be talked about."[2]

Existing campaign finance laws have lost much of their meaning, and prospects for meaningful change are remote. As a consequence, neither parties nor interest groups are much constrained in their fund-raising and spending behavior. Parties have more money than ever before and can be expected to expand their efforts as well. Court rulings now permit parties to engage in independent spending in the same manner as interest groups, and using soft money for issue advocacy advertisements is in vogue.

The meaning of all this for American representative democracy is unclear. In many ways party–interest group relations have been functionally altered, especially in that the party now has an enhanced electoral role as a fund-raiser. But in the process of becoming a vendor engaged in modern candidate-centered elections, the party has surrendered some of its traditional functions of grassroots activism and voter mobilization, which have been largely left to those organized interests with adequate resources to perform them.

National parties look suspiciously like special interests themselves, with their primary concern being to raise campaign resources for their parties' officeholders seeking reelection (the party of the incumbents), with little advice from party activists. When incumbents are threatened, both national parties may even cooperate with each other, as they did in 1987 in the face of a public outcry over congressional pay raises (the party chairs agreed not to offer financial support to challengers of those incumbents who had made the pay raise a campaign issue).

An electoral system based largely on the ability of parties and their candidates to raise funds from organized interests, especially through large contributions, inevitably clashes with the dominant notion of parties as representatives of mass interests and potential counterweights to the excessive demands of particular interests. Rather, the parties may well have become, as political scientist Thomas Ferguson has theorized, not much more than investment vehicles for wealthy interests who can choose to invest directly in candidates, or broadly in parties, or specifically in issue advocacy advertisements.

Interests, Information, and Policies:
Many Voices, Whose Tune?

If organized interests have changed their approaches to electoral politics, so too have they altered their strategies to affect governmental decisions. Although organized interests continue to lobby in time-honored ways within the corridors of Washington institutions, such as Congress and bureaucratic agencies, they have begun to spend more time shaping perceptions of problems and political agendas. In addition, they are devoting more and more attention to earlier stages of policy formulation, especially the fundamental defining and redefining of issues. Indeed, successfully defining conditions as problems (such as smog, learning disabilities, or global warming) often represents the single most important step in changing policies.

In the politics of problem definition, everyone can play by calling a press conference, releasing a study, going on a talk show, commissioning a poll, or buying an advertisement. There is no shortage in Washington either of well-defined problems or potential solutions, as the capital is awash in arguments and evidence that seek to define problems and set agendas. What is more difficult to understand very well is how certain definitions come to prevail within the context of political institutions that often, though not always, resist the consideration of new—or newly packaged—ideas.

As problem definition and agenda status become increasingly important elements of policy making, organized interests have stepped up their attempts to expand, restrict, or redirect conflict on given issues. The public interest and environmental movements of the 1960s often led the way in understanding these elements of political life, leaving business to catch up in the 1970s and 1980s. Jeffrey Berry, a long-time student of public interest groups, has concluded that citizen groups have driven the policy agenda since the 1960s, thus forcing business interests to respond to sets of issues developed by groups such as Common Cause and environmental organizations.[3]

Following on the heels of these agenda successes has been the institutionalization of interests within the government, especially when broad public concerns are at stake. For instance, many of the 1995 battles over the Contract with America placed legislators in sharp conflict with programs supported by members of government agencies, such as the Environmental Protection Agency. Moreover, many interests have found homes *within* the Congress in the form of caucuses composed of sitting legislators.

And there's the rub. *As more interests seek to define problems and push agenda items, more messages emanate from more sources.* For threatened interests, whether corporate, environmental, or professional, the decision to socialize a conflict (and to expand the attentive audience) has no meaning unless it can be accomplished. Even Ralph Nader, the past master of using the press to expand the scope of conflict, has recently found it difficult to attract media attention. Some interests can cut through the cacophony of voices; in particular, those in E. E. Schattschneider's "heavenly chorus" of affluent groups can—at a price—get their message across by spending lavishly on public relations campaigns or by buying advertising time and space. In addition, if such messages are directed toward legislators who have received substantial campaign contributions from these same interests, they typically reach an audience already inclined toward receptivity.

The emphasis on problem definition looms large when major public policy issues are on the table and tremendous uncertainty exists. Lots of substantive interests are in play, many competing scenarios are put forward, legislative decisions are always contingent, and public policy outcomes are often filled with unanticipated consequences. As cozy policy-making triangles have been replaced by loose, ill-defined policy communities, decision making under conditions of great uncertainty has become the rule, not the exception.

In policy battles, the capacity to obtain information and control its dissemination is the most important political power of all. Political scientist James Thurber echoes Schattschneider in arguing that if participants cannot resolve conflict on their own turf, "'outsiders' from other committees, agencies, bureaus, groups, the media, or the general public will take the issue away from them."[4] This scope-of-conflict perspective is extremely important to the dynamics of policy formulation, and it is also a source of the greatest type of uncertainty of all—conflict redefinition, as in changing a simple agricultural issue into a more complex environmental problem. The possibility of redefinition is exacerbated by the high stakes—often incredibly high—of policy decisions that may reshape entire sectors of the economy, such as health care and telecommunications. . . .

Although some corporate interests (such as Microsoft, until the 1990s) have resisted involvement in Washington politics, there has been a surge of activity since the late 1970s. As Jeffrey Birnbaum has observed, the growth of corporate (and trade association) lobbying makes good economic sense: "[Even] in relatively small changes to larger pieces of legislation . . . big money is made and lost. Careful *investment* in a Washington lobbyist can yield enormous returns in the form of taxes avoided or regulations curbed—an odd negative sort of calculation, but one that forms the basis of the economics of lobbying."[5]

The nature of high-stakes decisions makes such investment almost mandatory, given the potential for tremendous gains and losses. In addition, the usual cost-benefit logic that applies to most managerial decisions—lobbying extensively versus building a new plant or embarking on an ambitious new research project—does not apply in high-stakes circumstances, because the potential benefits or costs are so great that virtually any expenditure can be justified, even if its chance to affect the outcome is minuscule. Indeed, spending on a host of tactics—from election contributions to insider access to public relations campaigns—may represent a strategy designed as much to protect lobbyists from criticism by their corporate or trade associations as to influence a given decision.

It may be a mistake to make too much of a distinction between an organized interest spending money in investing in candidates through contributions and providing information to elected officials with lobbying, advertising, or public relations campaigns. Interests employ a wide array of tools in pressing for advantage. Nevertheless, information exchanges between interest groups and legislators are distinct from the seeking of influence through contributions or favors. One scholar, Jack Wright, has noted that interests

> achieve influence in the legislative process not by applying electoral or financial pressure, but by developing expertise about politics and policy and by strategically sharing this expertise with legislators through normal lobbying activities. . . . [Organized interests] can and do exercise substantial influence even without making campaign contributions and . . . contributions and other material gifts or favors are not the primary sources of interest group influence in the legislative process.[6]

Even if information, and not favors or contributions, reflects the basis for interest group influence, does that mean that money is unimportant? Or that all information is equal? Hardly. Inevitably, some interests have much greater resources to develop information that shapes policy debates. For this reason, a disproportionate share of the policy and political information that is collected reflects the views of well-heeled interests that subsidize think tanks, pay for surveys, and engage public relations firms.

Interests, Hyperpolitics, and the Permanent Campaign

At the turn of the twenty-first century, the outward appearance of the Washington lobbying community remains true to its manifestations in 1975 or 1985; the Gucci culture continues apace, with expensive suits and the constant buzz of the telephone call (cellular these days). In many ways, this appearance of stability is not deceptive at all. The big dogs of capital lobbying are still there—a Tommy Boggs or a Tom Korologos—trading on personal ties, political acuity, and the ability to raise a quick $10,000 (maybe even $100,000) with a word in the right ear at the right time. Favors are granted, favors are returned, and the quality of their political intelligence remains top flight.

At the same time, things are not the same. Some of the changes are obvious: the ability to create all varieties of grassroots pressure, a tactic raised to art form by Jack Bonner's firm;[7] the promise and uncertainty of the Internet (a recent survey reported that 97 percent of all legislative staff used the Internet to gather information); and the rash of policy-oriented television advertisements that have followed in the wake of the series of "Harry and Louise" commercials used in the health care debate. Moreover, the assault of issue-advocacy advertising in the 1996 congressional campaigns (in the wake of liberating court decisions that weakened restrictions on spending for such ads) may have ushered in an era of interest group–dominated electioneering. In addition, the entry of highly sophisticated information industry players into the political process (for example, Microsoft, a host of Silicon Valley firms, to say nothing of content providers such as Disney, which now owns ABC) may well lead to the politicization of many decisions over both the channels and the content of communication.

In general, we see three major trends taking shape and complementing each other. First, more interests are engaged in more kinds of behaviors to influence policy outcomes. Interests monitor more actions than they once did, and stand ready to swing into action more quickly when a red flag is raised (often by a lobbyist on retainer). Given the high stakes of governmental decisions, whether in a House committee or an EPA bureau, the monitoring–action combination is a worthwhile investment.

Second, there is little distinction, for most practical purposes, between "outside" and "inside" lobbying. Most effective influence relies on both. To be sure, a key provision can still find its way into a omnibus bill without a ripple, but battles over most major issues are fought simultaneously on multiple fronts. A call or fax from a House member's most important banker or editor or university president can be prompted by a lobbyist at the first sign of a problem in a committee hearing or, more likely, a casual conversation. Jack Bonner and a dozen other constituent-lobbying experts can construct a set of grassroots (or elite "grasstops") entreaties within a few days, if not a few hours. And a media buyer can target any sample of legislators for advertisements that run in their districts, thus ensuring that they know that their constituents and key Washington interests are watching their every action on an important bill.

Related to the diminished distinction between Washington and constituency-based lobbying is the increasing joint emphases on lobbying in state capitals and Washington. In particular, the tobacco settlement activity and the intensive campaigns of Microsoft to ward off antitrust actions in the states demonstrate how national and state politics are linked in an age of devolution. . . .

Third, and perhaps most dramatic, is the declining distinction between the politics of elections and the politics of policy making. Of course, in a democracy these are inextricably linked, and PACs may have solidified these ties since the 1970s. But these linkages have become much stronger—in many ways reflecting the "permanent campaign" of presidential elections–politics that emerged in the 1970s and 1980s. Blumenthal sees this as combining "image-making with strategic calculation. Under the permanent campaign government is turned into the perpetual campaign."[8] In the 1990s, many interests have come to see the combination of electoral and policy politics in much the same light, with the issue advocacy ads of 1996 serving as the initial demonstration of this new era. In addition, many interests are now viewing the "campaign" idea as one that defines their broader lobbying strategies and blurring the lines between electoral campaigns and public relations efforts.

All three of these trends—a move toward more activities, a lessened distinction between inside and outside lobbying, and the adoption of campaign-based strategies—come together in a 1998 business community initiative on international trade. Based on an initiative from the Commerce Department (and the tacit backing of a cautious White House), corporate advocates of free trade have embarked on a series of campaigns to argue publicly on behalf of free trade. As the *National Journal* reported, "The patrons of these pro-trade campaigns are typically multinational businesses, trade associations, lobbying groups and Washington think tanks, all called to action by Congress's declining support for . . . trade liberalization."[9] Responding to the growing strength of the much less well-funded loose coalition of labor, human rights, consumers, and environmental groups, the protrade interests, although not abandoning their insider initiatives, have reacted to their opponents' success in expanding the scope of the conflict over trade to issues such as domestic jobs, human rights, and environmental quality. Consider, for example, the actions of Cargill, the huge, privately held agriculture and financial services conglomerate. Historically, the firm has sought influence in the quiet ways, scarcely causing a ripple in public perceptions. But in 1998 the corporation sent 750 sets of videotapes, fact sheets, and sample speeches to its domestic plants and offices, so that its employees could make public pitches in community after community about the domestic impact of trade, especially in rural areas.[10]

At the same time, one thirty-year-old trade coalition (the less than aptly named Emergency Committee for American Trade) is sponsoring a campaign based on Cargill's efforts, while the Business Roundtable, another veteran group of top corporate leaders, "is spending a million dollars [in 1998] to shore up support of free trade in the districts of a dozen congressmen."[11] The Chamber of Commerce and the National Association of

Manufacturers have initiated similar efforts to offer their members information and analyses to buttress free trade arguments beyond the Beltway.

In addition, a host of think tanks, from the moderate Brookings Institution to the libertarian Cato Institute, have developed initiatives to provide higher quality information on the benefits of trade. On a related tack, the Washington-based Center for Strategic and International Studies has embarked on a pilot project in Tennessee to educate public officials, corporate leaders, academics, and students on the strategic importance of enhanced international trade.

The combination of many business organizations, the Commerce Department, a variety of think tanks, and congressional supporters illustrates the "campaign" nature of large-scale lobbying. The direction of influence is not clear, as business leaders respond to administration entreaties, but also hope to pressure the White House to support free trade aggressively. The lobbying is directed at community leaders and the public at large, but there is little capacity to measure its effectiveness. It does not seek, at least in 1998, to influence a particular piece of legislation. Rather, the campaign emphasizes an entire set of narratives on free trade that can be used by the executive branch, legislators, lobbyists, or grassroots advocates. . . .

Given such cacophony, coupled to high-stakes decisions, it is no wonder that those cultural icons Bill Gates and Big Bird have entered the political fray. Their respective interests, both economic and cultural, are great, and the costs of investing in lobbying, although substantial, pale before the potential benefits. But there is a cost to this extension of politics to much of our communication, what we choose to call *hyperpolitics*. If all information is seen as interested, as just one more story, then how do decision makers sort it all out? What voices cut through the "data smog" of a society that can cough up studies and stories at a moment's notice, and communicate them broadly or narrowly, as tactics suggest? Although some students of interest groups . . . see hopeful signs for a vigorous pluralism that accords major roles to consumers, public interest advocates, and environmentalists, we remain skeptical. The costs of lobbying in a hyperpolitics state are great, and the stakes are high. Money surely does not guarantee success, but the capacity to spend keeps well-heeled interests in the game, able to play the range of games that have come to define the politics of influence as we move further into the age of information.

NOTES

1. Jonathan D. Salant, "Cancer Group Gave to GOP, Democrats," *Kansas City Star,* March 30, 1998, A12.

2. Donna Cassata, "Independent Groups' Ads Increasingly Steer Campaigns," *CQ Weekly,* May 2, 1998, 1114.

3. Jeffery Berry, *The New Liberalism: The Rising Power of Citizen Groups* (Washington, D.C.: Brookings Institution, 1999).

4. James Thurber, *Divided Democracy* (Washington, D.C.: CQ Press), 336.

5. Jeffrey Birnbaum, *The Lobbyists* (New York: Times Books, 1993), 4, emphasis added.

6. John Wright, *Interest Groups and Congress* (Boston: Allyn and Bacon, 1996), 88.

7. Jack Bonner and his firm have changed the face of Washington lobbying to the extent that grassroots campaigns have become commonplace and available for purchase. More than most lobbyists, Bonner works to target grassroots efforts on key members of Congress.

8. Sidney Blumenthal, *The Permanent Campaign* (New York: Touchstone, 1982), 23.

9. Julie Kosterlitz, "Trade Crusade," *National Journal,* May 9, 1998, 1054. In addition to the specific citations noted here and later, the following paragraphs draw generally on this story.

10. Ibid., 1055.

11. Ibid.

13-4

The Money Culture

Elizabeth Drew

Money and politics, lobbying and campaign contributions, have long been intermingled in Washington politics. In the following essay Elizabeth Drew details the modern uses of money in lobbying and campaigns. Lobbying and contributing to campaigns, she finds, are still closely connected activities for interest groups. Organized interests and politicians have both responded to recent changes with remarkable inventiveness.

INDISPUTABLY, THE GREATEST change in Washington over the past twenty-five years—in its culture, in the way it does business, and the ever-burgeoning amount of business transactions that go on here—has been in the preoccupation with money.

Striving for and obtaining money has become the predominant activity—and not just in electoral politics—and its effects are pernicious. The culture of money dominates Washington as never before; money now rivals or even exceeds power as the preeminent goal. It affects the issues raised and their outcome; it has changed employment patterns in Washington; it has transformed politics; and it has subverted values. It has led good people to do things that are morally questionable, if not reprehensible. It has cut a deep gash, if not inflicted a mortal would, in the concept of public service.

Private interests have tried to influence legislative and administrative outcomes through the use of money for a long time. The great Daniel Webster was on retainer from the Bank of the United States and at the same time was one of its greatest defenders in the Congress. But never before in the modern age has political money played the pervasive role that it does now. By comparison, the Watergate period seems almost quaint.

Originally published in Elizabeth Drew, *The Corruption of American Politics: What Went Wrong and Why* (Secaucus, N.J.: Birch Lane Press, 1999), pp. 61–85. Reprinted by arrangement with Carol Publishing Group Inc.

THERE WAS A TIME when people came to Washington out of a spirit of public service and idealism. Engendering this spirit was one of John F. Kennedy's most important contributions. Then Richard Nixon, picking up from George Wallace, and then Ronald Reagan, in particular, derided "federal bureaucrats." The spirit of public service was stepped on, but not entirely extinguished.

But more than ever, Washington has become a place where people come or remain in order to benefit financially from their government service. (A similar thing could be said of journalists—and nonjournalists fresh out of government service—who package themselves as writers, television performers, and highly paid speakers at conventions.)

Probably not accidentally, the phenomenon of people cleaning up after, and from, government service also took on new proportions in the 1980s. (Several of Richard Nixon's alumni went to jail first.) The late Clark Clifford, the former Truman aide turned lawyer–wise man, minted money in his law office overlooking the White House. But Clifford was unusual for his time. Many of John F. Kennedy's alumni went on to—or back to—practicing law elsewhere, teaching, or doing philanthropic work. Jimmy Carter's alumni weren't in great demand. (Carter himself became an exemplary ex-President; unlike Gerald Ford and Ronald Reagan until he became too ill, Carter didn't use his former office to clean up, but continued his service in other ways.)

THERE USED TO BE a time when people joined presidential campaigns because they believed in the candidate. Now, an increasing number join campaigns with visions of the fame and fortune that might come their way afterward. The Reagan and Bush administrations produced several people who profited from their experience and contacts—but some of them, such as former Secretary of State James Baker, were wealthy before, and Baker probably would have flourished anyway.

Since his government service, Baker has done well as a partner in the Carlyle Group, a highly successful venture capital firm based in Washington (and which has attracted a number of former high administration officials), as a member of corporate boards, and as an attorney at his family's prosperous Houston firm. An institute at Rice University has been named after him. Like Henry Kissinger, Baker can open the door of international potentates for his clients and partners, and he also conducts business with these noteworthies. He specializes in Middle Eastern and Central Asian countries—for example, Kuwait and Azerbaijan—with which he built strong relationships as a result of the Gulf War.

Having worked for the Clinton White House, however, hasn't necessarily turned out to be particularly lucrative. An exception, of course, is the case of George Stephanopoulos, who became a famous public figure and a national heartthrob while he was still serving Clinton. When he left, he got a nearly $3 million book deal, plus a prominent television perch at ABC, plus a lot of well-paid public speaking engagements. But, in general, Clinton White House aides were not in great demand, and several spent a lot of time trying to arrange their postservice "packages." (People in this category do not take jobs so much as they put together packages.)

IN 1998, according to the requirements of the Lobbying Disclosure Act of 1995, there were close to 11,500 lobbyists wandering the halls of Congress. (Until the act went into effect, there were no real figures on how many lobbyists populated Washington.) However, this number isn't inclusive. A lot of people say they don't lobby—but they do something that seems a lot like it. Megafixer Clark Clifford solemnly maintained that he didn't lobby. Superlawyer Robert Strauss made the same claim. Perhaps these eminences were above betaking themselves to Capitol Hill to navigate the marble floors or to wait outside the Senate or House chamber, or a committee room, with the riffraff, hoping to nab a target, but they knew the power of their names and their phone calls and their social connections. And they could always send minions to do their bidding with the lawmakers or important staff members, who know who sent them.

In the past, law firms didn't engage in lobbying to the extent they do now, and sometimes the firms hired nonlawyers to do their influencing. And now there are small firms established for the purpose of lobbying just one member, or one Congressional committee; they're usually staffed by people who had been close to the member, in one case by a powerful congressman's reputed mistress.

MORE THAN EVER, corporations or other interests that want to influence the Congress hire former Members of Congress or their aides as lobbyists, in order to ingratiate themselves with the current members. The former members have distinct advantages: they can go on the floor of the House or Senate and use their chambers' official dining rooms; even better, former House members can use the House gym, where a lot of business gets done.

(A study by the *New York Times* found that in the 1970s only three percent of members who left Congress for one reason or another went to K Street—the downtown corridor that has come to symbolize the lawyer-lobbyist complex—and in the nineties twenty-three percent did so.)

The Buying of the Congress, a book by Charles Lewis of the Center for Public Integrity, published in 1998, said that from 1991 to 1996 at least fifteen percent of former Senate aides and at least fourteen percent of former senior House aides became registered lobbyists. The main sources of this pool of access-sharks were the "money committees," such as the House and Senate Commerce Committees, which handle such issues as banking and telecommunications. Sometimes the former aides so draw on their expertise and are so drawn into the legislative considerations that they in effect still act as staff members, writing legislation, except for a lot more money.

Sometimes a geographic region is spotted as an opportunity. In recent years, Latin America—with a growing economy, increased privatization, need for expensive "infrastructure" projects, and increased demand for U.S. goods (the second-largest market after Canada)—has become more and more attractive to Washington's lawyers and lobbyists. According to the *National Journal,* in the spring of 1998 former Clinton National Security Advisor Anthony Lake, who had supposedly returned to an academic life, and a former Commerce Department official, David Rothkopf, who had specialized in "emerging markets," formed their own consulting firm, which charged clients at least $250,000 a year for "strategic and political advice about investments in Latin America."

According to the same article, a Washington law firm, Verner, Liipfert, Bernhard, McPherson, and Hand, has fielded three of its former political stars—Bob Dole, Lloyd Bentsen, and Ann Richards—to drum up business in Latin America. So a former presidential candidate, a former vice-presidential candidate, and a former governor became, without apparent embarrassment, hustlers exploiting a new target of opportunity.

ANN WEXLER, one of Washington's premier lobbyists, knows a lot about how Washington has changed in the past twenty-five years. One day in the fall of 1997 she talked to me over lunch about how the new role of money has transformed Washington. Wexler, sixtyish, has short-cropped dark hair, brown eyes, and more energy than most people, in part because she enjoys life as well as the game. She has prospered as the head of her own firm, which she started the day after she left the Carter White House in January

1981. In 1983 she was astute enough to acquire as her partner Nancy Reynolds, who had worked for Ronald Reagan for ten years.

When she left the White House, Wexler, who had been in charge of "outreach"—working with outside groups in support of Carter's objectives—took with her what was believed to be the biggest Rolodex in town. She now has twenty-five lobbyists working with her, and in 1997 recruited as president former Representative Bob Walker, who had just retired from Congress and was one of Newt Gingrich's closest associates.

"This whole thing blew apart in the eighties, when congressmen could raise all this money," Wexler told me. "Before, they'd attend twenty-five-dollar barbecues."

"It was the development of PACs in the eighties—when people figured out that if they gave money through the PACs they could get access, they could get their phone calls returned. Just as the unions used dues for political activity, businesses began to use salary deductions for PACs. [Wexler's firm, like similar lobbying and law firms around town, has its own PAC.] The Hill figured it out. If you're a committee chairman, you could raise fifty thousand, even one hundred thousand dollars. Then they started leadership PACs—that's another extortion. Then the leader uses the money to try to gain higher office."

Under this last innovation, congressional leaders and would-be leaders and powerful committee chairmen created their own PACs, which they used to dole out money to win gratitude and advancement within their chamber—and to maintain power. Recent examples are former Senate Majority Leader George Mitchell and House Majority Whip Tom DeLay. DeLay's bestowing of campaign funds—especially on the class of 1994—helped him win his leadership post in 1995, and to maintain it.

One of the first things then–House Appropriations Committee chairman Bob Livingston, of Louisiana, did when he decided in the spring of 1998 that he would like to succeed Gingrich as Speaker was to establish his own PAC (B.O.B.S.PAC, for "building our bases"). As Appropriations chairman, Livingston was in a position to raise a great deal of money, and he did. Livingston contributed to over ninety Republican House candidates: $5,000 from his PAC, $1,000 from his own campaign funds (he usually ran for Congress virtually unopposed), and served as a conduit for earmarked checks from business PACs to Republican candidates.

Rivals within the same party for a higher leadership post compete to be the more beneficent. In 1998, Republican leaders raised a great deal more money than their Democratic counterparts did; they were the ones in power. Over the two-year election cycle, Republican leaders raised more than nineteen million dollars for fifty leadership PACs, while Democratic leaders raised a mere $328,000.

Wexler said, "We're dealing with a system where the members don't feel they can raise the money where they live. There's a panic among members. I get calls for money from people I've never heard of. The system's out of control."

THE ISSUE BEFORE the Senate in the spring of 1998 was a freighted one, a matter of historical importance. The question was whether to expand NATO, the North Atlantic Treaty Organization, founded after the Second World War to provide stability in Europe, which it had done successfully. The proposition was to include Poland, Hungary, and the Czech Republic, with other countries in Central Europe and the Baltics to follow in 2010.

There were strong reasons not to do so. Russia, whose cooperation the United States needed in all sorts of spheres (Bosnia, Kosovo, Iraq, and arms control, among others), and whose own stability was very much in the interest of the U.S., was vehemently against it. Russia saw a threat on its borders, and an insult. Moreover, by expanding NATO the original members became committed to the defense of countries or areas whose defense might lack public support. A successful alliance was in danger of being destabilized.

"We'll be back on a hair-trigger," said Senator Daniel Patrick Moynihan, who usually saw further than most of his colleagues. *New York Times* foreign affairs columnist Thomas L. Friedman in 1997 called the expansion "the Whitewater of the Clinton foreign policy."

By the time the matter reached the Senate floor in late April 1998, the Clinton Administration had so committed the United States to the new policy that to turn back would have been an embarrassing retreat—in the eyes of the country and our allies. The three countries had already been formally invited to join NATO. The administration had rushed into the policy without thinking it through—in large part to head off certain ethnic-American voting blocs from going to the Republicans, in particular to Bob Dole, who was espousing the expansion.

In turn, the administration used these groups to drum up support in the Senate for the expansion.

But there was another force behind the approval of NATO expansion: defense contractors. The enlarging of NATO promised a lucrative new market, a welcome boon after business had fallen off with the end of the cold war. Even the Contract with America, the Republican agenda presented by Newt Gingrich and others after they took over the House in the 1994 election, called for NATO expansion and encouraged greater "interoperability of military equipment." Translated, that meant that the new NATO members would have to buy sophisticated weapons from American defense companies. But since these countries couldn't afford them, according to Lars-Erik Nelson in the New York *Daily News,* the Pentagon had established a $15 billion fund to guarantee loans to these countries to buy the weapons.

According to a March 30, 1998, article in the *New York Times,* by Katharine Q. Seelye, a study done for the *Times* found that the six largest military contractors had spent $51 million on lobbying fees—which included not only the salaries of in-house lobbyists but also fees for others from outside the firms—from 1996 to the end of 1997. In that period, the six companies also expanded their contributions to congressional campaign committees. The defense industry was in fact the most generous contributor to the congressional campaigns, the *Times* said, having lavished $32.3 million on them since the collapse of communism in 1991.

Not all of the lobbying was for NATO expansion, of course, but that was the industry's main concern in those years, because of the lucrative new markets. If donations by computer and technology firms that do military work were added, the *Times* said, the total would "dwarf the lobbyist effort of any other industry."

The chief lobbying group on behalf of NATO expansion was the U.S. Committee to Expand NATO, whose president, Bruce L. Jackson, was also director of strategic planning for Lockheed Martin. The *Times* also said that arms manufacturers gave support to the ethnic groups who backed NATO membership for their native countries.

The Senate approved the expansion on April 30 overwhelmingly—by a vote of 80–19—after a few hours of debate spread over four days.

A GREAT DEAL more attention has been paid to the effects of the system on the politicians who raise money than on those who are asked for it. But some will talk about what befalls a contributor, or a potential one.

Nick Calio, the Republican lobbyist, who has some very large corporate clients, says that the rate of being hit up for money by Members of Congress has "increased significantly every year."

"Every request breeds another request," he adds. "If you show that you can produce, then you become a reservoir, and people come to dip in. And if you show any capacity to raise soft money and a crunch comes they come right back to you, because you've shown you can do it. And it gets difficult because you go back to the same people over and over again—your clients. And some people don't want to hear about it. They dive for cover when you call."

"Look at the list of Texas politicians," a former Republican Member of Congress said. "Texas has a long tradition of gaining power through using financial resources." He added that Dick Armey, the House Majority Leader, from Irving, Texas, as well as Tom DeLay, from Sugarland, Texas, just outside of Houston, "have used money to gain power." At the same time, another Texan, Bill Archer, of Houston, Texas, was chairman of the Ways and Means Committee, one of the most powerful committees in the House. The tradition of Texas leaders dispensing funds goes back to at least the late fifties, when Lyndon Johnson, of Texas, and Sam Rayburn, of Texas, ruled the Senate and the House respectively.

After the Republicans retook the House in 1994, DeLay became famous for keeping a list of contributors to the Republicans and refusing to grant audiences to anyone who hadn't forked over. He also tried to change what he saw—not inaccurately, given the forty-year Democratic domination of the House—as the Democratic-leaning culture of the lawyer-lobbyist community by refusing to see lobbyists who hadn't added Republicans to their firms after the Republican takeover. DeLay called this his "K Street Strategy."

In the fall of 1998, House Republican leaders, DeLay especially, brazenly objected to the naming, by the Electronic Industries Alliance, a major trade association, of a former Democratic congressman, David McCurdy, a moderate, as its president. A prominent soon-to-be-former Republican congressman, Bill Paxon, wanted the job. The association's board went ahead and named McCurdy to the post anyway. Gingrich, Armey, and DeLay ordered their staffs not to communicate with the association. Paxon was hired by the powerful law firm Akin, Gump, Strauss, Hauer & Feld, where he would join such eminent Democrats as Robert Strauss and Vernon Jordan.

In October of 1998, Representative John Linder, then chairman of the National Republican Congressional Committee, the political arm of the House Republicans, confirmed to *Roll Call*, a Capitol Hill newspaper, that the Republican leadership was blocking legislation of interest to the electronics association. The leaders were also spreading the word on K Street, he said, so that others would get the picture. Linder also said that he had told the National Association of Home Builders, one of the biggest and most powerful lobbying groups, that the Republican leaders would be less interested in working with them because they had hired a Democrat to run their organization.

MEMBERS OF CONGRESS—and the lobbyists who aim to please them—have come up with the relatively recent innovation of persuading people to donate money for university professorial chairs in their name when they retire.

I first heard of this a couple of years ago from the "Washington representative"—that is, lobbyist—for a major defense contractor, who was complaining about it to some of his counterparts. I later called him to ask how this gambit worked.

"Oh, man," he replied, "the bane of our existence." But first he started talking about another annoyance—the leadership PACs. He said, "One of the banes right now is the explosion of leadership PACs, in which leaders feel they have to curry favor with other members by giving them money. Now, even younger members feel that to get ahead they have to create a fund to butter up their own colleagues—especially if they don't have a tough reelection race—so that if there's a race for the leadership position or a committee chairmanship then you have chits you can call in. I can tell you that most industry PACs, like the one we have here, don't mind giving to members. It's money we've solicited from our employees and it's managed by the company's PAC board. We look at their records and see if we want to give to an incumbent. If it's someone we don't favor because of his voting record, we will go out and invite someone else to run." He said that the representatives of several military contractors, and some other corporate representatives as well ("we're all pretty close"), will get together to recruit a candidate.

"So there is this regular drumbeat for PAC money for people who are running, the drumbeat for leadership PACs, and then there's the drumbeat of the parties for soft money. Soft money is a bottomless pit. Each party has an entry fee [for attending their special events], usually fifteen thousand dollars. So we tend to throw fifteen thousand in the DNC pot, and the same for the RNC, and for the four party congressional committees—the Republican and Democratic House and Senate campaign committees. Usually, the money's for a dinner, so we probably contribute for six dinners. We tend to give a hundred thousand in soft money, and we get beat up as a poor contributor."

Then he turned to the subject of the chairs. "Now we're finding that not only do we support some members throughout their entire public life as long as they're helpful to us, but the year they retire there's a flurry of activity. It's now typical that when a member retires, the member thinks it's wonderful to have a chair endowed in his name at a university in his state. It's a big money deal, and we're usually very easy. Senior members who retire almost always get a university chair. It amounts to buying a table for a dinner for ten, fifteen, twenty thousand dollars—or they may ask for a hundred thousand or even a million. There's no limit. This is a charitable contribution to a university to endow a chair." (Therefore, it's tax deductible.)

He told me that a chair had been endowed for Sam Nunn, the former chairman of the Senate Armed Services Committee, at Emory University after he retired from the Senate in 1996. And he was expecting to be asked to contribute in the fall of 1998 when Strom Thurmond, age ninety-five, was to retire as chairman of the Senate Armed Services Committee. "Every company will be expected to throw in fifty to a hundred thousand dollars." Some chairs are dedicated by the lobbyists to a Member of Congress while he is still serving.

I asked the defense lobbyist what the point was of trying to please a member who was retiring. There were two reasons for doing so, he said. The first was—and this would be particularly applicable to defense contractors—it spreads goodwill in the state. "The bigger the company's presence in the state, the higher the contribution," he explained. "Second, it's another excuse to have a dinner where you can go elbow-to-elbow with a Member of Congress. We all do it."

Even if the member is going to retire?

"They have tons of their colleagues there, and it's a warm and fuzzy dinner."

The gift bans, or limits, enacted in recent years, including a limit on the price of meals that can be accepted, have driven lobbyists and members to find other avenues for purposeful socializing. So, besides the retirement dinners, special projects provide a means to please members of Congress and to spend a lobbyist's idea of "quality time" with them.

In 1995, Senator Daniel Inouye, the ranking Democrat on the Defense Appropriations Subcommittee, got the idea that the battleship U.S.S. *Missouri* should be towed from its mooring in Bremerton, Washington, to Pearl Harbor, in his home state of Hawaii, to be used as a memorial of the Japanese attack in 1941.

The defense-contractor lobbyist said, "There's a push within the industry to contribute funds to establish the *Missouri* as a memorial for visitors to the Pearl Harbor area. He [Inouye] gets folks to call the companies and ask for contributions to the memorial, and he gets great credit in the state. We also contribute to military museums in the states, and monuments and commemoratives."

And then there are the charitable dinners. "If you look at the dance cards around town," he told me, "there's the leukemia fund or the heart fund that members or members' wives have become associated with. You give for the dinner. It's a 501(c)(3) [tax deductible]. The charitable dinners become a way to spend time with a member.

"We spend several millions of dollars a year on contributions that aren't political."

Not precisely.

BUT OF LATE the interests and their favorite lawmakers—at least the most powerful ones—haven't waited for retirement to set up and contribute to a chair or, better yet, an "institute" in the politician's name. Thus, corporations can also curry favor with the politician by donating to a chair or institute while the politician is still in his prime.

Early in 1999 such an institute was being established in the name of Trent Lott at the University of Mississippi, his alma mater. Currying favor with the Senate majority leader through (tax-deductible) donations is obviously a good investment. The majority leader schedules legislation, appoints people to sensitive commissions, leans on committee chairmen to push certain bills—and this is just some of his power.

Among those who pledged large donations to the Trent Lott Leadership Institute were MCI WorldCom, a large telecommunications empire, which, under the law, could make direct donations to any federal politician of only $10,000 in PAC money. And MCI had a lot of concerns about congressional policymaking on telecommunications issues. Lott, for his part, appointed an MCI representative to a commission studying whether the Internet should be taxed. The plan was that major donors would have rooms named after them in the new building.

According to Congressional Quarterly, a similar institute had been established in the name of Jesse Helms, the North Carolina Republican and vengeful chairman of the Senate Foreign Relations Committee. Happily for Helms and Wingate College, his alma mater, foreign funds—supposedly illegal in American elections—could be donated to this enterprise. According to Congressional Quarterly, among those foreign governments that had contributed were Taiwan ($225,000) and Kuwait ($100,000).

And the University of Louisville has established the McConnell Center for the Study of Leadership, and a chair named the "McConnell Chair in Leadership," for the Kentucky Senator and ardent foe of reforming the campaign finance system. The university declines to reveal the donors.

Via such worthy-sounding and ego-enhancing projects, the possibilities for the politicians shaking down access- and favor-seekers, as well as corporations and foreign governments seeking access or favors, are substantial.

ANOTHER HIGHLY successful Washington lobbyist said, "One of the things that is amazing to me is the charities." Senators' wives, he said, "have wonderful charities. I mean, great, heart-tugging charities."

"When Senator So-and-so's wife calls your office and puts her arm around your neck about this wonderful charity and a black-tie event in the Mayflower Hotel ballroom, you get the drift. It's tables, not tickets, ten thousand to fifteen thousand a table. If you want to be a platinum donor, or an underwriter of the dinner, you give twenty-five thousand. You give a hundred thousand and you might get to sit next to the senator."

I asked about the benefits to the lobbyists of all this.

The lobbyist replied, "The senator probably feels he's done good works, and you give the money because, one, you want to be looked on favorably by the senator's wife and, two, it's part of the game around town called 'buying access.'"

VICE PRESIDENT Al Gore established a fund for a chair at the University of Tennessee in the name of his late sister, Nancy. In its early years, the fundraising for the chair was run by Peter Knight, Gore's chief fund-raiser in 1992, campaign manager in 1996, and in between and since a prosperous lawyer-lobbyist, and a major fund-raiser for Gore's campaign for the presidential election in 2000. After controversy inevitably arose over Knight's role in raising money for the chair, the fund-raising was taken over by the University of Tennessee.

A FORMER DEMOCRATIC congressman, a man still in his forties, had joined one of Washington's largest law firms. Over lunch in March 1997, he said, "Two things have changed so dramatically in the last dozen years: the severity of this town and the money chase. It goes together. All the races are about ethics—the other guy's ethics. They weren't like that before—going through people's financial records. Campaigns changed from the mid-eighties on—the harsher the better."

In his current position at a well-heeled law firm, the former congressman said, "I get an average of two calls a day" from candidates seeking money. "Our own PAC is one of the largest in the country—it's just huge. We're in play. We're popular. The CEO of our biggest client called the managing partner of the firm the other day, and we sent over fifteen thousand for a table at a Republican dinner. The money flow in the last half-dozen years is so much greater than it had been."

THE FORM OF LOBBYING has shifted in the last few years. The definitions have become more vague. People who call themselves consultants say they do not lobby. But they can make a ton of money planning strategies for influencing Congress, which usually involves P.R. of some sort: ad campaigns, press conferences. Consultants are hired by companies and trade associations to offer what is generally called "strategic advice." A person who would seem to be a lobbyist told me that he very rarely goes to Capitol Hill. "It depends on how you position yourself," he said. "Now it's more a matter of assessing the situation; we can't operate without a strategy." There are now so many consultants in Washington that a couple of years ago a friend of mine, himself a consultant, was hired by a large corporation to sort out its numerous consultants.

A man who was flourishing in the consulting business in Washington told me in 1998, "You see more and more people getting into the business and you think it's very competitive. But it's not. There's so much business. There are a lot of companies who have representation in Washington today who didn't have it before. Microsoft had no one until 1995; now it has about sixty [representatives]. Even if other companies' increases in consultants aren't as dramatic as Microsoft's, there's a long list of them."

THE FUND-RAISERS that take place on Capitol Hill virtually every night that Congress is in session—usually a half dozen a night—are commonplace, but there are of late new, more ingenious mechanisms for raising and donating money.

The Capitol Hill fund-raisers have the benefit of convenience, of course. They're held close enough to the Capitol itself that members can rush across the street and down two or three blocks to the Capitol Hill Club (for the Republicans) and the National Democratic Club (for the Democrats) between votes. Many of the fund-raisers for individual members of Congress are sponsored by interest groups.

On September 9, 1998, there was an Insurance Industry Meet and Greet for candidate Greg Walden, a challenger for a congressional seat in Oregon; it was held at La Colline, an elegant French restaurant near Capitol Hill. On September 16, there was Congressman Dan Miller's Florida Citrus Breakfast (cost, $500) at Miller's home on Capitol Hill. On September 17, there was a Cigar and Wine Tasting Reception for candidate Mark Nielson, a Republican challenger from Connecticut, hosted by the Associated Builders and Contractors (cost $1,000 for a PAC and $500 for an individual). On September 22, the American Trucking Association held a reception for Representative John Peterson, a Pennsylvania Republican. Actually, in September, the Trucking Association sponsored three fund-raisers for Republicans and one for a Democrat.

On the whole, few fund-raisers for Democrats were sponsored by interest groups. The Republicans controlled the Congress, after all. Yet Democrats nearly kept up with the Republicans in the number of fund-raising events that September: thirty-seven for the Republicans and thirty for the Democrats.

Thomas Boggs's law firm, Patton Boggs, occupies an entire nine-story building on M Street, N.W.—prime real estate. Boggs's office, on the top floor, opens onto a large balcony and has a splendid view of Washington west to Georgetown. Two things about Boggs's office caught my attention: the expensive paintings and the large stack of pink phone slips on his desk. Boggs, indisputably one of Washington's top superlawyer-lobbyists, is large, heavyset, with a round, pinkish face, blue eyes, dark wavy hair, and a look of prosperity, down to his Gucci loafers. When we spoke in the summer of 1998 about fund-raisers, Boggs said, "I go to a bunch of them."

Why?

"Just to show up and say, 'I like you. You're a good guy.' And to network. That's far more important. If a tax bill is being written up, people there will know what's in the tax bill. It doesn't matter so much who is the member the fund-raiser is for, but he's the catalyst for getting us there."

Boggs laughingly explained, "The best time for a member to hold a fund-raiser is right after a recess, because nobody has seen anybody. September is a big month, it's like going back to school."

Boggs's firm itself holds a host of fund-raisers. Another lobbyist says, "They must have events every single day. I get a half-dozen invitations a month from them." Boggs laughed and said, "He's probably right."

But methods of fund-raising have taken new forms in recent years. People in lobbying firms also raise money for Members of Congress by conveniently bringing together in intimate groups the member who is being helped (with money) and the client who wants help from him. Some Members of Congress hire their own professional fund-raisers, who work from computerized lists. Some lobbying firms even put themselves on contract to raise money for a Member of Congress.

"It's a little bit shady," one lobbyist said. "They're in effect working for that member and for their client."

Patrick Griffin, who headed the Clinton White House congressional liaison office from January 1994 until February 1996, and then returned to the lobbying firm he had started in 1987, told me that he doesn't go to the fund-raisers on the Hill, because he doesn't have to.

"I just send the money," he said, and he laid out his own approach to fund-raising. "I have fund-raisers all the time—sometimes jointly with somebody. I'll have a lunch for a member where I can raise ten thousand dollars. I'll have ten, fifteen people at most. You bring in your client. That's more effective than the big gang-bang." It's a more convenient way to discuss business.

Griffin continued, "Some interests don't have enough money to contribute to everyone they're interested in, so they might contribute to the party committees, who then invite them on a golfing or skiing weekend, where a number of members might be present. People see you around, and you get quality time with the members."

THE POPULAR CONCEPTION is that money is exchanged for a vote, but while that no doubt happens sometimes, there are subtler ways by which a Member of Congress can attract—and help—donors. "All we really expect is access," one lobbyist said to me. He was playing it down a bit, but access is the gate to influence. And there is much to try to affect besides actual votes in the Congress. Regulations by government agencies, over which Members of Congress can have powerful influence, can be just as important. An affected industry may be struggling to head off the promulgation of a new rule, and it might seek legislation, or other forms of pressure, that would prevent it. A lobbyist gave me a not-so-hypothetical example: a senator who has historically been for side A might agree to be helpful to side B—"because he doesn't want to completely alienate them and he might even get their support"—by asking the agency for a study before the rule is issued. This gives side B time to carry on its campaign.

"Does the money then come in from side B?" I asked.

"That's why he does it," the lobbyist replied.

This lobbyist said, "A lot of it isn't visible. Members can be responsive to lobbyists' needs without having to support their legislation in the end. A member can make a client or company happy by looking like he's trying—making a phone call to an agency, asking a question at a hearing, writing a letter. You might try to find a way to neutralize someone.

"The point is," the lobbyist continued, "money isn't all about votes. There are a lot of ways to make people happy. The sophisticated lobbyist and the sophisticated member understand that."

LATELY, INDIRECT WAYS of using money to influence a Member of Congress have come into vogue. A lobbyist for very big interests told me, "What does a savvy lobbyist do? He remembers that the most important thing for a Member of Congress is to get reelected." So the lobbyist would point out the "back-home reason" for a member to vote a certain way. To reinforce the "back-home" argument, lobbyists have created grass-roots support, or the appearance of it, for the corporation's or industry's position.

This approach, pioneered by the lobbyist Ann Wexler, has spawned another new industry in Washington: whole companies whose sole reason for being is to stir up grass-roots support for their client's position. Professional political operatives are hired to mobilize the local citizenry around an issue—economic, environmental—that affects, directly or indirectly, the client's business. Such groups are often organized to counter environmentalists who are objecting to a new plant or supporting a certain regulation.

The people, organized from outside, are encouraged to call on their representative in Washington or in his home district; to write letters, send faxes, make phone calls, organize town meetings, get someone in the area to write a letter to the editor, or even an op-ed piece—all to create the illusion of "grass-roots support." Even the National Association of Broadcasters, which ostensibly represents local stations but is dominated by the networks and their owned-and-operated stations, has retained a Washington company specializing in "grass roots."

But despite the importance of this relatively new form of influence/pressure, another lobbyist told me, it has to be paired with money. Pat Griffin said, "You can do money alone, but it helps to have grass-roots support. You can have money without grass roots, but not the other way around."

Of course, organizing and executing a campaign is expensive in itself. So these "grass roots" efforts, sown and nurtured from Washington, are another, indirect, and sometimes deceptive, way for interests to spend money to further their agenda.

As the "grass roots" method became widely used, a still newer approach was added, as was a new term in the lobbyists' liturgy, "grass tops."

"Grass tops" are the opinion-makers in a town or an area who are called on to help the cause of a lobbyist or local company. A lobbyist said, "Sometimes they have to be induced, and sometimes they're paid—that's not uncommon." These "grass roots" and "grass tops" efforts, in which Washington pros stir up, and even pay, people who might not be motivated to take action on their own are sometimes referred to by the more honest—or cynical—lobbyists as "Astroturf."

A lobbyist explained, "New techniques get invented as old ones get discounted."

GIVEN ITS COMBINED money and power and ability to create ostensible grass-roots activity, the broadcast industry has become, in the words of Senator John McCain, "the most powerful industry in Washington." The broadcasters have been able to resist McCain's efforts to get them to provide free airtime for political campaigns or to pay anything at all for their ultravaluable use of the traditional broadcast spectrum, making the United States one of the few countries that gives away the broadcast spectrum—a public asset—for nothing. (Parts of the spectrum for more specialized uses, such as cell phones and paging systems, are now auctioned off in order to bring in government revenue.) The broadcasters have also been able to fend off any serious impositions on the money they make off political advertising—even though they are required to offer such advertising at a reduced fee.

SOMETIMES THE ISSUE giving rise to a "grass roots" effort is largely manufactured. In one instance in the mid-nineties, involving state regulation of securities, a lobbyist who was involved said, "A campaign was manufactured on an issue that wasn't fully drawn, but the lobbying campaign forced it to be drawn. It had all the elements of the most sophisticated campaigns. The industry was willing to put aside fifteen to twenty million for it. This was an example of a completely manufactured crisis and solution."

He continued, "Sometimes you're trying to convince the Congress that there's a groundswell, but there's nobody behind it. If you have to make it up, you hope you don't get found out. It's like the Wizard of Oz—there's nobody there but you and the smoke and the whistle."

FROM TIME TO TIME, to the delight of "downtown" Washington, there's a big legislative fight that engages armies of lobbyists and consultants on both sides. For them, such titanic clashes are heaven-sent.

The Telecommunications Competition and Deregulation Act of 1995 was a classic. The purpose of the legislation, which was backed by Speaker Gingrich and by Vice President Gore, was to open up the telecommunications industry to competition. It would affect the general public a great deal because it dealt with how we are entertained, how we get news, how we're educated, how we communicate with each other. But those, of course, were not the questions that Congress was addressing.

Al Sykes, who was chairman of the Federal Communications Commission during the Bush Administration and is now president of Hearst News Media and Technology, said, "The issues became company versus company or industry versus industry, where in the final analysis there should be only one constituency—the public."

The fight unleashed vast amounts of money in contributions to the Members of Congress. It was also a vehicle for raising a great deal of soft money for both national parties, for all four congressional campaign committees (Republican and Democratic House and Senate), and for the state parties at the direction of the national parties. In the 1995–96 election cycle, during which numerous telecommunications issues were still being considered, the telecommunications industry gave three times as much soft money as it had in the previous election cycle. "Darling," said one lobbyist who was involved, "no other issue created more soft money."

The telecommunications fight pitted competing economic interests— long-distance telephone (MCI, AT&T, Sprint, GTE) against regional Bells, cable, Hollywood, broadcasters (large vs. small)—as they fought over the spoils. The interest that was hardly heard in the struggle was the public's.

A former telecommunications official said, "When the Congress gets into specific industry legislation, most members don't know much about it, and neither does the public, so members are much more pushed and pulled by the lobbying campaign. Look at members of the Communications sub-committees; they get large amounts of money from their local carrier, and a long-distance carrier, and a competitive carrier, and the cellular business. That works in favor of nobody doing anything because members don't want to 'work against our friends,' or you get a hodgepodge, butchered legislation. The 1995 act was butchered legislation."

Members of Congress have for the past couple of decades openly referred to the committees that handle telecommunications issues—the House and Senate Commerce Committees—as "lucrative" committees on which to serve, right up there with the tax-writing House Ways and Means and Senate Finance committees.

The selling point of the telecommunications bill was that it would "benefit the consumer" by creating more competition, and thus the market would lower prices. But so far the result has been mergers more than additional competition, and there's been no significant reduction of prices.

Senator McCain told me that he had opposed the telecommunications bill. "I thought it wasn't deregulatory, it was regulatory. Everyone from the Vice President to the congressional leaders said it was the greatest thing to happen to consumers. The result? Phone rates have gone up. Cable rates have gone up. The bill took care of every special interest in the communications industry, except for the average person who owns a telephone or watches cable or makes a long-distance call."

PERHAPS THE LONGEST-RUNNING jamboree has been the struggle between commercial banks and investment banks over something called the Glass-Steagall Act, which was passed in 1933, in the wake of the 1929 crash. The idea was to keep banks out of the stock market. Their participation in the market was one of the reasons cited for the 1929 crash—whether rightly or wrongly has never been resolved. The law also prevented commercial banks from getting into venture banking, and ever since the law was enacted the commercial banks have fought to enter the investment, bond, and insurance businesses. The fight over changing the law has gone on for at least two decades and has involved masses of lobbyists on both sides.

The money that poured in became a strong incentive for Members of Congress *not* to resolve the impasse. The financial, insurance, and securities industries combined are among the largest contributors to their campaigns: the Center for Responsive Politics, a monitoring group, said that during the 1997–98 election cycle the financial businesses, through their PACs or through individual donations, on both sides of the issue contributed over $70 million in hard and soft money to Members of Congress, the political parties, leadership PACs, and anywhere else they could put it (more to Republicans than Democrats). And individual donors associated with the financial service industry contributed almost $62 million to federal candidates, PACs, and federal parties for the 1998 election. Of course, "grass-roots" operations were created to carry on the war between the wealthy institutions.

A lobbyist for very large interests told me, "Senator Y is either for or against repealing Glass-Steagall. If you are for keeping Glass-Steagall the way it is, then you are friends with investment bankers; if you are for changing Glass-Steagall, your friends are the commercial banks.

"In the midst of trying to convince the senator which side of Glass-Steagall to be on, the senator calls you to buy a ticket or take a table for a dinner. If you're the corporate head of General Motors, what's ten thousand dollars? Most of them have dinners where the senator pats you on the fanny and says, 'Thanks, pal.'"

The lobbyist continued, "All this money. A man or woman in Congress has tens of thousands of issues to address. They are banged on by people on both sides of that issue. By meeting with all the groups involved they've created a constituency for money. They keep lists of those who have lobbied them, and go back to them to solicit their help in their campaign.

"I would have to conclude that in a lot of the fights there are no real people involved. Sometimes the outcome little affects the average citizen. It's a battle of corporations. You can get into an abstract discussion about the effects on the economy. Bunk. It's a decision between the very wealthy and the very rich. That's true of Glass-Steagall. It was true of the struggle between the Hollywood studios and the television networks over syndication rights and production. That Ping-Pong match lasted over twenty years."

A merger between Citicorp, a major bank, and Travelers Group, which dealt with securities and insurance, announced in early April 1998, required a change in Glass-Steagall. Egged on by lobbyists in support of the merger, the Congress decided to take another look at the law. In May, the House, by a one-vote margin that reflected the balance of power of the interests, passed a revision of the act. Senator Alfonse D'Amato had opposed changing Glass-Steagall in the past. But when the merger of two of his largest corporate constituents was announced, D'Amato, the chairman of the Senate Banking Committee and up for reelection in 1998, said he wasn't interested in having the Senate take up the matter until after the election. That way, the money would keep flowing.

The lobbyist said, "That's what everyone out here on K Street thinks." Thus, with the banking system in increasing turmoil as the industry was changing through mergers and the international financial system threw numerous shocks into it, Congress held off acting so as not to cut off lucrative sources of campaign funds. D'Amato received $2.9 million from both sides of the financial industry in the 1997–98 election cycle.

THERE IS, among lobbyists, a theological argument of sorts over whether it is better to give hard money (limited amounts) or soft (unlimited amounts). Because of the rise in the collection and use of soft money in recent years, the issue of PACs has almost been forgotten. But their continuing utility hasn't been lost on the lobbyists.

David Rehr is the vice president for public affairs for the National Beer Wholesalers Association, which is particularly powerful because there are beer wholesalers in virtually every congressional district.

Rehr told me, "We don't do soft money. It's a bottomless pit. It's never enough. Both sides play you against each other. Hard money is much more valuable, because it actually goes for electing someone. Giving a candidate ten thousand dollars [$5,000 in a primary and $5,000 in the general election] directly is much more useful. Soft money is more amorphous. If you go up to Congressman John Smith and say, 'John, we're going to give you ten thousand dollars,' it's much more valuable to him than if you give an amorphous fifty thousand in soft money to the national committee. The only way you get attention with soft money is it has to be really big: three hundred, four hundred, five hundred thousand, a million—that gets people's attention."

In a document—with holes punched for insertion in members' fund-raising notebooks—in the National Republican Congressional Committee's March–April 1998 newsletter for Republican members and their allies, Rehr sets forth "Six Steps to Maximize PAC Receipts Before November 1998." It provided an interesting window on the world of business contributions.

Rehr wrote, "At the NBWA, we generally receive ten to thirty invitations for events per week, dozens of telephone calls from professional PAC fund-raisers . . . and requests from other corporate and business association representatives serving on incumbents' PAC steering committees. . . . The growth of so-called 'Leadership PACs' in both the House and Senate has further increased the competition for PAC dollars. You need to elevate yourself above your peers to maximize your PAC support. . . . As an incumbent you have tremendous resources to maximize your PAC support from the business community."

In the past couple of years, some corporations have decided to stop giving soft money, for similar reasons. The money is unaccountable; there's now more scrutiny of big soft-money donors; there's no end to the requests; and a donation of hard money directly to a candidate is more welcome. But most of these corporations planned to put more soft money into "issue ads" for the 1998 race, another indirect way of influencing the Congress.

The Business Roundtable, an organization of the two hundred largest U.S. companies, increased, by about $300,000 per company, the amounts the members paid for dues, and ran ads against the "Patients' Bill of Rights," to reform managed-care programs, and against an international agreement reached in Kyoto, in 1998, to reduce the hazards of climate change. The Business Roundtable spent $5 million on issue ads alone in 1998.

But if one wants to please a presidential candidate, or party chairman, or chairman of one of the congressional campaign committees, soft money is in order because it's easier to get hold of and can be raised from individuals and labor unions and corporations in large amounts. And, at the least, big donors get access. Big-time donors or fund-raisers are also willing to steer money, as directed, to states where the President needs help. And, as was shown in 1996, they receive gratitude, access, and perhaps more.

A FORMER DEMOCRATIC Member of Congress said, "What's so often misunderstood about the way we finance our campaigns is it doesn't affect big decisions, such as how to fix Social Security. It's the smaller things, which don't get reported—on spending bills, on tax bills, on authorization bills."

As an example, a proposal that the government charge meat packers fees for inspecting meat and poultry has never been enacted. The impasse has continued despite recent incidents of meat and poultry causing health crises—*E. coli,* salmonella. But the meat and poultry industry have strongly opposed paying a fee to upgrade the inspection system. And they have opposed giving the government authority to level criminal fines on meat packers and poultry producers, and the Congress has rejected giving that authority.

"The opposition is bipartisan," says someone familiar with the politics of these issues. "These things die in the Agriculture Committees, which are made up of people who represent agricultural interests. The committees generally reflect one perspective. So these proposals don't get the free flow of debate. That's where the power of money is.

"By and large, it's in the secondary issues—the ones that may affect the public the most. These are the issues where Members of Congress are less free because of the financing of campaigns."

ONE WEARY LOBBYIST says, "When I retire, I'll never write another check. I do it now because it's the cost of doing business."

14

The News Media

Communication is essential to democracy. Citizens must be able to monitor their distant representatives in order to make informed decisions at the polls, and politicians have a vested interest in explaining their actions to those who will decide their future. Thus far, we have identified numerous avenues of communication: election campaigns, direct appeals by presidents and other politicians, and interest group newsletters, to name a few. Much of the two-way communication between politicians and voters occurs through the news media—that is, information gathered by reporters and editors and conveyed through newspapers, magazines, television, and increasingly the Internet. The Framers included a sweeping "freedom of the press" provision in the First Amendment to ensure that citizens would be provided with information about the actions of their representatives by independent agents. In self-recognition of their special political role, members of the news media frequently refer to themselves as the "fourth branch" of government.

The phrase "fourth branch" connotes more about the political status of the news media than its essential function to representative democracy. Politicians and members of the news media engage one another politically, in that each set of actors needs something from the other to achieve different and frequently incompatible goals. Politicians wish the news media to portray them and their positions on the issues in a favorable light. News reporters need information that makes for a good story. And because no news professional wants to be viewed as a publicist for a politician, journalists desire the kind of information that will reassure their audience they are presenting an objective view. As a consequence, there is a tension in the relationship, as both sides compete and cooperate to define the news. The essays that follow examine these political relations more closely.

14-1

Is Journalism Hopelessly Cynical?

Michael Schudson

The history of the news media reveals a set of institutions that are continually in flux, as professional journalists and their news organizations adapt to changes in communications technology, the business environment within which they compete, and the political setting they report to their audience. Journalistic adaptations of the past quarter-century have produced a rapid rise in negative news about politics and a growing tone of cynicism in political reporting. Michael Schudson's article below calls attention to a rarely noted irony—that the news media's coverage of politics is growing simultaneously more cynical and more comprehensive and credible, and for some of the same reasons. Schudson's explanation focuses on the growing professional autonomy of journalists and a worldwide change in political culture.

BY PROFESSION, journalists are supposed to be great cynics. Someone else's tragedy is their scoop, someone else's private moment is their opportunity for page one. Every politician's vaporous pronouncement exists only to be skewered.

The long-standing image of the journalist as cynic is contradicted by another image that is equally well-traveled—the journalist as reformer and romantic. In this image, journalists are forever young; with red, white, and blue always in their eyes; and with their typewriters (or computers) powered by a quest to right wrongs and speak truths to power.

The latter image is alive and well, at least at J-school commencements and the occasional convention of news practitioners. But in the broader public eye, and among scholars of the media, the picture of the journalist as romantic is said to be out of date. Critics of the American press—and the

This paper is based on an earlier essay, "Social Origins of Press Cynicism in Portraying Politics," published in *American Behavioral Scientist*, volume 42, number 6 (March 1999), 998–1008. Reprinted by permission.

world press, for that matter—have in recent years agreed on two overarching propositions:

1. political reporting is increasingly cynical and promotes cynicism in the audience;
2. the product of news institutions is increasingly "infotainment," a concoction governed by entertainment values more than news judgment.

Both of these claims are generally correct. Of course, they do not apply to all of the news media, and they do not apply equally across news institutions. Moreover, it is hard to judge if these developments are mild or severe: How much cynicism is too much? When is an interest in entertainment a legitimate effort to relate a complex situation as a compelling story? And when does the quest for sensation overtake the effort to tell a story?

My concern is not to press the issue of measuring trends toward cynicism and infotainment more precisely. Nor is it to define when enough is enough. Rather, it is to pose an uncomfortable possibility: That there's no reversing these trends. In fact, many of the most self-conscious efforts of journalists to improve their work may augment, rather than dampen, such criticism. The trends can perhaps be contained, they can be policed, but there's no going home again.

Political cynicism is a cynicism of the reporter's mind; infotainment is a cynicism of the corporate soul. As both conspire to promote in the public a cynical understanding of politics, the media have developed a character and style that corrode our civic culture. That's the last thing most journalists intend—so why is it happening?

Toward Cynicism and Entertainment

Before going on to explain the changes in journalism, I will first quickly document their direction. In *Out of Order* (1993), Thomas Patterson has made a strong case for the growth of cynicism in political reporting. He has argued that the press has developed an "antipolitics bias." Three of his points seem especially telling. First, he finds a growing trend from 1960 to 1992 in the newsweeklies of reporting bad news rather than good. In 1960, 75 percent of evaluative references to Kennedy and Nixon were positive; in 1992 only 40 percent of evaluative references were positive for Clinton or Bush.

Second, journalists leave the impression that politicians will promise anything to get elected. They neglect to mention the political science studies that show that politicians generally work hard for and often make good on their campaign pledges.

Third, journalists see political careers as more oriented to politics as a game than to politics as policy. The game schema directs attention to conflicts and to a few individuals, not to social conditions and the larger interests individuals may represent. For instance, over time journalists have shifted from reporting candidates' speeches to reporting the strategic moves behind them (and often not saying much at all about the speeches themselves). From 1960 to 1992, there has been a progressive increase in *New York Times* political stories that emphasize a "game" framework or schema rather than a "policy" one.

As for the plunge of journalism into the entertainment business, this is an old complaint, but new conditions make it more convincing. A 1998 study produced by the Committee of Concerned Journalists found a deterioration in issues coverage in television, newspaper, and news magazine journalism between 1977 and 1997, with a declining attention to policy issues and an increasing attention to scandal. In 1977, in a sample of stories from leading newspapers and news magazines, 32 percent of stories were "traditional" in their emphasis on policy or political process and 15 percent concerned personalities, scandal, lifestyle, and human interest. In 1997, "traditional" news was down to 26 percent and feature news up to 43 percent.

Political news, it appears, demeans and diminishes what citizens may hope from politics, and this has become increasingly true over the past thirty years. I have focused on America, but this is a world-wide phenomenon. Reporting styles around the world have grown more informal, more intimate, more critical, and more cynically detached or distanced in the past two generations. British television interviewing changed from a style formal and deferential toward politicians to a more aggressive and critical style that makes politicians more visibly and immediately answerable to the public. Japanese broadcasting changed in a similar direction in recent years, partly under the influence of news anchor Kume Hiroshi. As political scientist Ellis Krauss put it, Hiroshi's "alienated cynicism and critical stance toward society and government" appears to have charmed a younger, more urban, and more alienated generation. His style moved toward a type of politics "more cynical and populist" than the old bureaucratic conservatism, but one that "offers little in the way of the framing of real political alternatives" (Krauss 2000)

Meanwhile, there is a new investigative aggressiveness in Latin American journalism. In Brazil, Argentina, and Peru, revelation of government scandals emerges not from old-fashioned partisan journalism but from a new, more entertainment-oriented journalism that adopts stock narratives and a telenovela personality-focused moralizing style. The results do not contribute to a public accounting of the moral order but come from and reinforce cultural pessimism. Scandal becomes a form of entertainment, at best, and contributes to political cynicism.

In the United States, nothing better illustrates these trends than the saturation coverage of the Monica Lewinsky scandal. But Monica coverage may help us see behind the apparent cynicism of the press. Monica coverage was overdetermined. Monicagate depended on the existence of the special prosecutor's office created in Title VI of the Ethics in Government Act of 1978, the chief legislative legacy of Watergate (and one, as it happens, that was opposed by most of the chief legal figures in Watergate, including Watergate special prosecutors Archibald Cox, Leon Jaworski, and Henry Ruth). It depended also on the media's having overlearned a Watergate lesson—that where there's smoke, there's fire. This is especially true of our leading news outlets. The *New York Times* relentlessly promoted the Whitewater story for years, and both the *Washington Post* and the *New York Times* repeatedly editorialized in favor of pursuing the impeachment inquiry. Finally, it depended on the erosion of a public–private distinction once well understood. This is a result of a variety of factors—first and foremost, the successful entrance of a feminist agenda onto the political scene. Feminists took as their watchword in the early 1970s that "the personal is political." Boy, is it ever.

The Reasons Why

The Lewinsky example raises a troubling question. The conditions that made Monicagate possible included (1) the institutionalization of high standards for government ethics and new operations for pursuing government corruption; (2) aggressive investigative journalism; and (3) the recognition of the ways in which domains once considered part of private life have public dimensions and public implications. In other words, three developments one might well judge to be improvements in public life contributed centrally to one of the most sordid episodes of modern media culture.

For all of the faults of media today, Americans have more information, and more credible information, than ever. People today have unprecedented access to careful, conscientious, analytically sound, crisply presented information about national and world affairs. (Their access to local news was never very good. It is pretty bad today, but I am not sure it is any worse than before.)

Highly educated citizens have access to especially rich information. Twenty-four percent of college graduates "sometimes" listen to NPR news. There was no NPR before 1970. Twenty-eight percent of graduates sometimes watch C-SPAN. There was no C-SPAN until 1979. Some two-thirds of college graduates sometimes watch CNN, which did not exist until 1980. Half of college graduates sometimes read the *Wall Street Journal*, the *New York Times*, or *USA Today*; the *Times* did not have a national edition with national distribution until the 1970s and *USA Today* began only in 1982 (Center for Media and Public Affairs 1997, 15–47).

How can it be that the news has grown more cynical, more infotainment-oriented, and at the same time more comprehensive and credible? Three underlying trends in journalism help account for all of these developments.

Growing Professional Interventionism

The ties between news institutions and parties began to weaken near the end of the nineteenth century. With more and more news institutions run by mega-corporations and not by egomaniacal capitalist adventurers, the straightforward use of the press to advance the political interests of an individual, faction, or party have been progressively reduced. Reporters and editors have taken on greater authority, relative to ownership. They have also taken on greater authority relative to their own sources. They are less likely to defer to official authority than they were a generation ago. Vietnam, Watergate, the adversary culture of the 1960s, the revulsion in the media toward Ronald Reagan's photo opportunities and George Bush's cynically flag-waving victory over Michael Dukakis all contributed to a self-consciousness in journalism about both its possibilities and its pitfalls.

One sign of the new interventionism is the now famous shrinking of the "soundbite" in television news. In national network coverage of elections, the average length of time a candidate spoke uninterruptedly on camera was 43 seconds in 1968; by 1988, it was 9 seconds. This has generally been understood to mean that television news has grown worse and worse, more and more trivial, but this was not the conclusion of communication scholar Daniel Hallin, who did some of the original soundbite research in the first place. His conclusion was simply that television news had become more "mediated"—that is, journalists intervene with growing frequency in order to provide a compact and dramatic story. What did this mean for the overall quality of television news? Hallin found an increase in "horse-race" coverage from 1968 to 1988, a measure of the growing "game" or "strategy" orientation others have criticized, and so confirmed everyone's worst fears. But he *also* found an increase in the coverage of "issues," showing that television news is doing exactly what the media critics think it should be doing. How can both kinds of coverage increase at the same time? The answer is that television journalists offer a more highly structured, thematic story. There is less wasted motion, less silence, more rapid-fire editing.

Meanwhile, news stories have grown longer. In a recent study of ten newspapers in 1964 and in 1999, where in the earlier paper there was typically only one A-section story that ran twenty inches or more, today there are three; in 1964 there were typically thirty-six A-section stories under six inches, today only thirteen. Local, national, and international news represents only 24 percent of the news hole in today's papers rather than 35 percent in 1964—but the news hole has doubled during this period, thus making the total amount of news in the daily papers today significantly greater than it was in the early 1960s (Stepp 1999).

Thematizing

Media critic Paul Weaver has observed that television news is more inclined to "tell a story" than newspaper news. Both television and newspaper news are "essentially melodramatic accounts of current events," Weaver wrote. But television news is "far more coherently organized and tightly unified" compared to the newspaper story that still has an inverted pyramid organization in which the news account ends with a whimper, not a bang. The newspaper story has no teleological drive to wrap things up; in fact, after the opening paragraph or "lead," which can be read as a complete capsule story in itself, the rest of the story may be presented in very loose and only semicoherent order. The newspaper story is designed not to be read in its entirety, whereas the television story is meant to achieve its significance only as a full and finished object that keeps the viewer tuned in throughout. The newspaper story may confine itself to reporting an event, uninflected by any effort to give it meaning or analysis. The television story, in contrast, "inevitably . . . goes into, beneath or beyond the ostensive event to fix upon something else—a process, mood, trend, condition, irony, relationship, or whatever else seems a suitable theme in the circumstances" (Weaver 1981).

The effort of the television news story to thematize is hard to satisfy in an age suspicious of grand narrative and in an age when the Cold War is no longer available to provide a default narrative frame. So news institutions work overtime to put what they print into some kind of coherent analytic framework. Very often, this means putting the news into historical perspective. Where we do not have master narratives, we have at least some residual faith in the coherence of chronology. There is an increase, not a decrease, in news institutions' framing of current events in historical terms.

Growing News Coherence

A century ago competing newspapers in the same city featured front-page stories that their rivals did not even carry in the back pages. There was little urgency in journalism about coming up with "the" picture of that day's reality. News institutions now monitor one another all the time. CNN is a permanent presence in the newsrooms of daily newspapers. News magazines and newspapers preview their next editions on Web sites that reporters and editors at other news institutions examine almost the moment they are available. Newspapers advertise the next day's stories on cable news stations. The result is interinstitutional news coherence. Literary or film critics have talked of intertextuality for a long time; now news intertextuality is an electronic reality, not an accidental outcome of wars that draw reporters to the same hotel or power centers that draw them to the same bars in a capital city. News is a widely distributed, seamless intertext.

This follows in part from the domination of television in the news system. As Weaver suggested, because television journalism insists on thematic coherence, it "gives credence to the idea that there exists in America a single, coherent national agenda which can be perceived as such by any reasonable and well-intentioned person." This has intensified with (1) national news distribution—the *New York Times* News Service, CNN, *USA Today*, National Public Radio, and others—and (2) the growing importance of Washington news from the time of the Kennedy administration and Vietnam War to the present. The Vietnam War created modern television news as nothing else had before it. Since Vietnam, more news comes from Washington. Various factors contribute to this—the growing role of the federal government in everyday life, the growing celebrity of national television journalists, the improved technological capacity of satellite-borne television signals, and the growing corporatization of the press. More newspapers are owned by nonlocals and run by nonlocals with incentives to rise in the national organization rather than ties to local power structures or sentimental attachment to local roots. All of this not only nationalizes news but enlarges the possibilities for cynicism. When news is local, it typically remains personal, friendly, upbeat, gossipy, homey, and it very rarely probes local power structures or the assumptions—religious, ethnic, or otherwise—of local cultures. Nationalizing news distances journalists from their audiences, for better and for worse.

Growing interinstitutional news coherence is matched by a significant increase in intrainstitutional news coherence. News reporting seeks in each news institution a new comprehensiveness and cultural inclusiveness. If you walked into a newsroom fifty years ago, you would most likely not have seen any blacks or other racial minorities, and the only women you would have encountered would have been writing on the society page. (There were black journalists, but almost all of them worked for the several hundred black newspapers in the country.) The mainstream press conscientiously, if belatedly, sought to hire and promote black Americans and to cover news and views of minorities. Not only are there now minorities and women in the newsroom, but there is an acknowledged norm that stories of special interest to these groups are legitimate general-interest news stories.

Conclusion

Amid a veritable deluge of public information, people—especially young people—exhibit a declining interest in it. According to a 1996 survey conducted for the Radio and Television News Directors Foundation, 65 percent of people over 50 think it is "very important" to keep up with the news, compared to 55 percent of those 30–49 and 40 percent of those 18–29. Not everyone lives up to their ideals, of course. Only 51 percent of those over 50 say that they follow government and public affairs "most of the time," as did 29 percent of those 30–49 and 19 percent of those 18–29. Women in every age group are significantly less likely than men to follow government and public affairs—only 12 percent of women 18–29 claim that they do so (compared to 26 percent of men in this age group).

Young people have long lagged behind older people in following the news, but there has been a decrease over time. In 1965, 67 percent of those 21–35 read a newspaper the day before being surveyed; in 1990, only 30 percent. For the 30–49 age group, the percentage who read a newspaper the prior day dropped from 73 percent to 44 percent, and for those over 50, from 74 percent to 55 percent.

Publishers are alarmed. Their newspapers still turn handsome profits, but they are losing their audience. Every newspaper faces this reality. Urging the newspaper press to higher standards isn't much use if it should lead even more people to desert the habit of reading. So the print media become even more thematizing, professionally interventionist, more coherent, more cynical, and more entertainment-oriented.

There is no reason to suppose journalists are by personality or character more cynical than in the past. Institutional and cultural changes are more than enough in themselves to explain the cynical turn. Journalists today are unwilling to rely exclusively on official statements as they once did. Their own professional culture pushes them to be analytical and judgmental—for literary (thematizing) reasons, for cultural reasons (a society-wide growing distrust of established authority), for political reasons (the decline of the Cold War metanarrative for news), and for commercial reasons (fear of losing an audience). And of course, journalists are every bit as susceptible as the next person to the powerful political moods of the day. Whether it is Reagan to Clinton or Kohl to Shröder or Thatcher to Blair, the political mood takes government's proper role to be sustaining and encouraging the forces of the market. This leads to a naturalization of antigovernment talk, especially in the government itself, and journalists cannot help but reproduce this in their own work.

It is all very well to urge that news adopt a "policy" framework rather than a "game–strategy" framework for political news, but enacting this recommendation in the face of the journalism culture's best (as well as worst) instincts is another matter. The news media represent the nation and the world well, perhaps all too well, submitting to the moods of the hour rather than scrutinizing them. It will take more than a new journalistic diction to resist today's cynical undertow.

REFERENCES

Center for Media and Public Affairs. 1997. *What the People Want from the Press* (Washington, D.C.: Center for Media and Public Affairs).

Krauss, Ellis. 2000. *Broadcasting Politics in Japan: NHK and Television News* (Ithaca: Cornell University Press).

Patterson, Thomas. 1993. *Out of Order* (New York: Knopf).

Stepp, Carl Sessions. 1999. "The State of the American Newspaper: Then and Now," *American Journalism Review,* September, 60–75.

Weaver, Paul. 1981. "TV News and Newspaper News," in *Understanding Television,* ed. Richard P. Adler (New York: Praeger), 272–293.

14-2

Market Research and the Audience for Political News

Doug Underwood

*Facing stiff competition for the public's attention, the print and televi-
sion news media have recently become more attuned to market forces.
They carefully monitor the preferences of their audience as they design
the format and plan the content of their daily news. The news media's
greater attentiveness to marketing, Doug Underwood argues, has contributed to a shift in news coverage of politics. This trend, along with
changes in communication technology, has generated news programming that emphasizes the entertainment value of news over comprehensive coverage.*

PETE SCHULBERG, the television reporter for the Portland *Oregonian*, recently performed a content analysis that confirmed what many have already observed about local broadcast television news: coverage of politics
and government has virtually disappeared from the local television airwaves, crowded out by coverage of crime, sports, weather, lifestyles, and
the other audience-grabbing topics that now make up the local television
news formula.

Schulberg analyzed the late night newscasts of the five Portland area
over-the-airwaves local television stations during a five-day period in March
of 1997. The percentage of coverage devoted to issues (including stories
about government, politics, the law, social discourse, and the environment)
amounted to as little as 0.5 percent of the news coverage on one station up
to a maximum of 7.6 percent on another. On three of the stations, less air
time was devoted to issues coverage than any other topic area, including
coverage of animals (which Schulberg defined as stories focusing on four-
legged creatures, birds, fish, and pets).

"It's a sign of the times: If you want to hear about the national political
scene, catch Leno's monologue or David Letterman's 'Top 10 List'—

Excerpted from Doris Graber, Denis McQuail, and Pippa Norris, eds., *The Politics of News, the News of Politics* (Washington, D.C.: CQ Press, 1998), pp. 171–192.

because you won't find it on your favorite station's late news," wrote Schulberg. ". . . The late news is a place where stories involving animals often dwarf matters of social and economic significance."[1]

While this is happening at the local television level, the news departments of the national television networks have been cutting back their news operations in the nation's capital and overseas since the mid-1980s, when new corporate ownership began ruthlessly downsizing the news staffs at all three major news networks (CBS, NBC, and ABC). This has left network television news dominated by "marketeers" who are trying to hold dwindling network audiences through the mass appeal of "infotainment," explains Penn Kimball in his study of the network cutbacks.[2]

Daily newspapers, too, have been reflecting the trend in less coverage of nuts-and-bolts government news in favor of more stories tailored to perceived audience taste. Carl Sessions Stepp, in his 1992 article "Of the People, By the People, Bore the People," says that three factors—the shrinking news hole in many newspapers, the increased attention to lifestyle and leisure topics, and the perception that the public lacks an appetite for mundane copy about government—have led to less government coverage. "Journalists clearly believe that the public's eyes glaze over when the topic is government and politics," he writes.

Stepp says that some journalists, particularly those at large newspapers, are emphasizing quality over quantity in government coverage and experimenting with new approaches to make government coverage more interesting for readers, which he sees as a good thing. But he adds, "Don't rule out a period of retreat during which resource-hungry publishers defang watchdog journalists and snatch reporters and space from the government desk. Using public alienation as the excuse."[3]

Shrinking Government News on Television

Television news—local television, in particular—has never been very interested in covering the routine activities of government and politics. Communications research going back to the 1970s has established that local television news tends to cover dramatic happenings rather than government meetings or economic trends and issues.[4] The reasons for this are fairly obvious. The demands of television as a medium for visuals, ratings-grabbing news formulas, and emotion-laden themes tend to preclude coverage of the complex issues that make up governmental and political life. Television is an entertainment medium first and foremost—and that, rather than coverage of substance, tends to be the goal of most local television news reporting. Based on his 1990 case study of four western local news operations, media researcher John McManus concluded that 56 percent of the stories he analyzed were inaccurate or misleading. "There is economic logic to these distortions," he says. The coverage is designed to maximize viewer appeal, cut down the cost of reporting, or oversimplify matters so the story can be told in two minutes.[5]

In recent years this trend has grown more pronounced as local, over-the-airwaves television news operations—under pressure from declining ratings, cable competitors, and alternative news networks—have adopted sensationalistic, tabloid formulas to hold their audience. Local television has become the leading force in moving mainstream American journalism away from coverage of public affairs and into ratings-driven content that is mostly about "violent crime, abandoned warehouse fires, and cutesy features," as the *American Journalism Review* described it in an article entitled, "Bad News: Why Is Local TV News So Bad?"[6] In this environment, serious coverage of local government or politics has virtually disappeared from the airwaves.[7]

Most local television stations emphasize hot-button controversy, promote other shows and devote a lot of time to teasers for upcoming stories, and tend to tout the lurid, sensational, and the touchy-feely. A few have launched all-news cable companion channels that devote time to serious public issues. However, these operations, for the most part, have very small news staffs and little market share in most communities compared with the traditional, free, over-the-airwaves local television stations with their "hook-em-and-hold-em" news formulas.

"The old joke about local news is that 'if it bleeds, it leads,'" writes Phyllis Kaniss, the assistant dean of the Annenberg School for Communication at the University of Pennsylvania. "But it is the corollary that should concern us: if it doesn't bleed—or choke with emotion—it doesn't air. Unfortunately, most matters of public consequence fail to pass the blood-and-tears litmus test of local television news."[8]

Television network news has a serious news tradition established by Edward R. Murrow and other early television journalists. Compared with local news, traditionally it has been much more sober-minded and responsible in its coverage of government and politics, and particularly news that emanates from Washington, D.C., and foreign capitals. The networks still cover a fair amount of national politics, although with vastly shorter sound-bites and political stories than thirty years ago.[9] Facing ominous ratings problems and competitive pressures, the three major over-the-airwaves network news programs have reduced their focus on serious public affairs news in recent years. Television network executives, to insert more entertainment value into their programming, have slashed news reporting staffs and closed foreign bureaus, ceased the production of public affairs documentaries, and replaced serious news items with audience-friendly feature stories and "news about you" items.[10] Much of the effort at network news departments is now aimed at the networks' "news magazines," which are designed to draw audience through their use of hidden cameras, ambush interviews, and hyped-up and sensationalized video. These news magazines are modeled after CBS-TV's highly popular "60 Minutes," which demonstrated to the networks that aggressive reporting could be a money-maker. These news magazines have produced some good, award-winning journalism, but they also have tended to tailor their investigations to what will draw an audience. Their reports of wrongdoing, particularly when it involves government or politics, can be exaggerated and lacking in perspective.

Many people get their impressions of government from television news. Therefore, the tendency of television news to emphasize ratings-oriented crime and celebrity coverage, portray government in a negative light, and to ignore the complex elements of public issues has had a deeply distorting impact upon the public consciousness. In documenting these changes and cutbacks at the network level, Penn Kimball laments that everything from Congress to federal bureaucratic agencies to foreign affairs coverage has fallen victim to economic imperatives. "What is going on in network television is a redefinition of news, driven by financial considerations and ratings," Kimball says. "News is what networks feel they can afford to cover and what will get on the air as determined by ratings. The wall of separation between the business side and the news side, which had always been under siege, has now been significantly breached."[11]

Shrinking Government News in Newspapers

Researchers and scholars have only begun to examine the implications of this shift to market-based journalism at newspapers—and particularly the implications for the traditional public service mission of journalism as a watchdog of government. When it comes to daily newspapers, much of the evidence for the cutback in government and political coverage is anecdotal and supported largely by the impressions of journalists and editors involved in government coverage.

One of the few research studies to attempt to quantify this phenomenon is a master's thesis at the University of Washington by former Tacoma (Wash.) *News Tribune* political reporter Jerry Pugnetti. He determined that between the early 1980s and the early 1990s six of Washington State's seven major daily newspapers cut back significantly their coverage of legislative news. These six Washington dailies carried between 27 and 51 percent fewer legislative items in 1991–1992 than they did in 1981–1982, a trend he blamed upon the greater employment of product marketing strategies by newspapers, the intensified use of market research throughout the industry, and the adoption of "reader-driven" news values. "Once reader surveys are conducted, anecdotal evidence suggests that editors and news organization managers who interpret the research perceive that readers are bored with news about government," Pugnetti concludes.[12]

For generations, those interested in public affairs have relied largely upon daily newspapers for whatever in-depth coverage of government and politics is done by the media. Daily newspaper staffs are larger than their broadcast counterparts, and the traditions of newspaper journalism call for more aggressive scrutiny of the public sector. After the advent of television, daily newspapers came to see their role as providing the in-depth and analytical coverage that broadcast news did not. Although the public often doesn't realize it, daily newspapers are at the base of the information pyramid in the modern media age, and much of the serious news and information that is used by broadcasters, rewritten by the wire services, and repackaged by new media providers originates in newspaper reporting.

Despite these traditions, there has been a de-emphasis in coverage of routine political and government news at daily newspapers, too. This shift fits with a general pattern in news coverage away from traditional beat structures—such as local government, the legislature, agencies, and politics—toward "relevant" topics that are intended to touch what matters in readers' personal, family, and professional lives. In daily newspapers this move has resulted in a softer, lifestyle, "reader-friendly" definition of news with a focus on topics like parenting, women's careers, real estate, consumer affairs, personal finance, health and fitness, medical advice, and technology, and with formats designed to make the newspaper more accessible to time-pressed readers.[13] In recent years, many daily newspapers have put a stronger emphasis upon local issues coverage that they believe will appeal to the parochial interest of readers. But theme, team, and trend coverage—planned out in editorial meetings and packaged with high concept art and graphics—has become the fashion over old-style, cover-the-meetings, keep-track-of-the-bureaucracy, and grind-out-the-copy local beat reporting. The end result often has meant less attention to government by daily newspapers, particularly the hum-drum activities of agencies and legislative bodies that once was the staple of news coverage. When news of politics or government is reported, it tends to be focused on controversy, scandal, partisan bickering, or the efforts by politicians and campaign consultants to manipulate public opinion. This new focus on the "spin" and the "hype" and the "horse race" aspect of modern media-driven politics is no coincidence in a news industry now driven by its own audience polling. At the same time, much of the routine detail about local or state government activity has disappeared from the columns of daily newspapers. "We're covering a great deal less of the turn-of-the-wheel kind of [government coverage]," admits Davis "Buzz" Merritt, Jr., executive editor of the *Wichita Eagle*. "Nobody gives a damn." [14]

Modern management trends are also working against the traditional patterns of coverage of government and politics. At many newspapers, today's "holistic" approach to news means that newsroom management hierarchies have been flattened, reporters have been put on writing teams that coordinate their activities with designers and graphic artists, and new theme-oriented beats—like Quality of Life, Community Roots, Leisure, Transactions, City Life, and Governance—have replaced the old-style public affairs–oriented beats of courts, cops, city council, state legislature, and so on that have been around since the days of the nineteenth century. The journalists who pay attention to government these days often work in an environment where newsrooms are administered tightly by careerist manager-technocrats dedicated to the media corporation's values; where the consequences of market research are everywhere in evidence; where trendy new concepts like "circular management" and "newsrooms without walls" govern newsroom work life; and where editors may have titles like "change facilitator" or "team leader" rather than the old-fashioned "city editor." Although there are signs that more investigative reporting is being done than in the past, it tends to be institutionalized around the newspaper's planning, packaging, and prize-winning goals. Investigative teams

often carry out the kind of projects that can be micromanaged by news executives and promoted to meet the news organization's marketing strategy.

Whether newspapers' coverage of government and politics in the environment of market-research–driven journalism is better in quality, or worse,
is hardly a settled matter, given the paucity of research into the subject. Carl
Sessions Stepp, for example, applauds the efforts by some newspapers to
move away from the mundane, process-oriented government stories that
used to dominate the news pages and toward more sophisticated and creative ways of making governmental and political activity lively for readers.
Still, he worries that the press's longstanding devotion to public service
might "recede into oblivion, supplanted by a market-driven allegiance to the
tony and the trendy." [15] Pugnetti, in his analysis of Washington State newspapers, concludes that enterprise reporting on legislative matters actually dropped slightly in quantity from the early 1980s to the early 1990s.[16]

Many of the reporters who cover government and politics also worry
that, if they don't stay in regular contact with their government sources,
they will grow isolated from the issues, and the potential stories, that per-
colate through government life. Those reporters still covering traditional
government beats often complain that the preplanned and micromanaged
story packages—so much the rage in newsrooms these days—cannot compensate for regular and sustained reporting about public bodies and the bureaucracy. "If we're not there and if these people (in government) don't
know we are out there, there may become a greater tendency on the part of
politicians to cut corners or take money or not do their jobs," warns
Jonathan Salant, a Washington, D.C., correspondent for two Syracuse, New
York, newspapers, the *Herald-Journal* and the *Post-Standard*. "If we're not
there, all people are going to know is what politicians send out in press releases and newsletters." [17]

The Move to Market-Driven Journalism

The trend toward less government coverage is largely explained by the tight
hold of market research on the news business. Audience research pressures
are most severe in television. The TV ratings system has created a ruthless
and instantaneous feed-back mechanism to judge viewers' responses. Consultants circulate throughout the business helping local television news directors apply formula-based solutions to juicing up their news content to

lure viewers. Market research also has deeply affected the newspaper business. Newspaper executives now regularly survey their readers about their tastes and interests and then retailor their news content, their newspaper format, and their newsroom beat systems to meet those perceived interests.

Academic studies and articles in professional journals document the move by news organizations to use more marketing and readership research in their news content and newsroom management decisions. Critics of this trend generally lament that market-based journalism has led to superficial news coverage, investment in trendy management programs rather than journalistic resources, a focus on design and marketing gimmicks at the expense of journalistic substance, and an emphasis on corporate and bottom-line goals rather than the practice of good journalism.[18] Supporters, in turn, argue that the move to market-oriented journalism is simply a necessary adjustment to demographic, economic, and technological change in a competitive world where consumer preferences must be gauged and where close attention to audience interests doesn't have to come at the expense of sound journalism. The greater emphasis upon graphics, design, packaging, and reader relevance is what is needed to attract a busy and distracted and video-oriented audience increasingly focused on personal and life-style issues, popular culture, and electronic forms of entertainment and information, they say.[19]

Washington Post media critic Howard Kurtz analyzed the Boca Raton (Fla.) *News,* owned by Knight-Ridder. The company experimented with redesigning the newspaper around light features and reader-relevant news. Some editors disdain traditional public affairs coverage; *News* editor Wayne Ezell is one of them. Kurtz quotes Ezell as boasting that the paper covers "a lot less government stuff." Ezell, according to Kurtz, contrasted his paper's coverage of rising champagne prices with a story about a housing scandal in the *Miami Herald*. " 'Champagne Prices Soon to Explode'—we're the only paper in America to do an eight-inch story on that," Ezell said. "For baby boomers who go to a lot of champagne parties, that's more interesting than whatever Jack Kemp had to say today."[20] Still, Ezell maintains that market-based changes can be instituted without damaging coverage. "Just because you use graphics, . . . just because you give lots of lists, just because you are breaking things up to make things easier to grasp, doesn't mean you're treating the topics superficially. . . . You can be reader-friendly without being superficial," he insists.[21]

Kurtz takes a different approach. "The problem with dumbing-down newspapers is that we're talking down to people, and they know it. . . . My own view is that newspaper salvation lies in the opposite direction, with detailed, compelling reports on controversial subjects that simply can't be found elsewhere. . . . Those who insist on shrinking the news into ever-smaller digests will eventually digest themselves out of existence."[22]

In reality, the move toward market-oriented journalism is a continuation of a long historical trend that has seen American journalism grow more commercialized, more focused on audience interests, and more fixated on profit making.[23] American journalism originally flourished in the partisan political atmosphere of the colonial and post-colonial press. Caustic and satiric commentary about government and politics filled the pages of newspapers published by important figures such as Alexander Hamilton, Benjamin Franklin, and Franklin's brother, James. The partisan press so loathed by President Thomas Jefferson (1801–1809) came to full flower later under the patronage appointments and government printing contracts passed out to his journalistic cronies by President Andrew Jackson (1829–1837). For more than fifty years, the partisan press dominated the American journalistic landscape.

The partisan formula, however, was modified with the coming of the cheap, mass market, commercial newspapers—known as the Penny Press—in the 1830s. James Gordon Bennett and other early commercial newspaper editors pioneered the use of entertainment and sensationalism to capture the attention of a large and growing urban audience. They also focused heavily upon government and politics. Bennett, who did some of the earliest coverage of Washington, D.C., made government and political coverage a featured part of his *New York Herald*.

For commercial reasons, as much as anything, Bennett and his fellow Penny Press editors developed the daily newspaper as an independent, nonpartisan voice that served as a watchdog—and often harsh critic—of government. The roots of the adversarial relationship between the press and government can be found in this period. The commercial newspapers of the nineteenth century—echoing the dislike of many Americans for politicians—covered the public sector intensely, but often in ways that helped to exacerbate the hostility the public felt toward government.

In the late nineteenth and early twentieth century, the newspaper crusade, which generally had government as its target, came to fruition. The journalistic mission began to be identified with the cause of the common person. To enhance circulation as much as to promote civic good, publishers

Joseph Pulitzer, William Randolph Hearst, and E. W. Scripps developed the notion of the newspaper investigation as part of a package that emphasized entertainment, high society gossip, and sensationalistic coverage of crime and the courts. This tradition was reinforced by the populist and progressive movements, which brought reform to many communities and—with their emphasis upon honest, open, and meritocratic government—heavily influenced, and still influence, the values of journalists, as media sociologist Herbert Gans has pointed out.[24]

The muckraking period in the early twentieth century permanently affixed in the imagination of American journalists the concept of the reporter as a watchdog of government and as a force for reform. Although muckraking as a movement died out around the time of World War I, its premises have continued to motivate reform-oriented journalists throughout the twentieth century. Time and again its influence has reappeared. Consider, for example, the exposes of government misdeeds by investigative columnists I. F. Stone, Drew Pearson, and Jack Anderson; the Watergate probe by *Washington Post* reporters Bob Woodward and Carl Bernstein; and the national security and military investigations of Seymour Hersh.

It is also true that much of the coverage of government and politics throughout American history has been placid and credulous, little challenging the agenda of politicians and the government bureaucracy. Since the advent of the public relations industry in the nineteenth century, government and political forces have grown ever more sophisticated in finding ways to manipulate press coverage to their benefit. Studies have shown that a high proportion of news in news columns and broadcast reports originates with public relations sources.[25] With the growing influence of television in political campaigns, politicians and political candidates have become adept at packaging and presenting media events in ways that the press finds irresistible.

As newspapers, television, and other media organizations have cut back news-gathering staff, the agencies of government (as well as those of business and other institutions) have increased their public relations ranks. This is one of the quiet stories of the late twentieth century. Reporters are outnumbered, as they have been throughout the century, by the public relations agents of government and business. With the growing corporate control of news organizations and the greater market orientation of the media, many of these public relations officials have found it easy to market their prepackaged images to media corporations. As Mark Hertsgaard put it in his study of the public relations–savvy administration of Ronald Reagan, media corporations now treat the news largely as "a commodity to be bought and sold."[26] News about government that isn't sensationalized, spun by public relations impresarios, or shaped by audience marketing formulas often does not draw the attention of modern news executives.

What Does the Audience Really Want?

Ironically, news executives may not be right in their assumption that the public finds political and government news—including coverage of routine political and government matters—to be devoid of interest. For example, media research guru Leo Bogart consistently has found high levels of public interest in government-related news, and he has long complained that news executives really don't know their readers. Editors tend to believe the public is more interested in sports, entertainment, cultural, and fashion news than it is, Bogart believes. Professional news people, he says, have a tendency to "substantially" underestimate the public's interest in state, national, government and political, and international news.[27]

At the same time, Bogart's research, like many of the studies of readers' tastes, can make it very hard to interpret exactly what the public does want in its media coverage. Despite showing a strong interest in local, state, national, and international news, the readers surveyed by Bogart rated action line columns, feature stories, news summaries, comic strips, astrology columns, and homemaking features as much more important than did newspaper editors, and readers showed considerably less interest in news interpretation and a diversity of political commentators than did editors.[28] Much of their audience research is held as proprietary information by news organizations, but when pressed editors will often acknowledge that they, too, get such contradictory responses from their readers. When polled, readers seldom urge news executives to cut back on government or political coverage. However, many editors have come to believe that readers say this only because they don't want to appear uninformed or lacking in civic-mindedness.[29]

The conclusion that readers want their news and information in more personal, relevant, and easily digested fashion (whether research fully supported this conclusion or not) set the tone for the "reader-driven" journalism movement of the late 1970s and 1980s. More recently, researchers have begun to question whether the news industry has been moving too vigorously in the direction of "journalism lite." The presentation of these studies at journalism conventions in the late 1980s and early 1990s has led some newspaper executives to rethink matters. Perhaps they may have gone too far in emphasizing life-styles, short stories, and design gimmicks. This move, they now believe, has alienated traditional readers in a vain effort to attract a marginal, television-oriented audience that is unlikely to stick with newspapers anyway.

For example, researcher Ruth Clark, who helped launch the reader-driven journalism movement with her 1980s research calling for more self-elp and help-me-cope information in newspapers, later toned down her advice by warning editors that readers also wanted hard news, real facts, and coverage of serious social and world problems.[30] Another study showed that some prestige newspapers were rejecting the design-gimmicks-and-quick-read strategy of *USA Today* and instead banking their future on building readership among the more informed and educated population that looks to newspapers for in-depth, contextual coverage of public affairs.[31]

For two years, Melinda Hawley, a media researcher at the University of Georgia, studied thirty people who had dropped their subscription to the Knight-Ridder–owned Columbus (Ga.) *Ledger-Enquirer.* Her in-depth research raised doubts about the strategy of newspaper editors who have reduced their focus on governmental and political news. The former subscribers overwhelmingly listed dissatisfaction with the newspaper's content as their reason for dropping the newspaper. The ex-readers complained of parochialism, superficiality, the overreliance upon trivial fluff and redundant wire copy, and the employment of inexpert and inaccurate reporters as reasons for abandoning the *Ledger-Enquirer,* which Hawley described as a "lively, colorful" newspaper that had adopted many of the trendy, cosmetic strategies for attracting readers. Hawley's recommendation, which she prepared for the Cox Institute for Newspaper Management Studies, was that newspapers should expand state, national, and international coverage, cut out trivial items, and replace them with meaningful local news. In particular, she said, don't assume that readers care little about governmental and political news.[32]

Clearly, the unabated four-decade-long circulation stagnation of daily newspapers—as well as the audience loss suffered by the major television networks and over-the-airwaves, local television stations—have left many

news executives uncertain about how successful their use of market research has been in gaining or retaining readers. But despite studies that cast
doubt on the effectiveness of such a market-oriented strategy, it is difficult
to change editors' minds about the value of such an approach in solving
journalism's problems.

Market research–fixated news executives have a tendency to perpetuate
myths among themselves, particularly when they fit their presuppositions
and their prejudices. This tendency, says media researcher Randal Beam in
his survey of 167 daily newspaper editors, helps to explain why editors tend
to focus on readers' wants and needs and to adopt market-oriented strategies as they grow more uncertain about the nature of their audience and
their business environment. And yet Beam notes that there is only a "tenuous link" between the objective conditions of the marketplace and the editors' perceived solutions for trying to respond to readers' interests. "Editors'
uncertainty may be affected more by what's going on in their organization . . . than in the community that the paper serves," Beam concludes.[33]

The Debate among Professionals

Interestingly, some of the best journalists in the business echo the concerns
of their market-oriented editors. They, too, worry that traditional news
coverage of government—particularly the standard beat coverage of council meetings, legislative committees, and zoning board hearings—may now
seem irrelevant to modern readers. But journalists' reasons for worrying
about this, and their solutions to making public affairs coverage more relevant to the audience, are often very different from those of their bottom-
line oriented bosses.

Pulitzer Prize–winning investigative reporter Jim Steele of the *Philadelphia Inquirer* notes that "there are no boring government stories, but there
are a lot of boring reporters and editors." [34] Other journalists agree that
routine public affairs journalism handled in uninspired and unimaginative
ways should be replaced with more investigative reporting and interpretive
analysis that puts government activities into a broader, deeper, and more
meaningful context. By doing imaginative and in-depth journalism that
demonstrates to readers why government matters to their lives, Steele and
his partner, Donald Barlett, have gained widespread acclaim. Their series,
America: What Went Wrong?, showed the way government and tax decisions

in the 1980s harmed the American middle class. It won applause from newspaper executives struggling to find ways to connect with readers.[35]

In fact, the work of Barlett and Steele at the Knight-Ridder–owned *Inquirer* is often pointed to by those who say it is unfair to label reader-relevant journalism as necessarily shallow and superficial. A company like Knight-Ridder, they say, is open to experimentation at all levels in ways to relate to readers. While supporting Barlett and Steele in their long and expensive investigations, Knight-Ridder also sponsored the experiment in "Pink Flamingo" journalism, as it was scornfully labeled at the Boca Raton *News* (after the newspaper's colorful, YUPPY-friendly masthead). It also launched a company-wide "customer-obsession" campaign under James Batten, the Knight-Ridder chairman in the late 1980s.[36]

During the early 1990s, Knight-Ridder came in for stinging criticism of its staff cutbacks at its many respected newspapers, but CEO P. Anthony Ridder is convinced that attempts to increase profits to satisfy stockholders can be balanced with good journalism. "There should be absolutely no doubt that I am trying to improve the financial performance of the company," Ridder told the *American Journalism Review.* "But that doesn't mean that the quality of journalism has to suffer. It's this simplistic notion that you can't chew gum and walk at the same time."[37]. . .

Escaping Market-Driven Journalism

Public Journalism

Probably the most controversial development in the move back toward journalism with a civic conscience has been the "public journalism" movement. It has attempted to reconnect newspapers to their communities by promoting involvement by journalists in the community agenda-setting process.

"Buzz" Merritt, a leader of the movement, has been crusading for a kind of journalism that he believes would help counter public apathy and revitalize public life. At the *Wichita Eagle,* Merritt put into practice many of the ideas of Jay Rosen, a communications academic at New York University. Rosen has encouraged journalists to develop a symbiotic, rather than adversarial, relationship with government and to work with citizens and public officials rather than stand disinterestedly on the sidelines commenting about, but not helping to solve, community problems. "It is no coincidence that the decline in journalism and the decline in public life have happened at the same time," Merritt writes. "In modern society, they are codependent: Public life needs the information and perspective that journalism can provide, and journalism needs a viable public life because without it there is no need for journalism." [38]

Merritt is a critic of the market-oriented approach to journalism—despite the fact that some critics see the public journalism movement, with its efforts to involve citizens in helping to set the agenda for news coverage, as subtly linked to reader-driven journalism. "Our first response to eroding numbers was to spend countless hours and dollars analyzing the declines and devising ways to chase down readers in their manifold and ever-changing life niches," Merritt writes. ". . . We were treating people as consumers to be sought, as potential readers or at-risk readers; as a commodity rather than as a public." [39]

Some news organizations and media analysts—most notably *U.S. News and World Report* editor James Fallows—have endorsed Merritt's and Rosen's call for public journalism. In his book *Breaking the News*, Fallows complains that the media's adversarial approach to government coverage has fed public cynicism and alienation.[40] Public journalism has received a cold shoulder, however, from many top editors who resist the notion that journalists should become activists in trying to solve the problems of society. From the critics' perspective, public journalism clearly offends traditional journalistic notions of detachment and objectivity.

Many editors believe that public journalism should simply be seen as a more sophisticated form of the "good news," chamber-of-commerce oriented journalism that has long been a mainstay at certain newspapers. "Our central mission is to report the news, to set priorities, to analyze but not to shape or direct events or outcomes," says Jane R. Eisner, editorial page editor of the *Philadelphia Inquirer*. "Subsume or diminish the central mission, and we become like any other player in society, like any other politician, interest group, do-gooder, thief. I am not willing to relinquish this unique role." [41]

The New Media

Political Campaigns. One of the interesting political stories of the 1990s has been the way that politicians, members of the public, and alternative media outfits have used person-to-person forms of new media technologies to circumvent the public relations wizards, sound-bite–oriented editors, and political pundits who increasingly frame American political discourse. Direct, interactive, and personal forms of new media technology—ranging from C-SPAN to the Internet to talk radio to alternative television networks—now exercise enormous influence in political campaigns.

The 1992 presidential race, in particular, was hailed in many quarters for its new approach. Candidates Ross Perot and Bill Clinton used talk radio, town meetings, in-depth television advertisements, and appearances on non-network television (for example, MTV) to get their message directly across to voters. These developments were widely seen as a refreshing change from the catch phrases and attack ads that the television networks and political strategists use to shape the debate. The new media implicitly challenged the assumption that Americans were too bored, jaded, or indifferent to politics to pay attention to anything but the ever briefer soundbites or the crassest forms of negative advertising.

The developments of the 1992 campaign, in fact, raise a host of questions about poll- and market-driven media's focus upon voter surveys and political advertising in their coverage of campaigns. Like campaign strategists, many media executives came to believe that people pay little attention to politics unless it is packaged in ways that appeal to the short attention span of an audience largely uninterested in the complexity of public issues. But in the 1992 presidential campaign, Ross Perot's issue-oriented television ads found a large and ready audience. Many of these same news executives have been forced into the realization that a significant portion of the public is disgusted with the media's heavy focus upon staged media events, race horse polls, and commentary about political strategy rather than in-depth, issues-oriented coverage of campaigns. Newspapers' efforts to establish "truth-in-political-advertising" columns are just one reflection of the way journalists have responded to a public fed up with the negative and distorted aspects of modern television-age campaigning.

The Internet and News. Sadly, the advent of interactive news reporting on the Internet—hailed by some as the populist and democratic alternative to traditional, one-directional media—may not greatly improve the flow of serious government and political coverage. Despite its much-touted entry into the news business, Microsoft is putting much of its local focus on the development of "Sidewalk," an interactive electronic service that will give subscribers access to information about restaurants, entertainment, and recreation. Thus far, the efforts to put news onto the Internet (ranging from the newspaper industry's attempts to go on-line to alliances like Microsoft and NBC TV's news department, known as MS-NBC) have led to only modest audience interest. Few see general news coverage, and certainly government news, as a big revenue producer in the bifurcated marketplace of on-line information. In fact, the Internet—with its bias toward interactive communications, its tendency to appeal to fragmented interest groups, and its capacity for the instant measurement of hits to a Web site—may prove to be even more market-driven than traditional media have become. The Internet will expand around Web sites that can lure the most traffic. This, of course, could ultimately test the drawing power of government and political news. But at the same time, the Internet may only demonstrate that the on-line world won't prove to be the best environment for news of public affairs. . . .

Pressures on New Media. Quality news coverage in the world of new media is under increasing pressure as the traditional mass media news outlets, which the public has relied upon for the serious monitoring of government and politics, face ever greater threats from new media competitors. The competition from these new, on-line computer services is not only chipping away at traditional media's revenue base; it also is forcing traditional media companies to divert staff to their own divisions on new media.

Information about public affairs is not proving to be a growth area of these new divisions. Instead, on-line journalism is expanding around entertainment and restaurant information, classified and personals advertising, auto and real estate marketing, and other interactive, consumer-oriented services. Society has come to take for granted the existence of staffs of news professionals employed by daily newspapers and (to a lesser degree) television stations. These professionals gather and report much of the news about government and politics. With the movement of staff and resources in the direction of new media, the prospects for good public affairs coverage may only dim in the years ahead.

Radio serves as a prime example of what can happen when the marketplace alone dictates the nature of public affairs programming. After the federal government deregulated the industry in the 1980s, most commercial radio stations—which had been the subject of strong government pressure to do news programming—laid off news staff and did away with news reports. The radio dial is finely divided across a large spectrum of narrowly targeted audiences. And radio executives felt that the economics of the business no longer justified news or public affairs programming. The all-news stations that have sprung up may provide comfort to some. But the cutbacks in news staff and the disappearance of news and public affairs coverage on most commercial radio stations are alarming. This means that an industry that is struggling to gain market share in a highly segmented field—as is the case with virtually all new media organizations—may find little incentive to include public affairs coverage in the mix.

Nevertheless, the citizen who desires to follow government and politics in our information-saturated culture has a multitude of places to turn: CNN, C-SPAN, specialty magazines, public television, National Public Radio, Web sites, and cable programming that offer direct access to state and local government proceedings and data. Also available are newspapers that range from electronic versions of one's local daily to the *New York Times,* forums for citizens interested in public journalism, and all-news and talk radio. The combined forces of new computer technology, new media marketplace economics, global media conglomerate expansion, and an upsurge in public demand for direct participation in government offer unprecedented access to news and information relating to government and politics, even if it comes to us in radically new ways. These days citizens access information less through the professional commentary and reporting of the traditional channels of mass media and more through the search process that they must perform to comprehend the activities of the public sector amid a welter of new informational choices.

No matter what the promise of the new communications technologies, it is unlikely to compensate for the loss of attention paid to public life by the journalists who work in traditional, commercial, mainstream media organizations. The percentage of journalists who rank as important the key elements of the public service mission of journalism—investigating government claims, analyzing complex problems, and discussing national policy—has dropped considerably since the early 1970s.[42] And this decline may increase as more journalists are diverted from the dull, old-fashioned task of monitoring government into the sexy, new interactive fields being pursued by new media ventures. In an increasingly market-driven media environment, as well as one growing fragmented through the proliferation of new media channels, the future of news coverage of government and politics— at least, intelligent, serious, informed news coverage—is problematic at best. Internet "flaming," radio talk-show opinionating, and direct on-line and cable access to government proceedings may be a substitute for substantive journalism coverage in the minds of some, but they are unlikely to ever be a meaningful replacement. A democracy still needs solid facts, sound reporting, and intelligent journalistic analysis from committed news professionals to base its judgments.

Conclusion

Still the current experimentation in reporting of government and politics offers signs of hope. Interest in quality writing and creative approaches to government coverage is growing. There is a new commitment to investigative reporting and data-based journalism. Other positive signs include the debate over the public journalism movement, the growth of all-news channels, and the efforts to set the record straight on negative political advertising. All of these developments provide at least some counterbalance to the forces of marketplace journalism that threaten to erode the bedrock public service traditions and the government watchdog role of the American media. But once editors have decided that regular and sustained coverage of government and politics isn't a major priority of the public—and thus of their news organizations—it is going to be no easy task to turn around the trends that are contributing to diminished coverage of public life.

No doubt there will always be a market for creative, enterprising, and intrepid journalism that focuses on the public sector. But will mainstream commercial media organizations—in their quest to follow perceived changes in public taste—continue to provide the solid and substantial coverage of politics and government that they have defined as their role in the past? The respect of its readers or its viewers is one of the most elusive factors for any news outlet to gauge in its audience research. Although news organizations have been desperately trying to please their audience, there are signs that the public has been turned off by the shallow, superficial, and sensationalistic aspects of "journalism lite." In the next century, real marketplace journalism may try to satisfy the public's appetite for serious monitoring of government and politics and public affairs. There are indications that at least some news organizations are beginning to see that their future lies in this direction. One can only hope that the trend takes firmer root.

NOTES

1. Pete Schulberg, "How Much News Is There on the News?" *The Oregonian*, April 9, 1997, B1. Schulberg's findings generally have been confirmed by more extensive research about local television news. In its recent survey of 100 local newscasts across the nation, the Rocky Mountain Media Watch found that 43 percent of all news airtime was devoted to crime, disaster, war, or terrorism. This watchdog group determined that less than 2.5 percent of the total news time was devoted to public issues like education, arts, science, children, poverty, and civil rights. See Steve Johnson, "How Low Can TV News Go?" *Columbia Journalism Review* 36, no. 2 (July/August 1997): 25.

2. Penn Kimball, *Downsizing the News: Network Cutbacks in the Nation's Capital* (Washington, D.C.: The Woodrow Wilson Center Press, 1994), 4.

3. Carl Sessions Stepp, "Of the People, By the People, Bore the People," *Washington Journalism Review* 14, no. 2 (March 1992): 24–26.

4. John H. McManus, "What Kind of Commodity Is News?" *Communication Research* 19, no. 6 (December 1992): 798.

5. John H. McManus, "Local TV News: Not A Pretty Picture," *Columbia Journalism Review* 29, no. 1 (May/June 1990): 43.

6. "Bad News: Why Is Local TV News So Bad?" *American Journalism Review* 15, no. 7 (September 1993): 18.

7. Doug Underwood, "News or Hype?" *Seattle Post-Intelligencer,* October 3, 1993, E1, E3.

8. Phyllis Kaniss, "Too Few Reporters," *American Journalism Review* 15, no. 7 (September 1993): 20.

9. Kiku Adatto, *Picture Perfect: The Art and Artifice of Public Image Making* (New York: Basic, 1993), 2, 25, 58, 170.

10. Andie Tucher, "You News," *Columbia Journalism Review* 36, no. 1 (May/June 1997): 26–31. See also Peter J. Boyer, *Who Killed CBS?: The Undoing of America's Number One News Network* (New York: Random House, 1988); and Ken Auletta, *Three Blind Mice: How the TV Networks Lost Their Way* (New York: Random House, 1991).

11. Kimball, *Downsizing,* 165.

12. Jerry Pugnetti, *The Forgotten Statehouse: A Comparative Content Analysis of Newspaper Coverage of the Washington State Legislature,* Master's Thesis, University of Washington, 1994, see chaps. four and five. For the six newspapers over the same period, Pugnetti's study also showed a reduction in the news hole devoted to legislative coverage—ranging from 11 percent to 44 percent.

13. Stepp, "When Readers Design the News," *Washington Journalism Review* 13, no. 3 (April 1991): 20–24.

14. Stepp, "Bore the People," 24.

15. Ibid.

16. Pugnetti, *Forgotten Statehouse,* see chap. four. Not all researchers agree that news content based on researching readers' preferences has led to less attention to public affairs. For example, Randal Beam, a researcher at Indiana University, surveyed 167 daily

newspaper editors in 1991. The editors reported that readership research played a lesser role in their decisions about how to cover international affairs, the national government, and local government, or how to structure their beat system, than it did in their decisions involving comics, entertainment, business, and sports coverage. See Beam, "How Newspapers Use Readership Research," *Newspaper Research Journal* 16, no. 2 (Spring 1995): 31–32. Surveys that simply ask editors how marketing research influences their news judgments may have their limitations, however. News executives may not be forthcoming on a touchy subject about which they have received criticism over the years.

17. Stepp, "Bore the People," 26.

18. Doug Underwood, *When MBAs Rule the Newsroom: How the Marketers and Managers Are Reshaping Today's Media* (New York: Columbia University Press, 1993); John H. McManus, *Market-Driven Journalism: Let the Citizen Beware?* (Thousand Oaks, Calif.: Sage, 1994); James D. Squires, *Read All About It!: The Corporate Takeover of America's Newspapers* (New York: Times Books, 1993); Howard Kurtz, *Media Circus: The Trouble with America's Newspapers* (New York: Times Books, 1993).

19. David Pearce Demers, *The Menace of the Corporate Newspaper: Fact or Fiction?* (Ames: Iowa State University Press, 1996); Michael Fancher, "The Metamorphosis of the Newspaper Editor," *Gannett Center Journal* 1, no. 1 (Spring 1987): 69–80; John Morton, "Newspaper Business Grows Up At Last," *American Journalism Review* 15, no. 9 (November 1993): 48; Philip Meyer, *The Newspaper Survival Book: An Editor's Guide to Marketing Research* (Bloomington: Indiana University Press, 1985); Mary Alice Bagby, "Transforming Newspapers for Readers," *Presstime* 13, no. 4 (April 1991): 18–25; and Susan Miller, "American Dailies and the Drive to Capture Lost Readers," *Gannett Center Journal* 1, no. 1 (Spring 1987): 56–68.

20. Kurtz, *Media Circus,* 348.

21. Jay Taylor, "Success Stories: Two Projects Change Newspapers Nationwide," *Quill* 81, no. 4 (May 1993): 26.

22. Kurtz, *Media Circus,* 341.

23. For the historical perspective on American newspaper coverage of government and politics, see Frank Luther Mott, *American Journalism: A History of Newspapers in the United States through 260 Years: 1690 to 1950* (New York: MacMillan, 1950) and Michael Schudson, *Discovering the News: A Social History of American Newspapers* (New York: Basic, 1978). See also Gerald J. Baldasty, *The Commercialization of News in the Nineteenth Century* (Madison: University of Wisconsin Press, 1992).

24. Herbert J. Gans, *Deciding What's News: A Study of CBS Evening News, NBC Nightly News, Newsweek, and Time* (New York: Vintage, 1980), 68–69.

25. Gerald Stone, *Examining Newspapers: What Research Reveals about America's Newspapers* (Newbury Park, Calif.: Sage, 1987), 40–42.

26. Mark Hertsgaard, *On Bended Knee: The Press and the Reagan Presidency* (New York: Farrar Straus Giroux, 1988), 52.

27. Leo Bogart, *Press and Public: Who Reads What, When, Where, and Why in American Newspapers* (Hillsdale, N.J.: Erlbaum, 1989), 312–314.

28. Ibid., 260.

29. Bogart also is aware that readers often say they read things in the newspaper, or want things there, that they don't really pay much attention to. Readers, he adds, want to be good citizens, and they often express expectations about the content of their newspapers that go beyond their own personal needs and interests. Ibid., 332, 339.

30. Ruth Clark, *Changing Needs of Changing Readers* (Reston, Va.: American Newspaper Publishers Association, 1980); and Ruth Clark, *Relating to Readers in the '80s* (Washington, D.C.: American Society of Newspaper Editors, 1984).

31. George Albert Gladney, "The McPaper Revolution?: *USA Today*–style Innovation at Large U.S. Dailies," *Newspaper Research Journal* 13, nos. 1 and 2 (Winter/Spring 1992): 54–71.

32. Melinda D. Hawley, *Dropping the Paper: Losing Loyalists at the Local Level* (Athens, Ga.: James M. Cox Jr. Institute for Newspaper Management Studies, 1992). Hawley's study included mostly people of baby boom age and only one ex-subscriber under age 25, which is the group whose lack of newspaper reading habits is most worrisome to news executives. Hawley also indicated that the ex-readers' criticisms and their expectations of the local newspaper were influenced by the availability of the larger metro dailies in Atlanta.

33. Randal Beam, "How Perceived Environmental Uncertainty Influences the Marketing Orientation of U.S. Daily Newspapers," *Journalism and Mass Communication Quarterly* 73, no. 2 (Summer 1996): 298.

34. Taylor, "Success Stories," 25.

35. Donald L. Barlett and James B. Steele, *America: What Went Wrong?* (Kansas City, Mo.: Andrews and McMeel, 1992).

36. John Sedgwick, "Putting the Customers First: How CEO Jim Batten Gets Knight-Ridder Employees to Think Like Marketers," *Business Month* 133, no. 6 (June 1989): 28–35.

37. Susan Paterno, "Whither Knight-Ridder?" *American Journalism Review* 18, no. 1 (January/February 1996): 20.

38. Davis "Buzz" Merritt, *Public Journalism and Public Life: Why Telling the News Is Not Enough* (Hillsdale, N.J.: Erlbaum, 1995), 3–5, 6; and Jay Rosen, *Getting the Connections Right: Public Journalism and the Troubles in the Press* (New York: Twentieth Century Fund Press, 1996).

39. Merritt, *Public Journalism,* 66–67.

40. James Fallows, *Breaking the News: How the Media Undermine American Democracy* (New York: Pantheon, 1996).

41. Mike Hoyt, "Are You Now or Will You Ever Be, A Civic Journalist?" *Columbia Journalism Review* 39, no. 3 (September/October 1995): 29.

42. David H. Weaver and G. Cleveland Wilhoit, *The American Journalist in the 1990s: U.S. News People at the End of an Era* (Mahwah, N.J.: Erlbaum, 1996), 135–137.

14-3

Beaten

WASHINGTON BUREAUS HAVE LARGELY ABANDONED AGENCIES

John Herbers and James McCartney

*Print and broadcast news organizations both ensure that they system-
atically cover regular sources of important news by assigning reporters
to certain agencies and offices, referred to as "beats." Every major news
agency, for example, has an established White House correspondent.
Expecting routine coverage, and trying to influence it, political organizations such as the White House assign staff to feed stories to the reporters on their beat. The White House press secretary's office (whose
staff generally exceeds two dozen) continually offers photo opportunities and feeds reporters information that portrays the president in a favorable light. Beats are venerable institutions, and when they work well
they allow both politicians and the news media to achieve their different
goals. The next essay, by John Herbers and James McCartney, finds the
modern beat system deteriorating in both the scope and quality of its
coverage of the national government.*

Interior Secretary Has to Hit the Road to Find Reporters Willing to Listen

IN 1995, Interior Secretary Bruce Babbitt was trying to let the world know
what dire things would be in store for the national park system if hundreds
of millions of dollars in proposed budget cuts were actually adopted, but he
seemed to be getting nowhere with Congress—or, frankly, with the Washington press corps. So Babbitt took to the road.

Excerpted from article forthcoming in *American Journalism Review*. Reprinted by permission of
American Journalism Review.

He went bass fishing on Chickamauga Lake in southeastern Tennessee. He canoed along the Little Miami River in Ohio. He spoke before St. Louis' shimmering Gateway Arch. At every stop, Babbitt found local media receptive to his story, one wherein he cast Republican congressmen as villains for wanting, in effect, to shutter some of the country's hundreds of National Park Service sites. "We had 28 stories in New Jersey papers alone," recalls Stephanie Hanna, a department press assistant. The blitz worked. After this regional drumbeat, the national media began paying genuine attention to Babbitt's admonitions, and the budgetary threat to the parks passed. Now, you can read Babbitt's tour as a savvy exercise in public relations, which it surely was. But you can also read it as a commentary on the shifting, uneasy state of Washington press coverage today.

The Department of Interior controls the use of 500 million acres of public land, including a national park system that attracts 275 million visitors a year. It oversees the U.S. Geological Service, the U.S. Fish and Wildlife Service, the Bureau of Land Management and the Bureau of Indian Affairs. Day in and day out, Babbitt's department is involved in such lightning-rod issues as mining, logging, water rights and the protection of endangered species. And there are no newspaper reporters assigned full time to cover Interior. None.

This is a marked departure from the past, when the *Denver Post* and at least a handful of other Western papers thought it important to have someone more or less stationed in Washington to keep an eye on the region's biggest landholder. Now they largely endeavor to cover Interior from their hometowns. In any event, the department has learned its lesson. Today when it seeks to generate news, Interior bypasses Washington altogether. If Babbitt wants to talk about efforts to save the condor, for instance, he'll do it in California. Or he'll fly to Florida to discuss preservation of the Everglades—this despite the fact that both stories have much more than regional significance. The secretary's assistant, Michael Gauldin, says department officials have realized that if enough regional outlets pay attention to a given story, the national press just may follow. "We'd rather appear in the *Washington Post* through AP, coming from the out side," he says.

So far the strategy seems to be working—for Interior, anyway. Whether it works for the public is a far more dubious proposition, considering that under this system the "news" is basically whatever the department decides it is, and there are no reporters left to tell us otherwise.

Un-Covered

The Washington press corps has always been as susceptible to fad and fancy as the politicians they cover. The practices of daily journalism inside the Beltway evolve with the times and with changing media mores, and we're clearly in such a transition now. In today's confused, hypercompetitive environment, Washington's newspaper bureaus are struggling to define their basic mission, and in the process they have fundamentally altered what their reporters are covering and how they are deployed. So it is that some federal departments have witnessed a steep slide in beat coverage. At the same time, the number of Washington journalists covering business and finance has exploded. Tracking economic trends now far overshadows the once strong commitment of the capital press to social concerns such as poverty and equal opportunity under the law.

To help assess this evolution, the Project on the State of the American Newspaper recently surveyed newspaper and wire service beats at 19 federal departments and agencies, most of which have some direct influence on everyday life. How has the newspaper industry's commitment to covering these entities—as measured by full-time, or nearly full-time, beats—changed in the '90s? We found that in eight cases (the departments of Interior, State, Agriculture, Labor and Veterans' Affairs, the Supreme Court, the Federal Aviation Administration and the Nuclear Regulatory Commission) that commitment is clearly down, sometimes to the point of nonexistence. In seven other cases—most having to do with business and finance, but also the technology, health and science fields—coverage has increased. And in four cases, the commitment appears to be roughly the same as it was a decade ago.

Peek behind the numbers and you find other notable, and sometimes worrisome, trends. For one, it can scarcely be reassuring how much the newspaper industry has come to rely on just four key outlets—the *New York Times, Washington Post, Los Angeles Times* and Associated Press—to monitor vast portions of the federal government. (And that's just the major agencies we're talking about, much less the more arcane and virtually ignored specialty bureaucracies like the Federal Maritime Commission or the National Institute of Standards and Technology.) Conversely, many chains that reach huge segments of the reading public—Gannett, MediaNews, Cox and Scripps Howard alone sell 20 percent of America's daily papers—constitute a proportionately tiny fraction of the capital press corps.

The irony here is that more reporters are prowling Washington than ever. But that's not because the mainstream media have laid on thousands of extra people. To some extent it's due to a proliferation of newsletters, trade magazines and specialty publications running the gamut from *Army Times* to *Women's Wear Daily*. Mostly, though, the capital boom is attributable to an appetite for business news that in the '90s has become seemingly insatiable. Reuters, for instance, employs nearly 150 reporters and editors in its Washington office alone. Bloomberg News Service, which didn't even exist a decade ago, has nearly 60—or roughly three times that of such newspaper bureaus as Cox or McClatchy. Bridge News, formerly Knight Ridder Financial, stays abreast of federal activities moving the commodities and capital markets with 30 Washington journalists.

More people means more heat, and more pressure on the newspaper bureaus to somehow keep up. That pressure is the driving force behind the two most dramatic changes in Washington journalism, both of which involve the way reporters are being used. First, there has been a distinct move away from "covering buildings," jargon for the traditional practice of tying a specific beat to a specific agency. More and more beats today are built around broad themes—national security, law, science, economics—in which the reporters have the latitude to flit from agency to agency in pursuit of stories. So one day may find a national security correspondent at the State Department, the next day at CIA headquarters, and the day after that the Pentagon.

The second major shift involves a concentrated push to get reporters in Washington to write stories with strong angles for the reader back home. "Local, local, local," says Clark Hoyt, vice president for news for Knight Ridder and former chief of its Washington bureau. "Local news is the heart of the franchise. . . . If you look at reader research, the thing that readers are most intensively interested in is, first, local—my area, my neighborhood."

The fact is, Washington, with its multitude of public and private research agencies, increasingly is seen as a center for information rather than a center of government—and the new Washington journalism reflects this thinking. Virtually all the increase in coverage of business and economic affairs, for example, is based on a search for statistics and other information with little regard for what is happening within the agencies that produce it. But this evolution comes with some risk. If no one is covering Washington's "buildings," who will cultivate the kind of deep sources it takes to really know what's going on inside them? If everyone is looking for stories with "local angles," how many serious national stories will go unreported? If in trying to differentiate themselves from their electronic brethren Washington's print reporters become fixated with personalities or political process or today's spin, who will monitor actual governance on behalf of the public?

Instant Analysis

To understand the extent of these changes it is useful to look back to a time, before Monica Lewinsky was born, when presidents often were treated with a respect akin to kings, when reporters fought for the chance to travel with the secretary of state, when government actions weren't widely discussed until they had been read on the front page of the day's paper or heard on the nightly news. News from Washington was often high drama. It was about life-and-death issues of moment, not cynical gamesmanship. It seemed to matter.

Citizens were best connected to Washington by their local newspapers through the news dispatches, analyses and columns of their paper's staff in the capital, with numerous regional papers competing with their larger and more influential counterparts for leaks and exclusive information. In the process, they were able to follow and judge, at least to some extent, the policies and actions of the national government. Not anymore. Except for papers in the biggest markets, most dailies have drastically reduced the amount of foreign and national news they publish. Washington has scarcely been immune. "We are no longer there waiting for the call from the red phone," says Charles Lewis, Hearst's Washington bureau chief. "The Cold War for 50 years defined Washington coverage . . . but when it ended, it changed the relevance of Washington."

In terms of journalistic coverage, this truth is perhaps most evident at the State Department, where standing press representation is way down from its Vietnam-era peak. In the past decade, however, a kindred erosion has occurred throughout official Washington. With relative peace abroad and unprecedented prosperity at home, the Washington bureaus of many major papers, such as those of the *Detroit News, Chicago Sun-Times* and *Denver Post,* have virtually abandoned efforts to personally report national news stories. Even papers in such labor-conscious communities as Detroit, Milwaukee and St. Louis no longer maintain a regular presence at the Labor Department.

All these newspapers see their current mission as much more difficult than in the past because of the pressures to do more analysis of news events and to go behind the issues involved—and to do it all instantly, since they now compete with a daunting array of electronic media. "News is very different in the CNN era than in the pre-CNN era," says Carl Leubsdorf, Washington bureau chief of the *Dallas Morning News.* Andrew Glass, senior correspondent for Cox and its former bureau chief, elaborates: "In the old days, on the first day we would report what happened. On the second day, we would tell what the reaction was. On the third day, we would analyze what it means. Now CNN tells you what happened and five minutes later some professor from Fordham University is telling you what it means. That's the problem. We have to find a way to package it all the first day or we're out of business."

"If we tried today to do traditional coverage in the traditional way, it would be ignored," Glass continues. "The papers wouldn't run it."

Therefore an increasing number of chains and newspapers—Cox, Hearst, Newhouse, the *Los Angeles Times,* the *Boston Globe,* Cleveland's *Plain Dealer,* Copley and Scripps Howard, to name just a few—don't do it the traditional way. They have revamped their Washington bureaus to cover trends and issues that might take a reporter to a full gamut of government agencies and out into the country. Under these circumstances, they are more than willing to leave much of the "basic" Washington coverage— what the White House said, or the Supreme Court decreed, yesterday—to the wires and news services of the largest papers.

One of those wire service standbys, AP's veteran State Department correspondent Barry Schweid, finds the new culture deeply distressing. "The papers are trying hard to get away from hard news," he says. Even those reporters still assigned to State are less and less visible. They come around occasionally to pick up transcripts of old briefings and follow up anything of interest they might find, Schweid says, but he believes important news is being lost in the process.

One reason why is that bureaucratic Washington, taking its cue from the White House and Congress, is decidedly more sophisticated about managing the flow of news. When officials want something publicized, everything is scripted. And when they don't, they are much more adroit at keeping unpleasantness under wraps. . . .

The Little Picture

Even in those gauzy days when Washington's influential newspaper bureaus had the capital essentially to themselves, not every chain felt the obligation—or wanted the considerable expense—of fielding widespread beat coverage of the federal government. One that has shouldered the obligation through the years is Knight Ridder, which has maintained one of Washington's largest and more prestigious bureaus.

But even here the combined pressures of budget and competition increasingly are being brought to bear. The Knight Ridder bureau has just embarked on its second reorganization in seven years. The 1992 restructuring was traumatic enough, leading to a number of notable departures of seasoned journalists, a sharp redefinition of its essential mission and a change of beats and coverage areas. The company contends that the impending changes amount to little more than an adjustment of existing course, but others fear they promise to be more sweeping than ever, and an even more pronounced departure from the bureau's hard-news tradition. . . .

The notion of covering Washington through a local prism is everywhere as embattled papers focus on what they perceive to be their biggest competitive edge. Another case in point: the *Detroit News.* After the Persian Gulf War in 1991, says former Washington Bureau Chief James Gannon, editors in Detroit seemed to lose interest in covering government, politics or diplomacy. "The appetite in Detroit for that kind of news was minimal. . . . If it didn't have a local angle, they didn't want it."

Needless to say, Washington offers up local angles everywhere you turn. It is common practice for a bureau to staff the Supreme Court only when it is considering an appeal from a case of regional interest, or to report on new legislation only when a local member of Congress is its author. Of course, to some extent news from Washington with a local connection has always been prized copy back home. A host of small and medium-sized newspapers have long had reporters in the capital primarily to follow the home state's congressional delegation. In the '60s a story circulated in the House and Senate press galleries about a regional wire service reporter assigned to cover only Texas developments. One day a member of the House fell dead in the underground corridor leading to his office. The reporter, one of the first to happen along, saw the dead man's face and promptly went on his way. Asked why he didn't call his desk, he replied, "Well, he wasn't from Texas."

That yarn sounds less outrageous today, as what once was considered provincialism has become an established way of doing business. In recent years, a number of energetic new bureau chiefs have arrived on the scene armed with reader surveys and directives from their home offices determined to alter the way Washington is reported. Much of their criticism of past practices was well-founded: too many reporters standing around waiting for handouts, too much cozying up to high officials, too much redundancy in reporting among papers and agencies with little originality in news dispatches, too much allowing government officials to set the news agenda, too much pack journalism.

Deborah Howell, Washington chief for Newhouse, was one of the pioneers in structuring a bureau designed to avoid traditional beats and to focus on issues believed to be of greater reader interest. But she makes no claim that her 40-person bureau is covering Washington. Newhouse editors believed they received adequate hard news coverage from Washington from many other sources; they made clear to her that "they did not want another version of the story of the day. They wanted something different."

To say the least, many of her beats are not traditional. Among them are money and jobs; race and ethnicity; family and children; violence; cyberspace; the American scene; and "doing good." Howell believes the bureau's primary function should be focused on enterprise stories that nobody else has, and claims considerable success. "I want to have important trend stories," she says.

. . . [M]ake no mistake: Washington is still very much in business. For all the efforts to shrink the vast bureaucracy, despite the return of so much power to the states, official Washington continues to exert a huge impact on people's lives. "The demise of big government has been greatly exaggerated," says Doyle McManus, who runs the Washington bureau of the *L.A. Times.* "I'm actually surprised at how obsolete we aren't."

Proving a Negative

The inherent problem in assessing the impact of the new Washington coverage is what we don't see—stories reporters never find, or ones they do but cannot get printed. Morton Mintz keeps a fat file of occurrences he considers important but were never printed, or were buried on back pages of the major newspapers he reads.

Mintz had a distinguished career as an investigative reporter for the *Washington Post* (among other big stories, he alerted consumers to the dangers of thalidomide in the early '60s), and today he is a kind of conscience-scold who directs his ire in long memos and op-ed pieces. Last fall, writing in *The Nation,* he observed: "In the four months ending in mid-September, for example, news of deliberate, even criminal, corporate misconduct with dire consequences for people and the environment—news that could be plucked from the wires like plums from a tree—too often drew either scant attention or none at all. Some great newspapers shrink-wrapped these stories into brief, one-shot items, causing them to sink without a trace. No follow-up, no commentary, no editorials."

One of several examples Mintz cited occurred last summer, when the *St. Paul Pioneer Press* "drew on Minnesota tobacco-industry documents to expose 13 well-credentialed scientists who took more than $156,000 from the industry for writing letters—or signing letters written or edited by tobacco law firms—discrediting links between secondhand smoke and lung cancer." The *Washington Post* ran an AP summary, he said, while the *New York Times, Wall Street Journal* and *Los Angeles Times* carried nothing at all. . . .

14-4

Low Score

James B. Kelleher

Even when it functions properly, the beat system may fail to keep readers fully informed of the actions of politicians and bureaucrats. Sometimes news is reported in a two-step process, in which key stories are first spotted, not by the national press, but by more specialized news organizations that keep a sharp eye out for news that most affects their audience. In the following essay James Kelleher recounts an instance in which this arrangement, at times a salutary division of labor, failed to alert the public about important changes in federal education policy. The reluctance of the New York Times *and the* Washington Post *to adequately cover the story, even after it "broke" in their own pages, cautions us against optimism that the process will provide us with the news.*

WHEN THE DEPARTMENT of Education produced a guide that warned educators who rely heavily on standardized exams for admissions or promotions that they might be violating federal law—who got the story right?

A) *The Chronicle of Higher Education*
B) *Los Angeles Times*
C) *The New York Times*
D) *The Washington Post*
E) *The Wall Street Journal*
F) none of the above

The proposed guide, "Nondiscrimination in High-Stakes Testing: A Resource Guide," presented what the Education Department's Office of Civil Rights (OCR) characterized as a synthesis of existing law on the subject. Its key passage read, in part:

> The use of any educational test which has a significant disparate impact on members of any particular race, national origin, or sex is discrimina-

tory, and a violation of Title VI and/or Title IX, respectively, unless it is
educationally necessary and there is no practicable form of assessment
which meets the educational institution's needs and would have less of a
disparate impact.

Not to worry, the OCR told journalists who bothered to inquire about the
document. The guide, a draft four years in the making, broke no new legal
ground, the office said. No big deal.

Because many journalists bought this line they didn't cover the story. As
a result, most readers first heard about it not through news stories, but via
op-ed pieces mostly written by anti–affirmative-action conservatives.

The guide was a big deal indeed to many in education circles, including
the American Council on Education, representing almost 2,000 colleges
and universities, and the College Board and Educational Testing Service,
which respectively sponsor and produce the well-known SAT test. The
reason? As a group, African Americans and Latinos score lower than
whites on standardized tests, and women tend to score lower than men
on math tests. Standardized tests clearly have a "disparate" impact on
these groups. So the guide, its critics said, serves as a federal warning to
educational institutions not to rely on such tests. Or a how-to-sue map if
they do.

To Patrick Healy, political editor at the *Chronicle of Higher Education*, a
respected weekly that covers colleges and universities, the uproar in educational circles made the guide "an important national story." Higher
education sources he spoke to thought it staked out a hard-line position
in the contentious debate on the role affirmative action plays in education. They used words, he said, like "unprecedented, extraordinary." With
the next issue of the *Chronicle* already in the mail, Healy broke the story
on the weekly's Web site (http://chronicle.merit.edu) on May 17, following up with a more comprehensive account in the print issue dated
May 28.

Then . . . nothing. Or almost nothing, at least on news pages. Between
May 17, when the *Chronicle* broke the story, and June 9, when the *Los Angeles Times* briefly mentioned the controversy in a B2 news column, the only
major daily to touch the standardized testing tale in its news pages was the
Wall Street Journal (which ran a solid A2 piece on May 26). Neither the *Los
Angeles Times* nor the *New York Times* has a Washington education correspondent, but both papers say their silence on the guide was more a question of judgment than a missed story. "The *Chronicle* had a different

interpretation of the importance of this than we did," says Tami Dennis, interim education editor at the *Los Angeles Times*. "Yeah, it had education insiders upset, but how much of a difference was that going to make, really?"

David Corcoran, the education editor of the *New York Times*, says his initial reaction to the story was, "this is interesting, but what have they actually done?" Reporter Steven Holmes told him that "the story was less clear-cut than it seemed," Corcoran says. "He wanted to take some time to explore it more."

Into this news void rode the op-ed writers, who complained about the guide throughout May and prompted congressional hearings about it in late June. John Leo was first, with a column—"The Feds Strike Back"—that ran in the New York *Daily News* May 22 and in *U.S. News & World Report* May 31. He was followed by Stephen Balch in the *New York Post* (May 23), John O'Sullivan in the *Chicago Sun-Times* (May 25), Peter Schrag in the *Sacramento Bee* (May 26), and a series of editorials in the *Wall Street Journal, Detroit News, Indianapolis Star,* and *Washington Times*.

So readers mostly got one side of a complicated debate. Meanwhile, because the *Chronicle* was the first paper to report the story, press discussion about the guide was framed almost entirely in terms of higher education. But standardized tests—and their "disparate impact"—may be more important in the K–12 sphere, where foes of "social promotion" are embracing the idea of make-or-break proficiency tests that would determine whether students move up.

The *New York Times* did a news story about the guide on June 12, only after Abigail Thernstrom, co-author of *America in Black and White,* had thundered against the proposed guidelines in a June 10 piece on the *Times*'s op-ed page. Holmes's June 12 story, essentially a round-up of the hostile reaction to the guide, oddly included "news stories in education journals" as among the work published by "anti–affirmative-action conservatives."

When the debate became the subject of congressional hearings before Michigan Republican Representative Peter Hoekstra's education subcommittee on June 22, only *USA Today,* the *Chronicle of Higher Education,* and a college-paper wire service covered them. The *Washington Post* continued to ignore the story, leaving its readers to understand the issue via a June 12 op-ed piece—"Coerced Diversity"—by the iconoclastic Nat Hentoff. Not even Hentoff was happy with that circumstance. "The *Washington Post*," he says, "blew it."